The Reconstruction Amendments

The Reconstruction Amendments

Peter Nicolas
William L. Dwyer Chair in Law
Adjunct Professor of Gender, Women and Sexuality Studies
University of Washington

Carolina Academic Press
Durham, North Carolina

ISBN 978-1-5310-1875-7
eISBN 978-1-5310-1876-4
LCCN 2020937494

Carolina Academic Press
700 Kent Street
Durham, NC 27701
Telephone (919) 489-7486
Fax (919) 493-5668
www.caplaw.com

Printed in the United States of America

Contents

Table of Principal Cases

Preface

In 2010—my last year as the Academic Dean at the University of Washington School of Law—one of my final responsibilities was to find a faculty member to teach Constitutional Law II, our rights-based constitutional law course covering the Reconstruction Amendments. After knocking on countless doors, I finally came to the conclusion that the only way the course was going to be taught was if I taught it myself.

Although teaching a new law school course is always a challenge, this new course presented a particularly acute challenge—I never learned the material in law school! In the 1997–98 academic year, I took constitutional law as a 2L at Harvard Law School. The course was designed as a comprehensive constitutional law course that covered structural constitutional law; the Equal Protection and Due Process Clauses of the Fourteenth Amendment; and the First Amendment. My professor was very intelligent and was very pleasant to interact with. But he had a near obsession with the Interstate Commerce Clause and other structural aspects of constitutional law. Indeed, several weeks of the course were devoted to the Interstate Commerce Clause alone!

On the syllabus immediately following the Interstate Commerce Clause was a light at the end of the tunnel: a unit on the Fourteenth Amendment. We had four cases assigned to us: *Bowers v. Hardwick* (sodomy laws); *Romer v. Evans* (sexual orientation discrimination); *Planned Parenthood of Southeastern Pennsylvania v. Casey* (abortion); and *Washington v. Glucksberg* (physician-assisted suicide). In preparation for the single day (!) devoted to these cases, I read and re-read them, taking copious notes and trying to make sense of the diametrically opposed majority and dissenting opinions. As a gay male slowly making his way out of the closet, I was particularly intrigued to learn more about the Court's decisions in *Bowers* and *Romer*.

On the appointed day, I arrived in class ready to discuss the cases. Our professor started class by continuing the discussion of the Interstate Commerce Clause from the previous day. As he continued to discuss the fine points of that Clause, I watched in horror as the clock quickly ticked its way toward the end of the class period. With five minutes to go, our professor turned to the four cases and said, "These cases all involve highly controversial issues, and people have very strong emotions about the issues they raise, and we're not going to talk about them." That, in a nutshell, was my formal education on the Reconstruction Amendments.

In 2000, I was hired as an assistant professor at the University of Washington School of Law. I taught a variety of subjects in my first few years, including evidence, federal courts, conflict of laws, and international civil litigation. During my second year as a law professor, the LGBT student group at the law school asked me to help them get a course on sexual orientation, gender identity, and the law through the curriculum approval process. I succeeded in doing so, and began to teach the course the following year. In the process of teaching that course, I slowly began to develop my understanding of rights-based constitutional law.

In 2011, I was scheduled to teach Constitutional Law II twice. Both times, I assigned my students one of the many established and well-regarded textbooks in constitutional law. However, I found teaching from the book to be problematic for several reasons. First, like nearly all constitutional law textbooks, it was general in nature, with chapters devoted to all aspects of constitutional law, including structural issues; the Reconstruction Amendments; and the First Amendment. This made the book huge, and as a result, very expensive for students. Moreover, to keep it from being even bigger and more expensive, all of the chapters were heavily edited, with key historical cases omitted or reduced to references in notes and even the main cases severely truncated. As a result, I was constantly supplementing the book with my own, lightly edited versions of the cases.

That initial step of supplementing the textbook I was using began what has been a nearly ten-year process of writing this textbook on the Reconstruction Amendments—and *only* the Reconstruction Amendments. The book has a number of features that I believe will make it attractive to anyone teaching or enrolled in a rights-based constitutional law course:

- *Length*—At under 700 pages, the book is about one-third the length of most of the constitutional law textbooks on the market. As a result, it is also far less expensive.
- *Depth*—Because this book is *solely* focused on the Reconstruction Amendments, it examines them in much greater depth than do most constitutional law textbooks.
- *Reverse Engineering*—As I indicated above, I did not know that much about rights-based constitutional law when I set out to write this book. I was only familiar with the most recent cases on hot-button issues, so I started with those cases, and then read all the cases referenced within those cases. I continued this process until I arrived at the earliest cases interpreting the Reconstruction Amendments. As a result of this reverse engineering, I figured out which historical cases students needed to be exposed to in order to make sense of modern constitutional law decisions, and included those in the book.
- *Cohesive*—This is the third law school textbook I have written, all of which have been solo projects. Most textbooks, and especially most constitutional law textbooks, are written by multiple authors, many of whom have succeeded earlier groups of authors who have since passed away. While the collective knowledge brings a lot to the table, one often feels as they go from chapter to chapter that they are moving from one book to another, because often the chapters are written by

different people with different approaches. Because I wrote this book from start to finish, movement from one chapter to the next should feel seamless.

- *Historical Approach*—This book is, for the most part, organized in a historical rather than a purely topical order. Thus, the first chapter begins with a case from the 1700s while the final chapters contain cases from 2020. Thus, rather than briefly focusing on a given doctrinal principle before moving on to the next one, never to return, this book returns to each doctrinal principle multiple times in concert with doctrinal developments over time. This historical approach has the advantage of providing insight into how changes in the Court's composition and philosophy over time have impacted all aspects of rights-based constitutional law.
- *Viewpoint Neutral*—If we are being fully honest with ourselves, most law professors are somewhere between left-of-center and extremely left-of-center, and are not always careful about separating their views of what the law *should* be from what the law *is*. As I tell my constitutional law students on the first day of class, most of these decisions are closely divided because there are compelling arguments to be made on both sides of the issue. Accordingly, I have tried to present the materials in a balanced way so as to make sure liberal and conservative constitutional philosophies are given equal consideration.
- *Problem-Solving Exercises*—Law students are very good at learning and reciting doctrine, but find applying doctrine—especially constitutional doctrine—particularly challenging. Drawing on the success of my problem-based approach to evidence law in my evidence textbook, the last seven chapters of this textbook contain over a dozen detailed problems designed to help students apply their knowledge to hypothetical scenarios—some of which are loosely based on actual scenarios and some of which are a part of my wild constitutional imagination but all of which will help students master their skills in applying constitutional doctrine.

I want to thank a number of people who have helped make it possible for me to complete this project. Chief among them is Cindy Fester—the Publications Editor at my law school—who meticulously edited this book from cover to cover. I also wish to thank TJ Smithers, who shepherded the book through the publication process at Carolina Academic Press. In addition, I wish to thank my colleague Professor Kathryn Watts, who has taught out of a draft of this textbook twice and has provided me with detailed feedback. Finally, I wish to thank a decade worth of students—whom I have taught using skeletal forms of this textbook—for engaging in spirited discussions of the materials that has helped me to refine the textbook into what you have before you today.

PETER NICOLAS
Seattle, Washington

September 2020

The Reconstruction Amendments

Chapter 1

Pre-Reconstruction (1789–1865)

The focus of this book is on the Reconstruction Amendments—the Thirteenth, Fourteenth, and Fifteenth Amendments—which were approved by Congress and ratified by the States between 1865 and 1870, just as the Civil War was drawing to a close.

Yet it is impossible to understand the impact of the Reconstruction Amendments without some understanding of the constitutional scheme that the Amendments built upon and to some degree modified. Among the issues raised and addressed in the Court's pre-Reconstruction cases are the following:

- Does the U.S. Constitution protect only those rights *explicitly* enumerated therein, or are there additional, unenumerated rights that it also protects?
- Do the provisions of the Bill of Rights constrain the conduct of all levels of government, or do they merely constrain the conduct of the *federal* government?
- In what ways did the provisions of the original U.S. Constitution protect the rights of enslavers,* and how robustly did the Court interpret those provisions?

The following three cases address these issues and together provide a snapshot of the U.S. Constitution prior to Reconstruction. As you read these cases, focus not only on the specific holdings of the decisions themselves, but also the interpretative tools that the Court uses in each of these three cases to assist it in interpreting somewhat ambiguous constitutional provisions.

A. Unenumerated Rights

Calder v. Bull

3 U.S. 386 (1798)

[At issue in this case is a challenge to the constitutionality of a Connecticut law. The Court decides to uphold the law, but in the course of their opinions, Justices Chase and Iredell express diametrically different views on whether the Court has

* Traditionally, the terms "slavery," "slaves," and "slave owners" have been used to refer to the institution of slavery and the individuals involved. To respect the humanity of those who have been enslaved, and in accordance with modern style guides, this book will instead use the terms "enslavement," "enslaved persons," and "enslavers" unless the term appears in an original source such as a statute, case, or constitutional provision, or is part of a legal term of art (such as the "Fugitive Slave Clause.")

the power to hold a law unconstitutional even if it violates no express prohibition in the U.S. Constitution.]

CHASE, *Justice*. . . .

I cannot subscribe to the *omnipotence* of a *State* Legislature, or that it is *absolute and without control*; although its authority should not be *expressly* restrained by the *Constitution*, or *fundamental law*, of the State. The people of the *United States* erected their Constitutions, or forms of government, to establish justice, to promote the general welfare, to secure the blessings of liberty; and to protect their *persons* and *property* from violence. The purposes for which men enter into society will determine the *nature* and *terms* of the *social* compact; and as *they* are the foundation of the *legislative* power, *they* will decide what are the *proper* objects of it: The *nature*, and *ends* of *legislative* power will limit the *exercise* of it. This *fundamental* principle flows from the very nature of our free *Republican* governments, that no man should be compelled to do what the laws do *not* require; *nor to refrain from acts which the laws permit*. There are acts which the *Federal*, or *State*, Legislature cannot do, *without exceeding their authority*. There are certain *vital* principles in our *free Republican governments*, which will determine and over-rule an *apparent and flagrant* abuse of *legislative* power; as to authorize *manifest injustice by positive law*; or to take away that security for *personal liberty*, or *private property*, for the protection whereof the government was established. An ACT of the Legislature (for I cannot call it a *law*) contrary to the *great first principles* of the *social compact*, cannot be considered a *rightful exercise of legislative authority*. The obligation of a law in governments established on *express compact, and on republican principles*, must be determined by the *nature of the power*, on which it is founded. A few instances will suffice to explain what I mean. A law that punished a citizen for an *innocent* action, or, in other words, for an act, which, when done, was in violation of no *existing* law; a law that destroys, or impairs, the *lawful private* contracts of citizens; a law that makes a man *a Judge in his own cause*; or a law that takes *property* from A. and gives it to B: It is against all reason and justice, for a people to entrust a Legislature with SUCH powers; and, therefore, it cannot be presumed that they have done it. The *genius*, the *nature*, and the *spirit*, of our State Governments, amount to a prohibition of *such acts of legislation*; and the *general principles of law and reason* forbid them. The Legislature may enjoin, permit, forbid, and punish; they may declare *new* crimes; and establish rules of conduct for *all* its citizens in *future* cases; they may *command* what is right, and *prohibit* what is wrong; but they cannot change *innocence* into *guilt*; or punish *innocence* as a *crime*; or violate the right of an *antecedent lawful private contract*; or the *right of private property*. To maintain that our Federal, or State, Legislature *possesses such powers*, if they had not been *expressly* restrained; would, in my opinion, be a *political heresy*, altogether inadmissible in our *free republican governments*. . . .

IREDELL, *Justice*. . . .

If, then, a government, composed of Legislative, Executive and Judicial departments, were established, by a Constitution, which imposed no limits on the legislative power, the consequence would inevitably be, that whatever the legislative power chose to enact, would be lawfully enacted, and the judicial power could never interpose to pronounce it void. It is true, that some speculative jurists have held, that a legislative act against natural justice must, in itself, be void; but I cannot think that, under such a government, any Court of Justice would possess a power to declare it so. Sir *William Blackstone*, having put the strong case of an act of Parliament, which should authorise a man to try his own cause, explicitly adds, that even in that case, "there is no court that has power to defeat the intent of the Legislature, when couched in such evident and express words, as leave no doubt whether it was the intent of the Legislature, or no." 1 *Bl. Com.* 91.

In order, therefore, to guard against so great an evil, it has been the policy of all the *American* states, which have, individually, framed their state constitutions since the revolution, and of the people of the *United States*, when they framed the Federal Constitution, to define with precision the objects of the legislative power, and to restrain its exercise within marked and settled boundaries. If any act of Congress, or of the Legislature of a state, violates those constitutional provisions, it is unquestionably void; though, I admit, that as the authority to declare it void is of a delicate and awful nature, the Court will never resort to that authority, but in a clear and urgent case. If, on the other hand, the Legislature of the Union, or the Legislature of any member of the Union, shall pass a law, within the general scope of their constitutional power, the Court cannot pronounce it to be void, merely because it is, in their judgment, contrary to the principles of natural justice. The ideas of natural justice are regulated by no fixed standard: the ablest and the purest men have differed upon the subject; and all that the Court could properly say, in such an event, would be, that the Legislature (possessed of an equal right of opinion) had passed an act which, in the opinion of the judges, was inconsistent with the abstract principles of natural justice....

[The opinions of Justices Paterson and Cushing are omitted.]

Notes and Questions

1. The dispute between Justices Chase and Iredell builds upon an earlier dispute between English jurists Sir Edward Coke and Sir William Blackstone over the power of judges to invalidate an Act of Parliament making a man a Judge in his own case, a type of law referred to by Justice Chase in his opinion. Although Coke was of the opinion that such a law could be invalidated by an English court because it was unreasonable, Blackstone was of the view that if Parliament clearly and positively enacted an unreasonable law—even one that made a man a judge in his own case—the courts have no power to declare it void. *See* John V. Orth, Due Process of Law: A Brief History 15-32 (Univ. of Kansas Press 2003). As you will see in the chapters that follow, the dispute over the ability of judges to invalidate laws that violate no *express* provision of the U.S. Constitution continues into the present.

2. In the course of his opinion, Justice Chase lists four categories of laws that he believes exceed legislative authority: *ex post facto* laws; laws impairing lawful private

contracts; laws that make a man a Judge in his own cause; and finally, a law that takes property from A, and gives it to B. What, if anything, distinguishes the first three categories on his list from the final category? Stated somewhat differently, might Justice Iredell agree with Justice Chase with respect to the first three categories but not with respect to the final category? In this regard, consider the extent to which laws of these four types are addressed in the text of the U.S. Constitution in whole or part.

3. Assuming that Justice Chase is correct that the courts are empowered to recognize and enforce unenumerated constitutional rights, two further questions need to be addressed. First, is there any provision of the U.S. Constitution that provides textual support for courts to enforce unenumerated rights? Second, what do courts look to in order to determine the existence and scope of such unenumerated rights? As you examine cases in future chapters regarding unenumerated rights, keep an eye out for the many ways in which members of the U.S. Supreme Court answer these questions.

B. Scope of the Bill of Rights

Barron v. City of Baltimore

32 U.S. 243 (1833)

Mr. Chief Justice Marshall delivered the opinion of the court....

The plaintiff in error contends that [his case] comes within that clause in the fifth amendment to the constitution, which inhibits the taking of private property for public use, without just compensation. He insists that this amendment being in favour of the liberty of the citizen, ought to be so construed as to restrain the legislative power of a state, as well as that of the United States....

The question thus presented is, we think, of great importance, but not of much difficulty.

The constitution was ordained and established by the people of the United States for themselves, for their own government, and not for the government of the individual states. Each state established a constitution for itself, and, in that constitution, provided such limitations and restrictions on the powers of its particular government as its judgment dictated. The people of the United States framed such a government for the United States as they supposed best adapted to their situation, and best calculated to promote their interests. The powers they conferred on this government were to be exercised by itself; and the limitations on power, if expressed in general terms, are naturally, and, we think, necessarily applicable to the government created by the instrument. They are limitations of power granted in the instrument itself; not of distinct governments, framed by different persons and for different purposes.

If these propositions be correct, the fifth amendment must be understood as restraining the power of the general government, not as applicable to the states....

The counsel for the plaintiff in error insists that the constitution was intended to secure the people of the several states against the undue exercise of power by their respective state governments; as well as against that which might be attempted by their general government. In support of this argument he relies on the inhibitions contained in the tenth section of the first article.

We think, that section affords a strong if not a conclusive argument in support of the opinion already indicated by the court.

The preceding section contains restrictions which are obviously intended for the exclusive purpose of restraining the exercise of power by the departments of the general government. Some of them use language applicable only to congress: others are expressed in general terms. The third clause, for example, declares that "no bill of attainder or ex post facto law shall be passed." No language can be more general; yet the demonstration is complete that it applies solely to the government of the United States. . . . [T]he succeeding section, the avowed purpose of which is to restrain state legislation, contains in terms the very prohibition. It declares that "no state shall pass any bill of attainder or ex post facto law." This provision, then, of the ninth section, however comprehensive its language, contains no restriction on state legislation.

The ninth section having enumerated, in the nature of a bill of rights, the limitations intended to be imposed on the powers of the general government, the tenth proceeds to enumerate those which were to operate on the state legislatures. These restrictions are brought together in the same section, and are by express words applied to the states. . . . Perceiving that in a constitution framed by the people of the United States for the government of all, no limitation of the action of government on the people would apply to the state government, unless expressed in terms; the restrictions contained in the tenth section are in direct words so applied to the states. . . .

If the original constitution, in the ninth and tenth sections of the first article, draws this plain and marked line of discrimination between the limitations it imposes on the powers of the general government, and on those of the state; if in every inhibition intended to act on state power, words are employed which directly express that intent; some strong reason must be assigned for departing from this safe and judicious course in framing the amendments, before that departure can be assumed. . . .

Had the framers of these amendments intended them to be limitations on the powers of the state governments, they would have imitated the framers of the original constitution, and have expressed that intention. Had congress engaged in the extraordinary occupation of improving the constitutions of the several states by affording the people additional protection from the exercise of power by their own governments in matters which concerned themselves alone, they would have declared this purpose in plain and intelligible language.

But it is universally understood, it is a part of the history of the day, that the great revolution which established the constitution of the United States, was not effected without immense opposition. Serious fears were extensively entertained that those powers . . . deemed essential to union . . . might be exercised in a manner dangerous to liberty. In almost every convention by which the constitution was adopted, amendments to guard against the abuse of power were recommended. These amendments demanded security against the apprehended encroachments of the general government—not against those of the local governments.

In compliance with a sentiment thus generally expressed, to quiet fears thus extensively entertained, amendments were proposed by the required majority in congress, and adopted by the states. These amendments contain no expression indicating an intention to apply them to the state governments. This court cannot so apply them.

We are of opinion that the provision in the fifth amendment to the constitution, declaring that private property shall not be taken for public use without just compensation, is intended solely as a limitation on the exercise of power by the government of the United States, and is not applicable to the legislation of the states. . . .

Notes and Questions

1. Note that the text of most provisions of the Bill of Rights, including the Fifth Amendment at issue in *Barron*, are written in general terms in describing the rights at issue and thus are not as a textual matter necessarily limited to the actions of the federal government. What interpretive tools did the *Barron* Court employ to read in a non-textual limitation on the scope of the provisions of the Bill of Rights?

2. One provision of the Bill of Rights, the First Amendment, differs from most provisions of the Bill of Rights in that textually it does seem to be limited to the actions of the federal government. The First Amendment opens with the phrase "*Congress* shall make no law. . . ." Given that the First Amendment contains this textual limitation while the remaining provisions of the Bill of Rights do not, is there not an equally persuasive argument to that employed in *Barron* that the remaining provisions of the Bill of Rights *do* apply to the actions of state governments?

C. Enslavement

Two key provisions of the U.S. Constitution, while not using words such as "slavery," "slaves," or "enslavement"—in part because many of the Framers were embarrassed by the use of those terms—were inserted into the Constitution to protect the institution at the behest of Southern States.

First, Congress's power to restrict the importation of enslaved persons by the states was limited. Article I, Section 9, Clause 1 of the U.S. Constitution prohibited Congress from enacting any law prior to 1808 limiting the migration or importation of "such Persons as any of the States now existing shall think proper to admit," a euphemism for enslaved persons. Article V of the U.S. Constitution made this limitation on Congress's power an unamendable part of the U.S. Constitution prior to 1808.

Second, with full knowledge that some states would permit enslavement and others would be free states, the U.S. Constitution made clear that an enslaved person could not obtain freedom by escaping to a free state. Article IV, Section 2, Clause 3, commonly referred to as the Fugitive Slave Clause, obligated states to return persons "held to Service or Labour"—another euphemism for enslaved persons—to the states they came from.

Prior to the Civil War, opponents of enslavement attempted to chip away at the institution. At the state level, for example, Pennsylvania—a free state—made it a *crime* within the state to seize and attempt to return an enslaved person to her enslaver. A constitutional challenge was brought to the Pennsylvania law, and the U.S. Supreme Court, in *Prigg v. Pennsylvania*, 41 U.S. 539 (1842), declared the law unconstitutional, citing the Fugitive Slave Clause.

Two aspects of the Court's decision in *Prigg* are noteworthy, and relevant as you consider subsequent Court decisions and the interpretive tools used therein, especially the Court's post-Civil War cases interpreting the scope of the newly enacted Reconstruction Amendments. First, the *Prigg* Court, like the *Barron* Court, relied extensively on history in deciding how to interpret the scope of the constitutional provision at issue. Specifically, the Court noted that the Fugitive Slave Clause was considered vital to the Southern States, and that without its inclusion the Union would not have been formed. Second, the *Prigg* Court's historical finding that the Clause was designed to prevent free states from obstructing or abolishing the rights of enslavers led it to robustly interpret its language, concluding that it would do so in such a way that would "fully and completely effectuate the whole objects of it."

Congress also engaged in legislative activity designed to slow the growth of enslavement in the United States. First, effective January 1, 1808—the first day permitted by Article I, Section 9, Clause 1 of the U.S. Constitution—Congress banned the further importation of enslaved persons into the United States. Second, in 1820, Congress enacted the Missouri Compromise, which admitted Missouri as a state that permitted enslavement, Maine as a free state, and prohibited enslavement north and west of Missouri (the Louisiana Territory). In the case that follows, *Dred Scott*, the U.S. Supreme Court addressed the constitutionality of the Missouri Compromise.

Dred Scott v. Sandford

60 U.S. 393 (1857)

[Dred Scott was born an enslaved person. His enslaver eventually took him and his family to a free state (Illinois) and a free territory (Upper Louisiana) and eventually back to Missouri (a state that permitted enslavement). After his enslaver died, Scott sued the executor of his enslaver's estate in federal court, invoking the court's diversity jurisdiction (with Scott claiming to be a citizen of Missouri and the defendant a citizen of New York).

In the following excerpt, the Court first addresses the question whether Scott is a "citizen" as that term is used in the Constitution, and thus whether the federal courts have jurisdiction to adjudicate his suit pursuant to the Constitution's grant of diversity jurisdiction over "Controversies . . . between Citizens of different States." The Court then proceeds to address the question whether the Missouri Compromise—under which Scott arguably became free when his enslaver took him to the territory deemed free by that legislation—was a constitutional exercise of legislative power by Congress.]

Mr. Chief Justice TANEY delivered the opinion of the court. . . .

The question is simply this: Can a negro, whose ancestors were imported into this country, and sold as slaves, become a member of the political community formed and brought into existence by the Constitution of the United States, and as such become entitled to all the rights, and privileges, and immunities, guarantied by that instrument to the citizen? One of which rights is the privilege of suing in a court of the United States in the cases specified in the Constitution. . . .

The words "people of the United States" and "citizens" are synonymous terms, and mean the same thing. They both describe the political body who, according to our republican institutions, form the sovereignty, and who hold the power and conduct the Government through their representatives. They are what we familiarly call the "sovereign people," and every citizen is one of this people, and a constituent member of this sovereignty. The question before us is, whether the class of persons described in the plea in abatement compose a portion of this people, and are constituent members of this sovereignty? We think they are not, and that they are not included, and were not intended to be included, under the word "citizens" in the Constitution, and can therefore claim none of the rights and privileges which that instrument provides for and secures to citizens of the United States. On the contrary, they were at that time considered as a subordinate and inferior class of beings, who had been subjugated by the dominant race, and, whether emancipated or not, yet remained subject to their authority, and had no rights or privileges but such as those who held the power and the Government might choose to grant them. . . .

In discussing this question, we must not confound the rights of citizenship which a State may confer within its own limits, and the rights of citizenship as a member of the Union. It does not by any means follow, because he has all the rights and privileges of a citizen of a State, that he must be a citizen of the United States. . . .

It becomes necessary, therefore, to determine who were citizens of the several States when the Constitution was adopted. And in order to do this, we must recur to the Governments and institutions of the thirteen colonies, when they separated from Great Britain and formed new sovereignties, and took their places in the family of independent nations. We must inquire who, at that time, were recognized as the people or citizens of a State, whose rights and liberties had been outraged by the English Government; and who declared their independence, and assumed the powers of Government to defend their rights by force of arms.

In the opinion of the court, the legislation and histories of the times, and the language used in the Declaration of Independence, show, that neither the class of persons who had been imported as slaves, nor their descendants, whether they had become free or not, were then acknowledged as a part of the people, nor intended to be included in the general words used in that memorable instrument....

[The Court proceeds to survey laws in place in the colonies which drew distinctions based on race—such as laws prohibiting and punishing interracial marriage—without distinguishing between slaves and free African Americans.]

We refer to these historical facts for the purpose of showing the fixed opinions concerning that race, upon which the statesmen of that day spoke and acted. It is necessary to do this, in order to determine whether the general terms used in the Constitution of the United States, as to the rights of man and the rights of the people, was intended to include them, or to give to them or their posterity the benefit of any of its provisions.

The language of the Declaration of Independence is equally conclusive:

It begins by declaring that, "when in the course of human events it becomes necessary for one people to dissolve the political bands which have connected them with another, and to assume among the powers of the earth the separate and equal station to which the laws of nature and nature's God entitle them, a decent respect for the opinions of mankind requires that they should declare the causes which impel them to the separation."

It then proceeds to say: "We hold these truths to be self-evident: that all men are created equal; that they are endowed by their Creator with certain unalienable rights; that among them is life, liberty, and the pursuit of happiness; that to secure these rights, Governments are instituted, deriving their just powers from the consent of the governed."

The general words above quoted would seem to embrace the whole human family, and if they were used in a similar instrument at this day would be so understood. But it is too clear for dispute, that the enslaved African race were not intended to be included, and formed no part of the people who framed and adopted this declaration; for if the language, as understood in that day, would embrace them, the conduct of the distinguished men who framed the Declaration of Independence would have been utterly and flagrantly inconsistent with the principles they asserted; and instead of the sympathy of mankind, to which they so confidently appealed, they would have deserved and received universal rebuke and reprobation.

Yet the men who framed this declaration were great men—high in literary acquirements—high in their sense of honor, and incapable of asserting principles inconsistent with those on which they were acting. They perfectly understood the meaning of the language they used, and how it would be understood by others; and they knew that it would not in any part of the civilized world be supposed to embrace the negro race, which, by common consent, had been excluded from civilized Governments and the family of nations, and doomed to slavery. They spoke and acted according to the then established doctrines and principles, and in the ordinary language of the day, and no one misunderstood them. The unhappy black race were separated from the white by indelible marks, and laws long before established, and were never thought of or spoken of except as property, and when the claims of the owner or the profit of the trader were supposed to need protection. . . .

The brief preamble sets forth by whom it was formed, for what purposes, and for whose benefit and protection. It declares that it is formed by the *people* of the United States; that is to say, by those who were members of the different political communities in the several States; and its great object is declared to be to secure the blessings of liberty to themselves and their posterity. It speaks in general terms of the *people* of the United States, and of *citizens* of the several States, when it is providing for the exercise of the powers granted or the privileges secured to the citizen. It does not define what description of persons are intended to be included under these terms, or who shall be regarded as a citizen and one of the people. It uses them as terms so well understood, that no further description or definition was necessary.

But there are two clauses in the Constitution which point directly and specifically to the negro race as a separate class of persons, and show clearly that they were not regarded as a portion of the people or citizens of the Government then formed.

One of these clauses reserves to each of the thirteen States the right to import slaves until the year 1808, if it thinks proper. And the importation which it thus sanctions was unquestionably of persons of the race of which we are speaking, as the traffic in slaves in the United States had always been confined to them. And by the other provision the States pledge themselves to each other to maintain the right of property of the master, by delivering up to him any slave who may have escaped from his service, and be found within their respective territories. By the first above-mentioned clause, therefore, the right to purchase and hold this property is directly sanctioned and authorized for twenty years by the people who framed the Constitution. And by the second, they pledge themselves to maintain and uphold the right of the master in the manner specified, as long as the Government they then formed should endure. And these two provisions show, conclusively, that neither the description of persons therein referred to, nor their descendants, were embraced in any of the other provisions of the Constitution; for certainly these two clauses were not intended to confer on them or their posterity the blessings of liberty, or any of the personal rights so carefully provided for the citizen. . . .

In the case before us, we have already decided that the Circuit Court erred in deciding that it had jurisdiction upon the facts admitted by the pleadings. And it appears that, in the further progress of the case, it acted upon the erroneous principle it had decided on the pleadings, and gave judgment for the defendant, where, upon the facts admitted in the exception, it had no jurisdiction. . . .

It is true that the result either way, by dismissal or by a judgment for the defendant, makes very little, if any, difference in a pecuniary or personal point of view to either party. But the fact that the result would be very nearly the same to the parties in either form of judgment, would not justify this court in sanctioning an error in the judgment which is patent on the record, and which, if sanctioned, might be drawn into precedent, and lead to serious mischief and injustice in some future suit. . . ..

In considering this part of the controversy, two questions arise: 1. Was [Dred Scott], together with his family, free in Missouri by reason of the stay in the territory of the United States hereinbefore mentioned? And 2. If they were not, is Scott himself free by reason of his removal to Rock Island, in the State of Illinois, as stated in the above admissions?

We proceed to examine the first question.

The act of Congress, upon which the plaintiff relies, declares that slavery and involuntary servitude, except as a punishment for crime, shall be forever prohibited in all that part of the territory ceded by France, under the name of Louisiana, which lies north of thirty-six degrees thirty minutes north latitude, and not included within the limits of Missouri. And the difficulty which meets us at the threshold of this part of the inquiry is, whether Congress was authorized to pass this law under any of the powers granted to it by the Constitution; for if the authority is not given by that instrument, it is the duty of this court to declare it void and inoperative, and incapable of conferring freedom upon any one who is held as a slave under the laws of any one of the States. . . .

But the power of Congress over the person or property of a citizen can never be a mere discretionary power under our Constitution and form of Government. The powers of the Government and the rights and privileges of the citizen are regulated and plainly defined by the Constitution itself. And when the Territory becomes a part of the United States, the Federal Government enters into possession in the character impressed upon it by those who created it. It enters upon it with its powers over the citizen strictly defined, and limited by the Constitution, from which it derives its own existence, and by virtue of which alone it continues to exist and act as a Government and sovereignty. It has no power of any kind beyond it; and it cannot, when it enters a Territory of the United States, put off its character, and assume discretionary or despotic powers which the Constitution has denied to it. It cannot create for itself a new character separated from the citizens of the United States, and the duties it owes them under the provisions of the Constitution. The Territory being a part of the United States, the Government and the citizen both enter it under the authority of the Constitution, with their respective rights defined and marked out; and the Federal Government can exercise no power over his person or property, beyond what that instrument confers, nor lawfully deny any right which it has reserved.

A reference to a few of the provisions of the Constitution will illustrate this proposition.

For example, no one, we presume, will contend that Congress can make any law in a Territory respecting the establishment of religion, or the free exercise thereof, or abridging the freedom of speech or of the press, or the right of the people of the Territory peaceably to assemble, and to petition the Government for the redress of grievances.

Nor can Congress deny to the people the right to keep and bear arms, nor the right to trial by jury, nor compel any one to be a witness against himself in a criminal proceeding.

These powers, and others, in relation to rights of person, which it is not necessary here to enumerate, are, in express and positive terms, denied to the General Government; and the rights of private property have been guarded with equal care. Thus the rights of property are united with the rights of person, and placed on the same ground by the fifth amendment to the Constitution, which provides that no person shall be deprived of life, liberty, and property, without due process of law. And an act of Congress which deprives a citizen of the United States of his liberty or property, merely because he came himself or brought his property into a particular Territory of the United States, and who had committed no offence against the laws, could hardly be dignified with the name of due process of law.

So, too, it will hardly be contended that Congress could by law quarter a soldier in a house in a Territory without the consent of the owner, in time of peace; nor in time of war, but in a manner prescribed by law. Nor could they by law forfeit the property of a citizen in a Territory who was convicted of treason, for a longer period than the life of the person convicted; nor take private property for public use without just compensation.

The powers over person and property of which we speak are not only not granted to Congress, but are in express terms denied, and they are forbidden to exercise them. And this prohibition is not confined to the States, but the words are general, and extend to the whole territory over which the Constitution gives it power to legislate, including those portions of it remaining under Territorial Government, as well as that covered by States. It is a total absence of power everywhere within the dominion of the United States, and places the citizens of a Territory, so far as these rights are concerned, on the same footing with citizens of the States, and guards them as firmly and plainly against any inroads which the General Government might attempt, under the plea of implied or incidental powers. And if Congress itself cannot do this—if it is beyond the powers conferred on the Federal Government—it will be admitted, we presume, that it could not authorize a Territorial Government to exercise them. It could confer no power on any local Government, established by its authority, to violate the provisions of the Constitution.

It seems, however, to be supposed, that there is a difference between property in a slave and other property, and that different rules may be applied to it in expounding the Constitution of the United States. And the laws and usages of nations, and the writings of eminent jurists upon the relation of master and slave and their mutual rights and duties, and the powers which Governments may exercise over it, have been dwelt upon in the argument.

But in considering the question before us, it must be borne in mind that there is no law of nations standing between the people of the United States and their Government, and interfering with their relation to each other. The powers of the

Government, and the rights of the citizen under it, are positive and practical regulations plainly written down. The people of the United States have delegated to it certain enumerated powers, and forbidden it to exercise others. It has no power over the person or property of a citizen but what the citizens of the United States have granted. And no laws or usages of other nations, or reasoning of statesmen or jurists upon the relations of master and slave, can enlarge the powers of the Government, or take from the citizens the rights they have reserved. And if the Constitution recognizes the right of property of the master in a slave, and makes no distinction between that description of property and other property owned by a citizen, no tribunal, acting under the authority of the United States, whether it be legislative, executive, or judicial, has a right to draw such a distinction, or deny to it the benefit of the provisions and guarantees which have been provided for the protection of private property against the encroachments of the Government.

Now, as we have already said in an earlier part of this opinion, upon a different point, the right of property in a slave is distinctly and expressly affirmed in the Constitution. The right to traffic in it, like an ordinary article of merchandise and property, was guarantied to the citizens of the United States, in every State that might desire it, for twenty years. And the Government in express terms is pledged to protect it in all future time, if the slave escapes from his owner. This is done in plain words—too plain to be misunderstood. And no word can be found in the Constitution which gives Congress a greater power over slave property, or which entitles property of that kind to less protection than property of any other description. The only power conferred is the power coupled with the duty of guarding and protecting the owner in his rights.

Upon these considerations, it is the opinion of the court that the act of Congress which prohibited a citizen from holding and owning property of this kind in the territory of the United States north of the line therein mentioned, is not warranted by the Constitution, and is therefore void; and that neither Dred Scott himself, nor any of his family, were made free by being carried into this territory; even if they had been carried there by the owner, with the intention of becoming a permanent resident.

We have so far examined the case, as it stands under the Constitution of the United States, and the powers thereby delegated to the Federal Government.

But there is another point in the case which depends on State power and State law. And it is contended, on the part of the plaintiff, that he is made free by being taken to Rock Island, in the State of Illinois, independently of his residence in the territory of the United States; and being so made free, he was not again reduced to a state of slavery by being brought back to Missouri.

Our notice of this part of the case will be very brief; for the principle on which it depends was decided in this court, upon much consideration, in the case of Strader et al. v. Graham, reported in 10th Howard, 82. In that case, the slaves had been taken from Kentucky to Ohio, with the consent of the owner, and afterwards brought back to Kentucky. And this court held that their *status* or condition, as free or slave, depended upon the laws of Kentucky, when they were brought back into that State, and not of Ohio; and that this court had no jurisdiction to revise the judgment of a State court upon its own laws. This was the point directly before the court, and the decision that this court had not jurisdiction turned upon it, as will be seen by the report of the case.

So in this case. As Scott was a slave when taken into the State of Illinois by his owner, and was there held as such, and brought back in that character, his *status*, as free or slave, depended on the laws of Missouri, and not of Illinois. . . .

Mr. Justice CURTIS dissenting. . . .

[W]hat positive prohibition exists in the Constitution, which restrained Congress from enacting a law in 1820 to prohibit slavery north of thirty-six degrees thirty minutes north latitude?

The only one suggested is that clause in the fifth article of the amendments of the Constitution which declares that no person shall be deprived of his life, liberty, or property, without due process of law. I will now proceed to examine the question, whether this clause is entitled to the effect thus attributed to it. It is necessary, first, to have a clear view of the nature and incidents of that particular species of property which is now in question.

Slavery, being contrary to natural right, is created only by municipal law. This is not only plain in itself, and agreed by all writers on the subject, but is inferable from the Constitution, and has been explicitly declared by this court. The Constitution refers to slaves as "persons held to service in one State, under the laws thereof." Nothing can more clearly describe a *status* created by municipal law. In Prigg v. Pennsylvania, (10 Pet., 611,) this court said: "The state of slavery is deemed to be a mere municipal regulation, founded on and limited to the range of territorial laws." . . . . I am not acquainted with any case or writer questioning the correctness of this doctrine.

The *status* of slavery is not necessarily always attended with the same powers on the part of the master. The master is subject to the supreme power of the State, whose will controls his action towards his slave, and this control must be defined and regulated by the manicipal law. In one State, as at one period of the Roman law, it may put the life of the slave into the hand of the master; others, as those of the United States, which tolerate slavery, may treat the slave as a person, when the master takes his life; while in others, the law may recognize a right of the slave to be protected from cruel treatment. In other words, the *status* of slavery embraces every condition, from that in which the slave is known to the law simply as a chattel, with no civil rights, to that in which he is recognized as a person for all purposes, save the compulsory power of directing and receiving the fruits of his labor. Which of these conditions shall attend the *status* of slavery, must depend on the municipal law which creates and upholds it.

And not only must the *status* of slavery be created and measured by municipal law, but the rights, powers, and obligations, which grow out of that *status*, must be defined, protected, and enforced, by such laws. The liability of the master for the torts and crimes of his slave, and of third persons for assaulting or injuring or harboring or kidnapping him, the forms and modes of emancipation and sale, their subjection to the debts of the master, succession by death of the master, suits for freedom, the capacity of the slave to be party to a suit, or to be a witness, with such police regulations as have existed in all civilized States where slavery has been tolerated, are among the subjects upon which municipal legislation becomes necessary when slavery is introduced.

Is it conceivable that the Constitution has conferred the right on every citizen to become a resident on the territory of the United States with his slaves, and there to hold them as such, but has neither made nor provided for any municipal regulations which are essential to the existence of slavery?

Is it not more rational to conclude that they who framed and adopted the Constitution were aware that persons held to service under the laws of a State are property only to the extent and under the conditions fixed by those laws; that they must cease to be available as property, when their owners voluntarily place them permanently within another jurisdiction, where no municipal laws on the subject of slavery exist; and that, being aware of these principles, and having said nothing to interfere with or displace them, or to compel Congress to legislate in any particular manner on the subject, and having empowered Congress to make all needful rules and regulations respecting the territory of the United States, it was their intention to leave to the discretion of Congress what regulations, if any, should be made concerning slavery therein? Moreover, if the right exists, what are its limits, and what are its conditions? If citizens of the United States have the right to take their slaves to a Territory, and hold them there as slaves, without regard to the laws of the Territory, I suppose this right is not to be restricted to the citizens of slaveholding States. A citizen of a State which does not tolerate slavery can hardly be denied the power of doing the same thing. And what law of slavery does either take with him to the Territory? If it be said to be those laws respecting slavery which existed in the particular State from which each slave last came, what an anomaly is this? Where else can we find, under the law of any civilized country, the power to introduce and permanently continue diverse systems of foreign municipal law, for holding persons in slavery? I say, not merely to introduce, but permanently to continue, these anomalies. For the offspring of the female must be governed by the foreign municipal laws to which the mother was subject; and when any slave is sold or passes by succession on the death of the owner, there must pass with him, by a species of subrogation, and as a kind of unknown *jus in re*, the foreign municipal laws which constituted, regulated, and preserved, the *status* of the slave before his exportation. Whatever theoretical importance may be now supposed to belong to the maintenance of such a right, I feel a perfect conviction that it would, if ever tried, prove to be as impracticable in fact, as it is, in my judgment, monstrous in theory.

I consider the assumption which lies at the basis of this theory to be unsound; not in its just sense, and when properly understood, but in the sense which has been attached to it. That assumption is, that the territory ceded by France was acquired for the equal benefit of all the citizens of the United States. I agree to the position. But it was acquired for their benefit in their collective, not their individual, capacities. It was acquired for their benefit, as an organized political society, subsisting as "the people of the United States," under the Constitution of the United States; to be administered justly and impartially, and as nearly as possible for the equal benefit of every individual citizen, according to the best judgment and discretion of the Congress; to whose power, as the Legislature of the nation which acquired it, the people of the United States have committed its administration. Whatever individual claims may be founded on local circumstances, or sectional differences of condition, cannot, in my opinion, be recognized in this court, without arrogating to the judicial branch of the Government powers not committed to it; and which, with all the unaffected respect I feel for it, when acting in its proper sphere, I do not think it fitted to wield.

Nor, in my judgment, will the position, that a prohibition to bring slaves into a Territory deprives any one of his property without due process of law, bear examination. . . .

It was certainly understood by the Convention which framed the Constitution, and has been so understood ever since, that, under the power to regulate commerce, Congress could prohibit the importation of slaves; and the exercise of the power was restrained till 1808. A citizen of the United States owns slaves in Cuba, and brings them to the United States, where they are set free by the legislation of Congress. Does this legislation deprive him of his property without due process of law? If so, what becomes of the laws prohibiting the slave trade? If not, how can a similar regulation respecting a Territory violate the fifth amendment of the Constitution? . . . .

[The concurring opinions of Justices Wayne, Nelson, Grier, Daniel, Campbell, and Catron, and the dissenting opinion of Justice McLean, are omitted.]

Notes and Questions

1. Could Dred Scott have avoided the jurisdictional problem by invoking federal question jurisdiction, which, unlike diversity jurisdiction, does not depend upon the citizenship of the parties? Even assuming that Scott could frame his suit as a "federal question," Congress did not confer general federal question jurisdiction on the lower federal courts until 1875, well after Mr. Scott's suit was brought. *See Merrell Dow Pharmaceuticals Inc. v. Thompson*, 478 U.S. 804, 807 & n.4 (1986).

2. What interpretative tools does the *Dred Scott* Court employ to determine that neither enslaved persons *nor their descendants* are "citizens"? Are they the same tools used by the Court in *Barron*?

3. Given the Court's conclusion that it lacked jurisdiction over the dispute, was it appropriate for the Court to proceed to consider the substantive questions at issue in

the case, including the constitutionality of the Missouri Compromise? *See* Michael Abramowicz & Maxwell Stearns, *Defining Dicta*, 57 Stan. L. Rev. 953, 980 & n. 83 (2005) (characterizing the merits holding in *Dred Scott* as dictum). *Cf. Steel Co. v. Citizens for a Better Environment*, 523 U.S. 83, 93–102 (1998) (rejecting concept of hypothetical jurisdiction for purpose of reaching merits).

4. The *Dred Scott* Court proceeds to reference a series of constitutional amendments that seem irrelevant to the controversy at hand, including the various provisions of the First through Fifth Amendments, before ultimately relying upon the Fifth Amendment's Due Process Clause. In what way is the law at issue a violation of Due Process? How does the Court's invocation of Due Process in this way differ from the irrelevant constitutional amendments it mentions prior to the Due Process Clause? What similarities are there between the reasoning process it employs and that employed by Justice Chase in *Calder*? Is the *Dred Scott* majority in effect treating the law at issue here as "a law that takes property from A and gives it to B," and if so, who are "A" and "B"?

5. Why does the Court conclude that the enslaver's act of taking Dred Scott and his family to Illinois, a free state, did not change the status of the relationship between enslaved persons and their enslaver? Is the Court's holding that the Constitution requires that Missouri rather than Illinois law be applied to determine the status? What provision of the U.S. Constitution provides a basis for such a holding?

6. Conservative politicians often describe *Dred Scott* as the worst decision issued by the U.S. Supreme Court. Why do you suppose they cite the case for that reason? Is it because the Court unnecessarily reached the substantive questions in a case for which the Court lacked jurisdiction, because it upheld enslavement, or for some other reason? *See, e.g.*, Justin Buckley Dyer, *The Substance of* Dred Scott *and* Roe v. Wade, 16 Geo. J.L. Pub Pol'y 421 (2018) (collecting sources explaining invocation of *Dred Scott* by conservatives as a "code word" for *Roe v. Wade* and the debate over abortion rights).

7. In subsequent chapters, you will see the Court invoking the Due Process Clauses to support a fundamental right to liberty of contract (*Lochner v. New York*) and to procure an abortion (*Roe v. Wade*). Consider the following effort to link these subsequent precedents to *Dred Scott*:

> Professor David Currie wrote that *Dred Scott* "was at least very possibly the first application of substantive due process in the Supreme Court, the original precedent for *Lochner v. New York* and *Roe v. Wade*. *Lochner* employed substantive due process to strike down a state law limiting the hours of work by bakery employees. *Roe* used substantive due process to create a constitutional right to abortion. *Lochner* and *Roe* have, therefore, a very ugly common ancestor. But once it is conceded that a judge may give the due process clause substantive content, *Dred Scott, Lochner*, and *Roe* are equally valid examples of constitutional law. You may or may not like the judge's politics

> or his morality, but you have conceded, so far as the Constitution is concerned, the legitimacy of his imposing that politics and morality upon you.

Robert H. Bork, The Tempting of America 32 (Simon & Schuster 1990). Do you agree that the Court in *Dred Scott* invokes the Due Process Clause substantively? If so, is it in fact indistinguishable from future cases such as *Lochner* and *Roe*? Reconsider this quotation and this question when you encounter those two decisions.

Chapter 2

Reconstruction and the Gilded Age (1865–1896)

In 1863—in the midst of the Civil War—President Abraham Lincoln issued the Emancipation Proclamation, an executive order grounded in the President's War Powers, declaring enslaved persons free in the states then rebelling against the Union.

As the Civil War drew to a close, Congress voted in January 1865 to send a new constitutional amendment to the states—which would become the Thirteenth Amendment—to outlaw enslavement nationwide. The Thirteenth Amendment was ratified by the requisite number of states in December 1865. In full, it provides as follows:

> **Section 1.** Neither slavery nor involuntary servitude, except as a punishment for crime whereof the party shall have been duly convicted, shall exist within the United States, or any place subject to their jurisdiction.
>
> **Section 2.** Congress shall have power to enforce this article by appropriate legislation.

Four months later, in April 1866, Congress enacted the Civil Rights Act of 1866. Section 1 of the Act declared all persons born in the United States (excepting those "subject to any foreign power" and "Indians not taxed") to be citizens of the United States. Section 1 went on to provide that citizens of every race or color, without regard to any previous condition of enslavement or involuntary servitude (except as a punishment for crime) shall have the same right in every state and territory as a white citizen to make and enforce contracts; to sue, be sued, and give evidence; to inherit, purchase, lease, sell, hold, and convey real and personal property; and to be subjected to like punishment and penalties for violations of law. Section 2 provided a criminal penalty for depriving people of the rights set forth in Section 1.

President Johnson vetoed the Civil Rights Act of 1866, but Congress overrode his veto. Nonetheless, there were doubts about whether the Thirteenth Amendment provided Congress with the constitutional authority to enact the Act. To assuage those doubts, two months later, in June 1866, Congress voted to send what would become the Fourteenth Amendment to the states. The Fourteenth Amendment was ratified by the requisite number of states in July 1868. The first and fifth sections of the Fourteenth Amendment provide as follows:

> **Section 1.** All persons born or naturalized in the United States, and subject to the jurisdiction thereof, are citizens of the United States and of the State

> wherein they reside. No State shall make or enforce any law which shall abridge the privileges or immunities of citizens of the United States; nor shall any State deprive any person of life, liberty, or property, without due process of law; nor deny to any person within its jurisdiction the equal protection of the laws.
>
> . . . .
>
> **Section 5.** The Congress shall have the power to enforce, by appropriate legislation, the provisions of this article.

In specific terms, the Fourteenth Amendment did not provide for a right of all persons, regardless of race, to vote. Indeed, Section 2 of the Fourteenth Amendment *arguably* left states free to disenfranchise African Americans, imposing a penalty in the form of reduced representation in Congress for states that refused to extend the franchise to all regardless of race, rather than prohibiting such discrimination outright:

> **Section 2.** Representatives shall be apportioned among the several states according to their respective numbers, counting the whole number of persons in each state, excluding Indians not taxed. But when the right to vote at any election for the choice of electors for President and Vice President of the United States, Representatives in Congress, the executive and judicial officers of a state, or the members of the legislature thereof, is denied to any of the male inhabitants of such state, being twenty-one years of age, and citizens of the United States, or in any way abridged, except for participation in rebellion, or other crime, the basis of representation therein shall be reduced in the proportion which the number of such male citizens shall bear to the whole number of male citizens twenty-one years of age in such state.

However, any doubts about the right of the newly freed African Americans to vote was laid to rest by what would become the Fifteenth Amendment. Sent to the states by Congress in February 1869 and ratified in February 1870, it provides as follows:

> **Section 1.** The right of citizens of the United States to vote shall not be denied or abridged by the United States or by any State on account of race, color, or previous condition of servitude.
>
> **Section 2.** The Congress shall have power to enforce this article by appropriate legislation.

During this period and in the years immediately thereafter, Congress enacted a number of pieces of legislation designed to protect the rights of the newly freed slaves.

Between 1870 and 1871, Congress enacted the Enforcement Act of 1870 (16 Stat. 140), the Force Act of 1871 (16 Stat. 433), and the Civil Rights Act of 1871 (17 Stat. 13) (sometimes referred to as the Ku Klux Klan Act of 1871 or the Enforcement Act of 1871). The Enforcement Act of 1870 made it a crime for public officers as well as private persons to obstruct the exercise of the right to vote, while the Force Act of 1871 provided for federal supervision of elections under certain circumstances. Section 1 of the Civil Rights Act of 1871 provided that those deprived "of any rights, privileges, or immunities secured by the Constitution of the United States" could bring a private civil cause of action against any person acting under color of law who deprived them of such rights, while Section 2 provided criminal sanctions and a private civil cause of action for, *inter alia*, private conspiracies to deprive people of their right to "equal protection of the laws" or to prevent them from voting.

The last major piece of civil rights legislation during this era was the Civil Rights Act of 1875. Section 1 of the Act provided in relevant part as follows:

> [A]ll persons within the jurisdiction of the United States shall be entitled to the full and equal enjoyment of the accommodations, advantages, facilities, and privileges of inns, public conveyances on land or water, theaters, and other places of public amusement; subject only to the conditions and limitations established by law, and applicable alike to citizens of every race and color, regardless of any previous condition of servitude.

Section 2 of the Act both provided a civil cause of action for violations of Section 1, and made violations of Section 1 a criminal offense. In addition, Section 4 of the act made it a criminal offense for "any officer or other person charged with any duty in the selection or summoning of jurors" to disqualify a person as a grand or petit juror due to race, color, or previous condition of servitude.

The cases that follow provide a snapshot of the Supreme Court's interpretation of the scope of the Reconstruction Amendments from their inception through the end of the Nineteenth Century. Indeed, during this era, virtually every key question regarding the Reconstruction Amendments was raised and—initially, but not necessarily definitively—answered. Among these key questions are:

- Do the Amendments only encompass conduct by government officials, or do they reach private conduct as well?
- Do the Amendments make the Bill of Rights applicable to the states?
- Do the Amendments provide a vehicle for protecting other, unenumerated rights?
- Do the Amendments provide protection for anyone other than African Americans? Do they, for example, apply to "reverse discrimination" against whites? Do they encompass discrimination on the basis of sex?
- What does "equal" mean as used in the Fourteenth Amendment?
- Do the Amendments encompass only intentional acts of discrimination, or do they also encompass actions that have discriminatory effects against a particular group?
- What is the substantive reach of the self-executing portions of the Amendments, and to what extent do their "enforcement" provisions give Congress the authority to legislate beyond what is self-executing?

A. The Court's First Look at the Reconstruction Amendments

The Court's first opportunity to interpret the scope of the Reconstruction Amendments came in 1873, when the Court decided a series of cases entitled *The Slaughter-House Cases*. The issue in these cases seems on its face far removed from the concerns that motivated the enactment of the Reconstruction Amendments: they involved a challenge to a state law granting a single private corporation a monopoly over livestock landing and slaughterhouse operations in the city. However, relying on the text of the newly enacted Reconstruction Amendments, the challengers had clever arguments for why the law constituted an "involuntary servitude" in violation of the Thirteenth Amendment, and why it also violated the Equal Protection, Due Process, and Privileges or Immunities Clauses of the Fourteenth Amendment. In the course of dispensing with the plaintiffs' constitutional challenges, the Court made significant holdings regarding the scope of the Reconstruction Amendments that have had a lasting impact on their interpretation to this day.

The Slaughter-House Cases

83 U.S. 36 (1873)

[Challenge brought by association of butchers against a law that gave a private corporation a monopoly over livestock landing and slaughterhouse operations in New Orleans, requiring that the butchers land and slaughter animals at that location and nowhere else.]

Mr. Justice MILLER . . . delivered the opinion of the court. . . .

The plaintiffs in error . . . allege that the statute is a violation of the Constitution of the United States in these several particulars:

> That it creates an involuntary servitude forbidden by the thirteenth article of amendment;
>
> That it abridges the privileges and immunities of citizens of the United States;
>
> That it denies to the plaintiffs the equal protection of the laws; and,
>
> That it deprives them of their property without due process of law; contrary to the provisions of the first section of the fourteenth article of amendment.

This court is thus called upon for the first time to give construction to these articles. . . .

The most cursory glance at these articles discloses a unity of purpose, when taken in connection with the history of the times, which cannot fail to have an important bearing on any question of doubt concerning their true meaning. . . .

The institution of African slavery, as it existed in about half the States of the Union, and the contests pervading the public mind for many years, between those who desired its curtailment and ultimate extinction and those who desired additional safeguards for its security and perpetuation, culminated in the effort, on the part of most of the States in which slavery existed, to separate from the Federal government, and to resist its authority. This constituted the war of the rebellion, and whatever auxiliary causes may have contributed to bring about this war, undoubtedly the overshadowing and efficient cause was African slavery.

In that struggle slavery, as a legalized social relation, perished. . . . The proclamation of President Lincoln expressed an accomplished fact as to a large portion of the insurrectionary districts, when he declared slavery abolished in them all. But the war being over, those who had succeeded in re-establishing the authority of the Federal government were not content to permit this great act of emancipation to rest on the actual results of the contest or the proclamation of the Executive, both of which might have been questioned in after times, and they determined to place this main and most valuable result in the Constitution of the restored Union as one of its fundamental articles. Hence the thirteenth article of amendment of that instrument. Its two short sections seem hardly to admit of construction, so vigorous is their expression and so appropriate to the purpose we have indicated. . . .

To withdraw the mind from the contemplation of this grand yet simple declaration of the personal freedom of all the human race within the jurisdiction of this government—a declaration designed to establish the freedom of four millions of slaves—and with a microscopic search endeavor to find in it a reference to servitudes, which may have been attached to property in certain localities, requires an effort, to say the least of it.

That a personal servitude was meant is proved by the use of the word "involuntary," which can only apply to human beings. The exception of servitude as a punishment for crime gives an idea of the class of servitude that is meant. The word servitude is of larger meaning than slavery, as the latter is popularly understood in this country, and the obvious purpose was to forbid all shades and conditions of African slavery. It was very well understood that in the form of apprenticeship for long terms, as it had been practiced in the West India Islands, on the abolition of slavery by the English government, or by reducing the slaves to the condition of serfs attached to the plantation, the purpose of the article might have been evaded, if only the word slavery had been used. . . .

The process of restoring to their proper relations with the Federal government and with the other States those which had sided with the rebellion, undertaken under the proclamation of President Johnson in 1865, and before the assembling of Congress, developed the fact that, notwithstanding the formal recognition by those States of the abolition of slavery, the condition of the slave race would, without further protection of the Federal government, be almost as bad as it was before. Among the first acts of legislation adopted by several of the States in the legislative bodies which claimed to be in their normal relations with the Federal government, were laws which imposed upon the colored race onerous disabilities and burdens, and curtailed their rights in the pursuit of life, liberty, and property to such an extent that their freedom was of little value, while they had lost the protection which they had received from their former owners from motives both of interest and humanity.

They were in some States forbidden to appear in the towns in any other character than menial servants. They were required to reside on and cultivate the soil without the right to purchase or own it. They were excluded from many occupations of gain, and were not permitted to give testimony in the courts in any case where a white man was a party. It was said that their lives were at the mercy of bad men, either because the laws for their protection were insufficient or were not enforced.

These circumstances, whatever of falsehood or misconception may have been mingled with their presentation, forced upon the statesmen who had conducted the Federal government in safety through the crisis of the rebellion, and who supposed that by the thirteenth article of amendment they had secured the result of their labors, the conviction that something more was necessary in the way of constitutional protection to the unfortunate race who had suffered so much. They accordingly passed through Congress the proposition for the fourteenth amendment, and they declined to treat as restored to their full participation in the government of the Union the States which had been in insurrection, until they ratified that article by a formal vote of their legislative bodies.

Before we proceed to examine more critically the provisions of this amendment, on which the plaintiffs in error rely, let us complete and dismiss the history of the recent amendments, as that history relates to the general purpose which pervades them all. A few years' experience satisfied the thoughtful men who had been the authors of the other two amendments that, notwithstanding the restraints of those articles on the States, and the laws passed under the additional powers granted to Congress, these were inadequate for the protection of life, liberty, and property, without which freedom to the slave was no boon. They were in all those States denied the right of suffrage. The laws were administered by the white man alone. It was urged that a race of men distinctively marked as was the negro, living in the midst of another and dominant race, could never be fully secured in their person and their property without the right of suffrage.

Hence the fifteenth amendment, which declares that "the right of a citizen of the United States to vote shall not be denied or abridged by any State on account of race, color, or previous condition of servitude." The negro having, by the fourteenth amendment, been declared to be a citizen of the United States, is thus made a voter in every State of the Union.

We repeat, then, in the light of this recapitulation of events, almost too recent to be called history, but which are familiar to us all; and on the most casual examination of the language of these amendments, no one can fail to be impressed with the one pervading purpose found in them all, lying at the foundation of each, and without which none of them would have been even suggested; we mean the freedom of the slave race, the security and firm establishment of that freedom, and the protection of the newly-made freeman and citizen from the oppressions of those who had formerly exercised unlimited dominion over him. It is true that only the fifteenth amendment, in terms, mentions the negro by speaking of his color and his slavery. But it is just as true that each of the other articles was addressed to the grievances of that race, and designed to remedy them as the fifteenth.

We do not say that no one else but the negro can share in this protection. Both the language and spirit of these articles are to have their fair and just weight in any question of construction. Undoubtedly while negro slavery alone was in the mind of the Congress which proposed the thirteenth article, it forbids any other kind of slavery, now or hereafter. If Mexican peonage or the Chinese coolie labor system shall develop slavery of the Mexican or Chinese race within our territory, this amendment may safely be trusted to make it void. And so if other rights are assailed by the States which properly and necessarily fall within the protection of these articles, that protection will apply, though the party interested may not be of African descent. But what we do say, and what we wish to be understood is, that in any fair and just construction of any section or phrase of these amendments, it is necessary to look to the purpose which we have said was the pervading spirit of them all, the evil which they were designed to remedy, and the process of continued addition to the Constitution, until that purpose was supposed to be accomplished, as far as constitutional law can accomplish it.

The first section of the fourteenth article, to which our attention is more specially invited, opens with a definition of citizenship—not only citizenship of the United States, but citizenship of the States. No such definition was previously found in the Constitution, nor had any attempt been made to define it by act of Congress. . . . But it had been held by this court, in the celebrated Dred Scott case, only a few years before the outbreak of the civil war, that a man of African descent, whether a slave or not, was not and could not be a citizen of a State or of the United States. This decision, while it met the condemnation of some of the ablest statesmen and constitutional lawyers of the country, had never been overruled; and if it was to be accepted as a constitutional limitation of the right of citizenship, then all the negro race who had recently been made freemen, were still, not only not citizens, but were incapable of becoming so by anything short of an amendment to the Constitution.

To remove this difficulty primarily, and to establish a clear and comprehensive definition of citizenship which should declare what should constitute citizenship of the United States, and also citizenship of a State, the first clause of the first section was framed.

> "All persons born or naturalized in the United States, and subject to the jurisdiction thereof, are citizens of the United States and of the State wherein they reside."

The first observation we have to make on this clause is, that it puts at rest both the questions which we stated to have been the subject of differences of opinion. It declares that persons may be citizens of the United States without regard to their citizenship of a particular State, and it overturns the Dred Scott decision by making *all persons* born within the United States and subject to its jurisdiction citizens of the United States. That its main purpose was to establish the citizenship of the negro can admit of no doubt. The phrase, "subject to its jurisdiction" was intended to exclude from its operation children of ministers, consuls, and citizens or subjects of foreign States born within the United States.

The next observation is more important in view of the arguments of counsel in the present case. It is, that the distinction between citizenship of the United States and citizenship of a State is clearly recognized and established. Not only may a man be a citizen of the United States without being a citizen of a State, but an important element is necessary to convert the former into the latter. He must reside within the State to make him a citizen of it, but it is only necessary that he should be born or naturalized in the United States to be a citizen of the Union. . . .

We think this distinction and its explicit recognition in this amendment of great weight in this argument, because the next paragraph of this same section, which is the one mainly relied on by the plaintiffs in error, speaks only of privileges and immunities of citizens of the United States, and does not speak of those of citizens of the several States. . . .

The language is, "No State shall make or enforce any law which shall abridge the privileges or immunities of citizens of *the United States*." It is a little remarkable, if this clause was intended as a protection to the citizen of a State against the legislative power of his own State, that the word citizen of the State should be left out when it is so carefully used, and used in contradistinction to citizens of the United States, in the very sentence which precedes it. . . .

Of the privileges and immunities of the citizen of the United States, and of the privileges and immunities of the citizen of the State, and what they respectively are, we will presently consider; but we wish to state here that it is only the former which are placed by this clause under the protection of the Federal Constitution, and that the latter, whatever they may be, are not intended to have any additional protection by this paragraph of the amendment.

If, then, there is a difference between the privileges and immunities belonging to a citizen of the United States as such, and those belonging to the citizen of the State as such the latter must rest for their security and protection where they have heretofore rested; for they are not embraced by this paragraph of the amendment.

The first occurrence of the words "privileges and immunities" in our constitutional history, is to be found in the fourth of the articles of the old Confederation. . . .

In the Constitution of the United States, which superseded the Articles of Confederation, the corresponding provision is found in section two of the fourth article, in the following words: "The citizens of each State shall be entitled to all the privileges and immunities of citizens of the several States." . . . .

Fortunately we are not without judicial construction of this clause of the Constitution. The first and the leading case on the subject is that of *Corfield* v. *Coryell*, decided by Mr. Justice Washington in the Circuit Court for the District of Pennsylvania in 1823.

"The inquiry," he says, "is, what are the privileges and immunities of citizens of the several States? We feel no hesitation in confining these expressions to those privileges and immunities which are *fundamental;* which belong of right to the citizens of all free governments, and which have at all times been enjoyed by citizens of the several States which compose this Union, from the time of their becoming free, independent, and sovereign. What these fundamental principles are, it would be more tedious than difficult to enumerate. They may all, however, be comprehended under the following general heads: protection by the government, with the right to acquire and possess property of every kind, and to pursue and obtain happiness and safety, subject, nevertheless, to such restraints as the government may prescribe for the general good of the whole."

This definition of the privileges and immunities of citizens of the States is adopted in the main by this court in the recent case of *Ward* v. *Maryland* . . . . The description, when taken to include others not named, but which are of the same general character, embraces nearly every civil right for the establishment and protection of which organized government is instituted. They are, in the language of Judge Washington, those rights which the fundamental. Throughout his opinion, they are spoken of as rights belonging to the individual as a citizen of a State. They are so spoken of in the constitutional provision which he was construing. And they have always been held to be the class of rights which the State governments were created to establish and secure. . . .

The constitutional provision there alluded to did not create those rights, which it called privileges and immunities of citizens of the States. It threw around them in that clause no security for the citizen of the State in which they were claimed or exercised. Nor did it profess to control the power of the State governments over the rights of its own citizens.

Its sole purpose was to declare to the several States, that whatever those rights, as you grant or establish them to your own citizens, or as you limit or qualify, or impose restrictions on their exercise, the same, neither more nor less, shall be the measure of the rights of citizens of other States within your jurisdiction.

It would be the vainest show of learning to attempt to prove by citations of authority, that up to the adoption of the recent amendments, no claim or pretence was set up that those rights depended on the Federal government for their existence or protection, beyond the very few express limitations which the Federal Constitution imposed upon the States—such, for instance, as the prohibition against ex post facto laws, bills of attainder, and laws impairing the obligation of contracts. But with the exception of these and a few other restrictions, the entire domain of the privileges and immunities of citizens of the States, as above defined, lay within the constitutional and legislative power of the States, and without that of the Federal government. Was it the purpose of the fourteenth amendment, by the simple declaration that no State should make or enforce any law which shall abridge the privileges and immunities of *citizens of the United States*, to transfer the security and protection of all the civil rights which we have mentioned, from the States to the Federal government? And where it is declared that Congress shall have the power to enforce that article, was it intended to bring within the power of Congress the entire domain of civil rights heretofore belonging exclusively to the States?

All this and more must follow, if the proposition of the plaintiffs in error be sound.... [W]hen, as in the case before us, these consequences are so serious, so far-reaching and pervading, so great a departure from the structure and spirit of our institutions; when the effect is to fetter and degrade the State governments by subjecting them to the control of Congress, in the exercise of powers heretofore universally conceded to them of the most ordinary and fundamental character; when in fact it radically changes the whole theory of the relations of the State and Federal governments to each other and of both these governments to the people; the argument has a force that is irresistible, in the absence of language which expresses such a purpose too clearly to admit of doubt.

We are convinced that no such results were intended by the Congress which proposed these amendments, nor by the legislatures of the States which ratified them.

Having shown that the privileges and immunities relied on in the argument are those which belong to citizens of the States as such, and that they are left to the State governments for security and protection, and not by this article placed under the special care of the Federal government, we may hold ourselves excused from defining the privileges and immunities of citizens of the United States which no State can abridge, until some case involving those privileges may make it necessary to do so.

But lest it should be said that no such privileges and immunities are to be found if those we have been considering are excluded, we venture to suggest some which own their existence to the Federal government, its National character, its Constitution, or its laws.

One of these is ... said to be the right of the citizen of this great country, protected by implied guarantees of its Constitution, "to come to the seat of government to assert any claim he may have upon that government, to transact any business he may have with it, to seek its protection, to share its offices, to engage in administering its functions. He has the right of free access to its seaports, through which all operations of foreign commerce are conducted, to the subtreasuries, land offices, and courts of justice in the several States." ....

Another privilege of a citizen of the United States is to demand the care and protection of the Federal government over his life, liberty, and property when on the high seas or within the jurisdiction of a foreign government.... The right to use the navigable waters of the United States, however they may penetrate the territory of the several States, all rights secured to our citizens by treaties with foreign nations, are dependent upon citizenship of the United States, and not citizenship of a State.

One of these privileges is conferred by the very article under consideration. It is that a citizen of the United States can, of his own volition, become a citizen of any State of the Union by a *bonâ fide* residence therein, with the same rights as other citizens of that State. To these may be added the rights secured by the thirteenth and fifteenth articles of amendment, and by the other clause of the fourteenth, next to be considered.

But it is useless to pursue this branch of the inquiry, since we are of opinion that the rights claimed by these plaintiffs in error, if they have any existence, are not privileges and immunities of citizens of the United States within the meaning of the clause of the fourteenth amendment under consideration. . . .

The argument has not been much pressed in these cases that the defendant's charter deprives the plaintiffs of their property without due process of law, or that it denies to them the equal protection of the law. The first of these paragraphs has been in the Constitution since the adoption of the fifth amendment, as a restraint upon the Federal power. It is also to be found in some form of expression in the constitutions of nearly all the States, as a restraint upon the power of the States. This law then, has practically been the same as it now is during the existence of the government, except so far as the present amendment may place the restraining power over the States in this matter in the hands of the Federal government.

We are not without judicial interpretation, therefore, both State and National, of the meaning of this clause. And it is sufficient to say that under no construction of that provision that we have ever seen, or any that we deem admissible, can the restraint imposed by the State of Louisiana upon the exercise of their trade by the butchers of New Orleans be held to be a deprivation of property within the meaning of that provision.

> "Nor shall any State deny to any person within its jurisdiction the equal protection of the laws."

In the light of the history of these amendments, and the pervading purpose of them, which we have already discussed, it is not difficult to give a meaning to this clause. The existence of laws in the States where the newly emancipated negroes resided, which discriminated with gross injustice and hardship against them as a class, was the evil to be remedied by this clause, and by it such laws are forbidden.

If, however, the States did not conform their laws to its requirements, then by the fifth section of the article of amendment Congress was authorized to enforce it by suitable legislation. We doubt very much whether any action of a State not directed by way of discrimination against the negroes as a class, or on account of their race, will ever be held to come within the purview of this provision. It is so clearly a provision for that race and that emergency, that a strong case would be necessary for its application to any other. But as it is a State that is to be dealt with, and not alone the validity of its laws, we may safely leave that matter until Congress shall have exercised its power, or some case of State oppression, by denial of equal justice in its courts, shall have claimed a decision at our hands. . . .

Mr. Justice FIELD, dissenting. . . .

The [Fourteenth] amendment was adopted to obviate objections which had been raised and pressed with great force to the validity of the Civil Rights Act, and to place the common rights of American citizens under the protection of the National government. . . .

The amendment does not attempt to confer any new privileges or immunities upon citizens, or to enumerate or define those already existing. It assumes that there are such privileges and immunities which belong of right to citizens as such, and ordains that they shall not be abridged by State legislation. If this inhibition has no reference to privileges and immunities of this character, but only refers, as held by the majority of the court in their opinion, to such privileges and immunities as were before its adoption specially designated in the Constitution or necessarily implied as belonging to citizens of the United States, it was a vain and idle enactment, which accomplished nothing, and most unnecessarily excited Congress and the people on its passage. . . .

What, then, are the privileges and immunities which are secured against abridgment by State legislation?

In the first section of the Civil Rights Act Congress has given its interpretation to these terms, or at least has stated some of the rights which, in its judgment, these terms include; it has there declared that they include the right "to make and enforce contracts, to sue, be parties and give evidence, to inherit, purchase, lease, sell, hold, and convey real and personal property, and to full and equal benefit of all laws and proceedings for the security of person and property." That act, it is true, was passed before the fourteenth amendment, but the amendment was adopted, as I have already said, to obviate objections to the act, or, speaking more accurately, I should say, to obviate objections to legislation of a similar character, extending the protection of the National government over the common rights of all citizens of the United States. Accordingly, after its ratification, Congress re-enacted the act under the belief that whatever doubts may have previously existed of its validity, they were removed by the amendment.

The terms, privileges and immunities, are not new in the amendment; they were in the Constitution before the amendment was adopted. They are found in the second section of the fourth article, which declares that "the citizens of each State shall be entitled to all privileges and immunities of citizens in the several States," and they have been the subject of frequent consideration in judicial decisions. In *Corfield* v. *Coryell*, Mr. Justice Washington said he had "no hesitation in confining these expressions to those privileges and immunities which were, in their nature, fundamental; which belong of right to citizens of all free governments, and which have at all times been enjoyed by the citizens of the several States which compose the Union, from the time of their becoming free, independent, and sovereign;" and, in considering what those fundamental privileges were, he said that perhaps it would be more tedious than difficult to enumerate them, but that they might be "all comprehended under the following general heads: protection by the government; the enjoyment of life and liberty, with the right to acquire and possess property of every kind, and to pursue and obtain happiness and safety, subject, nevertheless, to such restraints as the government may justly prescribe for the general good of the whole." This appears to me to be a sound construction of the clause in question. The privileges and immunities designated are those *which of right belong to the citizens of all free governments.* Clearly among these must be placed the right to pursue a lawful employment in a lawful manner, without other restraint than such as equally affects all persons. In the discussions in Congress upon the passage of the Civil Rights Act repeated reference was made to this language of Mr. Justice Washington. It was cited by Senator Trumbull with the observation that it enumerated the very rights belonging to a citizen of the United States set forth in the first section of the act, and with the statement that all persons born in the United States, being declared by the act citizens of the United States, would thenceforth be entitled to the rights of citizens, and that these were the great fundamental rights set forth in the act; and that they were set forth "as appertaining to every freeman." . . . .

What the clause in question did for the protection of the citizens of one State against hostile and discriminating legislation of other States, the fourteenth amendment does for the protection of every citizen of the United States against hostile and discriminating legislation against him in favor of others, whether they reside in the same or in different States. If under the fourth article of the Constitution equality of privileges and immunities is secured between citizens of different States, under the fourteenth amendment the same equality is secured between citizens of the United States. . . .

This equality of right, with exemption from all disparaging and partial enactments, in the lawful pursuits of life, throughout the whole country, is the distinguishing privilege of citizens of the United States. To them, everywhere, all pursuits, all professions, all avocations are open without other restrictions than such as are imposed equally upon all others of the same age, sex, and condition. The State may prescribe such regulations for every pursuit and calling of life as will promote the public health, secure the good order and advance the general prosperity of society, but when once prescribed, the pursuit or calling must be free to be followed by every citizen who is within the conditions designated, and will conform to the regulations. This is the fundamental idea upon which our institutions rest; and unless adhered to in the legislation of the country our government will be a republic only in name. The fourteenth amendment, in my judgment, makes it essential to the validity of the legislation of every State that this equality of right should be respected. . . .

Mr. Justice BRADLEY, also dissenting. . . .

[T]he Declaration of Independence, which was the first political act of the American people in their independent sovereign capacity, lays the foundation of our National existence upon this broad proposition: "That all men are created equal; that they are endowed by their Creator with certain inalienable rights; that among these are life, liberty, and the pursuit of happiness." Here again we have the great threefold division of the rights of freemen, asserted as the rights of man. Rights to life, liberty, and the pursuit of happiness are equivalent to the rights of life, liberty, and property. These are the fundamental rights which can only be taken away by due process of law, and which can only be interfered with, or the enjoyment of which can only be modified, by lawful regulations necessary or proper for the mutual good of all; and these rights, I contend, belong to the citizens of every free government.

For the preservation, exercise, and enjoyment of these rights the individual citizen, as a necessity, must be left free to adopt such calling, profession, or trade as may seem to him most conducive to that end. Without this right he cannot be a freeman. This right to choose one's calling is an essential part of that liberty which it is the object of government to protect; and a calling, when chosen, is a man's property and right. Liberty and property are not protected where these rights are arbitrarily assailed.

I think sufficient has been said to show that citizenship is not an empty name, but that, in this country at least, it has connected with it certain incidental rights, privileges, and immunities of the greatest importance. And to say that these rights and immunities attach only to State citizenship, and not to citizenship of the United States, appears to me to evince a very narrow and insufficient estimate of constitutional history and the rights of men, not to say the rights of the American people. . . .

It is pertinent to observe that both the clause of the Constitution referred to [Article IV, Sec. 2], and Justice Washington in his comment on it, speak of the privileges and immunities of citizens *in* a State; not of citizens *of* a State. It is the privileges and immunities of citizens, that is, of citizens as such, that are to be accorded to citizens of other States when they are found in any State; or, as Justice Washington says, "privileges and immunities which are, in their nature, fundamental; which belong, of right, to the citizens of all free governments." . . . .

If my views are correct with regard to what are the privileges and immunities of citizens, it follows conclusively that any law which establishes a sheer monopoly, depriving a large class of citizens of the privilege of pursuing a lawful employment, does abridge the privileges of those citizens.

The amendment also prohibits any State from depriving any person (citizen or otherwise) of life, liberty, or property, without due process of law.

In my view, a law which prohibits a large class of citizens from adopting a lawful employment, or from following a lawful employment previously adopted, does deprive them of liberty as well as property, without due process of law. Their right of choice is a portion of their liberty; their occupation is their property. Such a law also deprives those citizens of the equal protection of the laws, contrary to the last clause of the section. . . .

It is futile to argue that none but persons of the African race are intended to be benefited by this amendment. They may have been the primary cause of the amendment, but its language is general, embracing all citizens, and I think it was purposely so expressed.

The mischief to be remedied was not merely slavery and its incidents and consequences; but that spirit of insubordination and disloyalty to the National government which had troubled the country for so many years in some of the States, and that intolerance of free speech and free discussion which often rendered life and property insecure, and led to much unequal legislation. The amendment was an attempt to give voice to the strong National yearning for that time and that condition of things, in which American citizenship should be a sure guaranty of safety, and in which every citizen of the United States might stand erect on every portion of its soil, in the full enjoyment of every right and privilege belonging to a freeman, without fear of violence or molestation.

But great fears are expressed that this construction of the amendment will lead to enactments by Congress interfering with the internal affairs of the States, and establishing therein civil and criminal codes of law for the government of the citizens, and thus abolishing the State governments in everything but name; or else, that it will lead the Federal courts to draw to their cognizance the supervision of State tribunals on every subject of judicial inquiry, on the plea of ascertaining whether the privileges and immunities of citizens have not been abridged.

In my judgment no such practical inconveniences would arise. Very little, if any, legislation on the part of Congress would be required to carry the amendment into effect. Like the prohibition against passing a law impairing the obligation of a contract, it would execute itself. The point would be regularly raised, in a suit at law, and settled by final reference to the Federal court. As the privileges and immunities protected are only those fundamental ones which belong to every citizen, they would soon become so far defined as to cause but a slight accumulation of business in the Federal courts. Besides, the recognized existence of the law would prevent its frequent violation. But even if the business of the National courts should be increased, Congress could easily supply the remedy by increasing their number and efficiency. The great question is, What is the true construction of the amendment? When once we find that, we shall find the means of giving it effect. The argument from inconvenience ought not to have a very controlling influence in questions of this sort. The National will and National interest are of far greater importance. . . .

Mr. Justice SWAYNE, dissenting. . . .

The first eleven amendments to the Constitution were intended to be checks and limitations upon the government which that instrument called into existence. They had their origin in a spirit of jealousy on the part of the States, which existed when the Constitution was adopted. . . . These amendments are a new departure, and mark an important epoch in the constitutional history of the country. They trench directly upon the power of the States, and deeply affect those bodies. They are, in this respect, at the opposite pole from the first eleven. . . .

The language employed [in the Fourteenth Amendment] is unqualified in its scope. There is no exception in its terms, and there can be properly none in their application. . . . No distinction is intimated on account of race or color. . . . The protection provided was not intended to be confined to those of any particular race or class, but to embrace equally all races, classes, and conditions of men. It is objected that the power conferred is novel and large. The answer is that the novelty was known and the measure deliberately adopted. . . . The construction adopted by the majority of my brethren is, in my judgment, much too narrow. It defeats, by a limitation not anticipated, the intent of those by whom the instrument was framed and of those by whom it was adopted. . . . By the Constitution, as it stood before the war, ample protection was given against oppression by the Union, but little was given against wrong and oppression by the States. That want was intended to be supplied by this amendment. . . .

Notes and Questions

1. The Reconstruction Amendments use rather broad language—such as "involuntary servitude" and "equal protection"—that if interpreted literally would make them potentially sweeping in scope. What interpretive tools does the *Slaughter-House Cases* Court use to limit their scope? Is the limitation justified? In what way is it similar to and different from the Court's interpretive tools employed in Chapter 1?

2. What, according to the majority and dissenting opinions, is the relationship (if any) between the Privileges and Immunities Clause of Article IV and the Privileges or Immunities Clause of the Fourteenth Amendment? What efficacy does the Privileges or Immunities Clause of the Fourteenth Amendment have under the majority's approach?

3. The majority notes that the Reconstruction Amendments were ratified by many states as a result of pressure from the federal government, which conditioned readmission to the United States on ratification of the Amendments. In addition, many of the legislatures in the South that ratified the Amendments were alternative "loyal" state governments that had been recognized by President Lincoln in lieu of what were the actual state governments. Should either of these facts cast doubt on whether the Amendments were lawfully ratified? *See generally* John Harrison, *The Lawfulness of the Reconstruction Amendments*, 68 U. Chi. L. Rev. 375 (2001).

4. Recently, some politicians have indicated a desire to eliminate so-called "birthright citizenship" for those born in the United States to foreign citizens, such as children born to Mexican immigrants who have entered the United States unlawfully. Is there language in the *Slaughter-House Cases* that would provide support for such an effort? *See generally* Gerald Walpin et al., *Birthright Citizenship: Two Perspectives*, 17 Fed. Soc. Rev. 9 (2016).

B. Sex and the Reconstruction Amendments

The day after the Court issued its decision in the *Slaughter-House Cases*, it issued a decision in *Bradwell v. Illinois*, 83 U.S. 130 (1873), rejecting a claim by a married woman that denying her a license to practice law violated the Privileges or

Immunities Clause of the Fourteenth Amendment. Justice Bradley—who dissented vigorously in the *Slaughter-House Cases*—wrote a concurring opinion upholding the state's decision to deny the plaintiff her license:

> The claim that, under the fourteenth amendment of the Constitution, which declares that no State shall make or enforce any law which shall abridge the privileges and immunities of citizens of the United States, the statute law of Illinois, or the common law prevailing in that State, can no longer be set up as a barrier against the right of females to pursue any lawful employment for a livelihood (the practice of law included), assumes that it is one of the privileges and immunities of women as citizens to engage in any and every profession, occupation, or employment in civil life.
>
> It certainly cannot be affirmed, as an historical fact, that this has ever been established as one of the fundamental privileges and immunities of the sex. On the contrary, the civil law, as well as nature herself, has always recognized a wide difference in the respective spheres and destinies of man and woman. Man is, or should be, woman's protector and defender. The natural and proper timidity and delicacy which belongs to the female sex evidently unfits it for many of the occupations of civil life. The constitution of the family organization, which is founded in the divine ordinance, as well as in the nature of things, indicates the domestic sphere as that which properly belongs to the domain and functions of womanhood. The harmony, not to say identity, of interest and views which belong, or should belong, to the family institution is repugnant to the idea of a woman adopting a distinct and independent career from that of her husband. So firmly fixed was this sentiment in the founders of the common law that it became a maxim of that system of jurisprudence that a woman had no legal existence separate from her husband, who was regarded as her head and representative in the social state; and, notwithstanding some recent modifications of this civil status, many of the special rules of law flowing from and dependent upon this cardinal principle still exist in full force in most States. One of these is, that a married woman is incapable, without her husband's consent, of making contracts which shall be binding on her or him. This very incapacity was one circumstance which the Supreme Court of Illinois deemed important in rendering a married woman incompetent fully to perform the duties and trusts that belong to the office of an attorney and counsellor.
>
> It is true that many women are unmarried and not affected by any of the duties, complications, and incapacities arising out of the married state, but these are exceptions to the general rule. The paramount destiny and mission of woman are to fulfil the noble and benign offices of wife and mother. This is the law of the Creator. And the rules of civil society must be adapted to the general constitution of things, and cannot be based upon exceptional cases.

> The humane movements of modern society, which have for their object the multiplication of avenues for woman's advancement, and of occupations adapted to her condition and sex, have my heartiest concurrence. But I am not prepared to say that it is one of her fundamental rights and privileges to be admitted into every office and position, including those which require highly special qualifications and demanding special responsibilities. In the nature of things it is not every citizen of every age, sex, and condition that is qualified for every calling and position. It is the prerogative of the legislator to prescribe regulations founded on nature, reason, and experience for the due admission of qualified persons to professions and callings demanding special skill and confidence. This fairly belongs to the police power of the State; and, in my opinion, in view of the peculiar characteristics, destiny, and mission of woman, it is within the province of the legislature to ordain what offices, positions, and callings shall be filled and discharged by men, and shall receive the benefit of those energies and responsibilities, and that decision and firmness which are presumed to predominate in the sterner sex.

Bradwell, 83 U.S. at 140-42 (Bradley, J., concurring).

The *Bradwell* decision, as well as the decision that follows, kicked off a one hundred year period in which the Court rejected virtually every effort to invoke the Reconstruction Amendments to guard against discrimination on the basis of sex.

Minor v. Happersett

88 U.S. 162 (1875)

The CHIEF JUSTICE delivered the opinion of the court.

The question is presented in this case, whether, since the adoption of the fourteenth amendment, a woman, who is a citizen of the United States and of the State of Missouri, is a voter in that State, notwithstanding the provision of the constitution and laws of the State, which confine the right of suffrage to men alone. . . .

The argument is, that as a woman, born or naturalized in the United States and subject to the jurisdiction thereof, is a citizen of the United States and of the State in which she resides, she has the right of suffrage as one of the privileges and immunities of her citizenship, which the State cannot by its laws or constitution abridge.

There is no doubt that women may be citizens. They are persons, and by the fourteenth amendment "all persons born or naturalized in the United States and subject to the jurisdiction thereof" are expressly declared to be "citizens of the United States and of the State wherein they reside." But, in our opinion, it did not need this amendment to give them that position. . . .

[S]ex has never been made one of the elements of citizenship in the United States. In this respect men have never had an advantage over women. The same laws precisely apply to both. The fourteenth amendment did not affect the citizenship of women any more than it did of men. In this particular, therefore, the rights of Mrs. Minor do not depend upon the amendment. She has always been a citizen from her birth, and entitled to all the privileges and immunities of citizenship. The amendment prohibited the State, of which she is a citizen, from abridging any of her privileges and immunities as a citizen of the United States; but it did not confer citizenship on her. That she had before its adoption.

If the right of suffrage is one of the necessary privileges of a citizen of the United States, then the constitution and laws of Missouri confining it to men are in violation of the Constitution of the United States, as amended, and consequently void. The direct question is, therefore, presented whether all citizens are necessarily voters.

The Constitution does not define the privileges and immunities of citizens. For that definition we must look elsewhere. In this case we need not determine what they are, but only whether suffrage is necessarily one of them.

It certainly is nowhere made so in express terms. The United States has no voters in the States of its own creation. The elective officers of the United States are all elected directly or indirectly by State voters. The members of the House of Representatives are to be chosen by the people of the States, and the electors in each State must have the qualifications requisite for electors of the most numerous branch of the State legislature. Senators are to be chosen by the legislatures of the States, and necessarily the members of the legislature required to make the choice are elected by the voters of the State. Each State must appoint in such manner, as the legislature thereof may direct, the electors to elect the President and Vice-President. . . .

The amendment did not add to the privileges and immunities of a citizen. It simply furnished an additional guaranty for the protection of such as he already had. No new voters were necessarily made by it. . . .

It is clear, therefore, we think, that the Constitution has not added the right of suffrage to the privileges and immunities of citizenship as they existed at the time it was adopted. This makes it proper to inquire whether suffrage was coextensive with the citizenship of the States at the time of its adoption. . . .

When the Federal Constitution was adopted, all the States, with the exception of Rhode Island and Connecticut, had constitutions of their own. . . . Upon an examination of those constitutions we find that in no State were all citizens permitted to vote. Each State determined for itself who should have that power. . . .

In this condition of the law in respect to suffrage in the several States it cannot for a moment be doubted that if it had been intended to make all citizens of the United States voters, the framers of the Constitution would not have left it to implication. So important a change in the condition of citizenship as it actually existed, if intended, would have been expressly declared. . . .

[B]y the very terms of the amendment we have been considering (the fourteenth), "Representatives shall be apportioned among the several States according to their respective numbers, counting the whole number of persons in each State, excluding Indians not taxed. But when the right to vote at any election for the choice of electors for President and Vice-President of the United States, representatives in Congress, the executive and judicial officers of a State, or the members of the legislature thereof, is denied to any of the male inhabitants of such State, being twenty-one years of age and citizens of the United States, or in any way abridged, except for participation in the rebellion, or other crimes, the basis of representation therein shall be reduced in the proportion which the number of such male citizens shall bear to the whole number of male citizens twenty-one years of age in such State." Why this, if it was not in the power of the legislature to deny the right of suffrage to some male inhabitants? And if suffrage was necessarily one of the absolute rights of citizenship, why confine the operation of the limitation to male inhabitants? Women and children are, as we have seen, "persons." They are counted in the enumeration upon which the apportionment is to be made, but if they were necessarily voters because of their citizenship unless clearly excluded, why inflict the penalty for the exclusion of males alone? Clearly, no such form of words would have been selected to express the idea here indicated if suffrage was the absolute right of all citizens.

And still again, after the adoption of the fourteenth amendment, it was deemed necessary to adopt a fifteenth, as follows: "The right of citizens of the United States to vote shall not be denied or abridged by the United States, or by any State, on account of race, color, or previous condition of servitude." The fourteenth amendment had already provided that no State should make or enforce any law which should abridge the privileges or immunities of citizens of the United States. If suffrage was one of these privileges or immunities, why amend the Constitution to prevent its being denied on account of race, &c.? Nothing is more evident than that the greater must include the less, and if all were already protected why go through with the form of amending the Constitution to protect a part? . . . .

Certainly, if the courts can consider any question settled, this is one. For nearly ninety years the people have acted upon the idea that the Constitution, when it conferred citizenship, did not necessarily confer the right of suffrage. If uniform practice long continued can settle the construction of so important an instrument as the Constitution of the United States confessedly is, most certainly it has been done here. Our province is to decide what the law is, not to declare what it should be. . . .

Notes and Questions

1. What interpretive tools does the *Minor* Court use to limit the scope of the Fourteenth Amendment? How is that similar to and different from the interpretive tools used by the Court in Chapter 1 and in *The Slaughter-House Cases*?

2. While *Minor* may seem unjust from our modern eyes, does it not seem consistent with the text and history of the Fourteenth Amendment? After all, although early advocates of women's rights—such as Susan B. Anthony and Elizabeth Cady Stanton—initially worked side-by-side with male abolitionists, they felt betrayed when the Fourteenth Amendment was drafted in the way that it was, and ultimately

worked to *defeat* its enactment as a result. *See* Joellen Lind, *Dominance and Democracy: The Legacy of Woman Suffrage for the Voting Right*, 5 UCLA Women's L.J. 103, 164 (1994). Does not that history suggest that the *Minor* Court is interpreting the Amendment exactly as its drafters intended, which was what angered people like Anthony and Stanton so much?

3. Is not the Court's unwillingness to invoke the Reconstruction Amendments to protect against sex discrimination consistent with the Court's statement in *The Slaughter-House Cases* regarding the Equal Protection Clause that "We doubt very much whether any action of a State not directed by way of discrimination against the negroes as a class, or on account of their race, will ever be held to come within the purview of this provision. It is so clearly a provision for that race and that emergency, that a strong case would be necessary for its application to any other."?

C. State versus Private Action

United States v. Cruikshank

92 U.S. 542 (1876)

Mr. Chief Justice Waite delivered the opinion of the court.

[This case grew out of the Colfax massacre, which followed a dispute between Democrats and Republicans in a contested gubernatorial election in Louisiana, resulting in the deaths of over 100 people, nearly all of whom were African American. Specifically at issue in this case is a criminal prosecution under the Enforcement Act of 1870, Section 6, for banding or conspiring to deprive a citizen of their constitutional rights, specifically, their First and Second Amendment rights as well as their rights to due process and equal protection.]

The general charge in the first eight counts is that of "banding," and in the second eight, that of "conspiring" together to injure, oppress, threaten, and intimidate Levi Nelson and Alexander Tillman, citizens of the United States, of African descent and persons of color, with the intent thereby to hinder and prevent them in their free exercise and enjoyment of rights and privileges "granted and secured" to them "in common with all other good citizens of the United States by the constitution and laws of the United States."

The offences provided for by the statute in question do not consist in the mere "banding" or "conspiring" of two or more persons together, but in their banding or conspiring with the intent, or for any of the purposes, specified. To bring this case under the operation of the statute, therefore, it must appear that the right, the enjoyment of which the conspirators intended to hinder or prevent, was one granted or secured by the constitution or laws of the United States. If it does not so appear, the criminal matter charged has not been made indictable by any act of Congress. . . .

We now proceed to an examination of the indictment, to ascertain whether the several rights, which it is alleged the defendants intended to interfere with, are such as had been in law and in fact granted or secured by the constitution or laws of the United States.

The first and ninth counts state the intent of the defendants to have been to hinder and prevent the citizens named in the free exercise and enjoyment of their "lawful right and privilege to peaceably assemble together with each other and with other citizens of the United States for a peaceful and lawful purpose." The right of the people peaceably to assemble for lawful purposes existed long before the adoption of the Constitution of the United States. In fact, it is, and always has been, one of the attributes of citizenship under a free government.... It is found wherever civilization exists. It was not, therefore, a right granted to the people by the Constitution.... Only such existing rights were committed by the people to the protection of Congress as came within the general scope of the authority granted to the national government.

The first amendment to the Constitution prohibits Congress from abridging "the right of the people to assemble and to petition the government for a redress of grievances." This, like the other amendments proposed and adopted at the same time, was not intended to limit the powers of the State governments in respect to their own citizens, but to operate upon the National government alone. *Barron* v. *The City of Baltimore*. It is now too late to question the correctness of this construction....

The particular amendment now under consideration assumes the existence of the right of the people to assemble for lawful purposes, and protects it against encroachment by Congress. The right was not created by the amendment; neither was its continuance guaranteed, except as against congressional interference. For their protection in its enjoyment, therefore, the people must look to the States. The power for that purpose was originally placed there, and it has never been surrendered to the United States....

The second and tenth counts are equally defective. The right there specified is that of "bearing arms for a lawful purpose." This is not a right granted by the Constitution. Neither is it in any manner dependent upon that instrument for its existence. The second amendment declares that it shall not be infringed; but this, as has been seen, means no more than that it shall not be infringed by Congress....

The third and eleventh counts are even more objectionable. They charge the intent to have been to deprive the citizens named, they being in Louisiana, "of their respective several lives and liberty of person without due process of law." This is nothing else than alleging a conspiracy to falsely imprison or murder citizens of the United States, being within the territorial jurisdiction of the State of Louisiana....

The fourteenth amendment prohibits a State from depriving any person of life, liberty, or property, without due process of law; but this adds nothing to the rights of one citizen as against another. It simply furnishes an additional guaranty against any encroachment by the States upon the fundamental rights which belong to every citizen as a member of society....

The fourth and twelfth counts charge. . . . nothing more than that the defendants conspired to prevent certain citizens of the United States, being within the State of Louisiana, from enjoying the equal protection of the laws of the State and of the United States.

The fourteenth amendment prohibits a State from denying to any person within its jurisdiction the equal protection of the laws; but this provision does not, any more than the one which precedes it, and which we have just considered, add any thing to the rights which one citizen has under the Constitution against another. The equality of the rights of citizens is a principle of republicanism. Every republican government is in duty bound to protect all its citizens in the enjoyment of this principle, if within its power. That duty was originally assumed by the States; and it still remains there. The only obligation resting upon the United States is to see that the States do not deny the right. This the amendment guarantees, but no more. The power of the national government is limited to the enforcement of this guaranty. . . .

[The dissenting opinion of Justice Clifford is omitted.]

The Civil Rights Cases

109 U.S. 3 (1883)

[At issue in this case is a challenge to the constitutionality of Sections 1 and 2 of the Civil Rights Act of 1875, which prohibited racial discrimination by places of public accommodation.]

MR. JUSTICE BRADLEY delivered the opinion of the court. . . .

The essence of the law is, not to declare broadly that all persons shall be entitled to the full and equal enjoyment of the accommodations, advantages, facilities, and privileges of inns, public conveyances, and theatres; but that such enjoyment shall not be subject to any conditions applicable only to citizens of a particular race or color, or who had been in a previous condition of servitude. In other words, it is the purpose of the law to declare that, in the enjoyment of the accommodations and privileges of inns, public conveyances, theatres, and other places of public amusement, no distinction shall be made between citizens of different race or color, or between those who have, and those who have not, been slaves. . . .

Has Congress constitutional power to make such a law? Of course, no one will contend that the power to pass it was contained in the Constitution before the adoption of the last three amendments. The power is sought, first, in the Fourteenth Amendment, and the views and arguments of distinguished Senators, advanced whilst the law was under consideration, claiming authority to pass it by virtue of that amendment, are the principal arguments adduced in favor of the power. . . .

The first section of the Fourteenth Amendment . . . is prohibitory in its character, and prohibitory upon the States. . . . Individual invasion of individual rights is not the subject-matter of the amendment. It has a deeper and broader scope. It nullifies and makes void all State legislation, and State action of every kind, which impairs the privileges and immunities of citizens of the United States, or which injures them in life, liberty or property without due process of law, or which denies to any of them the equal protection of the laws. It not only does this, but, in order that the national will, thus declared, may not be a mere *brutum fulmen*, the last section of the amendment invests Congress with power to enforce it by appropriate legislation. To enforce what? To enforce the prohibition. To adopt appropriate legislation for correcting the effects of such prohibited State laws and State acts, and thus to render them effectually null, void, and innocuous. This is the legislative power conferred upon Congress, and this is the whole of it. It does not invest Congress with power to legislate upon subjects which are within the domain of State legislation; but to provide modes of relief against State legislation, or State action, of the kind referred to. It does not authorize Congress to create a code of municipal law for the regulation of private rights; but to provide modes of redress against the operation of State laws, and the action of State officers[,] executive or judicial, when these are subversive of the fundamental rights specified in the amendment. Positive rights and privileges are undoubtedly secured by the Fourteenth Amendment; but they are secured by way of prohibition against State laws and State proceedings affecting those rights and privileges, and by power given to Congress to legislate for the purpose of carrying such prohibition into effect: and such legislation must necessarily be predicated upon such supposed State laws or State proceedings, and be directed to the correction of their operation and effect. . . .

And so in the present case, until some State law has been passed, or some State action through its officers or agents has been taken, adverse to the rights of citizens sought to be protected by the Fourteenth Amendment, no legislation of the United States under said amendment, nor any proceeding under such legislation, can be called into activity: for the prohibitions of the amendment are against State laws and acts done under State authority. Of course, legislation may, and should be, provided in advance to meet the exigency when it arises; but it should be adapted to the mischief and wrong which the amendment was intended to provide against; and that is, State laws, or State action of some kind, adverse to the rights of the citizen secured by the amendment. . . . It is absurd to affirm that, because the rights of life, liberty and property (which include all civil rights that men have), are by the amendment sought to be protected against invasion on the part of the State without due process of law, Congress may therefore provide due process of law for their vindication in every case; and that, because the denial by a State to any persons, of the equal protection of the laws, is prohibited by the amendment, therefore Congress may establish laws for their equal protection. In fine, the legislation which Congress is authorized to adopt in this behalf is not general legislation upon the rights of the citizen, but corrective legislation, that is, such as may be necessary and proper for counteracting such laws as the States may adopt or enforce, and which, by the amendment, they are prohibited from making or enforcing, or such acts and proceedings as the States may commit or take, and which, by the amendment, they are prohibited from committing or taking. . . .

An inspection of the law shows that it makes no reference whatever to any supposed or apprehended violation of the Fourteenth Amendment on the part of the States. It is not predicated on any such view. It proceeds *ex directo* to declare that certain acts committed by individuals shall be deemed offences, and shall be prosecuted and punished by proceedings in the courts of the United States. It does not profess to be corrective of any constitutional wrong committed by the States; it does not make its operation to depend upon any such wrong committed. It applies equally to cases arising in States which have the justest laws respecting the personal rights of citizens, and whose authorities are ever ready to enforce such laws, as to those which arise in States that may have violated the prohibition of the amendment. In other words, it steps into the domain of local jurisprudence, and lays down rules for the conduct of individuals in society towards each other, and imposes sanctions for the enforcement of those rules, without referring in any manner to any supposed action of the State or its authorities.

If this legislation is appropriate for enforcing the prohibitions of the amendment, it is difficult to see where it is to stop. Why may not Congress with equal show of authority enact a code of laws for the enforcement and vindication of all rights of life, liberty, and property? If it is supposable that the States may deprive persons of life, liberty, and property without due process of law (and the amendment itself does suppose this) why should not Congress proceed at once to prescribe due process of law for the protection of every one of these fundamental rights, in every possible case, as well as to prescribe equal privileges in inns, public conveyances, and theatres. The truth is, that the implication of a power to legislate in this manner is based upon the assumption that if the states are forbidden to legislate or act in a particular way on a particular subject, and power is conferred upon Congress to enforce the prohibition, this gives Congress power to legislate generally upon that subject, and not merely power to provide modes of redress against such State legislation or action. The assumption is certainly unsound. It is repugnant to the Tenth Amendment of the Constitution, which declares that powers not delegated to the United States by the Constitution, nor prohibited by it to the States, are reserved to the States respectively or to the people.

We have not overlooked the fact that the fourth section of the act now under consideration has been held by this court to be constitutional. That section declares "that no citizen, possessing all other qualifications which are or may be prescribed by law, shall be disqualified for service as grand or petit juror in any court of the United States, or of any State, on account of race, color, or previous condition of servitude; and any officer or other person charged with any duty in the selection or summoning of jurors who shall exclude or fail to summon any citizen for the cause aforesaid, shall, on conviction thereof, be deemed guilty of a misdemeanor, and be fined not more than five thousand dollars." In Ex parte *Virginia*, 100 U.S. 339, it was held that an indictment against a State officer under this section for excluding persons of color from the jury list is sustainable. But a moment's attention to its terms will show that the section is entirely corrective in its character. Disqualifications for service on juries are only created by the law, and the first part of the section is aimed at certain disqualifying laws, namely, those which make mere race or color a disqualification; and the second clause is directed against those who, assuming to use the authority of the State government, carry into effect such a rule of disqualification. In the Virginia case, the State, through its officer, enforced a rule of disqualification which the law was intended to abrogate and counteract. Whether the statute book of the State actually laid down any such rule of disqualification, or not, the State, through its officer, enforced such a rule: and it is against such State action, through its officers and agents, that the last clause of the section is directed. This aspect of the law was deemed sufficient to divest it of any unconstitutional character, and makes it differ widely from the first and second sections of the same act which we are now considering....

In this connection it is proper to state that civil rights, such as are guaranteed by the Constitution against State aggression, cannot be impaired by the wrongful acts of individuals, unsupported by State authority in the shape of laws, customs, or judicial or executive proceedings. The wrongful act of an individual, unsupported by any such authority, is simply a private wrong, or a crime of that individual; an invasion of the rights of the injured party, it is true, whether they affect his person, his property, or his reputation; but if not sanctioned in some way by the State, or not done under State authority, his rights remain in full force, and may presumably be vindicated by resort to the laws of the State for redress. An individual cannot deprive a man of his right to vote, to hold property, to buy and to sell, to sue in the courts, or to be a witness or a juror; he may, by force or fraud, interfere with the enjoyment of the right in a particular case; he may commit an assault against the person, or commit murder, or use ruffian violence at the polls, or slander the good name of a fellow citizen; but, unless protected in these wrongful acts by some shield of State law or State authority, he cannot destroy or injure the right; he will only render himself amenable to satisfaction or punishment; and amenable therefor to the laws of the State where the wrongful acts are committed. Hence, in all those cases where the Constitution seeks to protect the rights of the citizen against discriminative and unjust laws of the State by prohibiting such laws, it is not individual offences, but abrogation and denial of rights, which it denounces, and for which it clothes the Congress with power to provide a remedy. This abrogation and denial of rights, for which the States alone were or could be responsible, was the great seminal and fundamental wrong which was intended to be remedied. And the remedy to be provided must necessarily be predicated upon that wrong. It must assume that in the cases provided for, the evil or wrong actually committed rests upon some State law or State authority for its excuse and perpetration....

If the principles of interpretation which we have laid down are correct, as we deem them to be, ... it is clear that the law in question cannot be sustained by any grant of legislative power made to Congress by the Fourteenth Amendment....

We have discussed the question presented by the law on the assumption that a right to enjoy equal accommodation and privileges in all inns, public conveyances, and places of public amusement, is one of the essential rights of the citizen which no State can abridge or interfere with. Whether it is such a right, or not, is a different question which, in the view we have taken of the validity of the law on the ground already stated, it is not necessary to examine.

We have also discussed the validity of the law in reference to cases arising in the States only; and not in reference to cases arising in the Territories or the District of Columbia, which are subject to the plenary legislation of Congress in every branch of municipal regulation. Whether the law would be a valid one as applied to the Territories and the District is not a question for consideration in the cases before us: they all being cases arising within the limits of States. And whether Congress, in the exercise of its power to regulate commerce among the several States, might or might not pass a law regulating rights in public conveyances passing from one State to another, is also a question which is not now before us, as the sections in question are not conceived in any such view.

But the power of Congress to adopt direct and primary, as distinguished from corrective legislation, on the subject in hand, is sought, in the second place, from the Thirteenth Amendment, which abolishes slavery. This amendment declares "that neither slavery, nor involuntary servitude, except as a punishment for crime, whereof the party shall have been duly convicted, shall exist within the United States, or any place subject to their jurisdiction;" and it gives Congress power to enforce the amendment by appropriate legislation.

This amendment, as well as the Fourteenth, is undoubtedly self-executing without any ancillary legislation, so far as its terms are applicable to any existing state of circumstances. By its own unaided force and effect it abolished slavery, and established universal freedom. Still, legislation may be necessary and proper to meet all the various cases and circumstances to be affected by it, and to prescribe proper modes of redress for its violation in letter or spirit. And such legislation may be primary and direct in its character; for the amendment is not a mere prohibition of State laws establishing or upholding slavery, but an absolute declaration that slavery or involuntary servitude shall not exist in any part of the United States.

It is true that slavery cannot exist without law, any more than property in lands and goods can exist without law and, therefore the Thirteenth Amendment may be regarded as nullifying all State laws which establish or uphold slavery. But it has a reflex character also, establishing and decreeing universal civil and political freedom throughout the United States; and it is assumed, that the power vested in Congress to enforce the article by appropriate legislation, clothes Congress with power to pass all laws necessary and proper for abolishing all badges and incidents of slavery in the United States: and upon this assumption it is claimed, that this is sufficient authority for declaring by law that all persons shall have equal accommodations and privileges in all inns, public conveyances, and places of public amusement; the argument being that the denial of such equal accommodations and privileges is, in itself, a subjection to a species of servitude within the meaning of the amendment. Conceding the major proposition to be true, that Congress has a right to enact all necessary and proper laws for the obliteration and prevention of slavery with all its badges and incidents, is the minor proposition also true, that the denial to any person of admission to the accommodations and privileges of an inn, a public conveyance, or a theatre, does subject that person to any form of servitude, or tend to fasten upon him any badge of slavery? . . . .

Where does any slavery or servitude, or badge of either, arise from such an act of denial? Whether it might not be a denial of a right which, if sanctioned by the state law, would be obnoxious to the prohibitions of the Fourteenth Amendment, is another question. But what has it to do with the question of slavery?

It may be that by the Black Code (as it was called) in the times when slavery prevailed, the proprietors of inns and public conveyances were forbidden to receive persons of the African race, because it might assist slaves to escape from the control of their masters. This was merely a means of preventing such escapes, and was no part of the servitude itself. . . .

The long existence of African slavery in this country gave us very distinct notions of what it was, and what were its necessary incidents. Compulsory service of the slave for the benefit of the master, restraint of his movements except by the master's will, disability to hold property, to make contracts, to have a standing in court, to be a witness against a white person, and such like burdens and incapacities, were the inseparable incidents of the institution. Severer punishments for crimes were imposed on the slave than on free persons guilty of the same offences. Congress, as we have seen, by the Civil Rights Bill of 1866, passed in view of the Thirteenth Amendment, before the Fourteenth was adopted, undertook to wipe out these burdens and disabilities, the necessary incidents of slavery, constituting its substance and visible form; and to secure to all citizens of every race and color, and without regard to previous servitude, those fundamental rights which are the essence of civil freedom, namely, the same right to make and enforce contracts, to sue, be parties, give evidence, and to inherit, purchase, lease, sell and convey property, as is enjoyed by white citizens. Whether this legislation was fully authorized by the Thirteenth Amendment alone, without the support which it afterwards received from the Fourteenth Amendment, after the adoption of which it was re-enacted with some additions, it is not necessary to inquire. It is referred to for the purpose of showing that at that time (in 1866) Congress did not assume, under the authority given by the Thirteenth Amendment, to adjust what may be called the social rights of men and races in the community; but only to declare and vindicate those fundamental rights which appertain to the essence of citizenship, and the enjoyment or deprivation of which constitutes the essential distinction between freedom and slavery.

We must not forget that the province and scope of the Thirteenth and Fourteenth Amendments are different; the former simply abolished slavery: the latter prohibited the States from abridging the privileges or immunities of citizens of the United States; from depriving them of life, liberty, or property without due process of law, and from denying to any the equal protection of the laws. The amendments are different, and the powers of Congress under them are different. What congress has power to do under one, it may not have power to do under the other. Under the Thirteenth Amendment, it has only to do with slavery and its incidents. Under the Fourteenth Amendment, it has power to counteract and render nugatory all State laws and proceedings which have the effect to abridge any of the privileges or immunities of citizens of the United States, or to deprive them of life, liberty or property without due process of law, or to deny to any of them the equal protection of the laws. Under the Thirteenth Amendment, the legislation, so far as necessary or proper to eradicate all forms and incidents of slavery and involuntary servitude, may be direct and primary, operating upon the acts of individuals, whether sanctioned by State legislation or not; under the Fourteenth, as we have already shown, it must necessarily be, and can only be, corrective in its character, addressed to counteract and afford relief against State regulations or proceedings.

The only question under the present head, therefore, is, whether the refusal to any persons of the accommodations of an inn, or a public conveyance, or a place of public amusement, by an individual, and without any sanction or support from any State law or regulation, does inflict upon such persons any manner of servitude, or form of slavery, as those terms are understood in this country? Many wrongs may be obnoxious to the prohibitions of the Fourteenth Amendment which are not, in any just sense, incidents or elements of slavery. Such, for example, would be the taking of private property without due process of law; or allowing persons who have committed certain crimes (horse stealing, for example) to be seized and hung by the *posse comitatus* without regular trial; or denying to any person, or class of persons, the right to pursue any peaceful avocations allowed to others. What is called class legislation would belong to this category, and would be obnoxious to the prohibitions of the Fourteenth Amendment, but would not necessarily be so to the Thirteenth when not involving the idea of any subjection of one man to another. The Thirteenth Amendment has respect, not to distinctions of race, or class, or color, but to slavery. The Fourteenth Amendment extends its protection to races and classes, and prohibits any State legislation which has the effect of denying to any race or class, or to any individual, the equal protection of the laws.

Now, conceding, for the sake of the argument, that the admission to an inn, a public conveyance, or a place of public amusement, on equal terms with all other citizens, is the right of every man and all classes of men, is it any more than one of those rights which the states by the Fourteenth Amendment are forbidden to deny to any person? And is the Constitution violated until the denial of the right has some State sanction or authority? Can the act of a mere individual, the owner of the inn, the public conveyance or place of amusement, refusing the accommodation, be justly regarded as imposing any badge of slavery or servitude upon the applicant, or only as inflicting an ordinary civil injury, properly cognizable by the laws of the State, and presumably subject to redress by those laws until the contrary appears?

After giving to these questions all the consideration which their importance demands, we are forced to the conclusion that such an act of refusal has nothing to do with slavery or involuntary servitude, and that if it is violative of any right of the party, his redress is to be sought under the laws of the State; or if those laws are adverse to his rights and do not protect him, his remedy will be found in the corrective legislation which Congress has adopted, or may adopt, for counteracting the effect of State laws, or State action, prohibited by the Fourteenth Amendment. It would be running the slavery argument into the ground to make it apply to every act of discrimination which a person may see fit to make as to the guests he will entertain, or as to the people he will take into his coach or cab or car, or admit to his concert or theatre, or deal with in other matters of intercourse or business. Innkeepers and public carriers, by the laws of all the States, so far as we are aware, are bound, to the extent of their facilities, to furnish proper accommodation to all unobjectionable persons who in good faith apply for them. If the laws themselves make any unjust discrimination, amenable to the prohibitions of the Fourteenth Amendment, Congress has full power to afford a remedy under that amendment and in accordance with it.

When a man has emerged from slavery, and by the aid of beneficent legislation has shaken off the inseparable concomitants of that state, there must be some stage in the progress of his elevation when he takes the rank of a mere citizen, and ceases to be the special favorite of the laws, and when his rights as a citizen, or a man, are to be protected in the ordinary modes by which other men's rights are protected. There were thousands of free colored people in this country before the abolition of slavery, enjoying all the essential rights of life, liberty and property the same as white citizens; yet no one, at that time, thought that it was any invasion of his personal status as a freeman because he was not admitted to all the privileges enjoyed by white citizens, or because he was subjected to discriminations in the enjoyment of accommodations in inns, public conveyances and places of amusement. Mere discriminations on account of race or color were not regarded as badges of slavery. If, since that time, the enjoyment of equal rights in all these respects has become established by constitutional enactment, it is not by force of the Thirteenth Amendment (which merely abolishes slavery), but by force of the [Fourteenth] and Fifteenth Amendments.

On the whole, we are of opinion, that no countenance of authority for the passage of the law in question can be found in either the Thirteenth or Fourteenth Amendment of the Constitution; and no other ground of authority for its passage being suggested, it must necessarily be declared void, at least so far as its operation in the several States is concerned....

MR. JUSTICE HARLAN dissenting.

The opinion in these cases proceeds, as it seems to me, upon grounds entirely too narrow and artificial. I cannot resist the conclusion that the substance and spirit of the recent amendments of the Constitution have been sacrificed by a subtle and ingenious verbal criticism....

The Thirteenth Amendment, it is conceded, did something more than to prohibit slavery as an *institution*, resting upon distinctions of race, and upheld by positive law. My brethren admit that it established and decreed universal *civil freedom* throughout the United States. But did the freedom thus established involve nothing more than exemption from actual slavery? Was nothing more intended than to forbid one man from owning another as property? Was it the purpose of the nation simply to destroy the institution, and then remit the race, theretofore held in bondage, to the several States for such protection, in their civil rights, necessarily growing out of freedom, as those States, in their discretion, might choose to provide? Were the States against whose protest the institution was destroyed, to be left free, so far as national interference was concerned, to make or allow discriminations against that race, as such, in the enjoyment of those fundamental rights which by universal concession, inhere in a state of freedom? . . . .

That there are burdens and disabilities which constitute badges of slavery and servitude, and that the power to enforce by appropriate legislation the Thirteenth Amendment may be exerted by legislation of a direct and primary character, for the eradication, not simply of the institution, but of its badges and incidents, are propositions which ought to be deemed indisputable. . . . I do not contend that the Thirteenth Amendment invests Congress with authority, by legislation, to define and regulate the entire body of the civil rights which citizens enjoy, or may enjoy, in the several States. But I hold that since slavery, as the court has repeatedly declared, was the moving or principal cause of the adoption of that amendment, and since that institution rested wholly upon the inferiority, as a race, of those held in bondage, their freedom necessarily involved immunity from, and protection against, all discrimination against them, because of their race, in respect of such civil rights as belong to freemen of other races. Congress, therefore, under its express power to enforce that amendment, by appropriate legislation, may enact laws to protect that people against the deprivation, *because of their race*, of any civil rights granted to other freemen in the same State; and such legislation may be of a direct and primary character, operating upon States, their officers and agents, and, also, upon, at least, such individuals and corporations as exercise public functions and wield power and authority under the State. . . .

Congress has not, in these matters, entered the domain of State control and supervision. It does not, as I have said, assume to prescribe the general conditions and limitations under which inns, public conveyances, and places of public amusement, shall be conducted or managed. It simply declares, in effect, that since the nation has established universal freedom in this country, for all time, there shall be no discrimination, based merely upon race or color, in respect of the accommodations and advantages of public conveyances, inns, and places of public amusement.

I am of the opinion that such discrimination practised by corporations and individuals in the exercise of their public or quasi-public functions is a badge of servitude the imposition of which Congress may prevent under its power, by appropriate legislation, to enforce the Thirteenth Amendment; and, consequently, without reference to its enlarged power under the Fourteenth Amendment, the act of March 1, 1875, is not, in my judgment, repugnant to the Constitution.

It remains now to consider these cases with reference to the power Congress has possessed since the adoption of the Fourteenth Amendment. . . .

The theory of the opinion of the majority of the court—the foundation upon which their reasoning seems to rest—is, that the general government cannot, in advance of hostile State laws or hostile State proceedings, actively interfere for the protection of any of the rights, privileges, and immunities secured by the Fourteenth Amendment. It is said that such rights, privileges, and immunities are secured by way of *prohibition* against State laws and State proceedings affecting such rights and privileges, and by power given to Congress to legislate for the purpose of carrying *such prohibition* into effect; also, that congressional legislation must necessarily be predicated upon such supposed State laws or State proceedings, and be directed to the correction of their operation and effect. . . .

The assumption that this amendment consists wholly of prohibitions upon State laws and State proceedings in hostility to its provisions, is unauthorized by its language. The first clause of the first section—"All persons born or naturalized in the United States, and subject to the jurisdiction thereof, are citizens of the United States, and of the State wherein they reside"—is of a distinctly affirmative character. In its application to the colored race, previously liberated, it created and granted, as well citizenship of the United States, as citizenship of the State in which they respectively resided. . . .

The citizenship thus acquired, by that race, in virtue of an affirmative grant from the nation, may be protected, not alone by the judicial branch of the government, but by congressional legislation of a primary direct character; this, because the power of Congress is not restricted to the enforcement of prohibitions upon State laws or State action. It is, in terms distinct and positive, to enforce "the *provisions* of *this article*" of amendment; not simply those of a prohibitive character, but the provisions—*all* of the provisions—affirmative and prohibitive, of the amendment. It is, therefore, a grave misconception to suppose that the fifth section of the amendment has reference exclusively to express prohibitions upon State laws or State action. . . .

But what was secured to colored citizens of the United States—as between them and their respective States—by the national grant to them of State citizenship? With what rights, privileges, or immunities did this grant from the nation invest them? There is one, if there be no others—exemption from race discrimination in respect of any civil right belonging to citizens of the white race in the same State. That, surely, is their constitutional privilege when within the jurisdiction of other States. And such must be their constitutional right, in their own State, unless the recent amendments be "splendid baubles," thrown out to delude those who deserved fair and generous treatment at the hands of the nation. . . .

If, then, exemption from discrimination, in respect of civil rights, is a new constitutional right, secured by the grant of State citizenship to colored citizens of the United States—and I do not see how this can now be questioned—why may not the nation, by means of its own legislation of a primary direct character, guard, protect, and enforce that right? It is a right and privilege which the nation conferred....

If the grant to colored citizens of the United States of citizenship in their respective States, imports exemption from race discrimination, in their States, in respect of such civil rights as belong to citizenship, then, to hold that the amendment remits that right to the States for their protection, primarily, and stays the hands of the nation, until it is assailed by State laws or State proceedings, is to adjudge that the amendment, so far from enlarging the powers of Congress—as we have heretofore said it did—not only curtails them, but reverses the policy which the general government has pursued from its very organization.... In view of the circumstances under which the recent amendments were incorporated into the Constitution, and especially in view of the peculiar character of the new rights they created and secured, it ought not to be presumed that the general government has abdicated its authority, by national legislation, direct and primary in its character, to guard and protect privileges and immunities secured by that instrument. Such an interpretation of the Constitution ought not to be accepted if it be possible to avoid it. Its acceptance would lead to this anomalous result: that whereas, prior to the amendments, Congress, with the sanction of this court, passed the most stringent laws—operating directly and primarily upon States and their officers and agents, as well as upon individuals—in vindication of slavery and the right of the master, it may not now, by legislation of a like primary and direct character, guard, protect, and secure the freedom established, and the most essential right of the citizenship granted, by the constitutional amendments. With all respect for the opinion of others, I insist that the national legislature may, without transcending the limits of the Constitution, do for human liberty and the fundamental rights of American citizenship, what it did, with the sanction of this court, for the protection of slavery and the rights of the masters of fugitive slaves. If fugitive slave laws, providing modes and prescribing penalties, whereby the master could seize and recover his fugitive slave, were legitimate exercises of an implied power to protect and enforce a right recognized by the Constitution, why shall the hands of Congress be tied, so that—under an express power, by appropriate legislation, to enforce a constitutional provision granting citizenship—it may not, by means of direct legislation, bring the whole power of this nation to bear upon States and their officers, and upon such individuals and corporations exercising public functions as assume to abridge, impair, or deny rights confessedly secured by the supreme law of the land? ....

It was said of the case of *Dred Scott* v. *Sandford*, that this court, there overruled the action of two generations, virtually inserted a new clause in the Constitution, changed its character, and made a new departure in the workings of the federal government. I may be permitted to say that if the recent amendments are so construed that Congress may not, in its own discretion, and independently of the action or non-action of the States, provide, by legislation of a direct character, for the security of rights created by the national Constitution; if it be adjudged that the obligation to protect the fundamental privileges and immunities granted by the Fourteenth

Amendment to citizens residing in the several states, rests, primarily, not on the nation, but on the States; if it be further adjudged that individuals and corporations, exercising public functions, or wielding power under public authority, may, without liability to direct primary legislation on the part of Congress, make the race of citizens the ground for denying them that equality of civil rights which the Constitution ordains as a principle of republican citizenship; then, not only the foundations upon which the national supremacy has always securely rested will be materially disturbed, but we shall enter upon an era of constitutional law, when the rights of freedom and American citizenship cannot receive from the nation that efficient protection which heretofore was unhesitatingly accorded to slavery and the rights of the master.

But if it were conceded that the power of Congress could not be brought into activity until the rights specified in the act of 1875 had been abridged or denied by some State law or State action, I maintain that the decision of the court is erroneous. There has been adverse State action within the Fourteenth Amendment as heretofore interpreted by this court. I allude to *Ex parte Virginia, supra*. It appears, in that case, that one Cole, judge of a county court, was charged with the duty, by the laws of Virginia, of selecting grand and petit jurors. The law of the State did not authorize or permit him, in making such selections, to discriminate against colored citizens because of their race. But he was indicted in the federal court, under the act of 1875, for making such discriminations. The attorney general of Virginia contended before us that the State had done its duty, and had not authorized or directed that county judge to do what he was charged with having done; that the state had not denied to the colored race the equal protection of the laws; and that consequently the act of Cole must be deemed his individual act, in contravention of the will of the State. Plausible as this argument was, it failed to convince this court, and after saying that the Fourteenth Amendment had reference to the political body denominated a State, "by whatever instruments or in whatever modes that action may be taken," and that a State acts by its legislative, executive, and judicial authorities, and can act in no other way, we proceeded:

> "The constitutional provision, therefore, must mean that no agency of the State, or of the officers or agents by whom its powers are exerted, shall deny to any person within its jurisdiction the equal protection of the laws. Whoever, by virtue of public position under a State government, deprives another of property, life, or liberty without due process of law, or denies or takes away the equal protection of the laws, violates the constitutional inhibition; and, as he acts under the name and for the State, and is clothed with the State's power, his act is that of the State. This must be so, or the constitutional prohibition has no meaning. Then the State has clothed one of its agents with power to annul or evade it. But the constitutional amendment was ordained for a purpose. It was to secure equal rights to all persons, and, to insure to all persons the enjoyment of such rights, power was given to Congress to enforce its provisions by appropriate legislation. Such

> legislation must act upon persons, not upon the abstract thing denominated a State, but upon the persons who are the agents of the State, in the denial of the rights which were intended to be secured."

In every material sense applicable to the practical enforcement of the Fourteenth Amendment, railroad corporations, keepers of inns, and managers of places of public amusement are agents or instrumentalities of the State, because they are charged with duties to the public, and are amenable, in respect of their duties and functions, to governmental regulation. It seems to me that, within the principle settled in *Ex parte Virginia*, a denial, by these instrumentalities of the State, to the citizen, because of his race, of that equality of civil rights secured to him by law, is a denial by the State, within the meaning of the Fourteenth Amendment. If it be not, then that race is left, in respect of the civil rights in question, practically at the mercy of corporations and individuals wielding power under the States.

But the court says that Congress did not, in the act of 1866, assume, under the authority given by the Thirteenth Amendment, to adjust what may be called the social rights of men and races in the community. I agree that government has nothing to do with social, as distinguished from technically legal, rights of individuals. No government ever has brought, or ever can bring, its people into social intercourse against their wishes. Whether one person will permit or maintain social relations with another is a matter with which government has no concern. I agree that if one citizen chooses not to hold social intercourse with another, he is not and cannot be made amenable to the law for his conduct in that regard; for even upon grounds of race, no legal right of a citizen is violated by the refusal of others to maintain merely social relations with him. What I affirm is that no State, nor the officers of any State, nor any corporation or individual wielding power under State authority for the public benefit or the public convenience, can, consistently either with the freedom established by the fundamental law, or with that equality of civil rights which now belongs to every citizen, discriminate against freemen or citizens, in those civil rights, because of their race, or because they once labored under the disabilities of slavery imposed upon them as a race. The rights which Congress, by the act of 1875, endeavored to secure and protect are legal, not social rights. The right, for instance, of a colored citizen to use the accommodations of a public highway, upon the same terms as are permitted to white citizens, is no more a social right than his right, under the law, to use the public streets of a city or a town, or a turnpike road, or a public market, or a post office, or his right to sit in a public building with others, of whatever race, for the purpose of hearing the political questions of the day discussed. Scarcely a day passes without our seeing in this court-room citizens of the white and black races sitting side by side, watching the progress of our business. It would never occur to any one that the presence of a colored citizen in a court-house or court-room, was an invasion of the social rights of white persons who may frequent such places. And yet, such a suggestion would be quite as sound in law—I say it with all respect—as is the suggestion that the claim of a colored citizen to use, upon the same terms as is permitted to white citizens, the accommodations of public highways, or public inns, or places of public amusement, established under the license of the law, is an invasion of the social rights of the white race....

It is, I submit, scarcely just to say that the colored race has been the special favorite of the laws. The statute of 1875, now adjudged to be unconstitutional, is for the benefit of citizens of every race and color. What the nation, through Congress, has sought to accomplish in reference to that race, is—what had already been done in every State of the Union for the white race—to secure and protect rights belonging to them as freemen and citizens; nothing more.... The one underlying purpose of congressional legislation has been to enable the black race to take the rank of mere citizens.... If the constitutional amendments be enforced, according to the intent with which, as I conceive, they were adopted, there cannot be, in this republic, any class of human beings in practical subjection to another class, with power in the latter to dole out to the former just such privileges as they may choose to grant....

Notes and Questions

1. In *The Civil Rights Cases*, the majority and dissenting opinions have starkly different views regarding whether state action is required to make out a Fourteenth Amendment claim. Each claims textual support for its conclusion. Which argument do you find to be more persuasive?

2. Even accepting that state action is a requirement of the Fourteenth Amendment, the majority and dissenting opinions in *The Civil Rights Cases* have different conceptions of what constitutes state action. In what ways do the two opinions differ in their definition of the concept?

3. In *The Civil Rights Cases*, is the Court interpreting Section 1 of the Fourteenth Amendment, Section 5, or both?

4. In contrast to the Fourteenth Amendment, the majority in *The Civil Rights Cases* acknowledges that the Thirteenth Amendment reaches private action. Moreover, the majority suggests that, pursuant to Section 2 of the Thirteenth Amendment, Congress can prohibit not merely enslavement, but also its badges or incidents. What are "badges" and "incidents" of enslavement? And on what basis does the Court conclude that the conduct targeted by the Civil Rights Act of 1875 is neither a badge nor an incident of enslavement?

5. In attempting to define the scope of Congress's power under Section 2 of the Thirteenth Amendment, the majority in *The Civil Rights Cases* relies heavily on the scope of the Civil Rights Act of 1866. What is the significance of that Act in defining the contours of the Thirteenth Amendment?

6. Earlier in the same year that the Court struck down the Civil Rights Act of 1875, it also struck down Section 2 of the Civil Rights Act of 1871, which, *inter alia*, criminalized private conspiracies to deprive people of their right to "equal protection of the laws" or to prevent them from voting. In *United States v. Harris*, 106 U.S. 629 (1883), the Court rejected the claims that Congress had the power under either the Thirteenth or Fourteenth Amendments to enact the law. So far as Sections 1 and 5

of the Fourteenth Amendment was concerned, the Court relied on its earlier decisions in *United States v. Cruikshank* and *Virginia v. Rives* for the conclusion that it only encompasses *state* action. *Id.* at 637-640. So far as the Thirteenth Amendment was concerned, the Court reasoned as follows:

> Our conclusion is based on the fact that the provisions of [Section 2] are broader than the Thirteenth Amendment would justify. Under that section it would be an offence for two or more white persons to conspire, & c., for the purpose of depriving another white person of the equal protection of the laws. It would be an offence for two or more colored persons, enfranchised slaves, to conspire with the same purpose against a white citizen or against another colored citizen who had never been a slave. Even if the amendment is held to be directed against the action of private individuals, as well as against the action of the States and United States, the law under consideration covers cases both within and without the provisions of the amendment. It covers any conspiracy between two free white men against another free white man to deprive him of any right accorded him by the laws of the State or of the United States. A law under which two or more free white private citizens could be punished for conspiring or going in disguise for the purpose of depriving another free white citizen of a right accorded by the law of the State to all classes of persons—as, for instance, the right to make a contract, bring a suit, or give evidence—clearly cannot be authorized by the amendment which simply prohibits slavery and involuntary servitude. . . .
>
> There is another view which strengthens this conclusion. If Congress has constitutional authority under the Thirteenth Amendment to punish a conspiracy between two persons to do an unlawful act, it can punish the act itself, whether done by one or more persons.
>
> A private person cannot make constitutions or laws, nor can he with authority construe them, nor can he administer or execute them. The only way, therefore, in which one private person can deprive another of the equal protection of the laws is by the commission of some offence against the laws which protect the rights of persons, as by theft, burglary, arson, libel, assault, or murder. If, therefore, we hold that [the statute] is warranted by the Thirteenth Amendment, we should, by virtue of that amendment, accord to Congress the power to punish every crime by which the right of any person to life, property, or reputation is invaded. Thus, under a provision of the Constitution which simply abolished slavery and involuntary servitude, we should, with few exceptions, invest Congress with power over the whole catalogue of crimes. A construction of the amendment which leads to such a result is clearly unsound.

Id. at 641-643.

7. The year after *The Civil Rights Cases* and *Harris*, the Supreme Court upheld the constitutionality of provisions of the Enforcement Act of 1870 and the Civil Rights

Act of 1871 as applied to private individuals conspiring to prevent an African-American from voting in a congressional election. In *Ex Parte Yarbrough*, 110 U.S. 651 (1884), the Court relied on the fact that the right to vote in congressional elections is granted by the Constitution in Article I, Section 2, and thus that Congress has the power to enforce that right under the Necessary and Proper Clause of Article I, Section 8, Clause 18. *Id.* at 658-664. Yet part of the decision appeared to suggest that the Fifteenth Amendment might play a role as well:

> The Fifteenth Amendment of the Constitution, by its limitation on the power of the states in the exercise of their right to prescribe the qualifications of voters in their own elections, and by its limitation of the power of the United States over that subject, clearly shows that the right of suffrage was considered to be of supreme importance to the national government, and was not intended to be left within the exclusive control of the States. . . .
>
> While it is quite true, as was said by this court in *United States* v. *Reese*, 92 U.S. 214, that this article gives no affirmative right to the colored man to vote, and is designed primarily to prevent discrimination against him whenever the right to vote may be granted to others, it is easy to see that under some circumstances it may operate as the immediate source of a right to vote. In all cases where the former slave-holding States had not removed from their Constitutions the words "white man" as a qualification for voting, this provision did, in effect, confer on him the right to vote, because, being paramount to the State law, and a part of the State law, it annulled the discriminating word "white," and thus left him in the enjoyment of the same right as white persons. And such would be the effect of any future constitutional provision of a State which should give the right of voting exclusively to white people, whether they be men or women. *Neal* v. *Delaware*, 103 U.S. 370.
>
> In such cases this fifteenth article of amendment does, *proprio vigore*, substantially confer on the negro the right to vote, and Congress has the power to protect and enforce that right.

Id. at 664-665.

D. Racial Equality and the Reconstruction Amendments

The Slaughter-House Cases strongly hinted that the primary if not sole focus of the Reconstruction Amendments generally and the Equal Protection Clause in particular was on racial discrimination and, more specifically, discrimination against African-Americans. Unlike *The Slaughter-House Cases*, racial discrimination figures prominently in the following four cases. Although this leads the Court to strike down the challenged laws in two of the cases, the Court upholds racially discriminatory laws in the other two cases. Together, the separate opinions in each of these four cases provide a variety of different theories regarding the nature of the equality guaranteed by the Equal Protection Clause.

Strauder v. West Virginia

100 U.S. 303 (1880)

[An African-American man convicted and sentenced for murder challenged the constitutionality of a West Virginia law preventing African-Americans from serving on juries.]

MR. JUSTICE STRONG delivered the opinion of the court. . . .

In this court, several errors have been assigned . . . first, whether, by the Constitution and laws of the United States, every citizen of the United States has a right to a trial of an indictment against him by a jury selected and impanelled without discrimination against his race or color, because of race or color. . . .

It is to be observed that the first of these questions is not whether a colored man, when an indictment has been preferred against him, has a right to a grand or a petit jury composed in whole or in part of persons of his own race or color, but it is whether, in the composition or selection of jurors by whom he is to be indicted or tried, all persons of his race or color may be excluded by law, solely because of their race or color, so that by no possibility can any colored man sit upon the jury.

The questions are important, for they demand a construction of the recent amendments of the Constitution. . . . The Fourteenth Amendment ordains that "all persons born or naturalized in the United States and subject to the jurisdiction thereof are citizens of the United States and of the State wherein they reside. No State shall make or enforce any laws which shall abridge the privileges or immunities of citizens of the United States, nor shall any State deprive any person of life, liberty, or property, without due process of law, nor deny to any person within its jurisdiction the equal protection of the laws."

This is one of a series of constitutional provisions having a common purpose; namely, securing to a race recently emancipated, a race that through many generations had been held in slavery, all the civil rights that the superior race enjoy. The true spirit and meaning of the amendments, as we said in the *Slaughter-House Cases*, cannot be understood without keeping in view the history of the times when they were adopted, and the general objects they plainly sought to accomplish. At the time when they were incorporated into the Constitution, it required little knowledge of human nature to anticipate that those who had long been regarded as an inferior and subject race would, when suddenly raised to the rank of citizenship, be looked upon with jealousy and positive dislike, and that State laws might be enacted or enforced to perpetuate the distinctions that had before existed. Discriminations against them had been habitual. It was well known that in some States laws making such discriminations then existed, and others might well be expected. The colored race, as a race, was abject and ignorant, and in that condition was unfitted to command the respect of those who had superior intelligence. Their training had left them mere children, and as such they needed the protection which a wise government extends to those who are unable to protect themselves. They especially needed protection against unfriendly action in the States where they were resident. It was in view of these considerations the Fourteenth Amendment was framed and adopted. It was designed to assure to the colored race the enjoyment of all the civil rights that under the law are enjoyed by white persons, and to give to that race the protection of the general government, in that enjoyment, whenever it should be denied by the States. It not only gave citizenship and the privileges of citizenship to persons of color, but it denied to any State the power to withhold from them the equal protection of the laws, and authorized Congress to enforce its provisions by appropriate legislation. To quote the language used by us in the *Slaughter-House Cases*, "No one can fail to be impressed with the one pervading purpose found in all the amendments, lying at the foundation of each, and without which none of them would have been suggested,—we mean the freedom of the slave race, the security and firm establishment of that freedom, and the protection of the newly made freeman and citizen from the oppressions of those who had formerly exercised unlimited dominion over them." So again: "The existence of laws in the States where the newly emancipated negroes resided, which discriminated with gross injustice and hardship against them as a class, was the evil to be remedied, and by it [the Fourteenth Amendment] such laws were forbidden. If, however, the States did not conform their laws to its requirements, then, by the fifth section of the article of amendment, Congress was authorized to enforce it by suitable legislation." And it was added, "We doubt very much whether any action of a State, not directed by way of discrimination against the negroes, as a class, will ever be held to come within the purview of this provision."

If this is the spirit and meaning of the amendment, whether it means more or not, it is to be construed liberally, to carry out the purposes of its framers. It ordains that no State shall make or enforce any laws which shall abridge the privileges or immunities of citizens of the United States (evidently referring to the newly made citizens, who, being citizens of the United States, are declared to be also citizens of the State in which they reside). It ordains that no State shall deprive any person of life, liberty, or property, without due process of law, or deny to any person within its jurisdiction the equal protection of the laws. What is this but declaring that the law in the States shall be the same for the black as for the white; that all persons, whether colored or white, shall stand equal before the laws of the States, and, in regard to the colored race, for whose protection the amendment was primarily designed, that no discrimination shall be made against them by law because of their color? The words of the amendment, it is true, are prohibitory, but they contain a necessary implication of a positive immunity, or right, most valuable to the colored race,—the right to exemption from unfriendly legislation against them distinctively as colored,—exemption from legal discriminations, implying inferiority in civil society, lessening the security of their enjoyment of the rights which others enjoy, and discriminations which are steps towards reducing them to the condition of a subject race.

That the West Virginia statute respecting juries—the statute that controlled the selection of the grand and petit jury in the case of the plaintiff in error—is such a discrimination ought not to be doubted. Nor would it be if the persons excluded by it were white men. If in those States where the colored people constitute a majority of the entire population a law should be enacted excluding all white men from jury service, thus denying to them the privilege of participating equally with the blacks in the administration of justice, we apprehend no one would be heard to claim that it would not be a denial to white men of the equal protection of the laws. Nor if a law should be passed excluding all naturalized Celtic Irishmen, would there be any doubt of its inconsistency with the spirit of the amendment. The very fact that colored people are singled out and expressly denied by a statute all right to participate in the administration of the law, as jurors, because of their color, though they are citizens, and may be in other respects fully qualified, is practically a brand upon them, affixed by the law, an assertion of their inferiority, and a stimulant to that race prejudice which is an impediment to securing to individuals of the race that equal justice which the law aims to secure to all others.

The right to a trial by jury is guaranteed to every citizen of West Virginia by the Constitution of that State, and the constitution of juries is a very essential part of the protection such a mode of trial is intended to secure. The very idea of a jury is a body of men composed of the peers or equals of the person whose rights it is selected or summoned to determine; that is, of his neighbors, fellows, associates, persons having the same legal status in society as that which he holds. Blackstone, in his Commentaries, says, "The right of trial by jury, or the country, is a trial by the peers of every Englishman, and is the grand bulwark of his liberties, and is secured to him by the Great Charter." It is also guarded by statutory enactments intended to make impossible what Mr. Bentham called "packing juries." It is well known that prejudices often exist against particular classes in the community, which sway the judgment of jurors, and which, therefore, operate in some cases to deny to persons of those classes the full enjoyment of that protection which others enjoy. Prejudice in a local community is held to be a reason for a change of venue. The framers of the constitutional amendment must have known full well the existence of such prejudice and its likelihood to continue against the manumitted slaves and their race, and that knowledge was doubtless a motive that led to the amendment. By their manumission and citizenship the colored race became entitled to the equal protection of the laws of the States in which they resided; and the apprehension that through prejudice they might be denied that equal protection, that is, that there might be discrimination against them, was the inducement to bestow upon the national government the power to enforce the provision that no State shall deny to them the equal protection of the laws. Without the apprehended existence of prejudice that portion of the amendment would have been unnecessary, and it might have been left to the States to extend equality of protection.

In view of these considerations, it is hard to see why the statute of West Virginia should not be regarded as discriminating against a colored man when he is put upon trial for an alleged criminal offence against the State. It is not easy to comprehend how it can be said that while every white man is entitled to a trial by a jury selected from persons of his own race or color, or, rather, selected without discrimination against his color, and a negro is not, the latter is equally protected by the law with the former. Is not protection of life and liberty against race or color prejudice, a right, a legal right, under the constitutional amendment? And how can it be maintained that compelling a colored man to submit to a trial for his life by a jury drawn from a panel from which the State has expressly excluded every man of his race, because of color alone, however well qualified in other respects, is not a denial to him of equal legal protection?

We do not say that within the limits from which it is not excluded by the amendment a State may not prescribe the qualifications of its jurors, and in so doing make discriminations. It may confine the selection to males, to freeholders, to citizens, to persons within certain ages, or to persons having educational qualifications. We do not believe the Fourteenth Amendment was ever intended to prohibit this. Looking at its history, it is clear it had no such purpose. Its aim was against discrimination because of race or color. As we have said more than once, its design was to protect an emancipated race, and to strike down all possible legal discriminations against those who belong to it. To quote further from [the *Slaughter-House Cases*]: "In giving construction to any of these articles [amendments], it is necessary to keep the main purpose steadily in view." "It is so clearly a provision for that race and that emergency, that a strong case would be necessary for its application to any other." We are not now called upon to affirm or deny that it had other purposes.

The Fourteenth Amendment makes no attempt to enumerate the rights it designed to protect. It speaks in general terms, and those are as comprehensive as possible. Its language is prohibitory; but every prohibition implies the existence of rights and immunities, prominent among which is an immunity from inequality of legal protection, either for life, liberty, or property. Any State action that denies this immunity to a colored man is in conflict with the Constitution. . . .

[The dissenting opinion of Justice Field is omitted.]

Notes and Questions

1. What theory of equality does the *Strauder* Court endorse? Is it a theory of color blindness? An anti-subordination approach? A guarantee of equal outcomes? Of equal treatment?

2. How important is the nature of the right in this case to the outcome? Stated somewhat differently, is every racially discriminatory law likely to be struck down under the Equal Protection Clause, or are those that touch on important rights, such as the right to a trial by jury, more likely to be declared unconstitutional?

3. Recall that in *The Slaughter-House Cases*, the Court hinted that the Equal Protection Clause might only be applicable to laws that discriminate on the basis of

race and, more specifically, against African-Americans. Does *Strauder* reinforce or undercut this aspect of the *The Slaughter-House Cases*?

4. In a companion case to *Strauder*, the Court, in *Virginia v. Rives*, 100 U.S. 313 (1880), rejected an argument that the Equal Protection Clause requires that a jury be composed of persons of the defendant's race:

> It *is* a right to which every colored man is entitled, that, in the selection of jurors to pass upon his life, liberty, or property, there shall be no exclusion of his race, and no discrimination against them because of their color. But this is a different thing from the right which it is asserted was denied to the petitioners by the State court, viz. a right to have the jury composed in part of colored men. A mixed jury in a particular case is not essential to the equal protection of the laws, and the right to it is not given by any law of Virginia, or by any Federal statute. It is not, therefore, guaranteed by the Fourteenth Amendment. . . .

Id. at 322-323. However, in *Neal v. Delaware*, 103 U.S. 370 (1881), the Court suggested that *extreme* evidence of discriminatory effect in the jury selection process *could* constitute a violation of the Equal Protection Clause:

> The showing thus made, including, as it did, the fact (so generally known that the court felt obliged to take judicial notice of it) that no colored citizen had ever been summoned as a juror in the courts of the State,—although its colored population exceeded twenty thousand in 1870, and in 1880 exceeded twenty-six thousand, in a total population of less than one hundred and fifty thousand,—presented a *prima facie* case of denial, by the officers charged with the selection of grand and petit jurors, of that equality of protection which has been secured by the Constitution and laws of the United States. It was, we think, under all the circumstances, a violent presumption which the State court indulged, that such uniform exclusion of that race from juries, during a period of many years, was solely because, in the judgment of those officers, fairly exercised, the black race in Delaware were utterly disqualified, by want of intelligence, experience, or moral integrity, to sit on juries. The action of those officers in the premises is to be deemed the act of the State; and the refusal of the State court to redress the wrong by them committed was a denial of a right secured to the prisoner by the Constitution and laws of the United States.

Id. at 397.

5. In another companion case to *Strauder*, *Ex Parte Virginia*, 100 U.S. 339 (1880), the Court rejected an argument that because the Fourteenth Amendment requires *state* action, it does not apply to a situation in which a state official—a judge in that case—acts contrary to state law by discriminating on the basis of race even though state law does not permit or authorize such discrimination:

> We have said the prohibitions of the Fourteenth Amendment are addressed to the States. They are, "No *State* shall make or enforce a law which shall

> abridge the privileges or immunities of citizens of the United States, . . . nor deny to any person within its jurisdiction the equal protection of the laws." They have reference to actions of the political body denominated a State, by whatever instruments or in whatever modes that action may be taken. A State acts by its legislative, its executive, or its judicial authorities. It can act in no other way. The constitutional provision, therefore, must mean that no agency of the State, or of the officers or agents by whom its powers are exerted, shall deny to any person within its jurisdiction the equal protection of the laws. Whoever, by virtue of public position under a State government, deprives another of property, life, or liberty, without due process of law, or denies or takes away the equal protection of the laws, violates the constitutional inhibition; and as he acts in the name and for the State, and is clothed with the State's power, his act is that of the State. This must be so, or the constitutional prohibition has no meaning. Then the State has clothed one of its agents with power to annul or to evade it.

Id. at 346-347.

Pace v. Alabama

106 U.S. 583 (1883)

[At issue in this case is a challenge to the constitutionality of Alabama's statutory scheme for criminally punishing people living together in adultery or fornication. Under that statutory scheme, adultery or fornication occurring between "any white person and any negro" is punished more severely than when the conduct involves two people of the same race.]

Mr. Justice Field delivered the opinion of the court. . . .

The counsel of the plaintiff in error compares sects. 4184 and 4189 of the Code of Alabama, and assuming that the latter relates to the same offense as the former, and prescribes a greater punishment for it, because one of the parties is a negro, or of negro descent, claims that a discrimination is made against the colored person in the punishment designated, which conflicts with the clause of the Fourteenth Amendment prohibiting a State from denying to any person within its jurisdiction the equal protection of the laws.

The counsel is undoubtedly correct in his view of the purpose of the clause of the amendment in question, that it was to prevent hostile and discriminating State legislation against any person or class of persons. Equality of protection under the laws implies not only accessibility by each one, whatever his race, on the same terms with others to the courts of the country for the security of his person and property, but that in the administration of criminal justice he shall not be subjected, for the same offence, to any greater or different punishment. Such was the view of Congress in the enactment of the Civil Rights Act of May 31, 1870, c. 114, after the adoption of the amendment. That act, after providing that all persons within the jurisdiction of the United States shall have the same right, in every State and Territory, to make and enforce contracts, to sue, be parties, give evidence, and to the full and equal benefit of all laws and proceedings for the security of person and property as is enjoyed by white citizens, declares, in sect. 16, that they "shall be subject to like punishment, pains, penalties, taxes, licenses, and exactions of every kind and none other, any law, statute, ordinance, regulation, or custom to the contrary notwithstanding."

The defect in the argument of counsel consists in his assumption that any discrimination is made by the laws of Alabama in the punishment provided for the offence for which the plaintiff in error was indicted when committed by a person of the African race and when committed by a white person. The two sections of the code cited are entirely consistent. The one prescribes, generally, a punishment for an offence committed between persons of different sexes; the other prescribes a punishment for an offence which can only be committed where the two sexes are of different races. There is in neither section any discrimination against either race. Sect. 4184 equally includes the offence when the persons of the two sexes are both white and when they are both black. Sect. 4189 applies the same punishment to both offenders, the white and the black. Indeed, the offence against which this latter section is aimed cannot be committed without involving the persons of both races in the same punishment. Whatever discrimination is made in the punishment prescribed in the two sections is directed against the offence designated and not against the person of any particular color or race. The punishment of each offending person, whether white or black, is the same.

Notes and Questions

1. What theory of equality does the *Pace* Court endorse? Is it a theory of color blindness? An anti-subordination approach? A guarantee of equal outcomes? Of equal treatment? How does this compare with the approach taken in *Strauder*?

2. The *Pace* Court concludes that there is no racial discrimination because if a Caucasian and an African American engage in adultery or fornication together, they are punished equally. But is the Court making the right comparison? Consider Charlie, an African-American male who is admired by both Wanda, an African-American female and Lisa, a Caucasian female. If Wanda and Lisa both engage in an act of adultery or fornication with Charlie, Lisa will be subjected to more severe punishment than Wanda. Is there not racial discrimination in the disparate punishments given to Lisa and Wanda for engaging in the same conduct?

3. If *Pace* is correct in its notion of equality, what does that say about the constitutionality of laws banning interracial marriage? About segregated schools?

Yick Wo v. Hopkins

118 U.S. 356 (1886)

Mr. Justice Matthews delivered the opinion of the court....

The ordinance drawn in question in the present case ... does not prescribe a rule and conditions for the regulation of the use of property for laundry purposes, to which all similarly situated may conform. It allows without restriction the use for such purposes of buildings of brick or stone; but, as to wooden buildings, constituting nearly all those in previous use, it divides the owners or occupiers into two classes, not having respect to their personal character and qualifications for the business, nor the situation and nature and adaptation of the buildings themselves, but merely by an arbitrary line, on one side of which are those who are permitted to pursue their industry by the mere will and consent of the supervisors, and on the other those from whom that consent is withheld, at their mere will and pleasure. . . .

The rights of the petitioners, as affected by the proceedings of which they complain, are not less, because they are aliens and subjects of the Emperor of China. . . .

The Fourteenth Amendment to the Constitution is not confined to the protection of citizens. It says: "Nor shall any State deprive any person of life, liberty, or property without due process of law; nor deny to any person within its jurisdiction the equal protection of the laws." These provisions are universal in their application, to all persons within the territorial jurisdiction, without regard to any differences of race, of color, or of nationality; and the equal protection of the laws is a pledge of the protection of equal laws. . . .

It is contended on the part of the petitioners, that the ordinances for violations of which they are severally sentenced to imprisonment, are void on their face, as being within the prohibitions of the Fourteenth Amendment; and, in the alternative, if not so, that they are void by reason of their administration, operating unequally, so as to punish in the present petitioners what is permitted to others as lawful, without any distinction of circumstances—an unjust and illegal discrimination, it is claimed, which, though not made expressly by the ordinances is made possible by them.

When we consider the nature and the theory of our institutions of government, the principles upon which they are supposed to rest, and review the history of their development, we are constrained to conclude that they do not mean to leave room for the play and action of purely personal and arbitrary power. . . . For, the very idea that one man may be compelled to hold his life, or the means of living, or any material right essential to the enjoyment of life, at the mere will of another, seems to be intolerable in any country where freedom prevails, as being the essence of slavery itself.

There are many illustrations that might be given of this truth, which would make manifest that it was self-evident in the light of our system of jurisprudence. The case of the political franchise of voting is one. Though not regarded strictly as a natural right, but as a privilege merely conceded by society according to its will, under certain conditions, nevertheless it is regarded as a fundamental political right, because preservative of all rights. . . .

In the present cases we are not obliged to reason from the probable to the actual, and pass upon the validity of the ordinances complained of, as tried merely by the opportunities which their terms afford, of unequal and unjust discrimination in their administration. For the cases present the ordinances in actual operation, and the facts shown establish an administration directed so exclusively against a particular class of persons as to warrant and require the conclusion, that, whatever may have been the intent of the ordinances as adopted, they are applied by the public authorities charged with their administration, and thus representing the State itself, with a mind so unequal and oppressive as to amount to a practical denial by the State of that equal protection of the laws which is secured to the petitioners, as to all other persons, by the broad and benign provisions of the Fourteenth Amendment to the Constitution of the United States. Though the law itself be fair on its face and impartial in appearance, yet, if it is applied and administered by public authority with an evil eye and an unequal hand, so as practically to make unjust and illegal discriminations between persons in similar circumstances, material to their rights, the denial of equal justice is still within the prohibition of the Constitution. This principle of interpretation has been sanctioned by this court in *Henderson v. Mayor of New York*, 92 U.S. 259; *Chy Luny v. Freeman*, 92 U.S. 275; *Ex parte Virginia*, 100 U.S. 339; *Neal v. Delaware*, 103 U.S. 370; and *Soon Hing v. Crowley*, 113 U. S. 703.

The present cases, as shown by the facts disclosed in the record, are within this class. It appears that both petitioners have complied with every requisite, deemed by the law or by the public officers charged with its administration, necessary for the protection of neighboring property from fire, or as a precaution against injury to the public health. No reason whatever, except the will of the supervisors, is assigned why they should not be permitted to carry on, in the accustomed manner, their harmless and useful occupation, on which they depend for a livelihood. And while this consent of the supervisors is withheld from them and from two hundred others who have also petitioned, all of whom happen to be Chinese subjects, eighty others, not Chinese subjects, are permitted to carry on the same business under similar conditions. The fact of this discrimination is admitted. No reason for it is shown, and the conclusion cannot be resisted, that no reason for it exists except hostility to the race and nationality to which the petitioners belong, and which in the eye of the law is not justified. The discrimination is, therefore, illegal, and the public administration which enforces it is a denial of the equal protection of the laws and a violation of the Fourteenth Amendment of the Constitution. The imprisonment of the petitioners is, therefore, illegal, and they must be discharged. . . .

Notes and Questions

1. At the very least, *Yick Wo* stands for the proposition that a facially neutral law that is administered in a racially discriminatory manner violates the Equal Protection Clause. Under *Yick Wo*, is it always necessary to have direct evidence of discriminatory administration? Or can extreme discriminatory effects, standing alone, violate the Equal Protection Clause under *Yick Wo*? In this regard, what is the significance of the Court's citation to *Neal v. Delaware*?

2. Two additional aspects of *Yick Wo* are noteworthy. First, it makes clear that, in contrast to the Privileges or Immunities Clause, the protections of the Equal

Protection and Due Process Clauses are not limited to citizens, but extend to all *persons*. Second, *Yick Wo* marks the first time that the Equal Protection Clause has been successfully invoked by someone who is not African-American, thus suggesting broader application than the Court hinted at in *The Slaughter-House Cases.*

Plessy v. Ferguson

163 U.S. 537 (1896)

Mr. Justice Brown . . . delivered the opinion of the court.

This case turns upon the constitutionality of an act of the General Assembly of the State of Louisiana, passed in 1890, providing for separate railway carriages for the white and colored races. . . .

The information filed in the criminal District Court charged in substance that Plessy, being a passenger between two stations within the State of Louisiana, was assigned by officers of the company to the coach used for the race to which he belonged, but he insisted upon going into a coach used by the race to which he did not belong. Neither in the information nor plea was his particular race or color averred.

The petition for the writ of prohibition averred that petitioner was seven eighths Caucasian and one eighth African blood; that the mixture of colored blood was not discernible in him, and that he was entitled to every right, privilege and immunity secured to citizens of the United States of the white race; and that, upon such theory, he took possession of a vacant seat in a coach where passengers of the white race were accommodated, and was ordered by the conductor to vacate said coach and take a seat in another assigned to persons of the colored race, and having refused to comply with such demand he was forcibly ejected with the aid of a police officer, and imprisoned in the parish jail to answer a charge of having violated the above act.

The constitutionality of this act is attacked upon the ground that it conflicts both with the Thirteenth Amendment of the Constitution, abolishing slavery, and the Fourteenth Amendment, which prohibits certain restrictive legislation on the part of the States.

1. That it does not conflict with the Thirteenth Amendment, which abolished slavery and involuntary servitude, except as a punishment for crime, is too clear for argument. Slavery implies involuntary servitude—a state of bondage; the ownership of mankind as a chattel, or at least the control of the labor and services of one man for the benefit of another, and the absence of a legal right to the disposal of his own person, property and services. . . .

A statute which implies merely a legal distinction between the white and colored races—a distinction which is founded in the color of the two races, and which must always exist so long as white men are distinguished from the other race by color—has no tendency to destroy the legal equality of the two races, or reestablish a state of involuntary servitude. . . .

2. By the Fourteenth Amendment, all persons born or naturalized in the United States, and subject to the jurisdiction thereof, are made citizens of the United States and of the State wherein they reside; and the States are forbidden from making or enforcing any law which shall abridge the privileges or immunities of citizens of the United States, or shall deprive any person of life, liberty or property without due process of law, or deny to any person within their jurisdiction the equal protection of the laws. . . .

The object of the amendment was undoubtedly to enforce the absolute equality of the two races before the law, but in the nature of things it could not have been intended to abolish distinctions based upon color, or to enforce social, as distinguished from political equality, or a commingling of the two races upon terms unsatisfactory to either. Laws permitting, and even requiring, their separation in places where they are liable to be brought into contact do not necessarily imply the inferiority of either race to the other, and have been generally, if not universally, recognized as within the competency of the state legislatures in the exercise of their police power. The most common instance of this is connected with the establishment of separate schools for white and colored children, which have been held to be a valid exercise of the legislative power even by courts of States where the political rights of the colored race have been longest and most earnestly enforced. . . .

Similar laws have been enacted by Congress under its general power of legislation over the District of Columbia, as well as by the legislatures of many of the States, and have been generally, if not uniformly, sustained by the courts.

Laws forbidding the intermarriage of the two races may be said in a technical sense to interfere with the freedom of contract, and yet have been universally recognized as within the police power of the State.

The distinction between laws interfering with the political equality of the negro and those requiring the separation of the two races in schools, theatres, and railway carriages has been frequently drawn by this court. Thus in *Strauder v. West Virginia*, 100 U.S. 303, it was held that a law of West Virginia limiting to white male persons, 21 years of age and citizens of the State, the right to sit upon juries, was a discrimination which implied a legal inferiority in civil society, which lessened the security of the right of the colored race, and was a step toward reducing them to a condition of servility. . . .

In this connection, it is also suggested by the learned counsel for the plaintiff in error that the same argument that will justify the state legislature in requiring railways to provide separate accommodations for the two races will also authorize them to require separate cars to be provided for people whose hair is of a certain color, or who are aliens, or who belong to certain nationalities, or to enact laws requiring colored people to walk upon one side of the street, and white people upon the other, or requiring white men's houses to be painted white, and colored men's black, or their vehicles or business signs to be of different colors, upon the theory that one side of the street is as good as the other, or that a house or vehicle of one color is as good as one of another color. The reply to all this is that every exercise of the police power must be reasonable, and extend only to such laws as are enacted in good faith for the promotion [of] the public good, and not for the annoyance or oppression of a particular class. Thus in *Yick Wo v. Hopkins*, 118 U.S. 356, it was held by this court that a municipal ordinance of the city of San Francisco, to regulate the carrying on of public laundries within the limits of the municipality, violated the provisions of the Constitution of the United States, if it conferred upon the municipal authorities arbitrary power, at their own will, and without regard to discretion, in the legal sense of the term, to give or withhold consent as to persons or places, without regard to the competency of the persons applying, or the propriety of the places selected for the carrying on of the business. It was held to be a covert attempt on the part of the municipality to make an arbitrary and unjust discrimination against the Chinese race. . . .

So far, then, as a conflict with the Fourteenth Amendment is concerned, the case reduces itself to the question whether the statute of Louisiana is a reasonable regulation, and with respect to this there must necessarily be a large discretion on the part of the legislature. In determining the question of reasonableness it is at liberty to act with reference to the established usages, customs, and traditions of the people, and with a view to the promotion of their comfort, and the preservation of the public peace and good order. Gauged by this standard, we cannot say that a law which authorizes or even requires the separation of the two races in public conveyances is unreasonable, or more obnoxious to the Fourteenth Amendment than the acts of Congress requiring separate schools for colored children in the District of Columbia, the constitutionality of which does not seem to have been questioned, or the corresponding acts of state legislatures.

We consider the underlying fallacy of the plaintiff's argument to consist in the assumption that the enforced separation of the two races stamps the colored race with a badge of inferiority. If this be so, it is not by reason of anything found in the act, but solely because the colored race chooses to put that construction upon it. The argument necessarily assumes that if, as has been more than once the case, and is not unlikely to be so again, the colored race should become the dominant power in the state legislature, and should enact a law in precisely similar terms, it would thereby relegate the white race to an inferior position. We imagine that the white race, at least, would not acquiesce in this assumption. The argument also assumes that social prejudices may be overcome by legislation, and that equal rights cannot be secured to the negro except by an enforced commingling of the two races. We cannot accept this proposition. If the two races are to meet upon terms of social equality, it must be the result of natural affinities, a mutual appreciation of each other's merits and a voluntary consent of individuals.... Legislation is powerless to eradicate racial instincts or to abolish distinctions based upon physical differences, and the attempt to do so can only result in accentuating the difficulties of the present situation. If the civil and political rights of both races be equal one cannot be inferior to the other civilly or politically. If one race be inferior to the other socially, the Constitution of the United States cannot put them upon the same plane.

It is true that the question of the proportion of colored blood necessary to constitute a colored person, as distinguished from a white person, is one upon which there is a difference of opinion in the different States, some holding that any visible admixture of black blood stamps the person as belonging to the colored race; others that it depends upon the preponderance of blood; and still others that the predominance of white blood must only be in the proportion of three fourths. But these are questions to be determined under the laws of each State and are not properly put in issue in this case....

Mr. Justice Harlan dissenting....

In respect of civil rights, common to all citizens, the Constitution of the United States does not, I think, permit any public authority to know the race of those entitled to be protected in the enjoyment of such rights....

It was said in argument that the statute of Louisiana does not discriminate against either race, but prescribes a rule applicable alike to white and colored citizens. But this argument does not meet the difficulty. Every one knows that the statute in question had its origin in the purpose, not so much to exclude white persons from railroad cars occupied by blacks, as to exclude colored people from coaches occupied by or assigned to white persons.... The fundamental objection, therefore, to the statute is that it interferes with the personal freedom of citizens.... If a white man and a black man choose to occupy the same public conveyance on a public highway, it is their right to do so, and no government, proceeding alone on grounds of race, can prevent it without infringing the personal liberty of each....

If a State can prescribe, as a rule of civil conduct, that whites and blacks shall not travel as passengers in the same railroad coach, why may it not so regulate the use of the streets of its cities and towns as to compel white citizens to keep on one side of a street and black citizens to keep on the other? Why may it not, upon like grounds, punish whites and blacks who ride together in street cars or in open vehicles on a public road or street? Why may it not require sheriffs to assign whites to one side of a court-room and blacks to the other? And why may it not also prohibit the commingling of the two races in the galleries of legislative halls or in public assemblages convened for the consideration of the political questions of the day? Further, if this statute of Louisiana is consistent with the personal liberty of citizens, why may not the state require the separation in railroad coaches of native and naturalized citizens of the United States, or of Protestants and Roman Catholics? . . . .

The white race deems itself to be the dominant race in this country. And so it is, in prestige, in achievements, in education, in wealth, and in power. So, I doubt not, it will continue to be for all time, if it remains true to its great heritage and holds fast to the principles of constitutional liberty. But in view of the Constitution, in the eye of the law, there is in this country no superior, dominant, ruling class of citizens. There is no caste here. Our Constitution is color-blind, and neither knows nor tolerates classes among citizens. In respect of civil rights, all citizens are equal before the law. The humblest is the peer of the most powerful. The law regards man as man, and takes no account of his surroundings or of his color when his civil rights as guaranteed by the supreme law of the land are involved. It is, therefore, to be regretted that this high tribunal, the final expositor of the fundamental law of the land, has reached the conclusion that it is competent for a State to regulate the enjoyment by citizens of their civil rights solely upon the basis of race.

In my opinion, the judgment this day rendered will, in time, prove to be quite as pernicious as the decision made by this tribunal in the *Dred Scott* case. . . .

The recent amendments of the Constitution, it was supposed, had eradicated these principles from our institutions. . . . The present decision, it may well be apprehended, will not only stimulate aggressions, more or less brutal and irritating, upon the admitted rights of colored citizens, but will encourage the belief that it is possible, by means of state enactments, to defeat the beneficent purposes which the people of the United States had in view when they adopted the recent amendments of the Constitution, by one of which the blacks of this country were made citizens of the United States and of the States in which they respectively reside, and whose privileges and immunities, as citizens, the States are forbidden to abridge. Sixty millions of whites are in no danger from the presence here of eight millions of blacks. The destinies of the two races, in this country, are indissolubly linked together, and the interests of both require that the common government of all shall not permit the seeds of race hate to be planted under the sanction of law. What can more certainly arouse race hate, what more certainly create and perpetuate a feeling of distrust between these races, than state enactments, which, in fact, proceed on the ground that colored citizens are so inferior and degraded that they cannot be allowed to sit in public coaches occupied by white citizens? That, as all will admit, is the real meaning of such legislation as was enacted in Louisiana. . . .

There is a race so different from our own that we do not permit those belonging to it to become citizens of the United States. Persons belonging to it are, with few exceptions, absolutely excluded from our country. I allude to the Chinese race. But by the statute in question, a Chinaman can ride in the same passenger coach with white citizens of the United States, while citizens of the black race in Louisiana, many of whom, perhaps, risked their lives for the preservation of the Union, who are entitled, by law, to participate in the political control of the State and nation, who are not excluded, by law or by reason of their race, from public stations of any kind, and who have all the legal rights that belong to white citizens, are yet declared to be criminals, liable to imprisonment, if they ride in a public coach occupied by citizens of the white race. . . .

If laws of like character should be enacted in the several States of the Union, the effect would be in the highest degree mischievous. Slavery, as an institution tolerated by law, would, it is true, have disappeared from our country, but there would remain a power in the States, by sinister legislation, to interfere with the full enjoyment of the blessings of freedom; to regulate civil rights, common to all citizens, upon the basis of race; and to place in a condition of legal inferiority a large body of American citizens, now constituting a part of the political community called the People of the United States, for whom, and by whom through representatives, our government is administered. . . .

Notes and Questions

1. What theory of equality do the *Plessy* majority and dissenting opinions endorse? Is it a theory of color blindness? An anti-subordination approach? A guarantee of equal outcomes? Of equal treatment? How does this compare with the Court's approach in *Strauder* and *Pace*?

2. Just as in *The Civil Rights Cases*, the *Plessy* Court distinguishes between political and social equality. How clear is the distinction between those two categories?

3. Given *Pace*, how surprising is the outcome in *Plessy*? Given *Plessy*, can it be said that laws banning interracial marriage or segregated schools are unconstitutional?

4. Note how race is constructed under the law at issue in this case. Mr. Plessy, who is 7/8 European and only 1/8 African, viewed himself as white, but the law defines him as "colored." Indeed, in addition to his equality claims, Mr. Plessy also asserted that the reputation of belonging to the white race is "property," and that the law, by treating him as "colored," deprived him of that property. *See Plessy*, 163 U.S. at 549. The Court responded to this claim as follows:

> Conceding this to be so, for the purposes of this case, we are unable to see how this statute deprives him of, or in any way affects his right to such property. . . . [I]f he be a colored man, and he be so assigned, he has been deprived of no property, since he is not lawfully entitled to the reputation of being a White man.

Id. How persuasive is Mr. Plessy's alternative claim? The Court's response?

Chapter 3

The Rise and (Partial) Fall of Substantive Due Process

A. Economic Substantive Due Process

In the years following *The Slaughter-House Cases*, the Court—in a series of cases—suggested in dicta that the Due Process Clauses of the Fifth and Fourteenth Amendments might serve as a basis for invalidating legislation that interfered with what might be termed economic liberty. Thus, for example, in *Munn v. Illinois*, 94 U.S. 113 (1877), the Court indicated that "[u]nder some circumstances" government regulations on the use of one's property or the price for using one's property might be deemed a deprivation of private property without due process of law. *Id.* at 125.

In *Allgeyer v. Louisiana*, 165 U.S. 578 (1897), the Court invoked the Due Process Clause of the Fourteenth Amendment to declare unconstitutional a state law regulating contracting for insurance:

> [W]e think the statute is a violation of the Fourteenth Amendment of the Federal Constitution, in that it deprives the defendants of their liberty without due process of law.... The liberty mentioned in that amendment means not only the right of the citizen to be free from the mere physical restraint of his person, as by incarceration, but the term is deemed to embrace the right of the citizen to be free in the enjoyment of all his faculties; to be free to use them in all lawful ways; to live and work where he will; to earn his livelihood by any lawful calling; to pursue any livelihood or avocation, and for that purpose to enter into all contracts which may be proper, necessary and essential to his carrying out to a successful conclusion the purposes above mentioned....
>
> [W]e do not intend to hold that in no such case can the State exercise its police power. When and how far such power may be legitimately exercised with regard to these subjects must be left for determination to each case as it arises.

Id. at 589-590.

In the following case, the Court relied on *Allgeyer* to set forth an interpretation of the Due Process Clause that eventually would result in the invalidation of hundreds of state and federal laws regulating wages, hours, and working conditions.

Lochner v. New York

198 U.S. 45 (1905)

[At issue in this case is a challenge to the constitutionality of a New York law that makes it a crime for an employer to require or permit an employee in a bakery to work more than sixty hours per week or more than ten hours per day.]

Mr. Justice Peckham . . . delivered the opinion of the court. . . .

The statute necessarily interferes with the right of contract between the employer and employees, concerning the number of hours in which the latter may labor in the bakery of the employer. The general right to make a contract in relation to his business is part of the liberty of the individual protected by the Fourteenth Amendment of the Federal Constitution. *Allgeyer* v. *Louisiana*, 165 U.S. 578. Under that provision no State can deprive any person of life, liberty or property without due process of law. The right to purchase or to sell labor is part of the liberty protected by this amendment, unless there are circumstances which exclude the right. There are, however, certain powers, existing in the sovereignty of each State in the Union, somewhat vaguely termed police powers, the exact description and limitation of which have not been attempted by the courts. Those powers, broadly stated and without, at present, any attempt at a more specific limitation, relate to the safety, health, morals and general welfare of the public. Both property and liberty are held on such reasonable conditions as may be imposed by the governing power of the State in the exercise of those powers, and with such conditions the Fourteenth Amendment was not designed to interfere. . . .

It must, of course, be conceded that there is a limit to the valid exercise of the police power by the State. There is no dispute concerning this general proposition. Otherwise the Fourteenth Amendment would have no efficacy and the legislatures of the States would have unbounded power, and it would be enough to say that any piece of legislation was enacted to conserve the morals, the health or the safety of the people; such legislation would be valid, no matter how absolutely without foundation the claim might be. The claim of the police power would be a mere pretext—become another and delusive name for the supreme sovereignty of the State to be exercised free from constitutional restraint. This is not contended for. In every case that comes before this court, therefore, where legislation of this character is concerned and where the protection of the Federal Constitution is sought, the question necessarily arises: Is this a fair, reasonable and appropriate exercise of the police power of the State, or is it an unreasonable, unnecessary and arbitrary interference with the right of the individual to his personal liberty or to enter into those contracts in relation to labor which may seem to him appropriate or necessary for the support of himself and his family? Of course the liberty of contract relating to labor includes both parties to it. The one has as much right to purchase as the other to sell labor.

This is not a question of substituting the judgment of the court for that of the legislature. If the act be within the power of the State it is valid, although the judgment of the court might be totally opposed to the enactment of such a law. But the question would still remain: Is it within the police power of the State?, and that question must be answered by the court.

The question whether this act is valid as a labor law, pure and simple, may be dismissed in a few words. There is no reasonable ground for interfering with the liberty of person or the right of free contract, by determining the hours of labor, in the occupation of a baker. There is no contention that bakers as a class are not equal in intelligence and capacity to men in other trades or manual occupations, or that they are not able to assert their rights and care for themselves without the protecting arm of the State, interfering with their independence of judgment and of action. They are in no sense wards of the State. Viewed in the light of a purely labor law, with no reference whatever to the question of health, we think that a law like the one before us involves neither the safety, the morals nor the welfare of the public, and that the interest of the public is not in the slightest degree affected by such an act. The law must be upheld, if at all, as a law pertaining to the health of the individual engaged in the occupation of a baker. . . .

We think the limit of the police power has been reached and passed in this case. There is, in our judgment, no reasonable foundation for holding this to be necessary or appropriate as a health law to safeguard the public health or the health of the individuals who are following the trade of a baker. If this statute be valid, and if, therefore, a proper case is made out in which to deny the right of an individual, *sui juris*, as employer or employee, to make contracts for the labor of the latter under the protection of the provisions of the Federal Constitution, there would seem to be no length to which legislation of this nature might not go. . . .

We think that there can be no fair doubt that the trade of a baker, in and of itself, is not an unhealthy one to that degree which would authorize the legislature to interfere with the right to labor, and with the right of free contract on the part of the individual, either as employer or employee. In looking through statistics regarding all trades and occupations, it may be true that the trade of a baker does not appear to be as healthy as some other trades, and is also vastly more healthy than still others. To the common understanding the trade of a baker has never been regarded as an unhealthy one. Very likely physicians would not recommend the exercise of that or of any other trade as a remedy for ill health. Some occupations are more healthy than others, but we think there are none which might not come under the power of the legislature to supervise and control the hours of working therein, if the mere fact that the occupation is not absolutely and perfectly healthy is to confer that right upon the legislative department of the Government. It might be safely affirmed that almost all occupations more or less affect the health. There must be more than the mere fact of the possible existence of some small amount of unhealthiness to warrant legislative interference with liberty. It is unfortunately true that labor, even in any department, may possibly carry with it the seeds of unhealthiness. But are we all, on that account, at the mercy of legislative majorities? A printer, a tinsmith, a locksmith, a carpenter, a cabinetmaker, a dry goods clerk, a bank's, a lawyer's or a physician's clerk, or a clerk in almost any kind of business, would all come under the power of the legislature, on this assumption. No trade, no occupation, no mode of earning one's living, could escape this all-pervading power, and the acts of the legislature in limiting the hours of labor in all employments would be valid, although such limitation might seriously cripple the ability of the laborer to support himself and his family....

It is also urged, pursuing the same line of argument, that it is to the interest of the State that its population should be strong and robust, and therefore any legislation which may be said to tend to make people healthy must be valid as health laws, enacted under the police power. If this be a valid argument and a justification for this kind of legislation, it follows that the protection of the Federal Constitution from undue interference with liberty of person and freedom of contract is visionary, wherever the law is sought to be justified as a valid exercise of the police power. Scarcely any law but might find shelter under such assumptions, and conduct, properly so called, as well as contract, would come under the restrictive sway of the legislature. Not only the hours of employees, but the hours of employers, could be regulated, and doctors, lawyers, scientists, all professional men, as well as athletes and artisans, could be forbidden to fatigue their brains and bodies by prolonged hours of exercise, lest the fighting strength of the State be impaired. We mention these extreme cases because the contention is extreme....

It was further urged on the argument that restricting the hours of labor in the case of bakers was valid because it tended to cleanliness on the part of the workers, as a man was more apt to be cleanly when not overworked, and if cleanly then his "output" was also more likely to be so. What has already been said applies with equal force to this contention. We do not admit the reasoning to be sufficient to justify the claimed right of such interference. The State in that case would assume the position of a supervisor, or *pater familias*, over every act of the individual, and its right of governmental interference with his hours of labor, his hours of exercise, the character thereof, and the extent to which it shall be carried would be recognized and upheld. In our judgment it is not possible in fact to discover the connection between the number of hours a baker may work in the bakery and the healthful quality of the bread made by the workman. The connection, if any exist, is too shadowy and thin to build any argument for the interference of the legislature. If the man works ten hours a day it is all right, but if ten and a half or eleven his health is in danger and his bread may be unhealthful, and, therefore, he shall not be permitted to do it. This, we think, is unreasonable and entirely arbitrary. When assertions such as we have adverted to become necessary in order to give, if possible, a plausible foundation for the contention that the law is a "health law," it gives rise to at least a suspicion that there was some other motive dominating the legislature than the purpose to subserve the public health or welfare....

It is impossible for us to shut our eyes to the fact that many of the laws of this character, while passed under what is claimed to be the police power for the purpose of protecting the public health or welfare, are, in reality, passed from other motives. We are justified in saying so when, from the character of the law and the subject upon which it legislates, it is apparent that the public health or welfare bears but the most remote relation to the law. The purpose of a statute must be determined from the natural and legal effect of the language employed; and whether it is or is not repugnant to the Constitution of the United States must be determined from the natural effect of such statutes when put into operation, and not from their proclaimed purpose. The court looks beyond the mere letter of the law in such cases. *Yick Wo* v. *Hopkins*, 118 U. S. 356.

It is manifest to us that the limitation of the hours of labor as provided for in this section of the statute under which the indictment was found, and the plaintiff in error convicted, has no such direct relation to and no such substantial effect upon the health of the employee, as to justify us in regarding the section as really a health law. It seems to us that the real object and purpose were simply to regulate the hours of labor between the master and his employees (all being men, *sui juris*), in a private business, not dangerous in any degree to morals or in any real and substantial degree to the health of the employees. Under such circumstances the freedom of master and employee to contract with each other in relation to their employment, and in defining the same, cannot be prohibited or interfered with, without violating the Federal Constitution. . . .

Mr. Justice Harlan, with whom Mr. Justice White and Mr. Justice Day concurred, dissenting. . . .

Granting then that there is a liberty of contract which cannot be violated even under the sanction of direct legislative enactment, but assuming, as according to settled law we may assume, that such liberty of contract is subject to such regulations as the State may reasonably prescribe for the common good and the well-being of society, what are the conditions under which the judiciary may declare such regulations to be in excess of legislative authority and void? Upon this point there is no room for dispute; for, the rule is universal that a legislative enactment, Federal or state, is never to be disregarded or held invalid unless it be, beyond question, plainly and palpably in excess of legislative power. . . . If there be doubt as to the validity of the statute, that doubt must therefore be resolved in favor of its validity, and the courts must keep their hands off, leaving the legislature to meet the responsibility for unwise legislation. If the end which the legislature seeks to accomplish be one to which its power extends, and if the means employed to that end, although not the wisest or best, are yet not plainly and palpably unauthorized by law, then the court cannot interfere. In other words, when the validity of a statute is questioned, the burden of proof, so to speak, is upon those who assert it to be unconstitutional. . . .

I do not stop to consider whether any particular view of this economic question presents the sounder theory. What the precise facts are it may be difficult to say. It is enough for the determination of this case, and it is enough for this court to know, that the question is one about which there is room for debate and for an honest difference of opinion. There are many reasons of a weighty, substantial character, based upon the experience of mankind, in support of the theory that, all things considered, more than ten hours' steady work each day, from week to week, in a bakery or confectionery establishment, may endanger the health, and shorten the lives of the workmen, thereby diminishing their physical and mental capacity to serve the State and to provide for those dependent upon them.

If such reasons exist that ought to be the end of this case, for the State is not amenable to the judiciary, in respect of its legislative enactments, unless such enactments are plainly, palpably, beyond all question, inconsistent with the Constitution of the United States. We are not to presume that the State of New York has acted in bad faith. Nor can we assume that its legislature acted without due deliberation, or that it did not determine this question upon the fullest attainable information, and for the common good. We cannot say that the state has acted without reason nor ought we to proceed upon the theory that its action is a mere sham....

I take leave to say that the New York statute, in the particulars here involved, cannot be held to be in conflict with the Fourteenth Amendment, without enlarging the scope of the Amendment far beyond its original purpose and without bringing under the supervision of this court matters which have been supposed to belong exclusively to the legislative departments of the several states when exerting their conceded power to guard the health and safety of their citizens by such regulations as they in their wisdom deem best.... A decision that the New York statute is void under the Fourteenth Amendment will, in my opinion, involve consequences of a far-reaching and mischievous character; for such a decision would seriously cripple the inherent power of the States to care for the lives, health and well-being of their citizens. Those are matters which can be best controlled by the States....

Mr. Justice Holmes dissenting....

This case is decided upon an economic theory which a large part of the country does not entertain. If it were a question whether I agreed with that theory, I should desire to study it further and long before making up my mind. But I do not conceive that to be my duty, because I strongly believe that my agreement or disagreement has nothing to do with the right of a majority to embody their opinions in law.... The Fourteenth Amendment does not enact Mr. Herbert Spencer's Social Statics.... [A] constitution is not intended to embody a particular economic theory, whether of paternalism and the organic relation of the citizen to the State or of *laissez faire*. It is made for people of fundamentally differing views, and the accident of our finding certain opinions natural and familiar or novel and even shocking ought not to conclude our judgment upon the question whether statutes embodying them conflict with the Constitution of the United States....

I think that the word liberty in the Fourteenth Amendment is perverted when it is held to prevent the natural outcome of a dominant opinion, unless it can be said that a rational and fair man necessarily would admit that the statute proposed would infringe fundamental principles as they have been understood by the traditions of our people and our law. It does not need research to show that no such sweeping condemnation can be passed upon the statute before us. A reasonable man might think it a proper measure on the score of health. Men whom I certainly could not pronounce unreasonable would uphold it as a first instalment of a general regulation of the hours of work. . . .

Notes and Questions

1. How does the Court get from *The Slaughter-House Cases*' rejection of a due process right to pursue the common occupations of life to *Lochner*'s endorsement of such a right? *Lochner* cites *Allgeyer*, the case excerpted at the start of this chapter. In turn, *Allgeyer* relied on Justice Bradley's *concurring* opinion in *Butchers' Union Slaughterhouse Co. v. Crescent City Live-Stock Landing Co.*, 111 U.S. 746 (1884), where he wrote for himself on grounds very different from those stated in the majority opinion. And in *Butchers' Union*, Justice Bradley relied upon his own *dissenting* opinion in *The Slaughter-House Cases*! Thus, through this series of interlocking citations, the Court transformed a dissent in one opinion into the majority opinion in a subsequent one. For a critical examination of this stealth form of transforming constitutional law, *see* Peter Nicolas, *Reconstruction*, 10 U.C. Irvine L. Rev. 937 (2020).

2. Recall that in *Calder*, the Court spoke of laws that take from A and give to B. Can *Lochner* be characterized as such a law? If so, who are "A" and "B"? *See* John V. Orth, Due Process of Law: A Brief History 60-65 (Univ. of Kansas Press 2003).

3. What are the purported rationales for the law at issue in *Lochner*, and upon what does the Court rely in determining that these rationales are insufficient to justify the statute's infringement upon liberty? Are legislatures or courts better equipped to make such findings?

4. What is the significance of the *Lochner* Court's citation to *Yick Wo*? What might be the "other motives" to which the majority refers? For an argument that the law at issue in *Lochner* was enacted at the behest of large bakeries—which were already paying higher wages and limiting hours as a result of their unionized workforces—to make it harder for smaller non-unionized bakeries to compete with them, *see* David E. Bernstein, Rehabilitating *Lochner*: Defending Individual Rights Against Progressive Reform 23 (Univ. of Chicago Press 2011). For criticism of this argument, *see* Ian Millhiser, *The Most Incompetent Branch*, 23 Geo. Mason L. Rev. 507, 511–12 (2016).

5. Just as Justice Bradley's contrasting views in dissent in *The Slaughter-House Cases* and his concurring opinion in *Bradwell* suggested a double standard between men and women so far as the Privileges or Immunities Clause was concerned, so the Court's initial cases post-*Lochner* suggested a double standard under the Due Process Clause. Thus, in *Muller v. Oregon*, 208 U.S. 412 (1908), the Court upheld a state law limiting the number of hours per day a woman could work, distinguishing *Lochner* as follows:

> That woman's physical structure and the performance of maternal functions place her at a disadvantage in the struggle for subsistence is obvious. This is especially true when the burdens of motherhood are upon her. Even

when they are not, by abundant testimony of the medical fraternity continuance for a long time on her feet at work, repeating this from day to day, tends to injurious effects upon the body, and as healthy mothers are essential to vigorous offspring, the physical well-being of woman becomes an object of public interest and care in order to preserve the strength and vigor of the race.

Still again, history discloses the fact that woman has always been dependent upon man. He established his control at the outset by superior physical strength, and this control in various forms, with diminishing intensity, has continued to the present. As minors, though not to the same extent, she has been looked upon in the courts as needing especial care that her rights may be preserved. Education was long denied her, and while now the doors of the schoolroom are opened and her opportunities for acquiring knowledge are great, yet even with that and the consequent increase of capacity for business affairs it is still true that in the struggle for subsistence she is not an equal competitor with her brother. Though limitations upon personal and contractual rights may be removed by legislation, there is that in her disposition and habits of life which will operate against a full assertion of those rights. She will still be where some legislation to protect her seems necessary to secure a real equality of right. Doubtless there are individual exceptions, and there are many respects in which she has an advantage over him; but looking at it from the viewpoint of the effort to maintain an independent position in life, she is not upon an equality. Differentiated by these matters from the other sex, she is properly placed in a class by herself, and legislation designed for her protection may be sustained, even when like legislation is not necessary for men and could not be sustained. It is impossible to close one's eyes to the fact that she still looks to her brother and depends upon him. Even though all restrictions on political, personal and contractual rights were taken away, and she stood, so far as statutes are concerned, upon an absolutely equal plane with him, it would still be true that she is so constituted that she will rest upon and look to him for protection; that her physical structure and a proper discharge of her maternal functions—having in view not merely her own health, but the well-being of the race—justify legislation to protect her from the greed as well as the passion of man. The limitations which this statute places upon her contractual powers, upon her right to agree with her employer as to the time she shall labor, are not imposed solely for her benefit, but also largely for the benefit of all. Many words cannot make this plainer. The two sexes differ in structure of body, in the functions to be performed by each, in the amount of physical strength, in the capacity for long-continued labor, particularly when done standing, the influence of vigorous health upon the future well-being of the race, the self-reliance which enables one to assert full rights, and in the capacity to maintain the struggle for subsistence. This difference

> justifies a difference in legislation and upholds that which is designed to compensate for some of the burdens which rest upon her.

Id. at 421-423. In *Quong Wing v. Kirkendall*, 223 U.S. 59 (1912), the Court relied on *Muller* to uphold—against an Equal Protection Clause challenge brought by a man—a statute that exempted small laundries operated by women from a license tax:

> If the state. . . . finds a ground of distinction in sex, that is not without precedent. It has been recognized with regard to hours of work. *Muller v. Oregon*, 208 U.S. 412. It is recognized in the respective rights of husband and wife in land during life, in the inheritance after the death of the spouse. Often it is expressed in the time fixed for coming of age. If Montana deems it advisable to put a lighter burden upon women than upon men with regard to an employment that our people commonly regard as more appropriate for the former, the Fourteenth Amendment does not interfere by creating a fictitious equality where there is a real difference. The particular points at which that difference shall be emphasized by legislation are largely in the power of the State.

Id. at 63. In 1919, Congress voted to send to the states what would become the Nineteenth Amendment. The Amendment, which was ratified by the states in 1920, provides as follows:

> The right of citizens of the United States to vote shall not be denied or abridged by the United States or by any state on account of sex.
>
> Congress shall have power to enforce this article by appropriate legislation.

To what extent did the Nineteenth Amendment undermine the basis for *Muller* distinguishing *Lochner*? In *Adkins v. Children's Hospital*, 261 U.S. 525 (1923), the Court relied on this development in declaring unconstitutional a law establishing a minimum wage for women:

> In the *Muller* case the validity of an Oregon statute, forbidding the employment of any female in certain industries more than ten hours during any one day was upheld. The decision proceeded upon the theory that the difference between the sexes may justify a different rule respecting hours of labor in the case of women than in the case of men. It is pointed out that these consist in differences of physical structure, especially in respect of the maternal functions, and also in the fact that historically woman has always been dependent upon man, who has established his control by superior physical strength. . . . But the ancient inequality of the sexes, otherwise than physical, as suggested in the *Muller* case has continued "with diminishing intensity." In view of the great—not to say revolutionary—changes which have taken place since that utterance, in the contractual, political and civil status of women, culminating in the Nineteenth Amendment, it is not unreasonable to say that these differences have now come almost, if not quite, to the vanishing point. In this aspect of the matter, while the physical differences must be recognized in appropriate cases, and legislation fixing

> hours or conditions of work may properly take them into account, we cannot accept the doctrine that women of mature age, *sui juris*, require or may be subjected to restrictions upon their liberty of contract which could not lawfully be imposed in the case of men under similar circumstances. To do so would be to ignore all the implications to be drawn from the present day trend of legislation, as well as that of common thought and usage, by which woman is accorded emancipation from the old doctrine that she must be given special protection or be subjected to special restraint in her contractual and civil relationships.

Id. at 552-553.

* * *

The Court was much criticized in the years following the *Lochner* decision. Indeed, the decision and its aftermath was the impetus for President Roosevelt's so-called "court-packing plan," under which the President would have had the power to appoint up to an additional six Justices to the Court.

The following decision—*West Coast Hotel Co. v. Parrish*—overrules *Adkins v. Children's Hospital* and represents the so-called "switch in time that saved nine." It represents the end of the *Lochner* era and the ushering in of a more deferential standard of review under the Due Process Clause.

West Coast Hotel Co. v. Parrish

300 U.S. 379 (1937)

[At issue in this case is the constitutionality of a Washington State statute establishing a minimum wage for women only.]

Mr. Chief Justice Hughes delivered the opinion of the Court. . . .

The state court has refused to regard the decision in the *Adkins* case as determinative and has pointed to our decisions both before and since that case as justifying its position. We are of the opinion that this ruling of the state court demands on our part a reexamination of the *Adkins* case. The importance of the question, in which many States having similar laws are concerned, the close division by which the decision in the *Adkins* case was reached, and the economic conditions which have supervened, and in the light of which the reasonableness of the exercise of the protective power of the State must be considered, make it not only appropriate, but we think imperative, that in deciding the present case the subject should receive fresh consideration. . . .

The principle which must control our decision is not in doubt. The constitutional provision invoked is the due process clause of the Fourteenth Amendment governing the States, as the due process clause invoked in the *Adkins* case governed Congress. In each case the violation alleged by those attacking minimum wage regulation for women is deprivation of freedom of contract. What is this freedom? The Constitution does not speak of freedom of contract. It speaks of liberty and prohibits the deprivation of liberty without due process of law. In prohibiting that deprivation the Constitution does not recognize an absolute and uncontrollable liberty. Liberty in each of its phases has its history and connotation. But the liberty safeguarded is liberty in a social organization which requires the protection of law against the evils which menace the health, safety, morals and welfare of the people. Liberty under the Constitution is thus necessarily subject to the restraints of due process, and regulation which is reasonable in relation to its subject and is adopted in the interests of the community is due process. . . .

The minimum wage to be paid under the Washington statute is fixed after full consideration by representatives of employers, employees and the public. It may be assumed that the minimum wage is fixed in consideration of the services that are performed in the particular occupations under normal conditions. Provision is made for special licenses at less wages in the case of women who are incapable of full service. The statement of Mr. Justice Holmes in the *Adkins* case is pertinent: "This statute does not compel anybody to pay anything. It simply forbids employment at rates below those fixed as the minimum requirement of health and right living. It is safe to assume that women will not be employed at even the lowest wages allowed unless they earn them, or unless the employer's business can sustain the burden. In short the law in its character and operation is like hundreds of so-called police laws that have been upheld." 261 U.S. [525], p. 570. And Chief Justice Taft forcibly pointed out the consideration which is basic in a statute of this character: "Legislatures which adopt a requirement of maximum hours or minimum wages may be presumed to believe that when sweating employers are prevented from paying unduly low wages by positive law they will continue their business, abating that part of their profits, which were wrung from the necessities of their employees, and will concede the better terms required by the law; and that while in individual cases hardship may result, the restriction will enure to the benefit of the general class of employees in whose interest the law is passed, and so to that of the community at large." *Id.*, p.563.

We think that the views thus expressed are sound and that the decision in the *Adkins* case was a departure from the true application of the principles governing the regulation by the State of the relation of employer and employed. Those principles have been reenforced by our subsequent decisions. Thus in *Radice v. New York*, 264 U.S. 292, we sustained the New York statute which restricted the employment of women in restaurants at night. In *O'Gorman & Young v. Hartford Fire Insurance Co.*, 282 U.S. 251, which upheld an act regulating the commissions of insurance agents, we pointed to the presumption of the constitutionality of a statute dealing with a subject within the scope of the police power and to the absence of any factual foundation of record for deciding that the limits of power had been transcended. In *Nebbia v. New York*, 291 U.S. 502, dealing with the New York statute providing for minimum prices for milk, the general subject of the regulation of the use of private property and of the making of private contracts received an exhaustive examination and we again declared that if such laws "have a reasonable relation to a proper legislative purpose, and are neither arbitrary nor discriminatory, the requirements of due process are satisfied"; that "with the wisdom of the policy adopted, with the adequacy or practicability of the law enacted to forward it, the courts are both incompetent and unauthorized to deal"; that "times without number we have said that the legislature is primarily the judge of the necessity of such an enactment, that every possible presumption is in favor of its validity, and that though the court may hold views inconsistent with the wisdom of the law, it may not be annulled unless palpably in excess of legislative power." *Id.*, pp. 537, 538.

With full recognition of the earnestness and vigor which characterize the prevailing opinion in the *Adkins* case, we find it impossible to reconcile that ruling with these well-considered declarations. What can be closer to the public interest than the health of women and their protection from unscrupulous and overreaching employers? And if the protection of women is a legitimate end of the exercise of state power, how can it be said that the requirement of the payment of a minimum wage fairly fixed in order to meet the very necessities of existence is not an admissible means to that end? The legislature of the State was clearly entitled to consider the situation of women in employment, the fact that they are in the class receiving the least pay, that their bargaining power is relatively weak, and that they are the ready victims of those who would take advantage of their necessitous circumstances. The legislature was entitled to adopt measures to reduce the evils of the "sweating system," the exploiting of workers at wages so low as to be insufficient to meet the bare cost of living, thus making their very helplessness the occasion of a most injurious competition. The legislature had the right to consider that its minimum wage requirements would be an important aid in carrying out its policy of protection. The adoption of similar requirements by many States evidences a deepseated conviction both as to the presence of the evil and as to the means adapted to check it. Legislative response to that conviction cannot be regarded as arbitrary or capricious, and that is all we have to decide. Even if the wisdom of the policy be regarded as debatable and its effects uncertain, still the legislature is entitled to its judgment.

There is an additional and compelling consideration which recent economic experience has brought into a strong light. The exploitation of a class of workers who are in an unequal position with respect to bargaining power and are thus relatively defenceless against the denial of a living wage is not only detrimental to their health and well being but casts a direct burden for their support upon the community. What these workers lose in wages the taxpayers are called upon to pay. The bare cost of living must be met. We may take judicial notice of the unparalleled demands for relief which arose during the recent period of depression and still continue to an alarming extent despite the degree of economic recovery which has been achieved. It is unnecessary to cite official statistics to establish what is of common knowledge through the length and breadth of the land. While in the instant case no factual brief has been presented, there is no reason to doubt that the State of Washington has encountered the same social problem that is present elsewhere. The community is not bound to provide what is in effect a subsidy for unconscionable employers.

The community may direct its law-making power to correct the abuse which springs from their selfish disregard of the public interest. The argument that the legislation in question constitutes an arbitrary discrimination, because it does not extend to men, is unavailing. This Court has frequently held that the legislative authority, acting within its proper field, is not bound to extend its regulation to all cases which it might possibly reach. The legislature "is free to recognize degrees of harm and it may confine its restrictions to those classes of cases where the need is deemed to be clearest." If "the law presumably hits the evil where it is most felt, it is not to be overthrown because there are other instances to which it might have been applied." There is no "doctrinaire requirement" that the legislation should be couched in all embracing terms. This familiar principle has repeatedly been applied to legislation which singles out women, and particular classes of women, in the exercise of the State's protective power. Their relative need in the presence of the evil, no less than the existence of the evil itself, is a matter for the legislative judgment.

Our conclusion is that the case of *Adkins v. Children's Hospital, supra*, should be, and it is, overruled. . . .

[The dissenting opinion of Justice Sutherland is omitted.]

Notes and Questions

1. At issue in *Williamson v. Lee Optical*, 348 U.S. 483 (1955), was the constitutionality of a state law making it unlawful for any person to fit eyeglass lenses except a licensed optometrist or ophthalmologist. The effect of the law was to forbid opticians from fitting or duplicating lenses without a prescription from an ophthalmologist or optometrist.

In upholding the statute's constitutionality, the Court confirmed the degree of deference due to legislators in considering due process challenges in the post-*Lochner* era:

> The Oklahoma law may exact a needless, wasteful requirement in many cases. But it is for the legislature, not the courts, to balance the advantages and disadvantages of the new requirement. It appears that in many cases the optician can easily supply the new frames or new lenses without reference to the old written prescription. It also appears that many written prescriptions contain no directive data in regard to fitting spectacles to the face. But in some cases the directions contained in the prescription are essential, if the glasses are to be fitted so as to correct the particular defects of vision or alleviate the eye condition. The legislature might have concluded that the frequency of occasions when a prescription is necessary was sufficient to justify this regulation of the fitting of eyeglasses. Likewise, when it is necessary to duplicate a lens, a written prescription may or may not be necessary. But the legislature might have concluded that one was needed often enough to require one in every case. Or the legislature may have concluded that eye examinations were so critical, not only

> for correction of vision but also for detection of latent ailments or diseases, that every change in frames and every duplication of a lens should be accompanied by a prescription from a medical expert. To be sure, the present law does not require a new examination of the eyes every time the frames are changed or the lenses duplicated. For if the old prescription is on file with the optician, he can go ahead and make the new fitting or duplicate the lenses. But the law need not be in every respect logically consistent with its aims to be constitutional. It is enough that there is an evil at hand for correction, and that it might be thought that the particular legislative measure was a rational way to correct it.
>
> The day is gone when this Court uses the Due Process Clause of the Fourteenth Amendment to strike down state laws, regulatory of business and industrial conditions, because they may be unwise, improvident, or out of harmony with a particular school of thought. We emphasize again what Chief Justice Waite said in *Munn v. Illinois*, 94 U.S. 113, 134 "For protection against abuses by legislatures the people must resort to the polls, not to the courts."

Id. at 487-488.

2. What was wrong with the *Lochner* approach? Is it so bad to have courts carefully scrutinizing legislative rationales under the Due Process Clause? After all, historically and still today, legislative bodies invoke rather dubious rationales for enacting laws. Can one oppose *Lochner* and still support serious judicial scrutiny for certain types of laws, such as those restricting abortion, same-sex marriage, and the like? If so, how?

B. Incorporation

Recall from Chapter 1 that in *Barron v. Baltimore*, the U.S. Supreme Court rejected the contention that the provisions of the Bill of Rights applied to the actions of state governments, relying on their text, structure, and history to conclude that they were applicable solely to the actions of the federal government. Recall as well from Chapter 2 that after the adoption of the Reconstruction Amendments, the Court in *United States v. Cruikshank* re-confirmed its holding in *Barron*.

Yet while *Barron* and its progeny made clear that the provisions of the Bill of Rights did not apply against the states *of their own force*, another theory became available after the adoption of the Reconstruction Amendments: that the latter, and in particular the Fourteenth Amendment, somehow "incorporated" some or all of the provisions of the Bill of Rights and in turn made them applicable against the states.

In a series of twentieth century decisions, including *Twining v. New Jersey*, 211 U.S. 78 (1908) and *Palko v. Connecticut*, 302 U.S. 319 (1937), the Court, in reliance on *The Slaughter-House Cases*, rejected reliance on the Privileges or Immunities Clause as a basis for incorporating and applying the Bill of Rights against the states. It also rejected the argument that the Due Process Clause incorporated the Bill of Rights *in toto*. But the Court acknowledged that the Due Process Clause could serve as a vehicle for recognizing analogous protections as against the states. According to the *Twining* Court, "[i]f this is so, it is not because those rights are enumerated in the first eight Amendments, but because they are of such a nature that they are included in the conception of due process of law." According to the *Palko* Court, whether such rights were included in the conception of due process of law depended upon whether they were "implicit in the concept of ordered liberty" such that "neither liberty nor justice would exist if they were sacrificed."

The meaning of these and other lofty phrases used by the Court in the process of determining whether to incorporate and apply provisions of the Bill of Rights against the states is considered in more detail below in the *McDonald* case. But before taking a look at *McDonald*, it is worth examining some alternative approaches to incorporation that have been proposed by other Justices of the Court. In the following case, the Justices spar on the theoretical rationale for incorporating the provisions of the Bill of Rights against the states. As you compare their approaches, consider what is at stake in selecting one approach over the other, not just where incorporation of the Bill of Rights is involved, but where other, unenumerated rights may be at stake.

Adamson v. California

332 U.S. 46 (1947)

MR. JUSTICE REED delivered the opinion of the Court.

The appellant, Adamson, a citizen of the United States, was convicted, without recommendation for mercy, by a jury in a Superior Court of the State of California of murder in the first degree.... The provisions of California law which were challenged in the state proceedings as invalid under the Fourteenth Amendment to the Federal Constitution.... permit the failure of a defendant to explain or to deny evidence against him to be commented upon by court and by counsel and to be considered by court and jury....

We shall assume, but without any intention thereby of ruling upon the issue, that permission by law to the court, counsel and jury to comment upon and consider the failure of defendant "to explain or to deny by his testimony any evidence or facts in the case against him" would infringe defendant's privilege against self-incrimination under the Fifth Amendment if this were a trial in a court of the United States under a similar law....

The due process clause of the Fourteenth Amendment, however, does not draw all the rights of the federal Bill of Rights under its protection. That contention was made and rejected in *Palko v. Connecticut*, 302 U.S. 319, 323. It was rejected with citation of the cases excluding several of the rights, protected by the Bill of Rights, against infringement by the National Government. Nothing has been called to our attention that either the framers of the Fourteenth Amendment or the states that adopted

[it] intended its due process clause to draw within its scope the earlier amendments to the Constitution. *Palko* held that such provisions of the Bill of Rights as were "implicit in the concept of ordered liberty," became secure from state interference by the clause. But it held nothing more.

[The opinion goes on to conclude, in reliance on both *Palko* and *Twining*, that the state law at issue does not violate the Due Process Clause of the Fourteenth Amendment.]

Mr. Justice Frankfurter, concurring. . . .

Between the incorporation of the Fourteenth Amendment into the Constitution and the beginning of the present membership of the Court—a period of seventy years—the scope of that Amendment was passed upon by forty-three judges. Of all these judges, only one, who may respectfully be called an eccentric exception, ever indicated the belief that the Fourteenth Amendment was a shorthand summary of the first eight Amendments theretofore limiting only the Federal Government, and that due process incorporated those eight Amendments as restrictions upon the powers of the States. Among these judges were not only those who would have to be included among the greatest in the history of the Court, but—it is especially relevant to note—they included those whose services in the cause of human rights and the spirit of freedom are the most conspicuous in our history. It is not invidious to single out Miller, Davis, Bradley, Waite, Matthews, Gray, Fuller, Holmes, Brandeis, Stone and Cardozo (to speak only of the dead) as judges who were alert in safeguarding and promoting the interests of liberty and human dignity through law. But they were also judges mindful of the relation of our federal system to a progressively democratic society and therefore duly regardful of the scope of authority that was left to the States even after the Civil War. And so they did not find that the Fourteenth Amendment, concerned as it was with matters fundamental to the pursuit of justice, fastened upon the States procedural arrangements which, in the language of Mr. Justice Cardozo, only those who are "narrow or provincial" would deem essential to "a fair and enlightened system of justice." *Palko v. Connecticut*, 302 U.S. 319, 325. To suggest that it is inconsistent with a truly free society to begin prosecutions without an indictment, to try petty civil cases without the paraphernalia of a common law jury, to take into consideration that one who has full opportunity to make a defense remains silent is, in de Tocqueville's phrase, to confound the familiar with the necessary.

The short answer to the suggestion that the provision of the Fourteenth Amendment, which ordains "nor shall any State deprive any person of life, liberty, or property, without due process of law," was a way of saying that every State must thereafter initiate prosecutions through indictment by a grand jury, must have a trial by a jury of twelve in criminal cases, and must have trial by such a jury in common law suits where the amount in controversy exceeds twenty dollars, is that it is a strange way of saying it. It would be extraordinarily strange for a Constitution to convey such specific commands in such a roundabout and inexplicit way. . . . Those reading the English language with the meaning which it ordinarily conveys, those conversant with the political and legal history of the concept of due process, those sensitive to the relations of the States to the central government as well as the relation of some of the provisions of the Bill of Rights to the process of justice, would hardly recognize the Fourteenth Amendment as a cover for the various explicit provisions of the first eight Amendments.... The notion that the Fourteenth Amendment was a covert way of imposing upon the States all the rules which it seemed important to Eighteenth Century statesmen to write into the Federal Amendments, was rejected by judges who were themselves witnesses of the process by which the Fourteenth Amendment became part of the Constitution. Arguments that may now be adduced to prove that the first eight Amendments were concealed within the historic phrasing of the Fourteenth Amendment were not unknown at the time of its adoption. A surer estimate of their bearing was possible for judges at the time than distorting distance is likely to vouchsafe. Any evidence of design or purpose not contemporaneously known could hardly have influenced those who ratified the Amendment. Remarks of a particular proponent of the Amendment, no matter how influential, are not to be deemed part of the Amendment. What was submitted for ratification was his proposal, not his speech. Thus, at the time of the ratification of the Fourteenth Amendment the constitutions of nearly half of the ratifying States did not have the rigorous requirements of the Fifth Amendment for instituting criminal proceedings through a grand jury. It could hardly have occurred to these States that by ratifying the Amendment they uprooted their established methods for prosecuting crime and fastened upon themselves a new prosecutorial system.

Indeed, the suggestion that the Fourteenth Amendment incorporates the first eight Amendments as such is not unambiguously urged.... There is suggested merely a selective incorporation of the first eight Amendments into the Fourteenth Amendment. Some are in and some are out, but we are left in the dark as to which are in and which are out. Nor are we given the calculus for determining which go in and which stay out. If the basis of selection is merely that those provisions of the first eight Amendments are incorporated which commend themselves to individual justices as indispensable to the dignity and happiness of a free man, we are thrown back to a merely subjective test. The protection against unreasonable search and seizure might have primacy for one judge, while trial by a jury of twelve for every claim above twenty dollars might appear to another as an ultimate need in a free society. In the history of thought "natural law" has a much longer and much better founded meaning and justification than such subjective selection of the first eight Amendments for incorporation into the Fourteenth. If all that is meant is that due process contains within itself certain minimal standards which are "of the very essence of a scheme of ordered liberty," *Palko v. Connecticut*, 302 U.S. 319, 325, putting upon this Court the duty of applying these standards from time to time, then we have merely arrived at the insight which our predecessors long ago expressed....

It may not be amiss to restate the pervasive function of the Fourteenth Amendment in exacting from the States observance of basic liberties. The Amendment neither comprehends the specific provisions by which the founders deemed it appropriate to restrict the federal government nor is it confined to them. The Due Process

Clause of the Fourteenth Amendment has an independent potency, precisely as does the Due Process Clause of the Fifth Amendment in relation to the Federal Government. It ought not to require argument to reject the notion that due process of law meant one thing in the Fifth Amendment and another in the Fourteenth. The Fifth Amendment specifically prohibits prosecution of an "infamous crime" except upon indictment; it forbids double jeopardy; it bars compelling a person to be a witness against himself in any criminal case; it precludes deprivation of "life, liberty, or property, without due process of law. . . ." Are Madison and his contemporaries in the framing of the Bill of Rights to be charged with writing into it a meaningless clause? To consider "due process of law" as merely a shorthand statement of other specific clauses in the same amendment is to attribute to the authors and proponents of this Amendment ignorance of, or indifference to, a historic conception which was one of the great instruments in the arsenal of constitutional freedom which the Bill of Rights was to protect and strengthen.

A construction which gives to due process no independent function but turns it into a summary of the specific provisions of the Bill of Rights would, as has been noted, tear up by the roots much of the fabric of law in the several States, and would deprive the States of opportunity for reforms in legal process designed for extending the area of freedom. It would assume that no other abuses would reveal themselves in the course of time than those which had become manifest in 1791. Such a view not only disregards the historic meaning of "due process." It leads inevitably to a warped construction of specific provisions of the Bill of Rights to bring within their scope conduct clearly condemned by due process but not easily fitting into the pigeon-holes of the specific provisions. It seems pretty late in the day to suggest that a phrase so laden with historic meaning should be given an improvised content consisting of some but not all of the provisions of the first eight Amendments, selected on an undefined basis, with improvisation of content for the provisions so selected.

And so, when, as in a case like the present, a conviction in a State court is here for review under a claim that a right protected by the Due Process Clause of the Fourteenth Amendment has been denied, the issue is not whether an infraction of one of the specific provisions of the first eight Amendments is disclosed by the record. The relevant question is whether the criminal proceedings which resulted in conviction deprived the accused of the due process of law to which the United States Constitution entitled him. Judicial review of that guaranty of the Fourteenth Amendment inescapably imposes upon this Court an exercise of judgment upon the whole course of the proceedings in order to ascertain whether they offend those canons of decency and fairness which express the notions of justice of English-speaking peoples even toward those charged with the most heinous offenses. These standards of justice are not authoritatively formulated anywhere as though they were prescriptions in a pharmacopoeia. But neither does the application of the Due Process Clause imply that judges are wholly at large. The judicial judgment in applying the Due Process Clause must move within the limits of accepted notions of justice and is not to be based upon the idiosyncrasies of a merely personal judgment.

The fact that judges among themselves may differ whether in a particular case a trial offends accepted notions of justice is not disproof that general rather than idiosyncratic standards are applied....

Mr. Justice Black, dissenting.

I agree that if *Twining* be reaffirmed, the result reached might appropriately follow. But I would not reaffirm the *Twining* decision. I think that decision and the "natural law" theory of the Constitution upon which it relies degrade the constitutional safeguards of the Bill of Rights and simultaneously appropriate for this Court a broad power which we are not authorized by the Constitution to exercise....

The first ten amendments were proposed and adopted largely because of fear that Government might unduly interfere with prized individual liberties. The people wanted and demanded a Bill of Rights written into their Constitution. The amendments embodying the Bill of Rights were intended to curb all branches of the Federal Government in the fields touched by the amendments—Legislative, Executive, and Judicial....

But these limitations were not expressly imposed upon state court action. In 1833, *Barron v. Baltimore* was decided by this Court.... In deciding the particular point raised, the Court there said that it could not hold that the first eight amendments applied to the states. This was the controlling constitutional rule when the Fourteenth Amendment was proposed in 1866.

My study of the historical events that culminated in the Fourteenth Amendment, and the expressions of those who sponsored and favored, as well as those who opposed its submission and passage, persuades me that one of the chief objects that the provisions of the Amendment's first section, separately, and as a whole, were intended to accomplish was to make the Bill of Rights, applicable to the states. With full knowledge of the import of the *Barron* decision, the framers and backers of the Fourteenth Amendment proclaimed its purpose to be to overturn the constitutional rule that case had announced. This historical purpose has never received full consideration or exposition in any opinion of this Court interpreting the Amendment....

For this reason, I am attaching to this dissent an appendix which contains a résumé, by no means complete, of the Amendment's history. In my judgment that history conclusively demonstrates that the language of the first section of the Fourteenth Amendment, taken as a whole, was thought by those responsible for its submission to the people, and by those who opposed its submission, sufficiently explicit to guarantee that thereafter no state could deprive its citizens of the privileges and protections of the Bill of Rights.... And I further contend that the "natural law" formula which the Court uses to reach its conclusion in this case should be abandoned as an incongruous excrescence on our Constitution. I believe that formula to be itself a violation of our Constitution, in that it subtly conveys to courts, at the expense of legislatures, ultimate power over public policies in fields where no specific provision of the Constitution limits legislative power. And my belief seems to be in accord with the views expressed by this Court, at least for the first two decades after the Fourteenth Amendment was adopted.

In 1872, four years after the Amendment was adopted, the *Slaughter-House* cases came to this Court. The Court was not presented in that case with the evidence which showed that the special sponsors of the Amendment in the House and Senate had expressly explained one of its principal purposes to be to change the Constitution as construed in *Barron v. Baltimore,* and make the Bill of Rights applicable to the states. Nor was there reason to do so. For the state law under consideration in the *Slaughter-House* cases was only challenged as one which authorized a monopoly, and the brief for the challenger properly conceded that there was "no direct constitutional provision against a monopoly." The argument did not invoke any specific provision of the Bill of Rights, but urged that the state monopoly statute violated "the natural right of a person" to do business and engage in his trade or vocation. On this basis, it was contended that "bulwarks that have been erected around the investments of capital are impregnable against state legislation." These natural law arguments, so suggestive of the premises on which the present due process formula rests, were flatly rejected by a majority of the Court in the *Slaughter-House* cases. What the Court did hold was that the privileges and immunities clause of the Fourteenth Amendment only protected from state invasion such rights as a person has because he is a citizen of the United States. The Court enumerated some, but refused to enumerate all of these national rights. The majority of the Court emphatically declined the invitation of counsel to hold that the Fourteenth Amendment subjected all state regulatory legislation to continuous censorship by this Court in order for it to determine whether it collided with this Court's opinion of "natural" right and justice. In effect, the *Slaughter-House* cases rejected the very natural justice formula the Court today embraces. The Court did not meet the question of whether the safeguards of the Bill of Rights were protected against state invasion by the Fourteenth Amendment. . . .

[Justice Black here discusses the *Lochner* line of cases.]

The foregoing constitutional doctrine, judicially created and adopted by expanding the previously accepted meaning of "due process," marked a complete departure from the *Slaughter-House* philosophy of judicial tolerance of state regulation of business activities. Conversely, the new formula contracted the effectiveness of the Fourteenth Amendment as a protection from state infringement of individual liberties enumerated in the Bill of Rights. Thus the Court's second-thought interpretation of the Amendment was an about-face from the *Slaughter-House* interpretation and represented a failure to carry out the avowed purpose of the Amendment's sponsors. . . .

The *Twining* decision, rejecting the compelled testimony clause of the Fifth Amendment, and indeed rejecting all the Bill of Rights, is the end product of one phase of this philosophy. . . .

At the same time that the *Twining* decision held that the states need not conform to the specific provisions of the Bill of Rights, it consolidated the power that the Court had assumed under the due process clause by laying even broader foundations for the Court to invalidate state and even federal regulatory legislation. . . .

I cannot consider the Bill of Rights to be an outworn 18th Century "strait jacket" as the *Twining* opinion did. Its provisions may be thought outdated abstractions by some. And it is true that they were designed to meet ancient evils. But they are the same kind of human evils that have emerged from century to century wherever excessive power is sought by the few at the expense of the many. In my judgment the people of no nation can lose their liberty so long as a Bill of Rights like ours survives and its basic purposes are conscientiously interpreted, enforced and respected so as to afford continuous protection against old, as well as new, devices and practices which might thwart those purposes. I fear to see the consequences of the Court's practice of substituting its own concepts of decency and fundamental justice for the language of the Bill of Rights as its point of departure in interpreting and enforcing that Bill of Rights. If the choice must be between the selective process of the *Palko* decision applying some of the Bill of Rights to the States, or the *Twining* rule applying none of them, I would choose the *Palko* selective process. But rather than accept either of these choices, I would follow what I believe was the original purpose of the Fourteenth Amendment—to extend to all the people of the nation the complete protection of the Bill of Rights. To hold that this Court can determine what, if any, provisions of the Bill of Rights will be enforced, and if so to what degree, is to frustrate the great design of a written Constitution. . . .

MR. JUSTICE MURPHY, with whom MR. JUSTICE RUTLEDGE concurs, dissenting.

While in substantial agreement with the views of MR. JUSTICE BLACK, I have one reservation and one addition to make.

I agree that the specific guarantees of the Bill of Rights should be carried over intact into the first section of the Fourteenth Amendment. But I am not prepared to say that the latter is entirely and necessarily limited by the Bill of Rights. Occasions may arise where a proceeding falls so far short of conforming to fundamental standards of procedure as to warrant constitutional condemnation in terms of a lack of due process despite the absence of a specific provision in the Bill of Rights. . . .

McDonald v. City of Chicago

561 U.S. 742 (2010)

Justice Alito announced the judgment of the Court and delivered the opinion of the Court with respect to Parts I, II-A, II-B, II-D, III-A, and III-B, in which The Chief Justice, Justice Scalia, Justice Kennedy, and Justice Thomas join, and an opinion with respect to Parts II-C, IV, and V, in which The Chief Justice, Justice Scalia, and Justice Kennedy join.

Two years ago, in *District of Columbia v. Heller,* 554 U.S. 570 (2008), we held that the Second Amendment protects the right to keep and bear arms for the purpose of self-defense, and we struck down a District of Columbia law that banned the possession of handguns in the home. The city of Chicago (City) and the village of Oak Park, a Chicago suburb, have laws that are similar to the District of Columbia's, but Chicago and Oak Park argue that their laws are constitutional because the Second Amendment has no application to the States. We have previously held that most of the provisions of the Bill of Rights apply with full force to both the Federal Government and the States. Applying the standard that is well established in our case law, we hold that the Second Amendment right is fully applicable to the States....

II

....

B

The Bill of Rights, including the Second Amendment, originally applied only to the Federal Government. In *Barron ex rel. Tiernan v. Mayor of Baltimore,* 7 Pet. 243 (1833), the Court, in an opinion by Chief Justice Marshall, explained that this question was "of great importance" but "not of much difficulty." *Id.*, at 247. In less than four pages, the Court firmly rejected the proposition that the first eight Amendments operate as limitations on the States, holding that they apply only to the Federal Government.

The constitutional Amendments adopted in the aftermath of the Civil War fundamentally altered our country's federal system. The provision at issue in this case, § 1 of the Fourteenth Amendment, provides, among other things, that a State may not abridge "the privileges or immunities of citizens of the United States" or deprive "any person of life, liberty, or property, without due process of law."

Four years after the adoption of the Fourteenth Amendment, this Court was asked to interpret the Amendment's reference to "the privileges or immunities of citizens of the United States." The *Slaughter-House Cases, supra,* involved challenges to a Louisiana law permitting the creation of a state-sanctioned monopoly on the butchering of animals within the city of New Orleans. Justice Samuel Miller's opinion for the Court concluded that the Privileges or Immunities Clause protects only those rights "which owe their existence to the Federal government, its National character, its Constitution, or its laws." *Id.,* at 79. The Court held that other fundamental rights—rights that predated the creation of the Federal Government and that "the

State governments were created to establish and secure"—were not protected by the Clause. *Id.*, at 76.

In drawing a sharp distinction between the rights of federal and state citizenship, the Court relied on two principal arguments. First, the Court emphasized that the Fourteenth Amendment's Privileges or Immunities Clause spoke of "the privileges or immunities of *citizens of the United States*," and the Court contrasted this phrasing with the wording in the first sentence of the Fourteenth Amendment and in the Privileges and Immunities Clause of Article IV, both of which refer to *state* citizenship.[5] (Emphasis added.) Second, the Court stated that a contrary reading would "radically chang[e] the whole theory of the relations of the State and Federal governments to each other and of both these governments to the people," and the Court refused to conclude that such a change had been made "in the absence of language which expresses such a purpose too clearly to admit of doubt." *Id.*, at 78. Finding the phrase "privileges or immunities of citizens of the United States" lacking by this high standard, the Court reasoned that the phrase must mean something more limited.

Under the Court's narrow reading, the Privileges or Immunities Clause protects such things as the right

> "to come to the seat of government to assert any claim [a citizen] may have upon that government, to transact any business he may have with it, to seek its protection, to share its offices, to engage in administering its functions . . . [and to] become a citizen of any State of the Union by a *bona fide* residence therein, with the same rights as other citizens of that State."

Finding no constitutional protection against state intrusion of the kind envisioned by the Louisiana statute, the Court upheld the statute. . . .

Today, many legal scholars dispute the correctness of the narrow *Slaughter-House* interpretation. . . .

Three years after the decision in the *Slaughter–House Cases*, the Court decided *Cruikshank*. . . . In that case, the Court reviewed convictions stemming from the infamous Colfax Massacre in Louisiana on Easter Sunday 1873. Dozens of blacks, many unarmed, were slaughtered by a rival band of armed white men. Cruikshank himself allegedly marched unarmed African–American prisoners through the streets and then had them summarily executed. Ninety-seven men were indicted for participating in the massacre, but only nine went to trial. Six of the nine were acquitted of all charges; the remaining three were acquitted of murder but convicted under the Enforcement Act of 1870, 16 Stat. 140, for banding and conspiring

5. The first sentence of the Fourteenth Amendment makes "[a]ll persons born or naturalized in the United States and subject to the jurisdiction thereof . . . citizens of the United States *and of the State wherein they reside*." (Emphasis added.) The Privileges and Immunities Clause of Article IV provides that "[t]he Citizens of each State shall be entitled to all Privileges and Immunities of *Citizens in the several States*." (Emphasis added.)

together to deprive their victims of various constitutional rights, including the right to bear arms.

The Court reversed all of the convictions, including those relating to the deprivation of the victims' right to bear arms. The Court wrote that the right of bearing arms for a lawful purpose "is not a right granted by the Constitution" and is not "in any manner dependent upon that instrument for its existence." "The second amendment," the Court continued, "declares that it shall not be infringed; but this . . . means no more than that it shall not be infringed by Congress." *Ibid.* "Our later decisions in *Presser v. Illinois*, 116 U.S. 252, 265 (1886), and *Miller v. Texas*, 153 U.S. 535, 538 (1894), reaffirmed that the Second Amendment applies only to the Federal Government." *Heller*, 554 U.S., at 620 n. 23.

C

. . . .In petitioners' view, the Privileges or Immunities Clause protects all of the rights set out in the Bill of Rights, as well as some others, but petitioners are unable to identify the Clause's full scope. Nor is there any consensus on that question among the scholars who agree that the *Slaughter-House Cases*' interpretation is flawed.

We see no need to reconsider that interpretation here. For many decades, the question of the rights protected by the Fourteenth Amendment against state infringement has been analyzed under the Due Process Clause of that Amendment and not under the Privileges or Immunities Clause. We therefore decline to disturb the *Slaughter-House* holding.

At the same time, however, this Court's decisions in *Cruikshank*, *Presser*, and *Miller* do not preclude us from considering whether the Due Process Clause of the Fourteenth Amendment makes the Second Amendment right binding on the States. *See Heller*, 554 U.S., at 620 n. 23. None of those cases "engage[d] in the sort of Fourteenth Amendment inquiry required by our later cases." *Ibid.* As explained more fully below, *Cruikshank*, *Presser*, and *Miller* all preceded the era in which the Court began the process of "selective incorporation" under the Due Process Clause, and we have never previously addressed the question whether the right to keep and bear arms applies to the States under that theory.

Indeed, *Cruikshank* has not prevented us from holding that other rights that were at issue in that case are binding on the States through the Due Process Clause. In *Cruikshank*, the Court held that the general "right of the people peaceably to assemble for lawful purposes," which is protected by the First Amendment, applied only against the Federal Government and not against the States. Nonetheless, over 60 years later the Court held that the right of peaceful assembly was a "fundamental righ[t] . . . safeguarded by the due process clause of the Fourteenth Amendment." *De Jonge v. Oregon*, 299 U.S. 353, 364 (1937). We follow the same path here and thus consider whether the right to keep and bear arms applies to the States under the Due Process Clause.

D

1

In the late 19th century, the Court began to consider whether the Due Process Clause prohibits the States from infringing rights set out in the Bill of Rights. Five features of the approach taken during the ensuing era should be noted.

First, the Court viewed the due process question as entirely separate from the question whether a right was a privilege or immunity of national citizenship. See *Twining v. New Jersey,* 211 U.S. 78, 99 (1908).

Second, the Court explained that the only rights protected against state infringement by the Due Process Clause were those rights "of such a nature that they are included in the conception of due process of law." *Ibid.* While it was "possible that some of the personal rights safeguarded by the first eight Amendments against National action [might] also be safeguarded against state action," the Court stated, this was "not because those rights are enumerated in the first eight Amendments." *Twining, supra,* at 99.

The Court used different formulations in describing the boundaries of due process. For example, in *Twining,* the Court referred to "immutable principles of justice which inhere in the very idea of free government which no member of the Union may disregard." 211 U.S., at 102. In *Snyder v. Massachusetts,* 291 U.S. 97, 105 (1934), the Court spoke of rights that are "so rooted in the traditions and conscience of our people as to be ranked as fundamental." And in *Palko,* the Court famously said that due process protects those rights that are "the very essence of a scheme of ordered liberty" and essential to "a fair and enlightened system of justice." 302 U.S., at 325.

Third, in some cases decided during this era the Court "can be seen as having asked, when inquiring into whether some particular procedural safeguard was required of a State, if a civilized system could be imagined that would not accord the particular protection." *Duncan v. Louisiana,* 391 U.S. 145, 149, n. 14 (1968). Thus, in holding that due process prohibits a State from taking private property without just compensation, the Court described the right as "a principle of natural equity, recognized by all temperate and civilized governments, from a deep and universal sense of its justice." *Chicago, B. & Q.R. Co., supra,* at 238. Similarly, the Court found that due process did not provide a right against compelled incrimination in part because this right "has no place in the jurisprudence of civilized and free countries outside the domain of the common law." *Twining, supra,* at 113.

Fourth, the Court during this era was not hesitant to hold that a right set out in the Bill of Rights failed to meet the test for inclusion within the protection of the Due Process Clause. The Court found that some such rights qualified. But others did not.

Finally, even when a right set out in the Bill of Rights was held to fall within the conception of due process, the protection or remedies afforded against state infringement sometimes differed from the protection or remedies provided against abridgment by the Federal Government. . . .

2

An alternative theory regarding the relationship between the Bill of Rights and § 1 of the Fourteenth Amendment was championed by Justice Black. This theory held that § 1 of the Fourteenth Amendment totally incorporated all of the provisions of the Bill of Rights. See, *e.g., Adamson, supra,* at 71-72 (Black, J., dissenting); *Duncan, supra,* at 166 (Black, J., concurring). As Justice Black noted, the chief congressional proponents of the Fourteenth Amendment espoused the view that the Amendment made the Bill of Rights applicable to the States and, in so doing, overruled this Court's decision in *Barron. Adamson, supra,* at 72 (dissenting opinion). Nonetheless, the Court never has embraced Justice Black's "total incorporation" theory.

3

While Justice Black's theory was never adopted, the Court eventually moved in that direction by initiating what has been called a process of "selective incorporation," *i.e.,* the Court began to hold that the Due Process Clause fully incorporates particular rights contained in the first eight Amendments.

The decisions during this time abandoned three of the previously noted characteristics of the earlier period. The Court made it clear that the governing standard is not whether *any* "civilized system [can] be imagined that would not accord the particular protection." *Duncan,* 391 U.S., at 149, n. 14. Instead, the Court inquired whether a particular Bill of Rights guarantee is fundamental to *our* scheme of ordered liberty and system of justice. *Id.,* at 149, and n. 14; see also *id.,* at 148 (referring to those "fundamental principles of liberty and justice which lie at the base of all *our* civil and political institutions").

The Court also shed any reluctance to hold that rights guaranteed by the Bill of Rights met the requirements for protection under the Due Process Clause. The Court eventually incorporated almost all of the provisions of the Bill of Rights. Only a handful of the Bill of Rights protections remain unincorporated.[13]

Finally, the Court abandoned "the notion that the Fourteenth Amendment applies to the States only a watered-down, subjective version of the individual guarantees of the Bill of Rights," stating that it would be "incongruous" to apply different standards "depending on whether the claim was asserted in a state or federal court."

---

13. In addition to the right to keep and bear arms (and the Sixth Amendment right to a unanimous jury verdict, see n. 14, *infra*), the only rights not fully incorporated are (1) the Third Amendment's protection against quartering of soldiers; (2) the Fifth Amendment's grand jury indictment requirement; (3) the Seventh Amendment right to a jury trial in civil cases; and (4) the Eighth Amendment's prohibition on excessive fines.

We never have decided whether the Third Amendment or the Eighth Amendment's prohibition of excessive fines applies to the States through the Due Process Clause.

Our governing decisions regarding the Grand Jury Clause of the Fifth Amendment and the Seventh Amendment's civil jury requirement long predate the era of selective incorporation.

Malloy, 378 U.S., at 10-11. Instead, the Court decisively held that incorporated Bill of Rights protections "are all to be enforced against the States under the Fourteenth Amendment according to the same standards that protect those personal rights against federal encroachment." *Id.*, at 10.[14]

Employing this approach, the Court overruled earlier decisions in which it had held that particular Bill of Rights guarantees or remedies did not apply to the States.

III

With this framework in mind, we now turn directly to the question whether the Second Amendment right to keep and bear arms is incorporated in the concept of due process. In answering that question, as just explained, we must decide whether the right to keep and bear arms is fundamental to *our* scheme of ordered liberty, *Duncan,* 391 U.S., at 149, or as we have said in a related context, whether this right is "deeply rooted in this Nation's history and tradition," *Washington v. Glucksberg,* 521 U.S. 702, 721 (1997).

A

Our decision in *Heller* points unmistakably to the answer. Self-defense is a basic right, recognized by many legal systems from ancient times to the present day, and in *Heller,* we held that individual self-defense is "the *central component*" of the Second Amendment right. Explaining that "the need for defense of self, family, and property is most acute" in the home, we found that this right applies to handguns because they are "the most preferred firearm in the nation to 'keep' and use for protection of one's home and family." Thus, we concluded, citizens must be permitted "to use [handguns] for the core lawful purpose of self-defense."

Heller makes it clear that this right is "deeply rooted in this Nation's history and tradition." *Glucksberg, supra,* at 721. *Heller* explored the right's origins, noting that the 1689 English Bill of Rights explicitly protected a right to keep arms for self-defense,

14. There is one exception to this general rule. The Court has held that although the Sixth Amendment right to trial by jury requires a unanimous jury verdict in federal criminal trials, it does not require a unanimous jury verdict in state criminal trials. See *Apodaca v. Oregon,* 406 U.S. 404 (1972); see also *Johnson v. Louisiana,* 406 U.S. 356 (1972) (holding that the Due Process Clause does not require unanimous jury verdicts in state criminal trials). But that ruling was the result of an unusual division among the Justices, not an endorsement of the two-track approach to incorporation. In *Apodaca,* eight Justices agreed that the Sixth Amendment applies identically to both the Federal Government and the States. See *Johnson, supra,* at 395 (Brennan, J., dissenting). Nonetheless, among those eight, four Justices took the view that the Sixth Amendment does not require unanimous jury verdicts in either federal or state criminal trials, *Apodaca,* 406 U.S., at 406 (plurality opinion), and four other Justices took the view that the Sixth Amendment requires unanimous jury verdicts in federal and state criminal trials, *id.*, at 414-415 (Stewart, J., dissenting); *Johnson, supra,* at 381-382 (Douglas, J., dissenting). Justice Powell's concurrence in the judgment broke the tie, and he concluded that the Sixth Amendment requires juror unanimity in federal, but not state, cases. *Apodaca,* therefore, does not undermine the well-established rule that incorporated Bill of Rights protections apply identically to the States and the Federal Government.

and that by 1765, Blackstone was able to assert that the right to keep and bear arms was "one of the fundamental rights of Englishmen."

Blackstone's assessment was shared by the American colonists. As we noted in *Heller*, King George III's attempt to disarm the colonists in the 1760's and 1770's "provoked polemical reactions by Americans invoking their rights as Englishmen to keep arms."

The right to keep and bear arms was considered no less fundamental by those who drafted and ratified the Bill of Rights. "During the 1788 ratification debates, the fear that the federal government would disarm the people in order to impose rule through a standing army or select militia was pervasive in Antifederalist rhetoric." *Heller*, *supra*, at 598. Federalists responded, not by arguing that the right was insufficiently important to warrant protection but by contending that the right was adequately protected by the Constitution's assignment of only limited powers to the Federal Government. Thus, Antifederalists and Federalists alike agreed that the right to bear arms was fundamental to the newly formed system of government. But those who were fearful that the new Federal Government would infringe traditional rights such as the right to keep and bear arms insisted on the adoption of the Bill of Rights as a condition for ratification of the Constitution. This is surely powerful evidence that the right was regarded as fundamental in the sense relevant here.

This understanding persisted in the years immediately following the ratification of the Bill of Rights. In addition to the four States that had adopted Second Amendment analogues before ratification, nine more States adopted state constitutional provisions protecting an individual right to keep and bear arms between 1789 and 1820. Founding-era legal commentators confirmed the importance of the right to early Americans. . . .

B

1

. . . .

After the Civil War, many of the over 180,000 African Americans who served in the Union Army returned to the States of the old Confederacy, where systematic efforts were made to disarm them and other blacks. . . .

Union Army commanders took steps to secure the right of all citizens to keep and bear arms, but the 39th Congress concluded that legislative action was necessary. Its efforts to safeguard the right to keep and bear arms demonstrate that the right was still recognized to be fundamental.

The most explicit evidence of Congress' aim appears in § 14 of the Freedmen's Bureau Act of 1866, which provided that "the right . . . to have full and equal benefit of all laws and proceedings concerning personal liberty, personal security, and the acquisition, enjoyment, and disposition of estate, real and personal, *including the constitutional right to bear arms*, shall be secured to and enjoyed by all the citizens . . . without respect to race or color, or previous condition of slavery." 14 Stat. 176-177 (emphasis added). Section 14 thus explicitly guaranteed that "all the citizens," black and white, would have "the constitutional right to bear arms."

The Civil Rights Act of 1866, 14 Stat. 27, which was considered at the same time as the Freedmen's Bureau Act, similarly sought to protect the right of all citizens to keep and bear arms. Section 1 of the Civil Rights Act guaranteed the "full and equal benefit of all laws and proceedings for the security of person and property, as is enjoyed by white citizens." *Ibid*. This language was virtually identical to language in § 14 of the Freedmen's Bureau Act. . . .

Congress, however, ultimately deemed these legislative remedies insufficient. . . .

In debating the Fourteenth Amendment, the 39th Congress referred to the right to keep and bear arms as a fundamental right deserving of protection. . . .

Evidence from the period immediately following the ratification of the Fourteenth Amendment only confirms that the right to keep and bear arms was considered fundamental. In an 1868 speech addressing the disarmament of freedmen, Representative Stevens emphasized the necessity of the right: "Disarm a community and you rob them of the means of defending life. Take away their weapons of defense and you take away the inalienable right of defending liberty." "The fourteenth amendment, now so happily adopted, settles the whole question." Cong. Globe, 40th Cong., 2d Sess., 1967 [1868]. And in debating the Civil Rights Act of 1871, Congress routinely referred to the right to keep and bear arms and decried the continued disarmament of blacks in the South. Finally, legal commentators from the period emphasized the fundamental nature of the right.

The right to keep and bear arms was also widely protected by state constitutions at the time when the Fourteenth Amendment was ratified. In 1868, 22 of the 37 States in the Union had state constitutional provisions explicitly protecting the right to keep and bear arms. Quite a few of these state constitutional guarantees, moreover, explicitly protected the right to keep and bear arms as an individual right to self-defense. What is more, state constitutions adopted during the Reconstruction era by former Confederate States included a right to keep and bear arms. A clear majority of the States in 1868, therefore, recognized the right to keep and bear arms as being among the foundational rights necessary to our system of Government.

In sum, it is clear that the Framers and ratifiers of the Fourteenth Amendment counted the right to keep and bear arms among those fundamental rights necessary to our system of ordered liberty. . . .

[The concurring opinions of Justices Thomas and Scalia, and the dissenting opinion of Justices Stevens and Breyer, are omitted].

Notes and Questions

1. In footnote 13, the *McDonald* Court identifies a handful of provisions of the Bill of Rights that have yet to be incorporated, including the Excessive Fines Clause.

In 2019, the Court held that the Excessive Fines Clause was incorporated by the Fourteenth Amendment as well. *See Timbs v. Indiana*, 139 S. Ct. 682 (2019).

2. In *McDonald*, the Court indicates the general rule that incorporated provisions of the Bill of Rights are applied against the states in exactly the same way as they are applied against the federal government, but identifies in footnote 14 a glaring exception to this general rule so far as the requirement of a unanimous jury in criminal trials is concerned. In 2020, the U.S. Supreme Court eliminated this exception, overruling the cases cited in footnote 14. *See Ramos v. Louisiana*, 140 S. Ct. 1390 (2020).

3. In *McDonald*, and again in *Timbs* and *Ramos*, Justice Thomas agreed with the result, but argued that the Fourteenth Amendment's Privileges or Immunities Clause, rather than the Due Process Clause, was the appropriate vehicle for incorporating and applying provisions of the Bill of Rights against the states. Justice Thomas's opinion is examined in closer detail in Chapter 20.

4. Of the various approaches to incorporation outlined in the *Adamson* case, which approach has the Court adopted as a formal matter? As an informal one? Does it seem likely that, when presented with the question in the future, the Court will deem any provision of the Bill of Rights *not* to be incorporated?

5. Under the approach endorsed in *McDonald*, what is the Court supposed to look at to determine whether or not a provision of the Bill of Rights is incorporated? How malleable is the test? In this regard, consider that four Justices in *McDonald*, purporting to apply the same test, arrived at the opposite conclusion.

6. The *McDonald* Court repeatedly cites *Washington v. Glucksberg*, which it refers to as "a related context." *Glucksberg*, which will be examined in Chapter 16, considers a claim that there is an unenumerated fundamental right to physician-assisted suicide. What does this connection suggest about the true underlying debate amongst the Justices in *Adamson*?

7. In *Adamson*, Justice Frankfurter asserts that only one Justice—who he refers to as an "eccentric exception"—has endorsed the concept of total incorporation. While one might think he is referring to Justice Black, he is in fact referring to the first Justice Harlan. *See* Hon. Joseph R. Weisberger, *The Selective Incorporation Process and Judicial Activism*, 59-APR R.I. B.J. 13, 15 (2011). In any event, arguably his count was low not only as a historical matter but also taking into account the Justices dissenting in *Adamson*. *See* Jerold H. Israel, *Selective Incorporation: Revisited*, 71 Geo. L.J. 253, 257 & n.22 (1982).

C. The Transitional Cases

As indicated in Part A of this chapter, *West Coast Hotel* spelled the end of the *Lochner* era, and in the aftermath of *West Coast Hotel*, all of the *Lochner* era decisions have been overruled except for two: *Meyer v. Nebraska* and *Pierce v. Society of Sisters*.

These two decisions, which are excerpted below, appear at first glance to be of a piece with *Lochner*—relying on liberty of contract—and thus it is unclear why they, too, are no longer good law. Yet if you read them carefully, you will see that the decisions contain not only economic, but also non-economic, rationales for their conclusions. Moreover, although not explicit in the decisions themselves, there may be ways of thinking about the laws at stake not in general liberty terms but rather in terms of the classes of persons targeted by the laws.

Meyer v. Nebraska

262 U.S. 390 (1923)

MR. JUSTICE McREYNOLDS delivered the opinion of the Court.

Plaintiff in error was tried and convicted in the District Court for Hamilton County, Nebraska, under an information which charged that on May 25, 1920, while an instructor in Zion Parochial School, he unlawfully taught the subject of reading in the German language to Raymond Parpart, a child of ten years, who had not attained and successfully passed the eighth grade. The information is based upon "An act relating to the teaching of foreign languages in the State of Nebraska," approved April 9, 1919 . . . .

The problem for our determination is whether the statute as construed and applied unreasonably infringes the liberty guaranteed to the plaintiff in error by the Fourteenth Amendment. . . .

While this Court has not attempted to define with exactness the liberty thus guaranteed, the term has received much consideration and some of the included things have been definitely stated. Without doubt, it denotes not merely freedom from bodily restraint but also the right of the individual to contract, to engage in any of the common occupations of life, to acquire useful knowledge, to marry, establish a home and bring up children, to worship God according to the dictates of his own conscience, and generally to enjoy those privileges long recognized at common law as essential to the orderly pursuit of happiness by free men. The established doctrine is that this liberty may not be interfered with, under the guise of protecting the public interest, by legislative action which is arbitrary or without reasonable relation to some purpose within the competency of the State to effect. Determination by the legislature of what constitutes proper exercise of police power is not final or conclusive but is subject to supervision by the courts. . . .

Plaintiff in error taught this language in school as part of his occupation. His right thus to teach and the right of parents to engage him so to instruct their children, we think, are within the liberty of the Amendment.

The challenged statute forbids the teaching in school of any subject except in English; also the teaching of any other language until the pupil has attained and successfully passed the eighth grade, which is not usually accomplished before the age of twelve. The Supreme Court of the State has held that "the so-called ancient or dead languages:" are not "within the spirit or the purpose of the act." Latin, Greek, Hebrew are not proscribed; but German, French, Spanish, Italian and every other alien speech are within the ban. Evidently the legislature has attempted materially to interfere with the calling of modern language teachers, with the opportunities of pupils to acquire knowledge, and with the power of parents to control the education of their own.

It is said the purpose of the legislation was to promote civic development by inhibiting training and education of the immature in foreign tongues and ideals before they could learn English and acquire American ideals; and "that the English language should be and become the mother tongue of all children reared in this State." It is also affirmed that the foreign born population is very large, that certain communities commonly use foreign words, follow foreign leaders, move in a foreign atmosphere, and that the children are thereby hindered from becoming citizens of the most useful type and the public safety is imperiled.

That the State may do much, go very far, indeed, in order to improve the quality of its citizens, physically, mentally and morally, is clear; but the individual has certain fundamental rights which must be respected. The protection of the Constitution extends to all, to those who speak other languages as well as to those born with English on the tongue. Perhaps it would be highly advantageous if all had ready understanding of our ordinary speech, but this cannot be coerced by methods which conflict with the Constitution—a desirable end cannot be promoted by prohibited means. . . .

No emergency has arisen which renders knowledge by a child of some language other than English so clearly harmful as to justify its inhibition with the consequent infringement of rights long freely enjoyed. We are constrained to conclude that the statute as applied is arbitrary and without reasonable relation to any end within the competency of the State.

As the statute undertakes to interfere only with teaching which involves a modern language, leaving complete freedom as to other matters, there seems no adequate foundation for the suggestion that the purpose was to protect the child's health by limiting his mental activities. It is well known that proficiency in a foreign language seldom comes to one not instructed at an early age, and experience shows that this is not injurious to the health, morals or understanding of the ordinary child. . . .

Notes and Questions

1. *Meyer* was followed two years later by *Pierce v. Society of Sisters*, 268 U.S. 510 (1925). At issue in *Pierce* was a challenge to the constitutionality of a state law requiring children to attend *public* school between the ages of 8 and 16 brought by a private religious school. In deeming the law unconstitutional, the Court held as follows:

> The inevitable practical result of enforcing the Act under consideration would be destruction of appellees' primary schools, and perhaps all other private primary schools for normal children within the State of Oregon. These parties are engaged in a kind of undertaking not inherently harmful, but long regarded as useful and meritorious. Certainly there is nothing in the present records to indicate that they have failed to discharge their obligations to patrons, students or the State. And there are no peculiar circumstances or present emergencies which demand extraordinary measures relative to primary education.
>
> Under the doctrine of *Meyer v. Nebraska*, 262 U. S. 390, we think it entirely plain that the Act of 1922 unreasonably interferes with the liberty of parents and guardians to direct the upbringing and education of children under their control. As often heretofore pointed out, rights guaranteed by the Constitution may not be abridged by legislation which has no reasonable relation to some purpose within the competency of the State. The fundamental theory of liberty upon which all governments in this Union repose excludes any general power of the State to standardize its children by forcing them to accept instruction from public teachers only. The child is not the mere creature of the State; those who nurture him and direct his destiny have the right, coupled with the high duty, to recognize and prepare him for additional obligations.

Id. at 534-535.

2. As indicated in the introduction to this Part, *Meyer* and *Pierce* are the only *Lochner*-era decisions that remain good law today. In the cases that follow in subsequent chapters, keep an eye out for the various ways in which the Court recharacterizes the Court's holdings in these two cases to unmoor them from *Lochner*'s liberty of contract theory.

Chapter 4

Traditional Equal Protection Review

The Equal Protection Clause of the Fourteenth Amendment commands:

> No State shall . . . deny to any person within its jurisdiction the equal protection of the laws.

Unlike the Due Process Clause of the Fourteenth Amendment, the Equal Protection Clause—in terms—finds no counterpart in the Fifth Amendment, or indeed in any other part of the U.S. Constitution applicable to the federal government.

The Equal Protection Clause has long posed an interpretive quandary for courts. Taken at face value, it could be viewed as a command for *strict* equality, meaning that government could *never* draw distinctions amongst people, but would have to treat everyone precisely the same. While at first glance that might seem like a positive, consider for just a moment the many ways in which government *routinely* classifies people and treats people in those classes differently:

- *Classifications based on age*—Government routinely draws lines on the basis of age, establishing a minimum age for obtaining a driver's license, purchasing or consuming tobacco products or alcohol, or obtaining social security and other governmental benefits.
- *Classifications based on income*—Government routinely draws lines on the basis of income, imposing differential tax rates depending upon income and providing public assistance benefits only for those below certain income thresholds.
- *Classifications based on intellectual ability*—Government routinely draws lines on the basis of ability, admitting into state colleges and universities only those whose grade-point averages and standardized test scores exceed certain thresholds, and providing differential financial aid in the form of merit scholarships based on ability.
- *Classifications based on physical ability*—Government routinely specifies certain types of physical characteristics (height, weight, strength) for performing certain types of jobs, such as those in law enforcement or the military.

If the term "equal" as used in the Equal Protection Clause were to command strict equality, all such government classifications would be deemed unconstitutional, even though virtually everyone would agree that the sorts of line drawing described above seem very sensible. The U.S. Supreme Court has thus acknowledged that "[t]he Fourteenth Amendment's promise that no person shall be denied the equal protection of the laws must coexist with the practical necessity that most legislation classifies for one purpose or another, with resulting disadvantage to various groups or persons," and its case law has sought to "reconcile the principle with the reality." *Romer v. Evans*, 517 U.S. 620, 631 (1996).

Recall that the Court—in its first decision interpreting the Equal Protection Clause—suggested a limitation based on the history that motivated Congress to enact it and the States to ratify it:

> We doubt very much whether any action of a State not directed by way of discrimination against the negroes as a class, or on account of their race, will ever be held to come within the purview of this provision. It is so clearly a provision for that race and that emergency, that a strong case would be necessary for its application to any other.

The Slaughter-House Cases, 83 U.S. 36, 81 (1873).

Recall, too, that even within the realm of racial discrimination, the Court—in its early decisions—invoked history as a basis for interpreting the command of "equal" treatment in a rather narrow fashion. Thus, in *Plessy v. Ferguson*, 163 U.S. 537 (1896), the Court held the doctrine of "separate but equal" to be consistent with the Equal Protection Clause.

As you saw in Chapter 3, in the years and decades immediately following *Plessy*, litigants and the Court switched their focus away from the equality-based arguments of the Equal Protection Clause to the rights-based arguments of the Due Process Clause. Indeed, just one year after *Plessy* was decided, the Court kicked off the so-called *Lochner* era with its decision in *Allgeyer v. Louisiana*, 165 U.S. 578 (1897).

To be sure, litigants continued to invoke the Equal Protection Clause during the *Lochner* era, yet they continued to be rebuffed. Ultimately, in a series of cases beginning at the close of the *Lochner* era and persisting through the modern era, the Court has made clear that—at least where matters of social or economic policy are involved—it will apply the same, deferential standard of review without regard to whether challenges are brought pursuant to the Due Process Clauses or the Equal Protection Clause.

United States v. Carolene Products Co.

304 U.S. 144 (1938)

Mr. Justice Stone delivered the opinion of the Court.

The question for decision is whether the 'Filled Milk Act' of Congress of March 4, 1923, which prohibits the shipment in interstate commerce of skimmed milk compounded with any fat or oil other than milk fat, so as to resemble milk or cream ... infringes the Fifth Amendment.

Appellee raises no valid objection to the present statute by arguing that its prohibition has not been extended to oleomargarine or other butter substitutes in which vegetable fats or oils are substituted for butter fat. The Fifth Amendment has no equal protection clause, and even that of the Fourteenth, applicable only to the states, does not compel their Legislatures to prohibit all like evils, or none. A Legislature may hit at an abuse which it has found, even though it has failed to strike at another. . . .

[T]he existence of facts supporting the legislative judgment is to be presumed, for regulatory legislation affecting ordinary commercial transactions is not to be pronounced unconstitutional unless in the light of the facts made known or generally assumed it is of such a character as to preclude the assumption that it rests upon some rational basis within the knowledge and experience of the legislators.[4]

Where the existence of a rational basis for legislation whose constitutionality is attacked depends upon facts beyond the sphere of judicial notice, such facts may properly be made the subject of judicial inquiry, and the constitutionality of a statute predicated upon the existence of a particular state of facts may be challenged by showing to the court that those facts have ceased to exist. Similarly we recognize that the constitutionality of a statute, valid on its face, may be assailed by proof of facts tending to show that the statute as applied to a particular article is without support in reason because the article, although within the prohibited class, is so different from others of the class as to be without the reason for the prohibition, though the effect of such proof depends on the relevant circumstances of each case, as for example the administrative difficulty of excluding the article from the regulated class. But by their very nature such inquiries, where the legislative judgment is drawn in question, must be restricted to the issue whether any state of facts either known or which could reasonably be assumed affords support for it. . . .

[The concurring opinion of Justice Butler is omitted.]

4. There may be narrower scope for operation of the presumption of constitutionality when legislation appears on its face to be within a specific prohibition of the Constitution, such as those of the first ten Amendments, which are deemed equally specific when held to be embraced within the Fourteenth.

It is unnecessary to consider now whether legislation which restricts those political processes which can ordinarily be expected to bring about repeal of undesirable legislation, is to be subjected to more exacting judicial scrutiny under the general prohibitions of the Fourteenth Amendment than are most other types of legislation. [The Court here cites cases addressing the constitutionality of restrictions upon the right to vote; restraints upon the dissemination of information; interferences with political organizations; and prohibitions of peaceable assembly.]

Nor need we enquire whether similar considerations enter into the review of statutes directed at particular religious, Pierce v. Society of Sisters, 268 U.S. 510, or national, Meyer v. Nebraska, 262 U.S. 390, or racial minorities: whether prejudice against discrete and insular minorities may be a special condition, which tends seriously to curtail the operation of those political processes ordinarily to be relied upon to protect minorities, and which may call for a correspondingly more searching judicial inquiry.

Notes and Questions

1. As *Carolene Products* notes, unlike the Fourteenth Amendment, applicable only to state and local governmental actors, the provisions of the U.S. Constitution applicable to federal governmental actors in terms contains no equal protection guarantee. Does this mean that the federal government is free to engage in racial and other forms of class-based discrimination? If not, what basis is there for applying a comparable restriction to the actions of the federal government?

2. Footnote 4 of *Carolene Products* contains a number of caveats to the general rule announced in the text, situations in which the Court may apply a more exacting form of judicial scrutiny under the Equal Protection Clause. The Court cites its earlier decisions in *Meyer v. Nebraska* and *Pierce v. Society of Sisters* in support of its conclusion that a more exacting form of scrutiny may be applicable where religious or national minorities are targeted by a law. Is that a fair reading of those two cases?

Railway Express Agency v. New York

336 U.S. 106 (1949)

Mr. Justice Douglas delivered the opinion of the Court.

Section 124 of the Traffic Regulations of the City of New York promulgated by the Police Commissioner provides:

> "No person shall operate, or cause to be operated, in or upon any street an advertising vehicle; provided that nothing herein contained shall prevent the putting of business notices upon business delivery vehicles, so long as such vehicles are engaged in the usual business or regular work of the owner and not used merely or mainly for advertising."

Appellant is engaged in a nation-wide express business. It operates about 1,900 trucks in New York City and sells the space on the exterior sides of these trucks for advertising. That advertising is for the most part unconnected with its own business. It was convicted in the magistrates court and fined. The judgment of conviction was sustained in the Court of Special Sessions. . . .

The Court of Special Sessions concluded that advertising on vehicles using the streets of New York City constitutes a distraction to vehicle drivers and to pedestrians alike and therefore affects the safety of the public in the use of the streets. We do not sit to weigh evidence on the due process issue in order to determine whether the regulation is sound or appropriate; nor is it our function to pass judgment on its wisdom. We would be trespassing on one of the most intensely local and specialized of all municipal problems if we held that this regulation had no relation to the traffic problem of New York City. It is the judgment of the local authorities that it does have such a relation. And nothing has been advanced which shows that to be palpably false.

The question of equal protection of the laws is pressed more strenuously on us. It is pointed out that the regulation draws the line between advertisements of products sold by the owner of the truck and general advertisements. It is argued that unequal treatment on the basis of such a distinction is not justified by the aim and purpose of the regulation. It is said, for example, that one of appellant's trucks carrying the advertisement of a commercial house would not cause any greater distraction of pedestrians and vehicle drivers than if the commercial house carried the same advertisement on its own truck. Yet the regulation allows the latter to do what the former is forbidden from doing. It is therefore contended that the classification which the regulation makes has no relation to the traffic problem since a violation turns not on what kind of advertisements are carried on trucks but on whose trucks they are carried.

That, however, is a superficial way of analyzing the problem, even if we assume that it is premised on the correct construction of the regulation. The local authorities may well have concluded that those who advertised their own wares on their trucks do not present the same traffic problem in view of the nature or extent of the advertising which they use. It would take a degree of omniscience which we lack to say that such is not the case. If that judgment is correct, the advertising displays that are exempt have less incidence on traffic than those of appellants.

We cannot say that that judgment is not an allowable one. Yet if it is, the classification has relation to the purpose for which it is made and does not contain the kind of discrimination against which the Equal Protection Clause affords protection. It is by such practical considerations based on experience rather than by theoretical inconsistencies that the question of equal protection is to be answered. And the fact that New York City sees fit to eliminate from traffic this kind of distraction but does not touch what may be even greater ones in a different category, such as the vivid displays on Times Square, is immaterial. It is no requirement of equal protection that all evils of the same genus be eradicated or none at all. . . .

[The concurring opinion of Justice Jackson is omitted.]

Lee Optical of Oklahoma v. Williamson

348 U.S. 483 (1955)

Mr. Justice Douglas delivered the opinion of the Court.

This suit was instituted in the District Court to have an Oklahoma law declared unconstitutional and to enjoin state officials from enforcing it. . . .

The District Court . . . held invalid under the Due Process Clause of the Fourteenth Amendment the portions of § 2 which make it unlawful for any person not a licensed optometrist or ophthalmologist to fit lenses to a face or to duplicate or replace into frames lenses or other optical appliances, except upon written prescriptive authority of an Oklahoma licensed ophthalmologist or optometrist.

An ophthalmologist is a duly licensed physician who specializes in the care of the eyes. An optometrist examines eyes for refractive error, recognizes (but does not treat) diseases of the eye, and fills prescriptions for eyeglasses. The optician is an artisan qualified to grind lenses, fill prescriptions, and fit frames.

The effect of § 2 is to forbid the optician from fitting or duplicating lenses without a prescription from an ophthalmologist or optometrist. In practical effect, it means that no optician can fit old glasses into new frames or supply a lens, whether it be a new lens or one to duplicate a lost or broken lens, without a prescription. . . .

The Oklahoma law may exact a needless, wasteful requirement in many cases. But it is for the legislature, not the courts, to balance the advantages and disadvantages of the new requirement. It appears that in many cases the optician can easily supply the new frames or new lenses without reference to the old written prescription. It also appears that many written prescriptions contain no directive data in regard to fitting spectacles to the face. But in some cases the directions contained in the prescription are essential, if the glasses are to be fitted so as to correct the particular defects of vision or alleviate the eye condition. The legislature might have concluded that the frequency of occasions when a prescription is necessary was sufficient to justify this regulation of the fitting of eyeglasses. Likewise, when it is necessary to duplicate a lens, a written prescription may or may not be necessary. But the legislature might have concluded that one was needed often enough to require one in every case. Or the legislature may have concluded that eye examinations were so critical, not only for correction of vision but also for detection of latent ailments or diseases, that every change in frames and every duplication of a lens should be accompanied by a prescription from a medical expert. To be sure, the present law does not require a new examination of the eyes every time the frames are changed or the lenses duplicated. For if the old prescription is on file with the optician, he can go ahead and make the new fitting or duplicate the lenses. But the law need not be in every respect logically consistent with its aims to be constitutional. It is enough that there is an evil at hand for correction, and that it might be thought that the particular legislative measure was a rational way to correct it.

The day is gone when this Court uses the Due Process Clause of the Fourteenth Amendment to strike down state laws, regulatory of business and industrial conditions, because they may be unwise, improvident, or out of harmony with a particular school of thought. . . .

Secondly, the District Court held that it violated the Equal Protection Clause of the Fourteenth Amendment to subject opticians to this regulatory system and to exempt, as § 3 of the Act does, all sellers of ready-to-wear glasses. The problem of legislative classification is a perennial one, admitting of no doctrinaire definition. Evils in the same field may be of different dimensions and proportions, requiring different remedies. Or so the legislature may think. Or the reform may take one step at a time, addressing itself to the phase of the problem which seems most acute to the legislative mind. The legislature may select one phase of one field and apply a remedy there, neglecting the others. The prohibition of the Equal Protection Clause goes no further than the invidious discrimination. We cannot say that that point has been reached here. For all this record shows, the ready-to-wear branch of this business may not loom large in Oklahoma or may present problems of regulation distinct from the other branch. . . .

Federal Communications Commission v. Beach Communications, Inc.

508 U.S. 307 (1993)

Justice Thomas delivered the opinion of the Court. . . .

I

The Cable Communications Policy Act of 1984 (Cable Act) amended the Communications Act of 1934 to establish a national framework for regulating cable television. . . . Congress provided for the franchising of cable systems by local governmental authorities, and prohibited any person from operating a cable system without a franchise, subject to certain exceptions. Section 602(7) of the Communications Act . . . determines the reach of the franchise requirement by defining the operative term "cable system." A cable system means any facility designed to provide video programming to multiple subscribers through "closed transmission paths," but does not include, *inter alia,*

> "a facility that serves only subscribers in 1 or more multiple unit dwellings under common ownership, control, or management, unless such facility or facilities us[e] any public right-of-way." § 602(7)(B), 47 U.S.C. § 522(7)(B) (1988 ed., Supp. V).

. . . .

This case arises out of an FCC proceeding clarifying the agency's interpretation of the term "cable system" as it is used in the Cable Act. In this proceeding, the Commission addressed the application of the exemption codified in § 602(7)(B) to satellite master antenna television (SMATV) facilities. Unlike a traditional cable television system, which delivers video programming to a large community of subscribers through coaxial cables laid under city streets or along utility lines, an SMATV system typically receives a signal from a satellite through a small satellite dish located on a rooftop and then retransmits the signal by wire to units within a building or complex of buildings. The Commission ruled that an SMATV system that serves multiple buildings via a network of interconnected physical transmission lines is a cable system, unless it falls within the §602(7)(B) exemption. Consistent with the plain terms of the statutory exemption, the Commission concluded that such an SMATV system is subject to the franchise requirement if its transmission lines interconnect separately owned and managed buildings or if its lines use or cross any public right-of-way.

Respondents Beach Communications, Inc., Maxtel Limited Partnership, Pacific Cablevision, and Western Cable Communications, Inc.—SMATV operators that would be subject to franchising under the Cable Act as construed by the Commission—petitioned the Court of Appeals for review. The Court of Appeals rejected respondents' statutory challenge to the Commission's interpretation, but a majority of the court found merit in the claim that §602(7) violates the implied equal protection guarantee of the Due Process Clause. In the absence of what it termed "the predominant rationale for local franchising" (use of public rights-of-way), the court saw no rational basis "[o]n the record," and was "unable to imagine" any conceivable basis, for distinguishing between those facilities exempted by the statute and those SMATV cable systems that link separately owned and managed buildings. The court remanded the record and directed the FCC to provide "additional 'legislative facts'" to justify the distinction.

A report subsequently filed by the Commission failed to satisfy the Court of Appeals.... In a second opinion, the majority... held that "the Cable Act violates the equal protection component of the Fifth Amendment, insofar as it imposes a discriminatory franchising requirement....

II

Whether embodied in the Fourteenth Amendment or inferred from the Fifth, equal protection is not a license for courts to judge the wisdom, fairness, or logic of legislative choices. In areas of social and economic policy, a statutory classification that neither proceeds along suspect lines nor infringes fundamental constitutional rights must be upheld against equal protection challenge if there is any reasonably conceivable state of facts that could provide a rational basis for the classification. See *Sullivan v. Stroop,* 496 U.S. 478, 485 (1990); *Bowen v. Gilliard,* 483 U.S. 587, 600–603 (1987); *United States Railroad Retirement Bd. v. Fritz,* 449 U.S. 166, 174–179 (1980); *Dandridge v. Williams,* 397 U.S. 471, 484–485 (1970). Where there are "plausible reasons" for Congress' action, "our inquiry is at an end." *United States Railroad Retirement Bd. v. Fritz, supra,* 449 U.S., at 179. This standard of review is a paradigm of judicial restraint. "The Constitution presumes that, absent some reason to infer antipathy, even improvident decisions will eventually be rectified by the democratic process and that judicial intervention is generally unwarranted no matter how unwisely we may think a political branch has acted." *Vance v. Bradley,* 440 U.S. 93, 97 (1979).

On rational-basis review, a classification in a statute such as the Cable Act comes to us bearing a strong presumption of validity, see *Lyng v. Automobile Workers,* 485 U.S. 360, 370 (1988), and those attacking the rationality of the legislative classification have the burden "to negative every conceivable basis which might support it," *Lehnhausen v. Lake Shore Auto Parts Co.,* 410 U.S. 356, 364 (1973). Moreover, because we never require a legislature to articulate its reasons for enacting a statute, it is entirely irrelevant for constitutional purposes whether the conceived reason for the challenged distinction actually motivated the legislature. *United States Railroad Retirement Bd. v. Fritz, supra,* 449 U.S., at 179. Thus, the absence of "'legislative facts'" explaining the distinction "[o]n the record," 294 U.S.App.D.C., at 389, has no significance in rational-basis analysis. See *Nordlinger v. Hahn,* 505 U.S. 1, 15 (1992) (equal protection "does not demand for purposes of rational-basis review that a legislature or governing decisionmaker actually articulate at any time the purpose or rationale supporting its classification"). In other words, a legislative choice is not subject to courtroom fact-finding and may be based on rational speculation unsupported by evidence or empirical data. See *Vance v. Bradley, supra,* 440 U.S., at 111. "'Only by faithful adherence to this guiding principle of judicial review of legislation is it possible to preserve to the legislative branch its rightful independence and its ability to function.'" *Lehnhausen, supra,* 410 U.S., at 365.

These restraints on judicial review have added force "where the legislature must necessarily engage in a process of line-drawing." *United States Railroad Retirement Bd. v. Fritz,* 449 U.S., at 179. Defining the class of persons subject to a regulatory requirement—much like classifying governmental beneficiaries—"inevitably requires that some persons who have an almost equally strong claim to favored treatment be placed on different sides of the line, and the fact [that] the line might have been drawn differently at some points is a matter for legislative, rather than judicial, consideration." The distinction at issue here represents such a line: By excluding from the definition of "cable system" those facilities that serve commonly owned or managed buildings without using public rights-of-way, § 602(7)(B) delineates the bounds of the regulatory field. Such scope-of-coverage provisions are unavoidable components of most economic or social legislation. In establishing the franchise requirement, Congress had to draw the line somewhere; it had to choose which facilities to franchise. This necessity renders the precise coordinates of the resulting legislative judgment virtually unreviewable, since the legislature must be allowed leeway to approach a perceived problem incrementally. See, *e.g., Williamson v. Lee Optical of Okla., Inc.,* 348 U.S. 483 (1955):

> "The problem of legislative classification is a perennial one, admitting of no doctrinaire definition. Evils in the same field may be of different dimensions and proportions, requiring different remedies. Or so the legislature may think. Or the reform may take one step at a time, addressing itself to the phase of the problem which seems most acute to the legislative mind.

> The legislature may select one phase of one field and apply a remedy there, neglecting the others. The prohibition of the Equal Protection Clause goes no further than the invidious discrimination."[7]

Applying these principles, we conclude that the common-ownership distinction is constitutional. There are at least two possible bases for the distinction; either one suffices. First, Congress borrowed § 602(7)(B) from pre-Cable Act regulations, and although the existence of a prior administrative scheme is certainly not necessary to the rationality of the statute, it is plausible that Congress also adopted the FCC's earlier rationale. Under that rationale, common ownership was thought to be indicative of those systems for which the costs of regulation would outweigh the benefits to consumers. Because the number of subscribers was a similar indicator, the Commission also exempted cable facilities that served fewer than 50 subscribers. In explaining both exemptions, the Commission stated:

> "[N]ot all [systems] can be subject to effective regulation with the resources available nor is regulation necessarily needed in every instance. A sensible regulatory program requires that a division between the regulated and unregulated be made in a manner which best conserves regulatory energies and allows the most cost effective use of available resources. In attempting to make this division, we have focused on subscriber numbers as well as the multiple unit dwelling indicia on the theory that the very small are inefficient to regulate and can safely be ignored in terms of their potential for impact on broadcast service to the public and on multiple unit dwelling facilities on the theory that this effectively establishes certain maximum size limitations."

This regulatory-efficiency model . . . provides a conceivable basis for the common-ownership exemption. A legislator might rationally assume that systems serving only commonly owned or managed buildings without crossing public rights-of-way would typically be limited in size or would share some other attribute affecting their impact on the welfare of cable viewers such that regulators could "safely ignor[e]" these systems.

Respondents argue that Congress did not intend common ownership to be a surrogate for small size, since Congress simultaneously rejected the FCC's 50-subscriber exemption by omitting it from the Cable Act. Whether the posited reason for the challenged distinction actually motivated Congress is "constitutionally irrelevant," *United States Railroad Retirement Bd. v. Fritz, supra,* 449 U.S., at 179, and, in any

7. See also *Dandridge v. Williams,* 397 U.S. 471, 485 (1970) (classification does not violate equal protection simply because it "is not made with mathematical nicety or because in practice it results in some inequality"); *Metropolis Theatre Co. v. Chicago,* 228 U.S. 61, 69–70 (1913) ("The problems of government are practical ones and may justify, if they do not require, rough accommodations—illogical, it may be, and unscientific"); *Heath & Milligan Mfg. Co. v. Worst,* 207 U.S. 338, 354 (1907) ("logical appropriateness of the inclusion or exclusion of objects or persons" and "exact wisdom and nice adaptation of remedies are not required").

event, the FCC's explanation indicates that both common ownership and number of subscribers were considered indicia of "very small" cable systems. . . .

Furthermore, small size is only one plausible ownership-related factor contributing to consumer welfare. Subscriber influence is another. Where an SMATV system serves a complex of buildings under common ownership or management, individual subscribers could conceivably have greater bargaining power vis-à-vis the cable operator (even if the number of dwelling units were large), since all the subscribers could negotiate with one voice through the common owner or manager. Such an owner might have substantial leverage, because he could withhold permission to operate the SMATV system on his property. He would also have an incentive to guard the interests of his tenants. Thus, there could be less need to establish regulatory safeguards for subscribers in commonly owned complexes. Respondents acknowledge such possibilities, and we certainly cannot say that these assumptions would be irrational.

There is a second conceivable basis for the statutory distinction. Suppose competing SMATV operators wish to sell video programming to subscribers in a group of contiguous buildings, such as a single city block, which can be interconnected by wire without crossing a public right-of-way. If all the buildings belong to one owner or are commonly managed, that owner or manager could freely negotiate a deal for all subscribers on a competitive basis. But if the buildings are separately owned and managed, the first SMATV operator who gains a foothold by signing a contract and installing a satellite dish and associated transmission equipment on one of the buildings would enjoy a powerful cost advantage in competing for the remaining subscribers: He could connect additional buildings for the cost of a few feet of cable, whereas any competitor would have to recover the cost of his own satellite headend facility. Thus, the first operator could charge rates well above his cost and still undercut the competition. This potential for effective monopoly power might theoretically justify regulating the latter class of SMATV systems and not the former.

III

The Court of Appeals quite evidently believed that the crossing or use of a public right-of-way is the only conceivable basis upon which Congress could rationally require local franchising of SMATV systems. As we have indicated, however, there are plausible rationales unrelated to the use of public rights-of-way for regulating cable facilities serving separately owned and managed buildings. The assumptions underlying these rationales may be erroneous, but the very fact that they are "arguable" is sufficient, on rational-basis review, to "immuniz[e]" the congressional choice from constitutional challenge. *Vance v. Bradley,* 440 U.S., at 112 . . . .

[The concurring opinion of Justice Stevens is omitted.]

Notes and Questions

1. *Beach Communications* is an accurate summary of the modern interpretation of the equal protection guarantee where non-suspect classifications are involved,

incorporating the Court's earlier opinions in *Railway Express* and *Lee Optical.* According to the *Beach Communications* Court, what justifies such deferential review of legislation? Moreover, given how deferential the standard is, can you imagine any law that would be deemed unconstitutional under its standard?

2. Like *Carolene Products, Beach Communications* notes the absence of a textual equal protection guarantee applicable to the federal government. Yet it nonetheless concludes that such a guarantee exists. What is the Court's basis for that conclusion?

3. *Carolene Products*, together with *West Coast Hotel Co.*—issued just one year earlier—generally foreclosed invocation of both the Equal Protection and Due Process Clauses in most instances. As we shall see in later chapters of this book, when the Court to some extent revives each of these clauses, in some instances a viable constitutional challenge can be brought under both clauses. In such instances, is it better for the Court to rely on one clause versus the other? Consider the following:

> The burden should rest heavily upon one who would persuade us to use the due process clause to strike down a substantive law or ordinance. Even its provident use against municipal regulations frequently disables all government—state, municipal and federal—from dealing with the conduct in question because the requirement of due process is also applicable to State and Federal Governments. Invalidation of a statute or an ordinance on due process grounds leaves ungoverned and ungovernable conduct which many people find objectionable.
>
> Invocation of the equal protection clause, on the other hand, does not disable any governmental body from dealing with the subject at hand. It merely means that the prohibition or regulation must have a broader impact. I regard it as a salutary doctrine that cities, states and the Federal Government must exercise their powers so as not to discriminate between their inhabitants except upon some reasonable differentiation fairly related to the object of regulation. This equality is not merely abstract justice. The framers of the Constitution knew, and we should not forget today, that there is no more effective practical guaranty against arbitrary and unreasonable government than to require that the principles of law which officials would impose upon a minority must be imposed generally. Conversely, nothing opens the door to arbitrary action so effectively as to allow those officials to pick and choose only a few to whom they will apply legislation and thus to escape the political retribution that might be visited upon them if larger numbers were affected. Courts can take no better measure to assure that laws will be just than to require that laws be equal in operation.

Railway Express Agency v. New York, 336 U.S. 106, 112–13 (1949) (Jackson, J., concurring).

Chapter 5

Race and the Rise of Equal Protection Review

As you saw in Chapter 4, in the post-*Lochner* era, the Court, as a general rule, applied an extremely deferential standard of review in equal protection cases. During that same period, a separate line of equal protection cases was developing a more stringent standard of review for cases involving race discrimination. This chapter examines the development of that standard, the roots of which can be found, ironically, in two infamous Supreme Court decisions upholding racial discrimination against persons of Japanese descent.

A. The Japanese Internment Cases

Hirabayashi v. United States

320 U.S. 81 (1943)

Mr. Chief Justice Stone delivered the opinion of the Court.

[Defendant, an American of Japanese ancestry, challenges the constitutionality of his conviction for violating a curfew order requiring all persons of Japanese ancestry residing in certain geographic areas of the United States labeled Military Areas No. 1 and 2 to be within their place of residence daily between the hours of 8:00 p.m. and 6:00 a.m.]

The actions taken must be appraised in the light of the conditions with which the President and Congress were confronted in the early months of 1942, many of which since disclosed, were then peculiarly within the knowledge of the military authorities. On December 7, 1941, the Japanese air forces had attacked the United States Naval Base at Pearl Harbor without warning....

The challenged orders were defense measures for the avowed purpose of safeguarding the military area in question, at a time of threatened air raids and invasion by the Japanese forces, from the danger of sabotage and espionage. As the curfew was made applicable to citizens residing in the area only if they were of Japanese ancestry, our inquiry must be whether in the light of all the facts and circumstances there was any substantial basis for the conclusion, in which Congress and the military commander united, that the curfew as applied was a protective measure necessary to meet the threat of sabotage and espionage which would substantially affect the war effort and which might reasonably be expected to aid a threatened enemy invasion. The alternative which appellant insists must be accepted is for the military authorities to impose the curfew on all citizens within the military area, or on none. In a case of threatened danger requiring prompt action, it is a choice between inflicting obviously needless hardship on the many, or sitting passive and unresisting in the presence of the threat. We think that constitutional government, in time of war, is not so powerless and does not compel so hard a choice if those charged with the responsibility of our national defense have reasonable ground for believing that the threat is real.

When the orders were promulgated there was a vast concentration, within Military Areas No. 1 and 2, of installations and facilities for the production of military equipment, especially ships and airplanes. . . .

In the critical days of March, 1942, the danger to our war production by sabotage and espionage in this area seems obvious. . . . Espionage by persons in sympathy with the Japanese Government had been found to have been particularly effective in the surprise attack on Pearl Harbor. At a time of threatened Japanese attack upon this country, the nature of our inhabitants' attachments to the Japanese enemy was consequently a matter of grave concern. Of the 126,000 persons of Japanese descent in the United States, citizens and non-citizens, approximately 112,000 resided in California, Oregon and Washington at the time of the adoption of the military regulations. Of these approximately two-thirds are citizens because born in the United States. Not only did the great majority of such persons reside within the Pacific Coast states but they were concentrated in or near three of the large cities, Seattle, Portland and Los Angeles, all in Military Area No. 1.

There is support for the view that social, economic and political conditions which have prevailed since the close of the last century, when the Japanese began to come to this country in substantial numbers, have intensified their solidarity and have in large measure prevented their assimilation as an integral part of the white population. In addition, large numbers of children of Japanese parentage are sent to Japanese language schools outside the regular hours of public schools in the locality. Some of these schools are generally believed to be sources of Japanese nationalistic propaganda, cultivating allegiance to Japan. Considerable numbers, estimated to be approximately 10,000, of American-born children of Japanese parentage have been sent to Japan for all or a part of their education.

Congress and the Executive, including the military commander, could have attributed special significance, in its bearing on the loyalties of persons of Japanese descent, to the maintenance by Japan of its system of dual citizenship. Children born in the United States of Japanese alien parents, and especially those children born before December 1, 1924, are under many circumstances deemed, by Japanese law, to be citizens of Japan. . . .

The large number of resident alien Japanese, approximately one-third of all Japanese inhabitants of the country, are of mature years and occupy positions of influence in

Japanese communities. The association of influential Japanese residents with Japanese Consulates has been deemed a ready means for the dissemination of propaganda and for the maintenance of the influence of the Japanese Government with the Japanese population in this country.

As a result of all these conditions affecting the life of the Japanese, both aliens and citizens, in the Pacific Coast area, there has been relatively little social intercourse between them and the white population. The restrictions, both practical and legal, affecting the privileges and opportunities afforded to persons of Japanese extraction residing in the United States, have been sources of irritation and may well have tended to increase their isolation, and in many instances their attachments to Japan and its institutions.

Viewing these data in all their aspects, Congress and the Executive could reasonably have concluded that these conditions have encouraged the continued attachment of members of this group to Japan and Japanese institutions. These are only some of the many considerations which those charged with the responsibility for the national defense could take into account in determining the nature and extent of the danger of espionage and sabotage, in the event of invasion or air raid attack. The extent of that danger could be definitely known only after the event and after it was too late to meet it. Whatever views we may entertain regarding the loyalty to this country of the citizens of Japanese ancestry, we cannot reject as unfounded the judgment of the military authorities and of Congress that there were disloyal members of that population, whose number and strength could not be precisely and quickly ascertained. We cannot say that the war-making branches of the Government did not have ground for believing that in a critical hour such persons could not readily be isolated and separately dealt with, and constituted a menace to the national defense and safety, which demanded that prompt and adequate measures be taken to guard against it. . . .

But appellant insists that the exercise of the power is inappropriate and unconstitutional because it discriminates against citizens of Japanese ancestry, in violation of the Fifth Amendment. The Fifth Amendment contains no equal protection clause and it restrains only such discriminatory legislation by Congress as amounts to a denial of due process. Congress may hit at a particular danger where it is seen, without providing for others which are not so evident or so urgent.

Distinctions between citizens solely because of their ancestry are by their very nature odious to a free people whose institutions are founded upon the doctrine of equality. For that reason, legislative classification or discrimination based on race alone has often been held to be a denial of equal protection. We may assume that these considerations would be controlling here were it not for the fact that the danger of espionage and sabotage, in time of war and of threatened invasion, calls upon the military authorities to scrutinize every relevant fact bearing on the loyalty of populations in the danger areas. Because racial discriminations are in most circumstances irrelevant and therefore prohibited, it by no means follows that, in dealing with the perils of war, Congress and the Executive are wholly precluded from taking into account those facts and circumstances which are relevant to measures for our national defense and for the successful prosecution of the war, and which may in fact place citizens of one ancestry in a different category from others. . . . The adoption by Government, in the crisis of war and of threatened invasion, of measures for the public safety, based upon the recognition of facts and circumstances which indicate that a group of one national extraction may menace that safety more than others, is not wholly beyond the limits of the Constitution and is not to be condemned merely because in other and in most circumstances racial distinctions are irrelevant. . . .

We have stated in detail facts and circumstances with respect to the American citizens of Japanese ancestry residing on the Pacific Coast. . . . We cannot say that these facts and circumstances, considered in the particular war setting, could afford no ground for differentiating citizens of Japanese ancestry from other groups in the United States. The fact alone that attack on our shores was threatened by Japan rather than another enemy power set these citizens apart from others who have no particular associations with Japan. . . .

We need not now attempt to define the ultimate boundaries of the war power. We decide only the issue as we have defined it—we decide only that the curfew order as applied, and at the time it was applied, was within the boundaries of the war power. In this case it is enough that circumstances within the knowledge of those charged with the responsibility for maintaining the national defense afforded a rational basis for the decision which they made. Whether we would have made it is irrelevant. . . .

Mr. Justice Murphy, concurring. . . .

Distinctions based on color and ancestry are utterly inconsistent with our traditions and ideals. They are at variance with the principles for which we are now waging war. We cannot close our eyes to the fact that for centuries the Old World has been torn by racial and religious conflicts and has suffered the worst kind of anguish because of inequality of treatment for different groups. There was one law for one and a different law for another. Nothing is written more firmly into our law than the compact of the Plymouth voyagers to have just and equal laws. . . .

Today is the first time, so far as I am aware, that we have sustained a substantial restriction of the personal liberty of citizens of the United States based upon the accident of race or ancestry. . . . The result is the creation in this country of two classes of citizens for the purposes of a critical and perilous hour—to sanction discrimination between groups of United States citizens on the basis of ancestry. In my opinion this goes to the very brink of constitutional power.

Except under conditions of great emergency a regulation of this kind applicable solely to citizens of a particular racial extraction would not be regarded as in accord with the requirement of due process of law contained in the Fifth Amendment. . . . It is true that the Fifth Amendment, unlike the Fourteenth, contains no guarantee of equal protection of the laws. It is also true that even the guaranty of equal protection of the laws allows a measure of reasonable classification. It by no means follows, however, that there may not be discrimination of such an injurious character in the application of laws as to amount to a denial of due process of law as that term is used in the Fifth Amendment. I think that point is dangerously approached when we have one law for the majority of our citizens and another for those of a particular racial heritage.

In view, however, of the critical military situation which prevailed on the Pacific Coast area in the spring of 1942, and the urgent necessity of taking prompt and effective action to secure defense installations and military operations against the risk of sabotage and espionage, the military authorities should not be required to conform to standards of regulatory action appropriate to normal times. . . . Modern war does not always wait for the observance of procedural requirements that are considered essential and appropriate under normal conditions. Accordingly I think that the military arm, confronted with the peril of imminent enemy attack and acting under the authority conferred by the Congress, made an allowable judgment at the time the curfew restriction was imposed. Whether such a restriction is valid today is another matter. . . .

[The concurring opinions of Justices Douglas and Rutledge are omitted.]

Korematsu v. United States

323 U.S. 214 (1944)

Mr. Justice Black delivered the opinion of the Court.

[Subsequent to the curfew at issue in *Hirabayshi*, the military issued a new order excluding all persons of Japanese ancestry from remaining within certain locations on the West Coast. Korematsu, an American citizen of Japanese descent, was convicted in a federal court for violating the exclusion order. He challenged the constitutionality of the exclusion order].

It should be noted, to begin with, that all legal restrictions which curtail the civil rights of a single racial group are immediately suspect. That is not to say that all such restrictions are unconstitutional. It is to say that courts must subject them to the most rigid scrutiny. Pressing public necessity may sometimes justify the existence of such restrictions; racial antagonism never can. . . .

In the light of the principles we announced in the *Hirabayashi* case, we are unable to conclude that it was beyond the war power of Congress and the Executive to exclude those of Japanese ancestry from the West Coast war area at the time they did. True, exclusion from the area in which one's home is located is a far greater deprivation than constant confinement to the home from 8 p.m. to 6 a.m. Nothing short of apprehension by the proper military authorities of the gravest imminent danger to the public safety can constitutionally justify either. But exclusion from a threatened area, no less than curfew, has a definite and close relationship to the prevention of espionage and sabotage. The military authorities, charged with the primary responsibility of defending our shores, concluded that curfew provided inadequate protection and ordered exclusion. They did so, as pointed out in our *Hirabayashi* opinion, in accordance with Congressional authority to the military to say who should, and who should not, remain in the threatened areas. . . .

Here, as in the *Hirabayashi* case, ". . . we cannot reject as unfounded the judgment of the military authorities and of Congress that there were disloyal members of that population, whose number and strength could not be precisely and quickly ascertained. We cannot say that the war-making branches of the Government did not have ground for believing that in a critical hour such persons could not readily be isolated and separately dealt with, and constituted a menace to the national defense and safety, which demanded that prompt and adequate measures be taken to guard against it."

Like curfew, exclusion of those of Japanese origin was deemed necessary because of the presence of an unascertained number of disloyal members of the group, most of whom we have no doubt were loyal to this country. It was because we could not reject the finding of the military authorities that it was impossible to bring about an immediate segregation of the disloyal from the loyal that we sustained the validity of the curfew order as applying to the whole group. In the instant case, temporary exclusion of the entire group was rested by the military on the same ground. The judgment that exclusion of the whole group was for the same reason a military imperative answers the contention that the exclusion was in the nature of group punishment based on antagonism to those of Japanese origin. That there were members of the group who retained loyalties to Japan has been confirmed by investigations made subsequent to the exclusion. Approximately five thousand American citizens of Japanese ancestry refused to swear unqualified allegiance to the United States and to renounce allegiance to the Japanese Emperor, and several thousand evacuees requested repatriation to Japan. . . .

Some of the members of the Court are of the view that evacuation and detention in an Assembly Center were inseparable. After May 3, 1942, the date of Exclusion Order No. 34, Korematsu was under compulsion to leave the area not as he would choose but via an Assembly Center. The Assembly Center was conceived as a part of the machinery for group evacuation. The power to exclude includes the power to do it by force if necessary. And any forcible measure must necessarily entail some degree of detention or restraint whatever method of removal is selected. But whichever view is taken, it results in holding that the order under which petitioner was convicted was valid.

It is said that we are dealing here with the case of imprisonment of a citizen in a concentration camp solely because of his ancestry, without evidence or inquiry concerning his loyalty and good disposition towards the United States. Our task would be simple, our duty clear, were this a case involving the imprisonment of a loyal citizen in a concentration camp because of racial prejudice. Regardless of the true nature of the assembly and relocation centers—and we deem it unjustifiable to call them concentration camps with all the ugly connotations that term implies—we are dealing specifically with nothing but an exclusion order. To cast this case into outlines of racial prejudice, without reference to the real military dangers which were presented, merely confuses the issue. Korematsu was not excluded from the Military Area because of hostility to him or his race. He was excluded because we are at war with the Japanese Empire, because the properly constituted military authorities feared an invasion of our West Coast and felt constrained to take proper security measures, because they decided that the military urgency of the situation demanded that all citizens of Japanese ancestry be segregated from the West Coast temporarily, and finally, because Congress, reposing its confidence in this time of war in our military leaders—as inevitably it must—determined that they should have the power to do just this. There was evidence of disloyalty on the part of some, the military authorities considered that the need for action was great, and time was short. We cannot—by availing ourselves of the calm perspective of hindsight—now say that at that time these actions were unjustified.

Mr. Justice Roberts.

I dissent, because I think the indisputable facts exhibit a clear violation of Constitutional rights.

This is not a case of keeping people off the streets at night as was *Kiyoshi Hirabayashi v. United States*, nor a case of temporary exclusion of a citizen from an area for his own safety or that of the community, nor a case of offering him an opportunity to go temporarily out of an area where his presence might cause danger to himself or to his fellows. On the contrary, it is the case of convicting a citizen as a punishment for not submitting to imprisonment in a concentration camp, based on his ancestry, and solely because of his ancestry, without evidence or inquiry concerning his loyalty and good disposition towards the United States. If this be a correct statement of the facts disclosed by this record, and facts of which we take judicial notice, I need hardly labor the conclusion that Constitutional rights have been violated....

Mr. Justice Murphy, dissenting.

This exclusion of "all persons of Japanese ancestry, both alien and non-alien," from the Pacific Coast area on a plea of military necessity in the absence of martial law ought not to be approved. Such exclusion goes over "the very brink of constitutional power" and falls into the ugly abyss of racism....

The judicial test of whether the Government, on a plea of military necessity, can validly deprive an individual of any of his constitutional rights is whether the deprivation is reasonably related to a public danger that is so "immediate, imminent, and impending" as not to admit of delay and not to permit the intervention of ordinary constitutional processes to alleviate the danger. Civilian Exclusion Order No. 34, banishing from a prescribed area of the Pacific Coast "all persons of Japanese ancestry, both alien and non-alien," clearly does not meet that test. Being an obvious racial discrimination, the order deprives all those within its scope of the equal protection of the laws as guaranteed by the Fifth Amendment. It further deprives these individuals of their constitutional rights to live and work where they will, to establish a home where they choose and to move about freely. In excommunicating them without benefit of hearings, this order also deprives them of all their constitutional rights to procedural due process. Yet no reasonable relation to an 'immediate, imminent, and impending' public danger is evident to support this racial restriction which is one of the most sweeping and complete deprivations of constitutional rights in the history of this nation in the absence of martial law. . . .

In adjudging the military action taken in light of the then apparent dangers, we must not erect too high or too meticulous standards; it is necessary only that the action have some reasonable relation to the removal of the dangers of invasion, sabotage and espionage. But the exclusion, either temporarily or permanently, of all persons with Japanese blood in their veins has no such reasonable relation. And that relation is lacking because the exclusion order necessarily must rely for its reasonableness upon the assumption that *all* persons of Japanese ancestry may have a dangerous tendency to commit sabotage and espionage and to aid our Japanese enemy in other ways. It is difficult to believe that reason, logic or experience could be marshalled in support of such an assumption. . . .

I dissent, therefore, from this legalization of racism. Racial discrimination in any form and in any degree has no justifiable part whatever in our democratic way of life. It is unattractive in any setting but it is utterly revolting among a free people who have embraced the principles set forth in the Constitution of the United States. All residents of this nation are kin in some way by blood or culture to a foreign land. Yet they are primarily and necessarily a part of the new and distinct civilization of the United States. They must accordingly be treated at all times as the heirs of the American experiment and as entitled to all the rights and freedoms guaranteed by the Constitution.

Mr. Justice Jackson, dissenting. . . .

Much is said of the danger to liberty from the Army program for deporting and detaining these citizens of Japanese extraction. But a judicial construction of the due process clause that will sustain this order is a far more subtle blow to liberty than the promulgation of the order itself. A military order, however unconstitutional, is not apt to last longer than the military emergency. Even during that period a succeeding commander may revoke it all. But once a judicial opinion rationalizes such an order to show that it conforms to the Constitution, or rather rationalizes the Constitution to show that the Constitution sanctions such an order, the Court for all time has validated the principle of racial discrimination in criminal procedure and of transplanting American citizens. The principle then lies about like a loaded weapon ready for the hand of any authority that can bring forward a plausible claim of an urgent need. Every repetition imbeds that principle more deeply in our law and thinking and expands it to new purposes. . . . A military commander may overstep the bounds of constitutionality, and it is an incident. But if we review and approve, that passing incident becomes the doctrine of the Constitution. There it has a generative power of its own, and all that it creates will be in its own image. Nothing better illustrates this danger than does the Court's opinion in this case.

In [*Hirabayashi*] we were urged to consider only that curfew feature, that being all that technically was involved, because it was the only count necessary to sustain Hirabayashi's conviction and sentence. We yielded, and the Chief Justice guarded the opinion as carefully as language will do. . . . However, in spite of our limiting words we did validate a discrimination of the basis of ancestry for mild and temporary deprivation of liberty. Now the principle of racial discrimination is pushed from support of mild measures to very harsh ones, and from temporary deprivations to indeterminate ones. And the precedent which it is said requires us to do so is *Hirabayashi*. The Court is now saying that in *Hirabayashi* we did decide the very things we there said we were not deciding. Because we said that these citizens could be made to stay in their homes during the hours of dark, it is said we must require them to leave home entirely; and if that, we are told they may also be taken into custody for deportation; and if that, it is argued they may also be held for some undetermined time in detention camps. How far the principle of this case would be extended before plausible reasons would play out, I do not know. . . .

[The concurring opinion of Justice Frankfurter is omitted.]

Notes and Questions

1. Obviously, the outcomes of the *Hirabayashi* and *Korematsu* decisions were unfavorable to the challengers in those cases. However, both cases contain strong language regarding the nature of the equal protection guarantee so far as race is concerned. As you read subsequent decisions, keep an eye out for the Court's selective quotation of that language in defining the scope of the equal protection guarantee.

2. In *Hirabayashi*, the challengers do not contend that the government is powerless to impose a curfew, but argue instead that the curfew should be applied to *everyone*, not merely those of Japanese ancestry. How does the Court's response to this argument compare with Justice Jackson's approach to equal protection as set forth in his separate opinion in *Railway Express* in Chapter 4?

3. Of what significance is it that the power being exercised in this case, the War Power, is one particularly committed in the U.S. Constitution to the executive's discretion? In other words, might it be the case that a stringent form of scrutiny usually applies when race is involved, but that standard is relaxed somewhat when certain types of discretionary powers are exercised by the legislative or executive branches?

4. In both of these cases, the challenge is to the conduct of the federal government. Recall that in terms the U.S. Constitution contains no equal protection guarantee applicable to the conduct of the federal government. How do the decisions nonetheless recognize an equal protection guarantee applicable to the federal government?

5. Setting aside the actual holdings in these two cases and focusing instead on the strong dicta, what exactly is it about race that justifies a more stringent level of scrutiny than the general standard articulated in cases such as *Carolene Products* and *Beach Communications?*

6. Do the Court's decisions in *Hirabayashi* and *Korematsu* remain good law today? In *Trump v. Hawaii*, 138 S.Ct. 2392, 2423 (2018), the majority rejected the dissent's effort to draw an analogy between a Presidential Proclamation denying admission to the United States to those from certain countries and the relocation orders at issue in *Korematsu*, and went on to comment on the latter's continuing efficacy:

> The dissent's reference to *Korematsu*, however, affords this Court the opportunity to make express what is already obvious: *Korematsu* was gravely wrong the day it was decided, has been overruled in the court of history, and—to be clear—"has no place in law under the Constitution." 323 U.S., at 248 (Jackson, J., dissenting).

7. Recall that in *Lochner*, the Court did not take the government's purported interests at face value, but instead engaged in its own independent analysis of the factual assertion that long hours were detrimental to the health of employees and the general public. In contrast, in *Hirabayashi* and *Korematsu*, the Court accepts the government's factual assertions regarding the dangers posed by those of Japanese ancestry at face value. In considering the appropriate level of deference to give, of what significance is it that declassified documents subsequently showed that the federal government had lied to the Supreme Court about the purported dangers posed by those of Japanese ancestry? *See* Eric Yamamato, *Racial Reparations: Japanese American Redress and African American Claims*, 40 B.C. L. Rev. 477, 489–90 (1998).

B. "Separate" But "Equal" Revisited

Recall from Chapter 3 that in *Plessy*, the Court upheld the doctrine of "separate" but "equal" in the context of railroad transportation. In the six decades following *Plessy*, African-American litigants were able to achieve modest victories in challenging segregated legal regimes on equal protection grounds. Those victories were based not on the fact that facilities for Caucasians and African Americans were separate—*Plessy* had endorsed that—but rather on the ground that the segregated facilities were not, in fact, equal.

For example, in *McCabe v. Atchison, Topeka & Santa Fe Ry.*, 235 U.S. 151 (1914), the Court struck down an Oklahoma law that required trains to have separate coach sections for Caucasians and African Americans but permitted the trains to have dining and sleeping cars solely for Caucasians. The Court held that this was not equal, and that it did not matter that market demand among African Americans for dining and sleeping cars was not enough to justify a separate facility for them. And in *Missouri ex rel. Gaines v. Canada*, 305 U.S. 337 (1938), the Court rejected an effort by Missouri to deny African Americans admission to the Caucasian-only state law school. Missouri had agreed to provide financial aid to African American citizens to attend out-of-state law schools that admitted African Americans, but the

Court found this to be insufficient. According to the Court, in determining whether "equal" facilities were offered to African Americans and Caucasians alike, the key was what options were available *within* the state itself.

These successes, while important, were nonetheless limited. First, separate facilities were rarely *ever* equal, and efforts to litigate the inequality were expensive, time consuming, and not always successful. Second, and significantly, even if the quality of the physical facilities was formally equal, that did not create true equality and dignity for African Americans.

In a key decision toward the end of the *Plessy* era, the Court acknowledged this second weakness of separate facilities. At issue in *Sweatt v. Painter*, 339 U.S. 629 (1950) was the constitutionality of Texas denying admission to African-American students at the University of Texas Law School. Unlike in *Missouri ex rel. Gaines*, Texas had set up a separate law school within the state for African Americans, and had made significant efforts to equalize the facilities. Yet the *Sweatt* Court, in addition to noting that the facilities remained unequal, also focused on intangible differences between the two schools:

> What is more important, the University of Texas Law School possesses to a far greater degree those qualities which are incapable of objective measurement but which make for greatness in a law school. Such qualities, to name but a few, include reputation of the faculty, experience of the administration, position and influence of the alumni, standing in the community, traditions and prestige. It is difficult to believe that one who had a free choice between these law schools would consider the question close.

339 U.S., at 634. Moreover, in a paragraph that seemed to undercut the efficacy of *Pace v. Alabama*, the *Sweatt* Court rejected the state's appeal to the superficial equality of the segregated regime:

> It may be argued that excluding petitioner from that school is no different from excluding white students from the new law school. This contention overlooks realities. It is unlikely that a member of a group so decisively in the majority, attending a school with rich traditions and prestige which only a history of consistently maintained excellence could command, would claim that the opportunities afforded him for legal education were unequal to those held open to petitioner.

339 U.S., at 634-35. The *Sweatt* Court thus ordered Texas to admit African Americans to the University of Texas Law School.

A few years after deciding *Sweatt*, the Court granted certiorari in a series of cases involving segregated primary and secondary public schools. Among these cases was *Brown v. Board of Education*, which involved separate schools for African Americans and Caucasians in Kansas, South Carolina, Virginia, and Delaware, as well as *Bolling v. Sharp*, which involved a challenge to segregated schools in the District of Columbia.

Brown v. Board of Education

347 U.S. 483 (1954)

MR. CHIEF JUSTICE WARREN delivered the opinion of the Court.

These cases come to us from the States of Kansas, South Carolina, Virginia, and Delaware. They are premised on different facts and different local conditions, but a common legal question justifies their consideration together in this consolidated opinion.

In each of the cases, minors of the Negro race, through their legal representatives, seek the aid of the courts in obtaining admission to the public schools of their community on a nonsegregated basis. In each instance, they have been denied admission to schools attended by white children under laws requiring or permitting segregation according to race. This segregation was alleged to deprive the plaintiffs of the equal protection of the laws under the Fourteenth Amendment. In each of the cases other than the Delaware case, a three-judge federal district court denied relief to the plaintiffs on the so-called "separate but equal" doctrine announced by this Court in *Plessy v. Ferguson*, 163 U.S. 537. Under that doctrine, equality of treatment is accorded when the races are provided substantially equal facilities, even though these facilities be separate. In the Delaware case, the Supreme Court of Delaware adhered to that doctrine, but ordered that the plaintiffs be admitted to the white schools because of their superiority to the Negro schools.

The plaintiffs contend that segregated public schools are not "equal" and cannot be made "equal," and that hence they are deprived of the equal protection of the laws. Because of the obvious importance of the question presented, the Court took jurisdiction. Argument was heard in the 1952 Term, and reargument was heard this Term on certain questions propounded by the Court.

Reargument was largely devoted to the circumstances surrounding the adoption of the Fourteenth Amendment in 1868. It covered exhaustively consideration of the Amendment in Congress, ratification by the states, then existing practices in racial segregation, and the views of proponents and opponents of the Amendment. This discussion and our own investigation convince us that, although these sources cast some light, it is not enough to resolve the problem with which we are faced. At best, they are inconclusive. The most avid proponents of the post-War Amendments undoubtedly intended them to remove all legal distinctions among "all persons born or naturalized in the United States." Their opponents, just as certainly, were antagonistic to both the letter and the spirit of the Amendments and wished them to have the most limited effect. What others in Congress and the state legislatures had in mind cannot be determined with any degree of certainty.

An additional reason for the inconclusive nature of the Amendment's history, with respect to segregated schools, is the status of public education at that time. In the South, the movement toward free common schools, supported by general taxation, had not yet taken hold. Education of white children was largely in the hands of private groups. Education of Negroes was almost nonexistent, and practically all of the race were illiterate. In fact, any education of Negroes was forbidden by law in some states. Today, in contrast, many Negroes have achieved outstanding success in the arts and sciences as well as in the business and professional world. It is true that public school education at the time of the Amendment had advanced further in the North, but the effect of the Amendment on Northern States was generally ignored in the congressional debates. Even in the North, the conditions of public education did not approximate those existing today. The curriculum was usually rudimentary; ungraded schools were common in rural areas; the school term was but three months a year in many states; and compulsory school attendance was virtually unknown. As a consequence, it is not surprising that there should be so little in the history of the Fourteenth Amendment relating to its intended effect on public education.

In the first cases in this Court construing the Fourteenth Amendment, decided shortly after its adoption, the Court interpreted it as proscribing all state-imposed discriminations against the Negro race.[5] The doctrine of "separate but equal" did not make its appearance in this court until 1896 in the case of *Plessy v. Ferguson*, *supra*, involving not education but transportation. American courts have since labored with the doctrine for over half a century. In this Court, there have been six cases involving the "separate but equal" doctrine in the field of public education.... In more recent cases, all on the graduate school level, inequality was found in that specific benefits enjoyed by white students were denied to Negro students of the same educational qualifications. *Missouri ex rel. Gaines v. Canada*, 305 U.S. 337; *Sipuel v. Board of Regents of University of Oklahoma*, 332 U.S. 631; *Sweatt v. Painter*, 339 U.S. 629; *McLaurin v. Oklahoma State Regents*, 339 U.S. 637. In none of these cases was it necessary to re-examine the doctrine to grant relief to the Negro plaintiff. And in *Sweatt v. Painter*, *supra*, the Court expressly reserved decision on the question whether *Plessy v. Ferguson* should be held inapplicable to public education.

In the instant cases, that question is directly presented. Here, unlike *Sweatt v. Painter*, there are findings below that the Negro and white schools involved have been equalized, or are being equalized, with respect to buildings, curricula, qualifications and salaries of teachers, and other 'tangible' factors. Our decision, therefore, cannot turn on merely a comparison of these tangible factors in the Negro and white schools involved in each of the cases. We must look instead to the effect of segregation itself on public education.

---

5. In re Slaughter-House Cases, 1873, 16 Wall. 36, 67-72; Strauder v. West Virginia, 1880, 100 U.S. 303, 307-308. See also Virginia v. Rives, 1879, 100 U.S. 313; Ex parte Virginia, 1879, 100 U.S. 339, 344-345.

In approaching this problem, we cannot turn the clock back to 1868 when the Amendment was adopted, or even to 1896 when *Plessy v. Ferguson* was written. We must consider public education in the light of its full development and its present place in American life throughout the Nation. Only in this way can it be determined if segregation in public schools deprives these plaintiffs of the equal protection of the laws.

Today, education is perhaps the most important function of state and local governments. Compulsory school attendance laws and the great expenditures for education both demonstrate our recognition of the importance of education to our democratic society. It is required in the performance of our most basic public responsibilities, even service in the armed forces. It is the very foundation of good citizenship. Today it is a principal instrument in awakening the child to cultural values, in preparing him for later professional training, and in helping him to adjust normally to his environment. In these days, it is doubtful that any child may reasonably be expected to succeed in life if he is denied the opportunity of an education. Such an opportunity, where the state has undertaken to provide it, is a right which must be made available to all on equal terms.

We come then to the question presented: Does segregation of children in public schools solely on the basis of race, even though the physical facilities and other "tangible" factors may be equal, deprive the children of the minority group of equal educational opportunities? We believe that it does.

In *Sweatt v. Painter, supra* (339 U.S. 629), in finding that a segregated law school for Negroes could not provide them equal educational opportunities, this Court relied in large part on "those qualities which are incapable of objective measurement but which make for greatness in a law school." In *McLaurin v. Oklahoma State Regents, supra* (339 U.S. 637), the Court, in requiring that a Negro admitted to a white graduate school be treated like all other students, again resorted to intangible considerations: ". . . his ability to study, to engage in discussions and exchange views with other students, and, in general, to learn his profession." Such considerations apply with added force to children in grade and high schools. To separate them from others of similar age and qualifications solely because of their race generates a feeling of inferiority as to their status in the community that may affect their hearts and minds in a way unlikely ever to be undone. The effect of this separation on their educational opportunities was well stated by a finding in the Kansas case by a court which nevertheless felt compelled to rule against the Negro plaintiffs:

> "Segregation of white and colored children in public schools has a detrimental effect upon the colored children. The impact is greater when it has the sanction of the law; for the policy of separating the races is usually interpreted as denoting the inferiority of the negro group. A sense of inferiority affects the motivation of a child to learn. Segregation with the sanction of law, therefore, has a tendency to (retard) the educational and mental development of Negro children and to deprive them of some of the benefits they would receive in a racial(ly) integrated school system"

Whatever may have been the extent of psychological knowledge at the time of *Plessy v. Ferguson*, this finding is amply supported by modern authority.[11] Any language in *Plessy v. Ferguson* contrary to this finding is rejected.

We conclude that in the field of public education the doctrine of 'separate but equal' has no place. Separate educational facilities are inherently unequal. Therefore, we hold that the plaintiffs and others similarly situated for whom the actions have been brought are, by reason of the segregation complained of, deprived of the equal protection of the laws guaranteed by the Fourteenth Amendment. . . .

Bolling v. Sharpe

347 U.S. 497 (1954)

Mr. Chief Justice Warren delivered the opinion of the Court.

This case challenges the validity of segregation in the public schools of the District of Columbia. The petitioners, minors of the Negro race, allege that such segregation deprives them of due process of law under the Fifth Amendment. They were refused admission to a public school attended by white children solely because of their race. . . .

We have this day held that the Equal Protection Clause of the Fourteenth Amendment prohibits the states from maintaining racially segregated public schools. The legal problem in the District of Columbia is somewhat different, however. The Fifth Amendment, which is applicable in the District of Columbia, does not contain an equal protection clause as does the Fourteenth Amendment which applies only to the states. But the concepts of equal protection and due process, both stemming from our American ideal of fairness, are not mutually exclusive. The "equal protection of the laws" is a more explicit safeguard of prohibited unfairness than "due process of law," and, therefore, we do not imply that the two are always interchangeable phrases. But, as this Court has recognized, discrimination may be so unjustifiable as to be violative of due process.

Classifications based solely upon race must be scrutinized with particular care, since they are contrary to our traditions and hence constitutionally suspect.[3] . . . .

Although the Court has not assumed to define "liberty" with any great precision, that term is not confined to mere freedom from bodily restraint. Liberty under law extends to the full range of conduct which the individual is free to pursue, and

11. K. B. Clark, Effect of Prejudice and Discrimination on Personality Development (Midcentury White House Conference on Children and Youth, 1950); Witmer and Kotinsky, Personality in the Making (1952), c. VI; Deutscher and Chein, The Psychological Effects of Enforced Segregation: A Survey of Social Science Opinion, 26 J.Psychol. 259 (1948); Chein, What are the Psychological Effects of Segregation Under Conditions of Equal Facilities?, 3 Int. J. Opinion and Attitude Res. 229 (1949); Brameld, Educational Costs, in Discrimination and National Welfare (MacIver, ed., 1949), 44-48; Frazier, The Negro in the United States (1949), 674-681. And see generally Myrdal, An American Dilemma (1944).

3. *Korematsu v. United States*, 323 U.S. 214, 216; *Hirabayashi v. United States*, 320 U.S. 81, 100.

it cannot be restricted except for a proper governmental objective. Segregation in public education is not reasonably related to any proper governmental objective, and thus it imposes on Negro children of the District of Columbia a burden that constitutes an arbitrary deprivation of their liberty in violation of the Due Process Clause.

In view of our decision that the Constitution prohibits the states from maintaining racially segregated public schools, it would be unthinkable that the same Constitution would impose a lesser duty on the Federal Government. We hold that racial segregation in the public schools of the District of Columbia is a denial of the due process of law guaranteed by the Fifth Amendment to the Constitution. . . .

Notes and Questions

1. Why didn't the *Brown* Court simply cite *Korematsu* for the proposition that "the most rigid scrutiny" applied? In other words, what is it about the two situations that makes them arguably distinguishable from one another?

2. Is *Brown* overruling or distinguishing *Plessy*? In other words, is this a case about the constitutionality of racial segregation generally, the right to education independent of racial segregation, or the two combined?

3. What role does history play in the Court's interpretation of the Reconstruction Amendments? How does this compare with the role of history in earlier decisions?

4. The *Brown* Court relies on *Sweatt* for the proposition that differences in intangible factors are relevant in the constitutional analysis. What, exactly, are those intangible differences in *Brown*? What is the Court's basis for so finding?

5. The *Bolling* Court engages in what is sometimes referred to as "reverse incorporation" to conclude that the Fifth Amendment's Due Process Clause incorporates an equal protection guarantee analogous to that contained within the Fourteenth Amendment. Is that a persuasive argument? If Due Process includes a guarantee of "equal protection," why did the drafters of the Fourteenth Amendment include a separate Equal Protection Clause? In any event, is the *Bolling* Court's holding that this equal protection guarantee implied from the Fifth Amendment's Due Process Clause is *always* co-extensive with that of the Fourteenth Amendment's Equal Protection Clause?

C. *Pace v. Alabama* Revisited

Recall from Chapter 3 that the Court's 19th century cases took a narrow view of the Equal Protection Clause, upholding laws restricting the mixing of the races on the ground that the laws at issue even-handedly applied to whites and blacks alike. As noted in the previous section, in the realm of education, the Court retreated from this superficial definition of equality.

Nonetheless, laws restricting certain types of comingling of the races—including marriage and sexual intimacy—remained on the books in many states, buoyed by decisions such as *Pace v. Alabama* and the statements in many U.S. Supreme Court cases tacitly approving of laws restricting interracial marriage. The two cases that follow, decided approximately one decade after *Brown*, revisit *Pace*'s notion of superficial equality where such so-called "social rights" are concerned.

McLaughlin v. Florida

379 U.S. 184 (1964)

Mr. Justice White delivered the opinion of the Court.

At issue in this case is the validity of a conviction under § 798.05 of the Florida statutes, providing that:

> "Any negro man and white woman, or any white man and negro woman, who are not married to each other, who shall habitually live in and occupy in the nighttime the same room shall each be punished by imprisonment not exceeding twelve months, or by fine not exceeding five hundred dollars."

Because the section applies only to a white person and a Negro who commit the specified acts and because no couple other than one made up of a white and a Negro is subject to conviction upon proof of the elements comprising the offense it proscribes, we hold § 798.05 invalid as a denial of the equal protection of the laws guaranteed by the Fourteenth Amendment.

The challenged statute is a part of chapter 798 entitled "Adultery and Fornication." Section 798.01 forbids living in adultery and § 798.02 proscribes lewd cohabitation. Both sections are of general application, both require proof of intercourse to sustain a conviction, and both authorize imprisonment up to two years. Section 798.03 also of general application, proscribes fornication and authorizes a three-month jail sentence. The fourth section of the chapter, 798.04, makes criminal a white person and a Negro's living together in adultery or fornication. A one-year prison sentence is authorized. The conduct it reaches appears to be the same as is proscribed under the first two sections of the chapter. Section 798.05, the section at issue in this case, applies only to a white person and a Negro who habitually occupy the same room at nighttime. This offense, however, is distinguishable from the other sections of the chapter in that it is the only one which does not require proof of intercourse along with the other elements of the crime....

I.

....

In this situation, *Pace v. Alabama*, *supra*, is relied upon as controlling authority. In our view, however, *Pace* represents a limited view of the Equal Protection Clause which has not withstood analysis in the subsequent decisions of this Court.... Under *Pace* the Alabama law regulating the conduct of both Negroes and whites satisfied the Equal Protection Clause since it applied equally to and among the members of the class which it reached without regard to the fact that the statute did not reach other types of couples performing the identical conduct and without any necessity to justify the difference in penalty established for the two offenses. Because each of the Alabama laws applied equally to those to whom it was applicable, the different treatment accorded interracial and intraracial couples was irrelevant.

This narrow view of the Equal Protection Clause was soon swept away. While acknowledging the currency of the view that "if the law deals alike with all of a certain class" it is not obnoxious to the Equal Protection Clause and that "as a general proposition, this is undeniably true," the Court in *Gulf, C. & S.F.R. Co. v. Ellis*, 165 U.S. 150, 155, said that it was "equally true that such classification cannot be made arbitrarily. . . ." . . . .

Judicial inquiry under the Equal Protection Clause, therefore, does not end with a showing of equal application among the members of the class defined by the legislation. The courts must reach and determine the question whether the classifications drawn in a statute are reasonable in light of its purpose—in this case, whether there is an arbitrary or invidious discrimination between those classes covered by Florida's cohabitation law and those excluded. That question is what *Pace* ignored and what must be faced here.

Normally, the widest discretion is allowed the legislative judgment in determining whether to attack some, rather than all, of the manifestations of the evil aimed at; and normally that judgment is given the benefit of every conceivable circumstance which might suffice to characterize the classification as reasonable rather than arbitrary and invidious. But we deal here with a classification based upon the race of the participants, which must be viewed in light of the historical fact that the central purpose of the Fourteenth Amendment was to eliminate racial discrimination emanating from official sources in the States. This strong policy renders racial classifications "constitutionally suspect," *Bolling v. Sharpe*, 347 U.S. 497, 499; and subject to the "most rigid scrutiny," *Korematsu v. United States*, 323 U.S. 214, 216; and "in most circumstances irrelevant" to any constitutionally acceptable legislative purpose, *Hirabayashi v. United States*, 320 U.S. 81, 100. Thus it is that racial classifications have been held invalid in a variety of contexts. See, *e.g.*, *Virginia Board of Elections v. Hamm*, 379 U.S. 19 (designation of race in voting and property records); *Anderson v. Martin*, 375 U.S. 399 (designation of race on nomination papers and ballots); *Watson v. City of Memphis*, 373 U.S. 526 (segregation in public parks and playgrounds); *Brown v. Board of Education*, 349 U.S. 294 (segregation in public schools).

We deal here with a racial classification embodied in a criminal statute. In this context, where the power of the State weighs most heavily upon the individual or the group, we must be especially sensitive to the policies of the Equal Protection Clause which, as reflected in congressional enactments dating from 1870, were intended to secure "the full and equal benefit of all laws and proceedings for the security of persons and property" and to subject all persons "to like punishment, pains, penalties, taxes, licenses, and exactions of every kind, and to no other."

Our inquiry, therefore, is whether there clearly appears in the relevant materials some overriding statutory purpose requiring the proscription of the specified conduct when engaged in by a white person and a Negro, but not otherwise. . . .

The State in its brief in this Court, however, says that the legislative purpose of § 798.05, like the other sections of chapter 798, was to prevent breaches of the basic concepts of sexual decency. . . .

We find nothing in this suggested legislative purpose, however, which makes it essential to punish promiscuity of one racial group and not that of another. There is no suggestion that a white person and a Negro are any more likely habitually to occupy the same room together than the white or the Negro couple or to engage in illicit intercourse if they do. Sections 798.01-798.05 indicate no legislative conviction that promiscuity by the interracial couple presents any particular problems requiring separate or different treatment if the suggested over-all policy of the chapter is to be adequately served. Sections 798.01-798.03 deal with adultery, lewd cohabitation and fornication, in that order. All are of general application. Section 798.04 prohibits a white and a Negro from living in a state of adultery or fornication and imposes a lesser period of imprisonment than does either § 798.01 or § 798.02, each of which is applicable to all persons. Simple fornication by the interracial couple is covered only by the general provision of § 798.03. This is not, therefore, a case where the class defined in the law is that from which "the evil mainly is to be feared," *Patsone v. Pennsylvania*, 232 U.S. 138, 144; or where the "[e]vils in the same field may be of different dimensions and proportions, requiring different remedies," *Williamson v. Lee Optical*, 348 U.S. 483, 489; or even one where the State has done as much as it can as fast as it can, *Buck v. Bell*, 274 U.S. 200, 208. That a general evil will be partially corrected may at times, and without more, serve to justify the limited application of a criminal law; but legislative discretion to employ the piecemeal approach stops short of permitting a State to narrow statutory coverage to focus on a racial group. Such classifications bear a far heavier burden of justification. "When the law lays an unequal hand on those who have committed intrinsically the same quality of offense and sterilizes one and not the other, it has made as an invidious a discrimination as if it had selected a particular race or nationality for oppressive treatment." *Skinner v. Oklahoma*, 316 U.S. 535, 541.

II.

Florida's remaining argument is related to its law against interracial marriage, Fla. Stat.Ann. § 741.11, which, in the light of certain legislative history of the Fourteenth Amendment, is said to be immune from attack under the Equal Protection Clause. Its interracial cohabitation law, § 798.05, is likewise valid, it is argued, because it is ancillary to and serves the same purpose as the miscegenation law itself.

We reject this argument, without reaching the question of the validity of the State's prohibition against interracial marriage or the soundness of the arguments rooted in the history of the Amendment. For even if we posit the constitutionality of the ban against the marriage of a Negro and a white, it does not follow that the cohabitation law is not to be subjected to independent examination under the Fourteenth Amendment....

There is involved here an exercise of the state police power which trenches upon the constitutionally protected freedom from invidious official discrimination based on race. Such a law, even though enacted pursuant to a valid state interest, bears a heavy burden of justification, as we have said, and will be upheld only if it is necessary, and not merely rationally related, to the accomplishment of a permissible state policy. Those provisions of chapter 798 which are neutral as to race express a general and strong state policy against promiscuous conduct, whether engaged in by those who are married, those who may marry or those who may not. These provisions, if enforced, would reach illicit relations of any kind and in this way protect the integrity of the marriage laws of the State, including what is claimed to be a valid ban on interracial marriage. These same provisions, moreover, punish premarital sexual relations as severely or more severely in some instances than do those provisions which focus on the interracial couple. Florida has offered no argument that the State's policy against interracial marriage cannot be as adequately served by the general, neutral, and existing ban on illicit behavior as by a provision such as § 798.05 which singles out the promiscuous interracial couple for special statutory treatment. In short, it has not been shown that § 798.05 is a necessary adjunct to the State's ban on interracial marriage. We accordingly invalidate § 798.05 without expressing any views about the State's prohibition of interracial marriage, and reverse these convictions.

Mr. Justice Stewart, with whom Mr. Justice Douglas joins, concurring.

I concur in the judgment and agree with most of what is said in the Court's opinion. But the Court implies that a criminal law of the kind here involved might be constitutionally valid if a State could show 'some overriding statutory purpose.' This is an implication in which I cannot join, because I cannot conceive of a valid legislative purpose under our Constitution for a state law which makes the color of a person's skin the test of whether his conduct is a criminal offense.... There might be limited room under the Equal Protection Clause for a civil law requiring the keeping of racially segregated public records for statistical or other valid public purposes. But we deal here with a criminal law which imposes criminal punishment. And I think it is simply not possible for a state law to be valid under our Constitution which makes the criminality of an act depend upon the race of the actor. Discrimination of that kind is invidious per se.

[The concurring opinion of Justice Harlan is omitted.]

Notes and Questions

1. Overruling *Pace* is a key aspect of *McLaughlin* because under *Pace*, there is no racial discrimination and thus no basis for applying anything more than traditional rational basis scrutiny. *McLaughlin*, in contrast, finds that the law at issue discriminates on the basis of race and thus apples a more robust level of scrutiny. What, exactly, is

the level of scrutiny that the *McLaughlin* majority applies? How does that compare with the level of scrutiny that Justice Stewart suggests in his separate concurrence?

2. How significant is it to the decision that what is involved in this case is a *criminal* statute? Would the scrutiny be as searching if criminal consequences did not attach to the conduct at issue?

3. How significant is the *right* at issue to the outcome in this case, namely, the right to engage in sexual intimacy with the person of one's choosing? Does that make the scrutiny more robust than it might be if something more trivial were at stake?

4. Note that even though heightened scrutiny applies, that does not necessarily mean that the law is unconstitutional, at least under the majority's approach. Rather, it means that it must be supported by sufficiently strong reasons. What are the reasons proffered by the state, and why are they not deemed by the Court to be sufficiently persuasive to justify the law?

5. Does *McLaughlin* directly or indirectly cast doubt on the constitutionality of laws restricting inter-racial marriage?

Loving v. Virginia

388 U.S. 1 (1967)

Mr. Chief Justice Warren delivered the opinion of the Court.

This case presents a constitutional question never addressed by this Court: whether a statutory scheme adopted by the State of Virginia to prevent marriages between persons solely on the basis of racial classifications violates the Equal Protection and Due Process Clauses of the Fourteenth Amendment. For reasons which seem to us to reflect the central meaning of those constitutional commands, we conclude that these statutes cannot stand consistently with the Fourteenth Amendment.

In June 1958, two residents of Virginia, Mildred Jeter, a Negro woman, and Richard Loving, a white man, were married in the District of Columbia pursuant to its laws. Shortly after their marriage, the Lovings returned to Virginia and established their marital abode in Caroline County. At the October Term, 1958, of the Circuit Court of Caroline County, a grand jury issued an indictment charging the Lovings with violating Virginia's ban on interracial marriages. On January 6, 1959, the Lovings pleaded guilty to the charge and were sentenced to one year in jail; however, the trial judge suspended the sentence for a period of 25 years on the condition that the Lovings leave the State and not return to Virginia together for 25 years. He stated in an opinion that:

> "Almighty God created the races white, black, yellow, malay and red, and he placed them on separate continents. And but for the interference with his arrangement there would be no cause for such marriages. The fact that he separated the races shows that he did not intend for the races to mix."

After their convictions, the Lovings took up residence in the District of Columbia. On November 6, 1963, they filed a motion in the state trial court to vacate the judgment and set aside the sentence on the ground that the statutes which they had violated were repugnant to the Fourteenth Amendment. The motion not having been decided by October 28, 1964, the Lovings instituted a class action in the United States District Court for the Eastern District of Virginia requesting that a three-judge court be convened to declare the Virginia antimiscegenation statutes unconstitutional and to enjoin state officials from enforcing their convictions. On January 22, 1965, the state trial judge denied the motion to vacate the sentences, and the Lovings perfected an appeal to the Supreme Court of Appeals of Virginia. On February 11, 1965, the three-judge District Court continued the case to allow the Lovings to present their constitutional claims to the highest state court.

The Supreme Court of Appeals upheld the constitutionality of the antimiscegenation statutes and, after modifying the sentence, affirmed the convictions. The Lovings appealed this decision, and we noted probable jurisdiction on December 12, 1966.

The two statutes under which appellants were convicted and sentenced are part of a comprehensive statutory scheme aimed at prohibiting and punishing interracial marriages. The Lovings were convicted of violating § 20–58 of the Virginia Code:

> "*Leaving State to evade law.*—If any white person and colored person shall go out of this State, for the purpose of being married, and with the intention of returning, and be married out of it, and afterwards return to and reside in it, cohabiting as man and wife, they shall be punished as provided in § 20–59, and the marriage shall be governed by the same law as if it had been solemnized in this State. The fact of their cohabitation here as man and wife shall be evidence of their marriage."

Section 20–59, which defines the penalty for miscegenation, provides:

> "*Punishment for marriage.*—If any white person intermarry with a colored person, or any colored person intermarry with a white person, he shall be guilty of a felony and shall be punished by confinement in the penitentiary for not less than one nor more than five years."

Other central provisions in the Virginia statutory scheme are § 20–57, which automatically voids all marriages between "a white person and a colored person" without any judicial proceeding, and §§ 20–54 and 1–14 which, respectively, define "white persons" and "colored persons and Indians" for purposes of the statutory prohibitions.[4] The Lovings have never disputed in the course of this litigation that

---

4. Section 20–54 of the Virginia Code provides:
"*Intermarriage prohibited; meaning of term 'white persons.'*—It shall hereafter be unlawful for any white person in this State to marry any save a white person, or a person with no other admixture of blood than white and American Indian. For the purpose of this chapter, the term 'white person' shall apply only to such person as has no trace whatever of any blood other than Caucasian; but persons who have one-sixteenth or less of the blood of the American Indian and have no other non-Caucasic blood shall be deemed to

Mrs. Loving is a "colored person" or that Mr. Loving is a "white person" within the meanings given those terms by the Virginia statutes.

Virginia is now one of 16 States which prohibit and punish marriages on the basis of racial classifications. Penalties for miscegenation arose as an incident to slavery and have been common in Virginia since the colonial period. The present statutory scheme dates from the adoption of the Racial Integrity Act of 1924, passed during the period of extreme nativism which followed the end of the First World War. The central features of this Act, and current Virginia law, are the absolute prohibition of a "white person" marrying other than another "white person," a prohibition against issuing marriage licenses until the issuing official is satisfied that the applicants' statements as to their race are correct, certificates of "racial composition" to be kept by both local and state registrars, and the carrying forward of earlier prohibitions against racial intermarriage.

I.

In upholding the constitutionality of these provisions in the decision below, the Supreme Court of Appeals of Virginia referred to its 1955 decision in *Naim v. Naim*, as stating the reasons supporting the validity of these laws. In *Naim*, the state court concluded that the State's legitimate purposes were "to preserve the racial integrity of its citizens," and to prevent "the corruption of blood," "a mongrel breed of citizens," and "the obliteration of racial pride," obviously an endorsement of the doctrine of White Supremacy. The court also reasoned that marriage has traditionally been subject to state regulation without federal intervention, and, consequently, the regulation of marriage should be left to exclusive state control by the Tenth Amendment.

While the state court is no doubt correct in asserting that marriage is a social relation subject to the State's police power, *Maynard v. Hill*, 125 U.S. 190 (1888), the State does not contend in its argument before this Court that its powers to regulate marriage are unlimited notwithstanding the commands of the Fourteenth Amendment. Nor could it do so in light of *Meyer v. Nebraska*, 262 U.S. 390 (1923), and *Skinner v. Oklahoma*, 316 U.S. 535 (1942). Instead, the State argues that the meaning

---

be white persons. All laws heretofore passed and now in effect regarding the intermarriage of white and colored persons shall apply to marriages prohibited by this chapter." The exception for persons with less than one-sixteenth "of the blood of the American Indian" is apparently accounted for, in the words of a tract issued by the Registrar of the State Bureau of Vital Statistics, by "the desire of all to recognize as an integral and honored part of the white race the descendants of John Rolfe and Pocahontas * * *."

Section 1–14 of the Virginia Code provides:

["]*Colored persons and Indians defined.*—Every person in whom there is ascertainable any Negro blood shall be deemed and taken to be a colored person, and every person not a colored person having one fourth or more of American Indian blood shall be deemed an American Indian; except that members of Indian tribes existing in this Commonwealth having one fourth or more of Indian blood and less than one sixteenth of Negro blood shall be deemed tribal Indians."

of the Equal Protection Clause, as illuminated by the statements of the Framers, is only that state penal laws containing an interracial element as part of the definition of the offense must apply equally to whites and Negroes in the sense that members of each race are punished to the same degree. Thus, the State contends that, because its miscegenation statutes punish equally both the white and the Negro participants in an interracial marriage, these statutes, despite their reliance on racial classifications do not constitute an invidious discrimination based upon race. The second argument advanced by the State assumes the validity of its equal application theory. The argument is that, if the Equal Protection Clause does not outlaw miscegenation statutes because of their reliance on racial classifications, the question of constitutionality would thus become whether there was any rational basis for a State to treat interracial marriages differently from other marriages. On this question, the State argues, the scientific evidence is substantially in doubt and, consequently, this Court should defer to the wisdom of the state legislature in adopting its policy of discouraging interracial marriages.

Because we reject the notion that the mere "equal application" of a statute containing racial classifications is enough to remove the classifications from the Fourteenth Amendment's proscription of all invidious racial discriminations, we do not accept the State's contention that these statutes should be upheld if there is any possible basis for concluding that they serve a rational purpose. The mere fact of equal application does not mean that our analysis of these statutes should follow the approach we have taken in cases involving no racial discrimination where the Equal Protection Clause has been arrayed against a statute discriminating between the kinds of advertising which may be displayed on trucks in New York City, *Railway Express Agency, Inc. v. New York*, 336 U.S. 106 (1949), or an exemption in Ohio's ad valorem tax for merchandise owned by a non-resident in a storage warehouse, *Allied Stores of Ohio, Inc. v. Bowers*, 358 U.S. 522 (1959). In these cases, involving distinctions not drawn according to race, the Court has merely asked whether there is any rational foundation for the discriminations, and has deferred to the wisdom of the state legislatures. In the case at bar, however, we deal with statutes containing racial classifications, and the fact of equal application does not immunize the statute from the very heavy burden of justification which the Fourteenth Amendment has traditionally required of state statutes drawn according to race.

The State argues that statements in the Thirty-ninth Congress about the time of the passage of the Fourteenth Amendment indicate that the Framers did not intend the Amendment to make unconstitutional state miscegenation laws. Many of the statements alluded to by the State concern the debates over the Freedmen's Bureau Bill, which President Johnson vetoed, and the Civil Rights Act of 1866, 14 Stat. 27, enacted over his veto. While these statements have some relevance to the intention of Congress in submitting the Fourteenth Amendment, it must be understood that they pertained to the passage of specific statutes and not to the broader, organic purpose of a constitutional amendment. As for the various statements directly concerning the Fourteenth Amendment, we have said in connection with a related problem, that although these historical sources "cast some light" they are not sufficient to resolve the problem; "[a]t best, they are inconclusive. The most avid proponents of the post-War Amendments undoubtedly intended them to remove all legal distinctions among 'all persons born or naturalized in the United States.' Their opponents, just as certainly, were antagonistic to both the letter and the spirit of the Amendments and wished them to have the most limited effect." *Brown v. Board of Education of Topeka*, 347 U.S. 483, 489 (1954). See also *Strauder v. West Virginia*, 100 U.S. 303, 310 (1880). We have rejected the proposition that the debates in the Thirty-ninth Congress or in the state legislatures which ratified the Fourteenth Amendment supported the theory advanced by the State, that the requirement of equal protection of the laws is satisfied by penal laws defining offenses based on racial classifications so long as white and Negro participants in the offense were similarly punished. *McLaughlin v. Florida*, 379 U.S. 184 (1964).

The State finds support for its "equal application" theory in the decision of the Court in *Pace v. Alabama*, 106 U.S. 583 (1883). In that case, the Court upheld a conviction under an Alabama statute forbidding adultery or fornication between a white person and a Negro which imposed a greater penalty than that of a statute proscribing similar conduct by members of the same race. The Court reasoned that the statute could not be said to discriminate against Negroes because the punishment for each participant in the offense was the same. However, as recently as the 1964 Term, in rejecting the reasoning of that case, we stated "*Pace* represents a limited view of the Equal Protection Clause which has not withstood analysis in the subsequent decisions of this Court." *McLaughlin v. Florida*, *supra*, 379 U.S. at 188. As we there demonstrated, the Equal Protection Clause requires the consideration of whether the classifications drawn by any statute constitute an arbitrary and invidious discrimination. The clear and central purpose of the Fourteenth Amendment was to eliminate all official state sources of invidious racial discrimination in the States.

There can be no question but that Virginia's miscegenation statutes rest solely upon distinctions drawn according to race. The statutes proscribe generally accepted conduct if engaged in by members of different races. Over the years, this Court has consistently repudiated "[d]istinctions between citizens solely because of their ancestry" as being "odious to a free people whose institutions are founded upon the doctrine of equality." *Hirabayashi v. United States*, 320 U.S. 81, 100 (1943). At the very least, the Equal Protection Clause demands that racial classifications, especially suspect in criminal statutes, be subjected to the "most rigid scrutiny," *Korematsu v. United States*, 323 U.S. 214, 216 (1944), and, if they are ever to be upheld, they must be shown to be necessary to the accomplishment of some permissible state objective, independent of the racial discrimination which it was the object of the Fourteenth Amendment to eliminate. Indeed, two members of this Court have already stated that they "cannot conceive of a valid legislative purpose . . . which makes the color of a person's skin the test of whether his conduct is a criminal offense." *McLaughlin v. Florida*, *supra*, 379 U.S. at 198 (Stewart, J., joined by Douglas, J., concurring).

There is patently no legitimate overriding purpose independent of invidious racial discrimination which justifies this classification. The fact that Virginia prohibits only interracial marriages involving white persons demonstrates that the racial classifications must stand on their own justification, as measures designed to maintain White Supremacy.[11] We have consistently denied the constitutionality of measures which restrict the rights of citizens on account of race. There can be no doubt that restricting the freedom to marry solely because of racial classifications violates the central meaning of the Equal Protection Clause....

Mr. Justice Stewart, concurring.

I have previously expressed the belief that "it is simply not possible for a state law to be valid under our Constitution which makes the criminality of an act depend upon the race of the actor." *McLaughlin v. Florida*, 379 U.S. 184, 198 (concurring opinion). Because I adhere to that belief, I concur in the judgment of the Court.

Notes and Questions

1. What is the purported purpose of the law at issue in *Loving*? Is that purpose accomplished in an even-handed manner, and if not, is that significant to the Court's decision? Stated somewhat differently, might the outcome have been different had the law been drafted more tightly and without any exceptions?

2. Given *McLaughlin*, the outcome in *Loving* seems like a foregone conclusion, does it not? Together, what theory of equality do the *McLaughlin* and *Loving* Courts endorse, and how does it differ from the theories adopted by the Court in the 19th century?

3. As in *McLaughlin*, the law at issue in this case imposes criminal sanctions. How important is that to the decision? Stated somewhat differently, if a law merely denied marriage licenses to couples, but did not criminalize the act of somehow getting married, would it be subject to lesser scrutiny?

4. What level of scrutiny does the *Loving* Court apply, and why does it hold that the rationale for the law does not pass constitutional muster?

5. How important is the nature of the specific right at issue in this case, to wit, the right to marry? Recall that this was identified in *Meyer v. Nebraska*—a case cited in *Loving*—as one of the fundamental rights of man. In a separate section of the

---

11. Appellants point out that the State's concern in these statutes, as expressed in the words of the 1924 Act's title, "An Act to Preserve Racial Integrity," extends only to the integrity of the white race. While Virginia prohibits whites from marrying any nonwhite (subject to the exception for the descendants of Pocahontas), Negroes, Orientals, and any other racial class may intermarry without statutory interference. Appellants contend that this distinction renders Virginia's miscegenation statutes arbitrary and unreasonable even assuming the constitutional validity of an official purpose to preserve "racial integrity." We need not reach this contention because we find the racial classifications in these statutes repugnant to the Fourteenth Amendment, even assuming an even-handed state purpose to protect the "integrity" of all races.

opinion, excerpted in a later chapter, the Court considers the nature of the right at issue in *Loving* as an alternative rationale for striking the law down.

6. Note that both *McLaughlin* and *Loving* quote selectively from the Court's earlier decisions in *Korematsu* and *Hirabayashi*. In so doing, have they not transformed these cases—which both upheld stark instances of racial discrimination—into cases that stand for a rather different proposition? Is this approach virtuous or troublesome?

D. Private Bias as a Governmental Interest

As the Court has noted time and again, the equal protection guarantee regulates only the conduct of governmental actors, not private ones. It is thus not a violation of the equal protection guarantee for private actors to discriminate against someone because of their race. But what if the government makes racially conscious decisions that are grounded in private biases? The following case explores that issue, and also sets forth the modern form of the strict scrutiny test for assessing race-based classifications.

Palmore v. Sidoti

466 U.S. 429 (1984)

Chief Justice Burger delivered the opinion of the Court.

We granted certiorari to review a judgment of a state court divesting a natural mother of the custody of her infant child because of her remarriage to a person of a different race.

I

When petitioner Linda Sidoti Palmore and respondent Anthony J. Sidoti, both Caucasians, were divorced in May 1980 in Florida, the mother was awarded custody of their 3-year-old daughter.

In September 1981 the father sought custody of the child by filing a petition to modify the prior judgment because of changed conditions. The change was that the child's mother was then cohabiting with a Negro, Clarence Palmore, Jr., whom she married two months later. . . .

The court [] concluded that the best interests of the child would be served by awarding custody to the father. The court's rationale is contained in the following:

> "The father's evident resentment of the mother's choice of a black partner is not sufficient to wrest custody from the mother. It is of some significance, however, that the mother did see fit to bring a man into her home and carry on a sexual relationship with him without being married to him. Such action tended to place gratification of her own desires ahead of her concern for the child's future welfare. *This Court feels that despite the strides*

> *that have been made in bettering relations between the races in this country, it is inevitable that Melanie will, if allowed to remain in her present situation and attains school age and thus more vulnerable to peer pressures, suffer from the social stigmatization that is sure to come.*" App. to Pet. for Cert. 26–27 (emphasis added).

. . . .

II

A core purpose of the Fourteenth Amendment was to do away with all governmentally imposed discrimination based on race. . . . Such classifications are subject to the most exacting scrutiny; to pass constitutional muster, they must be justified by a compelling governmental interest and must be "necessary . . . to the accomplishment" of their legitimate purpose, *McLaughlin v. Florida*, 379 U.S. 184, 196 (1964). *See Loving v. Virginia*, 388 U.S. 1, 11 (1967).

The State, of course, has a duty of the highest order to protect the interests of minor children, particularly those of tender years. In common with most states, Florida law mandates that custody determinations be made in the best interests of the children involved. The goal of granting custody based on the best interests of the child is indisputably a substantial governmental interest for purposes of the Equal Protection Clause.

It would ignore reality to suggest that racial and ethnic prejudices do not exist or that all manifestations of those prejudices have been eliminated. There is a risk that a child living with a stepparent of a different race may be subject to a variety of pressures and stresses not present if the child were living with parents of the same racial or ethnic origin.

The question, however, is whether the reality of private biases and the possible injury they might inflict are permissible considerations for removal of an infant child from the custody of its natural mother. We have little difficulty concluding that they are not. The Constitution cannot control such prejudices but neither can it tolerate them. Private biases may be outside the reach of the law, but the law cannot, directly or indirectly, give them effect. . . .

The effects of racial prejudice, however real, cannot justify a racial classification removing an infant child from the custody of its natural mother found to be an appropriate person to have such custody. . . .

Notes and Questions

1. Recall that under rational basis review, there is an assessment of both the end that the government seeks to achieve with a law and the means employed to achieve it. Under traditional rational basis review, this review is highly deferential, requiring only a legitimate end and a rational relationship between the end sought and the means employed to achieve it. How, according to *Palmore*, does the strict scrutiny employed for race differ?

2. Is *Palmore*'s statement regarding private biases limited to private *racial* biases, or does it extend to other forms of private biases that are taken into account? Suppose instead that one of the divorced parents decided to marry someone of the same sex. Could a judge take private biases regarding sexual orientation into account in deciding to deny that parent custody? Would it likewise be subject to strict scrutiny?

3. Separate and apart from the racial classification at play in this case, is the nature of the right—the right to custody of one's child—an independent basis for applying heightened scrutiny under cases such as *Meyer v. Nebraska*? Of what significance is that in answering the question in the preceding note?

Chapter 6

The Fifteenth Amendment

Thus far, the focus of this book has been on the first two Reconstruction Amendments, the Thirteenth and Fourteenth Amendments. Yet in addition to restricting the civil and social rights of African Americans, state governments were also attempting to restrict their ability to vote. The cases that follow thus examine the scope of the Fifteenth Amendment, the first section of which provides that "[t]he right of citizens of the United States to vote shall not be denied or abridged by the United States or by any State on account of race, color, or previous condition of servitude." As you read these cases and the cases that follow in subsequent chapters, consider the following questions:

- Does the Fifteenth Amendment apply only to laws that explicitly deny the right to vote based on race, color, or previous condition of servitude, or does it also encompass laws that indirectly accomplish the same result?
- Does the Fifteenth Amendment apply only when governmental actors intend to deny the right to vote based on race, color, or previous condition of servitude, or does it also encompass laws that have a disparate impact on that right to vote?
- Section 2 gives Congress the power to enforce the Fifteenth Amendment by "appropriate legislation." How, if at all, does Congress's power under Section 2 differ from the self-executing provision of the Fifteenth Amendment set forth in Section 1?
- Is the Fifteenth Amendment the only provision of the Reconstruction Amendments that is applicable when the right to vote is at issue, or do other provisions, such as the Thirteenth or Fourteenth Amendments, play a role as well?

Guinn v. United States

238 U.S. 347 (1915)

Mr. Chief Justice White delivered the opinion of the court:

[At issue in this case is the constitutionality of an amendment to the Oklahoma Constitution requiring as a condition for voting that an individual "be able to read and write any section of the Constitution of the state of Oklahoma" but containing a proviso that "no person who was, on January 1st, 1866, or any time prior thereto, entitled to vote under any form of government, or who at that time resided in some foreign nation, and no lineal descendant of such person, shall be denied the right to register and vote because of his inability to so read and write sections of such Constitution."]

No question is raised by the government concerning the validity of the literacy test provided for in the amendment under consideration as an independent standard since the conclusion is plain that that test rests on the exercise of state judgment, and therefore cannot be here assailed either by disregarding the state's power to judge on the subject, or by testing its motive in enacting the provision. The real question involved, so the argument of the government insists, is the repugnancy of the standard which the amendment makes, based upon the conditions existing on January 1st, 1866, because on its face and inherently considering the substance of things, that standard is a mere denial of the restrictions imposed by the prohibitions of the 15th Amendment, and by necessary result re-creates and perpetuates the very conditions which the Amendment was intended to destroy....

The questions then are: (1) Giving to the propositions of the government the interpretation which the government puts upon them, and assuming that the suffrage provision has the significance which the government assumes it to have, is that provision as a matter of law repugnant to the 15th Amendment? which leads us, of course, to consider the operation and effect of the 15th Amendment. (2) If yes, has the assailed amendment in so far as it fixes a standard for voting as of January 1, 1866, the meaning which the government attributes to it? which leads us to analyze and interpret that provision of the amendment....

1. *The operation and effect of the 15th Amendment...*

(a) Beyond doubt the Amendment does not take away from the state governments in a general sense the power over suffrage which has belonged to those governments from the beginning, and without the possession of which power the whole fabric upon which the division of state and national authority under the Constitution and the organization of both governments rest would be without support, and both the authority of the nation and the state would fall to the ground. In fact, the very command of the Amendment recognizes the possession of the general power by the state, since the Amendment seeks to regulate its exercise as to the particular subject with which it deals.

(b) But it is equally beyond the possibility of question that the Amendment in express terms restricts the power of the United States or the states to abridge or deny the right of a citizen of the United States to vote on account of race, color, or previous condition of servitude. The restriction is coincident with the power and prevents its exertion in disregard to the command of the Amendment. But while this is true, it is true also that the Amendment does not change, modify, or deprive the states of their full power as to suffrage except, of course, as to the subject with which the Amendment deals and to the extent that obedience to its command is necessary. Thus the authority over suffrage which the states possess and the limitation which the Amendment imposes are co-ordinate and one may not destroy the other without bringing about the destruction of both.

(c) While in the true sense, therefore, the Amendment gives no right of suffrage, it was long ago recognized that in operation its prohibition might measurably have that effect; that is to say, that as the command of the Amendment was self-executing and reached without legislative action the conditions of discrimination against which it was aimed, the result might arise that, as a consequence of the striking down of a discrimination clause, a right of suffrage would be enjoyed by reason of the generic character of the provision which would remain after the discrimination was stricken out. *Ex parte Yarbrough*, 110 U. S. 651; *Neal v. Delaware*, 103 U. S. 370. A familiar illustration of this doctrine resulted from the effect of the adoption of the Amendment on state Constitutions in which, at the time of the adoption of the Amendment, the right of suffrage was conferred on all white male citizens, since by the inherent power of the Amendment the word "white" disappeared and therefore all male citizens, without discrimination on account of race, color, or previous condition of servitude, came under the generic grant of suffrage made by the state.

With these principles before us how can there be room for any serious dispute concerning the repugnancy of the standard based upon January 1, 1866 (a date which preceded the adoption of the 15th Amendment), if the suffrage provision fixing that standard is susceptible of the significance which the government attributes to it? Indeed, there seems no escape from the conclusion that to hold that there was even possibility for dispute on the subject would be but to declare that the 15th Amendment not only had not the self-executing power which it has been recognized to have from the beginning, but that its provisions were wholly inoperative because susceptible of being rendered inapplicable by mere forms of expression embodying no exercise of judgment and resting upon no discernible reason other than the purpose to disregard the prohibitions of the Amendment by creating a standard of voting which, on its face, was in substance but a revitalization of conditions which, when they prevailed in the past, had been destroyed by the self-operative force of the Amendment.

2. *The standard of January 1, 1866, fixed in the suffrage amendment and its significance.*

The inquiry, of course, here is, Does the amendment as to the particular standard which this heading embraces involve the mere refusal to comply with the commands of the 15th Amendment as previously stated? This leads us, for the purpose of the analysis, to recur to the text of the suffrage amendment. Its opening sentence fixes the literacy standard which is all-inclusive, since it is general in its expression and contains no word of discrimination on account of race or color or any other reason. This, however, is immediately followed by the provisions creating the standard based upon the condition existing on January 1, 1866, and carving out those coming under that standard from the inclusion in the literacy test which would have controlled them but for the exclusion thus expressly provided for. The provision is this:

> "But no person who was, on January 1st, 1866, or at any time prior thereto, entitled to vote under any form of government, or who at that time resided in some foreign nation, and no lineal descendant of such person, shall be

> denied that right to register and vote because of his inability to so read and write sections of such Constitution."

We have difficulty in finding words to more clearly demonstrate the conviction we entertain that this standard has the characteristics which the government attributes to it than does the mere statement of the text. It is true it contains no express words of an exclusion from the standard which it establishes of any person on account of race, color, or previous condition of servitude, prohibited by the 15th Amendment, but the standard itself inherently brings that result into existence since it is based purely upon a period of time before the enactment of the 15th Amendment, and makes that period the controlling and dominant test of the right of suffrage. In other words, we seek in vain for any ground which would sustain any other interpretation but that the provision, recurring to the conditions existing before the 15th Amendment was adopted and the continuance of which the 15th Amendment prohibited, proposed by in substance and effect lifting those conditions over to a period of time after the Amendment, to make them the basis of the right to suffrage conferred in direct and positive disregard of the 15th Amendment. And the same result, we are of opinion, is demonstrated by considering whether it is possible to discover any basis of reason for the standard thus fixed other than the purpose above stated. We say this because we are unable to discover how, unless the prohibitions of the 15th Amendment were considered, the slightest reason was afforded for basing the classification upon a period of time prior to the 15th Amendment. Certainly it cannot be said that there was any peculiar necromancy in the time named which engendered attributes affecting the qualification to vote which would not exist at another and different period unless the 15th Amendment was in view. . . .

3. ***The determination of the validity of the literacy test and the possibility of its surviving the disappearance of the 1866 standard with which it is associated in the suffrage amendment.***

No time need be spent on the question of the validity of the literacy test, considered alone, since, as we have seen, its establishment was but the exercise by the state of a lawful power vested in it, not subject to our supervision, and, indeed, its validity is admitted. . . .

Lassiter v. Northampton County Board of Elections

360 U.S. 45 (1959)

Mr. Justice Douglas delivered the opinion of the Court. . . .

Appellant, a Negro citizen of North Carolina, sued to have the literacy test for voters prescribed by that State declared unconstitutional and void. . . .

The Court in *Guinn v. United States* disposed of the question in a few words, "No time need be spent on the question of the validity of the literacy test, considered alone, since, as we have seen its establishment was but the exercise by the state of a lawful power vested in it not subject to our supervision, and indeed, its validity is admitted."

The States have long been held to have broad powers to determine the conditions under which the right of suffrage may be exercised.... So while the right of suffrage is established and guaranteed by the Constitution it is subject to the imposition of state standards which are not discriminatory and which do not contravene any restriction that Congress acting pursuant to its constitutional powers, has imposed....

We do not suggest that any standards which a State desires to adopt may be required of voters. But there is wide scope for exercise of its jurisdiction. Residence requirements, age, previous criminal record are obvious examples indicating factors which a State may take into consideration in determining the qualifications of voters. The ability to read and write likewise has some relation to standards designed to promote intelligent use of the ballot. Literacy and illiteracy are neutral on race, creed, color, and sex, as reports around the world show. Literacy and intelligence are obviously not synonymous. Illiterate people may be intelligent voters. Yet in our society where newspapers, periodicals, books, and other printed matter canvass and debate campaign issues, a State might conclude that only those who are literate should exercise the franchise....

Of course a literacy test, fair on its face, may be employed to perpetuate that discrimination which the Fifteenth Amendment was designed to uproot. No such influence is charged here.... The present requirement, applicable to members of all races, is that the prospective voter "be able to read and write any section of the Constitution of North Carolina in the English language." That seems to us to be one fair way of determining whether a person is literate, not a calculated scheme to lay springes for the citizen. Certainly we cannot condemn it on its face as a device unrelated to the desire of North Carolina to raise the standards for people of all races who cast the ballot.

Notes and Questions

1. Registration to vote in Oklahoma's 1914 general election had been based on the registration statute struck down in *Guinn*. Thereafter, the Oklahoma legislature enacted a new registration statute providing that those who had voted in the general election of 1914 automatically remained qualified voters, while everyone else had (with minor exceptions) a 12-day window in which to register, the consequence of a failure to register during that window being the permanent loss of the right to register and thus to vote. In *Lane v. Wilson*, 307 U.S. 268 (1939), the Court struck this down as violative of the Fifteenth Amendment:

> The Amendment nullifies sophisticated as well as simple-minded modes of discrimination. It hits onerous procedural requirements which effectively handicap exercise of the franchise by the colored race although the abstract right to vote may remain unrestricted as to race....
>
> [A]ll citizens who were qualified to vote in 1916 but had not voted in 1914 were required to register, save in the exceptional circumstances, between

> April 30 and May 11, 1916, and in default of such registration were perpetually disenfranchised. Exemption from this onerous provision was enjoyed by all who had registered in 1914. But this registration was held under the statute which was condemned in the *Guinn* case. Unfair discrimination was thus retained by automatically granting voting privileges for life to the white citizens whom the constitutional "grandfather clause" had sheltered while subjecting colored citizens to a new burden. The practical effect of the 1916 legislation was to accord to the members of the negro race who had been discriminated against in the outlawed registration system of 1914, not more than 12 days within which to reassert constitutional rights which this Court found in the *Guinn* case to have been improperly taken from them. We believe that the opportunity thus given negro voters to free themselves from the effects of discrimination to which they should never have been subjected was too cabined and confined. The restrictions imposed must be judged with reference to those for whom they were designed. It must be remembered that we are dealing with a body of citizens lacking the habits and traditions of political independence and otherwise living in circumstances which do not encourage initiative and enterprise. To be sure, in exceptional cases a supplemental period was available. But the narrow basis of the supplemental registration, the very brief normal period of relief for the persons and purposes in question, the practical difficulties, of which the record in this case gives glimpses, inevitable in the administration of such strict registration provisions, leave no escape from the conclusion that the means chosen as substitutes for the invalidated "grandfather clause" were themselves invalid under the Fifteenth Amendment. They operated unfairly against the very class on whose behalf the protection of the Constitution was here successfully invoked.

Id. at 275-277.

2. Does the *Guinn* Court address the constitutionality of a literacy test, standing alone? If so, how does it resolve that question? If it resolves that in the negative, what makes the scheme employed in *Guinn* unconstitutional? How does the *Lassiter* Court resolve that question? Under *Lassiter*, can a literacy test, standing alone, ever violate the Fifteenth Amendment?

3. If literacy tests do not, on their face, violate the Fifteenth Amendment, is Congress nonetheless empowered under Section 2 of the Fifteenth Amendment to prohibit their use? If so, how would Congress justify such a prohibition?

Gomillion v. Lightfoot

364 U.S. 339 (1960)

Mr. Justice Frankfurter delivered the opinion of the Court.

This litigation challenges the validity, under the United States Constitution, of Local Act No. 140, passed by the Legislature of Alabama in 1957, redefining the boundaries of the City of Tuskegee. . . . Petitioners' claim is that enforcement of the statute . . . will constitute a discrimination against them in violation of the Due Process and Equal Protection Clauses of the Fourteenth Amendment to the Constitution and will deny them the right to vote in defiance of the Fifteenth Amendment. . . .

The complaint, charging that Act 140 is a device to disenfranchise Negro citizens, alleges the following facts: Prior to Act 140 the City of Tuskegee was square in shape; the Act transformed it into a strangely irregular twenty-eight-sided figure as indicated in the diagram appended to this opinion. The essential inevitable effect of this redefinition of Tuskegee's boundaries is to remove from the city all save four or five of its 400 Negro voters while not removing a single white voter or resident. The result of the Act is to deprive the Negro petitioners discriminatorily of the benefits of residence in Tuskegee, including, *inter alia*, the right to vote in municipal elections.

These allegations, if proven, would abundantly establish that Act 140 was not an ordinary geographic redistricting measure even within familiar abuses of gerrymandering. If these allegations upon a trial remained uncontradicted or unqualified, the conclusion would be irresistible, tantamount for all practical purposes to a mathematical demonstration, that the legislation is solely concerned with segregating white and colored voters by fencing Negro citizens out of town so as to deprive them of their pre-existing municipal vote.

It is difficult to appreciate what stands in the way of adjudging a statute having this inevitable effect invalid in light of the principles by which this Court must judge, and uniformly has judged, statutes that, howsoever speciously defined, obviously discriminate against colored citizens. "The [Fifteenth] Amendment nullifies sophisticated as well as simple-minded modes of discrimination." *Lane v. Wilson*, 307 U.S. 268.

The complaint amply alleges a claim of racial discrimination. Against this claim the respondents have never suggested, either in their brief or in oral argument, any countervailing municipal function which Act 140 is designed to serve. . . .

The petitioners here complain that affirmative legislative action deprives them of their votes and the consequent advantages that the ballot affords. When a legislature thus singles out a readily isolated segment of a racial minority for special discriminatory treatment, it violates the Fifteenth Amendment. In no case involving unequal weight in voting distribution that has come before the Court did the decision sanction a differentiation on racial lines whereby approval was given to unequivocal withdrawal of the vote solely from colored citizens. . . .

A statute which is alleged to have worked unconstitutional deprivations of petitioners' rights is not immune to attack simply because the mechanism employed by the legislature is a redefinition of municipal boundaries. According to the allegations here made, the Alabama Legislature has not merely redrawn the Tuskegee city limits with incidental inconvenience to the petitioners; it is more accurate to say that it has deprived the petitioners of the municipal franchise and consequent rights and to that end it has incidentally changed the city's boundaries. While in form this is merely an act redefining metes and bounds, if the allegations are established, the inescapable human effect of this essay in geometry and geography is to despoil colored citizens, and only colored citizens, of their theretofore enjoyed voting rights. . . .

APPENDIX TO OPINION OF THE COURT.
CHART SHOWING TUSKEGEE, ALABAMA, BEFORE AND AFTER ACT 140

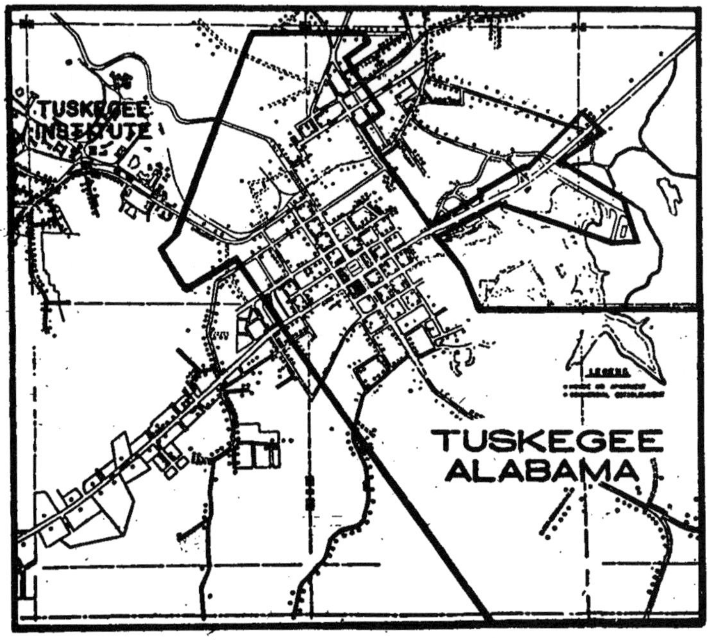

(The entire area of the square comprised the City prior to Act 140. The irregular black-bordered figure within the square represents the post-enactment city.)

Mr. Justice Whitaker, concurring.

I concur in the Court's judgment, but not in the whole of its opinion. It seems to me that the decision should be rested not on the Fifteenth Amendment, but rather on the Equal Protection Clause of the Fourteenth Amendment to the Constitution. I am doubtful that the averments of the complaint, taken for present purposes to be true, show a purpose by Act No. 140 to abridge petitioners' "right . . . to vote", in the Fifteenth Amendment sense. It seems to me that the "right . . . to vote" that is guaranteed by the Fifteenth Amendment is but the same right to vote as is enjoyed by all others within the same election precinct, ward or other political division. And, inasmuch as no one has the right to vote in a political division, or in a local election concerning only an area in which he does not reside, it would seem to follow that one's right to vote in Division A is not abridged by a redistricting that places his residence in Division B if he there enjoys the same voting privileges as all others in that Division, even though the redistricting was done by the State for the purpose of placing a racial group of citizens in Division B rather than A.

But it does seem clear to me that accomplishment of a State's purpose-to use the Court's phrase-of "fencing Negro citizens out of" Division A and into Division B is an unlawful segregation of races of citizens, in violation of the Equal Protection Clause of the Fourteenth Amendment, *Brown v. Board of Education*, 347 U.S. 483; *Cooper v. Aaron*, 358 U.S. 1 . . . .

Notes and Questions

1. Note that the challengers in *Gomillion* invoke both the Fourteenth and Fifteenth Amendments, and the Justices, while agreeing that the Act at issue is unconstitutional, split on which Amendment provides the basis for so concluding. Which opinion do you find more persuasive? Is invocation of the Fourteenth Amendment to protect a right to vote consistent with the Court's earlier decision in *Minor v. Happersett?*

2. Although the intent of the Alabama legislature in *Gomillion* seems likely, the Court does not cite direct evidence of the legislature's intent. It does, however, note the extreme discriminatory effect that the Act has on African Americans. Does that mean that proof of discriminatory intent is not always required to make out a Fifteenth Amendment claim, and that extreme discriminatory effects, standing alone, can suffice? What similarities are there between this case and the Court's earlier decision in *Yick Wo v. Hopkins*?

Chapter 7

Expanding the Concept of State Action

Recall from Chapter 2 that in *The Civil Rights Cases*, the Court placed an important limitation on the scope of the Fourteenth Amendment, holding that it applies only to state action, and thus is inapplicable to private conduct. The majority in *The Civil Rights Cases* found support for its conclusion in the text of the Fourteenth Amendment, which begins with the phrase "No state." The majority contrasted this with the broad language of the Thirteenth Amendment, which it held applicable to private as well as state action. Moreover, the majority in *The Civil Rights Cases* interpreted this textual limitation in Section 1 as relevant to interpreting Section 5 as well, and thus concluded that Congress could not invoke Section 5 to enact laws regulating private racial discrimination. Comparable language, limited to the actions of states and the federal government, is also present in the Fifteenth Amendment.

Justice Harlan's dissent in *The Civil Rights Cases*, while refusing to concede that state action was necessarily required under the Fourteenth Amendment, alternatively argued that the majority was interpreting the concept of state action too narrowly. In Justice Harlan's view, by licensing places of public accommodation to serve the public, there was sufficient state action in the background to bring the actions of places of public accommodation within the scope of the Fourteenth Amendment:

> In every material sense applicable to the practical enforcement of the Fourteenth Amendment, railroad corporations, keepers of inns, and managers of places of public amusement are agents or instrumentalities of the State, because they are charged with duties to the public, and are amenable, in respect of their duties and functions, to governmental regulation.

109 U.S., at 58-59. The Court has never retreated from its holding in *The Civil Rights Cases* that the Fourteenth Amendment is applicable only when state action is involved. However, over time, differing majorities on the Court have oscillated between narrow and broad conceptions of what constitutes "state action." The materials that follow examine the Court's state action decisions through the 1960s, a period marked by an increasingly expansive view of what constitutes state action.

A. Traditional Governmental Functions

We associate numerous functions with governmental entities, such as holding elections, operating prisons, managing municipalities, and operating court systems. To the extent the government performs these functions, they are subject to the strictures of the Fourteenth Amendment. But suppose they contract out these services to private actors, or simply permit private actors to perform these functions. Does that delegation of governmental authority to private actors allow those private actors to avoid scrutiny of their conduct under the Fourteenth Amendment, even if the exercise of those functions would be subjected to such scrutiny if performed directly by governmental actors? The following materials explore those questions.

Marsh v. Alabama

326 U.S. 501 (1946)

Mr. Justice Black delivered the opinion of the Court.

In this case we are asked to decide whether a State, consistently with the First and Fourteenth Amendments, can impose criminal punishment on a person who undertakes to distribute religious literature on the premises of a company-owned town contrary to the wishes of the town's management. The town, a suburb of Mobile, Alabama, known as Chickasaw, is owned by the Gulf Shipbuilding Corporation. Except for that it has all the characteristics of any other American town. The property consists of residential buildings, streets, a system of sewers, a sewage disposal plant and a "business block" on which business places are situated. A deputy of the Mobile County Sheriff, paid by the company, serves as the town's policeman. Merchants and service establishments have rented the stores and business places on the business block and the United States uses one of the places as a post office from which six carriers deliver mail to the people of Chickasaw and the adjacent area. The town and the surrounding neighborhood, which can not be distinguished from the Gulf property by anyone not familiar with the property lines, are thickly settled, and according to all indications the residents use the business block as their regular shopping center. To do so, they now, as they have for many years, make use of a company-owned paved street and sidewalk located alongside the store fronts in order to enter and leave the stores and the post office. Intersecting company-owned roads at each end of the business block lead into a four-lane public highway which runs parallel to the business block at a distance of thirty feet. There is nothing to stop highway traffic from coming onto the business block and upon arrival a traveler may make free use of the facilities available there. In short the town and its shopping district are accessible to and freely used by the public in general and there is nothing to distinguish them from any other town and shopping center except the fact that the title to the property belongs to a private corporation.

Appellant, a Jehovah's Witness, came onto the sidewalk we have just described, stood near the post-office and undertook to distribute religious literature. In the stores the corporation had posted a notice which read as follows: "This Is Private Property, and Without Written Permission, No Street, or House Vendor, Agent or Solicitation of Any Kind Will Be Permitted." Appellant was warned that she could not distribute the literature without a permit and told that no permit would be issued to her. She protested that the company rule could not be constitutionally applied so as to prohibit her from distributing religious writings. When she was asked to leave the sidewalk and Chickasaw she declined. The deputy sheriff arrested her and she was charged in the state court with violating Title 14, Section 426 of the 1940 Alabama Code which makes it a crime to enter or remain on the premises of another after having been warned not to do so. Appellant contended that to construe the state statute as applicable to her activities would abridge her right to freedom of press and religion contrary to the First and Fourteenth Amendments to the Constitution. This contention was rejected and she was convicted. . . .

Had the title to Chickasaw belonged not to a private but to a municipal corporation and had appellant been arrested for violating a municipal ordinance rather than a ruling by those appointed by the corporation to manage a company-town it would have been clear that appellant's conviction must be reversed. . . . [H]ad the people of Chickasaw owned all the homes, and all the stores, and all the streets, and all the sidewalks, all those owners together could not have set up a municipal government with sufficient power to pass an ordinance completely barring the distribution of religious literature. Our question then narrows down to this: Can those people who live in or come to Chickasaw be denied freedom of press and religion simply because a single company has legal title to all the town? For it is the state's contention that the mere fact that all the property interests in the town are held by a single company is enough to give that company power, enforceable by a state statute, to abridge these freedoms.

We do not agree that the corporation's property interests settle the question. The State urges in effect that the corporation's right to control the inhabitants of Chickasaw is coextensive with the right of a homeowner to regulate the conduct of his guests. We can not accept that contention. Ownership does not always mean absolute dominion. The more an owner, for his advantage, opens up his property for use by the public in general, the more do his rights become circumscribed by the statutory and constitutional rights of those who use it. Thus, the owners of privately held bridges, ferries, turnpikes and railroads may not operate them as freely as a farmer does his farm. Since these facilities are built and operated primarily to benefit the public and since their operation is essentially a public function, it is subject to state regulation. . . .

When we balance the Constitutional rights of owners of property against those of the people to enjoy freedom of press and religion, as we must here, we remain mindful of the fact that the latter occupy a preferred position. . . . In our view the circumstance that the property rights to the premises where the deprivation of liberty, here involved, took place, were held by others than the public, is not sufficient to justify the State's permitting a corporation to govern a community of citizens so as to restrict their fundamental liberties and the enforcement of such restraint by the application of a State statute. . . .

[The concurring opinion of Justice Frankfurter and the dissenting opinion of Justice Reed are omitted.]

Notes and Questions

1. Some language in *Marsh* is sweeping in nature, suggesting that the owner of private property can subject himself to constitutional scrutiny merely by opening up his property for use by the public. In this sense, the opinion resembles the broad conception of state action endorsed by Justice Harlan in *The Civil Rights Cases*. On the other hand, the Court cabins this somewhat by noting that the private actors it describes are performing "essentially a public function." If the latter is the correct interpretation of the opinion, what does one look to in order to determine whether something constitutes a public function?

2. How important were *appearances* in this case? In other words, how critical was it to the Court's decision that there was no clear demarcation between public and private property, and that by all appearances, the company town was a continuation of the surrounding public streets? Consider in this regard an effort to apply the strictures of the Fourteenth Amendment to Walt Disney World, which in many ways appears to be a small town:

> [T]he most obvious difference between this case and *Marsh* is that Disney World is not an open town fully accessible and available to all commerce. This private property is an amusement park to which admission is charged. . . . No one is permitted into the outer gates of Disney World except by consent of the owners.

United States v. Francoeur, 547 F.2d 891, 893-94 (5th Cir. 1977).

The White Primary Cases

In a series of cases decided between 1927 and 1953, the U.S. Supreme Court considered challenges to efforts to prevent African Americans from voting in primary elections in Texas. Initially, the exclusion was in terms a part of state law, with a Texas statute providing that "in no event shall a negro be eligible to participate in a Democratic Party primary election held in the State of Texas." In *Nixon v. Herndon*, 273 U.S. 536 (1927), the U.S. Supreme Court struck the statute down as a straightforward violation of the Fourteenth Amendment's Equal Protection Clause.

Thereafter, Texas enacted a new statute providing that "every political party in this State through its State Executive Committee shall have the power to prescribe the qualifications of its own members and shall in its own way determine who shall be qualified to vote or otherwise participate in such political party." In turn, the state executive committee of the Democratic Party adopted a resolution permitting only "white democrats" to vote in the 1928 primary. In *Nixon v. Condon*, 286 U.S. 73 (1932), the Court viewed this as a delegation of state power to the State Executive Committee, and thus treated the latter's actions as "state action" subject to the strictures of the Fourteenth Amendment and held the exclusion of African Americans unconstitutional.

Subsequently, the state Democratic Party—at its convention—adopted a resolution excluding African Americans from the primary election. Initially, the U.S. Supreme Court viewed the difference between the state executive committee of the party acting pursuant to direct delegation in a state statute and the party acting at its convention as constitutionally significant, viewing the former as state action but the latter being voluntary action by a private organization, the political party. *See Grovey v. Townsend*, 295 U.S. 45 (1935). But the Court reversed itself nine years later, holding in *Smith v. Allwright*, 321 U.S. 649 (1944), that the exclusion of African Americans by a political party is state action, and that it violates the Fifteenth Amendment:

> Primary elections are conducted by the party under state statutory authority. The county executive committee selects precinct election officials and the county, district or state executive committees, respectively, canvass the returns. These party committees or the state convention certify the party's candidates to the appropriate officers for inclusion on the official ballot for the general election. No name which has not been so certified may appear upon the ballot for the general election as a candidate of a political party....
>
> We think that this statutory system for the selection of party nominees for inclusion on the general election ballot makes the party which is required to follow these legislative directions an agency of the state in so far as it determines the participants in a primary election. The party takes its character as a state agency from the duties imposed upon it by state statutes; the duties do not become matters of private law because they are performed by a political party.... When primaries become a part of the machinery for choosing officials, state and national, as they have here, the same tests to determine the character of discrimination or abridgement should be applied to the primary as are applied to the general election. If the state requires a certain electoral procedure, prescribes a general election ballot made up of party nominees so chosen and limits the choice of the electorate in general elections for state offices, practically speaking, to those whose names appear on such a ballot, it endorses, adopts and enforces the discrimination against Negroes, practiced by a party entrusted by Texas law with the determination of the qualifications of participants in the primary. This is state action within the meaning of the Fifteenth Amendment.
>
> The United States is a constitutional democracy. Its organic law grants to all citizens a right to participate in the choice of elected officials without restriction by any state because of race. This grant to the people of the

> opportunity for choice is not to be nulified by a state through casting its electoral process in a form which permits a private organization to practice racial discrimination in the election. Constitutional rights would be of little value if they could be thus indirectly denied. *Lane v. Wilson*.
>
> The privilege of membership in a party may be, as this Court said in *Grovey v. Townsend*, no concern of a state. But when, as here, that privilege is also the essential qualification for voting in a primary to select nominees for a general election, the state makes the action of the party the action of the state.

321 U.S., at 663-69. In this sense, the White Primary Cases are in accord with *Marsh v. Alabama*. In both scenarios, what is at issue is the performance by a private actor of what is in essence a public function. In the case that follows, the Court addresses yet another, more subtle attempt to exclude African Americans from the process of selecting Democratic candidates for public office in Texas.

Terry v. Adams

345 U.S. 461 (1953)

Mr. Justice Black announced the judgment of the Court and an opinion in which Mr. Justice Douglas and Mr. Justice Burton join.

In *Smith v. Allwright*, we held that rules of the Democratic Party of Texas excluding Negroes from voting in the party's primaries violated the Fifteenth Amendment. While no state law directed such exclusion, our decision pointed out that many party activities were subject to considerable statutory control. This case raises questions concerning the constitutional power of a Texas county political organization called the Jaybird Democratic Association or Jaybird Party to exclude Negroes from its primaries on racial grounds. The Jaybirds deny that their racial exclusions violate the Fifteenth Amendment. They contend that the Amendment applies only to elections or primaries held under state regulation, that their association is not regulated by the state at all, and that it is not a political party but a self-governing voluntary club....

There was evidence that:

The Jaybird Association or Party was organized in 1889. Its membership was then and always has been limited to white people; they are automatically members if their names appear on the official list of county voters. It has been run like other political parties with an executive committee named from the county's voting precincts. Expenses of the party are paid by the assessment of candidates for office in its primaries. Candidates for county offices submit their names to the Jaybird Committee in accordance with the normal practice followed by regular political parties all over the country. Advertisements and posters proclaim that these candidates are running subject to the action of the Jaybird primary. While there is no legal compulsion on successful Jaybird candidates to enter Democratic primaries they have nearly always done so and with few exceptions since 1889 have run and won without opposition in the Democratic primaries and the general elections that followed. Thus the party has been the dominant political group in the county since organization, having endorsed every county-wide official elected since 1889.

It is apparent that Jaybird activities follow a plan purposefully designed to exclude Negroes from voting and at the same time to escape the Fifteenth Amendment's command that the right of citizens to vote shall neither be denied nor abridged on account of race. These were the admitted party purposes according to the [] testimony of the Jaybird's president. . . .

The District Court found that the Jaybird Association was a political organization or party; that the majority of white voters generally abide by the results of its primaries and support in the Democratic primaries the persons endorsed by the Jaybird primaries; and that the chief object of the Association has always been to deny Negroes any voice or part in the election of Fort Bend County officials. . . .

Clearly the Amendment includes any election in which public issues are decided or public officials selected. Just as clearly the Amendment excludes social or business clubs. . . .

It is significant that precisely the same qualifications as those prescribed by Texas entitling electors to vote at county-operated primaries are adopted as the sole qualifications entitling electors to vote at the county-wide Jaybird primaries with a single proviso—Negroes are excluded. Everyone concedes that such a proviso in the county-operated primaries would be unconstitutional. The Jaybird Party thus brings into being and holds precisely the kind of election that the Fifteenth Amendment seeks to prevent. When it produces the equivalent of the prohibited election, the damage has been done.

For a state to permit such a duplication of its election processes is to permit a flagrant abuse of those processes to defeat the purposes of the Fifteenth Amendment. The use of the county-operated primary to ratify the result of the prohibited election merely compounds the offense. It violates the Fifteenth Amendment for a state, by such circumvention, to permit within its borders the use of any device that produces an equivalent of the prohibited election.

The only election that has counted in this Texas county for more than fifty years has been that held by the Jaybirds from which Negroes were excluded. The Democratic primary and the general election have become no more than the perfunctory ratifiers of the choice that has already been made in Jaybird elections from which Negroes have been excluded. It is immaterial that the state does not control that part of this elective process which it leaves for the Jaybirds to manage. The Jaybird primary has become an integral part, indeed the only effective part, of the elective process that determines who shall rule and govern in the county. The effect of the whole procedure, Jaybird primary plus Democratic primary plus general election, is to do precisely that which the Fifteenth Amendment forbids—strip Negroes of every vestige of influence in selecting the officials who control the local county matters that intimately touch the daily lives of citizens. . . .

We affirm the District Court's holding that the combined Jaybird-Democratic-general election machinery has deprived these petitioners of their right to vote on account of their race and color. . . .

Mr. Justice Frankfurter. . . .

The Fifteenth Amendment, not the Fourteenth, outlawed discrimination on the basis of race or color with respect to the right to vote. . . . The command against such denial or abridgment is directed to the United States and to the individual States. Therefore, violation of this Amendment and the enactments passed in enforcement of it must involve the United States or a State. In this case the conduct that is assailed pertains to the election of local Texas officials. To find a denial or abridgment of the guaranteed voting right to colored citizens of Texas solely because they are colored, one must find that the State has had a hand in it.

The State, in these situations, must mean not private citizens but those clothed with the authority and the influence which official position affords. The application of the prohibition of the Fifteenth Amendment to "any State" is translated by legal jargon to read "State action." This phrase gives rise to a false direction in that it implies some impressive machinery or deliberative conduct normally associated with what orators call a sovereign state. The vital requirement is State responsibility—that somewhere, somehow, to some extent, there be an infusion of conduct by officials, panoplied with State power, into any scheme by which colored citizens are denied voting rights merely because they are colored.

As the action of the entire white voting community, the Jaybird primary is as a practical matter the instrument of those few in this small county who are politically active—the officials of the local Democratic party and, we may assume, the elected officials of the county. As a matter of practical politics, those charged by State law with the duty of assuring all eligible voters an opportunity to participate in the selection of candidates at the primary—the county election officials who are normally leaders in their communities—participate by voting in the Jaybird primary. They join the white voting community in proceeding with elaborate formality, in almost all respects parallel to the procedures dictated by Texas law for the primary itself, to express their preferences in a wholly successful effort to withdraw significance from the State-prescribed primary, to subvert the operation of what is formally the law of the State for primaries in this county. . . .

The State of Texas has entered into a comprehensive scheme of regulation of political primaries, including procedures by which election officials shall be chosen. The county election officials are thus clothed with the authority of the State to secure observance of the State's interest in "fair methods and a fair expression" of preferences in the selection of nominees. If the Jaybird Association, although not a political party, is a device to defeat the law of Texas regulating primaries, and if the electoral officials, clothed with State power in the county, share in that subversion, they cannot divest themselves of the State authority and help as participants in the scheme. . . .

This is not a case of occasional efforts to mass voting strength. Nor is this a case of boss-control, whether crudely or subtly exercised. Nor is this a case of spontaneous efforts by citizens to influence votes or even continued efforts by a fraction of the electorate in support of good government. This is a case in which county election officials have participated in and condoned a continued effort effectively to exclude Negroes from voting. . . .

Mr. Justice Clark, with whom The Chief Justice, Mr. Justice Reed, and Mr. Justice Jackson join, concurring. . . .

The Fifteenth Amendment secures the franchise exercised by citizens of the United States against abridgment by any state on the basis of race or color. In *Smith v. Allwright*, this Court held that the Democratic Party of itself, and perforce any other political party, is prohibited by that Amendment from conducting a racially discriminatory primary election. By the rule of that case, any 'part of the machinery for choosing officials' becomes subject to the Constitution's restraints. There, as here, we dealt with an organization that took the form of 'voluntary association' of unofficial character. But because in fact it functioned as a part of the state's electoral machinery, we held it controlled by the same constitutional limitations that ruled the official general election.

We agree with Chief District Judge Kennerly that the Jaybird Democratic Association is a political party whose activities fall within the Fifteenth Amendment's self-executing ban. Not every private club, association or league organized to influence public candidacies or political action must conform to the Constitution's restrictions on political parties. Certainly a large area of freedom permits peaceable assembly and concerted private action for political purposes to be exercised separately by white and colored citizens alike. More, however, is involved here.

The record discloses that the Jaybird Democratic Association operates as part and parcel of the Democratic Party, an organization existing under the auspices of Texas law. Each maintains the same basic qualification for membership: eligibility to vote under Texas law. Although the state Democratic Party in Texas since *Smith v. Allwright, supra*, no longer can restrict its membership to whites, the Jaybird Democratic Association bars Negroes from its ranks. In May of each election year it conducts a full-scale white primary in which each candidate campaigns for his candidacy subject to the action of that primary *and the Democratic primary of July*, linking the two primaries together. After gaining the Jaybird Democratic Association's endorsement, the announced winners after full publicity then file in the July Democratic primary. The record reveals that 3,910 eligible voters were listed in Fort Bend County in the presidential year 1944; though only 2,032 participated in the July primary under the Democratic banner, 3,790 members voted in the May balloting of the Jaybird Democratic Association. In 1946, an off-year for presidential balloting, eligible voters numbered 4,460; the Association's May primary polled 3,309 votes, and the Democratic July primary counted but 2,996. And while the lists in 1948, again a presidential year, show only 3,856 eligible electors in the County, the Jaybird primary mustered a total vote of 4,055, compared with 3,108 in the primary voting in July. Significantly, since 1889 the winners of the Jaybird Democratic Association balloting, with but a single exception shown by this record, ran unopposed and invariably won in the Democratic July primary and the subsequent general elections for county-wide office.

Quite evidently the Jaybird Democratic Association operates as an auxiliary of the local Democratic Party organization, selecting its nominees and using its machinery for carrying out an admitted design of destroying the weight and effect of Negro ballots in Fort Bend County. To be sure, the Democratic primary and the general election are nominally open to the colored elector. But his must be an empty vote cast after the real decisions are made. And because the Jaybird-indorsed nominee meets no opposition in the Democratic primary, the Negro minority's vote is nullified at the sole stage of the local political process where the bargaining and interplay of rival political forces would make it count.

The Jaybird Democratic Association device, as a result, strikes to the core of the electoral process in Fort Bend County. Whether viewed as a separate political organization or as an adjunct of the local Democratic Party, the Jaybird Democratic Association is the decisive power in the county's recognized electoral process. Over the years its balloting has emerged as the locus of effective political choice. Consonant with the broad and lofty aims of its Framers, the Fifteenth Amendment, as the Fourteenth, "refers to exertions of state power in all forms." *Shelley v. Kramer*, 334 U.S. 1, 20 (1948). Accordingly, when a state structures its electoral apparatus in a form which devolves upon a political organization the uncontested choice of public officials, that organization itself, in whatever disguise, takes on those attributes of government which draw the Constitution's safeguards in play....

Mr. Justice Minton, dissenting.

I am not concerned in the least as to what happens to the Jaybirds or their unworthy scheme. I am concerned about what this Court says is state action within the meaning of the Fifteenth Amendment to the Constitution. For, after all, this Court has power to redress a wrong under that Amendment only if the wrong is done by the State. That has been the holding of this Court since the earliest cases....

As I understand Mr. Justice Black's opinion, he would have this Court redress the wrong even if it was individual action alone. I can understand that praiseworthy position, but it seems to me it is not in accord with the Constitution. State action must be shown.

Mr. Justice Frankfurter recognizes that it must be state action but he seems to think it is enough to constitute state action if a state official participates in the Jaybird primary. That I cannot follow. For it seems clear to me that everything done by a person who is an official is not done officially and as a representative of the State. However, I find nothing in this record that shows the state or county officials participating in the Jaybird primary.

Mr. Justice Clark seems to recognize that state action must be shown. He finds state action in assumption, not in facts. This record will be searched in vain for one iota of state action sufficient to support an anemic inference that the Jaybird Association is in any way associated with or forms a part of or cooperates in any manner with the Democratic Party of the County or State, or with the State. It calls itself the Jaybird Democratic Association because its interest is only in the candidates of the Democratic Party in the county, a position understandable in Texas. . . .

What the Jaybird Association did here was to conduct as individuals, separate and apart from the Democratic Party or the State, a straw vote as to who should receive the Association's endorsement for county and precinct offices. It has been successful in seeing that those who receive its endorsement are nominated and elected. That is true of concerted action by any group. In numbers there is strength. In organization there is effectiveness. Often a small minority of stockholders control a corporation. Indeed, it is almost an axiom of corporate management that a small, cohesive group may control, especially in the larger corporations where the holdings are widely diffused. . . .

In the instant case, the State of Texas has provided for elections and primaries. This is separate and apart and wholly unrelated to the Jaybird Association's activities. Its activities are confined to one County where a group of citizens have appointed themselves the censors of those who would run for public offices. Apparently so far they have succeeded in convincing the voters of this County in most instances that their supported candidates should win. This seems to differ very little from situations common in many other places far north of the Mason-Dixon line, such as areas where a candidate must obtain the approval of a religious group. In other localities, candidates are carefully selected by both parties to give proper weight to Jew, Protestant and Catholic, and certain posts are considered the sole possession of certain ethnic groups. The propriety of these practices is something the courts sensibly have left to the good or bad judgment of the electorate. It must be recognized that elections and other public business are influenced by all sorts of pressures from carefully organized groups. We have pressure from labor unions, from the National Association of Manufacturers, from the Silver Shirts, from the National Association for the Advancement of Colored People, from the Ku Klux Klan and others. Far from the activities of these groups being properly labeled as state action, under either the Fourteenth or the Fifteenth Amendment, they are to be considered as attempts to influence or obtain state action.

The courts do not normally pass upon these pressure groups, whether their causes are good or bad, highly successful or only so-so. It is difficult for me to see how this Jaybird Association is anything but such a pressure group. Apparently it is believed in by enough people in Fort Bend County to obtain a majority of the votes for its approved candidates. This differs little from the situation in many parts of the "Bible Belt" where a church stamp of approval or that of the Anti-Saloon League must be put on any candidate who does not want to lose the election. . . .

In this case the majority have found that this pressure group's work does constitute state action. The basis of this conclusion is rather difficult to ascertain. Apparently it derives mainly from a dislike of the goals of the Jaybird Association. I share that dislike. I fail to see how it makes state action. I would affirm.

Notes and Questions

1. According to each of the opinions in *Terry*, what is the nature of the state action involved in this case? The Jaybird organization is not exercising delegated state power, is it? Does the state action in this case consist of state *inaction*? The participation by public officials (in their private capacities as citizens) in the Jaybird primary? The entanglement between the state democratic party (which is exercising delegated state power) and the Jaybird organization? Or are the Justices not focused on state action, but are instead focused on the effect that the Jaybird organization has on the voting rights of racial minorities?

B. Enforcement of Private Racism

Given the limitation of the Fourteenth and Fifteenth Amendments to state action, they play no role should a private actor choose to engage in a private act of racism. Thus, for example, it violates neither constitutional provision for a private homeowner to eject someone from his property because the person is African American, or to leave his daughter out of his will because she married an African American, or even to agree by contract not to sell his property to African Americans. But what if a private actor seeks the government's help to enforce his private act of racism? Under what circumstances, if any, does the government's enforcement of private racism constitute racially discriminatory state action?

Shelley v. Kraemer

334 U.S. 1 (1948)

MR. CHIEF JUSTICE VINSON delivered the opinion of the Court.

These cases present for our consideration questions relating to the validity of court enforcement of private agreements, generally described as restrictive covenants, which have as their purpose the exclusion of persons of designated race or color from the ownership or occupancy of real property. . . .

[In the two cases before the Court, the properties at issue were subject to private restrictive covenants barring the properties from being occupied by any person not of the Caucasian race. Caucasian owners sold the properties to African Americans, and owners of other property subject to the restrictive covenants brought suit to enforce the covenants. In both cases, the state courts enforced the covenants.]

I.

Whether the equal protection clause of the Fourteenth Amendment inhibits judicial enforcement by state courts of restrictive covenants based on race or color is a question which this Court has not heretofore been called upon to consider. . . .

It cannot be doubted that among the civil rights intended to be protected from discriminatory state action by the Fourteenth Amendment are the rights to acquire, enjoy, own and dispose of property. . . . Thus, § 1978 of the Revised Statutes, derived from § 1 of the Civil Rights Act of 1866 which was enacted by Congress while the Fourteenth Amendment was also under consideration, provides:

> "All citizens of the United States shall have the same right, in every State and Territory, as is enjoyed by white citizens thereof to inherit, purchase, lease, sell, hold, and convey real and personal property."

. . . .

It is likewise clear that restrictions on the right of occupancy of the sort sought to be created by the private agreements in these cases could not be squared with the requirements of the Fourteenth Amendment if imposed by state statute or local ordinance. . . .

But the present cases . . . do not involve action by state legislatures or city councils. Here the particular patterns of discrimination and the areas in which the restrictions are to operate, are determined, in the first instance, by the terms of agreements among private individuals. Participation of the State consists in the enforcement of the restrictions so defined. The crucial issue with which we are here confronted is whether this distinction removes these cases from the operation of the prohibitory provisions of the Fourteenth Amendment.

Since the decision of this Court in the *Civil Rights Cases*, the principle has become firmly embedded in our constitutional law that the action inhibited by the first section of the Fourteenth Amendment is only such action as may fairly be said to be that of the States. That Amendment erects no shield against merely private conduct, however discriminatory or wrongful.

We conclude, therefore, that the restrictive agreements standing alone cannot be regarded as a violation of any rights guaranteed to petitioners by the Fourteenth Amendment. So long as the purposes of those agreements are effectuated by voluntary adherence to their terms, it would appear clear that there has been no action by the State and the provisions of the Amendment have not been violated.

But here there was more. These are cases in which the purposes of the agreements were secured only by judicial enforcement by state courts of the restrictive terms of the agreements. . . .

II.

That the action of state courts and of judicial officers in their official capacities is to be regarded as action of the State within the meaning of the Fourteenth Amendment, is a proposition which has long been established by decisions of this Court. . . .

III.

. . . .

We have no doubt that there has been state action in these cases in the full and complete sense of the phrase. The undisputed facts disclose that petitioners were willing purchasers of properties upon which they desired to establish homes. The owners of the properties were willing sellers; and contracts of sale were accordingly consummated. It is clear that but for the active intervention of the state courts, supported by the full panoply of state power, petitioners would have been free to occupy the properties in question without restraint.

These are not cases, as has been suggested, in which the States have merely abstained from action, leaving private individuals free to impose such discriminations as they see fit. Rather, these are cases in which the States have made available to such individuals the full coercive power of government to deny to petitioners, on the grounds of race or color, the enjoyment of property rights in premises which petitioners are willing and financially able to acquire and which the grantors are willing to sell. The difference between judicial enforcement and nonenforcement of the restrictive covenants is the difference to petitioners between being denied rights of property available to other members of the community and being accorded full enjoyment of those rights on an equal footing. . . .

State action, as that phrase is understood for the purposes of the Fourteenth Amendment, refers to exertions of state power in all forms. . . .

Respondents urge, however, that since the state courts stand ready to enforce restrictive covenants excluding white persons from the ownership or occupancy of property covered by such agreements, enforcement of covenants excluding colored persons may not be deemed a denial of equal protection of the laws to the colored persons who are thereby affected. This contention does not bear scrutiny. The parties have directed our attention to no case in which a court, state or federal, has been called upon to enforce a covenant excluding members of the white majority from ownership or occupancy of real property on grounds of race or color. But there are more fundamental considerations. The rights created by the first section of the Fourteenth Amendment are, by its terms, guaranteed to the individual. The rights established are personal rights. It is, therefore, no answer to these petitioners to say that the courts may also be induced to deny white persons rights of ownership and occupancy on grounds of race or color. Equal protection of the laws is not achieved through indiscriminate imposition of inequalities. . . .

The historical context in which the Fourteenth Amendment became a part of the Constitution should not be forgotten. Whatever else the framers sought to achieve, it is clear that the matter of primary concern was the establishment of equality in the enjoyment of basic civil and political rights and the preservation of those rights from discriminatory action on the part of the States based on considerations of race or color. . . .

Notes and Questions

1. If you take *Shelley* for all it is worth, then any time a private actor seeks the assistance of the government in enforcing its private acts of racism, there is racially discriminatory state action within the meaning of the Fourteenth Amendment. Is there a way to limit the decision's scope? In this regard, consider whether there is a constitutionally significant distinction amongst each of the following four scenarios:

(a) Probate of a will of a white man is sought in a state court. The man has disinherited his daughter. Although the will does not disclose the reasons for doing so, there is evidence that he disinherited her because she married an African American man.

(b) Probate of a will of a white man is sought in a state court. The will contains a provision indicating that his daughter will inherit half of his estate "so long as she is not married to a black man at the time of my death, in which case she inherits nothing." At the time of the decedent's death, his daughter was married to an African American man.

(c) A homeowner throws an open party for the neighborhood. Three African Americans from the neighborhood show up. Known for his animosity toward African Americans, the homeowner asks them to leave, and when they refuse, he calls the police. When the police arrive, he points to the three African Americans and asks the police to remove them from his property.

(d) A homeowner throws an open party for the neighborhood. Several African Americans from the neighborhood show up. The homeowner asks them to leave, and when they refuse, he calls the police. When the police arrive, he asks the police to "remove all the blacks" from his property.

2. In what way does *Shelley* foreshadow the eventual overturning of *Pace v. Alabama*? Stated somewhat differently, is there not arguably superficial equality in *Shelley* comparable to the superficial equality found by the Court in *Pace*? How does the *Shelley* Court address that contention?

3. *Shelley* holds that voluntary enforcement of racially restrictive covenants by private persons does not violate the Fourteenth Amendment. Could Congress nonetheless prohibit such racially restrictive covenants pursuant to its powers under Section 2 of the Thirteenth Amendment or Section 5 of the Fourteenth Amendment? Reconsider this question when you read the materials in Chapter 9.

Bell v. Maryland

378 U.S. 226 (1964)

Mr. Justice Brennan delivered the opinion of the Court.

Petitioners, 12 Negro students, were convicted in a Maryland state court as a result of their participation in a "sit-in" demonstration at Hooper's restaurant in the City of Baltimore in 1960. The convictions were based on a record showing in summary that a group of 15 to 20 Negro students, including petitioners, went to Hooper's restaurant to engage in what their counsel describes as a "sit-in protest" because the restaurant would not serve Negroes. The "hostess," on orders of Mr. Hooper, the president of the corporation owning the restaurant, told them, "solely on the basis of their color," that they would not be served. Petitioners did not leave when requested to by the hostess and the manager; instead they went to tables, took seats, and refused to leave, insisting that they be served. On orders of Mr. Hooper the police were called, but they advised that a warrant would be necessary before they could arrest petitioners. Mr. Hooper then went to the police station and swore out warrants, and petitioners were accordingly arrested.

The statute under which the convictions were obtained was the Maryland criminal trespass law, § 577 of Art. 27 of the Maryland Code, 1957 edition, under which it is a misdemeanor to 'enter upon or cross over the land, premises or private property of any person or persons in this State after having been duly notified by the owner or his agent not to do so.' The convictions were affirmed by the Maryland Court of Appeals....

We do not reach the questions that have been argued under the Equal Protection and Due Process Clauses of the Fourteenth Amendment. It appears that a significant change has taken place in the applicable law of Maryland since these convictions were affirmed by the Court of Appeals....

[The Court goes on to suggest that there may be a state law basis for overturning the convictions, and remands the case to the state courts.]

Mr. Justice Douglas, with whom Mr. Justice Goldberg concurs as respects Parts II-V, for reversing and directing dismissal of the indictment.

I.

I reach the merits of this controversy. The issue is ripe for decision and petitioners, who have been convicted of asking for service in Hooper's restaurant, are entitled to an answer to their complaint here and now....

IV.

The problem in this case, and in the other sit-in cases before us, is presented as though it involved the situation of "a private operator conducting his own business on his own premises and exercising his own judgment" as to whom he will admit to the premises.

The property involved is not, however, a man's home or his yard or even his fields. Private property is involved, but it is property that is serving the public....

The problem with which we deal has no relation to opening or closing the door of one's home. The home of course is the essence of privacy, in no way dedicated to public use, in no way extending an invitation to the public. Some businesses, like the classical country store where the owner lives overhead or in the rear, make the store an extension, so to speak, of the home. But such is not this case. The facts of these sit-in cases have little resemblance to any institution of property which we customarily associate with privacy....

V.

....

State judicial action is as clearly "state" action as state administrative action. Indeed, we held in *Shelley v. Kraemer* that "State action, as that phrase is understood for the purposes of the Fourteenth Amendment, refers to exertions of state power in all forms."

That case involved suits in state courts to enforce restrictive covenants in deeds of residential property whereby the owner agreed that it should not be used or occupied by any person except a Caucasian. There was no state statute regulating the matter. That is, the State had not authorized by legislative enactment the use of restrictive covenants in residential property transactions; nor was there any administrative regulation of the matter. Only the courts of the State were involved. We held without dissent in an opinion written by Chief Justice Vinson that there was nonetheless state action within the meaning of the Fourteenth Amendment. . . .

Maryland's action against these Negroes was as authoritative as any case where the State in one way or another puts its full force behind a policy. The policy here was segregation in places of public accommodation; and Maryland enforced that policy with her police, her prosecutors, and her courts. . . .

The preferences involved in *Shelley v. Kraemer* and its companion cases were far more personal than the motivations of the corporate managers in the present case when they declined service to Negroes. Why should we refuse to let state courts enforce *apartheid* in residential areas of our cities but let state courts enforce *apartheid* in restaurants? If a court decree is state action in one case, it is in the other. Property rights, so heavily underscored, are equally involved in each case.

The customer in a restaurant is transitory; he comes and may never return. The colored family who buys the house next door is there for keeps—night and day. If "personal prejudices" are not to be the criterion in one case they should not be in the other. We should put these restaurant cases in line with *Shelley v. Kraemer*, holding that what the Fourteenth Amendment requires in restrictive covenant cases it also requires from restaurants.

Segregation of Negroes in the restaurants and lunch counters of parts of America is a relic of slavery. . . . When the state police, the state prosecutor, and the state courts unite to convict Negroes for renouncing that relic of slavery, the 'State' violates the Fourteenth Amendment. . . .

Mr. Justice Black, with whom Mr. Justice Harlan and Mr. Justice White, join, dissenting.

This case does not involve the constitutionality of any existing or proposed state or federal legislation requiring restaurant owners to serve people without regard to color. The crucial issue which the case does present but which the Court does not decide is whether the Fourteenth Amendment, of itself, forbids a State to enforce its trespass laws to convict a person who comes into a privately owned restaurant, is told that because of his color he will not be served, and over the owner's protest refuses to leave. We dissent from the Court's refusal to decide that question. For reasons stated, we think that the question should be decided and that the Fourteenth Amendment does not forbid this application of a State's trespass laws. . . .

Petitioners . . . contend that their conviction for trespass under the state statute was by itself the kind of discriminatory state action forbidden by the Fourteenth Amendment. This contention, on its face, has plausibility when considered along with general statements to the effect that under the Amendment forbidden "state action" may be that of the Judicial as well as of the Legislative or Executive Branch of Government. But a mechanical application of the Fourteenth Amendment to this case cannot survive analysis. The Amendment does not forbid a State to prosecute for crimes committed against a person or his property, however prejudiced or narrow the victim's views may be. Nor can whatever prejudice and bigotry the victim of a crime may have be automatically attributed to the State that prosecutes. Such a doctrine would not only be based on a fiction; it would also severely handicap a State's efforts to maintain a peaceful and orderly society. Our society has put its trust in a system of criminal laws to punish lawless conduct. To avert personal feuds and violent brawls it was led its people to believe and expect that wrongs against them will be vindicated in the courts. Instead of attempting to take the law into their own hands people have been taught to call for police protection to protect their rights wherever possible. It would betray our whole plan for a tranquil and orderly society to say that a citizen, because of his personal prejudices, habits, attitudes, or beliefs, is cast outside the law's protection and cannot call for the aid of officers sworn to uphold the law and preserve the peace. The worst citizen no less than the best is entitled to equal protection of the laws of his State and of his Nation. None of our past cases justifies reading the Fourteenth Amendment in a way that might well penalize citizens who are law-abiding enough to call upon the law and its officers for protection instead of using their own physical strength or dangerous weapons to preserve their rights. . . .

In concluding that mere judicial enforcement of the trespass law is not sufficient to impute to Maryland Hooper's refusal to serve Negroes, we are in accord with the Solicitor General's views as we understand them. He takes it for granted

> "that the mere fact of State intervention through the courts or other public authority in order to provide sanctions for a private decision is not enough to implicate the State for the purposes of the Fourteenth Amendment. . . . Where the only State involvement is color-blind support for every property-owner's exercise of the normal right to choose his business visitors or social guests, proof that the particular property-owner was motivated by racial or religious prejudice is not enough to convict the State of denying equal protection of the laws."

The Solicitor General also says:

> "The preservation of a free and pluralistic society would seem to require substantial freedom for private choice in social, business and professional associations. Freedom of choice means the liberty to be wrong as well as right, to be mean as well as noble, to be vicious as well as kind. And even if that view were questioned, the philosophy of federalism leaves an area for choice to the States and their people, when the State is not otherwise

involved, instead of vesting the only power of effective decision in the federal courts."

We, like the Solicitor General, reject the argument that the State's protection of Hooper's desire to choose customers on the basis of race by prosecuting trespassers is enough, standing alone, to deprive Hooper of his right to operate the property in his own way. . . .

Notes and Questions

1. In *Bell*, Justice Brennan's full opinion goes out of its way to avoid deciding the federal constitutional question by identifying a far-fetched state law ground for overturning the convictions. On remand, the state courts hold that the ground cited by Justice Brennan did not provide a basis for overturning the conviction, but they nonetheless overturned the conviction on other state law grounds. *See Bell v. State*, 204 A.2d 54 (1964).

2. In contrast to Justice Brennan, Justices Douglas and Black are eager to reach the constitutional question raised in the case. Which of the opinions do you find more persuasive? Is the scenario in *Bell* on all fours with *Shelley*, or is it somehow distinguishable? In considering this latter question, reconsider the hypotheticals in the note immediately following *Shelley*.

C. Entanglement with Private Racism

Burton v. Wilmington Parking Authority

365 U.S. 715 (1961)

MR. JUSTICE CLARK delivered the opinion of the Court.

In this action for declaratory and injunctive relief it is admitted that the Eagle Coffee Shoppe, Inc., a restaurant located within an off-street automobile parking building in Wilmington, Delaware, has refused to serve appellant food or drink solely because he is a Negro. The parking building is owned and operated by the Wilmington Parking Authority, an agency of the State of Delaware, and the restaurant is the Authority's lessee. Appellant claims that such refusal abridges his rights under the Equal Protection Clause of the Fourteenth Amendment to the United States Constitution. The Supreme Court of Delaware has held that Eagle was acting in "a purely private capacity" under its lease; that its action was not that of the Authority and was not, therefore, state action within the contemplation of the prohibitions contained in that Amendment. It also held that under 24 Del.Code § 1501,[1] Eagle was

1. The statute provides that: "No keeper of an inn, tavern, hotel, or restaurant, or other place of public entertainment or refreshment of travelers, guests, or customers shall be obliged, by law, to furnish entertainment or refreshment to persons whose reception or entertainment by him would

a restaurant, not an inn, and that as such it "is not required (under Delaware law) to serve any and all persons entering its place of business." ....

The Authority was created by the City of Wilmington.... The Authority has no power to pledge the credit of the State of Delaware but may issue its own revenue bonds which are tax exempt. Any and all property owned or used by the Authority is likewise exempt from state taxation.

The first project undertaken by the Authority was the erection of a parking facility on Ninth Street in downtown Wilmington....

Before it began actual construction of the facility, the Authority was advised by its retained experts that the anticipated revenue from the parking of cars and proceeds from sale of its bonds would not be sufficient to finance the construction costs of the facility. Moreover, the bonds were not expected to be marketable if payable solely out of parking revenues. To secure additional capital needed for its "debt-service" requirements, and thereby to make bond financing practicable, the Authority decided it was necessary to enter long-term leases with responsible tenants for commercial use of some of the space available in the projected "garage building." The public was invited to bid for these leases.

In April 1957 such a private lease, for 20 years and renewable for another 10 years, was made with Eagle Coffee Shoppe, Inc., for use as a "restaurant, dining room, banquet hall, cocktail lounge and bar and for no other use and purpose." The multi-level space of the building which was let to Eagle, although "within the exterior walls of the structure, has no marked public entrance leading from the parking portion of the facility into the restaurant proper ... (whose main entrance) is located on Ninth Street." .... Eagle spent some $220,000 to make the space suitable for its operation and, to the extent such improvements were so attached to realty as to become part thereof, Eagle to the same extent enjoys the Authority's tax exemption.

The Authority further agreed to furnish heat for Eagle's premises, gas service for the boiler room, and to make, at its own expense, all necessary structural repairs, all repairs to exterior surfaces except store fronts and any repairs caused by lessee's own act or neglect. The Authority retained the right to place any directional signs on the exterior of the let space which would not interfere with or obscure Eagle's display signs. Agreeing to pay an annual rental of $28,700, Eagle covenanted to 'occupy and use the leased premises in accordance with all applicable laws, statutes, ordinances and rules and regulations of any federal, state or municipal authority.' Its lease, however, contains no requirement that its restaurant services be made available to the general public on a nondiscriminatory basis, in spite of the fact that the Authority has power to adopt rules and regulations respecting the use of its facilities except any as would impair the security of its bondholders.

---

be offensive to the major part of his customers, and would injure his business. As used in this section, 'customer' includes all who have occasion for entertainment or refreshment."

Other portions of the structure were leased to other tenants, including a bookstore, a retail jeweler, and a food store. Upon completion of the building, the Authority located at appropriate places thereon official signs indicating the public character of the building, and flew from mastheads on the roof both the state and national flags.

In August 1958 appellant parked his car in the building and walked around to enter the restaurant by its front door on Ninth Street. Having entered and sought service, he was refused it. Thereafter he filed this declaratory judgment action....

The Civil Rights Cases "embedded in our constitutional law" the principle "that the action inhibited by the first section [Equal Protection Clause] of the Fourteenth Amendment is only such action as may fairly be said to be that of the States. That Amendment erects no shield against merely private conduct, however discriminatory or wrongful." Chief Justice Vinson in *Shelley v. Kraemer*.... It is clear, as it always has been since the *Civil Rights Cases*, that 'Individual invasion of individual rights is not the subject-matter of the amendment,' and that private conduct abridging individual rights does no violence to the Equal Protection Clause unless to some significant extent the State in any of its manifestations has been found to have become involved in it. Because the virtue of the right to equal protection of the laws could lie only in the breadth of its application, its constitutional assurance was reserved in terms whose imprecision was necessary if the right were to be enjoyed in the variety of individual-state relationships which the Amendment was designed to embrace. For the same reason, to fashion and apply a precise formula for recognition of state responsibility under the Equal Protection Clause is an "impossible task" which "This Court has never attempted." *Kotch v. Board of River Port Pilot Com'rs*, 330 U.S. 552, 556. Only by sifting facts and weighing circumstances can the nonobvious involvement of the State in private conduct be attributed its true significance....

The land and building were publicly owned. As an entity, the building was dedicated to "public uses" in performance of the Authority's "essential governmental functions." 22 Del.Code, §§ 501, 514. The costs of land acquisition, construction, and maintenance are defrayed entirely from donations by the City of Wilmington, from loans and revenue bonds and from the proceeds of rentals and parking services out of which the loans and bonds were payable. Assuming that the distinction would be significant, the commercially leased areas were not surplus state property, but constituted a physically and financially integral and, indeed, indispensable part of the State's plan to operate its project as a self-sustaining unit. Upkeep and maintenance of the building, including necessary repairs, were responsibilities of the Authority and were payable out of public funds. It cannot be doubted that the peculiar relationship of the restaurant to the parking facility in which it is located confers on each an incidental variety of mutual benefits. Guests of the restaurant are afforded a convenient place to park their automobiles, even if they cannot enter the restaurant directly from the parking area. Similarly, its convenience for diners may well provide additional demand for the Authority's parking facilities. Should any improvements effected in the leasehold by Eagle become part of the realty, there is no possibility of increased taxes being passed on to it since the fee is held by a tax-exempt government agency. Neither can it be ignored, especially in view of Eagle's affirmative allegation that for it to serve Negroes would injure its business, that profits earned by discrimination not only contribute to, but also are indispensable elements in, the financial success of a governmental agency.

Addition of all these activities, obligations and responsibilities of the Authority, the benefits mutually conferred, together with the obvious fact that the restaurant is operated as an integral part of a public building devoted to a public parking service, indicates that degree of state participation and involvement in discriminatory action which it was the design of the Fourteenth Amendment to condemn. It is irony amounting to grave injustice that in one part of a single building, erected and maintained with public funds by an agency of the State to serve a public purpose, all persons have equal rights, while in another portion, also serving the public, a Negro is a second-class citizen, offensive because of his race, without rights and unentitled to service, but at the same time fully enjoys equal access to nearby restaurants in wholly privately owned buildings. As the Chancellor pointed out, in its lease with Eagle the Authority could have affirmatively required Eagle to discharge the responsibilities under the Fourteenth Amendment imposed upon the private enterprise as a consequence of state participation. But no State may effectively abdicate its responsibilities by either ignoring them or by merely failing to discharge them whatever the motive may be. . . . By its inaction, the Authority, and through it the State, has not only made itself a party to the refusal of service, but has elected to place its power, property and prestige behind the admitted discrimination. The State has so far insinuated itself into a position of interdependence with Eagle that it must be recognized as a joint participant in the challenged activity, which, on that account, cannot be considered to have been so "purely private" as to fall without the scope of the Fourteenth Amendment.

Because readily applicable formulae may not be fashioned, the conclusions drawn from the facts and circumstances of this record are by no means declared as universal truths on the basis of which every state leasing agreement is to be tested. . . . Specifically defining the limits of our inquiry, what we hold today is that when a State leases public property in the manner and for the purpose shown to have been the case here, the proscriptions of the Fourteenth Amendment must be complied with by the lessee as certainly as though they were binding covenants written into the agreement itself. . . .

Mr. Justice Stewart, concurring.

I agree that the judgment must be reversed, but I reach that conclusion by a route much more direct than the one traveled by the Court. In upholding Eagle's right to deny service to the appellant solely because of his race, the Supreme Court of Delaware relied upon a statute of that State which permits the proprietor of a restaurant to refuse to serve "persons whose reception or entertainment by him would be offensive to the major part of his customers. . . ." There is no suggestion in the record that the appellant as an individual was such a person. The highest court of

Delaware has thus construed this legislative enactment as authorizing discriminatory classification based exclusively on color. Such a law seems to me clearly violative of the Fourteenth Amendment....

[The dissenting opinions of Justices Harlan and Frankfurter are omitted.]

Notes and Questions

1. The *Burton* Court refuses to set forth a precise formula for identifying state action, describing this as an "impossible task." If there is not a precise formula, are there factors identified by the *Burton* Court that help identify the presence or absence of state action? If so, what are those factors?

2. Recall that in *Marsh*, appearances seemed to be a relevant consideration. Are appearances equally relevant in this case? If so, how?

3. On what ground does Justice Stewart decide the case? How does that ground differ from the majority? Keep Justice Stewart's concurring opinion in mind as you read the final section in this chapter.

D. Encouragement of Private Racism

Anderson v. Martin

375 U.S. 399 (1964)

Mr. Justice Clark delivered the opinion of the Court....

I.

Appellants, residents of East Baton Rouge, Louisiana, are Negroes. Each sought election to the School Board of that parish in the 1962 Democratic Party primary election. Prior to the election they filed this suit against the Secretary of State of Louisiana seeking to enjoin the enforcement of Act 538 of the 1960 Louisiana Legislature, which requires the Secretary to print, in parentheses, the race of each candidate opposite his name on all ballots. Asserting that the statute violated, *inter alia*, the Fourteenth and Fifteenth Amendments, appellants sought both preliminary and permanent injunctions and a temporary restraining order.... We have concluded that the compulsory designation by Louisiana of the race of the candidate on the ballot operates as a discrimination against appellants and is therefore violative of the Fourteenth Amendment's Equal Protection Clause....

II.

At the outset it is well that we point out what this case does not involve. It has nothing whatever to do with the right of a citizen to cast his vote for whomever he chooses and for whatever reason he pleases or to receive all information concerning a candidate which is necessary to a proper exercise of his franchise. It has to do only with the right of a State to require or encourage its voters to discriminate upon the grounds of race. In the abstract, Louisiana imposes no restriction upon anyone's candidacy nor upon an elector's choice in the casting of his ballot. But by placing at racial label on a candidate at the most crucial stage in the electoral process—the instant before the vote is cast—the State furnishes a vehicle by which racial prejudice may be so aroused as to operate against one group because of race and for another. This is true because by directing the citizen's attention to the single consideration of race or color, the State indicates that a candidate's race or color is an important—perhaps paramount—consideration in the citizen's choice, which may decisively influence the citizen to cast his ballot along racial lines. Hence in a State or voting district where Negroes predominate, that race is likely to be favored by a racial designation on the ballot, while in those communities where other races are in the majority, they may be preferred. The vice lies not in the resulting injury but in the placing of the power of the State behind a racial classification that induces racial prejudice at the polls.

III.

. . . .

We see no relevance in the State's pointing up the race of the candidate as bearing upon his qualifications for office. . . .

The State contends that its Act is nondiscriminatory because the labeling provision applies equally to Negro and white. Obviously, Louisiana may not bar Negro citizens from offering themselves as candidates for public office, nor can it encourage its citizens to vote for a candidate solely on account of race. And that which cannot be done by express statutory prohibition cannot be done by indirection. Therefore, we view the alleged equality as superficial. Race is the factor upon which the statute operates and its involvement promotes the ultimate discrimination which is sufficient to make it invalid. . . .

Reitman v. Mulkey

387 U.S. 369 (1967)

Mr. Justice White delivered the opinion of the Court.

The question here is whether Art. I, s 26, of the California Constitution denies "to any person . . . the equal protection of the laws" within the meaning of the Fourteenth Amendment of the Constitution of the United States. Section 26 of Art. I, an initiated measure submitted to the people as Proposition 14 in a statewide ballot in 1964, provides in part as follows:

> "Neither the State nor any subdivision or agency thereof shall deny, limit or abridge, directly or indirectly, the right of any person, who is willing or desires to sell, lease or rent any part or all of his real property, to decline to sell, lease or rent such property to such person or persons as he, in his absolute discretion, chooses."

The real property covered by § 26 is limited to residential property and contains an exception for state-owned real estate. . . .

[The California Supreme Court] held that Art. I, § 26, was invalid as denying the equal protection of the laws guaranteed by the Fourteenth Amendment. . . .

We affirm the judgments of the California Supreme Court. We first turn to the opinion of that court in *Reitman*, which quite properly undertook to examine the constitutionality of § 26 in terms of its "immediate objective," its "ultimate effect" and its "historical context and the conditions existing prior to its enactment." . . . .

First, the court considered whether § 26 was concerned at all with private discriminations in residential housing. This involved a review of past efforts by the California Legislature to regulate such discriminations. The Unruh Act, Civ. Code §§ 51—52, on which respondents based their cases, was passed in 1959. The Hawkins Act, formerly Health & Safety Code §§ 35700–35741, followed and prohibited discriminations in publicly assisted housing. In 1961, the legislature enacted proscriptions against restrictive covenants. Finally, in 1963, came the Rumford Fair Housing Act, Health & Safety Code §§ 35700–35744, superseding the Hawkins Act and prohibiting racial discriminations in the sale or rental of any private dwelling containing more than four units. That act was enforceable by the State Fair Employment Practice Commission.

It was against this background that Proposition 14 was enacted. Its immediate design and intent, the California court said, were "to overturn state laws that bore on the right of private sellers and lessors to discriminate," the Unruh and Rumford Acts, and "to forestall future state action that might circumscribe this right." This aim was successfully achieved: the adoption of Proposition 14 "generally nullifies both the Rumford and Unruh Acts as they apply to the housing market," and establishes "a purported constitutional right to *privately* discriminate on grounds which admittedly would be unavailable under the Fourteenth Amendment *should state action* be involved."

Second, the court conceded that the State was permitted a neutral position with respect to private racial discriminations and that the State was not bound by the Federal Constitution to forbid them. But, because a significant state involvement in private discriminations could amount to unconstitutional state action, *Burton v. Wilmington Parking Authority*, the court deemed it necessary to determine whether Proposition 14 invalidly involved the State in racial discriminations in the housing market. Its conclusion was that it did.

To reach this result, the state court examined certain prior decisions in this Court in which discriminatory state action was identified. Based on these cases, it concluded that a prohibited state involvement could be found "even where the state can be charged with only encouraging," rather than commanding discrimination. Also of particular interest to the court was Mr. Justice Stewart's concurrence in *Burton v. Wilmington Parking Authority*, where it was said that the Delaware courts had construed an existing Delaware statute as "authorizing" racial discrimination in restaurants and that the statute was therefore invalid. To the California court "[t]he instant case presents an undeniably analogous situation" wherein the State had taken affirmative action designed to make private discriminations legally possible. Section 26 was said to have changed the situation from one in which discrimination was restricted "to one wherein it is encouraged, within the meaning of the cited decisions"; § 26 was legislative action "which authorized private discrimination" and made the State "at least a partner in the instant act of discrimination. . . ." The court could "conceive of no other purpose for an application of section 26 aside from authorizing the perpetration of a purported private discrimination. . . ." The judgment of the California court was that § 26 unconstitutionally involves the State in racial discriminations and is therefore invalid under the Fourteenth Amendment.

There is so sound reason for rejecting this judgment. Petitioners contend that the California court has misconstrued the Fourteenth Amendment since the repeal of any statute prohibiting racial discrimination, which is constitutionally permissible, may be said to "authorize" and "encourage" discrimination because it makes legally permissible that which was formerly proscribed. But, as we understand the California court, it did not posit a constitutional violation on the mere repeal of the Unruh and Rumford Acts. It did not read either our cases or the Fourteenth Amendment as establishing an automatic constitutional barrier to the repeal of an existing law prohibiting racial discriminations in housing; nor did the court rule that a State may never put in statutory form an existing policy of neutrality with respect to private discriminations. What the court below did was first to reject the notion that the State was required to have a statute prohibiting racial discriminations in housing. Second, it held the intent of § 26 was to authorize private racial discriminations in the housing market, to repeal the Unruh and Rumford Acts and to create a constitutional right to discriminate on racial grounds in the sale and leasing of real property. Hence, the court dealt with § 26 as though it expressly authorized and constitutionalized the private right to discriminate. Third, the court assessed the ultimate impact of § 26 in the California environment and concluded that the section would encourage and significantly involve the State in private racial discrimination contrary to the Fourteenth Amendment.

The California court could very reasonably conclude that § 26 would and did have wider impact than a mere repeal of existing statutes. Section 26 mentioned neither the Unruh nor Rumford Act in so many words. Instead, it announced the constitutional right of any person to decline to sell or lease his real property to anyone to whom he did not desire to sell or lease. Unruh and Rumford were thereby *pro tanto* repealed. But the section struck more deeply and more widely. Private discriminations in housing were now not only free from Rumford and Unruh but they also enjoyed a far different status than was true before the passage of those statutes. The right to discriminate, including the right to discriminate on racial grounds, was now embodied in the State's basic charter, immune from legislative, executive, or judicial regulation at any level of the state government. Those practicing racial discriminations need no longer rely solely on their personal choice. They could now invoke express constitutional authority, free from censure or interference of any kind from official sources. All individuals, partnerships, corporations and other legal entities, as well as their agents and representatives, could now discriminate with respect to their residential real property, which is defined as any interest in real property of any kind or quality, "irrespective of how obtained or financed," and seemingly irrespective of the relationship of the State to such interests in real property. Only the State is excluded with respect to property owned by it.

This Court has never attempted the "impossible task" of formulating an infallible test for determining whether the State "in any of its manifestations" has become significantly involved in private discriminations. "Only by sifting facts and weighing circumstances" on a case-by-case basis can a "nonobvious involvement of the State in private conduct be attributed its true significance." *Burton v. Wilmington Parking Authority*. Here the California court, armed as it was with the knowledge of the facts and circumstances concerning the passage and potential impact of § 26, and familiar with the milieu in which that provision would operate, has determined that the provision would involve the State in private racial discriminations to an unconstitutional degree. We accept this holding of the California court. . . .

[Our cases] exemplify the necessity for a court to assess the potential impact of official action in determining whether the State has significantly involved itself with invidious discriminations. Here we are dealing with a provision which does not just repeal an existing law forbidding private racial discriminations. Section 26 was intended to authorize, and does authorize, racial discrimination in the housing market. The right to discriminate is now one of the basic policies of the State. The California Supreme Court believes that the section will significantly encourage and involve the State in private discriminations. We have been presented with no persuasive considerations indicating that these judgments should be overturned.

Affirmed.

Mr. Justice Harlan, whom Mr. Justice Black, Mr. Justice Clark, and Mr. Justice Stewart join, dissenting. . . .

The facts of this case are simple and undisputed. The legislature of the State of California has in the last decade enacted a number of statutes restricting the right of private landowners to discriminate on the basis of such factors as race in the sale or rental of property. These laws aroused considerable opposition, causing certain groups to organize themselves and to take advantage of procedures embodied in the California Constitution permitting a "proposition" to be presented to the voters for a constitutional amendment. "Proposition 14" was thus put before the electorate in the 1964 election and was adopted by a vote of 4,526,460 to 2,395,747 . . . .

In the case at hand California, acting through the initiative and referendum, has decided to remain "neutral" in the realm of private discrimination affecting the sale or rental of private residential property; in such transactions private owners are now free to act in a discriminatory manner previously forbidden to them. In short, all that has happened is that California has effected a *pro tanto* repeal of its prior statutes forbidding private discrimination. This runs no more afoul of the Fourteenth Amendment than would have California's failure to pass any such antidiscrimination statutes in the first instance. The fact that such repeal was also accompanied by a constitutional prohibition against future enactment of such laws by the California Legislature cannot well be thought to affect, from a federal constitutional standpoint, the validity of what California has done. The Fourteenth Amendment does not reach such state constitutional action any more than it does a simple legislative repeal of legislation forbidding private discrimination. . . .

I.

The Court attempts to fit § 26 within the coverage of the Equal Protection Clause by characterizing it as in effect an affirmative call to residents of California to discriminate. The main difficulty with this viewpoint is that it depends upon a characterization of § 26 that cannot fairly be made. The provision is neutral on its face, and it is only by in effect asserting that this requirement of passive official neutrality is camouflage that the Court is able to reach its conclusion. . . .

A state enactment, particularly one that is simply permissive of private decision-making rather than coercive and one that has been adopted in this most democratic of processes, should not be struck down by the judiciary under the Equal Protection Clause without persuasive evidence of an invidious purpose or effect. . . .

II.

There is no question that the adoption of § 26, repealing the former state antidiscrimination laws and prohibiting the enactment of such state laws in the future, constituted "state action" within the meaning of the Fourteenth Amendment. The only issue is whether this provision impermissibly deprives any person of equal protection of the laws. As a starting point, it is clear that any statute requiring unjustified discriminatory treatment is unconstitutional. *E.g., Nixon v. Herndon*, 273 U.S. 536; *Brown v. Board of Education, supra*; *Peterson v. City of Greenville*, 373 U.S. 244. And it is no less clear that the Equal Protection Clause bars as well discriminatory governmental administration of a statute fair on its face. *E.g., Yick Wo v. Hopkins*, 118 U.S. 356. This case fits within neither of these two categories: Section 26 is by its terms inoffensive, and its provisions require no affirmative governmental enforcement of any sort. A third category of equal-protection cases, concededly more difficult to characterize, stands for the proposition that when governmental involvement in private discrimination reaches a level at which the State can be held responsible for the specific act of private discrimination, the strictures of the Fourteenth Amendment come into play. In dealing with this class of cases, the inquiry has been framed as whether the State has become "a joint participant in the challenged activity, which, on that account, cannot be considered to have been so 'purely private' as to fall without the scope of the Fourteenth Amendment." *Burton v. Wilmington Parking Authority*, 365 U.S. 715, 725 . . . .

It is true that standards in this area have not been definitely formulated, and that acts of discrimination have been included within the compass of the Equal Protection Clause not merely when they were compelled by a state statute or other governmental pressures, but also when they were said to be "induced" or "authorized" by the State. Most of these cases, however, can be approached in terms of the impact and extent of affirmative state governmental activities.... In situations such as these the focus has been on positive state cooperation or partnership in affirmatively promoted activities, an involvement that could have been avoided. Here, in contrast, we have only the straight-forward adoption of a neutral provision restoring to the sphere of free choice, left untouched by the Fourteenth Amendment, private behavior within a limited area of the racial problem. The denial of equal protection emerges only from the conclusion reached by the Court that the implementation of a new policy of governmental neutrality, embodied in a constitutional provision and replacing a former policy of antidiscrimination, has the effect of lending encouragement to those who wish to discriminate....

A moment of thought will reveal the far-reaching possibilities of the Court's new doctrine, which I am sure the Court does not intend. Every act of private discrimination is either forbidden by state law or permitted by it. There can be little doubt that such permissiveness—whether by express constitutional or statutory provision, or implicit in the common law—to some extent "encourages" those who wish to discriminate to do so. Under this theory "state action" in the form of laws that do nothing more than passively permit private discrimination could be said to tinge all private discrimination with the taint of unconstitutional state encouragement....

III.

I think that this decision is not only constitutionally unsound, but in its practical potentialities short-sighted. Opponents of state antidiscrimination statutes are now in a position to argue that such legislation should be defeated because, if enacted, it may be unrepealable....

[The concurring opinion of Justice Douglas is omitted.]

Notes and Questions

1. The state's desire to encourage private racism seems clear in *Anderson*. Is its intent equally clear in *Reitman*? How about in *Burton*?

2. Is there a constitutionally significant difference between never enacting anti-discrimination laws in the first instance, and enacting and then subsequently repealing those same laws? In other words, why is it constitutionally impermissible for a relatively progressive state such as California to experiment with anti-discrimination laws and later repeal them, but it is *not* constitutionally impermissible for a more conservative state to never enact such anti-discrimination laws in the first instance?

3. Of what significance is it that in *Reitman*, the state did not simply repeal the legislation, but also placed a constitutional barrier to its re-enactment? In other words, the challenged law made it significantly harder to enact such legislation in the future, because it now requires not merely persuading the legislature to enact anti-discrimination legislation; it also requires a repeal of the constitutional provision that prohibits enactment of such a statute.

Chapter 8

"Fundamental Rights" and the Rise of Equal Protection Review

Recall from Chapter 1 that since the nation's founding, Justices of the U.S. Supreme Court have been divided on the question whether the U.S. Constitution empowers them to recognize and enforce unenumerated rights. In *The Slaughter-House Cases*, the Court effectively closed the door to invoking the Fourteenth Amendment's Privileges or Immunities Clause to do so. And while it regularly invoked the Due Process Clauses of the Fifth and Fourteenth Amendments to do so during the *Lochner* period, the Court closed off that avenue for recognizing and enforcing unenumerated rights—at least temporarily—in *West Coast Hotel*.

Yet in the post-*Lochner* period, the Court began to consider a third basis for recognizing and enforcing such rights: the Equal Protection Clause. The materials that follow explore three different rights that the Court has recognized as fundamental under that Clause: the right to procreate, the right to vote, and the right to travel.

As you read these cases, see if you can identify the criteria, if any, that the Court identifies for recognizing a right as fundamental under the Equal Protection Clause. Moreover, identify the ways in which recognizing a right under the Equal Protection Clause has different consequences from recognizing one under the Due Process Clause. Finally, consider how this branch of equal protection jurisprudence differs from the class-based analysis you have examined thus far, and how it might benefit a group who is discriminated against in the exercise of a given right, but who is not entitled to the heightened scrutiny that the Court applies to race-based distinctions, or, as you will later see, to other suspect or quasi-suspect classifications.

A. The Right to Procreate

In 1927, the U.S. Supreme Court considered a constitutional challenge to a sterilization law brought on behalf of Carrie Buck, an allegedly intellectually disabled young lady living in an institution in Virginia. In *Buck v. Bell*, 274 U.S. 200 (1927), the Court upheld the law—which provided for the sterilization of institutionalized but not non-institutionalized intellectually disabled persons—against a class-based equal protection challenge as well as substantive and procedural due process challenges.

According to the *Buck* Court, Carrie Buck—as well as her mother and her child—were all "feeble-minded." This finding, according to an opinion written by Justice Holmes—a *Lochner* dissenter—gave the government enough of an interest to overcome a substantive due process challenge to the law:

> It is better for all the world, if instead of waiting to execute degenerate offspring for crime, or to let them starve for their imbecility, society can prevent those who are manifestly unfit from continuing their kind. The principle that sustains compulsory vaccination is broad enough to cover cutting the Fallopian tubes. Three generations of imbeciles are enough.

274 U.S., at 207. The *Buck* Court also dispensed with any procedural due process challenges to the law, noting that there existed a process of presenting a petition, review by a board, and an appeal before the sterilization surgery was performed.

Finally, the *Buck* Court rejected a class-based equal protection challenge to the sterilization law. According to Carrie Buck's attorneys, the equal protection problem arose because the law was applicable only to those intellectually disabled persons living in institutions, not those living outside of institutions. Describing class-based equal protection challenges as "the usual last resort of constitutional arguments," Justice Holmes rejected that claim as well:

> [T]he law does all that is needed when it does all that it can, indicates a policy, applies it to all within the lines, and seeks to bring within the lines all similary situated so far and so fast as its means allow. Of course so far as the operations enable those who otherwise must be kept confined to be returned to the world, and thus open the asylum to others, the equality aimed at will be more nearly reached.

274 U.S., at 208. As it turns out, Carrie Buck was not intellectually disabled at all. Subsequent investigations uncovered that she had been sent to an institution by her foster parents after she had become pregnant following a sexual assault committed against her by a relative of her foster parents. Moreover, the actual evidence of intellectual disability for Carrie Buck, her mother, and her child was very weak, consisting of IQ tests for her and her mother and an observation of her child by a social worker. Indeed, in 2002, Virginia's governor issued a posthumous apology to Carrie Buck. Yet if one is committed to enforcing only enumerated constitutional rights, Justice Holmes was probably correct to reject her constitutional claims. A thorough review of the U.S. Constitution's text will not reveal any enumerated right to procreate, and the Court's deferential review of her equal protection claim is consistent with its approach to equal protection challenges outside the context of race.

In the case that follows, the U.S. Supreme Court reconsiders the question whether there is a protected right to procreate, in a case challenging the mandatory sterilization of those convicted of certain felonies, considering an additional constitutional claim not considered in *Buck*.

Skinner v. Oklahoma

316 U.S. 535 (1942)

MR. JUSTICE DOUGLAS delivered the opinion of the Court.

This case touches a sensitive and important area of human rights. Oklahoma deprives certain individuals of a right which is basic to the perpetuation of a race—the right to have offspring. Oklahoma has decreed the enforcement of its law against petitioner, overruling his claim that it violated the Fourteenth Amendment....

The statute involved is Oklahoma's Habitual Criminal Sterilization Act. That Act defines an "habitual criminal" as a person who, having been convicted two or more times for crimes "amounting to felonies involving moral turpitude" either in an Oklahoma court or in a court of any other State, is thereafter convicted of such a felony in Oklahoma and is sentenced to a term of imprisonment in an Oklahoma penal institution. Machinery is provided for the institution by the Attorney General of a proceeding against such a person in the Oklahoma courts for a judgment that such person shall be rendered sexually sterile. Notice, an opportunity to be heard, and the right to a jury trial are provided. The issues triable in such a proceeding are narrow and confined. If the court or jury finds that the defendant is an "habitual criminal" and that he "may be rendered sexually sterile without detriment to his or her general health," then the court "shall render judgment to the effect that said defendant be rendered sexually sterile" by the operation of vasectomy in case of a male and of salpingectomy in case of a female. Only one other provision of the Act is material here and that is § 195 which provides that "offenses arising out of the violation of the prohibitory laws, revenue acts, embezzlement, or political offenses, shall not come or be considered within the terms of this Act." ....

Several objections to the constitutionality of the Act have been pressed upon us. It is urged that the Act cannot be sustained as an exercise of the police power in view of the state of scientific authorities respecting inheritability of criminal traits. It is argued that due process is lacking because under this Act, unlike the act upheld in *Buck v. Bell*, the defendant is given no opportunity to be heard on the issue as to whether he is the probable potential parent of socially undesirable offspring. It is also suggested that the Act is penal in character and that the sterilization provided for is cruel and unusual punishment and violative of the Fourteenth Amendment. We pass those points without intimating an opinion on them, for there is a feature of the Act which clearly condemns it. That is its failure to meet the requirements of the equal protection clause of the Fourteenth Amendment.

We do not stop to point out all of the inequalities in this Act. A few examples will suffice. In Oklahoma grand larceny is a felony. Larceny is grand larceny when the property taken exceeds $20 in value. Embezzlement is punishable "in the manner prescribed for feloniously stealing property of the value of that embezzled." Hence he who embezzles property worth more than $20 is guilty of a felony. A clerk who appropriates over $20 from his employer's till and a stranger who steals the same amount are thus both guilty of felonies. If the latter repeats his act and is convicted three times, he may be sterilized. But the clerk is not subject to the pains and penalties of the Act no matter how large his embezzlements nor how frequent his convictions. A person who enters a chicken coop and steals chickens commits a felony; and he may be sterilized if he is thrice convicted. If, however, he is a bailee of the property and fraudulently appropriates it, he is an embezzler. Hence no matter how habitual his proclivities for embezzlement are and no matter how often his conviction, he may not be sterilized. . . .

It was stated in *Buck v. Bell* that the claim that state legislation violates the equal protection clause of the Fourteenth Amendment is "the usual last resort of constitutional arguments." Under our constitutional system the States in determining the reach and scope of particular legislation need not provide "abstract symmetry." They may mark and set apart the classes and types of problems according to the needs and as dictated or suggested by experience. . . . Thus, if we had here only a question as to a State's classification of crimes, such as embezzlement or larceny, no substantial federal question would be raised. For a State is not constrained in the exercise of its police power to ignore experience which marks a class of offenders or a family of offenses for special treatment. . . . As stated in *Buck v. Bell*, ". . . the law does all that is needed when it does all that it can, indicates a policy, applies it to all within the lines, and seeks to bring within the lines all similarly situated so far and so fast as its means allow."

But the instant legislation runs afoul of the equal protection clause, though we give Oklahoma that large deference which the rule of the foregoing cases requires. We are dealing here with legislation which involves one of the basic civil rights of man. Marriage and procreation are fundamental to the very existence and survival of the race. The power to sterilize, if exercised, may have subtle, far-reaching and devastating effects. In evil or reckless hands it can cause races or types which are inimical to the dominant group to wither and disappear. There is no redemption for the individual whom the law touches. Any experiment which the State conducts is to his irreparable injury. He is forever deprived of a basic liberty. We mention these matters not to reexamine the scope of the police power of the States. We advert to them merely in emphasis of our view that strict scrutiny of the classification which a State makes in a sterilization law is essential, lest unwittingly or otherwise invidious discriminations are made against groups or types of individuals in violation of the constitutional guaranty of just and equal laws. The guaranty of "equal protection of the laws is a pledge of the protection of equal laws." *Yick Wo v. Hopkins*. When the law lays an unequal hand on those who have committed intrinsically the same quality of offense and sterilizes one and not the other, it has made as an invidious a discrimination as if it had selected a particular race or nationality for oppressive treatment. *Yick Wo v. Hopkins*. Sterilization of those who have thrice committed grand larceny with immunity for those who are embezzlers is a clear, pointed, unmistakable discrimination. Oklahoma makes no attempt to say that he who commits larceny by trespass or trick or fraud has biologically inheritable traits which he who commits embezzlement lacks. Oklahoma's line between larceny by fraud and embezzlement is determined, as we have noted, "with reference to the time when the fraudulent intent to convert the property to the taker's own use" arises. We have not the slightest basis for inferring that that line has any significance in eugenics nor that the inheritability of criminal traits follows the neat legal distinctions which the law has marked between those two offenses. In terms of fines and imprisonment the crimes of larceny and embezzlement rate the same under the Oklahoma code. Only when it comes to sterilization are the pains and penalties of the law different. The equal protection clause would indeed be a formula of empty words if such conspicuously artificial lines could be drawn. In *Buck v. Bell*, the Virginia statute was upheld though it applied only to feebleminded persons in institutions of the State. But it was pointed out that "so far as the operations enable those who otherwise must be kept confined to be returned to the world, and thus open the asylum to others, the equality aimed at will be more nearly reached." Here there is no such saving feature. Embezzlers are forever free. Those who steal or take in other ways are not. . . .

Mr. Chief Justice Stone concurring.

I concur in the result, but I am not persuaded that we are aided in reaching it by recourse to the equal protection clause.

If Oklahoma may resort generally to the sterilization of criminals on the assumption that their propensities are transmissible to future generations by inheritance, I seriously doubt that the equal protection clause requires it to apply the measure to all criminals in the first instance, or to none.

Moreover, if we must presume that the legislature knows—what science has been unable to ascertain—that the criminal tendencies of any class of habitual offenders are transmissible regardless of the varying mental characteristics of its individuals, I should suppose that we must likewise presume that the legislature, in its wisdom, knows that the criminal tendencies of some classes of offenders are more likely to be transmitted than those of others. And so I think the real question we have to consider is not one of equal protection, but whether the wholesale condemnation of a class to such an invasion of personal liberty, without opportunity to any individual to show that his is not the type of case which would justify resort to it, satisfies the demands of due process.

There are limits to the extent to which the presumption of constitutionality can be pressed, especially where the liberty of the person is concerned (*see United States v. Carolene Products Co.*, 304 U.S. 144, 152, n. 4) and where the presumption is resorted to only to dispense with a procedure which the ordinary dictates of prudence would seem to demand for the protection of the individual from arbitrary action. Although petitioner here was given a hearing to ascertain whether sterilization would be detrimental to his health, he was given none to discover whether his criminal tendencies are of an inheritable type. Undoubtedly a state may, after appropriate inquiry, constitutionally interfere with the personal liberty of the individual to prevent the transmission by inheritance of his socially injurious tendencies. *Buck v. Bell*. But until now we have not been called upon to say that it may do so without giving him a hearing and opportunity to challenge the existence as to him of the only facts which could justify so drastic a measure.

Science has found and the law has recognized that there are certain types of mental deficiency associated with delinquency which are inheritable. But the State does not contend—nor can there be any pretense—that either common knowledge or experience, or scientific investigation, has given assurance that the criminal tendencies of any class of habitual offenders are universally or even generally inheritable. In such circumstances, inquiry whether such is the fact in the case of any particular individual cannot rightly be dispensed with. Whether the procedure by which a statute carries its mandate into execution satisfies due process is a matter of judicial cognizance. A law which condemns, without hearing, all the individuals of a class to so harsh a measure as the present because some or even many merit condemnation, is lacking in the first principles of due process. And so, while the state may protect itself from the demonstrably inheritable tendencies of the individual which are injurious to society, the most elementary notions of due process would seem to require it to take appropriate steps to safeguard the liberty of the individual by affording him, before he is condemned to an irreparable injury in his person, some opportunity to show that he is without such inheritable tendencies. The state is called on to sacrifice no permissible end when it is required to reach its objective by a reasonable and just procedure adequate to safeguard rights of the individual which concededly the Constitution protects.

Mr. Justice Jackson, concurring....

Perhaps to employ a broad and loose scheme of classification would be permissible if accompanied by the individual hearings indicated by the Chief Justice. On the other hand, narrow classification with reference to the end to be accomplished by the Act might justify limiting individual hearings to the issue whether the individual belonged to a class so defined. Since this Act does not present these questions, I reserve judgment on them.

I also think the present plan to sterilize the individual in pursuit of a eugenic plan to eliminate from the race characteristics that are only vaguely identified and which in our present state of knowledge are uncertain as to transmissibility presents other constitutional questions of gravity. This Court has sustained such an experiment with respect to an imbecile, a person with definite and observable characteristics where the condition had persisted through three generations and afforded grounds for the belief that it was transmissible and would continue to manifest itself in generations to come. *Buck v. Bell*.

There are limits to the extent to which a legislatively represented majority may conduct biological experiments at the expense of the dignity and personality and natural powers of a minority-even those who have been guilty of what the majority define as crimes. But this Act falls down before reaching this problem, which I mention only to avoid the implication that such a question may not exist because not discussed. On it I would also reserve judgment.

Notes and Questions

1. For an excellent overview of the horrific history behind *Buck v. Bell*, see Paul A. Lombardo, Three Generations, No Imbeciles: Eugenics, The Supreme Court, and *Buck v. Bell* (Johns Hopkins Univ. Press 2010).

2. Why does the majority in *Skinner* opt to decide the case on equal protection grounds instead of—as the separate concurring opinions suggest—on substantive or procedural due process grounds? Might the Court majority—many of whose members had only recently voted to overrule *Lochner*—be reluctant to invoke the Due Process Clause for fear of seeming hypocritical? *See* Kenneth L. Karst, *The Liberties of Equal Citizens: Groups and the Due Process Clause*, 55 UCLA L. Rev. 99, 112, 123 (2007); G. Edward White, *The Anti-Judge: William O. Douglas and the Ambiguities of Individuality*, 74 Va. L. Rev. 17, 65–72 (1988).

3. How does the Court determine that the right at issue in this case is fundamental so as to justify the application of strict scrutiny? Does it cite any sources, or does it simply assert its fundamental nature?

4. What, exactly, is the right at issue in this case? The Court writes that "[m]arriage and procreation" are fundamental. What does marriage have to do with this case? Is the Court identifying two, independent fundamental rights—marriage and procreation—or are the two rights somehow linked?

5. What is the significance of the Court's citation to *Yick Wo*? In this light, consider that the decision was handed down in the midst of World War II, when Nazi Germany's racially based eugenics policies were exposed.

6. Does the right to procreate recognized in *Skinner* imply a corresponding right *not* to procreate, to wit, a right to use contraception or to procure an abortion? If not, what distinguishes the two rights from one another?

7. Does the *Skinner* Court distinguish or overrule its earlier decision in *Buck v. Bell*?

B. The Right to Vote

The original U.S. Constitution largely left the question of voter qualification to the states, even for federal elections. Thus, for example, Article I, § 2, cl. 1 provides that those voting for members of the U.S. House of Representatives "shall have the Qualifications for Electors of the most numerous Branch of the State Legislature," while Article II, § 1, cl. 2 provides that the electors for President and Vice-President are appointed by each state "in such Manner as the Legislature thereof may direct."

Recall as well that the Fourteenth Amendment did not directly prohibit discrimination by states in voting qualifications. Rather, Section 2 of the Fourteenth Amendment merely penalized states that denied the right to *males* twenty-one years of age or older with a reduction in representation in Congress. Indeed, it was this aspect of the Fourteenth Amendment that caused the Court in *Minor v. Happersett* to reject a claim that the Fourteenth Amendment's Privileges or Immunities Clause guaranteed women the right to vote.

Several constitutional amendments ratified after the Fourteenth Amendment addressed discrete aspects of the right to vote. The Fifteenth Amendment, ratified in 1870, prohibited denial of the right to vote on account of race, color, or previous condition of servitude. The Nineteenth Amendment, ratified in 1920, prohibited denial of the right to vote on account of sex. The Twenty-Fourth Amendment, ratified in 1964, prohibited denial of the right to vote for *federal* officials by reason of failure to pay a poll tax. Finally, the Twenty-Sixth Amendment, ratified in 1971, prohibited denial of the right to vote to those age eighteen or older.

Given all of these specific provisions dealing with the right to vote, and the precedent set forth in *Minor*, one might reasonably conclude that the Fourteenth Amendment plays no role so far as the right to vote is concerned. Nonetheless, in a series of cases, excerpted below, the Court invoked the Fourteenth Amendment's Equal Protection Clause as a basis for striking down laws restricting the right to vote that did not directly violate the Fifteenth, Nineteenth, Twenty-Fourth, or Twenty-Sixth Amendments.

Reynolds v. Sims

377 U.S. 533 (1964)

Mr. Chief Justice Warren delivered the opinion of the Court.

[At issue in this case is a challenge to the apportionment of seats in the two houses of the Alabama Legislature, with the plaintiffs contending that a failure to apportion legislative districts on a population basis violates the Equal Protection Clause.]

A predominant consideration in determining whether a State's legislative apportionment scheme constitutes an invidious discrimination violative of rights asserted under the Equal Protection Clause is that the rights allegedly impaired are individual and personal in nature.... Like *Skinner v. Oklahoma*, such a case "touches a sensitive and important area of human rights," and "involves one of the basic civil rights of man," presenting questions of alleged "invidious discriminations ... against groups or types of individuals in violation of the constitutional guaranty of just and equal laws." Undoubtedly, the right of suffrage is a fundamental matter in a free and democratic society. Especially since the right to exercise the franchise in a free and unimpaired manner is preservative of other basic civil and political rights, any alleged infringement of the right of citizens to vote must be carefully and meticulously scrutinized. Almost a century ago, in *Yick Wo v. Hopkins*, the Court referred to "the political franchise of voting' as 'a fundamental political right, because preservative of all rights."

Legislators represent people, not trees or acres. Legislators are elected by voters, not farms or cities or economic interests. As long as ours is a representative form of government, and our legislatures are those instruments of government elected directly by and directly representative of the people, the right to elect legislators in a free and unimpaired fashion is a bedrock of our political system. It could hardly be gainsaid that a constitutional claim had been asserted by an allegation that certain otherwise qualified voters had been entirely prohibited from voting for members of their state legislature. And, if a State should provide that the votes of citizens in one part of the State should be given two times, or five times, or 10 times the weight of votes of citizens in another part of the State, it could hardly be contended that the right to vote of those residing in the disfavored areas had not been effectively diluted. It would appear extraordinary to suggest that a State could be constitutionally permitted to enact a law providing that certain of the State's voters could vote two, five, or 10 times for their legislative representatives, while voters living elsewhere could vote only once. And it is inconceivable that a state law to the effect that, in counting votes for legislators, the votes of citizens in one part of the State would be multiplied by two, five, or 10, while the votes of persons in another area would be counted only at face value, could be constitutionally sustainable. Of course, the effect of state legislative districting schemes which give the same number of representatives to unequal numbers of constituents is identical. Overweighting and overvaluation of the votes of those living here has the certain effect of dilution and undervaluation of the votes of those living there. The resulting discrimination against those individual voters living in disfavored areas is easily demonstrable mathematically. Their right to vote is simply not the same right to vote as that of those living in a favored part of the State. Two, five, or 10 of them must vote before the effect of their voting is equivalent to that of their favored neighbor. Weighting the votes of citizens differently, by any method or means, merely because of where they happen to reside, hardly seems justifiable. One must be ever aware that the Constitution forbids "sophisticated as well as simpleminded modes of discrimination." *Lane v. Wilson*; *Gomillion v. Lightfoot*. . . .

[T]he concept of equal protection has been traditionally viewed as requiring the uniform treatment of persons standing in the same relation to the governmental action questioned or challenged. With respect to the allocation of legislative representation, all voters, as citizens of a State, stand in the same relation regardless of where they live. Any suggested criteria for the differentiation of citizens are insufficient to justify any discrimination, as to the weight of their votes, unless relevant to the permissible purposes of legislative apportionment. Since the achieving of fair and effective representation for all citizens is concededly the basic aim of legislative apportionment, we conclude that the Equal Protection Clause guarantees the opportunity for equal participation by all voters in the election of state legislators . . .

We hold that, as a basic constitutional standard, the Equal Protection Clause requires that the seats in both houses of a bicameral state legislature must be apportioned on a population basis. Simply stated, an individual's right to vote for state legislators is unconstitutionally impaired when its weight is in a substantial fashion diluted when compared with votes of citizens living on other parts of the State. . . .

By holding that as a federal constitutional requisite both houses of a state legislature must be apportioned on a population basis, we mean that the Equal Protection Clause requires that a State make an honest and good faith effort to construct districts, in both houses of its legislature, as nearly of equal population as is practicable. We realize that it is a practical impossibility to arrange legislative districts so that each one has an identical number of residents, or citizens, or voters. Mathematical exactness or precision is hardly a workable constitutional requirement....

Mr. Justice Harlan, dissenting....

Had the Court paused to probe more deeply into the matter, it would have found that the Equal Protection Clause was never intended to inhibit the States in choosing any democratic method they pleased for the apportionment of their legislatures. This is shown by the language of the Fourteenth Amendment taken as a whole, by the understanding of those who proposed and ratified it, and by the political practices of the States at the time the Amendment was adopted. It is confirmed by numerous state and congressional actions since the adoption of the Fourteenth Amendment, and by the common understanding of the Amendment as evidenced by subsequent constitutional amendments and decisions of this Court....

The Court relies exclusively on that portion of § 1 of the Fourteenth Amendment which provides that no State shall "deny to any person within its jurisdiction the equal protection of the laws," and disregards entirely the significance of § 2, which reads:

> "Representatives shall be apportioned among the several States according to their respective numbers, counting the whole number of persons in each State, excluding Indians not taxed. *But when the right to vote at any election for* the choice of electors for President and Vice President of the United States, Representatives in Congress, *the Executive and Judicial officers of a State, or the members of the Legislature thereof, is denied* to any of the male inhabitants of such State, being twenty-one years of age, and citizens of the United States, *or in any way abridged*, except for participation in rebellion, or other crime, the basis of representation therein shall be reduced in the proportion which the number of such male citizens shall bear to the whole number of male citizens twenty-one years of age in such State." (Emphasis added.)

....

Whatever one might take to be the application of these cases of the Equal Protection Clause if it stood alone, I am unable to understand the Court's utter disregard of the second section which expressly recognizes the States' power to deny "or in any way" abridge the right of their inhabitants to vote for "the members of the (State) Legislature," and its express provision of a remedy for such denial or abridgment. The comprehensive scope of the second section and its particular reference to the state legislatures preclude the suggestion that the first section was intended to have the result reached by the Court today....

The history of the adoption of the Fourteenth Amendment provides conclusive evidence that neither those who proposed nor those who ratified the Amendment believed that the Equal Protection Clause limited the power of the States to apportion their legislatures as they saw fit. Moreover, the history demonstrate that the intention to leave this power undisturbed was deliberate and was widely believed to be essential to the adoption of the Amendment.

[The dissent here proceeds to discuss the historical evidence in support of this conclusion.]

In this summary of what the majority ignores, note should be taken of the Fifteenth and Nineteenth Amendments. The former prohibited the States from denying or abridging the right to vote "on account of race, color, or previous condition of servitude." The latter, certified as part of the Constitution in 1920, added sex to the prohibited classifications. In *Minor v. Happersett*, this Court considered the claim that the right of women to vote was protected by the Privileges [or] Immunities Clause of the Fourteenth Amendment. The Court's discussion there of the significance of the Fifteenth Amendment is fully applicable here with respect to the Nineteenth Amendment as well.

> "And still again, after the adoption of the fourteenth amendment, it was deemed necessary to adopt a fifteenth, as follows: 'The right of citizens of the United States to vote shall not be denied or abridged by the United States, or by any State, on account of race, color, or previous condition of servitude.' The fourteenth amendment had already provided that no State should make or enforce any law which should abridge the privileges or immunities of citizens of the United States. If suffrage was one of these privileges or immunities, why amend the Constitution to prevent its being denied on account of race, &c.? Nothing is more evident than that the greater must include the less, and if all were already protected why go through with the form of amending the Constitution to protect a part?"

In the present case, we can go still further. If constitutional amendment was the only means by which all men and, later, women, could be guaranteed the right to vote at all, even for *federal* officers, how can it be that the far less obvious right to a particular kind of apportionment of *state* legislatures—a right to which is opposed a far more plausible conflicting interest of the State than the interest which opposes the general right to vote—can be conferred by judicial construction of the Fourteenth Amendment? Yet, unless one takes the highly implausible view that the Fourteenth Amendment controls methods of apportionment but leaves the right to vote itself unprotected, the conclusion is inescapable that the Court has, for purposes of these cases, relegated the Fifteenth and Nineteenth Amendments to the same limbo of constitutional anachronisms to which the second section of the Fourteenth Amendment has been assigned....

[The concurring opinion of Justice Clark and the opinion of Justice Stewart are omitted.]

Harper v. Virginia State Board of Elections

383 U.S. 663 (1966)

Mr. Justice Douglas delivered the opinion of the Court.

These are suits by Virginia residents to have declared unconstitutional Virginia's poll tax.[1] . . . .

[O]nce the franchise is granted to the electorate, lines may not be drawn which are inconsistent with the Equal Protection Clause of the Fourteenth Amendment. That is to say, the right of suffrage "is subject to the imposition of state standards which are not discriminatory and which do not contravene any restriction that Congress, acting pursuant to its constitutional powers, has imposed." *Lassiter v. Northampton County Board of Elections*. We were speaking there of a state literacy test which we sustained, warning that the result would be different if a literacy test, fair on its face, were used to discriminate against a class. But the *Lassiter* case does not govern the result here, because, unlike a poll tax, the "ability to read and write . . . has some relation to standards designed to promote intelligent use of the ballot."

We conclude that a State violates the Equal Protection Clause of the Fourteenth Amendment whenever it makes the affluence of the voter or payment of any fee an electoral standard. Voter qualifications have no relation to wealth nor to paying or not paying this or any other tax. . . .

Long ago in *Yick Wo v. Hopkins*, the Court referred to "the political franchise of voting' as a 'fundamental political right, because preservative of all rights." Recently in *Reynolds v. Sims*, we said, "Undoubtedly, the right of suffrage is a fundamental matter in a free and democratic society. Especially since the right to exercise the franchise in a free and unimpaired manner is preservative of other basic civil and political rights, any alleged infringement of the right of citizens to vote must be carefully and meticulously scrutinized." There we were considering charges that voters in one part of the State had greater representation per person in the State Legislature than voters in another part of the State. . . .

We say the same whether the citizen, otherwise qualified to vote, has $1.50 in his pocket or nothing at all, pays the fee or fails to pay it. The principle that denies the State the right to dilute a citizen's vote on account of his economic status or other such factors by analogy bars a system which excludes those unable to pay a fee to vote or who fail to pay.

It is argued that a State may exact fees from citizens for many different kinds of licenses; that if it can demand from all an equal fee for a driver's license, it can demand from all an equal poll tax for voting. But we must remember that the interest of the

1. Section 173 of Virginia's Constitution directs the General Assembly to levy an annual poll tax not exceeding $1.50 on every resident of the State 21 years of age and over (with exceptions not relevant here) . . . . Enforcement of poll taxes takes the form of disenfranchisement of those who do not pay. . . .

State, when it comes to voting, is limited to the power to fix qualifications. Wealth, like race, creed, or color, is not germane to one's ability to participate intelligently in the electoral process. Lines drawn on the basis of wealth or property, like those of race (*Korematsu v. United States*), are traditionally disfavored. To introduce wealth or payment of a fee as a measure of a voter's qualifications is to introduce a capricious or irrelevant factor. The degree of the discrimination is irrelevant. In this context—that is, as a condition of obtaining a ballot—the requirement of fee paying causes an "invidious" discrimination (*Skinner v. Oklahoma*) that runs afoul of the Equal Protection Clause. Levy "by the poll," as stated in *Breedlove v. Suttles*, is an old familiar form of taxation; and we say nothing to impair its validity so long as it is not made a condition to the exercise of the franchise. *Breedlove v. Suttles* sanctioned its use as "a prerequisite of voting." To that extent the *Breedlove* case is overruled.

We agree, of course, with Mr. Justice Holmes that the Due Process Clause of the Fourteenth Amendment "does not enact Mr. Herbert Spencer's Social Statics" (*Lochner v. New York*). Likewise, the Equal Protection Clause is not shackled to the political theory of a particular era. In determining what lines are unconstitutionally discriminatory, we have never been confined to historic notions of equality, any more than we have restricted due process to a fixed catalogue of what was at a given time deemed to be the limits of fundamental rights. Notions of what constitutes equal treatment for purposes of the Equal Protection Clause do change. This Court in 1896 held that laws providing for separate public facilities for white and Negro citizens did not deprive the latter of the equal protection and treatment that the Fourteenth Amendment commands. *Plessy v. Ferguson*. Seven of the eight Justices then sitting subscribed to the Court's opinion, thus joining in expressions of what constituted unequal and discriminatory treatment that sound strange to a contemporary ear. When, in 1954—more than a half-century later—we repudiated the "separate-but-equal" doctrine of *Plessy* as respects public education we stated: "In approaching this problem, we cannot turn the clock back to 1868 when the Amendment was adopted, or even to 1896 when *Plessy v. Ferguson* was written." *Brown v. Board of Education*.

In a recent searching re-examination of the Equal Protection Clause, we held, as already noted, that "the opportunity for equal participation by all voters in the election of state legislators" is required. *Reynolds v. Sims*. We decline to qualify that principle by sustaining this poll tax. Our conclusion, like that in *Reynolds v. Sims*, is founded not on what we think governmental policy should be, but on what the Equal Protection Clause requires.

We have long been mindful that where fundamental rights and liberties are asserted under the Equal Protection Clause, classifications which might invade or restrain them must be closely scrutinized and carefully confined. *See, e.g., Skinner v. Oklahoma*; *Reynolds v. Sims*.

Those principles apply here. For to repeat, wealth or fee paying has, in our view, no relation to voting qualifications; the right to vote is too precious, too fundamental to be so burdened or conditioned.

Mr. Justice Black, dissenting. . . .

It should be pointed out at once that the Court's decision is to no extent based on a finding that the Virginia law as written or as applied is being used as a device or mechanism to deny Negro citizens of Virginia the right to vote on account of their color. . . . If the record could support a finding that the law as written or applied has such an effect, the law would of course be unconstitutional as a violation of the Fourteenth and Fifteenth Amendments. . . . What the Court does hold is that the Equal Protection Clause necessarily bars all States from making payment of a state tax, any tax, a prerequisite to voting. . . .

Another reason for my dissent from the Court's judgment and opinion is that it seems to be using the old "natural-law-due-process formula" to justify striking down state laws as violations of the Equal Protection Clause. I have heretofore had many occasions to express my strong belief that there is no constitutional support whatever for this Court to use the Due Process Clause as though it provided a blank check to alter the meaning of the Constitution as written so as to add to it substantive constitutional changes which a majority of the Court at any given time believes are needed to meet present-day problems. Nor is there in my opinion any more constitutional support for this Court to use the Equal Protection Clause, as it has today, to write into the Constitution its notions of what it thinks is good governmental policy. . . .

Mr. Justice Harlan, whom Mr. Justice Stewart joins, dissenting.

The final demise of state poll taxes, already totally proscribed by the Twenty-Fourth Amendment with respect to federal elections and abolished by the States themselves in all but four States with respect to state elections, is perhaps in itself not of great moment. But that fact that the *coup de grace* has been administered by this Court instead of being left to the affected States or to the federal political process should be a matter of continuing concern to all interested in maintaining the proper role of this tribunal under our scheme of government. . . .

The Equal Protection Clause prevents States from arbitrarily treating people differently under their laws. Whether any such differing treatment is to be deemed arbitrary depends on whether or not it reflects an appropriate differentiating classification among those affected; the clause has never been thought to require equal treatment of all persons despite differing circumstances. The test evolved by this Court for determining whether an asserted justifying classification exists is whether such a classification can be deemed to be founded on some rational and otherwise constitutionally permissible state policy. This standard reduces to a minimum the likelihood that the federal judiciary will judge state policies in terms of the individual notions and predilections of its own members, and until recently it has been followed in all kinds of "equal protection" cases.[3]

3. I think the somewhat different application of the Equal Protection Clause to racial discrimination cases finds justification in the fact that insofar as that clause may embody a particular value in addition to rationality, the historical origins of the Civil War Amendments might attribute to racial equality this special status. . . .

Reynolds v. Sims, among its other breaks with the past, also marked a departure from these traditional and wise principles. Unless its "one man, one vote" thesis of state legislative apportionment is to be attributed to the unsupportable proposition that "Equal Protection" simply means indiscriminate equality, it seems inescapable that what *Reynolds* really reflected was but this Court's own views of how modern American representative government should be run. For it can hardly be thought that no other method of apportionment may be considered rational....

[T]oday in holding unconstitutional state poll taxes and property qualifications for voting ... the Court reverts to the highly subjective judicial approach manifested by *Reynolds*. In substance the Court's analysis of the equal protection issue goes no further than to say that the electoral franchise is "precious" and "fundamental," and to conclude that "[t]o introduce wealth or payment of a fee as a measure of a voter's qualifications is to introduce a capricious or irrelevant factor." These are of course captivating phrases, but they are wholly inadequate to satisfy the standard governing adjudication of the equal protection issue: Is there a rational basis for Virginia's poll tax as a voting qualification? I think the answer to that question is undoubtedly "yes."

Property qualifications and poll taxes have been a traditional part of our political structure. In the Colonies the franchise was generally a restricted one. Over the years these and other restrictions were gradually lifted, primarily because popular theories of political representation had changed. Often restrictions were lifted only after wide public debate. The issue of woman suffrage, for example, raised question of family relationships, of participation in public affairs, of the very nature of the type of society in which Americans wished to live; eventually a consensus was reached, which culminated in the Nineteenth Amendment no more than 45 years ago.

Similarly with property qualifications, it is only by fiat that it can be said, especially in the context of American history, that there can be no rational debate as to their advisability. Most of the early Colonies had them; many of the States have had them during much of their histories; and, whether one agrees or not, arguments have been and still can be made in favor of them. For example, it is certainly a rational argument that payment of some minimal poll tax promotes civic responsibility, weeding out those who do not care enough about public affairs to pay $1.50 or thereabouts a year for the exercise of the franchise. It is also arguable, indeed it was probably accepted as sound political theory by a large percentage of Americans through most of our history, that people with some property have a deeper stake in community affairs, and are consequently more responsible, more educated, more knowledgeable, more worthy of confidence, than those without means, and that the community and Nation would be better managed if the franchise were restricted to such citizens. Nondiscriminatory and fairly applied literacy tests, upheld by this Court in *Lassiter v. Northampton County Board of Elections*, find justification on very similar grounds.

These viewpoints, to be sure, ring hollow on most contemporary ears. Their lack of acceptance today is evidenced by the fact that nearly all of the States, left to their own devices, have eliminated property or poll-tax qualifications; by the cognate fact that Congress and three-quarters of the States quickly ratified the Twenty-Fourth Amendment; and by the fact that rules such as the "pauper exclusion" in Virginia law have never been enforced.

Property and poll-tax qualifications, very simply, are not in accord with current egalitarian notions of how a modern democracy should be organized. It is of course entirely fitting that legislatures should modify the law to reflect such changes in popular attitudes. However, it is all wrong, in my view, for the Court to adopt the political doctrines popularly accepted at a particular moment of our history and to declare all others to be irrational and invidious, barring them from the range of choice by reasonably minded people acting through the political process. It was not too long ago that Mr. Justice Holmes felt impelled to remind the Court that the Due Process Clause of the Fourteenth Amendment does not enact the *laissez-faire* theory of society, *Lochner v. New York*. The times have changed, and perhaps it is appropriate to observe that neither does the Equal Protection Clause of that Amendment rigidly impose upon America an ideology of unrestrained egalitarianism. . . .

Notes and Questions

1. For what purpose do the *Reynolds* and *Harper* Courts cite *Yick Wo*? Is that a fair characterization of the holding in *Yick Wo*, or does it seem more like dicta? How critical is *Yick Wo* to their conclusions that the right to vote is fundamental?

2. How can the Court's decisions in the *Reynolds* line of cases be harmonized with the Court's earlier decision in *Happersett*? Does the difference lie in the difference between the Privileges or Immunities Clause and the Equal Protection Clause? Or is it based on the fact that the Court up until this point has generally rejected all Fourteenth Amendment claims grounded in sex discrimination?

3. How persuasive is the *Harper* Court's distinction between literacy tests and poll taxes in terms of the strength of the governmental interest at stake? Are they not equally persuasive, or unpersuasive? Does it turn on the level of scrutiny being applied?

4. Is *Harper* a rights-based equal protection decision focused on the right to vote, a class-based equal protection decision focused on wealth discrimination, or an amalgam of the two? If the case is about wealth discrimination, does the case involve facial discrimination against the poor, or is there instead only a discriminatory effect on that class?

5. What is the nature of the right recognized in the *Reynolds* line of cases? Is it a freestanding universal guarantee that everyone has a right to vote for every type of public official, or a qualified right that turns on whether or not the government opts to make a position elective in nature? Consider the following:

> States do have latitude in determining whether certain public officials shall be selected by election or chosen by appointment and whether various questions shall be submitted to the voters. In fact, we have held that where a county school board is an administrative, not legislative, body, its members

> need not be elected. However, "once the franchise is granted to the electorate, lines may not be drawn which are inconsistent with the Equal Protection Clause of the Fourteenth Amendment." *Harper v. Virginia Bd. of Elections*. . . .
>
> For example, a city charter might well provide that the elected city council appoint a mayor who would have broad administrative powers. Assuming the council were elected consistent with the commands of the Equal Protection Clause, the delegation of power to the mayor would not call for this Court's exacting review. On the other hand, if the city charter made the office of mayor subject to an election in which only some resident citizens were entitled to vote, there would be presented a situation calling for our close review.

Kramer v. Union Free School Dist. No. 15, 395 U.S. 621, 629–30 (1969). *See also* Peter Nicolas, *Fundamental Rights in a Post-*Obergefell *World*, 27 Yale J.L. & Feminism 331, 358 (2016) ("In contrast to the enduring protection afforded fundamental rights protected by the Due Process Clause, fundamental rights protected by the Equal Protection Clause can be infringed upon or even eliminated by the government without raising any constitutional concerns, so long as the government does so evenhandedly and denies the right to everyone. Only if it infringes upon or denies the right to some individuals but not others is government's conduct subject to heightened scrutiny.").

6. What consequence does your answer to the questions posed in the previous note have for the right to procreate recognized in *Skinner*? In this regard, reconsider the separate opinions in *Skinner*, which suggested a decision on alternative grounds. Reconsider as well Justice Jackson's concurring opinion in *Railway Express*, in which he distinguished between deciding a case on due process versus equal protection grounds.

7. Is Justice Black correct in *Harper* to accuse the majority of reviving *Lochner* under the guise of the Equal Protection Clause? How, if at all, do the cases in this chapter differ from the repudiated *Locnher*-era cases?

8. What justifies heightened equal protection review for laws that restrict the right to vote? Consider the following justification:

> [T]he deference usually given to the judgment of legislators does not extend to decisions concerning which resident citizens may participate in the election of legislators and other public officials. Those decisions must be carefully scrutinized by the Court to determine whether each resident citizen has, as far as is possible, an equal voice in the selections. Accordingly, when we are reviewing statutes which deny some residents the right to vote, the general presumption of constitutionality afforded state statutes and the traditional approval given state classifications if the Court can conceive of a "rational basis" for the distinctions made are not applicable. *See Harper v. Virginia State Bd. of Elections*. The presumption of constitutionality and the

> approval given "rational" classifications in other types of enactments are based on an assumption that the institutions of state government are structured so as to represent fairly all the people. However, when the challenge to the statute is in effect a challenge of this basic assumption, the assumption can no longer serve as the basis for presuming constitutionality.

Kramer v. Union Free School Dist. No. 15, 395 U.S. 621, 627–28 (1969).

9. The 2000 election for U.S. President was extremely close, with the outcome potentially turning on the results of a recount of the vote in Florida. In a creative invocation of the *Reynolds* line of cases, a narrow conservative majority on the Court deemed the recount to be a violation of the fundamental right to vote:

> The individual citizen has no federal constitutional right to vote for electors for the President of the United States unless and until the state legislature chooses a statewide election as the means to implement its power to appoint members of the electoral college. U.S. Const., Art. II, § 1 . . . . The State, of course, after granting the franchise in the special context of Article II, can take back the power to appoint electors.
>
> The right to vote is protected in more than the initial allocation of the franchise. Equal protection applies as well to the manner of its exercise. Having once granted the right to vote on equal terms, the State may not, by later arbitrary and disparate treatment, value one person's vote over that of another. *See, e.g., Harper v. Virginia Bd. of Elections.* It must be remembered that "the right of suffrage can be denied by a debasement or dilution of the weight of a citizen's vote just as effectively as by wholly prohibiting the free exercise of the franchise." *Reynolds v. Sims*. . . .
>
> Much of the controversy seems to revolve around ballot cards designed to be perforated by a stylus but which, either through error or deliberate omission, have not been perforated with sufficient precision for a machine to register the perforations. In some cases a piece of the card—a chad—is hanging, say, by two corners. In other cases there is no separation at all, just an indentation.
>
> The Florida Supreme Court has ordered that the intent of the voter be discerned from such ballots. . . . The problem inheres in the absence of specific standards to ensure its equal application. . . .
>
> The want of those rules here has led to unequal evaluation of ballots in various respects. As seems to have been acknowledged at oral argument, the standards for accepting or rejecting contested ballots might vary not only from county to county but indeed within a single county from one recount team to another. . . .
>
> The recount process, in its features here described, is inconsistent with the minimum procedures necessary to protect the fundamental right of each voter in the special instance of a statewide recount under the authority of

> a single state judicial officer. Our consideration is limited to the present circumstances, for the problem of equal protection in election processes generally presents many complexities.

Bush v. Gore, 531 U.S. 98, 104–09 (2000). Note that in a reversal from the Court's decisions in *Reynolds* and *Harper*, in *Bush*, conservative Justices were in the majority arguing that a fundamental right was at stake, while the Court's four liberal Justices were in dissent contending otherwise. Does this state of affairs provide support for the view that fundamental rights jurisprudence is too malleable and subject to the political whims of the Court's majority?

C. The Right to Travel

Shapiro v. Thompson

394 U.S. 618 (1969)

Mr. Justice Brennan delivered the opinion of the Court.

These three appeals were restored to the calendar for reargument. Each is an appeal from a decision of a three-judge District Court holding unconstitutional a State or District of Columbia statutory provision which denies welfare assistance to residents of the State or District who have not resided within their jurisdictions for at least one year immediately preceding their applications for such assistance. We affirm the judgments of the District Courts in the three cases. . . .

II.

There is no dispute that the effect of the waiting-period requirement in each case is to create two classes of needy resident families indistinguishable from each other except that one is composed of residents who have resided a year or more, and the second of residents who have resided less than a year, in the jurisdiction. On the basis of this sole difference the first class is granted and the second class is denied welfare aid upon which may depend the ability of the families to obtain the very means to subsist—food, shelter, and other necessities of life. In each case, the

District Court found that appellees met the test for residence in their jurisdictions, as well as all other eligibility requirements except the requirement of residence for a full year prior to their applications. On reargument, appellees' central contention is that the statutory prohibition of benefits to residents of less than a year creates a classification which constitutes an invidious discrimination denying them equal protection of the laws. We agree. The interests which appellants assert are promoted by the classification either may not constitutionally be promoted by government or are not compelling governmental interests.

III.

Primarily, appellants justify the waiting-period requirement as a protective device to preserve the fiscal integrity of state public assistance programs. It is asserted that people who require welfare assistance during their first year of residence in a State are likely to become continuing burdens on state welfare programs. Therefore, the argument runs, if such people can be deterred from entering the jurisdiction by denying them welfare benefits during the first year, state programs to assist long-time residents will not be impaired by a substantial influx of indigent newcomers. . . .

We do not doubt that the one-year waiting period device is well suited to discourage the influx of poor families in need of assistance. An indigent who desires to migrate, resettle, find a new job, and start a new life will doubtless hesitate if he knows that he must risk making the move without the possibility of falling back on state welfare assistance during his first year of residence, when his need may be most acute. But the purpose of inhibiting migration by needy persons into the State is constitutionally impermissible.

This Court long ago recognized that the nature of our Federal Union and our constitutional concepts of personal liberty unite to require that all citizens be free to travel throughout the length and breadth of our land uninhibited by statutes, rules, or regulations which unreasonably burden or restrict this movement. . . .

We have no occasion to ascribe the source of this right to travel interstate to a particular constitutional provision.[8] It suffices that, as Mr. Justice Stewart said for the Court in *United States v. Guest*, 383 U.S. 745, 757–758 (1966):

---

8. In *Corfield v. Coryell*, 6 Fed.Cas. pp. 546, 552 (No. 3230) (C.C.E.D.Pa.1825), *Paul v. Virginia*, 8 Wall. (75 U.S.) 168, 180 (1869), and *Ward v. Maryland*, 12 Wall. (79 U.S.) 418, 430 (1871), the right to travel interstate was grounded upon the Privileges and Immunities Clause of Art. IV, § 2. In *Edwards v. California*, 314 U.S. 160, 181, 183–185 (1941) (Douglas and Jackson, JJ., concurring), and *Twining v. New Jersey*, *supra*, reliance was placed on the Privileges and Immunities Clause of the Fourteenth Amendment. In *Edwards v. California*, *supra*, and the *Passenger Cases*, 7 How. 283 (1849), a Commerce Clause approach was employed.

See also Kent v. Dulles, 357 U.S. 116, 125 (1958); *Aptheker v. Secretary of State*, 378 U.S. 500, 505–506 (1964); *Zemel v. Rusk*, 381 U.S. 1, 14 (1965), where the freedom of Americans to travel outside the country was grounded upon the Due Process Clause of the Fifth Amendment.

"The constitutional right to travel from one State to another . . . occupies a position fundamental to the concept of our Federal Union. It is a right that has been firmly established and repeatedly recognized.

". . . (The) right finds no explicit mention in the Constitution. The reason, it has been suggested, is that a right so elementary was conceived from the beginning to be a necessary concomitant of the stronger Union the Constitution created. In any event, freedom to travel throughout the United States has long been recognized as a basic right under the Constitution."

Thus, the purpose of deterring the in-migration of indigents cannot serve as justification for the classification created by the one-year waiting period, since that purpose is constitutionally impermissible. . . .

Appellants argue further that the challenged classification may be sustained as an attempt to distinguish between new and old residents on the basis of the contribution they have made to the community through the payment of taxes. . . . Appellants' reasoning would logically permit the State to bar new residents from schools, parks, and libraries or deprive them of police and fire protection. Indeed it would permit the State to apportion all benefits and services according to the past tax contributions of its citizens. The Equal Protection Clause prohibits such an apportionment of state services.

We recognize that a State has a valid interest in preserving the fiscal integrity of its programs. It may legitimately attempt to limit its expenditures, whether for public assistance, public education, or any other program. But a State may not accomplish such a purpose by invidious distinctions between classes of its citizens. . . .

IV.

Appellants next advance as justification certain administrative and related governmental objectives allegedly served by the waiting-period requirement. . . .

At the outset, we reject appellants' argument that a mere showing of a rational relationship between the waiting period and these four admittedly permissible state objectives will suffice to justify the classification. The waiting-period provision denies welfare benefits to otherwise eligible applicants solely because they have recently moved into the jurisdiction. But in moving from State to State or to the District of Columbia appellees were exercising a constitutional right, and any classification which serves to penalize the exercise of that right, unless shown to be necessary to promote a *compelling* governmental interest, is unconstitutional. *Cf. Skinner v. Oklahoma*.

[The Court concludes that none of the additional justifications for the law satisfy strict scrutiny.]

Mr. Justice Harlan, dissenting. . . .

In upholding the equal protection argument, the Court has applied an equal protection doctrine of relatively recent vintage: the rule that statutory classifications which either are based upon certain "suspect" criteria or affect "fundamental rights" will be held to deny equal protection unless justified by a "compelling" governmental interest.

The "compelling interest" doctrine, which today is articulated more explicitly than ever before, constitutes an increasingly significant exception to the long-established rule that a statute does not deny equal protection if it is rationally related to a legitimate governmental objective. The "compelling interest" doctrine has two branches. The branch which requires that classifications based upon "suspect" criteria be supported by a compelling interest apparently had its genesis in cases involving racial classifications, which have, at least since *Korematsu v. United States*, been regarded as inherently "suspect." The criterion of "wealth" apparently was added to the list of "suspects" as an alternative justification for the rationale in *Harper v. Virginia Bd. of Elections*. . . .

I think that this branch of the "compelling interest" doctrine is sound when applied to racial classifications, for historically the Equal Protection Clause was largely a product of the desire to eradicate legal distinctions founded upon race. However, I believe that the more recent extensions have been unwise. . . .

The second branch of the "compelling interest" principle is even more troublesome. For it has been held that a statutory classification is subject to the "compelling interest" test if the result of the classification may be to affect a "fundamental right," regardless of the basis of the classification. This rule was foreshadowed in *Skinner v. Oklahoma*, in which an Oklahoma statute providing for compulsory sterilization of "habitual criminals" was held subject to "strict scrutiny" mainly because it affected "one of the basic civil rights." After a long hiatus, the principle re-emerged in *Reynolds v. Sims*, in which state apportionment statutes were subjected to an unusually stringent test because "any alleged infringement of the right of citizens to vote must be carefully and meticulously scrutinized." . . . . This branch of the doctrine was also an alternate ground in *Harper v. Virginia Bd. of Elections*. . . .

I think this branch of the "compelling interest" doctrine particularly unfortunate and unnecessary. It is unfortunate because it creates an exception which threatens to swallow the standard equal protection rule. Virtually every state statute affects important rights. This Court has repeatedly held, for example, that the traditional equal protection standard is applicable to statutory classifications affecting such fundamental matters as the right to pursue a particular occupation, the right to receive greater or smaller wages or to work more or less hours, and the right to inherit property. Rights such as these are in principle indistinguishable from those involved here, and to extend the "compelling interest" rule to all cases in which such rights are affected would go far toward making this Court a "super-legislature." This branch of the doctrine is also unnecessary. When the right affected is one assured by the Federal Constitution, any infringement can be dealt with under the Due Process Clause. But when a statute affects only matters not mentioned in the Federal Constitution and is not arbitrary or irrational, I must reiterate that I know of nothing which entitles this Court to pick out particular human activities, characterize them as "fundamental," and give them added protection under an unusually stringent equal protection test. . . .

[The concurring opinion of Justice Stewart and the dissenting opinion of Chief Justice Warren are omitted.]

Notes and Questions

1. The Court, while somewhat unclear on the source of the right to travel, identifies various constitutional provisions *other than* the Equal Protection Clause. How, then, does the Equal Protection Clause come into play in this case, and why does the Court apply heightened equal protection scrutiny?

2. Does the entire line of cases presented in this chapter, as indicated by Justice Black in his *Harper* dissent and strongly implied by Justice Harlan in his *Shapiro* dissent, raise the very same sorts of problems that the *Lochner*-era cases raised? If not, how are the two lines of cases distinguishable?

Chapter 9

The Rise of Congressional Power to "Enforce" the Reconstruction Amendments

Recall from Chapter 2 that each of the three Reconstruction Amendments has a similarly worded provision giving Congress the power to "enforce" the Amendment by "appropriate" legislation. In *The Civil Rights Cases*, the Court considered the enforcement provisions of the Thirteenth and Fourteenth Amendments, and narrowly interpreted each in such a way as to make them of limited utility for justifying congressional legislation designed to combat racial and other forms of discrimination.

More specifically, the majority in *The Civil Rights Cases* did not seem to acknowledge that Congress had any power pursuant to the enforcement provisions that was broader than the self-executing provisions of the Reconstruction Amendments. Thus, with respect to Section 5 of the Fourteenth Amendment, the majority wrote:

> [T]he last section of the amendment invests Congress with power to enforce it by appropriate legislation. To enforce what? To enforce the prohibition.... This is the legislative power conferred upon Congress, and this is the whole of it.

109 U.S., at 11. Thus, because Section 1 of the Fourteenth Amendment encompassed only state action, the majority reasoned that Congress could only regulate state, not private, action pursuant to Section 5. Moreover, with respect to Section 2 of the Thirteenth Amendment, the majority *assumed* that it vested "Congress with power to pass all laws necessary and proper for abolishing all badges and incidents of slavery in the United States," but took a narrow view of "badges and incidents of slavery" that did not encompass exclusion from inns, places of public amusement, and the like.

As a direct consequence of *The Civil Rights Cases,* the enforcement provisions of the Thirteenth and Fourteenth Amendments lay dormant for some time as a means of supporting congressional authority to redress private discrimination. Thus, for example, when Congress enacted Title II of the Civil Rights Act of 1964—which outlawed discrimination in public accommodations on the basis of race—it was justified instead on the basis of Congress's Commerce Clause power. *See Heart of Atlanta Motel v. United States*, 379 U.S. 241 (1964); *Katzenbach v. McClung*, 379 U.S. 294 (1964)).

Although the Commerce Clause power as interpreted in *Heart of Atlanta Motel* and *McClung* filled an important gap left by the Court's decision in *The Civil Rights Cases*, it was of limited scope. Because successful invocation of the Commerce Clause power requires a showing of an impact on interstate commerce, that source of congressional power could thus not justify the regulation of purely intrastate discrimination.

Yet after nearly a century of dormancy, the U.S. Supreme Court breathed new life into the enforcement provisions of the Reconstruction Amendments in a series of decisions issued between 1966 and 1968. The first two of these cases upheld the Voting Rights Act of 1965 pursuant to Congress's power to enforce the Fourteenth and Fifteenth Amendments, while the third case upheld Congress's power to regulate private racial discrimination in the sale of real property. As you read each of these three cases, consider the following questions:

- What is the relationship between the scope of the enforcement provision and the self-executing provision of each Amendment? More specifically, to what extent can Congress regulate conduct pursuant to the enforcement provision of each Amendment that does not, standing alone, necessarily violate the self-executing provision?
- Is the relationship between the enforcement and self-executing provisions the same across all three Amendments? If not, how do they differ, and why?

A. The Fourteenth and Fifteenth Amendments

The Voting Rights Act of 1965 was a landmark piece of legislation enacted by Congress to combat disenfranchisement of racial and other minorities in certain parts of the United States, and contained a number of key features.

First, Section 4(a) of the Act suspended literacy tests or like devices prerequisite to voting for "covered jurisdictions." Moreover, Section 5 set forth a "preclearance" requirement for future changes to voting qualifications or procedures in covered jurisdictions. Under the preclearance procedure, a change could not go into effect unless approved by either the Attorney General of the United States or the federal district court in Washington, D.C. The standard for approving a preclearance request was a finding that the proposed change did not have the purpose *or* effect of reducing minority voting strength.

Sections 4(a) through 4(d) of the Act defined those areas that were "covered jurisdictions." Pursuant to those sections, a jurisdiction would be deemed covered under the act if on November 1, 1964, it maintained any test or device and had less than 50 percent of the voting-age population registered to vote or in which less than 50 percent of such persons voted in the 1964 presidential election. However, under the Act, such a jurisdiction would not remain covered indefinitely. Pursuant to the Act, they would no longer be deemed covered if five years had passed without the use of any tests or devices to abridge voting on racial grounds.

Finally, Section 4(e) of the Act prohibited literacy tests everywhere in the United States for those who had completed the sixth grade in a school in Puerto Rico in a language other than English.

Congress invoked Section 2 of the Fifteenth Amendment to justify its power to enact Sections 4(a) through 4(d) and Section 5 of the Act, and it invoked Section 5 of the Fourteenth Amendment to justify its power to enact Section 4(e) of the Act. In the two cases that follow, the Court upheld Congress's power to enact all of these provisions of the Act.

South Carolina v. Katzenbach

383 U.S. 301 (1966)

Mr. Chief Justice Warren delivered the opinion of the Court.

By leave of the Court, South Carolina has filed a bill of complaint, seeking a declaration that selected provisions of the Voting Rights Act of 1965 violate the Federal Constitution, and asking for an injunction against enforcement of these provisions by the Attorney General. . . .

The Voting Rights Act was designed by Congress to banish the blight of racial discrimination in voting, which has infected the electoral process in parts of our country for nearly a century. The Act creates stringent new remedies for voting discrimination where it persists on a pervasive scale, and in addition the statute strengthens existing remedies for pockets of voting discrimination elsewhere in the country. Congress assumed the power to prescribe these remedies from § 2 of the Fifteenth Amendment, which authorizes the National Legislature to effectuate by "appropriate" measures the constitutional prohibition against racial discrimination in voting. We hold that the sections of the Act which are properly before us are an appropriate means for carrying out Congress' constitutional responsibilities and are consonant with all other provisions of the Constitution. . . .

I.

The constitutional propriety of the Voting Rights Act of 1965 must be judged with reference to the historical experience which it reflects. Before enacting the measure, Congress explored with great care the problem of racial discrimination in voting. The House and Senate Committees on the Judiciary each held hearings for nine days and received testimony from a total of 67 witnesses. More than three full days were consumed discussing the bill on the floor of the House, while the debate in the Senate covered 26 days in all. At the close of these deliberations, the verdict of both chambers was overwhelming. The House approved the bill by a vote of 328-74, and the measure passed the Senate by a margin of 79-18.

Two points emerge vividly from the voluminous legislative history of the Act contained in the committee hearings and floor debates. First: Congress felt itself confronted by an insidious and pervasive evil which had been perpetuated in certain parts of our country through unremitting and ingenious defiance of the

Constitution. Second: Congress concluded that the unsuccessful remedies which it had prescribed in the past would have to be replaced by sterner and more elaborate measures in order to satisfy the clear commands of the Fifteenth Amendment....

The Fifteenth Amendment to the Constitution was ratified in 1870. Promptly thereafter Congress passed the Enforcement Act of 1870, which made it a crime for public officers and private persons to obstruct exercise of the right to vote. The statute was amended in the following year to provide for detailed federal supervision of the electoral process, from registration to the certification of returns. As the years passed and fervor for racial equality waned, enforcement of the laws became spotty and ineffective, and most of their provisions were repealed in 1894. The remnants have had little significance in the recently renewed battle against voting discrimination.

Meanwhile, beginning in 1890, the States of Alabama, Georgia, Louisiana, Mississippi, North Carolina, South Carolina, and Virginia enacted tests still in use which were specifically designed to prevent Negroes from voting. Typically, they made the ability to read and write a registration qualification and also required completion of a registration form. These laws were based on the fact that as of 1890 in each of the named States, more than two-thirds of the adult Negroes were illiterate while less than one-quarter of the adult whites were unable to read or write. At the same time, alternate tests were prescribed in all of the named States to assure that white illiterates would not be deprived of the franchise. These included grandfather clauses, property qualifications, "good character" tests, and the requirement that registrants "understand" or "interpret" certain matter.

The course of subsequent Fifteenth Amendment litigation in this Court demonstrates the variety and persistence of these and similar institutions designed to deprive Negroes of the right to vote. Grandfather clauses were invalidated in *Guinn v. United States*, 238 U.S. 347, and *Myers v. Anderson*, 238 U.S. 368. Procedural hurdles were struck down in *Lane v. Wilson*, 307 U.S. 268. The white primary was outlawed in *Smith v. Allwright*, 321 U.S. 649, and *Terry v. Adams*, 345 U.S. 461. Improper challenges were nullified in *United States v. Thomas*, 362 U.S. 58. Racial gerrymandering was forbidden by *Gomillion v. Lightfoot*, 364 U.S. 339. Finally, discriminatory application of voting tests was condemned in *Schnell v. Davis*, 336 U.S. 933; *Alabama v. United States*, 371 U.S. 37, and *Louisiana v. United States*, 380 U.S. 145.

According to the evidence in recent Justice Department voting suits, the latter stratagem is now the principal method used to bar Negroes from the polls.... Moreover, in almost all of these cases, the courts have held that the discrimination was pursuant to a widespread "pattern or practice." White applicants for registration have often been excused altogether from the literacy and understanding tests or have been given easy versions, have received extensive help from voting officials, and have been registered despite serious errors in their answers. Negroes, on the other hand, have typically been required to pass difficult versions of all the tests, without any outside assistance and without the slightest error. The good-morals requirement is so vague and subjective that it has constituted an open invitation to abuse at the hands of voting officials. Negroes obliged to obtain vouchers from registered voters have found it virtually impossible to comply in areas where almost no Negroes are on the rolls.

In recent years, Congress has repeatedly tried to cope with the problem by facilitating case-by-case litigation against voting discrimination. The Civil Rights Act of 1957 authorized the Attorney General to seek injunctions against public and private interference with the right to vote on racial grounds. Perfecting amendments in the Civil Rights Act of 1960 permitted the joinder of States as parties defendant, gave the Attorney General access to local voting records, and authorized courts to register voters in areas of systematic discrimination. Title I of the Civil Rights Act of 1964 expedited the hearing of voting cases before three-judge courts and outlawed some of the tactics used to disqualify Negroes from voting in federal elections.

Despite the earnest efforts of the Justice Department and of many federal judges, these new laws have done little to cure the problem of voting discrimination. According to estimates by the Attorney General during hearings on the Act, registration of voting-age Negroes in Alabama rose only from 14.2% to 19.4% between 1958 and 1964; in Louisiana it barely inched ahead from 31.7% to 31.8% between 1956 and 1965; and in Mississippi it increased only from 4.4% to 6.4% between 1954 and 1964. In each instance, registration of voting-age whites ran roughly 50 percentage points or more ahead of Negro registration. . . .

II.

The Voting Rights Act of 1965 reflects Congress' firm intention to rid the country of racial discrimination in voting. The heart of the Act is a complex scheme of stringent remedies aimed at areas where voting discrimination has been most flagrant. [The Court here provides a detailed explanation of Sections 4(a) through 4(d) and Section 5 of the Act.] . . . .

III.

These provisions of the Voting Rights Act of 1965 are challenged on the fundamental ground that they exceed the powers of Congress and encroach on an area reserved to the States by the Constitution. . . .

The ground rules for resolving this question are clear. The language and purpose of the Fifteenth Amendment, the prior decisions construing its several provisions, and the general doctrines of constitutional interpretation, all point to one fundamental principle. As against the reserved powers of the States, Congress may use any rational means to effectuate the constitutional prohibition of racial discrimination in voting. . . .

Section 1 of the Fifteenth Amendment declares that "[t]he right of citizens of the United States to vote shall not be denied or abridged by the United States or by any State on account of race, color, or previous condition of servitude." This declaration has always been treated as self-executing and has repeatedly been construed, without further legislative specification, to invalidate state voting qualifications or procedures which are discriminatory on their face or in practice. . . .

South Carolina contends that the cases cited above are precedents only for the authority of the judiciary to strike down state statutes and procedures—that to allow an exercise of this authority by Congress would be to rob the courts of their rightful constitutional role. On the contrary, § 2 of the Fifteenth Amendment expressly declares that "Congress shall have power to enforce this article by appropriate legislation." By adding this authorization, the Framers indicated that Congress was to be chiefly responsible for implementing the rights created in § 1. "It is the power of Congress which has been enlarged. Congress is authorized to enforce the prohibitions by appropriate legislation Some legislation is contemplated to make the (Civil War) amendments fully effective." *Ex parte Virginia*, 100 U.S. 339, 345. Accordingly, in addition to the courts, Congress has full remedial powers to effectuate the constitutional prohibition against racial discrimination in voting. . . .

The basic test to be applied in a case involving § 2 of the Fifteenth Amendment is the same as in all cases concerning the express powers of Congress with relation to the reserved powers of the States. Chief Justice Marshall laid down the classic formulation, 50 years before the Fifteenth Amendment was ratified:

> "Let the end be legitimate, let it be within the scope of the constitution, and all means which are appropriate, which are plainly adapted to that end, which are not prohibited, but consist with the letter and spirit of the constitution, are constitutional." *McCulloch v. Maryland*, 4 Wheat. 316, 421.

. . . .

IV.

Congress exercised its authority under the Fifteenth Amendment in an inventive manner when it enacted the Voting Rights Act of 1965. First: The measure prescribes remedies for voting discrimination which go into effect without any need for prior adjudication. This was clearly a legitimate response to the problem, for which there is ample precedent under other constitutional provisions. Congress had found that case-by-case litigation was inadequate to combat widespread and persistent discrimination in voting, because of the inordinate amount of time and energy required to overcome the obstructionist tactics invariably encountered in these lawsuits. After enduring nearly a century of systematic resistance to the Fifteenth Amendment, Congress might well decide to shift the advantage of time and inertia from the perpetrators of the evil to its victims. The question remains, of course, whether the specific remedies prescribed in the Act were an appropriate means of combatting the evil, and to this question we shall presently address ourselves.

Second: The Act intentionally confines these remedies to a small number of States and political subdivisions which in most instances were familiar to Congress by name. This, too, was a permissible method of dealing with the problem. Congress had learned that substantial voting discrimination presently occurs in certain sections of the country, and it knew no way of accurately forecasting whether the evil might spread elsewhere in the future. In acceptable legislative fashion, Congress chose to limit its attention to the geographic areas where immediate action seemed necessary. . . .

We now consider the related question of whether the specific States and political subdivisions within §4(b) of the Act were an appropriate target for the new remedies. South Carolina contends that the coverage formula is awkwardly designed in a number of respects and that it disregards various local conditions which have nothing to do with racial discrimination. These arguments, however, are largely beside the point. Congress began work with reliable evidence of actual voting discrimination in a great majority of the States and political subdivisions affected by the new remedies of the Act. The formula eventually evolved to describe these areas was relevant to the problem of voting discrimination, and Congress was therefore entitled to infer a significant danger of the evil in the few remaining States and political subdivisions covered by §4(b) of the Act. No more was required to justify the application to these areas of Congress' express powers under the Fifteenth Amendment. . . .

It is irrelevant that the coverage formula excludes certain localities which do not employ voting tests and devices but for which there is evidence of voting discrimination by other means. Congress had learned that widespread and persistent discrimination in voting during recent years has typically entailed the misuse of tests and devices, and this was the evil for which the new remedies were specifically designed. At the same time, through §§3, 6(a), and 13(b) of the Act, Congress strengthened existing remedies for voting discrimination in other areas of the country. Legislation need not deal with all phases of a problem in the same way, so long as the distinctions drawn have some basis in practical experience. See *Williamson v. Lee Optical Co.*, 348 U.S. 483, 488-489; *Railway Express Agency v. New York*, 336 U.S. 106. There are no States or political subdivisions exempted from coverage under §4(b) in which the record reveals recent racial discrimination involving tests and devices. This fact confirms the rationality of the formula.

Acknowledging the possibility of overbreadth, the Act provides for termination of special statutory coverage at the behest of States and political subdivisions in which the danger of substantial voting discrimination has not materialized during the preceding five years. . . .

We now arrive at consideration of the specific remedies prescribed by the Act for areas included within the coverage formula. South Carolina assails the temporary suspension of existing voting qualifications, reciting the rule laid down by *Lassiter v. Northampton County Bd. of Elections*, 360 U.S. 45, that literacy tests and related devices are not in themselves contrary to the Fifteenth Amendment. In that very case, however, the Court went on to say, "Of course a literacy test, fair on its face, may be employed to perpetuate that discrimination which the Fifteenth Amendment was designed to uproot." *Id.*, at 53. The record shows that in most of the States covered by the Act, including South Carolina, various tests and devices have been instituted with the purpose of disenfranchising Negroes, have been framed in such a way as to facilitate this aim, and have been administered in a discriminatory fashion for many years. Under these circumstances, the Fifteenth Amendment has clearly been violated.

The Act suspends literacy tests and similar devices for a period of five years from the last occurrence of substantial voting discrimination. This was a legitimate response to the problem, for which there is ample precedent in Fifteenth Amendment cases. Underlying the response was the feeling that States and political subdivisions which had been allowing white illiterates to vote for years could not sincerely complain about "dilution" of their electorates through the registration of Negro illiterates. Congress knew that continuance of the tests and devices in use at the present time, no matter how fairly administered in the future, would freeze the effect of past discrimination in favor of unqualified white registrants. Congress permissibly rejected the alternative of requiring a complete re-registration of all voters, believing that this would be too harsh on many whites who had enjoyed the franchise for their entire adult lives. . . .

The Act suspends new voting regulations pending scrutiny by federal authorities to determine whether their use would violate the Fifteenth Amendment. This may have been an uncommon exercise of congressional power, as South Carolina contends, but the Court has recognized that exceptional conditions can justify legislative measures not otherwise appropriate. Congress knew that some of the States covered by § 4(b) of the Act had resorted to the extraordinary stratagem of contriving new rules of various kinds for the sole purpose of perpetuating voting discrimination in the face of adverse federal court decrees. Congress had reason to suppose that these States might try similar maneuvers in the future in order to evade the remedies for voting discrimination contained in the Act itself. Under the compulsion of these unique circumstances, Congress responded in a permissibly decisive manner. . . .

The Act authorizes the appointment of federal examiners to list qualified applicants who are thereafter entitled to vote, subject to an expeditious challenge procedure. This was clearly an appropriate response to the problem, closely related to remedies authorized in prior cases. In many of the political subdivisions covered by § 4(b) of the Act, voting officials have persistently employed a variety of procedural tactics to deny Negroes the franchise, often in direct defiance or evasion of federal court decrees. Congress realized that merely to suspend voting rules which have been misused or are subject to misuse might leave this localized evil undisturbed. As for the briskness of the challenge procedure, Congress knew that in some of the areas affected, challenges had been persistently employed to harass registered Negroes. It chose to forestall this abuse, at the same time providing alternative ways for removing persons listed through error or fraud. In addition to the judicial challenge procedure, § 7(d) allows for the removal of names by the examiner himself, and § 11(c) makes it a crime to obtain a listing through fraud. . . .

After enduring nearly a century of widespread resistance to the Fifteenth Amendment, Congress has marshalled an array of potent weapons against the evil, with authority in the Attorney General to employ them effectively. Many of the areas directly affected by this development have indicated their willingness to abide by any restraints legitimately imposed upon them. We here hold that the portions of the Voting Rights Act properly before us are a valid means for carrying out the commands of the Fifteenth Amendment. Hopefully, millions of non-white Americans will now be able to participate for the first time on an equal basis in the government under which they live. We may finally look forward to the day when truly "[t]he right of citizens of the United States to vote shall not be denied or abridged by the United States or by any State on account of race, color, or previous condition of servitude."

The bill of complaint is dismissed.

[The opinion of Justice Black, concurring in part and dissenting in part, is omitted.]

Katzenbach v. Morgan

384 U.S. 641 (1966)

Mr. Justice Brennan delivered the opinion of the Court.

These cases concern the constitutionality of § 4(e) of the Voting Rights Act of 1965. That law, in the respects pertinent in these cases, provides that no person who has successfully completed the sixth primary grade in a public school in, or a private school accredited by, the Commonwealth of Puerto Rico in which the language of instruction was other than English shall be denied the right to vote in any election because of his inability to read or write English. Appellees, registered voters in New York City, brought this suit to challenge the constitutionality of § 4(e) insofar as it pro tanto prohibits the enforcement of the election laws of New York requiring an ability to read and write English as a condition of voting. Under these laws many of the several hundred thousand New York City residents who have migrated there from the Commonwealth of Puerto Rico had previously been denied the right to vote, and appellees attack § 4(e) insofar as it would enable many of these citizens to vote. . . .

We hold that, in the application challenged in these cases, § 4(e) is a proper exercise of the powers granted to Congress by § 5 of the Fourteenth Amendment and that by force of the Supremacy Clause, Article VI, the New York English literacy requirement cannot be enforced to the extent that it is inconsistent with § 4(e) . . . .

The Attorney General of the State of New York argues that an exercise of congressional power under § 5 of the Fourteenth Amendment that prohibits the enforcement of a state law can only be sustained if the judicial branch determines that the state law is prohibited by the provisions of the Amendment that Congress sought to enforce. More specifically, he urges that § 4(e) cannot be sustained as appropriate legislation to enforce the Equal Protection Clause unless the judiciary decides—even with the guidance of a congressional judgment—that the application of the English literacy requirement prohibited by § 4(e) is forbidden by the Equal Protection Clause itself. We disagree. Neither the language nor history of § 5 supports such a construction. As was said with regard to § 5 in *Ex parte Virginia*, 100 U.S. 339, 345.

"It is the power of Congress which has been enlarged. Congress is authorized to enforce the prohibitions by appropriate legislation. Some legislation is contemplated to make the amendments fully effective." A construction of § 5 that would require a judicial determination that the enforcement of the state law precluded by Congress violated the Amendment, as a condition of sustaining the congressional enactment, would depreciate both congressional resourcefulness and congressional responsibility for implementing the Amendment. It would confine the legislative power in this context to the insignificant role of abrogating only those state laws that the judicial branch was prepared to adjudge unconstitutional, or of merely informing the judgment of the judiciary by particularizing the "majestic generalities" of § 1 of the Amendment.

Thus our task in this case is not to determine whether the New York English literacy requirement as applied to deny the right to vote to a person who successfully completed the sixth grade in a Puerto Rican school violates the Equal Protection Clause. Accordingly, our decision in *Lassiter v. Northampton County Bd. of Election*, 360 U.S. 45, sustaining the North Carolina English literacy requirement as not in all circumstances prohibited by the first sections of the Fourteenth and Fifteenth Amendments, is inapposite. *Lassiter* did not present the question before us here: Without regard to whether the judiciary would find that the Equal Protection Clause itself nullifies New York's English literacy requirement as so applied, could Congress prohibit the enforcement of the state law by legislating under § 5 of the Fourteenth Amendment? In answering this question, our task is limited to determining whether such legislation is, as required by § 5, appropriate legislation to enforce the Equal Protection Clause.

By including § 5 the draftsmen sought to grant to Congress, by a specific provision applicable to the Fourteenth Amendment, the same broad powers expressed in the Necessary and Proper Clause, Art. I, § 8, cl. 18. The classic formulation of the reach of those powers was established by Chief Justice Marshall in *McCulloch v. Maryland*, 4 Wheat. 316, 421:

> "Let the end be legitimate, let it be within the scope of the constitution, and all means which are appropriate, which are plainly adapted to that end, which are not prohibited, but consist with the letter and spirit of the constitution, are constitutional."

Ex parte Virginia, 100 U.S., at 345-346, decided 12 years after the adoption of the Fourteenth Amendment, held that congressional power under § 5 had this same broad scope....

Section 2 of the Fifteenth Amendment grants Congress a similar power to enforce by "appropriate legislation" the provisions of that amendment; and we recently held in *South Carolina v. Katzenbach*, 383 U.S. 301, 326, that "[t]he basic test to be applied in a case involving § 2 of the Fifteenth Amendment is the same as in all cases concerning the express powers of Congress with relation to the reserved powers of the States." That test was identified as the one formulated in *McCulloch v. Maryland*.

Thus the *McCulloch v. Maryland* standard is the measure of what constitutes 'appropriate legislation' under § 5 of the Fourteenth Amendment. Correctly viewed, § 5 is a positive grant of legislative power authorizing Congress to exercise its discretion in determining whether and what legislation is needed to secure the guarantees of the Fourteenth Amendment.

We therefore proceed to the consideration whether § 4(e) is "appropriate legislation" to enforce the Equal Protection Clause, that is, under the *McCulloch v. Maryland* standard, whether § 4(e) may be regarded as an enactment to enforce the Equal Protection Clause, whether it is "plainly adapted to that end" and whether it is not prohibited by but is consistent with "the letter and spirit of the constitution."[10]

There can be no doubt that § 4(e) may be regarded as an enactment to enforce the Equal Protection Clause. Congress explicitly declared that it enacted § 4(e) "to secure the rights under the fourteenth amendment of persons educated in American-flag schools in which the predominant classroom language was other than English." The persons referred to include those who have migrated from the Commonwealth of Puerto Rico to New York and who have been denied the right to vote because of their inability to read and write English, and the Fourteenth Amendment rights referred to include those emanating from the Equal Protection Clause. More specifically, § 4(e) may be viewed as a measure to secure for the Puerto Rican community residing in New York nondiscriminatory treatment by government—both in the imposition of voting qualifications and the provision or administration of governmental services, such as public schools, public housing and law enforcement.

Section 4(e) may be readily seen as "plainly adapted" to furthering these aims of the Equal Protection Clause. The practical effect of § 4(e) is to prohibit New York from denying the right to vote to large segments of its Puerto Rican community. Congress has thus prohibited the State from denying to that community the right that is "preservative of all rights." *Yick Wo v. Hopkins*, 118 U.S. 356, 370. This enhanced political power will be helpful in gaining nondiscriminatory treatment in public services for the entire Puerto Rican community. Section 4(e) thereby enables the Puerto Rican minority better to obtain "perfect equality of civil rights and the equal protection of the laws." It was well within congressional authority to say that this need of the Puerto Rican minority for the vote warranted federal intrusion upon any state interests served by the English literacy requirement. It was for Congress, as the branch that made this judgment, to assess and weigh the various conflicting

---

10. Contrary to the suggestion of the dissent, § 5 does not grant Congress power to exercise discretion in the other direction and to enact "statutes so as in effect to dilute equal protection and due process decisions of this Court." We emphasize that Congress' power under § 5 is limited to adopting measures to enforce the guarantees of the Amendment; § 5 grants Congress no power to restrict, abrogate, or dilute these guarantees. Thus, for example, an enactment authorizing the States to establish racially segregated systems of education would not be—as required by § 5—a measure "to enforce" the Equal Protection Clause since that clause of its own force prohibits such state laws.

considerations—the risk or pervasiveness of the discrimination in governmental services, the effectiveness of eliminating the state restriction on the right to vote as a means of dealing with the evil, the adequacy or availability of alternative remedies, and the nature and significance of the state interests that would be affected by the nullification of the English literacy requirement as applied to residents who have successfully completed the sixth grade in a Puerto Rican school. It is not for us to review the congressional resolution of these factors. It is enough that we be able to perceive a basis upon which the Congress might resolve the conflict as it did. There plainly was such a basis to support § 4(e) in the application in question in this case. Any contrary conclusion would require us to be blind to the realities familiar to the legislators.

The result is no different if we confine our inquiry to the question whether § 4(e) was merely legislation aimed at the elimination of an invidious discrimination in establishing voter qualifications. We are told that New York's English literacy requirement originated in the desire to provide an incentive for non-English speaking immigrants to learn the English language and in order to assure the intelligent exercise of the franchise. Yet Congress might well have questioned, in light of the many exemptions provided, and some evidence suggesting that prejudice played a prominent role in the enactment of the requirement, whether these were actually the interests being served. Congress might have also questioned whether denial of a right deemed so precious and fundamental in our society was a necessary or appropriate means of encouraging persons to learn English, or of furthering the goal of an intelligent exercise of the franchise. Finally, Congress might well have concluded that as a means of furthering the intelligent exercise of the franchise, an ability to read or understand Spanish is as effective as ability to read English for those to whom Spanish-language newspapers and Spanish-language radio and television programs are available to inform them of election issues and governmental affairs. Since Congress undertook to legislate so as to preclude the enforcement of the state law, and did so in the context of a general appraisal of literacy requirements for voting, see *South Carolina v. Katzenbach*, *supra*, to which it brought a specially informed legislative competence, it was Congress' prerogative to weigh these competing considerations. Here again, it is enough that we perceive a basis upon which Congress might predicate a judgment that the application of New York's English literacy requirement to deny the right to vote to a person with a sixth grade education in Puerto Rican schools in which the language of instruction was other than English constituted an invidious discrimination in violation of the Equal Protection Clause. . . .

Mr. Justice Harlan, whom Mr. Justice Stewart joins, dissenting. . . .

The Court declares that since § 5 of the Fourteenth Amendment gives to the Congress power to "enforce" the prohibitions of the Amendment by "appropriate" legislation, the test for judicial review of any congressional determination in this area is simply one of rationality; that is, in effect, was Congress acting rationally in declaring that the New York statute is irrational? Although § 5 most certainly does give to the Congress wide powers in the field of devising remedial legislation to effectuate the Amendment's prohibition on arbitrary state action, I believe the Court has confused the issue of how much enforcement power Congress possesses under §5 with the distinct issue of what questions are appropriate for congressional determination and what questions are essentially judicial in nature.

When recognized state violations of federal constitutional standards have occurred, Congress is of course empowered by §5 to take appropriate remedial measures to redress and prevent the wrongs. See *Strauder v. West Virginia*, 100 U.S. 303. But it is a judicial question whether the condition with which Congress has thus sought to deal is in truth an infringement of the Constitution, something that is the necessary prerequisite to bringing the §5 power into play at all. Thus, in *Ex parte Virginia*, *supra*, involving a federal statute making it a federal crime to disqualify anyone from jury service because of race, the Court first held as a matter of constitutional law that "the Fourteenth Amendment secures, among other civil rights, to colored men, when charged with criminal offences against a State, an impartial jury trial, by jurors indifferently selected or chosen without discrimination against such jurors because of their color." 100 U.S. at 345. Only then did the Court hold that to enforce this prohibition upon state discrimination, Congress could enact a criminal statute of the type under consideration. . . .

A more recent Fifteenth Amendment case also serves to illustrate this distinction. In *South Carolina v. Katzenbach*, 383 U.S. 301, decided earlier this Term, we held certain remedial sections of this Voting Rights Act of 1965 constitutional under the Fifteenth Amendment, which is directed against deprivations of the right to vote on account of race. In enacting those sections of the Voting Rights Act the Congress made a detailed investigation of various state practices that had been used to deprive Negroes of the franchise. In passing upon the remedial provisions, we reviewed first the 'voluminous legislative history' as well as judicial precedents supporting the basic congressional finding that the clear commands of the Fifteenth Amendment had been infringed by various state subterfuges. Given the existence of the evil, we held the remedial steps taken by the legislature under the Enforcement Clause of the Fifteenth Amendment to be a justifiable exercise of congressional initiative.

Section 4(e), however, presents a significantly different type of congressional enactment. The question here is not whether the statute is appropriate remedial legislation to cure an established violation of a constitutional command, but whether there has in fact been an infringement of that constitutional command, that is, whether a particular state practice or, as here, a statute is so arbitrary or irrational as to offend the command of the Equal Protection Clause of the Fourteenth Amendment. That question is one for the judicial branch ultimately to determine. Were the rule otherwise, Congress would be able to qualify this Court's constitutional decisions under the Fourteenth and Fifteenth Amendments let alone those under other provisions of the Constitution, by resorting to congressional power under the Necessary and Proper Clause. In view of this Court's holding in *Lassiter*, *supra*, that an English literacy test is a permissible exercise of state supervision over its franchise, I do not think it is open to Congress to limit the effect of that decision as it has undertaken to do by § 4(e). In effect the Court reads § 5 of the Fourteenth Amendment as giving Congress the power to define the *substantive* scope of the Amendment. If that indeed be the true reach of § 5, then I do not see why Congress should not be able as well to exercise its § 5 "discretion" by enacting statutes so as in effect to dilute equal protection and due process decisions of this Court. In all such cases there is room for reasonable men to differ as to whether or not a denial of equal protection or due process has occurred, and the final decision is one of judgment. Until today this judgment has always been one for the judiciary to resolve.

I do not mean to suggest in what has been said that a legislative judgment of the type incorporated in § 4(e) is without any force whatsoever. Decisions on questions of equal protection and due process are based not on abstract logic, but on empirical foundations. To the extent "legislative facts" are relevant to a judicial determination, Congress is well equipped to investigate them, and such determinations are of course entitled to due respect. In *South Carolina v. Katzenbach*, *supra*, such legislative findings were made to show that racial discrimination in voting was actually occurring. Similarly, in *Heart of Atlanta Motel, Inc. v. United States*, 379 U.S. 241, and *Katzenbach v. McClung*, 379 U.S. 294, this Court upheld Title II of the Civil Rights Act of 1964 under the Commerce Clause. There again the congressional determination that racial discrimination in a clearly defined group of public accommodations did effectively impede interstate commerce was based on "voluminous testimony," 379 U.S., at 253, which had been put before the Congress and in the context of which it passed remedial legislation.

But no such factual data provide a legislative record supporting § 4(e) by way of showing that Spanish-speaking citizens are fully as capable of making informed decisions in a New York election as are English-speaking citizens. Nor was there any showing whatever to support the Court's alternative argument that § 4(e) should be viewed as but a remedial measure designed to cure or assure against unconstitutional discrimination of other varieties, e.g., in "public schools, public housing and law enforcement," 384 U.S., p. 652, to which Puerto Rican minorities might be subject in such communities as New York. . . .

Thus, we have here not a matter of giving deference to a congressional estimate, based on its determination of legislative facts, bearing upon the validity *vel non* of a statute, but rather what can at most be called a legislative announcement that Congress believes a state law to entail an unconstitutional deprivation of equal protection. Although this kind of declaration is of course entitled to the most respectful consideration, coming as it does from a concurrent branch and one that is knowledgeable in matters of popular political participation, I do not believe it lessens our responsibility to decide the fundamental issue of whether in fact the state enactment violates federal constitutional rights. . . .

To deny the effectiveness of this congressional enactment is not of course to disparage Congess' exertion of authority in the field of civil rights; it is simply to recognize that the Legislative Branch like the other branches of federal authority is subject to the governmental boundaries set by the Constitution. To hold, on this record, that § 4(e) overrides the New York literacy requirement seems to me tantamount to allowing the Fourteenth Amendment to swallow the State's constitutionally ordained primary authority in this field. For if Congress by what, as here, amounts to mere *ipse dixit* can set that otherwise permissible requirement partially at naught I see no reason why it could not also substitute its judgment for that of the States in other fields of their exclusive primary competence as well. . . .

[The concurring opinion of Justice Douglas is omitted.]

Notes and Questions

1. If *Lassiter* held that literacy tests do not *per se* violate Section 1 of the Fifteenth Amendment, how can the *South Carolina* Court justify Congress banning such tests pursuant to Section 2 of the Fifteenth Amendment? Does that suggest that Congress's enforcement power pursuant to Section 2 is significantly broader than the self-executing provisions of Section 1? Or is Congress's exercise of power in *South Carolina* under Section 2 justified by a factual finding of actual violations of Section 1?

2. What level of scrutiny does the *South Carolina* Court apply to Congress's exercise of its power to enforce the Fifteenth Amendment via Section 2? Note in this regard that the *South Carolina* Court cites *McCulloch v. Maryland*, *Lee Optical* and *Railway Express*.

3. What level of scrutiny does the *Morgan* Court apply to Congress's exercise of its power to enforce the Fourteenth Amendment via Section 5? Is it analogous to the way in which the Court interpreted the scope of Congress's power to enforce the Fifteenth Amendment via Section 2? Are there policy reasons why the scope of congressional power should be broader under one of these enforcement sections than the other, or does the equivalent text used in the two provisions justify a similarly broad interpretation of congressional power under each provision?

4. Is there a reading of *Morgan* that arguably puts it in conflict with the Court's decision in *Marbury v. Madison*, 5 U.S. 137 (1803), in which the Court declared that "[i]t is emphatically the province and duty of the judicial department to say what the law is."? In this regard, what is the significance, if any, of the Court's caveat in footnote 10?

5. Both *South Carolina* and *Morgan* can be read in ways that suggest breathtakingly sweeping congressional power pursuant to Section 5 of the Fourteenth Amendment and Section 2 of the Fifteenth Amendment. Is there a way to interpret the decisions in a way that more narrowly cabins the scope of congressional power under these enforcement provisions?

B. The Thirteenth Amendment

Jones v. Alfred H. Mayer Co.

392 U.S. 409 (1968)

MR. JUSTICE STEWART delivered the opinion of the Court.

In this case we are called upon to determine the scope and constitutionality of an Act of Congress, 42 U.S.C. § 1982, which provides that:

> "All citizens of the United States shall have the same right, in every State and Territory, as is enjoyed by white citizens thereof to inherit, purchase, lease, sell, hold, and convey real and personal property."

On September 2, 1965, the petitioners filed a complaint in the District Court for the Eastern District of Missouri, alleging that the respondents had refused to sell them a home in the Paddock Woods community of St. Louis County for the sole reason that petitioner Joseph Lee Jones is a Negro. Relying in part upon § 1982, the petitioners sought injunctive and other relief. The District Court sustained the respondents' motion to dismiss the complaint, and the Court of Appeals for the Eighth Circuit affirmed, concluding that § 1982 applies only to state action and does not reach private refusals to sell. . . . We hold that § 1982 bars *all* racial discrimination, private as well as public, in the sale or rental of property, and that the statute, thus construed, is a valid exercise of the power of Congress to enforce the Thirteenth Amendment.[5]

I.

At the outset, it is important to make clear precisely what this case does not involve. Whatever else it may be, 42 U.S.C. § 1982 is not a comprehensive open housing law. . . . the statute in this case deals only with racial discrimination and does not address itself to discrimination on grounds of religion or national origin. . . .

III.

We begin with the language of the statute itself. In plain and unambiguous terms, § 1982 grants to all citizens, without regard to race or color, "the same right" to purchase and lease property "as is enjoyed by white citizens." . . . .

On its face, therefore, § 1982 appears to prohibit *all* discrimination against Negroes in the sale or rental of property—discrimination by private owners as well as discrimination by public authorities. . . . Stressing what they consider to be the revolutionary implications of so literal a reading of § 1982, the respondents argue that Congress cannot possibly have intended any such result. Our examination of the relevant history, however, persuades us that Congress meant exactly what it said.

---

5. Because we have concluded that the discrimination alleged in the petitioners' complaint violated a federal statute that Congress had the power to enact under the Thirteenth Amendment, we find it unnecessary to decide whether that discrimination also violated the Equal Protection Clause of the Fourteenth Amendment.

IV.

[The Court here exhaustively reviews the history of Section 1982, which it notes was originally enacted as part of Section 1 of the Civil Rights Act of 1866. The Court notes that it was introduced in Congress shortly after the Thirteenth Amendment was ratified, and that it was described by its sponsor as a way to give effect to the declaration of freedom contained in the Thirteenth Amendment.]

V.

The remaining question is whether Congress has power under the Constitution to do what § 1982 purports to do: to prohibit all racial discrimination, private and public, in the sale and rental of property. Our starting point is the Thirteenth Amendment, for it was pursuant to that constitutional provision that Congress originally enacted what is now § 1982. The Amendment consists of two parts. Section 1 states:

> "Neither slavery nor involuntary servitude, except as a punishment for crime whereby the party shall have been duly convicted, shall exist within the United States, or any place subject to their jurisdiction."

Section 2 provides:

> "Congress shall have power to enforce this article by appropriate legislation."

As its text reveals, the Thirteenth Amendment "is not a mere prohibition of state laws establishing or upholding slavery, but an absolute declaration that slavery or involuntary servitude shall not exist in any part of the United States." Civil Rights Cases, 109 U.S. 3, 20. It has never been doubted, therefore, "that the power vested in Congress to enforce the article by appropriate legislation," *ibid.*, includes the power to enact laws "direct and primary, operating upon the acts of individuals, whether sanctioned by state legislation or not." *Id.*, at 23.[74]

Thus, the fact that § 1982 operates upon the unofficial acts of private individuals, whether or not sanctioned by state law, presents no constitutional problem. If Congress has power under the Thirteenth Amendment to eradicate conditions that prevent Negroes from buying and renting property because of their race or color, then no federal statute calculated to achieve that objective can be thought to exceed the constitutional power of Congress simply because it reaches beyond state action to regulate the conduct of private individuals. The constitutional question in this case, therefore, comes to this: Does the authority of Congress to enforce the Thirteenth Amendment "by appropriate legislation" include the power to eliminate all racial barriers to the acquisition of real and personal property? We think the answer to that question is plainly yes.

"By its own unaided force and effect," the Thirteenth Amendment "abolished slavery, and established universal freedom." Civil Rights Cases, 109 U.S. 3, 20. Whether

74. So it was, for example, that this Court unanimously upheld the power of Congress under the Thirteenth Amendment to make it a crime for one individual to compel another to work in order to discharge a debt. *Clyatt v. United States*, 197 U.S. 207.

or not the Amendment *itself* did any more than that—a question not involved in this case—it is at least clear that the Enabling Clause of that Amendment empowered Congress to do much more. For that clause clothed 'Congress with power to pass *all laws necessary and proper for abolishing all badges and incidents of slavery in the United States.*' *Ibid.* (Emphasis added.)

Those who opposed passage of the Civil Rights Act of 1866 argued in effect that the Thirteenth Amendment merely authorized Congress to dissolve the legal bond by which the Negro slave was held to his master. Yet many had earlier opposed the Thirteenth Amendment on the very ground that it would give Congress virtually unlimited power to enact laws for the protection of Negroes in every State. And the majority leaders in Congress—who were, after all, the authors of the Thirteenth Amendment—had no doubt that its Enabling Clause contemplated the sort of positive legislation that was embodied in the 1866 Civil Rights Act. Their chief spokesman, Senator Trumbull of Illinois, the Chairman of the Judiciary Committee, had brought the Thirteenth Amendment to the floor of the Senate in 1864. In defending the constitutionality of the 1866 Act, he argued that, if the narrower construction of the Enabling Clause were correct, then

> "the trumpet of freedom that we have been blowing throughout the land has given an 'uncertain sound,' and the promised freedom is a delusion. Such was not the intention of Congress, which proposed the constitutional amendment, nor is such the fair meaning of the amendment itself. . . . I have no doubt that under this provision . . . we may destroy all these discriminations in civil rights against the black man; and if we cannot, our constitutional amendment amounts to nothing. It was for that purpose that the second clause of that amendment was adopted, which says that Congress shall have authority, by appropriate legislation, to carry into effect the article prohibiting slavery. Who is to decide what that appropriate legislation is to be? The Congress of the United States; and it is for Congress to adopt such appropriate legislation as it may think proper, so that it be a means to accomplish the end."

Surely Senator Trumbull was right. Surely Congress has the power under the Thirteenth Amendment rationally to determine what are the badges and the incidents of slavery, and the authority to translate that determination into effective legislation. Nor can we say that the determination Congress has made is an irrational one. For this Court recognized long ago that, whatever else they may have encompassed, the badges and incidents of slavery—its "burdens and disabilities"—included restraints upon "those fundamental rights which are the essence of civil freedom, namely, the same right . . . to inherit, purchase, lease, sell and convey property, as is enjoyed by white citizens." *Civil Rights Cases*, 109 U.S. 3, 22.[78] Just as the Black

---

78. The Court did conclude in the *Civil Rights Cases* that "the act of . . . the owner of the inn, the public conveyance or place of amusement, refusing . . . accommodation" cannot be "justly regarded as imposing any badge of slavery or servitude upon the applicant." 109 U.S., at 24. "It

Codes, enacted after the Civil War to restrict the free exercise of those rights, were substitutes for the salve system, so the exclusion of Negroes from white communities became a substitute for the Black Codes. And when racial discrimination herds men into ghettos and makes their ability to buy property turn on the color of their skin, then it too is a relic of slavery.

Negro citizens, North and South, who saw in the Thirteenth Amendment a promise of freedom—freedom to "go and come at pleasure" and to "buy and sell when they please"—would be left with "a more paper guarantee" if Congress were powerless to assure that a dollar in the hands of a Negro will purchase the same thing as a dollar in the hands of a white man. At the very least, the freedom that Congress is empowered to secure under the Thirteenth Amendment includes the freedom to buy whatever a white man can buy, the right to live wherever a white man can live. If Congress cannot say that being a free man means at least this much, then the Thirteenth Amendment made a promise the Nation cannot keep.

Representative Wilson of Iowa was the floor manager in the House for the Civil Rights Act of 1866. In urging that Congress had ample authority to pass the pending bill, he recalled the celebrated words of Chief Justice Marshall in *McCulloch v. Maryland*, 4 Wheat. 316:

> "Let the end by legitimate, let it be within the scope of the constitution, and all means which are appropriate, which are plainly adapted to that end, which are not prohibited, but consist with the letter and spirit of the constitution, are constitutional."

"The end is legitimate," the Congressman said, "because it is defined by the Constitution itself. The end is the maintenance of freedom. . . . A man who enjoys the civil rights mentioned in this bill cannot be reduced to slavery. . . . This settles the appropriateness of this measure, and that settles its constitutionality."

We agree. The judgment is reversed.

---

would be running the slavery argument into the ground," the Court thought, "to make it apply to every act of discrimination which a person may see fit to make as to the guests he will entertain, or as to the people he will take into his coach or cab or car, or admit to his concert or theatre, or deal with in other matters of intercourse or business." *Id.*, at 24–25. Mr. Justice Harlan, dissented, expressing the view that "such discrimination practised by corporations and individuals in the exercise of their public or quasi-public functions is a badge of servitude the imposition of which congress may prevent under its power, by appropriate legislation, to enforce the thirteenth amendment." *Id.*, at 43.

Whatever the present validity of the position taken by the majority on that issue—a question rendered largely academic by Title II of the Civil Rights Act of 1964, 78 Stat. 243 (see *Heart of Atlanta Motel v. United States*, 379 U.S. 241; *Katzenbach v. McClung*, 379 U.S. 294)—we note that the entire Court agreed upon at least one proposition: The Thirteenth Amendment authorizes Congress not only to outlaw all forms of slavery and involuntary servitude but also to eradicate the last vestiges and incidents of a society half slave and half free, by securing to all citizens, of every race and color, "the same right to make and enforce contracts, to sue, be parties, give evidence, and to inherit, purchase, lease, sell and convey property, as is enjoyed by white citizens." 109 U.S., at 22. *Cf. id.*, at 35 (dissenting opinion) . . . .

[The concurring opinion of Justice Douglas and the dissenting opinion of Justice Harlan are omitted.]

Notes and Questions

1. In *Jones*, the trial court relied on the Court's decision in *Shelley v. Kraemer* to reject the plaintiffs' claims. *See Jones v. Alfred H. Mayer Co.*, 255 F. Supp. 115, 120 (1966). Is there an inconsistency between *Shelley* and *Jones*, or are the cases readily reconcilable?

2. Go back and re-read the sections of *The Civil Rights Cases* quoted by the majority in *Jones*? Is *Jones* accurately quoting its earlier decision, or are the quotes taken out of context?

3. Recall that in *The Civil Rights Cases*, the Court engaged in an independent analysis of what constituted a badge or incident of slavery. What role does the *Jones* Court hold is appropriate for the Court to play in addressing that question?

4. Eight years after *Jones* was decided, the Court, in *Runyon v. McCrary*, 427 U.S. 160 (1976) relied on *Jones* to uphold the constitutionality of 42 U.S.C. § 1981—which provides in pertinent part that "[a]ll persons within the jurisdiction of the United States shall have the same right in every State and Territory to make and enforce contracts . . . as is enjoyed by white citizens. . . ."—as applied to private schools that refused to admit students because they were African American. The Court in *Runyon* noted that Section 1981, like Section 1982, originated in Section 1 of the Civil Rights Act of 1866, and reasoned that "[t]he prohibition of racial discrimination that interferes with the making and enforcement of private educational services furthers goals closely analogous to those served . . . by § 1982's guarantee that 'a dollar in the hands of a Negro will purchase the same thing as a dollar in the hands of a white man.'" *Id.* at 179 (quoting *Jones*, 392 U.S., at 443).

5. In what way is Congress's power under Section 2 of the Thirteenth Amendment broader than its power under the Commerce Clause so far as anti-discrimination legislation is concerned? In what way is its power narrower?

6. Despite the Court's rather broad interpretation of Congress's power under Section 2 of the Thirteenth Amendment, the Court has rather narrowly interpreted the scope of Section 1 of the Amendment. In *United States v. Kozminski*, 487 U.S. 931 (1988), the Court summarized its Section 1 precedents as follows:

> [I]n every case in which this Court has found a condition of involuntary servitude, the victim had no available choice but to work or be subject to legal sanction. In *Clyatt v. United States,* 197 U.S. 207 (1905), for example, the Court recognized that peonage—a condition in which the victim is coerced by threat of legal sanction to work off a debt to a master—is involuntary servitude under the Thirteenth Amendment. *Id.,* at 215, 218. Similarly, in *United States v. Reynolds,* 235 U.S. 133 (1914), the Court held that "[c]ompulsion of . . . service by the constant fear of imprisonment under the criminal laws" violated "rights intended to be secured by the Thirteenth

Amendment." *Id.*, at 146, 150. In that case the Court struck down a criminal surety system under which a person fined for a misdemeanor offense could contract to work for a surety who would, in turn, pay the convict's fine to the State. The critical feature of the system was that that breach of the labor contract by the convict was a crime. The convict was thus forced to work by threat of criminal sanction. The Court has also invalidated state laws subjecting debtors to prosecution and criminal punishment for failing to perform labor after receiving an advance payment. *Pollock v. Williams,* 322 U.S. 4 (1944); *Taylor v. Georgia,* 315 U.S. 25 (1942); *Bailey v. Alabama,* 219 U.S. 219 (1911). The laws at issue in these cases made failure to perform services for which money had been obtained prima facie evidence of intent to defraud. The Court reasoned that "the State could not avail itself of the sanction of the criminal law to supply the compulsion [to enforce labor] any more than it could use or authorize the use of physical force." *Bailey, supra,* at 244.

Our precedents reveal that not all situations in which labor is compelled by physical coercion or force of law violate the Thirteenth Amendment. By its terms the Amendment excludes involuntary servitude imposed as legal punishment for a crime. Similarly, the Court has recognized that the prohibition against involuntary servitude does not prevent the State or Federal Governments from compelling their citizens, by threat of criminal sanction, to perform certain civic duties. See *Hurtado v. United States,* 410 U.S. 578, 589, n. 11 (1973) (jury service); *Selective Draft Law Cases,* 245 U.S. 366, 390 (1918) (military service); *Butler v. Perry, supra* (roadwork). Moreover, in *Robertson v. Baldwin,* 165 U.S. 275 (1897), the Court observed that the Thirteenth Amendment was not intended to apply to "exceptional" cases well established in the common law at the time of the Thirteenth Amendment, such as "the right of parents and guardians to the custody of their minor children or wards," *id.*, at 282, or laws preventing sailors who contracted to work on vessels from deserting their ships. *Id.*, at 288.

Putting aside such exceptional circumstances . . . our precedents clearly define a Thirteenth Amendment prohibition of involuntary servitude enforced by the use or threatened use of physical or legal coercion.

487 U.S., at 943-44.

Chapter 10

Equal Protection and the Reordering of the Political Process Doctrine

Recall that, toward the end of Chapter 7, you examined the Court's 1967 decision in *Reitman v. Mulkey*, in which the Court struck down as violating the Equal Protection Clause a voter initiative in California that both repealed existing open housing laws and prevented the enactment of such laws in the future. In declaring the law unconstitutional, the *Reitman* Court relied on its state action decisions in *Anderson* and *Burton* to conclude that the state of California was encouraging private actors to discriminate on the basis of race. This holding required two logical leaps. First, a leap from the race-neutral language of the initiative to the conclusion that it was about race. And second, a leap from that to a conclusion that the state was *encouraging* racial discrimination, as opposed to remaining neutral on the subject.

The notes following *Reitman* raised the question whether there was another way to think about the constitutional problem at stake in the case. In *Reitman*, the voters of California did more than merely repeal existing anti-discrimination laws. By enshrining the new provision into the state constitution, they erected a significant barrier for those hoping to get such legislation re-enacted in the future. After the initiative succeeded, supporters of such anti-discrimination laws had to do more than merely persuade the legislature to re-enact them; they would have to first undertake the significant step of getting the state constitution amended to remove the initiative at issue in *Reitman*.

In the cases that follow, the Court considers an alternative to the approach taken in *Reitman* that focuses not so much on whether the state is encouraging private discrimination, but instead on whether the erection of barriers to achieving political success for certain categories of laws creates an equal protection problem.

A. The Rise of the Political Process Doctrine

Hunter v. Erickson

393 U.S. 385 (1969)

MR. JUSTICE WHITE delivered the opinion of the Court.

The question in this case is whether the City of Akron, Ohio, has denied a Negro citizen, Nellie Hunter, the equal protection of its laws by amending the city charter to prevent the city council from implementing any ordinance dealing with racial, religious, or ancestral discrimination in housing without the approval of the majority of the voters of Akron.

The Akron City Council in 1964 enacted a fair housing ordinance premised on a recognition of the social and economic losses to society which flow from substandard, ghetto housing and its tendency to breed discrimination and segregation contrary to the policy of the city to "assure equal opportunity to all persons to live in decent housing facilities regardless of race, color, religion, ancestry or national origin." A Commission on Equal Opportunity in Housing was established by the ordinance....

Seeking to invoke this machinery which had been established by the city for her benefit, Nellie Hunter addressed a complaint to the Commission.... Mrs. Hunter's affidavit met with the reply that the fair housing ordinance was unavailable to her because the city charter had been amended to provide:

> "Any ordinance enacted by the Council of The City of Akron which regulates the use, sale, advertisement, transfer, listing assignment, lease, sublease or financing of real property of any kind or of any interest therein on the basis of race, color, religion, national origin or ancestry must first be approved by a majority of the electors voting on the question at a regular or general election before said ordinance shall be effective. Any such ordinance in effect at the time of the adoption of this section shall cease to be effective until approved by the electors as provided herein." Akron City Charter § 137.

The proposal for the charter amendment had been placed on the ballot at a general election upon petition of more than 10% of Akron's voters, and the amendment had been duly passed by a majority....

Akron argues that this case is unlike *Reitman v. Mulkey*, 387 U.S. 369 (1967) in that here the city charter declares no right to discriminate in housing, authorizes and encourages no housing discrimination, and places no ban on the enactment of fair housing ordinances. But we need not rest on *Reitman* to decide this case. Here, unlike *Reitman*, there was an explicitly racial classification treating racial housing matters differently from other racial and housing matters.

By adding § 137 to its Charter the City of Akron, which unquestionably wields state power,[4] not only suspended the operation of the existing ordinance forbidding housing discrimination, but also required the approval of the electors before any future ordinance could take effect.[5] Section 137 thus drew a distinction between those groups who sought the law's protection against racial, religious, or ancestral

---

4. See, *e.g., Evans v. Newton*, 382 U.S. 296 (1966); *Burton v. Wilmington Parking Authority*, 365 U.S. 715 (1961); *Shelley v. Kraemer*, 334 U.S. 1 (1948).

5. Thus we do not hold that mere repeal of an existing ordinance violates the Fourteenth Amendment.

discriminations in the sale and rental of real estate and those who sought to regulate real property transactions in the pursuit of other ends. Those who sought, or would benefit from, most ordinances regulating the real property market remained subject to the general rule: the ordinance would become effective 30 days after passage by the City Council, or immediately if passed as an emergency measure, and would be subject to referendum only if 10% of the electors so requested by filing a proper and timely petition. Passage by the Council sufficed unless the electors themselves invoked the general referendum provisions of the city charter. But for those who sought protection against racial bias, the approval of the City Council was not enough. A referendum was required by charter at a general or regular election, without any provision for use of the expedited special election ordinarily available. The Akron charter obviously made it substantially more difficult to secure enactment of ordinances subject to § 137.

Only laws to end housing discrimination based on "race, color, religion, national origin or ancestry" must run § 137's gantlet. It is true that the section draws no distinctions among racial and religious groups. Negroes and whites, Jews and Catholics are all subject to the same requirements if there is housing discrimination against them which they wish to end. But § 137 nevertheless disadvantages those who would benefit from laws barring racial, religious, or ancestral discriminations as against those who would bar other discriminations or who would otherwise regulate the real estate market in their favor. The automatic referendum system does not reach housing discrimination on sexual or political grounds, or against those with children or dogs, nor does it affect tenants seeking more heat or better maintenance from landlords, nor those seeking rent control, urban renewal, public housing, or new building codes.

Moreover, although the law on its face treats Negro and white, Jew and gentile in an identical manner, the reality is that the law's impact falls on the minority. The majority needs no protection against discrimination and if it did, a referendum might be bothersome but no more than that. Like the law requiring specification of candidates' race on the ballot, *Anderson v. Martin*, 375 U.S. 399 (1964), § 137 places special burden on racial minorities within the governmental process. This is no more permissible than denying them the vote, on an equal basis with others. The preamble to the open housing ordinance which was suspended by § 137 recited that the population of Akron consists of "people of different race, color, religion, ancestry or national origin, many of whom live in circumscribed and segregated areas, under substandard unhealthful, unsafe, unsanitary and overcrowded conditions, because of discrimination in the sale, lease, rental and financing of housing." Such was the situation in Akron. It is against this background that the referendum required by § 137 must be assessed.

Because the core of the Fourteenth Amendment is the prevention of meaningful and unjustified official distinctions based on race, racial classifications are "constitutionally suspect," *Bolling v. Sharpe*, 347 U.S. 497, 499 (1954), and subject to the "most rigid scrutiny," *Korematsu v. United States*, 323 U.S. 214, 216 (1944). They "bear a far heavier burden of justification" than other classifications, *McLaughlin v. Florida*, 379 U.S. 184, 194 (1964).

We are unimpressed with any of Akron's justifications for its discrimination. Characterizing it simply as a public decision to move slowly in the delicate area of race relations emphasizes the impact and burden of § 137, but does not justify it. The amendment was unnecessary either to implement a decision to go slowly, or to allow the people of Akron to participate in that decision.[7] Likewise, insisting that a State may distribute legislative power as it desires and that the people may retain for themselves the power over certain subjects may generally be true, but these principles furnish no justification for a legislative structure which otherwise would violate the Fourteenth Amendment.... Even though Akron might have proceeded by majority vote at town meeting on all its municipal legislation, it has instead chosen a more complex system. Having done so, the State may no more disadvantage any particular group by making it more difficult to enact legislation in its behalf than it may dilute any person's vote or give any group a smaller representation than another of comparable size.

We hold that § 137 discriminates against minorities, and constitutes a real, substantial, and invidious denial of the equal protection of the laws.

Reversed.

Mr. Justice Harlan, whom Mr. Justice Stewart joins, concurring.

At the outset, I think it well to sketch my constitutional approach to state statutes which structure the internal governmental process and which are challenged under the Equal Protection Clause of the Fourteenth Amendment. For equal protection purposes, I believe that laws which define the powers of political institutions fall into two classes. First, a statute may have the clear purpose of making it more difficult for racial and religious minorities to further their political aims. Like any other statute which is discriminatory on its face, such a law cannot be permitted to stand unless it can be supported by state interests of the most weighty and substantial kind.

Most laws which define the structure of political institutions, however, fall into a second class. They are designed with the aim of providing a just framework within which the diverse political groups in our society may fairly compete and are not enacted with the purpose of assisting one particular group in its struggle with its political opponents. Consider, for example, Akron's procedure which requires that almost any ordinance be submitted to a general referendum if 10% of the electorate signs an appropriate petition. This rule obviously does not have the purpose of protecting one particular group to the detriment of all others. It will sometimes operate in favor of one faction; sometimes in favor of another. Akron has adopted the referendum system because its citizens believe that whenever an action of the

---

7. The people of Akron had the power to initiate legislation, or to review council decisions, even before § 137. The procedural prerequisites for this popular action are perfectly reasonable, as the gathering of 10% of the voters' signatures in the course of passing § 137 illustrates.

City Council raises the emotional opposition of *any* significant group in the community, the people should have a right to decide the matter directly. Statutes of this type, which are grounded upon general democratic principle, do not violate the Equal Protection Clause simply because they occasionally operate to disadvantage Negro political interests. If a governmental institution is to be fair, one group cannot always be expected to win. If the Council's fair housing legislation were defeated at a referendum, Negroes would undoubtedly lose an important political battle, but they would not thereby be denied equal protection.

This same analysis applies to other institutions of government which are even more solidly rooted in our history than is the referendum. The existence of a bicameral legislature or an executive veto may on occasion make it more difficult for minorities to achieve favorable legislation; nevertheless, they may not be attacked on equal protection grounds since they are founded on neutral principles. Similarly, the rule which makes it relatively difficult to amend a state constitution is commonly justified on the theory that constitutional provisions should be more thoroughly scrutinized and more soberly considered than are simple statutory enactments. Here, too, Negroes may stand to gain by the rule if a fair housing law is made part of the constitution, or they may lose if the constitution adopts a position of strict neutrality on the question. See *Reitman v. Mulkey*, 387 U.S. 369, 389 (1967) (dissenting opinion of Harlan, J.). But even if Negroes are obliged to undertake the arduous task of amending the state constitution, they are not thereby denied equal protection. For the rule making constitutional amendment difficult is grounded in neutral principle.

In the case before us, however, the city of Akron has not attempted to allocate governmental power on the basis of any general principle. Here, we have a provision that has the clear purpose of making it more difficult for certain racial and religious minorities to achieve legislation that is in their interest. Since the charter amendment is discriminatory on its face, Akron must 'bear a far heavier burden of justification' than is required in the normal case. *McLaughlin v. Florida*, 379 U.S. 184, 194 (1964). And Akron has failed to sustain this burden. The city's principal argument in support of the charter amendment relies on the undisputed fact that fair housing legislation may often be expected to raise the passions of the community to their highest pitch. It was not necessary, however, to pass this amendment in order to assure that particularly sensitive issues will ultimately be decided by the general electorate. Akron has already provided a procedure, which is grounded in neutral principle, that requires a general referendum on this issue if 10% of the voters insist. If the prospect of fair housing legislation really arouses passionate opposition, the voters will have the final say. Consequently, the charter amendment will have its real impact only when fair housing does *not* arouse extraordinary controversy. This being the case, I can perceive no legitimate state interest which in any degree vindicates the action taken by the City here.

As I read the Court's opinion to be entirely consistent with the basic principles which I believe control this case, I join in it.

[The dissenting opinion of Justice Black is omitted.]

James v. Valtierra

402 U.S. 137 (1971)

Mr. Justice Black delivered the opinion of the Court.

These cases raise but a single issue. It grows out of the United States Housing Act of 1937, which established a federal housing agency authorized to make loans and grants to state agencies for slum clearance and low rent housing projects. In response, the California Legislature created in each county and city a public housing authority to take advantage of the financing made available by the federal Housing Act. At the time the federal legislation was passed the California Constitution had for many years reserved to the State's people the power to initiate legislation and to reject or approve by referendum any Act passed by the state legislature. The same section reserved to the electors of counties and cities the power of initiative and referendum over acts of local government bodies. In 1950, however, the State Supreme Court held that local authorities' decisions on seeking federal aid for public housing projects were "executive" and "administrative," not "legislative," and therefore the state constitution's referendum provisions did not apply to these actions. Within six months of that decision the California voters adopted Article XXXIV of the state constitution to bring public housing decisions under the State's referendum policy. The Article provided that no low-rent housing project should be developed, constructed, or acquired in any manner by a state public body until the project was approved by a majority of those voting at a community election....

The first paragraph in the District Court's decision stated simply: "We hold Article XXXIV to be unconstitutional. See *Hunter v. Erickson*...." The court below erred in relying on Hunter to invalidate Article XXXIV. Unlike the case before us, Hunter rested on the conclusion that Akron's referendum law denied equal protection by placing "special burdens on racial minorities within the governmental process." *Id.*, at 391. In *Hunter* the citizens of Akron had amended the city charter to require that any ordinance regulating real estate on the basis of race, color, religion, or national origin could not take effect without approval by a majority of those voting in a city election. The Court held that the amendment created a classification based upon race because it required that laws dealing with racial housing matters could take effect only if they survived a mandatory referendum while other housing ordinances took effect without any such special election....

Unlike the Akron referendum provision, it cannot be said that California's Article XXXIV rests on "distinctions based on race." *Id.*, at 391. The Article requires referendum approval for any low-rent public housing project, not only for projects which will be occupied by a racial minority. And the record here would not support any claim that a law seemingly neutral on its face is in fact aimed at a racial minority. Cf. *Gomillion v. Lightfoot*, 364 U.S. 339 (1960). The present case could be affirmed only by extending *Hunter*, and this we decline to do....

[A]ppellees contend that Article XXXIV denies them equal protection because it demands a mandatory referendum while many other referendums only take place upon citizen initiative. They suggest that the mandatory nature of the Article XXXIV referendum constitutes unconstitutional discrimination because it hampers persons desiring public housing from achieving their objective when no such roadblock faces other groups seeking to influence other public decisions to their advantage. But of course a lawmaking procedure that "disadvantages" a particular group does not always deny equal protection. Under any such holding, presumably a State would not be able to require referendums on any subject unless referendums were required on all, because they would always disadvantage some group. And this Court would be required to analyze governmental structures to determine whether a gubernatorial veto provision or a filibuster rule is likely to "disadvantage" any of the diverse and shifting groups that make up the American people.

Furthermore, an examination of California law reveals that persons advocating low-income housing have not been singled out for mandatory referendums while no other group must face that obstacle. Mandatory referendums are required for approval of state constitutional amendments, for the issuance of general obligation long-term bonds by local governments, and for certain municipal territorial annexations. California statute books contain much legislation first enacted by voter initiative, and no such law can be repealed or amended except by referendum. Some California cities have wisely provided that their public parks may not be alienated without mandatory referendums....

[The dissenting opinion of Justice Marshall is omitted.]

Washington v. Seattle School District No. 1

458 U.S. 457 (1982)

Justice Blackmun delivered the opinion of the Court....

I

A

Seattle School District No. 1 (District), which is largely coterminous with the city of Seattle, Wash., is charged by state law with administering 112 schools and educating approximately 54,000 public school students.... Because segregated housing patterns in Seattle have created racially imbalanced schools, the District historically has taken steps to alleviate the isolation of minority students; since 1963, it has permitted students to transfer from their neighborhood schools to help cure the District's racial imbalance....

In September 1977, the District implemented a "magnet" program, designed to alleviate racial isolation by enhancing educational offerings at certain schools, thereby encouraging voluntary student transfers. A "disproportionate amount of the overall movement" inspired by the program was undertaken by Negro students, however, and racial imbalance in the Seattle schools was found to have actually increased between the 1970–1971 and 1977–1978 academic years. The District therefore concluded that mandatory reassignment of students was necessary if racial isolation in its schools was to be eliminated. Accordingly, in March 1978, the School Board enacted the so-called "Seattle Plan" for desegregation. The plan, which makes extensive use of busing and mandatory reassignments, desegregates elementary schools by "pairing" and "triading" predominantly minority with predominantly white attendance areas, and by basing student assignments on attendance zones rather than on race. The racial makeup of secondary schools is moderated by "feeding" them from the desegregated elementary schools. . . .

B

In late 1977, shortly before the Seattle Plan was formally adopted by the District, a number of Seattle residents who opposed the desegregation strategies being discussed by the School Board formed an organization called the Citizens for Voluntary Integration Committee (CiVIC). This organization, which the District Court found "was formed because of its founders' opposition to The Seattle Plan," attempted to enjoin implementation of the Board's mandatory desegregation program through litigation in state court; when these efforts failed, CiVIC drafted a statewide initiative designed to terminate the use of mandatory busing for purposes of racial integration. This proposal, known as Initiative 350, provided that "no school board . . . shall directly or indirectly require any student to attend a school other than the school which is geographically nearest or next nearest the student's place of residence . . . and which offers the course of study pursued by such student. . . ." The initiative then set out, however, a number of broad exceptions to this requirement: a student may be assigned beyond his neighborhood school if he "requires special education, care or guidance," or if "there are health or safety hazards, either natural or man made, or physical barriers or obstacles . . . between the student's place of residence and the nearest or next nearest school," or if "the school nearest or next nearest to his place of residence is unfit or inadequate because of overcrowding, unsafe conditions or lack of physical facilities." Initiative 350 also specifically proscribed use of seven enumerated methods of "indirec[t]" student assignment—among them the redefinition of attendance zones, the pairing of schools, and the use of "feeder" schools—that are a part of the Seattle Plan. The initiative envisioned busing for racial purposes in only one circumstance: it did not purport to "prevent any court of competent jurisdiction from adjudicating constitutional issues relating to the public schools."

Its proponents placed Initiative 350 on the Washington ballot for the November 1978 general election. During the ensuing campaign, the District Court concluded, the leadership of CiVIC "acted legally and responsibly," and did not address "its appeals to the racial biases of the voters." At the same time, however, the court's findings demonstrate that the initiative was directed solely at desegregative busing in general, and at the Seattle Plan in particular. . . . In campaigning for the measure, CiVIC officials accurately represented that its passage would result in "no loss of school district flexibility other than in busing for desegregation purposes," and it is evident that the campaign focused almost exclusively on the wisdom of "forced busing" for integration.

On November 8, 1978, two months after the Seattle Plan went into effect, Initiative 350 passed by a substantial margin, drawing almost 66% of the vote statewide. . . .

II

The Equal Protection Clause of the Fourteenth Amendment guarantees racial minorities the right to full participation in the political life of the community. It is beyond dispute, of course, that given racial or ethnic groups may not be denied the franchise, or precluded from entering into the political process in a reliable and meaningful manner. But the Fourteenth Amendment also reaches "a political structure that treats all individuals as equals," *Mobile v. Bolden*, 446 U.S. 55, 84 (1980) (Stevens, J., concurring in judgment), yet more subtly distorts governmental processes in such a way as to place special burdens on the ability of minority groups to achieve beneficial legislation.

This principle received its clearest expression in *Hunter v. Erickson, supra*, a case that involved attempts to overturn antidiscrimination legislation in Akron, Ohio. . . .

In striking down the charter amendment, the *Hunter* Court recognized that, on its face, the provision "draws no distinctions among racial and religious groups." *Id.*, at 390. But it did differentiate "between those groups who sought the law's protection against racial . . . discriminatio[n] in the sale and rental of real estate and those who sought to regulate real property transactions in the pursuit of other ends," *ibid.*, thus "disadvantag[ing] those who would benefit from laws barring racial . . . discriminatio[n] as against those who would bar other discriminations or who would otherwise regulate the real estate market in their favor." *Id.*, at 391. In "reality," the burden imposed by such an arrangement necessarily "falls on the minority. The majority needs no protection against discrimination and if it did, a referendum might be bothersome but no more than that." *Ibid.* In effect, then, the charter amendment served as an "explicitly racial classification treating racial housing matters differently from other racial and housing matters." *Id.*, at 389. This made the amendment constitutionally suspect: "the State may no more disadvantage any *particular* group by making it more difficult to enact legislation in its behalf than it may dilute any person's vote or give any group a smaller representation than another of comparable size." *Id.*, at 393 (emphasis added) . . . .

As Justice Harlan noted while concurring in the Court's opinion in *Hunter*, laws structuring political institutions or allocating political power according to "neutral principles"—such as the executive veto, or the typically burdensome requirements for amending state constitutions—are not subject to equal protection attack, though they may "make it more difficult for minorities to achieve favorable legislation." 393 U.S., at 394. Because such laws make it more difficult for *every* group in the community to enact comparable laws, they "provid[e] a just framework within which the diverse political groups in our society may fairly compete." *Id.*, at 393. Thus, the political majority may generally restructure the political process to place obstacles in the path of everyone seeking to secure the benefits of governmental action. But a different analysis is required when the State allocates governmental power nonneutrally, by explicitly using the *racial* nature of a decision to determine the decisionmaking process. . . .

III

. . . . In our view, Initiative 350 must fall because it does "not attemp[t] to allocate governmental power on the basis of any general principle." *Hunter v. Erickson*, 393 U.S., at 395 (Harlan, J., concurring). Instead, it uses the racial nature of an issue to define the governmental decisionmaking structure, and thus imposes substantial and unique burdens on racial minorities.

A

Noting that Initiative 350 nowhere mentions "race" or "integration," appellants suggest that the legislation has no racial overtones; they maintain that *Hunter* is inapposite because the initiative simply permits busing for certain enumerated purposes while neutrally forbidding it for all other reasons. We find it difficult to believe that appellants' analysis is seriously advanced, however, for despite its facial neutrality there is little doubt that the initiative was effectively drawn for racial purposes. Neither the initiative's sponsors, nor the District Court, nor the Court of Appeals had any difficulty perceiving the racial nature of the issue settled by Initiative 350. Thus, the District Court found that the text of the initiative was carefully tailored to interfere only with desegregative busing. Proponents of the initiative candidly "represented that there would be no loss of school district flexibility other than in busing for desegregation purposes." And, as we have noted, Initiative 350 in fact allows school districts to bus their students "for most, if not all," of the nonintegrative purposes required by their educational policies. The Washington electorate surely was aware of this, for it was "assured" by CiVIC officials that "'99% of the school districts in the state'"—those that lacked mandatory integration programs—"would not be affected by the passage of 350." It is beyond reasonable dispute, then, that the initiative was enacted "'because of,' not merely 'in spite of,' its adverse effects upon" busing for integration. *Personnel Administrator of Massachusetts v. Feeney*, 442 U.S. 256, 279 (1979) . . . .

It undoubtedly is true, as the United States suggests, that the proponents of mandatory integration cannot be classified by race: Negroes and whites may be counted among both the supporters and the opponents of Initiative 350. And it should be equally clear that white as well as Negro children benefit from exposure to "ethnic and racial diversity in the classroom." But neither of these factors serves to distinguish *Hunter*, for we may fairly assume that members of the racial majority both favored and benefited from Akron's fair housing ordinance.

In any event, our cases suggest that desegregation of the public schools, like the Akron open housing ordinance, at bottom inures primarily to the benefit of the minority, and is designed for that purpose. . . .

It is undeniable that busing for integration—particularly when ordered by a federal court—now engenders considerably more controversy than does the sort of fair housing ordinance debated in *Hunter*. But in the absence of a constitutional violation, the desirability and efficacy of school desegregation are matters to be resolved through the political process. For present purposes, it is enough that minorities may consider busing for integration to be "legislation that is in their interest." *Hunter v. Erickson*, 393 U.S., at 395 (Harlan, J., concurring). Given the racial focus of Initiative 350, this suffices to trigger application of the *Hunter* doctrine.

B

We are also satisfied that the practical effect of Initiative 350 is to work a reallocation of power of the kind condemned in *Hunter*. The initiative removes the authority to address a racial problem—and only a racial problem—from the existing decisionmaking body, in such a way as to burden minority interests. Those favoring the elimination of *de facto* school segregation now must seek relief from the state legislature, or from the statewide electorate. Yet authority over all other student assignment decisions, as well as over most other areas of educational policy, remains vested in the local school board. Indeed, by specifically exempting from Initiative 350's proscriptions most nonracial reasons for assigning students away from their neighborhood schools, the initiative expressly requires those championing school integration to surmount a considerably higher hurdle than persons seeking comparable legislative action. As in *Hunter*, then, the community's political mechanisms are modified to place effective decisionmaking authority over a racial issue at a different level of government.[17] In a very obvious sense, the initiative thus "disadvantages those who would benefit from laws barring" *de facto* desegregation "as against those who . . . would otherwise regulate" student assignment decisions; "the reality is that the law's impact falls on the minority." *Hunter v. Erickson*, 393 U.S., at 391 . . . .

At the outset, it is irrelevant that the State might have vested all decisionmaking authority in itself, so long as the political structure it in fact erected imposes comparative burdens on minority interests. . . . And until the passage of Initiative 350, Washington law in fact had established the local school board, rather than the State, as the entity charged with making decisions of the type at issue here. . . .

Given this statutory structure, we have little difficulty concluding that Initiative 350 worked a major reordering of the State's educational decisionmaking process. Before adoption of the initiative, the power to determine what programs would most appropriately fill a school district's educational needs—including programs involving student assignment and desegregation—was firmly committed to the

17. . . . . The evil condemned by the *Hunter* Court was not the particular political obstacle of mandatory referenda imposed by the Akron charter amendment; it was, rather, the comparative structural burden placed on the political achievement of minority interests. Thus, in *Hunter*, the procedures for enacting racial legislation were modified in such a way as to place effective control in the hands of the citywide electorate. Similarly here, the power to enact racial legislation has been reallocated. In each case, the effect of the challenged action was to redraw decisionmaking authority over racial matters—and only over racial matters—in such a way as to place comparative burdens on minorities. . . .

local board's discretion.... After passage of Initiative 350, authority over all but one of those areas remained in the hands of the local board. By placing power over desegregative busing at the state level, then, Initiative 350 plainly "differentiates between the treatment of problems involving racial matters and that afforded other problems in the same area." *Lee v. Nyquist*, 318 F.Supp., at 718.[23]

C

To be sure, "the simple repeal or modification of desegregation or antidiscrimination laws, without more, never has been viewed as embodying a presumptively invalid racial classification." As Justice Harlan noted in *Hunter*, the voters of the polity may express their displeasure through an established legislative or referendum procedure when particular legislation "arouses passionate opposition." *Id.*, at 395 (concurring opinion). Had Akron's fair housing ordinance been defeated at a referendum, for example, "Negroes would undoubtedly [have lost] an important political battle, but they would not thereby [have been] denied equal protection." *Id.*, at 394.

Initiative 350, however, works something more than the "mere repeal" of a desegregation law by the political entity that created it. It burdens all future attempts to integrate Washington schools in districts throughout the State, by lodging decision-making authority over the question at a new and remote level of government....

IV

In the end, appellants are reduced to suggesting that *Hunter* has been effectively overruled by more recent decisions of this Court. As they read it, *Hunter* applied a simple "disparate impact" analysis: it invalidated a facially neutral ordinance because of the law's adverse effects upon racial minorities. Appellants therefore contend that *Hunter* was swept away, along with the disparate-impact approach to equal protection, in *Washington v. Davis*, 426 U.S. 229 (1976), and *Arlington Heights v. Metropolitan Housing Dev. Corp.*, 429 U.S. 252 (1977). Cf. *James v. Valtierra*, 402 U.S. 137 (1971).

---

23. Throughout his dissent, JUSTICE POWELL insists that the Court has created a "vested constitutional right to local decisionmaking," that under our holding "the people of the State of Washington apparently are forever barred from developing a different policy on mandatory busing where a school district previously has adopted one of its own," and that today's decision somehow raises doubts about "the authority of a State to abolish school boards altogether." These statements evidence a basic misunderstanding of our decision. Our analysis vests no rights, and has nothing to do with whether school board action predates that taken by the State. Instead, what we find objectionable about Initiative 350 is the comparative burden it imposes on minority participation in the political process—that is, the racial nature of the way in which it structures the *process* of decisionmaking. It is evident, then, that the horribles paraded by the dissent—which have nothing to do with the ability of minorities to participate in the process of self-government—are entirely unrelated to this case. It is equally clear, as we have noted at several points in our opinion, that the State remains free to vest all decisionmaking power in state officials, or to remove authority from local school boards in a race-neutral manner.

Appellants unquestionably are correct when they suggest that "purposeful discrimination is 'the condition that offends the Constitution,'" *Personnel Administrator of Massachusetts v. Feeney*, 442 U.S., at 274, for the "central purpose of the Equal Protection Clause . . . is the prevention of official conduct discriminating on the basis of race." *Washington v. Davis*, 426 U.S., at 239. Thus, when facially neutral legislation is subjected to equal protection attack, an inquiry into intent is necessary to determine whether the legislation in some sense was designed to accord disparate treatment on the basis of racial considerations. Appellants' suggestion that this analysis somehow conflicts with *Hunter*, however, misapprehends the basis of the *Hunter* doctrine. We have not insisted on a particularized inquiry into motivation in all equal protection cases: "A racial classification, regardless of purported motivation, is presumptively invalid and can be upheld only upon an extraordinary justification." *Personnel Administrator of Massachusetts v. Feeney*, 442 U.S., at 272. And legislation of the kind challenged in *Hunter* similarly falls into an inherently suspect category.

There is one immediate and crucial difference between *Hunter* and the cases cited by appellants. While decisions such as *Washington v. Davis* and *Arlington Heights* considered classifications facially unrelated to race, the charter amendment at issue in *Hunter* dealt in explicitly racial terms with legislation designed to benefit minorities "as minorities," not legislation intended to benefit some larger group of underprivileged citizens among whom minorities were disproportionately represented. This does not mean, of course, that every attempt to address a racial issue gives rise to an impermissible racial classification. But when the political process or the decisionmaking mechanism used to *address* racially conscious legislation—and only such legislation—is singled out for peculiar and disadvantageous treatment, the governmental action plainly "rests on 'distinctions based on race.'" *James v. Valtierra*, 402 U.S., at 141, quoting *Hunter v. Erickson*, 393 U.S., at 391. And when the State's allocation of power places unusual burdens on the ability of racial groups to enact legislation specifically designed to overcome the "special condition" of prejudice, the governmental action seriously "curtail[s] the operation of those political processes ordinarily to be relied upon to protect minorities." *United States v. Carolene Products Co.*, 304 U.S. 144, 153, n. 4 (1938). In a most direct sense, this implicates the judiciary's special role in safeguarding the interests of those groups that are "relegated to such a position of political powerlessness as to command extraordinary protection from the majoritarian political process." *San Antonio Independent School Dist. v. Rodriguez*, 411 U.S. 1, 28 (1973) . . . .

Certainly, a state requirement that "desegregation or antidiscrimination laws," *Crawford v. Los Angeles Board of Education*, 458 U.S., at 539, and only such laws, be passed by unanimous vote of the legislature would be constitutionally suspect. It would be equally questionable for a community to require that laws or ordinances "designed to ameliorate race relations or to protect racial minorities," *ibid.*, be confirmed by popular vote of the electorate as a whole, while comparable legislation is exempted from a similar procedure. The amendment addressed in *Hunter*—and, as we have explained, the legislation at issue here—was less obviously pernicious than are these examples, but was no different in principle. . . .

[The dissenting opinion of Justice Powell is omitted.]

Notes and Questions

1. Does this line of cases, and in particular the *James* case, hold that there is a constitutional claim available based on reordering the political process only when it is a *race*-based reordering? What if it instead was on some other basis, such as sex, sexual orientation or disability? Is it perhaps the case that the doctrine is available whenever heightened scrutiny would somehow be applicable under the Equal Protection Clause, such as when a suspect or quasi-suspect classification is at issue or a fundamental right is at stake?

2. Even if the challenged laws in these cases are about *race*, are they necessarily targeted at racial minorities? After all, the underlying laws at stake in both *Hunter* and *Washington* applied across-the-board to all races. Thus, for example, after the charter amendment in *Hunter*, laws protecting whites from racial discrimination could no longer be enacted. If in fact race neutral, why is heightened scrutiny in play? Is it based on a belief that racial minorities favor anti-discrimination laws and mandatory busing, and whites do not? If so, is that belief itself based on racial stereotypes?

3. In both *Hunter* and *Washington*, the Court is careful to say that more than mere repeal is involved. What, exactly, is the "more" that makes the challenged laws unconstitutional?

4. Not until *Romer v. Evans*, 517 U.S. 620 (1996), did the Court formally tie *Reitman* together with *Hunter* and *Washington*. There, the Court collectively referred to the three decisions as "our precedents involving discriminatory restructuring of governmental decisionmaking." *Romer*, 517 U.S. at 625. In *Romer*—which will be examined in detail in Chapter 18—the Court addressed the constitutionality of a Colorado constitutional amendment that repealed state and local laws prohibiting discrimination on the basis of sexual orientation and prohibited the subsequent enactment of such laws at either the state or local levels. Although the lower court relied on the Court's reordering of the political process cases, the *Romer* Court instead held that the law was unconstitutional for a different reason. Was the Court's reluctance to rely on the *Reitman-Hunter-Washington* line of cases tied to the fact that the law at issue in *Romer* was not race-based?

B. The End of the Political Process Doctrine?

Since its decision in *Washington*, the political process doctrine lay dormant in the U.S. Supreme Court, although it arose occasionally in the lower courts. In 2014, the Court re-examined the doctrine in the case that follows, and split heavily on the doctrine's continuing viability and scope.

Schuette v. Coalition to Defend Affirmative Action

572 U.S. 291 (2014)

JUSTICE KENNEDY announced the judgment of the Court and delivered an opinion, in which THE CHIEF JUSTICE and JUSTICE ALITO join. . . .

The Court in this case must determine whether an amendment to the Constitution of the State of Michigan, approved and enacted by its voters, is invalid under the Equal Protection Clause of the Fourteenth Amendment to the Constitution of the United States.

In 2003 the Court reviewed the constitutionality of two admissions systems at the University of Michigan, one for its undergraduate class and one for its law school. . . . Each admissions process permitted the explicit consideration of an applicant's race. In *Gratz,* the Court invalidated the undergraduate plan as a violation of the Equal Protection Clause. In *Grutter,* the Court found no constitutional flaw in the law school admission plan's more limited use of race-based preferences.

In response to the Court's decision in *Gratz,* the university revised its undergraduate admissions process, but the revision still allowed limited use of race-based preferences. After a statewide debate on the question of racial preferences in the context of governmental decisionmaking, the voters, in 2006, adopted an amendment to the State Constitution prohibiting state and other governmental entities in Michigan from granting certain preferences, including race-based preferences, in a wide range of actions and decisions. Under the terms of the amendment, race-based preferences cannot be part of the admissions process for state universities. That particular prohibition is central to the instant case.

The ballot proposal was called Proposal 2 and, after it passed by a margin of 58 percent to 42 percent, the resulting enactment became Article I, § 26, of the Michigan Constitution. . . .

In holding § 26 invalid in the context of student admissions at state universities, the Court of Appeals relied in primary part on *Seattle, supra,* which it deemed to control the case. But that determination extends *Seattle*'s holding in a case presenting quite different issues to reach a conclusion that is mistaken here. Before explaining this further, it is necessary to consider the relevant cases that preceded *Seattle* and the background against which *Seattle* itself arose.

Though it has not been prominent in the arguments of the parties, this Court's decision in *Reitman v. Mulkey,* 387 U.S. 369 (1967), is a proper beginning point for discussing the controlling decisions. In *Mulkey,* voters amended the California Constitution to prohibit any state legislative interference with an owner's prerogative to decline to sell or rent residential property on any basis. Two different cases gave rise to *Mulkey.* In one a couple could not rent an apartment, and in the other a couple were evicted from their apartment. Those adverse actions were on account of race. In both cases the complaining parties were barred, on account of race, from invoking the protection of California's statutes; and, as a result, they were unable to lease residential property. This Court concluded that the state constitutional provision was a denial of equal protection. The Court agreed with the California Supreme Court that the amendment operated to insinuate the State into the decision to discriminate by encouraging that practice. The Court noted the "immediate design and intent" of the amendment was to "establis[h] a purported constitutional right to privately discriminate." The Court agreed that the amendment "expressly authorized and constitutionalized the private right to discriminate." The effect of the state constitutional amendment was to "significantly encourage and involve the State in private racial discriminations." In a dissent joined by three other Justices, Justice Harlan disagreed with the majority's holding. The dissent reasoned that California, by the action of its voters, simply wanted the State to remain neutral in this area, so that the State was not a party to discrimination. That dissenting voice did not prevail against the majority's conclusion that the state action in question encouraged discrimination, causing real and specific injury.

The next precedent of relevance, *Hunter v. Erickson,* 393 U.S. 385 (1969), is central to the arguments the respondents make in the instant case. In *Hunter,* the Court for the first time elaborated what the Court of Appeals here styled the "political process" doctrine. There, the Akron City Council found that the citizens of Akron consisted of "'people of different race[s], . . . many of whom live in circumscribed and segregated areas, under sub-standard unhealthful, unsafe, unsanitary and overcrowded conditions, because of discrimination in the sale, lease, rental and financing of housing.'" To address the problem, Akron enacted a fair housing ordinance to prohibit that sort of discrimination. In response, voters amended the city charter to overturn the ordinance and to require that any additional antidiscrimination housing ordinance be approved by referendum. But most other ordinances "regulating the real property market" were not subject to those threshold requirements. The plaintiff, a black woman in Akron, Ohio, alleged that her real estate agent could not show her certain residences because the owners had specified they would not sell to black persons.

Central to the Court's reasoning in *Hunter* was that the charter amendment was enacted in circumstances where widespread racial discrimination in the sale and rental of housing led to segregated housing, forcing many to live in "'unhealthful, unsafe, unsanitary and overcrowded conditions.'" The Court stated: "It is against this background that the referendum required by [the charter amendment] must be assessed." Akron attempted to characterize the charter amendment "simply as a public decision to move slowly in the delicate area of race relations" and as a means "to allow the people of Akron to participate" in the decision. The Court rejected Akron's flawed "justifications for its discrimination," justifications that by their own terms had the effect of acknowledging the targeted nature of the charter amendment. The Court noted, furthermore, that the charter amendment was unnecessary as a general means of public control over the city council; for the people of Akron already were empowered to overturn ordinances by referendum. The Court found that the city charter amendment, by singling out antidiscrimination ordinances, "places special burden on racial minorities within the governmental process," thus becoming as impermissible as any other government action taken with the invidious intent to injure a racial minority. Justice Harlan filed a concurrence. He argued the city charter amendment "has the clear purpose of making it more difficult for certain racial and religious minorities to achieve legislation that is in their interest." But without regard to the sentence just quoted, *Hunter* rests on the unremarkable principle that the State may not alter the procedures of government to target racial minorities. The facts in *Hunter* established that invidious discrimination would be the necessary result of the procedural restructuring. Thus, in *Mulkey* and *Hunter*, there was a demonstrated injury on the basis of race that, by reasons of state encouragement or participation, became more aggravated.

Seattle is the third case of principal relevance here. There, the school board adopted a mandatory busing program to alleviate racial isolation of minority students in local schools. Voters who opposed the school board's busing plan passed a state initiative that barred busing to desegregate. The Court first determined that, although "white as well as Negro children benefit from" diversity, the school board's plan "inures primarily to the benefit of the minority." The Court next found that "the practical effect" of the state initiative was to "remov[e] the authority to address a racial problem—and only a racial problem—from the existing decisionmaking body, in such a way as to burden minority interests" because advocates of busing "now must seek relief from the state legislature, or from the statewide electorate." The Court therefore found that the initiative had "explicitly us[ed] the racial nature of a decision to determine the decisionmaking process."

Seattle is best understood as a case in which the state action in question (the bar on busing enacted by the State's voters) had the serious risk, if not purpose, of causing specific injuries on account of race, just as had been the case in *Mulkey* and *Hunter*. Although there had been no judicial finding of *de jure* segregation with respect to Seattle's school district, it appears as though school segregation in the district in the 1940's and 1950's may have been the partial result of school board policies that "permitted white students to transfer out of black schools while restricting the transfer of black students into white schools." *Parents Involved in Community Schools v. Seattle School Dist. No. 1*, 551 U.S. 701, 807–808 (2007) (Breyer, J., dissenting). In 1977, the National Association for the Advancement of Colored People (NAACP) filed a complaint with the Office for Civil Rights, a federal agency. The NAACP alleged that the school board had maintained a system of *de jure* segregation. Specifically, the complaint alleged "that the Seattle School Board had created or perpetuated unlawful racial segregation through, *e.g.*, certain school-transfer criteria, a construction program that needlessly built new schools in white areas, district line-drawing criteria, the maintenance of inferior facilities at black schools, the use of explicit racial criteria in the assignment of teachers and other staff, and a general pattern of delay in respect to the implementation of promised desegregation efforts." *Id.*, at 810. As part of a settlement with the Office for Civil Rights, the school board implemented the "Seattle Plan," which used busing and mandatory reassignments between elementary schools to reduce racial imbalance and which was the subject of the state initiative at issue in *Seattle*. See 551 U.S., at 807–812.

As this Court held in *Parents Involved*, the school board's purported remedial action would not be permissible today absent a showing of *de jure* segregation. That holding prompted JUSTICE BREYER to observe in dissent, as noted above, that one permissible reading of the record was that the school board had maintained policies to perpetuate racial segregation in the schools. In all events we must understand *Seattle* as *Seattle* understood itself, as a case in which neither the State nor the United States "challenge[d] the propriety of race-conscious student assignments for the purpose of achieving integration, even absent a finding of prior *de jure* segregation." In other words the legitimacy and constitutionality of the remedy in question (busing for desegregation) was assumed, and *Seattle* must be understood on that basis. *Seattle* involved a state initiative that "was carefully tailored to interfere only with desegregative busing." The *Seattle* Court, accepting the validity of the school board's busing remedy as a predicate to its analysis of the constitutional question, found that the State's disapproval of the school board's busing remedy was an aggravation of the very racial injury in which the State itself was complicit.

The broad language used in *Seattle*, however, went well beyond the analysis needed to resolve the case. The Court there seized upon the statement in Justice Harlan's concurrence in *Hunter* that the procedural change in that case had "the clear purpose of making it more difficult for certain racial and religious minorities to achieve legislation that is in their interest." That language, taken in the context of the facts in *Hunter*, is best read simply to describe the necessity for finding an equal protection violation where specific injuries from hostile discrimination were at issue. The *Seattle* Court, however, used the language from the *Hunter* concurrence to establish a new and far-reaching rationale. *Seattle* stated that where a government policy "inures primarily to the benefit of the minority" and "minorities . . . consider" the policy to be "'in their interest,'" then any state action that "place[s] effective decisionmaking authority over" that policy "at a different level of government" must be reviewed under strict scrutiny. In essence, according to the broad reading of *Seattle*, any state action with a "racial focus" that makes it "more difficult for certain racial minorities than for other groups" to "achieve legislation that is in their interest" is subject to strict scrutiny. It is this reading of *Seattle* that the Court of Appeals found to be controlling here. And that reading must be rejected.

The broad rationale that the Court of Appeals adopted goes beyond the necessary holding and the meaning of the precedents said to support it; and in the instant case neither the formulation of the general rule just set forth nor the precedents cited to authenticate it suffice to invalidate Proposal 2. The expansive reading of *Seattle* has no principled limitation and raises serious questions of compatibility with the Court's settled equal protection jurisprudence. To the extent *Seattle* is read to require the Court to determine and declare which political policies serve the "interest" of a group defined in racial terms, that rationale was unnecessary to the decision in *Seattle*; it has no support in precedent; and it raises serious constitutional concerns. That expansive language does not provide a proper guide for decisions and should not be deemed authoritative or controlling. The rule that the Court of Appeals elaborated and respondents seek to establish here would contradict central equal protection principles.

In cautioning against "impermissible racial stereotypes," this Court has rejected the assumption that "members of the same racial group—regardless of their age, education, economic status, or the community in which they live—think alike, share the same political interests, and will prefer the same candidates at the polls." *Shaw v. Reno,* 509 U.S. 630, 647 (1993); see also *Metro Broadcasting, Inc. v. FCC,* 497 U.S. 547, 636 (1990) (Kennedy, J., dissenting) (rejecting the "demeaning notion that members of . . . defined racial groups ascribe to certain 'minority views' that must be different from those of other citizens"). It cannot be entertained as a serious proposition that all individuals of the same race think alike. Yet that proposition would be a necessary beginning point were the *Seattle* formulation to control, as the Court of Appeals held it did in this case. And if it were deemed necessary to probe how some races define their own interest in political matters, still another beginning point would be to define individuals according to race. But in a society in which those lines are becoming more blurred, the attempt to define race-based categories also raises serious questions of its own. Government action that classifies individuals on the basis of race is inherently suspect and carries the danger of perpetuating the very racial divisions the polity seeks to transcend. Were courts to embark upon this venture not only would it be undertaken with no clear legal standards or accepted sources to guide judicial decision but also it would result in, or at least impose a high risk of, inquiries and categories dependent upon demeaning stereotypes, classifications of questionable constitutionality on their own terms.

Even assuming these initial steps could be taken in a manner consistent with a sound analytic and judicial framework, the court would next be required to determine the policy realms in which certain groups—groups defined by race—have a political interest. That undertaking, again without guidance from any accepted legal standards, would risk, in turn, the creation of incentives for those who support or oppose certain policies to cast the debate in terms of racial advantage or disadvantage. Thus could racial antagonisms and conflict tend to arise in the context of judicial decisions as courts undertook to announce what particular issues of public policy should be classified as advantageous to some group defined by race. This risk is inherent in adopting the *Seattle* formulation.

There would be no apparent limiting standards defining what public policies should be included in what *Seattle* called policies that "inur[e] primarily to the benefit of the minority" and that "minorities . . . consider" to be "'in their interest.'" Those who seek to represent the interests of particular racial groups could attempt to advance those aims by demanding an equal protection ruling that any number of matters be foreclosed from voter review or participation. In a nation in which governmental policies are wide ranging, those who seek to limit voter participation might be tempted, were this Court to adopt the *Seattle* formulation, to urge that a group they choose to define by race or racial stereotypes are advantaged or disadvantaged by any number of laws or decisions. Tax policy, housing subsidies, wage regulations, and even the naming of public schools, highways, and monuments are just a few examples of what could become a list of subjects that some organizations could insist should be beyond the power of voters to decide, or beyond the power of a legislature to decide when enacting limits on the power of local authorities or other governmental entities to address certain subjects. Racial division would be validated, not discouraged, were the *Seattle* formulation, and the reasoning of the Court of Appeals in this case, to remain in force. . . .

For reasons already discussed, *Mulkey, Hunter*, and *Seattle* are not precedents that stand for the conclusion that Michigan's voters must be disempowered from acting. Those cases were ones in which the political restriction in question was designed to be used, or was likely to be used, to encourage infliction of injury by reason of race. What is at stake here is not whether injury will be inflicted but whether government can be instructed not to follow a course that entails, first, the definition of racial categories and, second, the grant of favored status to persons in some racial categories and not others. The electorate's instruction to governmental entities not to embark upon the course of race-defined and race-based preferences was adopted, we must assume, because the voters deemed a preference system to be unwise, on account of what voters may deem its latent potential to become itself a source of the very resentments and hostilities based on race that this Nation seeks to put behind it. Whether those adverse results would follow is, and should be, the subject of debate. Voters might likewise consider, after debate and reflection, that programs designed to increase diversity—consistent with the Constitution—are a necessary part of progress to transcend the stigma of past racism.

This case is not about how the debate about racial preferences should be resolved. It is about who may resolve it. There is no authority in the Constitution of the United States or in this Court's precedents for the Judiciary to set aside Michigan laws that commit this policy determination to the voters. Deliberative debate on sensitive issues such as racial preferences all too often may shade into rancor. But that does not justify removing certain court-determined issues from the voters' reach. Democracy does not presume that some subjects are either too divisive or too profound for public debate. . . .

Justice Scalia, with whom Justice Thomas joins, concurring in the judgment. . . .

[T]he battleground for this case is not the constitutionality of race-based admissions—at least, not quite. Rather, it is the so-called political-process doctrine, derived from this Court's opinions in *Washington v. Seattle School Dist. No. 1*, 458 U.S. 457 (1982), and *Hunter v. Erickson*, 393 U.S. 385 (1969). I agree with those parts of the plurality opinion that repudiate this doctrine. But I do not agree with its reinterpretation of *Seattle* and *Hunter*, which makes them stand in part for the cloudy and doctrinally anomalous proposition that whenever state action poses "the serious risk . . . of causing specific injuries on account of race," it denies equal protection. . . .

I

A

The political-process doctrine has its roots in two of our cases. The first is *Hunter.* In 1964, the Akron City Council passed a fair-housing ordinance "'assur[ing] equal opportunity to all persons to live in decent housing facilities regardless of race, color, religion, ancestry or national origin.'" Soon after, the city's voters passed an amendment to the Akron City Charter stating that any ordinance enacted by the council that "'regulates'" commercial transactions in real property "'on the basis of race, color, religion, national origin or ancestry'"—including the already enacted 1964 ordinance—"must first be approved by a majority of the electors voting on the question" at a later referendum. The question was whether the charter amendment denied equal protection. Answering yes, the Court explained that "although the law on its face treats Negro and white, Jew and gentile in an identical manner, the reality is that the law's impact falls on the minority. The majority needs no protection against discrimination." By placing a "special burden on racial minorities within the governmental processes," the amendment "disadvantage[d]" a racial minority "by making it more difficult to enact legislation in its behalf."

The reasoning in *Seattle* is of a piece. Resolving to "eliminate all [racial] imbalance from the Seattle public schools," the city school board passed a mandatory busing and pupil-reassignment plan of the sort typically imposed on districts guilty of *de jure* segregation. A year later, the citizens of the State of Washington passed Initiative 350, which directed (with exceptions) that "'no school . . . shall directly or indirectly require any student to attend a school other than the school which is geographically nearest or next nearest the student's place of residence . . . and which offers the course of study pursued by such student,'" permitting only court-ordered race-based busing. The lower courts held Initiative 350 unconstitutional, and we affirmed, announcing in the prelude of our analysis—as though it were beyond debate—that the Equal Protection Clause forbade laws that "subtly distor[t] governmental processes in such a way as to place special burdens on the ability of minority groups to achieve beneficial legislation."

The first question in *Seattle* was whether the subject matter of Initiative 350 was a "'racial' issue," triggering *Hunter* and its process doctrine. It was "undoubtedly . . . true" that whites and blacks were "counted among both the supporters and the opponents of Initiative 350." It was "equally clear" that both white and black children benefitted from desegregated schools. Nonetheless, we concluded that desegregation "inures *primarily* to the benefit of the minority, and is designed for that purpose." (emphasis added). In any event, it was "enough that minorities may consider busing for integration to be 'legislation that is in their interest.'"

So we proceeded to the heart of the political-process analysis. We held Initiative 350 unconstitutional, since it removed "the authority to address a racial problem—and only a racial problem—from the existing decisionmaking body, in such a way as to burden minority interests." Although school boards in Washington retained authority over *other* student-assignment issues and over most matters of educational policy generally, under Initiative 350, minorities favoring race-based busing would have to "surmount a considerably higher hurdle" than the mere petitioning of a local assembly: They "now must seek relief from the state legislature, or from the statewide electorate," a "different level of government."

The relentless logic of *Hunter* and *Seattle* would point to a similar conclusion in this case. In those cases, one level of government exercised borrowed authority over an apparently "racial issue," until a higher level of government called the loan. So too here. In those cases, we deemed the revocation an equal-protection violation *regardless* of whether it facially classified according to race or reflected an invidious purpose to discriminate. Here, the Court of Appeals did the same.

The plurality sees it differently. Though it, too, disavows the political-process-doctrine basis on which *Hunter* and *Seattle* were decided, it does not take the next step of overruling those cases. Rather, it reinterprets them beyond recognition. *Hunter*, the plurality suggests, was a case in which the challenged act had "target[ed] racial minorities." Maybe, but the *Hunter* Court neither found that to be so nor considered it relevant, bypassing the question of intent entirely, satisfied that its newly minted political-process theory sufficed to invalidate the charter amendment.

As for *Seattle*, what was *really* going on, according to the plurality, was that Initiative 350 had the consequence (if not the purpose) of preserving the harms effected by prior *de jure* segregation. Thus, "the political restriction in question was designed to be used, or was likely to be used, to encourage infliction of injury by reason of race." That conclusion is derived not from the opinion but from recently discovered evidence that the city of Seattle had been a cause of its schools' racial imbalance all along: "Although there had been no judicial finding of *de jure* segregation with respect to Seattle's school district, it appears as though school segregation in the district in the 1940's and 1950's may have been the partial result of school board policies." That the district's effort to end racial imbalance had been stymied by Initiative 350 meant that the people, by passing it, somehow had become complicit in Seattle's equal-protection-denying status quo, whether they knew it or not. Hence, there was in *Seattle* a government-furthered "infliction of a specific"—and, presumably, constitutional—"injury."

Once again this describes what our opinion in *Seattle* might have been, but assuredly not what it was. The opinion assumes throughout that Seattle's schools suffered at most from *de facto* segregation—that is, segregation not the "product . . . of state action but of private choices," having no "constitutional implications," *Freeman*, 503 U.S., at 495–496. Nor did it anywhere state that the current racial imbalance was the (judicially remediable) effect of prior *de jure* segregation. Absence of *de jure* segregation or the effects of *de jure* segregation was a necessary premise of the *Seattle* opinion. That is what made the issue of busing and pupil reassignment a matter of political choice rather than judicial mandate. And precisely *because* it was a question for the political branches to decide, the manner—which is to say, the *process*—of its resolution implicated the Court's new process theory. The opinion itself says this: "[I]n the absence of a constitutional violation, the desirability and efficacy of school desegregation are matters to be resolved though the political process. For present purposes, it is enough [to hold reallocation of that political decision to a higher level unconstitutional] that minorities may consider busing for integration to be legislation that is in their interest." . . . .

B

Patently atextual, unadministrable, and contrary to our traditional equal-protection jurisprudence, *Hunter* and *Seattle* should be overruled.

The problems with the political-process doctrine begin with its triggering prong, which assigns to a court the task of determining whether a law that reallocates policymaking authority concerns a "racial issue." *Seattle* takes a couple of dissatisfying cracks at defining this crucial term. It suggests that an issue is racial if adopting one position on the question would "at bottom inur[e] primarily to the benefit of the minority, and is designed for that purpose." . . . .

No good can come of such random judicial musing. . . . For one thing, it involves judges in the dirty business of dividing the Nation "into racial blocs." . . . . What is worse, the exercise promotes the noxious fiction that, knowing only a person's color or ethnicity, we can be sure that he has a predetermined set of policy "interests," thus "reinforc[ing] the perception that members of the same racial group—regardless of their age, education, economic status, or the community in which they live—think alike, [and] share the same political interests." *Shaw v. Reno*, 509 U.S. 630, 647 (1993) . . . .

But that is not the "racial issue" prong's only defect. More fundamentally, it misreads the Equal Protection Clause to protect "particular group[s]," a construction that we have tirelessly repudiated in a "long line of cases understanding equal protection as a personal right." *Adarand Constructors, Inc. v. Pena*, 515 U.S. 200, 224, 230 (1995). It is a "basic principle that the Fifth and Fourteenth Amendments to the Constitution protect *persons*, not *groups*." *Id.* at 227. Yet *Seattle* insists that only those political-process alterations that burden racial *minorities* deny equal protection. . . . In the years since *Seattle*, we have repeatedly rejected "a reading of the guarantee of equal protection under which the level of scrutiny varies according to the ability of different groups to defend their interests in the representative process." *Richmond v. J.A. Croson Co.*, 488 U.S. 469, 495 (1989) . . . .

C

Moving from the appalling to the absurd, I turn now to the second part of the *Hunter–Seattle* analysis—which is apparently no more administrable than the first. This part of the inquiry directs a court to determine whether the challenged act "place[s] effective decisionmaking authority over [the] racial issue at a different level of government." . . . .

Taken to the limits of its logic, *Hunter–Seattle* is the gaping exception that nearly swallows the rule of structural state sovereignty. If indeed the Fourteenth Amendment forbids States to "place effective decisionmaking authority over" racial issues at "different level[s] of government," then it must be true that the Amendment's ratification in 1868 worked a partial ossification of each State's governing structure, rendering basically irrevocable the power of any subordinate state official who, the day *before* the Fourteenth Amendment's passage, happened to enjoy legislatively conferred authority over a "racial issue." Under the Fourteenth Amendment, that subordinate entity (suppose it is a city council) could itself take action on the issue, action either favorable or unfavorable to minorities. It could even reverse itself later. What it could not do, however, is redelegate its power to an even lower level of state government (such as a city-council committee) without forfeiting it, since the necessary effect of wresting it back would be to put an additional obstacle in the path of minorities. Likewise, no entity or official higher up the state chain (*e.g.,* a county board) could exercise authority over the issue. Nor, even, could the state legislature, or the people by constitutional amendment, revoke the legislative conferral of power to the subordinate, whether the city council, its subcommittee, or the county board. *Seattle*'s logic would create affirmative-action safe havens wherever subordinate officials in public universities (1) traditionally have enjoyed "effective decisionmaking authority" over admissions policy but (2) have not yet used that authority to prohibit race-conscious admissions decisions. The mere existence of a subordinate's discretion over the matter would work a kind of reverse pre-emption. . . .

II

I part ways with *Hunter, Seattle*, and (I think) the plurality for an additional reason: Each endorses a version of the proposition that a facially neutral law may deny equal protection solely because it has a disparate racial impact. Few equal-protection theories have been so squarely and soundly rejected. "An unwavering line of cases from this Court holds that a violation of the Equal Protection Clause requires state action motivated by discriminatory intent," *Hernandez v. New York,* 500 U.S. 352, 372–373 (1991) (O'Connor, J., concurring in judgment), and that "official action will not be held unconstitutional solely because it results in a racially disproportionate impact," *Arlington Heights v. Metropolitan Housing Development Corp.,* 429 U.S. 252, 264–265 (1977) . . . .

Notwithstanding our dozens of cases confirming the exceptionless nature of the *Washington v. Davis* rule, the plurality opinion leaves ajar an effects-test escape hatch modeled after *Hunter* and *Seattle*, suggesting that state action denies equal protection when it "ha[s] the *serious risk,* if not purpose, of causing specific injuries on account of race," or is either "designed to be used, or . . . *likely to be used,* to encourage infliction of injury by reason of race." Since these formulations enable a determination of an equal-protection violation where there is no discriminatory intent, they are inconsistent with the long *Washington v. Davis* line of cases. . . .

A law that "neither says nor implies that persons are to be treated differently on account of their race" is not a racial classification. . . .

Thus, the question in this case, as in every case in which neutral state action is said to deny equal protection on account of race, is whether the action reflects a racially discriminatory purpose. . . .

JUSTICE BREYER, concurring in the judgment. . . .

I agree with the plurality that the amendment is consistent with the Federal Equal Protection Clause. But I believe this for different reasons. . . .

First, we do not address the amendment insofar as it forbids the use of race-conscious admissions programs designed to remedy past exclusionary racial discrimination or the direct effects of that discrimination. Application of the amendment in that context would present different questions which may demand different answers. Rather, we here address the amendment only as it applies to, and forbids, programs that, as in *Grutter v. Bollinger*, 539 U.S. 306 (2003), rest upon "one justification": using "race in the admissions process" solely in order to "obtai[n] the educational benefits that flow from a diverse student body." . . . .

Hunter and *Seattle* involved efforts to manipulate the political process in a way not here at issue. Both cases involved a restructuring of the political process that changed the political level at which policies were enacted. In *Hunter*, decisionmaking was moved from the elected city council to the local electorate at large. And in *Seattle*, decisionmaking by an elected school board was replaced with decisionmaking by the state legislature and electorate at large.

This case, in contrast, does not involve a reordering of the *political* process; it does not in fact involve the movement of decisionmaking from one political level to another. Rather, here, Michigan law delegated broad policymaking authority to elected university boards, but those boards delegated admissions-related decisionmaking authority to unelected university faculty members and administrators. Although the boards unquestionably retained the *power* to set policy regarding race-conscious admissions, in *fact* faculty members and administrators set the race-conscious admissions policies in question. (It is often true that elected bodies—including, for example, school boards, city councils, and state legislatures—have the power to enact policies, but in fact delegate that power to administrators.) Although at limited times the university boards were advised of the content of their race-conscious admissions policies, to my knowledge no board voted to accept or reject any of those policies. Thus, unelected faculty members and administrators, not voters or their elected representatives, adopted the race-conscious admissions programs affected by Michigan's constitutional amendment. The amendment took decisionmaking authority away from these unelected actors and placed it in the hands of the voters.

Why does this matter? For one thing, considered conceptually, the doctrine set forth in *Hunter* and *Seattle* does not easily fit this case. In those cases minorities had participated in the political process and they had won. The majority's subsequent reordering of the political process repealed the minority's successes and made it more difficult for the minority to succeed in the future. The majority thereby diminished the minority's ability to participate meaningfully in the electoral process. But one cannot as easily characterize the movement of the decisionmaking mechanism at issue here—from an administrative process to an electoral process—as diminishing the minority's ability to participate meaningfully in the *political* process. There is no prior electoral process in which the minority participated.

For another thing, to extend the holding of *Hunter* and *Seattle* to reach situations in which decisionmaking authority is moved from an administrative body to a political one would pose significant difficulties. The administrative process encompasses vast numbers of decisionmakers answering numerous policy questions in hosts of different fields. Administrative bodies modify programs in detail, and decisionmaking authority within the administrative process frequently moves around—due to amendments to statutes, new administrative rules, and evolving agency practice. It is thus particularly difficult in this context for judges to determine when a change in the locus of decisionmaking authority places a comparative structural burden on a racial minority. And to apply *Hunter* and *Seattle* to the administrative process would, by tending to hinder change, risk discouraging experimentation, interfering with efforts to see when and how race-conscious policies work.

Finally, the principle that underlies *Hunter* and *Seattle* runs up against a competing principle, discussed above. This competing principle favors decisionmaking though the democratic process. Just as this principle strongly supports the right of the people, or their elected representatives, to adopt race-conscious policies for reasons of inclusion, so must it give them the right to vote not to do so.

As I have said, my discussion here is limited to circumstances in which decisionmaking is moved from an unelected administrative body to a politically responsive one, and in which the targeted race-conscious admissions programs consider race solely in order to obtain the educational benefits of a diverse student body. We need now decide no more than whether the Federal Constitution permits Michigan to apply its constitutional amendment in those circumstances. I would hold that it does. Therefore, I concur in the judgment of the Court.

Justice Sotomayor, with whom Justice Ginsburg joins, dissenting....

Hunter and *Seattle* vindicated a principle that is as elementary to our equal protection jurisprudence as it is essential: The majority may not suppress the minority's right to participate on equal terms in the political process. Under this doctrine, governmental action deprives minority groups of equal protection when it (1) has a racial focus, targeting a policy or program that "inures primarily to the benefit of the minority"; and (2) alters the political process in a manner that uniquely burdens racial minorities' ability to achieve their goals through that process....

And what now of the political-process doctrine? After the plurality's revision of *Hunter* and *Seattle*, it is unclear what is left. The plurality certainly does not tell us.

On this point, and this point only, I agree with Justice Scalia that the plurality has rewritten those precedents beyond recognition. . . .

[The concurring opinion of Chief Justice Roberts is omitted.]

Notes and Questions

1. Is Justice Kennedy's opinion a fair reading of the Court's decisions in *Reitman*, *Hunter*, and *Washington*? Note that Justices Scalia and Sotomayor, while arriving at starkly different conclusions, agree that the majority "has rewritten those precedents beyond recognition." Do you agree? Could it instead be said that Justice Kennedy is harmonizing *Hunter* and *Washington* with the *original* basis for the Court's decision in *Reitman*?

2. Given the split among the Justices, how would you reconcile this line of cases? Is there a constitutionally significant difference between banning affirmative action laws and anti-discrimination laws? Does it matter whether the affirmative action law is designed to address diversity or to remedy prior discrimination? In the case of affirmative action, would it matter if the policy was originally enacted by an *elected* local body? In this regard consider Justice Breyer's separate opinion, especially after reading the Court's later decisions regarding affirmative action in Chapter 17.

Chapter 11

The Rebirth of Substantive Due Process

A. Introduction

In the cases excerpted in earlier chapters, the Court has been grappling with *whether* it is empowered to recognize and enforce unenumerated rights; how to determine the substance of those rights; and the textual hook for exercising such a power. In the materials that you have read so far, the Justices have cycled through the Privileges or Immunities, Due Process, and Equal Protection Clauses of the Fourteenth Amendment in their search for a textual basis for recognizing and enforcing unenumerated rights.

In the case that follows, the Court considers the flip-side of the right to procreate recognized in *Skinner*, to wit, the right *not* to procreate. Specifically, it involves a challenge to the constitutionality of a law criminalizing the sale of contraceptives to married persons.

As you read the various opinions in the case, keep an eye out for three key aspects of the opinion. First, what constitutional text does each Justice identify as a basis for recognizing and enforcing the right at issue? Second, to the extent that the opinions rely on earlier precedents, are they faithfully characterizing the holdings of those decisions? Finally, separate and apart from the right at issue in this case, consider how you would apply the opinion when other rights are at stake, including the following:

- A law criminalizing the sale of contraceptives to unmarried persons;
- A law criminalizing adultery or sexual activity between unmarried persons;
- A law criminalizing sexual activity between persons of the same sex;
- A law prohibiting interracial marriage; and
- A law prohibiting same-sex marriage.

Griswold v. Connecticut

381 U.S. 479 (1965)

Mr. Justice Douglas delivered the opinion of the Court.

Appellant Griswold is Executive Director of the Planned Parenthood League of Connecticut. Appellant Buxton is a licensed physician and a professor at the Yale Medical School who served as Medical Director for the League at its Center in New

Haven—a center open and operating from November 1 to November 10, 1961, when appellants were arrested.

They gave information, instruction, and medical advice to *married persons* as to the means of preventing conception. They examined the wife and prescribed the best contraceptive device or material for her use. Fees were usually charged, although some couples were serviced free.

The statutes whose constitutionality is involved in this appeal are §§ 53–32 and 54–196 of the General Statutes of Connecticut (1958 rev.). The former provides:

> "Any person who uses any drug, medicinal article or instrument for the purpose of preventing conception shall be fined not less than fifty dollars or imprisoned not less than sixty days nor more than one year or be both fined and imprisoned."

Section 54–196 provides:

> "Any person who assists, abets, counsels, causes, hires or commands another to commit any offense may be prosecuted and punished as if he were the principal offender."

The appellants were found guilty as accessories and fined $100 each, against the claim that the accessory statute as so applied violated the Fourteenth Amendment. . . .

We think that appellants have standing to raise the constitutional rights of the married people with whom they had a professional relationship. . . . Certainly the accessory should have standing to assert that the offense which he is charged with assisting is not, or cannot constitutionally be a crime. . . .

The rights of husband and wife, pressed here, are likely to be diluted or adversely affected unless those rights are considered in a suit involving those who have this kind of confidential relation to them.

Coming to the merits, we are met with a wide range of questions that implicate the Due Process Clause of the Fourteenth Amendment. Overtones of some arguments suggest that *Lochner v. New York*, 198 U.S. 45, should be our guide. But we decline that invitation. . . . We do not sit as a super-legislature to determine the wisdom, need, and propriety of laws that touch economic problems, business affairs, or social conditions. This law, however, operates directly on an intimate relation of husband and wife and their physician's role in one aspect of that relation.

The association of people is not mentioned in the Constitution nor in the Bill of Rights. The right to educate a child in a school of the parents' choice—whether public or private or parochial—is also not mentioned. Nor is the right to study any particular subject or any foreign language. Yet the First Amendment has been construed to include certain of those rights.

By *Pierce v. Society of Sisters*, the right to educate one's children as one chooses is made applicable to the States by the force of the First and Fourteenth Amendments. By *Meyer v. Nebraska*, the same dignity is given the right to study the German language in a private school. In other words, the State may not, consistently with the spirit of the First Amendment, contract the spectrum of available knowledge. The right of freedom of speech and press includes not only the right to utter or to print, but the right to distribute, the right to receive, the right to read and freedom of inquiry, freedom of thought, and freedom to teach—indeed the freedom of the entire university community. Without those peripheral rights the specific rights would be less secure. And so we reaffirm the principle of the *Pierce* and the *Meyer* cases.

In *NAACP v. Alabama*, 357 U.S. 449, 462, we protected the "freedom to associate and privacy in one's associations," noting that freedom of association was a peripheral First Amendment right. Disclosure of membership lists of a constitutionally valid association, we held, was invalid "as entailing the likelihood of a substantial restraint upon the exercise by petitioner's members of their right to freedom of association." In other words, the First Amendment has a penumbra where privacy is protected from governmental intrusion. In like context, we have protected forms of "association" that are not political in the customary sense but pertain to the social, legal, and economic benefit of the members. . . .

The foregoing cases suggest that specific guarantees in the Bill of Rights have penumbras, formed by emanations from those guarantees that help give them life and substance. Various guarantees create zones of privacy. The right of association contained in the penumbra of the First Amendment is one, as we have seen. The Third Amendment in its prohibition against the quartering of soldiers "in any house" in time of peace without the consent of the owner is another facet of that privacy. The Fourth Amendment explicitly affirms the "right of the people to be secure in their persons, houses, papers, and effects, against unreasonable searches and seizures." The Fifth Amendment in its Self-Incrimination Clause enables the citizen to create a zone of privacy which government may not force him to surrender to his detriment. The Ninth Amendment provides: "The enumeration in the Constitution, of certain rights, shall not be construed to deny or disparage others retained by the people." . . . .

The present case, then, concerns a relationship lying within the zone of privacy created by several fundamental constitutional guarantees. And it concerns a law which, in forbidding the *use* of contraceptives rather than regulating their manufacture or sale, seeks to achieve its goals by means having a maximum destructive impact upon that relationship. Such a law cannot stand in light of the familiar principle, so often applied by this Court, that a "governmental purpose to control or prevent activities constitutionally subject to state regulation may not be achieved by means which sweep unnecessarily broadly and thereby invade the area of protected freedoms." Would we allow the police to search the sacred precincts of marital bedrooms for telltale signs of the use of contraceptives? The very idea is repulsive to the notions of privacy surrounding the marriage relationship.

We deal with a right of privacy older than the Bill of Rights—older than our political parties, older than our school system. Marriage is a coming together for better or for worse, hopefully enduring, and intimate to the degree of being sacred. It is an association that promotes a way of life, not causes; a harmony in living, not political faiths; a bilateral loyalty, not commercial or social projects. Yet it is an association for as noble a purpose as any involved in our prior decisions.

Reversed.

Mr. Justice Goldberg, whom The Chief Justice and Mr. Justice Brennan join, concurring.

I agree with the Court that Connecticut's birth-control law unconstitutionally intrudes upon the right of marital privacy, and I join in its opinion and judgment. Although I have not accepted the view that "due process" as used in the Fourteenth Amendment includes all of the first eight Amendments, I do agree that the concept of liberty protects those personal rights that are fundamental, and is not confined to the specific terms of the Bill of Rights. My conclusion that the concept of liberty is not so restricted and that it embraces the right of marital privacy though that right is not mentioned explicitly in the Constitution is supported both by numerous decisions of this Court, referred to in the Court's opinion, and by the language and history of the Ninth Amendment. In reaching the conclusion that the right of marital privacy is protected, as being within the protected penumbra of specific guarantees of the Bill of Rights, the Court refers to the Ninth Amendment. I add these words to emphasize the relevance of that Amendment to the Court's holding. . . .

This Court, in a series of decisions, has held that the Fourteenth Amendment absorbs and applies to the States those specifics of the first eight amendments which express fundamental personal rights. The language and history of the Ninth Amendment reveal that the Framers of the Constitution believed that there are additional fundamental rights, protected from governmental infringement, which exist alongside those fundamental rights specifically mentioned in the first eight constitutional amendments.

The Ninth Amendment reads, "The enumeration in the Constitution, of certain rights, shall not be construed to deny or disparage others retained by the people." The Amendment is almost entirely the work of James Madison. It was introduced in Congress by him and passed the House and Senate with little or no debate and virtually no change in language. It was proffered to quiet expressed fears that a bill of specifically enumerated rights could not be sufficiently broad to cover all essential rights and that the specific mention of certain rights would be interpreted as a denial that others were protected.

In presenting the proposed Amendment, Madison said:

> "It has been objected also against a bill of rights, that, by enumerating particular exceptions to the grant of power, it would disparage those rights which were not placed in that enumeration; and it might follow by implication, that those rights which were not singled out, were intended to be assigned into the hands of the General Government, and were consequently insecure. This is one of the most plausible arguments I have ever heard urged against the admission of a bill of rights into this system; but, I

> conceive, that it may be guarded against. I have attempted it, as gentlemen may see by turning to the last clause of the fourth resolution (the Ninth Amendment)." I Annals of Congress 439 (Gales and Seaton ed. 1834).

Mr. Justice Story wrote of this argument against a bill of rights and the meaning of the Ninth Amendment:

> "In regard to . . . [a] suggestion, that the affirmance of certain rights might disparage others, or might lead to argumentative implications in favor of other powers, it might be sufficient to say that such a course of reasoning could never be sustained upon any solid basis. . . . But a conclusive answer is, that such an attempt may be interdicted (as it has been) by a positive declaration in such a bill of rights that the enumeration of certain rights shall not be construed to deny or disparage others retained by the people." II Story, Commentaries on the Constitution of the United States 626-627 (5th ed. 1891).

He further stated, referring to the Ninth Amendment:

> "This clause was manifestly introduced to prevent any perverse or ingenious misapplication of the well-known maxim, that an affirmation in particular cases implies a negation in all others; and, *e converso*, that a negation in particular cases implies an affirmation in all others." *Id.*, at 651.

These statements of Madison and Story make clear that the Framers did not intend that the first eight amendments be construed to exhaust the basic and fundamental rights which the Constitution guaranteed to the people. . . .

The Ninth Amendment to the Constitution may be regarded by some as a recent discovery and may be forgotten by others, but since 1791 it has been a basic part of the Constitution which we are sworn to uphold. To hold that a right so basic and fundamental and so deep-rooted in our society as the right of privacy in marriage may be infringed because that right is not guaranteed in so many words by the first eight amendments to the Constitution is to ignore the Ninth Amendment and to give it no effect whatsoever. . . .

A dissenting opinion suggests that my interpretation of the Ninth Amendment somehow "broaden[s] the powers of this Court." With all due respect, I believe that it misses the import of what I am saying. I do not take the position . . . that the entire Bill of Rights is incorporated in the Fourteenth Amendment, and I do not mean to imply that the Ninth Amendment is applied against the States by the Fourteenth. Nor do I mean to state that the Ninth Amendment constitutes an independent source of rights protected from infringement by either the States or the Federal Government. Rather, the Ninth Amendment shows a belief of the Constitution's authors that fundamental rights exist that are not expressly enumerated in the first eight amendments and an intent that the list of rights included there not be deemed exhaustive. As any student of this Court's opinions knows, this Court has held, often unanimously, that the Fifth and Fourteenth Amendments protect certain fundamental personal liberties from abridgment by the Federal Government or the States. The Ninth Amendment simply shows the intent of the Constitution's authors that other fundamental personal rights should not be denied such protection or disparaged in any other way simply because they are not specifically listed in the first eight constitutional amendments. I do not see how this broadens the authority of the Court; rather it serves to support what this Court has been doing in protecting fundamental rights.

Nor am I turning somersaults with history in arguing that the Ninth Amendment is relevant in a case dealing with a *State's* infringement of a fundamental right. While the Ninth Amendment—and indeed the entire Bill of Rights—originally concerned restrictions upon *federal* power, the subsequently enacted Fourteenth Amendment prohibits the States as well from abridging fundamental personal liberties. And, the Ninth Amendment, in indicating that not all such liberties are specifically mentioned in the first eight amendments, is surely relevant in showing the existence of other fundamental personal rights, now protected from state, as well as federal, infringement. . . .

In determining which rights are fundamental, judges are not left at large to decide cases in light of their personal and private notions. Rather, they must look to the "traditions and [collective] conscience of our people" to determine whether a principle is "so rooted [there] . . . as to be ranked as fundamental." *Snyder v. Massachusetts*, 291 U.S. 97, 105 . . . .

The Connecticut statutes here involved deal with a particularly important and sensitive area of privacy—that of the marital relation and the marital home. This Court recognized in *Meyer v. Nebraska* that the right "to marry, establish a home and bring up children" was an essential part of the liberty guaranteed by the Fourteenth Amendment. 262 U.S., at 399. In *Pierce v. Society of Sisters*, 268 U.S. 510, the Court held unconstitutional an Oregon Act which forbade parents from sending their children to private schools because such an act "unreasonably interferes with the liberty of parents and guardians to direct the upbringing and education of children under their control." As this Court said in *Prince v. Massachusetts*, 321 U.S. 158, at 166, the *Meyer* and *Pierce* decisions "have respected the private realm of family life which the state cannot enter." . . . .

The entire fabric of the Constitution and the purposes that clearly underlie its specific guarantees demonstrate that the rights to marital privacy and to marry and raise a family are of similar order and magnitude as the fundamental rights specifically protected.

Although the Constitution does not speak in so many words of the right of privacy in marriage, I cannot believe that it offers these fundamental rights no protection. The fact that no particular provision of the Constitution explicitly forbids the State from disrupting the traditional relation of the family—a relation as old and as fundamental as our entire civilization—surely does not show that the Government was meant to have the power to do so. Rather, as the Ninth Amendment expressly recognizes, there are fundamental personal rights such as this one, which are protected from abridgment by the Government though not specifically mentioned in the Constitution. . . .

The logic of the dissents would sanction federal or state legislation that seems to me even more plainly unconstitutional than the statute before us. Surely the Government, absent a showing of a compelling subordinating state interest, could not decree that all husbands and wives must be sterilized after two children have been born to them. Yet by their reasoning such an invasion of marital privacy would not be subject to constitutional challenge because, while it might be "silly," no provision of the Constitution specifically prevents the Government from curtailing the marital right to bear children and raise a family. While it may shock some of my Brethren that the Court today holds that the Constitution protects the right of marital privacy, in my view it is far more shocking to believe that the personal liberty guaranteed by the Constitution does not include protection against such totalitarian limitation of family size, which is at complete variance with our constitutional concepts. Yet, if upon a showing of a slender basis of rationality, a law outlawing voluntary birth control by married persons is valid, then, by the same reasoning, a law requiring compulsory birth control also would seem to be valid. In my view, however, both types of law would unjustifiably intrude upon rights of marital privacy which are constitutionally protected.

In a long series of cases this Court has held that where fundamental personal liberties are involved, they may not be abridged by the States simply on a showing that a regulatory statute has some rational relationship to the effectuation of a proper state purpose. "Where there is a significant encroachment upon personal liberty, the State may prevail only upon showing a subordinating interest which is compelling." The law must be shown "necessary, and not merely rationally related to, the accomplishment of a permissible state policy."

Although the Connecticut birth-control law obviously encroaches upon a fundamental personal liberty, the State does not show that the law serves any "subordinating [state] interest which is compelling" or that it is "necessary . . . to the accomplishment of a permissible state policy." The State, at most, argues that there is some rational relation between this statute and what is admittedly a legitimate subject of state concern—the discouraging of extra-marital relations. It says that preventing the use of birth-control devices by married persons helps prevent the indulgence by some in such extra-marital relations. The rationality of this justification is dubious, particularly in light of the admitted widespread availability to all persons in the State of Connecticut, unmarried as well as married, of birth-control devices for the prevention of disease, as distinguished from the prevention of conception. But, in any event, it is clear that the state interest in safeguarding marital fidelity can be served by a more discriminately tailored statute, which does not, like the present one, sweep unnecessarily broadly, reaching far beyond the evil sought to be dealt with and intruding upon the privacy of all married couples. Here, as elsewhere, "[p]recision of regulation must be the touchstone in an area so closely touching our most precious freedoms." The State of Connecticut does have statutes, the constitutionality of which is beyond doubt, which prohibit adultery and fornication. These statutes demonstrate that means for achieving the same basic purpose of protecting marital fidelity are available to Connecticut without the need to "invade the area of protected freedoms."

Finally, it should be said of the Court's holding today that it in no way interferes with a State's proper regulation of sexual promiscuity or misconduct. As my Brother Harlan so well stated in his dissenting opinion in *Poe v. Ullman*.

> "Adultery, homosexuality and the like are sexual intimacies which the State forbids . . . but the intimacy of husband and wife is necessarily an essential and accepted feature of the institution of marriage, an institution which the State not only must allow, but which always and in every age it has fostered and protected. It is one thing when the State exerts its power either to forbid extra-marital sexuality . . . or to say who may marry, but it is quite another when, having acknowledged a marriage and the intimacies inherent in it, it undertakes to regulate by means of the criminal law the details of that intimacy."

In sum, I believe that the right of privacy in the marital relation is fundamental and basic—a personal right "retained by the people" within the meaning of the Ninth Amendment. Connecticut cannot constitutionally abridge this fundamental right, which is protected by the Fourteenth Amendment from infringement by the States. I agree with the Court that petitioners' convictions must therefore be reversed.

Mr. Justice Harlan, concurring in the judgment.

I fully agree with the judgment of reversal, but find myself unable to join the Court's opinion. The reason is that it seems to me to evince an approach to this case very much like that taken by my Brothers Black and Stewart in dissent, namely: the Due Process Clause of the Fourteenth Amendment does not touch this Connecticut statute unless the enactment is found to violate some right assured by the letter or penumbra of the Bill of Rights.

In other words, what I find implicit in the Court's opinion is that the "incorporation" doctrine may be used to *restrict* the reach of Fourteenth Amendment Due Process. For me this is just as unacceptable constitutional doctrine as is the use of the "incorporation" approach to *impose* upon the States all the requirements of the Bill of Rights as found in the provisions of the first eight amendments and in the decisions of this Court interpreting them.

In my view, the proper constitutional inquiry in this case is whether this Connecticut statute infringes the Due Process Clause of the Fourteenth Amendment because the enactment violates basic values "implicit in the concept of ordered liberty," *Palko v. Connecticut*, 302 U.S. 319, 325. For reasons stated at length in my dissenting opinion in *Poe v. Ullman*, I believe that it does. While the relevant inquiry may be aided by resort to one or more of the provisions of the Bill of Rights, it is not dependent on them or any of their radiations. The Due Process Clause of the Fourteenth Amendment stands, in my opinion, on its own bottom.

A further observation seems in order respecting the justification of my Brothers BLACK and STEWART for their "incorporation" approach to this case. Their approach does not rest on historical reasons, which are of course wholly lacking, but on the thesis that by limiting the content of the Due Process Clause of the Fourteenth Amendment to the protection of rights which can be found elsewhere in the Constitution, in this instance in the Bill of Rights, judges will thus be confined to "interpretation" of specific constitutional provisions, and will thereby be restrained from introducing their own notions of constitutional right and wrong into the "vague contours of the Due Process Clause."

While I could not more heartily agree that judicial "self restraint" is an indispensable ingredient of sound constitutional adjudication, I do submit that the formula suggested for achieving it is more hollow than real. "Specific" provisions of the Constitution, no less than "due process," lend themselves as readily to "personal" interpretations by judges whose constitutional outlook is simply to keep the Constitution in supposed "tune with the times" . . . .

Judicial self-restraint . . . will be achieved in this area, as in other constitutional areas, only by continual insistence upon respect for the teachings of history, solid recognition of the basic values that underlie our society, and wise appreciation of the great roles that the doctrines of federalism and separation of powers have played in establishing and preserving American freedoms. Adherence to these principles will not, of course, obviate all constitutional differences of opinion among judges, nor should it. Their continued recognition will, however, go farther toward keeping most judges from roaming at large in the constitutional field than will the interpolation into the Constitution of an artificial and largely illusory restriction on the content of the Due Process Clause.

MR. JUSTICE WHITE, concurring in the judgment.

In my view this Connecticut law as applied to married couples deprives them of "liberty" without due process of law, as that concept is used in the Fourteenth Amendment. I therefore concur in the judgment of the Court reversing these convictions under Connecticut's aiding and abetting statute. . . .

[S]tatutes regulating sensitive areas of liberty do, under the cases of this Court, require "strict scrutiny," *Skinner v. Oklahoma*, 316 U.S. 535, 541, and "must be viewed in the light of less drastic means for achieving the same basic purpose." *Shelton v. Tucker*, 364 U.S. 479, 488. "Where there is a significant encroachment upon personal liberty, the State may prevail only upon showing a subordinating interest which is compelling." *Bates v. Little Rock*, 361 U.S. 516, 524 . . . .

As I read the opinions of the Connecticut courts and the argument of Connecticut in this Court, the State claims but one justification for its anti-use statute. There is no serious contention that Connecticut thinks the use of artificial or external methods of contraception immoral or unwise in itself, or that the anti-use statute is founded upon any policy of promoting population expansion. Rather, the statute is said to serve the State's policy against all forms of promiscuous or illicit sexual relationships, be they premarital or extramarital, concededly a permissible and legitimate legislative goal.

Without taking issue with the premise that the fear of conception operates as a deterrent to such relationships in addition to the criminal proscriptions Connecticut has against such conduct, I wholly fail to see how the ban on the use of contraceptives by married couples in any way reinforces the State's ban on illicit sexual relationships. Connecticut does not bar the importation or possession of contraceptive devices; they are not considered contraband material under state law, and their availability in that State is not seriously disputed. The only way Connecticut seeks to limit or control the availability of such devices is through its general aiding and abetting statute whose operation in this context has been quite obviously ineffective and whose most serious use has been against birth-control clinics rendering advice to married, rather than unmarried, persons. Indeed, after over 80 years of the State's proscription of use, the legality of the sale of such devices to prevent disease has never been expressly passed upon, although it appears that sales have long occurred and have only infrequently been challenged. This "undeviating policy . . . throughout all the long years . . . bespeaks more than prosecutorial paralysis." *Poe v. Ullman*, 367 U.S. 497, 502. Moreover, it would appear that the sale of contraceptives to prevent disease is plainly legal under Connecticut law.

In these circumstances one is rather hard pressed to explain how the ban on use by married persons in any way prevents use of such devices by persons engaging in illicit sexual relations and thereby contributes to the State's policy against such relationships. Neither the state courts nor the State before the bar of this Court has tendered such an explanation. It is purely fanciful to believe that the broad proscription on use facilitates discovery of use by persons engaging in a prohibited relationship or for some other reason makes such use more unlikely and thus can be supported by any sort of administrative consideration. Perhaps the theory is that the flat ban on use prevents married people from possessing contraceptives and without the ready availability of such devices for use in the marital relationship, there will be no or less temptation to use them in extramarital ones. This reasoning rests on the premise that married people will comply with the ban in regard to their marital relationship, notwithstanding total nonenforcement in this context and apparent nonenforcibility, but will not comply with criminal statutes prohibiting extramarital affairs and the anti-use statute in respect to illicit sexual relationships, a premise whose validity has not been demonstrated and whose intrinsic validity is not very evident. At most the broad ban is of marginal utility to the declared objective. A statute limiting its prohibition on use to persons engaging in the prohibited relationship would serve the end posited by Connecticut in the same way, and with the same effectiveness, or ineffectiveness, as the broad anti-use statute under attack in this case. I find nothing in this record justifying the sweeping scope of this statute, with its telling effect on the freedoms of married persons, and therefore conclude that it deprives such persons of liberty without due process of law.

MR. JUSTICE BLACK, with whom MR. JUSTICE STEWART joins, dissenting. . . .

The Court talks about a constitutional "right of privacy" as though there is some constitutional provision or provisions forbidding any law ever to be passed which might abridge the "privacy" of individuals. But there is not. There are, of course, guarantees in certain specific constitutional provisions which are designed in part to protect privacy at certain times and places with respect to certain activities. Such, for example, is the Fourth Amendment's guarantee against "unreasonable searches and seizures." But I think it belittles that Amendment to talk about it as though it protects nothing but "privacy." To treat it that way is to give it a niggardly interpretation, not the kind of liberal reading I think any Bill of Rights provision should be given. The average man would very likely not have his feelings soothed any more by having his property seized openly than by having it seized privately and by stealth. He simply wants his property left alone. And a person can be just as much, if not more, irritated, annoyed and injured by an unceremonious public arrest by a policeman as he is by a seizure in the privacy of his office or home.

One of the most effective ways of diluting or expanding a constitutionally guaranteed right is to substitute for the crucial word or words of a constitutional guarantee another word or words, more or less flexible and more or less restricted in meaning. This fact is well illustrated by the use of the term "right of privacy" as a comprehensive substitute for the Fourth Amendment's guarantee against "unreasonable searches and seizures." "Privacy" is a broad, abstract and ambiguous concept which can easily be shrunken in meaning but which can also, on the other hand, easily be interpreted as a constitutional ban against many things other than searches and seizures. . . . I like my privacy as well as the next one, but I am nevertheless compelled to admit that government has a right to invade it unless prohibited by some specific constitutional provision. For these reasons I cannot agree with the Court's judgment and the reasons it gives for holding this Connecticut law unconstitutional. . . .

The due process argument which my Brothers HARLAN and WHITE adopt here is based, as their opinions indicate, on the premise that this Court is vested with power to invalidate all state laws that it consider to be arbitrary, capricious, unreasonable, or oppressive, or this Court's belief that a particular state law under scrutiny has no "rational or justifying" purpose, or is offensive to a "sense of fairness and justice." If these formulas based on "natural justice," or others which mean the same thing, are to prevail, they require judges to determine what is or is not constitutional on the basis of their own appraisal of what laws are unwise or unnecessary. The power to make such decisions is of course that of a legislative body. Surely it has to be admitted that no provision of the Constitution specifically gives such blanket power to courts to exercise such a supervisory veto over the wisdom and value of legislative policies and to hold unconstitutional those laws which they believe unwise or dangerous. I readily admit that no legislative body, state or national, should pass laws that can justly be given any of the invidious labels invoked as constitutional excuses to strike down state laws. But perhaps it is not too much to say that no legislative body ever does pass laws without believing that they will accomplish a sane, rational, wise and justifiable purpose. While I completely subscribe to the holding of *Marbury v. Madison*, 1 Cranch 137, and subsequent cases, that our Court has constitutional power to strike down statutes, state or federal, that violate commands of the Federal Constitution, I do not believe that we are granted power by the Due Process Clause or any other constitutional provision or provisions to measure constitutionality by our belief that legislation is arbitrary, capricious or unreasonable, or accomplishes no justifiable purpose, or is offensive to our own notions of "civilized standards of conduct." Such an appraisal of the wisdom of legislation is an attribute of the power to make laws, not of the power to interpret them. The use by federal courts of such a formula or doctrine or whatnot to veto federal or state laws simply takes away from Congress and States the power to make laws based on their own judgment of fairness and wisdom and transfers that power to this Court for ultimate determination—a power which was specifically denied to federal courts by the convention that framed the Constitution.

Of the cases on which my Brothers White and Goldberg rely so heavily, undoubtedly the reasoning of two of them supports their result here—as would that of a number of others which they do not bother to name.... The two they do cite and quote from, *Meyer v. Nebraska*, 262 U.S. 390, and *Pierce v. Society of Sisters*, 268 U.S. 510, were both decided in opinions by Mr. Justice McReynolds which elaborated the same natural law due process philosophy found in *Lochner v. New York*....

My Brother Goldberg has adopted the recent discovery that the Ninth Amendment as well as the Due Process Clause can be used by this Court as authority to strike down all state legislation which this Court thinks violates "fundamental principles of liberty and justice," or is contrary to the "traditions and [collective] conscience of our people." He also states, without proof satisfactory to me, that in making decisions on this basis judges will not consider "their personal and private notions." One may ask how they can avoid considering them. Our Court certainly has no machinery with which to take a Gallup Poll. And the scientific miracles of this age have not yet produced a gadget which the Court can use to determine what traditions are rooted in the "[collective] conscience of our people." Moreover, one would certainly have to look far beyond the language of the Ninth Amendment to find that the Framers vested in this Court any such awesome veto powers over lawmaking, either by the States or by the Congress. Nor does anything in the history of the Amendment offer any support for such a shocking doctrine. The whole history of the adoption of the Constitution and Bill of Rights points the other way, and the very material quoted by my Brother Goldberg shows that the Ninth Amendment was intended to protect against the idea that "by enumerating particular exceptions to the grant of power" to the Federal Government, "those rights which were not singled out, were intended to be assigned into the hands of the General Government [the United States], and were consequently insecure." That Amendment was passed, not to broaden the powers of this Court or any other department of "the General Government," but, as every student of history knows, to assure the people that the Constitution in all its provisions was intended to limit the Federal Government to the powers granted expressly or by necessary implication. If any broad, unlimited power to hold laws unconstitutional because they offend what this Court conceives to be the "[collective] conscience of our people" is vested in this Court by the Ninth Amendment, the Fourteenth Amendment, or any other provision of the Constitution, it was not given by the Framers, but rather has been bestowed on the Court by the Court. This fact is perhaps responsible for the peculiar phenomenon that for a period of a century and a half no serious suggestion was ever made that the Ninth Amendment, enacted to protect state powers against federal invasion, could be used as a weapon of federal power to prevent state legislatures from passing laws they consider appropriate to govern local affairs. Use of any such broad, unbounded judicial authority would make of this Court's members a day-to-day constitutional convention.

I repeat so as not to be misunderstood that this Court does have power, which it should exercise, to hold laws unconstitutional where they are forbidden by the Federal Constitution. My point is that there is no provision of the Constitution which either expressly or impliedly vests power in this Court to sit as a supervisory agency over acts of duly constituted legislative bodies and set aside their laws because of the Court's belief that the legislative policies adopted are unreasonable, unwise, arbitrary, capricious or irrational. The adoption of such a loose, flexible, uncontrolled standard for holding laws unconstitutional, if ever it is finally achieved, will amount to a great unconstitutional shift of power to the courts which I believe and am constrained to say will be bad for the courts and worse for the country. Subjecting federal and state laws to such an unrestrained and unrestrainable judicial control as to the wisdom of legislative enactments would, I fear, jeopardize the separation of governmental powers that the Framers set up and at the same time threaten to take away much of the power of States to govern themselves which the Constitution plainly intended them to have.

I realize that many good and able men have eloquently spoken and written, sometimes in rhapsodical strains, about the duty of this Court to keep the Constitution in tune with the times. The idea is that the Constitution must be changed from time to time and that this Court is charged with a duty to make those changes. For myself, I must with all deference reject that philosophy. The Constitution makers knew the need for change and provided for it. Amendments suggested by the people's elected representatives can be submitted to the people or their selected agents for ratification. That method of change was good for our Fathers, and being somewhat old-fashioned I must add it is good enough for me. And so, I cannot rely on the Due Process Clause or the Ninth Amendment or any mysterious and uncertain natural law concept as a reason for striking down this state law. The Due Process Clause with an "arbitrary and capricious" or "shocking to the conscience" formula was liberally used by this Court to strike down economic legislation in the early decades of this century, threatening, many people thought, the tranquility and stability of the Nation. See, *e.g.*, *Lochner v. New York*, 198 U.S. 45. That formula, based on subjective considerations of "natural justice," is no less dangerous when used to enforce this Court's views about personal rights than those about economic rights. . . .

MR. JUSTICE STEWART, whom MR. JUSTICE BLACK joins, dissenting.

Since 1879 Connecticut has had on its books a law which forbids the use of contraceptives by anyone. I think this is an uncommonly silly law. As a practical matter, the law is obviously unenforceable, except in the oblique context of the present case. As a philosophical matter, I believe the use of contraceptives in the relationship of marriage should be left to personal and private choice, based upon each individual's moral, ethical, and religious beliefs. As a matter of social policy, I think professional counsel about methods of birth control should be available to all, so that each individual's choice can be meaningfully made. But we are not asked in this case to say whether we think this law is unwise, or even asinine. We are asked to hold that it violates the United States Constitution. And that I cannot do.

In the course of its opinion the Court refers to no less than six Amendments to the Constitution: the First, the Third, the Fourth, the Fifth, the Ninth, and the Fourteenth. But the Court does not say which of these Amendments, if any, it thinks is infringed by this Connecticut law.

We *are* told that the Due Process Clause of the Fourteenth Amendment is not, as such, the "guide" in this case. With that much I agree. There is no claim that this law, duly enacted by the Connecticut Legislature, is unconstitutionally vague. There is no claim that the appellants were denied any of the elements of procedural due process at their trial, so as to make their convictions constitutionally invalid. And, as the Court says, the day has long passed since the Due Process Clause was regarded as a proper instrument for determining "the wisdom, need, and propriety" of state laws....

As to the First, Third, Fourth, and Fifth Amendments, I can find nothing in any of them to invalidate this Connecticut law, even assuming that all those Amendments are fully applicable against the States. It has not even been argued that this is a law "respecting an establishment of religion, or prohibiting the free exercise thereof." And surely, unless the solemn process of constitutional adjudication is to descend to the level of a play on words, there is not involved here any abridgment of "the freedom of speech, or of the press; or the right of the people peaceably to assemble, and to petition the Government for a redress of grievances." No soldier has been quartered in any house. There has been no search, and no seizure. Nobody has been compelled to be a witness against himself.

The Court also quotes the Ninth Amendment, and my Brother GOLDBERG's concurring opinion relies heavily upon it. But to say that the Ninth Amendment has anything to do with this case is to turn somersaults with history. The Ninth Amendment, like its companion the Tenth, which this Court held "states but a truism that all is retained which has not been surrendered," *United States v. Darby*, 312 U.S. 100, 124, was framed by James Madison and adopted by the States simply to make clear that the adoption of the Bill of Rights did not alter the plan that the *Federal* Government was to be a government of express and limited powers, and that all rights and powers not delegated to it were retained by the people and the individual States. Until today no member of this Court has ever suggested that the Ninth Amendment meant anything else, and the idea that a federal court could ever use the Ninth Amendment to annul a law passed by the elected representatives of the people of the State of Connecticut would have caused James Madison no little wonder.

What provision of the Constitution, then, does make this state law invalid? The Court says it is the right of privacy "created by several fundamental constitutional guarantees." With all deference, I can find no such general right of privacy in the Bill of Rights, in any other part of the Constitution, or in any case ever before decided by this Court.[7]

At the oral argument in this case we were told that the Connecticut law does not "conform to current community standards." But it is not the function of this Court to decide cases on the basis of community standards. We are here to decide cases "agreeably to the Constitution and laws of the United States." It is the essence of judicial duty to subordinate our own personal views, our own ideas of what legislation is wise and what is not. If, as I should surely hope, the law before us does not reflect the standards of the people of Connecticut, the people of Connecticut can freely exercise their true Ninth and Tenth Amendment rights to persuade their elected representatives to repeal it. That is the constitutional way to take this law off the books.

Notes and Questions

1. In his opinion in *Griswold*, Justice Douglas characterizes *Meyer* and *Pierce* as cases applying the First Amendment against the states via the Fourteenth Amendment. But neither *Meyer* nor *Pierce* even once cited the First Amendment. Indeed, at the time those cases were decided, the Court had not yet "incorporated" the First Amendment and deemed it applicable to the states via the Fourteenth Amendment. *See McDonald v. City of Chicago*, 561 U.S. 742, 764 n.12 (2010).

Moreover, despite the *Meyer* Court's broad statement regarding the right "to marry, establish a home and bring up children," it was—as Justice Black notes in his *Griswold* dissent—fundamentally an economic substantive due process case, focused on the rights of the teachers and the parents to contract with one another for services. *See Meyer*, 262 U.S. at 401 ("Plaintiff in error taught this language in school as part of his occupation. His right thus to teach and the right of parents to engage him so to instruct their children, we think, are within the liberty of the amendment.").

2. In *Griswold*, Justice Douglas tries mightily to avoid reliance on the Due Process Clause, given the stigma associated with the *Lochner*-era cases. But how successful is he in doing so? As indicated in the previous note, he relies on two *Lochner*-era cases, *Meyer* and *Pierce*. But beyond that, even accepting that the right to privacy is located within the penumbras of the Bill of Rights, he still needs a vehicle for applying that penumbral right against the states. After all, if the Bill of Rights does

7. . . . .The Court does not say how far the new constitutional right of privacy announced today extends. I suppose, however, that even after today a State can constitutionally still punish at least some offenses which are not committed in public.

not apply directly against the states without the aid of "incorporation" via the Due Process Clause of the Fourteenth Amendment, how could the penumbras of the Bill of Rights apply against the states?

3. How persuasive is Justice Douglas's argument in *Griswold* that, collectively, the First, Third, Fourth, Fifth and Ninth Amendments provide a more general constitutional right to "privacy"? Indeed, does not the fact that the framers provided protection for privacy in discrete circumstances suggest quite the opposite: that they did *not* intend to recognize a broader right to privacy?

In any event, even accepting that there exists a constitutional right to privacy, what limits are there on that right, and how are courts to determine those boundaries? After all, murder, sexual assault, and child abuse often occur in private—are those protected by the right to privacy? If not, what principle does Justice Douglas provide for deciding what is and is not protected?

4. If one is looking for textual support for the proposition that unenumerated constitutional rights exist, isn't Justice Goldberg exactly right in his concurring opinion in *Griswold* to focus on the Ninth Amendment? If the Ninth Amendment does not mean what Justice Goldberg represents it to mean, what, exactly, does it stand for?

5. In Justice Goldberg's view, what, exactly, is the *source* of the right at issue? On the one hand, he appears to reject the idea that he is incorporating the Ninth Amendment and applying it against the states via the Fourteenth Amendment. But is he not incorporating *something* and applying it against the states, and if so, what is that something?

6. How broad is the right to privacy recognized by Justices Douglas and Goldberg in *Griswold*? Justice Douglas speaks of the "privacy surrounding the marriage relationship"; does that mean the right to sexual privacy is not available to unmarried couples, whether same-sex or opposite-sex?

Although Justice Douglas does not provide any direct answers to these questions, Justice Goldberg does, making clear in his concurring opinion that states retain the ability to criminalize fornication (sexual intercourse engaged in by an unmarried person), adultery, and homosexuality, as well as the power to decide *who* may marry. What principled basis is there for drawing the line Justice Goldberg draws? Reconsider whether the line Justice Goldberg draws remains viable after reading the cases in the two sections that follow.

7. Although the focus of Justice Douglas's opinion is on marital privacy, and the fear that the police would "search the sacred precincts of marital bedrooms for telltale signs of the use of contraceptives," no such invasion of marital privacy occurred in this case. After all, the conduct at issue in this case—giving information, instruction, and medical advice about preventing contraception—did not take place within the privacy of the marital bedroom. That means, does it not, that not only do the specific guarantees of the Bill of Rights have penumbras, but the penumbras themselves have penumbras?

8. Both Justices Goldberg and White focus in their opinions in *Griswold* on the *level* of scrutiny that applies under the Due Process Clause when a fundamental right is

involved, namely, strict scrutiny. Justice Goldberg contrasts this with the normal level of scrutiny—rational basis—that is applicable for run-of-the mill substantive due process cases, as articulated in *Carolene Products* and *Lee Optical.* Note that there are two key differences between rational basis and strict scrutiny: the importance of the state's interest in enacting and enforcing the law, and the fit between the end the government seeks to achieve and the means used to accomplish it.

As laid out in their opinions, strict scrutiny requires a very strong state interest underlying the law—a "compelling" one—as well as a close ends-means fit, one that is "necessary" to accomplishing the goal. In contrast, rational basis scrutiny requires a minimal state interest—it need only be a "legitimate" or "proper" one—and the ends-means fit need only be "rational."

9. Isn't Justice Black right to note in his dissenting opinion in *Griswold* that the tests set forth by Justices Douglas, Goldberg, and Harlan are too open-ended to place any constraints on the Court? How, for example, can one tell whether something is so rooted in the traditions and collective conscience of the people so as to be ranked as fundamental? What does it mean to be "implicit in the concept of ordered liberty"? Indeed, why is this any different from the *Dred Scott* or *Lochner* Court's invocation of substantive due process?

10. Recall Justice Black's dissent in *Adamson v. California*, excerpted in Chapter 3 and decided nearly twenty years prior to *Griswold*, in which he argued strongly in favor of total incorporation of the Bill of Rights. Does it seem that Justice Blackman was contemplating cases such as *Griswold* when he penned his *Adamson* dissent?

11. As an alternative to the rights-based arguments employed in the various opinions in *Griswold*, is it possible to instead conceptualize the case as one involving class-based discrimination on the basis of sex? In contemplating the answer to that question, consider the types of contraceptives—particularly in 1965—that prevent the transmission of disease and thus that were exempt from the law. Would that have been a viable argument in the absence of an *intent* to discriminate on the basis of sex? In the absence of heightened equal protection scrutiny for sex-based classifications? Reconsider your answers to these questions after reading Chapters 12 and 15.

B. Marriage

Loving v. Virginia

388 U.S. 1 (1967)

Mr. Chief Justice Warren delivered the opinion of the Court.

[In an earlier portion of this opinion, excerpted in Chapter 5, the Court held that Virginia's statute criminalizing interracial marriage violated the Equal Protection Clause of the Fourteenth Amendment. In the following excerpt, the Court also addressed the question whether the statute violated the Due Process Clause.]

II.

These statutes also deprive the Lovings of liberty without due process of law in violation of the Due Process Clause of the Fourteenth Amendment. The freedom to marry has long been recognized as one of the vital personal rights essential to the orderly pursuit of happiness by free men.

Marriage is one of the "basic civil rights of man," fundamental to our very existence and survival. *Skinner v. Oklahoma*, 316 U.S. 535, 541 (1942). See also *Maynard v. Hill*, 125 U.S. 190 (1888). To deny this fundamental freedom on so unsupportable a basis as the racial classifications embodied in these statutes, classifications so directly subversive of the principle of equality at the heart of the Fourteenth Amendment, is surely to deprive all the State's citizens of liberty without due process of law. The Fourteenth Amendment requires that the freedom of choice to marry not be restricted by invidious racial discriminations. Under our Constitution, the freedom to marry or not marry, a person of another race resides with the individual and cannot be infringed by the State. . . .

[The concurring opinion of Justice Stewart is omitted.]

Notes and Questions

1. The *Loving* Court relies on *Skinner* (Chapter 8) for the proposition that marriage is a fundamental right protected by the Due Process Clause. Is that an accurate characterization of what *Skinner* held?

2. Is *Loving* consistent with the various opinions in *Griswold*? In contemplating your answer to this question, re-read the excerpt from Justice Harlan's dissent in *Poe v. Ullman*, quoted with approval in Justice Goldberg's concurring opinion (which Justice Harlan, who wrote separately in *Griswold*, would presumably also agree with).

3. If the *Loving* Court already decided that the law at issue violated the Equal Protection Clause because it made an unlawful race-based classification, why did it also reach the Due Process Clause claim? Did the Court not unnecessarily reach an additional constitutional issue? Or was it the synergy of the two aspects of the case—the race-based nature of the classification and the fact that it touched on an important right—that caused the case to come out as it did?

4. What consequences does this portion of the *Loving* opinion have for other types of restrictions on the right to marry, such as bans on same-sex marriage?

C. Contraception Revisited

Eisenstadt v. Baird

405 U.S. 438 (1972)

Mr. Justice BRENNAN delivered the opinion of the Court.

Appellee William Baird was convicted at a bench trial in the Massachusetts Superior Court under Massachusetts General Laws Ann., c. 272, § 21, first, for exhibiting contraceptive articles in the course of delivering a lecture on contraception to a group of students at Boston University and, second, for giving a young woman a package of Emko vaginal foam at the close of his address.[1] The Massachusetts Supreme Judicial Court unanimously set aside the conviction for exhibiting contraceptives on the ground that it violated Baird's First Amendment rights, but by a four-to-three vote sustained the conviction for giving away the foam....

Massachusetts General Laws Ann., c. 272, § 21, under which Baird was convicted, provides a maximum five-year term of imprisonment for "whoever... gives away... any drug, medicine, instrument or article whatever for the prevention of conception," except as authorized in § 21A. Under § 21A, "[a] registered physician may administer to or prescribe for any married person drugs or articles intended for the prevention of pregnancy or conception. [And a] registered pharmacist actually engaged in the business of pharmacy may furnish such drugs or articles to any married person presenting a prescription from a registered physician." As interpreted by the State Supreme Judicial Court, these provisions make it a felony for anyone, other than a registered physician or pharmacist acting in accordance with the terms of § 21A, to dispense any article with the intention that it be used for the prevention of conception. The statutory scheme distinguishes among three distinct classes of distributees—*first*, married persons may obtain contraceptives to prevent pregnancy, but only from doctors or druggists on prescription; *second*, single persons may not obtain contraceptives from anyone to prevent pregnancy; and, *third*, married or single persons may obtain contraceptives from anyone to prevent, not pregnancy, but the spread of disease....

We agree [with the Court of Appeals] that the goals of deterring premarital sex and regulating the distribution of potentially harmful articles cannot reasonably be regarded as legislative aims of §§ 21 and 21A. And we hold that the statute, viewed as a prohibition on contraception *per se*, violates the rights of single persons under the Equal Protection Clause of the Fourteenth Amendment....

II

The basic principles governing application of the Equal Protection Clause of the Fourteenth Amendment are familiar. As The Chief Justice only recently explained in *Reed v. Reed*, 404 U.S. 71, 75–76 (1971):

> "In applying that clause, this Court has consistently recognized that the Fourteenth Amendment does not deny to State the power to treat different classes of persons in different ways. The Equal Protection Clause of that amendment does, however, deny to State the power to legislate that different treatment be accorded to persons placed by a statute into different classes on the basis of criteria wholly unrelated to the objective of that statute. A classification 'must be reasonable, not arbitrary, and must rest

1. The Court of Appeals below described the recipient of the foam as "an unmarried adult woman." However, there is no evidence in the record about her marital status.

> upon some ground of difference having a fair and substantial relation to the object of the legislation, so that all persons similarly circumstanced shall be treated alike.'"

The question for our determination in this case is whether there is some ground of difference that rationally explains the different treatment accorded married and unmarried persons under Massachusetts General Laws Ann., c. 272, §§ 21 and 21A.[7] For the reasons that follow, we conclude that no such ground exists.

First. Section 21 stems from Mass. Stat.1879, c. 159, § 1, which prohibited without exception, distribution of articles intended to be used as contraceptives. In *Commonwealth v. Allison*, 227 Mass. 57, 62 (1917), the Massachusetts Supreme Judicial Court explained that the law's "plain purpose is to protect purity, to preserve chastity, to encourage continence and self restraint, to defend the sanctity of the home, and thus to engender in the State and nation a virile and virtuous race of men and women." Although the State clearly abandoned that purpose with the enactment of § 21A, at least insofar as the illicit sexual activities of married persons are concerned, the court reiterated in *Sturgis v. Attorney General*, that the object of the legislation is to discourage premarital sexual intercourse. Conceding that the State could, consistently with the Equal Protection Clause, regard the problems of extramarital and premarital sexual relations as "[e]vils . . . of different dimensions and proportions, requiring different remedies," *Williamson v. Lee Optical Co.*, 348 U.S. 483, 489 (1955), we cannot agree that the deterrence of premarital sex may reasonably be regarded as the purpose of the Massachusetts law.

It would be plainly unreasonable to assume that Massachusetts has prescribed pregnancy and the birth of an unwanted child as punishment for fornication, which is a misdemeanor under Massachusetts General Laws Ann., c. 272, § 18. Aside from the scheme of values that assumption would attribute to the State, it is abundantly clear that the effect of the ban on distribution of contraceptives to unmarried persons has at best a marginal relation to the proffered objective. What Mr. Justice Goldberg said in *Griswold v. Connecticut*, 381 U.S., at 498 (concurring opinion), concerning the effect of Connecticut's prohibition on the use of contraceptives in discouraging extramarital sexual relations, is equally applicable here. "The rationality of this justification is dubious, particularly in light of the admitted widespread availability to all persons in the State of Connecticut, unmarried as well as married, of birth-control devices for the prevention of disease, as distinguished from the prevention of conception." Like Connecticut's laws, §§ 21 and 21A do not at all regulate the distribution of contraceptives when they are to be used to prevent, not pregnancy, but the spread of disease. Nor, in making contraceptives available to married persons

---

7. Of course, if we were to conclude that the Massachusetts statute impinges upon fundamental freedoms under *Griswold*, the statutory classification would have to be not merely *rationally related* to a valid public purpose but *necessary* to the achievement of a *compelling* state interest. But just as in Reed v. Reed, 404 U.S. 71 (1971), we do not have to address the statute's validity under that test because the law fails to satisfy even the more lenient equal protection standard.

without regard to their intended use, does Massachusetts attempt to deter married persons from engaging in illicit sexual relations with unmarried persons. Even on the assumption that the fear of pregnancy operates as a deterrent to fornication, the Massachusetts statute is thus so riddled with exceptions that deterrence of premarital sex cannot reasonably be regarded as its aim.

Moreover, §§ 21 and 21A on their face have a dubious relation to the State's criminal prohibition on fornication. As the Court of Appeals explained, "Fornication is a misdemeanor [in Massachusetts], entailing a thirty dollar fine, or three months in jail. Massachusetts General Laws Ann. c. 272 § 18. Violation of the present statute is a felony, punishable by five years in prison. We find it hard to believe that the legislature adopted a statute carrying a five-year penalty for its possible, obviously by no means fully effective, deterrence of the commission of a ninety-day misdemeanor." Even conceding the legislature a full measure of discretion in fashioning means to prevent fornication, and recognizing that the State may seek to deter prohibited conduct by punishing more severely those who facilitate than those who actually engage in its commission, we, like the Court of Appeals, cannot believe that in this instance Massachusetts has chosen to expose the aider and abetter who simply *gives away* a contraceptive to *20* times the *90-day* sentence of the offender himself. The very terms of the State's criminal statutes, coupled with the *de minimis* effect of §§ 21 and 21A in deterring fornication, thus compel the conclusion that such deterrence cannot reasonably be taken as the purpose of the ban on distribution of contraceptives to unmarried persons.

Second. Section 21A was added to the Massachusetts General Laws by Stat. 1966, c. 265, § 1. The Supreme Judicial Court in *Commonwealth v. Baird*, held that the purpose of the amendment was to serve the health needs of the community by regulating the distribution of potentially harmful articles. It is plain that Massachusetts had no such purpose in mind before the enactment of § 21A. As the Court of Appeals remarked, "Consistent with the fact that the statute was contained in a chapter dealing with 'Crimes Against Chastity, Morality, Decency and Good Order,' it was cast only in terms of morals. A physician was forbidden to prescribe contraceptives even when needed for the protection of health." Nor did the Court of Appeals "believe that the legislature [in enacting § 21A] suddenly reversed its field and developed an interest in health. Rather, it merely made what it thought to be the precise accommodation necessary to escape the *Griswold* ruling."

Again, we must agree with the Court of Appeals. If health were the rationale of § 21A, the statute would be both discriminatory and overbroad. Dissenting in *Commonwealth v. Baird*, 355 Mass., at 758, Justices Whittemore and Cutter stated that they saw "in § 21 and § 21A, read together, no public health purpose. If there is need to have a physician prescribe (and a pharmacist dispense) contraceptives, that need is as great for unmarried persons as for married persons." The Court of Appeals added: "If the prohibition [on distribution to unmarried persons] . . . is to be taken to mean that the same physician who can prescribe for married patients does not have sufficient skill to protect the health of patients who lack a marriage certificate, or who may be currently divorced, it is illogical to the point of irrationality." Furthermore, we must join the Court of Appeals in noting that not all contraceptives are potentially dangerous. As a result, if the Massachusetts statute were a health measure, it would not only invidiously discriminate against the unmarried, but also be overbroad with respect to the married. . . .

But if further proof that the Massachusetts statute is not a health measure is necessary, the argument of Justice Spiegel, who also dissented in *Commonwealth v. Baird*, 355 Mass., at 759, is conclusive: "It is at best a strained conception to say that the Legislature intended to prevent the distribution of articles 'which may have undesirable, if not dangerous, physical consequences.' If that was the Legislature's goal, § 21 is not required" in view of the federal and state laws *already* regulating the distribution of harmful drugs. See Federal Food, Drug, and Cosmetic Act, § 503, 52 Stat. 1051, as amended, 21 U.S.C. § 353; Mass. Gen. Laws Ann., c. 94, § 187A, as amended. We conclude, accordingly, that, despite the statute's superficial earmarks as a health measure, health, on the face of the statute, may no more reasonably be regarded as its purpose than the deterrence of premarital sexual relations.

Third. If the Massachusetts statute cannot be upheld as a deterrent to fornication or as a health measure, may it, nevertheless, be sustained simply as a prohibition on contraception? The Court of Appeals analysis "led inevitably to the conclusion that, so far as morals are concerned, it is contraceptives per se that are considered immoral—to the extent that *Griswold* will permit such a declaration." The Court of Appeals went on to hold:

> "To say that contraceptives are immoral as such, and are to be forbidden to unmarried persons who will nevertheless persist in having intercourse, means that such persons must risk for themselves an unwanted pregnancy, for the child, illegitimacy, and for society, a possible obligation of support. Such a view of morality is not only the very mirror image of sensible legislation; we consider that it conflicts with fundamental human rights. In the absence of demonstrated harm, we hold it is beyond the competency of the state."

We need not and do not, however, decide that important question in this case because, whatever the rights of the individual to access to contraceptives may be, the rights must be the same for the unmarried and the married alike.

If under *Griswold* the distribution of contraceptives to married persons cannot be prohibited, a ban on distribution to unmarried persons would be equally impermissible. It is true that in *Griswold* the right of privacy in question inhered in the marital relationship. Yet the marital couple is not an independent entity with a mind and heart of its own, but an association of two individuals each with a separate intellectual and emotional makeup. If the right of privacy means anything, it is the right of the *individual*, married or single, to be free from unwarranted governmental intrusion into matters so fundamentally affecting a person as the decision whether to bear or beget a child.

On the other hand, if *Griswold* is no bar to a prohibition on the distribution of contraceptives, the State could not, consistently with the Equal Protection Clause, outlaw distribution to unmarried but not to married persons. In each case the evil, as perceived by the State, would be identical, and the underinclusion would be invidious....

We hold that by providing dissimilar treatment for married and unmarried persons who are similarly situated, Massachusetts General Laws Ann., c. 272, §§ 21 and 21A, violate the Equal Protection Clause....

MR. JUSTICE WHITE, with whom MR. JUSTICE BLACKMUN joins, concurring in the result....

Given Griswold v. Connecticut, and absent proof of the probable hazards of using vaginal foam, we could not sustain appellee's conviction had it been for selling or giving away foam to a married person. Just as in *Griswold*, where the right of married persons to use contraceptives was "diluted or adversely affected" by permitting a conviction for giving advice as to its exercise, so here, to sanction a medical restriction upon distribution of a contraceptive not proved hazardous to health would impair the exercise of the constitutional right.

That Baird could not be convicted for distributing Emko to a married person disposes of this case. Assuming, *arguendo*, that the result would be otherwise had the recipient been unmarried, nothing has been placed in the record to indicate her marital status. The State has maintained that marital status is irrelevant because an unlicensed person cannot legally dispense vaginal foam either to married or unmarried persons. This approach is plainly erroneous and requires the reversal of Baird's conviction; for on the facts of this case, it deprives us of knowing whether Baird was in fact convicted for making a constitutionally protected distribution of Emko to a married person....

Because this case can be disposed of on the basis of settled constitutional doctrine, I perceive no reason for reaching the novel constitutional question whether a State may restrict or forbid the distribution of contraceptives to the unmarried.

[The concurring opinion of Justice Douglas, and the dissenting opinion of Chief Justice Burger, are omitted.]

Notes and Questions

1. Is *Eisenstadt* applying rational basis scrutiny or some form of heightened scrutiny? In this regard, consider whether the Court's analysis of the statute's constitutionality is more akin to the standard employed in *Lochner* or to that employed in *Lee Optical* and *Beach Communications*. Note in this regard that the *Eisenstadt* Court quotes from a case entitled *Reed v. Reed* that uses somewhat different language than that employed in *Lee Optical* and *Beach Communications*. *Reed* is examined in closer detail in Chapter 12.

2. Is *Eisenstadt* an equal protection case, a substantive due process case, or both? Asked somewhat differently, do you suppose the case would have turned out

differently if a "lesser" right were at issue? After all, government discriminates against unmarried couples in all sorts of ways, such as by denying them the income tax advantages given to married couples. If the Court had before it a challenge to the income tax preference for married couples, do you think the decision would have come out the same way?

3. Toward the end of the opinion, the *Eisenstadt* majority broadens its focus from contraception specifically to the more general "decision whether to bear or beget a child." What consequence does that broader framing of the right at stake have for other types of laws that might be challenged? More generally, in considering rights-based claims, how narrowly or broadly should the Court frame the right at issue, and what consequence does that framing have for the outcome of the case, particularly given the sources that the Court relies upon to determine whether or not a given unenumerated right is entitled to constitutional protection?

D. Abortion

Roe v. Wade

410 U.S. 113 (1973)

Mr. Justice Blackmun delivered the opinion of the Court.

This Texas federal appeal and its Georgia companion, *Doe v. Bolton*, 410 U.S. 179, present constitutional challenges to state criminal abortion legislation. The Texas statutes under attack here are typical of those that have been in effect in many States for approximately a century. The Georgia statutes, in contrast, have a modern cast and are a legislative product that, to an extent at least, obviously reflects the influences of recent attitudinal change, of advancing medical knowledge and techniques, and of new thinking about an old issue.

We forthwith acknowledge our awareness of the sensitive and emotional nature of the abortion controversy, of the vigorous opposing views, even among physicians, and of the deep and seemingly absolute convictions that the subject inspires. One's philosophy, one's experiences, one's exposure to the raw edges of human existence, one's religious training, one's attitudes toward life and family and their values, and the moral standards one establishes and seeks to observe, are all likely to influence and to color one's thinking and conclusions about abortion.

In addition, population growth, pollution, poverty, and racial overtones tend to complicate and not to simplify the problem.

Our task, of course, is to resolve the issue by constitutional measurement, free of emotion and of predilection. We seek earnestly to do this, and, because we do, we have inquired into, and in this opinion place some emphasis upon, medical and medical-legal history and what that history reveals about man's attitudes toward the abortion procedure over the centuries. We bear in mind, too, Mr. Justice Holmes' admonition in his now-vindicated dissent in *Lochner v. New York*, 198 U.S. 45, 76 (1905):

> "[The Constitution] is made for people of fundamentally differing views, and the accident of our finding certain opinions natural and familiar, or novel, and even shocking, ought not to conclude our judgment upon the question whether statutes embodying them conflict with the Constitution of the United States."

I

The Texas statutes that concern us here . . . make it a crime to "procure an abortion," as therein defined, or to attempt one, except with respect to "an abortion procured or attempted by medical advice for the purpose of saving the life of the mother." Similar statutes are in existence in a majority of the States.

Texas first enacted a criminal abortion statute in 1854. This was soon modified into language that has remained substantially unchanged to the present time. The final article in each of these compilations provided the same exception, as does the present Article 1196, for an abortion by "medical advice for the purpose of saving the life of the mother."

II

Jane Roe,[4] a single woman who was residing in Dallas County, Texas, instituted this federal action in March 1970 against the District Attorney of the county. She sought a declaratory judgment that the Texas criminal abortion statutes were unconstitutional on their face, and an injunction restraining the defendant from enforcing the statutes.

Roe alleged that she was unmarried and pregnant; that she wished to terminate her pregnancy by an abortion "performed by a competent, licensed physician, under safe, clinical conditions"; that she was unable to get a "legal" abortion in Texas because her life did not appear to be threatened by the continuation of her pregnancy; and that she could not afford to travel to another jurisdiction in order to secure a legal abortion under safe conditions. She claimed that the Texas statutes were unconstitutionally vague and that they abridged her right of personal privacy, protected by the First, Fourth, Fifth, Ninth, and Fourteenth Amendments. By an amendment to her complaint Roe purported to sue "on behalf of herself and all other women" similarly situated. . . .

V

The principal thrust of appellant's attack on the Texas statutes is that they improperly invade a right, said to be possessed by the pregnant woman, to choose to terminate her pregnancy. Appellant would discover this right in the concept of personal

---

4. The name is a pseudonym.

"liberty" embodied in the Fourteenth Amendment's Due Process Clause; or in personal marital, familial, and sexual privacy said to be protected by the Bill of Rights or its penumbras, see *Griswold v. Connecticut*, 381 U.S. 479 (1965); *Eisenstadt v. Baird*, 405 U.S. 438 (1972); *id.*, at 460 (White, J., concurring in result); or among those rights reserved to the people by the Ninth Amendment, *Griswold v. Connecticut*, 381 U.S., at 486 (Goldberg, J., concurring). Before addressing this claim, we feel it desirable briefly to survey, in several aspects, the history of abortion, for such insight as that history may afford us, and then to examine the state purposes and interests behind the criminal abortion laws.

VI

It perhaps is not generally appreciated that the restrictive criminal abortion laws in effect in a majority of States today are of relatively recent vintage. Those laws, generally proscribing abortion or its attempt at any time during pregnancy except when necessary to preserve the pregnant woman's life, are not of ancient or even of common-law origin. Instead, they derive from statutory changes effected, for the most part, in the latter half of the 19th century.

[The Court reviews ancient attitudes toward abortion as well as those contained in the Hippocratic Oath.]

3. *The common law.* It is undisputed that at common law, abortion performed *before* "quickening"—the first recognizable movement of the fetus *in utero*, appearing usually from the 16th to the 18th week of pregnancy—was not an indictable offense. The absence of a common-law crime for pre-quickening abortion appears to have developed from a confluence of earlier philosophical, theological, and civil and canon law concepts of when life begins. These disciplines variously approached the question in terms of the point at which the embryo or fetus became "formed" or recognizably human, or in terms of when a "person" came into being, that is, infused with a "soul" or "animated." A loose consensus evolved in early English law that these events occurred at some point between conception and live birth. This was "mediate animation." Although Christian theology and the canon law came to fix the point of animation at 40 days for a male and 80 days for a female, a view that persisted until the 19th century, there was otherwise little agreement about the precise time of formation or animation. There was agreement, however, that prior to this point the fetus was to be regarded as part of the mother, and its destruction, therefore, was not homicide. Due to continued uncertainty about the precise time when animation occurred, to the lack of any empirical basis for the 40–80-day view, and perhaps to Aquinas' definition of movement as one of the two first principles of life, Bracton focused upon quickening as the critical point. The significance of quickening was echoed by later common-law scholars and found its way into the received common law in this country.

Whether abortion of a *quick* fetus was a felony at common law, or even a lesser crime, is still disputed. . . .

[The Court reviews the English common law's attitudes toward abortion.]

5. *The American law.* In this country, the law in effect in all but a few States until mid-19th century was the pre-existing English common law. Connecticut, the first State to enact abortion legislation, adopted in 1821 that part of Lord Ellenborough's Act that related to a woman "quick with child." The death penalty was not imposed. Abortion before quickening was made a crime in that State only in 1860. In 1828, New York enacted legislation that, in two respects, was to serve as a model for early anti-abortion statutes. First, while barring destruction of an unquickend fetus as well as a quick fetus, it made the former only a misdemeanor, but the latter second-degree manslaughter. Second, it incorporated a concept of therapeutic abortion by providing that an abortion was excused if it "shall have been necessary to preserve the life of such mother, or shall have been advised by two physicians to be necessary for such purpose." By 1840, when Texas had received the common law, only eight American States had statutes dealing with abortion. It was not until after the War Between the States that legislation began generally to replace the common law. Most of these initial statutes dealt severely with abortion after quickening but were lenient with it before quickening. Most punished attempts equally with completed abortions. While many statutes included the exception for an abortion thought by one or more physicians to be necessary to save the mother's life, that provision soon disappeared and the typical law required that the procedure actually be necessary for that purpose.

Gradually, in the middle and late 19th century the quickening distinction disappeared from the statutory law of most States and the degree of the offense and the penalties were increased. By the end of the 1950's a large majority of the jurisdictions banned abortion, however and whenever performed, unless done to save or preserve the life of the mother. The exceptions, Alabama and the District of Columbia, permitted abortion to preserve the mother's health. Three States permitted abortions that were not "unlawfully" performed or that were not "without lawful justification," leaving interpretation of those standards to the courts. In the past several years, however, a trend toward liberalization of abortion statutes has resulted in adoption, by about one-third of the States, of less stringent laws. . . .

It is thus apparent that at common law, at the time of the adoption of our Constitution, and throughout the major portion of the 19th century, abortion was viewed with less disfavor than under most American statutes currently in effect. Phrasing it another way, a woman enjoyed a substantially broader right to terminate a pregnancy than she does in most States today. At least with respect to the early stage of pregnancy, and very possibly without such a limitation, the opportunity to make this choice was present in this country well into the 19th century. Even later, the law continued for some time to treat less punitively an abortion procured in early pregnancy.

[The Court proceeds to summarize the positions of the American Medical Association, the American Public Health Association, and the American Bar Association.]

VII

Three reasons have been advanced to explain historically the enactment of criminal abortion laws in the 19th century and to justify their continued existence.

It has been argued occasionally that these laws were the product of a Victorian social concern to discourage illicit sexual conduct. Texas, however, does not advance this justification in the present case, and it appears that no court or commentator has taken the argument seriously. The appellants and *amici* contend, moreover, that this is not a proper state purpose at all and suggest that, if it were, the Texas statutes are overbroad in protecting it since the law fails to distinguish between married and unwed mothers.

A second reason is concerned with abortion as a medical procedure. When most criminal abortion laws were first enacted, the procedure was a hazardous one for the woman. This was particularly true prior to the development of antisepsis. Antiseptic techniques, of course, were based on discoveries by Lister, Pasteur, and others first announced in 1867, but were not generally accepted and employed until about the turn of the century. Abortion mortality was high. Even after 1900, and perhaps until as late as the development of antibiotics in the 1940's, standard modern techniques such as dilation and curettage were not nearly so safe as they are today. Thus, it has been argued that a State's real concern in enacting a criminal abortion law was to protect the pregnant woman, that is, to restrain her from submitting to a procedure that placed her life in serious jeopardy.

Modern medical techniques have altered this situation. Appellants and various *amici* refer to medical data indicating that abortion in early pregnancy, that is, prior to the end of the first trimester, although not without its risk, is now relatively safe. Mortality rates for women undergoing early abortions, where the procedure is legal, appear to be as low as or lower than the rates for normal childbirth. Consequently, any interest of the State in protecting the woman from an inherently hazardous procedure, except when it would be equally dangerous for her to forgo it, has largely disappeared. Of course, important state interests in the areas of health and medical standards do remain. The State has a legitimate interest in seeing to it that abortion, like any other medical procedure, is performed under circumstances that insure maximum safety for the patient. This interest obviously extends at least to the performing physician and his staff, to the facilities involved, to the availability of aftercare, and to adequate provision for any complication or emergency that might arise. The prevalence of high mortality rates at illegal "abortion mills" strengthens, rather than weakens, the State's interest in regulating the conditions under which abortions are performed. Moreover, the risk to the woman increases as her pregnancy continues. Thus, the State retains a definite interest in protecting the woman's own health and safety when an abortion is proposed at a late stage of pregnancy,

The third reason is the State's interest—some phrase it in terms of duty—in protecting prenatal life. Some of the argument for this justification rests on the theory that a new human life is present from the moment of conception. The State's interest and general obligation to protect life then extends, it is argued, to prenatal life. Only when the life of the pregnant mother herself is at stake, balanced against the life she carries within her, should the interest of the embryo or fetus not prevail. Logically, of course, a legitimate state interest in this area need not stand or fall on acceptance of the belief that life begins at conception or at some other point prior to life birth. In assessing the State's interest, recognition may be given to the less rigid claim that as long as at least *potential* life is involved, the State may assert interests beyond the protection of the pregnant woman alone.

Parties challenging state abortion laws have sharply disputed in some courts the contention that a purpose of these laws, when enacted, was to protect prenatal life. Pointing to the absence of legislative history to support the contention, they claim that most state laws were designed solely to protect the woman. Because medical advances have lessened this concern, at least with respect to abortion in early pregnancy, they argue that with respect to such abortions the laws can no longer be justified by any state interest. There is some scholarly support for this view of original purpose. The few state courts called upon to interpret their laws in the late 19th and early 20th centuries did focus on the State's interest in protecting the woman's health rather than in preserving the embryo and fetus. Proponents of this view point out that in many States, including Texas, by statute or judicial interpretation, the pregnant woman herself could not be prosecuted for self-abortion or for cooperating in an abortion performed upon her by another. They claim that adoption of the "quickening" distinction through received common law and state statutes tacitly recognizes the greater health hazards inherent in late abortion and impliedly repudiates the theory that life begins at conception.

It is with these interests, and the weight to be attached to them, that this case is concerned.

VIII

The Constitution does not explicitly mention any right of privacy. In a line of decisions, however . . . the Court has recognized that a right of personal privacy, or a guarantee of certain areas or zones of privacy, does exist under the Constitution. . . . These decisions make it clear that only personal rights that can be deemed "fundamental" or "implicit in the concept of ordered liberty," *Palko v. Connecticut*, 302 U.S. 319, 325 (1937), are included in this guarantee of personal privacy. They also make it clear that the right has some extension to activities relating to marriage, *Loving v. Virginia*, 388 U.S. 1, 12 (1967); procreation, *Skinner v. Oklahoma*, 316 U.S. 535, 541–542 (1942); contraception, *Eisenstadt v. Baird*, 405 U.S., at 453-454; id., at 460, 463-465 (White, J., concurring in result); family relationships, *Prince v. Massachusetts*, 321 U.S. 158, 166 (1944); and child rearing and education, *Pierce v. Society of Sisters*, 268 U.S. 510, 535 (1925), *Meyer v. Nebraska*, *supra*.

This right of privacy, whether it be founded in the Fourteenth Amendment's concept of personal liberty and restrictions upon state action, as we feel it is, or, as the District Court determined, in the Ninth Amendment's reservation of rights to the people, is broad enough to encompass a woman's decision whether or not to terminate her pregnancy. The detriment that the State would impose upon the pregnant woman by denying this choice altogether is apparent. Specific and direct harm medically diagnosable even in early pregnancy may be involved. Maternity, or additional offspring, may force upon the woman a distressful life and future. Psychological harm may be imminent. Mental and physical health may be taxed by child care. There is also the distress, for all concerned, associated with the unwanted child, and there is the problem of bringing a child into a family already unable, psychologically and otherwise, to care for it. In other cases, as in this one, the additional difficulties and continuing stigma of unwed motherhood may be involved. All these are factors the woman and her responsible physician necessarily will consider in consultation.

On the basis of elements such as these, appellant and some *amici* argue that the woman's right is absolute and that she is entitled to terminate her pregnancy at whatever time, in whatever way, and for whatever reason she alone chooses. With this we do not agree. Appellant's arguments that Texas either has no valid interest at all in regulating the abortion decision, or no interest strong enough to support any limitation upon the woman's sole determination, are unpersuasive. The Court's decisions recognizing a right of privacy also acknowledge that some state regulation in areas protected by that right is appropriate. As noted above, a State may properly assert important interests in safeguarding health, in maintaining medical standards, and in protecting potential life. At some point in pregnancy, these respective interests become sufficiently compelling to sustain regulation of the factors that govern the abortion decision. The privacy right involved, therefore, cannot be said to be absolute. In fact, it is not clear to us that the claim asserted by some *amici* that one has an unlimited right to do with one's body as one pleases bears a close relationship to the right of privacy previously articulated in the Court's decisions. The Court has refused to recognize an unlimited right of this kind in the past.

We, therefore, conclude that the right of personal privacy includes the abortion decision, but that this right is not unqualified and must be considered against important state interests in regulation....

Where certain "fundamental rights" are involved, the Court has held that regulation limiting these rights may be justified only by a "compelling state interest," and that legislative enactments must be narrowly drawn to express only the legitimate state interests at stake....

IX

....

A. The appellee and certain *amici* argue that the fetus is a "person" within the language and meaning of the Fourteenth Amendment. In support of this, they outline at length and in detail the well-known facts of fetal development. If this suggestion of personhood is established, the appellant's case, of course, collapses, for the fetus' right to life would then be guaranteed specifically by the Amendment....

The Constitution does not define "person" in so many words. Section 1 of the Fourteenth Amendment contains three references to "person." The first, in defining "citizens," speaks of "persons born or naturalized in the United States." The word also appears both in the Due Process Clause and in the Equal Protection Clause. "Person" is used in other places in the Constitution: in the listing of qualifications for Representatives and Senators, Art, I, § 2, cl. 2, and § 3, cl. 3; in the Apportionment Clause, Art. I, § 2, cl. 3; in the Migration and Importation provision, Art. I, § 9, cl. 1; in the Emolument Clause, Art, I, § 9, cl. 8; in the Electros provisions, Art. II, § 1, cl. 2, and the superseded cl. 3; in the provision outlining qualifications for the office of President, Art. II, § 1, cl. 5; in the Extradition provisions, Art. IV, § 2, cl. 2, and the superseded Fugitive Slave Clause 3; and in the Fifth, Twelfth, and Twenty-second Amendments, as well as in §§ 2 and 3 of the Fourteenth Amendment. But in nearly all these instances, the use of the word is such that it has application only postnatally. None indicates, with any assurance, that it has any possible prenatal application.[54]

All this, together with our observation, *supra*, that throughout the major portion of the 19th century prevailing legal abortion practices were far freer than they are today, persuades us that the word "person," as used in the Fourteenth Amendment, does not include the unborn. . . .

B. The pregnant woman cannot be isolated in her privacy. She carries an embryo and, later, a fetus, if one accepts the medical definitions of the developing young in the human uterus. The situation therefore is inherently different from marital intimacy, or bedroom possession of obscene material, or marriage, or procreation, or education, with which *Eisenstadt* and *Griswold*, *Stanley*, *Loving*, *Skinner* and *Pierce* and *Meyer* were respectively concerned. As we have intimated above, it is reasonable and appropriate for a State to decide that at some point in time another interest, that of health of the mother or that of potential human life, becomes significantly involved. The woman's privacy is no longer sole and any right of privacy she possesses must be measured accordingly.

Texas urges that, apart from the Fourteenth Amendment, life begins at conception and is present throughout pregnancy, and that, therefore, the State has a compelling interest in protecting that life from and after conception. We need not resolve the difficult question of when life begins. When those trained in the respective disciplines of medicine, philosophy, and theology are unable to arrive at any consensus,

54. When Texas urges that a fetus is entitled to Fourteenth Amendment protection as a person, it faces a dilemma. Neither in Texas nor in any other State are all abortions prohibited. Despite broad proscription, an exception always exists. The exception contained in Art. 1196, for an abortion procured or attempted by medical advice for the purpose of saving the life of the mother, is typical. But if the fetus is a person who is not to be deprived of life without due process of law, and if the mother's condition is the sole determinant, does not the Texas exception appear to be out of line with the Amendment's command?

There are other inconsistencies between Fourteenth Amendment status and the typical abortion statute. It has already been pointed out that in Texas the woman is not a principal or an accomplice with respect to an abortion upon her. If the fetus is a person, why is the woman not a principal or an accomplice? Further, the penalty for criminal abortion specified by Art. 1195 is significantly less than the maximum penalty for murder prescribed by Art. 1257 of the Texas Penal Code. If the fetus is a person, may the penalties be different?

the judiciary, at this point in the development of man's knowledge, is not in a position to speculate as to the answer.

It should be sufficient to note briefly the wide divergence of thinking on this most sensitive and difficult question. There has always been strong support for the view that life does not begin until live birth. This was the belief of the Stoics. It appears to be the predominant, though not the unanimous, attitude of the Jewish faith. It may be taken to represent also the position of a large segment of the Protestant community, insofar as that can be ascertained; organized groups that have taken a formal position on the abortion issue have generally regarded abortion as a matter for the conscience of the individual and her family. As we have noted, the common law found greater significance in quickening. Physicians and their scientific colleagues have regarded that event with less interest and have tended to focus either upon conception, upon live birth, or upon the interim point at which the fetus becomes "viable," that is, potentially able to live outside the mother's womb, albeit with artificial aid. Viability is usually placed at about seven months (28 weeks) but may occur earlier, even at 24 weeks. The Aristotelian theory of "mediate animation," that held sway throughout the Middle Ages and the Renaissance in Europe, continued to be official Roman Catholic dogma until the 19th century, despite opposition to this "ensoulment" theory from those in the Church who would recognize the existence of life from the moment of conception. The latter is now, of course, the official belief of the Catholic Church. As one brief *amicus* discloses, this is a view strongly held by many non-Catholics as well, and by many physicians. Substantial problems for precise definition of this view are posed, however, by new embryological data that purport to indicate that conception is a "process" over time, rather than an event, and by new medical techniques such as menstrual extraction, the "morning-after" pill, implantation of embryos, artificial insemination, and even artificial wombs.

In areas other than criminal abortion, the law has been reluctant to endorse any theory that life, as we recognize it, begins before live birth or to accord legal rights to the unborn except in narrowly defined situations and except when the rights are contingent upon live birth. For example, the traditional rule of tort law denied recovery for prenatal injuries even though the child was born alive. That rule has been changed in almost every jurisdiction. In most States, recovery is said to be permitted only if the fetus was viable, or at least quick, when the injuries were sustained, though few courts have squarely so held. In a recent development, generally opposed by the commentators, some States permit the parents of a stillborn child to maintain an action for wrongful death because of prenatal injuries. Such an action, however, would appear to be one to vindicate the parents' interest and is thus consistent with the view that the fetus, at most, represents only the potentiality of life. Similarly, unborn children have been recognized as acquiring rights or interests by way of inheritance or other devolution of property, and have been represented by guardians *ad litem*. Perfection of the interests involved, again, has generally been contingent upon live birth. In short, the unborn have never been recognized in the law as persons in the whole sense.

X

In view of all this, we do not agree that, by adopting one theory of life, Texas may override the rights of the pregnant woman that are at stake. We repeat, however, that the State does have an important and legitimate interest in preserving and protecting the health of the pregnant woman, whether she be a resident of the State or a non-resident who seeks medical consultation and treatment there, and that it has still *another* important and legitimate interest in protecting the potentiality of human life. These interests are separate and distinct. Each grows in substantiality as the woman approaches term and, at a point during pregnancy, each becomes "compelling."

With respect to the State's important and legitimate interest in the health of the mother, the "compelling" point, in the light of present medical knowledge, is at approximately the end of the first trimester. This is so because of the now-established medical fact . . . that until the end of the first trimester mortality in abortion may be less than mortality in normal childbirth. It follows that, from and after this point, a State may regulate the abortion procedure to the extent that the regulation reasonably relates to the preservation and protection of maternal health. Examples of permissible state regulation in this area are requirements as to the qualifications of the person who is to perform the abortion; as to the licensure of that person; as to the facility in which the procedure is to be performed, that is, whether it must be a hospital or may be a clinic or some other place of less-than-hospital status; as to the licensing of the facility; and the like.

This means, on the other hand, that, for the period of pregnancy prior to this "compelling" point, the attending physician, in consultation with his patient, is free to determine, without regulation by the State, that, in his medical judgment, the patient's pregnancy should be terminated. If that decision is reached, the judgment may be effectuated by an abortion free of interference by the State.

With respect to the State's important and legitimate interest in potential life, the "compelling" point is at viability. This is so because the fetus then presumably has the capability of meaningful life outside the mother's womb. State regulation protective of fetal life after viability thus has both logical and biological justifications. If the State is interested in protecting fetal life after viability, it may go so far as to proscribe abortion during that period, except when it is necessary to preserve the life or health of the mother.

Measured against these standards, Art. 1196 of the Texas Penal Code, in restricting legal abortions to those "procured or attempted by medical advice for the purpose of saving the life of the mother," sweeps too broadly. The statute makes no distinction between abortions performed early in pregnancy and those performed later, and it limits to a single reason, "saving" the mother's life, the legal justification for the procedure. The statute, therefore, cannot survive the constitutional attack made upon it here. . . .

XI

To summarize and to repeat:

1. A state criminal abortion statute of the current Texas type, that excepts from criminality only a *life-saving* procedure on behalf of the mother, without regard to pregnancy stage and without recognition of the other interests involved, is violative of the Due Process Clause of the Fourteenth Amendment.

(a) For the stage prior to approximately the end of the first trimester, the abortion decision and its effectuation must be left to the medical judgment of the pregnant woman's attending physician.

(b) For the stage subsequent to approximately the end of the first trimester, the State, in promoting its interest in the health of the mother, may, if it chooses, regulate the abortion procedure in ways that are reasonably related to maternal health.

(c) For the stage subsequent to viability, the State in promoting its interest in the potentiality of human life may, if it chooses, regulate, and even proscribe, abortion except where it is necessary, in appropriate medical judgment, for the preservation of the life or health of the mother.

2. The State may define the term "physician," as it has been employed in the preceding paragraphs of this Part XI of this opinion, to mean only a physician currently licensed by the State, and may proscribe any abortion by a person who is not a physician as so defined. . . .

This holding, we feel, is consistent with the relative weights of the respective interests involved, with the lessons and examples of medical and legal history, with the lenity of the common law, and with the demands of the profound problems of the present day. The decision leaves the State free to place increasing restrictions on abortion as the period of pregnancy lengthens, so long as those restrictions are tailored to the recognized state interests. The decision vindicates the right of the physician to administer medical treatment according to his professional judgment up to the points where important state interests provide compelling justifications for intervention. Up to those points, the abortion decision in all its aspects is inherently, and primarily, a medical decision, and basic responsibility for it must rest with the physician. If an individual practitioner abuses the privilege of exercising proper medical judgment, the usual remedies, judicial and intra-professional, are available.

XII

Our conclusion that Art. 1196 is unconstitutional means, of course, that the Texas abortion statutes, as a unit, must fall. The exception of Art. 1196 cannot be struck down separately, for then the State would be left with a statute proscribing all abortion procedures no matter how medically urgent the case. . . .

Mr. Justice Rehnquist, dissenting. . . .

If the Court means by the term "privacy" no more than that the claim of a person to be free from unwanted state regulation of consensual transactions may be a form of "liberty" protected by the Fourteenth Amendment, there is no doubt that similar claims have been upheld in our earlier decisions on the basis of that liberty. I agree . . . that the "liberty," against deprivation of which without due process the Fourteenth Amendment protects, embraces more than the rights found in the Bill of Rights. But that liberty is not guaranteed absolutely against deprivation, only against deprivation without due process of law. The test traditionally applied in the area of social and economic legislation is whether or not a law such as that challenged has a rational relation to a valid state objective. *Williamson v. Lee Optical Co.*, 348 U.S. 483, 491 (1955). The Due Process Clause of the Fourteenth Amendment undoubtedly does place a limit, albeit a broad one, on legislative power to enact laws such as this. If the Texas statute were to prohibit an abortion even where the mother's life is in jeopardy, I have little doubt that such a statute would lack a rational relation to a valid state objective under the test stated in *Williamson*. But the Court's sweeping invalidation of any restrictions on abortion during the first trimester is impossible to justify under that standard, and the conscious weighing of competing factors that the Court's opinion apparently substitutes for the established test is far more appropriate to a legislative judgment than to a judicial one.

The Court eschews the history of the Fourteenth Amendment in its reliance on the "compelling state interest" test. But the Court adds a new wrinkle to this test by transposing it from the legal considerations associated with the Equal Protection Clause of the Fourteenth Amendment to this case arising under the Due Process Clause of the Fourteenth Amendment. Unless I misapprehend the consequences of this transplanting of the "compelling state interest test," the Court's opinion will accomplish the seemingly impossible feat of leaving this area of the law more confused than it found it.

While the Court's opinion quotes from the dissent of Mr. Justice Holmes in *Lochner v. New York*, 198 U.S. 45, 74 (1905), the result it reaches is more closely attuned to the majority opinion of Mr. Justice Peckham in that case. As in *Lochner* and similar cases applying substantive due process standards to economic and social welfare legislation, the adoption of the compelling state interest standard will inevitably require this Court to examine the legislative policies and pass on the wisdom of these policies in the very process of deciding whether a particular state interest put forward may or may not be "compelling." The decision here to break pregnancy into three distinct terms and to outline the permissible restrictions the State may impose in each one, for example, partakes more of judicial legislation than it does of a determination of the intent of the drafters of the Fourteenth Amendment.

The fact that a majority of the States reflecting, after all the majority sentiment in those States, have had restrictions on abortions for at least a century is a strong indication, it seems to me, that the asserted right to an abortion is not "so rooted in the traditions and conscience of our people as to be ranked as fundamental," *Snyder v. Massachusetts*, 291 U.S. 97, 105 (1934) . . . .

Even if one were to agree that the case that the Court decides were here, and that the enunciation of the substantive constitutional law in the Court's opinion were proper, the actual disposition of the case by the Court is still difficult to justify. The Texas statute is struck down *in toto*, even though the Court apparently concedes that at later periods of pregnancy Texas might impose these selfsame statutory limitations on abortion. My understanding of past practice is that a statute found to be invalid as applied to a particular plaintiff, but not unconstitutional as a whole, is not simply "struck down" but is, instead, declared unconstitutional as applied to the fact situation before the Court. . . .

[The concurring opinions of Chief Justice Burger and Justices Douglas and Stewart, and the dissenting opinion of Justice White, are omitted.]

Notes and Questions

1. Can you articulate the *Roe* Court's test for determining the scope of unenumerated rights? In other words, in thinking about the application of *Roe* outside the context of abortion, what would its test be for determining whether to recognize other unenumerated rights?

2. How persuasive is the Court's decision to draw fixed lines at the ends of the first and second trimesters of pregnancy? To what extent are its conclusions based on then-existing technology, and if so, what impact would (or should) later advances in technology have on the Court's test?

3. Are there analogies between what the Court did in *Dred Scott* and what it did in *Roe*? Of course, as discussed above, both cases are known as substantive due process cases. But beyond that, both cases reject a claim of personhood as a way of resolving the claims raised in the cases. In other words, is it fair to note that, just as *Dred Scott* held that slaves and their descendants are not citizens under the constitution, so too fetuses are not persons? In this regard, reconsider the excerpt from Judge Bork's book in Chapter 1, immediately following the excerpt from *Dred Scott*.

4. If the state has an interest in potential life, why does that interest not justify state interference in the abortion decision before the point of "viability"? Indeed, wouldn't a state interest in potential life justify the bans on contraception use at issue in cases such as *Griswold* and *Eisenstadt*?

5. The *Roe* Court, like the *Griswold* Court, grounds its holding in the right to privacy. Accepting that that there is a constitutionally protected zone of privacy, is the claim to "privacy" as strong in *Roe* as it was in *Griswold*? Does the Court's definition of privacy turn on where the conduct occurs? Who is present when the conduct occurs? Or is privacy defined solely by the type of conduct at issue, without regard to where or in whose presence it takes place?

6. The *Roe* Court grounds the right to privacy in the Due Process Clause, and cites a number of its prior precedents in describing the scope of that privacy right,

including *Loving*, *Skinner*, *Pierce*, and *Meyer*. Is the *Roe* Court accurately characterizing the actual holdings in these earlier precedents?

7. Does *Roe* necessarily follow from the line of substantive due process cases that precede it? Recall that in *Griswold*, the Court spoke of a right to *marital* privacy, and addressed the issue of contraception. Jane Roe, however, was an unmarried woman, and the act of abortion is different in kind, is it not, from the use of contraception? To what extent does the *Eisenstadt* decision aid in linking *Roe* to *Griswold*?

8. The laws at issue in both *Griswold* and *Eisenstadt* were to some extent outliers in that at the time of those decisions, those laws were inconsistent with the laws of virtually every other state. In contrast, at the time *Roe* was decided, nearly every state regulated or prohibited abortion in some way. Of what significance is that distinction? Stated somewhat differently, what role do history and tradition play in the Court's substantive due process analysis? To the extent they play a role, which historical time periods are relevant?

9. Is it significant in *Roe* that the abortion laws at issue, while widespread at the time of the decision, represented a stark departure from historical practice in the United States, under which abortion was largely unregulated? In this sense, can the protection of the Due Process Clauses be said to be backward looking, protecting against modern incursions on practices that have attained the *de facto* status of being a right due to longstanding state inaction? If so, why does state inaction justify granting such conduct the status of being a protected right? Moreover, if this is an accurate of how the Due Process Clauses function, how likely is it that the Clauses will serve as a viable vehicle for challenging laws that have a robust historical pedigree, such as those criminalizing consensual sodomy? On the other hand, did not the anti-miscegenation laws at issue in *Loving* have a robust historical pedigree as well?

10. The *Roe* Court acknowledges two state interests that it holds can be compelling at certain points in time: the health of the pregnant woman and the potential life of the fetus. Is the Court's holding that those are the *only* possible governmental interests that can ever be compelling, or are those merely the relevant ones raised by the government in *Roe*? Suppose that in a future case, the government raises a different interest, such as an interest in preventing fetal pain or sex-selective abortions? Does anything in *Roe* foreclose consideration of such an interest as one sufficiently compelling to infringe upon the abortion right?

11. In dissent, Justice Rehnquist accuses the majority of embracing the *Lochner* majority's discredited approach. Does he have a fair point? Is the Court any more qualified to dig into the science of abortion than it was to opine on the health and safety of the baking profession? Is there a way to justify *Roe* while still endorsing the Court's general post-*Lochner* hands-off approach when the Due Process Clauses are invoked?

Chapter 12

Sex Discrimination and the Rise of Equal Protection Review

As demonstrated by the cases in the earlier chapters, in the first hundred years after ratification of the Fourteenth Amendment, the U.S. Supreme Court rejected all efforts to challenge sex discrimination under the Fourteenth Amendment, without regard to the clause invoked. Nonetheless, advocates for sex equality persisted in bringing constitutional challenges to laws that drew distinctions on the basis of sex. In bringing those challenges, advocates for sex equality focused their efforts on the Equal Protection Clause.

The cases that follow demonstrate a remarkable evolution in the Court's equal protection jurisprudence for sex-based classifications. Over the course of U.S. history, the Court has vacillated between applying traditional rational basis scrutiny, strict scrutiny, and just about everything in between to sex-based classifications. As you read these cases, consider the following questions:

- Setting precedent to one side, what level of scrutiny is appropriate for sex-based classifications? Is sex akin to race—justifying strict scrutiny—or should traditional rational basis review apply? Or does it occupy a middle zone necessitating a new level of scrutiny?
- Assuming that heightened scrutiny is appropriate in assessing the constitutionality of laws that discriminate against women, should that same heightened standard apply to laws that discriminate against men?
- Is the concept of "sex"—as discussed in the line of cases that follow—broad enough to encompass discrimination on the basis of sexual orientation or gender identity?
- What factors does the Court look to in deciding whether or not to apply heightened scrutiny to a given classification?
- How is the Court able to undo the first 100 years of its sex-based Fourteenth Amendment jurisprudence without actually overruling any cases?

A. Traditional Rational Basis Review

Goesaert v. Cleary

335 U.S. 464 (1948)

MR. JUSTICE FRANKFURTER delivered the opinion of the Court.

As part of the Michigan system for controlling the sale of liquor, bartenders are required to be licensed in all cities having a population of 50,000, or more, but no female may be so licensed unless she be "the wife or daughter of the male owner" of a licensed liquor establishment.... The claim ... is that Michigan cannot forbid females generally from being barmaids and at the same time make an exception in favor of the wives and daughters of the owners of liquor establishments. Beguiling as the subject is, it need not detain us long. To ask whether or not the Equal Protection of the Laws Clause of the Fourteenth Amendment barred Michigan from making the classification the State has made between wives and daughters of owners of liquor places and wives and daughters of non-owners, is one of those rare instances where to state the question is in effect to answer it.

We are, to be sure, dealing with a historic calling. We meet the alewife, sprightly and ribald, in Shakespeare, but centuries before him she played a role in the social life of England. The Fourteenth Amendment did not tear history up by the roots, and the regulation of the liquor traffic is one of the oldest and most untrammeled of legislative powers. Michigan could, beyond question, forbid all women from working behind a bar. This is so despite the vast changes in the social and legal position of women. The fact that women may now have achieved the virtues that men have long claimed as their prerogatives and now indulge in vices that men have long practiced, does not preclude the States from drawing a sharp line between the sexes, certainly, in such matters as the regulation of the liquor traffic. The Constitution does not require legislatures to reflect sociological insight, or shifting social standards, any more than it requires them to keep abreast of the latest scientific standards.

While Michigan may deny to all women opportunities for bartending, Michigan cannot play favorites among women without rhyme or reasons. The Constitution in enjoining the equal protection of the laws upon States precludes irrational discrimination as between persons or groups of persons in the incidence of a law. But the Constitution does not require situations "which are different in fact or opinion to be treated in law as though they were the same." Since bartending by women may, in the allowable legislative judgment, give rise to moral and social problems against which it may devise preventive measures, the legislature need not go to the full length of prohibition if it believes that as to a defined group of females other factors are operating which either eliminate or reduce the moral and social problems otherwise calling for prohibition. Michigan evidently believes that the oversight assured through ownership of a bar by a barmaid's husband or father minimizes hazards that may confront a barmaid without such protecting oversight. This Court is certainly not in a position to gainsay such belief by the Michigan legislature. If it is entertainable, as we think it is, Michigan has not violated its duty to afford equal protection of its laws. We cannot cross-examine either actually or argumentatively the mind of Michigan legislators nor question their motives. Since the line they have drawn is not without a basis in reason, we cannot give ear to the suggestion that the real impulse behind this legislation was an unchivalrous desire of male bartenders to try to monopolize the calling....

MR. JUSTICE RUTLEDGE, with whom MR. JUSTICE DOUGLAS and MR. JUSTICE MURPHY join, dissenting.

While the equal protection clause does not require a legislature to achieve "abstract symmetry" or to classify with "mathematical nicety," that clause does require lawmakers to refrain from invidious distinctions of the sort drawn by the statute challenged in this case.

The statute arbitrarily discriminates between male and female owners of liquor establishments. A male owner, although he himself is always absent from his bar, may employ his wife and daughter as barmaids. A female owner may neither work as a barmaid herself nor employ her daughter in that position, even if a man is always present in the establishment to keep order. This inevitable result of the classification belies the assumption that the statute was motivated by a legislative solicitude for the moral and physical well-being of women who, but for the law, would be employed as barmaids. Since there could be no other conceivable justification for such discrimination against women owners of liquor establishments, the statute should be held invalid as a denial of equal protection.

Hoyt v. Florida

368 U.S. 57 (1961)

MR. JUSTICE HARLAN delivered the opinion of the Court.

Appellant, a woman, has been convicted in Hillsborough County, Florida, of second degree murder of her husband. On this appeal ... from the Florida Supreme Court's affirmance of the judgment of conviction, we noted probable jurisdiction to consider appellant's claim that her trial before an all-male jury violated rights assured by the Fourteenth Amendment. The claim is that such jury was the product of a state jury statute which works an unconstitutional exclusion of women from jury service....

In the selection of jurors Florida has differentiated between men and women in two respects. It has given women an absolute exemption from jury duty based solely on their sex, no similar exemption obtaining as to men. And it has provided for its effectuation in a manner less onerous than that governing exemptions exercisable by men: women are not to be put on the jury list unless they have voluntarily registered for such service; men, on the other hand, even if entitled to an exemption, are to be included on the list unless they have filed a written claim of exemption as provided by law.

In neither respect can we conclude that Florida's statute is not 'based on some reasonable classification,' and that it is thus infected with unconstitutionality. Despite the enlightened emancipation of women from the restrictions and protections of bygone years, and their entry into many parts of community life formerly considered to be reserved to men, woman is still regarded as the center of home and family life. We cannot say that it is constitutionally impermissible for a State, acting in pursuit of the general welfare, to conclude that a woman should be relieved from the civic duty of jury service unless she herself determines that such service is consistent with her own special responsibilities....

It is true, of course, that Florida could have limited the exemption, as some other States have done, only to women who have family responsibilities. But we cannot regard it as irrational for a state legislature to consider preferable a broad exemption, whether born of the State's historic public policy or of a determination that it would not be administratively feasible to decide in each individual instance whether the family responsibilities of a prospective female juror were serious enough to warrant an exemption.

Likewise we cannot say that Florida could not reasonably conclude that full effectuation of this exemption made it desirable to relieve women of the necessity of affirmatively claiming it, while at the same time requiring of men an assertion of the exemptions available to them. Moreover, from the standpoint of its own administrative concerns the State might well consider that it was "impractical to compel large numbers of women, who have an absolute exemption, to come to the clerk's office for examination since they so generally assert their exemption." *Fay v. New York*, *supra*, 332 U.S. at 277 ....

We cannot hold this statute as written offensive to the Fourteenth Amendment....

[The concurring opinion of Chief Justice Warren is omitted.]

Notes and Questions

1. To what extent are the decisions in *Goesaert* and *Hoyt* based on stereotypes about the typical qualities of men versus women, stereotypes that may have *some* basis in fact but are not true of all or even most men and women?

2. In *Goesaert* and *Hoyt*, does the Court identify the actual purpose behind the law, or is it merely hypothesizing a rationale for the law?

3. What is the nature of the discriminatory classification in *Goesaert*? Is it discrimination between males and females who desire to be bartenders? Is it discrimination between females who are the wife or daughter of a male bar owner and who desire to be bartenders and females who are not the wife or daughter of a male bar owner and who desire to be bartenders? Or is it discrimination between male bar owners—who are able to work in their own bars or have their wives or daughters work there—and female bar owners, who can neither work in their own bars nor employ their daughters?

4. In a case, such as *Hoyt*, where the claim is that jurors of a particular race, sex, or other classification are being kept off the jury, *whose* equal protection rights are at stake, those of the excluded jurors, those of a party who is negatively impacted by that discrimination because they share that same characteristic, or both?

5. The *Goesaert* and *Hoyt* decisions are consistent with the Court's general approach to equal protection claims embodied in cases such as *Lee Optical* and *Beach Communications*. Are there reasons why sex-based classifications, like race-based ones, should be subject to a more searching form of scrutiny? If so, what are those reasons?

B. Transitional Rational Basis Plus Review

Reed v. Reed

404 U.S. 71 (1971)

MR. CHIEF JUSTICE BURGER delivered the opinion of the Court.

Richard Lynn Reed, a minor, died intestate in Ada County, Idaho, on March 29, 1967 . . . . Approximately seven months after Richard's death, his mother, appellant Sally Reed, filed a petition in the Probate Court of Ada County, seeking appointment as administratrix of her son's estate. Prior to the date set for a hearing on the mother's petition, appellee Cecil Reed, the father of the decedent, filed a competing petition seeking to have himself appointed administrator of the son's estate. The probate court held a joint hearing on the two petitions and thereafter ordered that letters of administration be issued to appellee Cecil Reed upon his taking the oath and filing the bond required by law. The court treated §§ 15-312 and 15-314 of the Idaho Code as the controlling statutes and read those sections as compelling a preference for Cecil Reed because he was a male.

Section 15-312 designates the persons who are entitled to administer the estate of one who dies intestate. In making these designations, that section lists 11 classes of persons who are so entitled and provides, in substance, that the order in which those classes are listed in the section shall be determinative of the relative rights of competing applicants for letters of administration. One of the 11 classes so enumerated is "[t]he father or mother" of the person dying intestate. Under this section then appellant and appellee, being members of the same entitlement class, would seem to have been equally entitled to administer their son's estate. Section 15-314 provides, however, that

> "[o]f several persons claiming and equally entitled (under § 15-312) to administer, males must be preferred to females, and relatives of the whole to those of the half blood."

[The decision was appealed and eventually affirmed by the Idaho Supreme Court.]

Sally Reed thereupon appealed for review by this Court. . . . Having examined the record and considered the briefs and oral arguments of the parties, we have concluded that the arbitrary preference established in favor of males by § 15-314 of the Idaho Code cannot stand in the face of the Fourteenth Amendment's command that no State deny the equal protection of the laws to any person within its jurisdiction....

Section 15-314 is restricted in its operation to those situations where competing applications for letters of administration have been filed by both male and female members of the same entitlement class established by § 15-312. In such situations, § 15-314 provides that different treatment be accorded to the applicants on the basis of their sex; it thus establishes a classification subject to scrutiny under the Equal Protection Clause.

In applying that clause, this Court has consistently recognized that the Fourteenth Amendment does not deny to States the power to treat different classes of persons in different ways. The Equal Protection Clause of that amendment does, however, deny to States the power to legislate that different treatment be accorded to persons placed by a statute into different classes on the basis of criteria wholly unrelated to the objective of that statute. A classification "must be reasonable, not arbitrary, and must rest upon some ground of difference having a fair and substantial relation to the object of the legislation, so that all persons similarly circumstanced shall be treated alike." *Royster Guano Co. v. Virginia*, 253 U.S. 412, 415 (1920). The question presented by this case, then, is whether a difference in the sex of competing applicants for letters of administration bears a rational relationship to a state objective that is sought to be advanced by the operation of §§ 15-312 and 15-314.

In upholding the latter section, the Idaho Supreme Court concluded that its objective was to eliminate one area of controversy when two or more persons, equally entitled under § 15-312, seek letters of administration and thereby present the probate court "with the issue of which one should be named." The court also concluded that where such persons are not of the same sex, the elimination of females from consideration "is neither an illogical nor arbitrary method devised by the legislature to resolve an issue that would otherwise require a hearing as to the relative merits ... of the two or more petitioning relatives...."

Clearly the objective of reducing the workload on probate courts by eliminating one class of contests is not without some legitimacy. The crucial question, however, is whether § 15-314 advances that objective in a manner consistent with the command of the Equal Protection Clause. We hold that it does not. To give a mandatory preference to members of either sex over members of the other, merely to accomplish the elimination of hearings on the merits, is to make the very kind of arbitrary legislative choice forbidden by the Equal Protection Clause of the Fourteenth Amendment; and whatever may be said as to the positive values of avoiding intrafamily controversy, the choice in this context may not lawfully be mandated solely on the basis of sex....

Notes and Questions

1. Is the *Reed* Court applying the same type of rational basis scrutiny employed in cases such as *Lee Optical* and *Beach Communications*? Note that the language used

by the Court to describe the standard is somewhat different and not nearly as deferential. Indeed, the case upon which *Reed* relies—*Royster Guano*—was decided during the height of the *Lochner* era and prior to the Court's announced deferential approach to equal protection claims in *Carolene Products*. Recall as well that the *Eisenstadt* Court, which relied on *Reed*, likewise appeared to be applying something more robust than traditional rational basis review. Why would the *Reed* Court make it appear as though it was doing one thing (applying rational basis review) when it was in fact applying a more robust form of judicial scrutiny?

2. Can you hypothesize a rationale for the Idaho law that would withstand traditional rational basis scrutiny? Given the era in which the case was decided, would it not be fair to say that men were generally more knowledgeable about business matters relevant to administering an estate, thus justifying a preference for males over females? Although based on stereotypes about men and women, would that be any different from the reasoning employed by the Court in *Goesaert* and *Hoyt*?

C. Strict Scrutiny

Around the time of the *Reed* decision, a young lawyer by the name of Ruth Bader Ginsburg was litigating sex discrimination cases in the lower federal courts. In 1972, relying on *Reed* and representing a male client, she succeeded in persuading the U.S. Court of Appeals for the 10th Circuit to declare unconstitutional on equal protection grounds a deduction in the tax code that was available only to women, not men. *See Moritz v. Commissioner of Internal Revenue*, 469 F.2d 466 (1972). A year later, in the following case, she persuaded a plurality of the Court to hold strict scrutiny applicable to sex-based classifications.

Frontiero v. Richardson

411 U.S. 677 (1973)

Mr. Justice Brennan announced the judgment of the Court in an opinion in which Mr. Justice Douglas, Mr. Justice White, and Mr. Justice Marshall join.

The question before us concerns the right of a female member of the uniformed services to claim her spouse as a "dependent" for the purposes of obtaining increased quarters allowances and medical and dental benefits under 37 U.S.C. §§ 401, 403, and 10 U.S.C. §§ 1072, 1076, on an equal footing with male members. Under these statutes, a serviceman may claim his wife as a "dependent" without regard to whether she is in fact dependent upon him for any part of her support. A servicewoman, on the other hand, may not claim her husband as a "dependent" under these programs unless he is in fact dependent upon her for over one-half of his support. Thus, the question for decision is whether this difference in treatment constitutes an unconstitutional discrimination against servicewomen in violation of the Due Process Clause of the Fifth Amendment....

I

. . . .

Appellant Sharron Frontiero, a lieutenant in the United States Air Force, sought increased quarters allowances, and housing and medical benefits for her husband, appellant Joseph Frontiero, on the ground that he was her "dependent." Although such benefits would automatically have been granted with respect to the wife of a male member of the uniformed services, appellant's application was denied because she failed to demonstrate that her husband was dependent on her for more than one-half of his support. Appellants then commenced this suit, contending that, by making this distinction, the statutes unreasonably discriminate on the basis of sex in violation of the Due Process Clause of the Fifth Amendment.[5] In essence, appellants asserted that the discriminatory impact of the statutes is twofold: first, as a procedural matter, a female member is required to demonstrate her spouse's dependency, while no such burden is imposed upon male members; and, second, as a substantive matter, a male member who does not provide more than one-half of his wife's support receives benefits, while a similarly situated female member is denied such benefits. Appellants therefore sought a permanent injunction against the continued enforcement of these statutes and an order directing the appellees to provide Lieutenant Frontiero with the same housing and medical benefits that a similarly situated male member would receive.

Although the legislative history of these statutes sheds virtually no light on the purposes underlying the differential treatment accorded male and female members, a majority of the three-judge District Court surmised that Congress might reasonably have concluded that, since the husband in our society is generally the "breadwinner" in the family—and the wife typically the "dependent" partner—"it would be more economical to require married female members claiming husbands to prove actual dependency than to extend the presumption of dependency to such members." Indeed, given the fact that approximately 99% of all members of the uniformed services are male, the District Court speculated that such differential treatment might conceivably lead to a "considerable saving of administrative expense and manpower."

II

At the outset, appellants contend that classifications based upon sex, like classifications based upon race, alienage, and national origin, are inherently suspect and must therefore be subjected to close judicial scrutiny. We agree and, indeed, find at least implicit support for such an approach in our unanimous decision only last Term in *Reed v. Reed*, 404 U.S. 71 (1971).

5. "[W]hile the Fifth Amendment contains no equal protection clause, it does forbid discrimination that is 'so unjustifiable as to be violative of due process.'" *Schneider v. Rusk*, 377 U.S. 163, 168 (1964); see *Shapiro v. Thompson*, 394 U.S. 618, 641–642 (1969); *Bolling v. Sharpe*, 347 U.S. 497 (1954).

In *Reed*, the Court considered the constitutionality of an Idaho statute providing that, when two individuals are otherwise equally entitled to appointment as administrator of an estate, the male applicant must be preferred to the female. Appellant, the mother of the deceased, and appellee, the father, filed competing petitions for appointment as administrator of their son's estate. Since the parties, as parents of the deceased, were members of the same entitlement class the statutory preference was invoked and the father's petition was therefore granted. Appellant claimed that this statute, by giving a mandatory preference to males over females without regard to their individual qualifications, violated the Equal Protection Clause of the Fourteenth Amendment.

The Court noted that the Idaho statute "provides that different treatment be accorded to the applicants on the basis of their sex; it thus establishes a classification subject to scrutiny under the Equal Protection Clause." Under "traditional" equal protection analysis, a legislative classification must be sustained unless it is "patently arbitrary" and bears no rational relationship to a legitimate governmental interest.

In an effort to meet this standard, appellee contended that the statutory scheme was a reasonable measure designed to reduce the workload on probate courts by eliminating one class of contests. Moreover, appellee argued that the mandatory preference for male applicants was in itself reasonable since "men [are] as a rule more conversant with business affairs than . . . women."[10] Indeed, appellee maintained that "it is a matter of common knowledge, that women still are not engaged in politics, the professions, business or industry to the extent that men are."[11] And the Idaho Supreme Court, in upholding the constitutionality of this statute, suggested that the Idaho Legislature might reasonably have "concluded that in general men are better qualified to act as an administrator than are women."

Despite these contentions, however, the Court held the statutory preference for male applicants unconstitutional. In reaching this result, the Court implicitly rejected appellee's apparently rational explanation of the statutory scheme, and concluded that, by ignoring the individual qualifications of particular applicants, the challenged statute provide "dissimilar treatment for men and women who are . . . similarly situated." The Court therefore held that, even though the State's interest in achieving administrative efficiency "is not without some legitimacy," "[t]o give a mandatory preference to members of either sex over members of the other, merely to accomplish the elimination of hearings on the merits, is to make the very kind of arbitrary legislative choice forbidden by the [Constitution] . . . ." This departure from "traditional" rational-basis analysis with respect to sex-based classifications is clearly justified.

---

10. Brief for Appellee in No. 70–4, O.T. 1971, *Reed v. Reed*, p. 12.

11. *Id.*, at 12-13.

There can be no doubt that our Nation has had a long and unfortunate history of sex discrimination. Traditionally, such discrimination was rationalized by an attitude of "romantic paternalism" which, in practical effect, put women, not on a pedestal, but in a cage. Indeed, this paternalistic attitude became so firmly rooted in our national consciousness that, 100 years ago, a distinguished Member of this Court was able to proclaim:

> "Man is, or should be, women's protector and defender. The natural and proper timidity and delicacy which belongs to the female sex evidently unfits it for many of the occupations of civil life. The constitution of the family organization, which is founded in the divine ordinance, as well as in the nature of things, indicates the domestic sphere as that which properly belongs to the domain and functions of womanhood. The harmony, not to say identity, of interests and views which belong, or should belong, to the family institution is repugnant to the idea of a woman adopting a distinct and independent career from that of her husband....
>
> "... The paramount destiny and mission of woman are to fulfil the noble and benign offices of wife and mother. This is the law of the Creator." *Bradwell v. Illinois*, 16 Wall. 130, 141 (1873) (Bradley, J., concurring).

As a result of notions such as these, our statute books gradually became laden with gross, stereotyped distinctions between the sexes and, indeed, throughout much of the 19th century the position of women in our society was, in many respects, comparable to that of blacks under the pre-Civil War slave codes. Neither slaves nor women could hold office, serve on juries, or bring suit in their own names, and married women traditionally were denied the legal capacity to hold or convey property or to serve as legal guardians of their own children. And although blacks were guaranteed the right to vote in 1870, women were denied even that right—which is itself "preservative of other basic civil and political rights"—until adoption of the Nineteenth Amendment half a century later.

It is true, of course, that the position of women in America has improved markedly in recent decades. Nevertheless, it can hardly be doubted that, in part because of the high visibility of the sex characteristic, women still face pervasive, although at times more subtle, discrimination in our educational institutions, in the job market and, perhaps most conspicuously, in the political arena.[17]

Moreover, since sex, like race and national origin, is an immutable characteristic determined solely by the accident of birth, the imposition of special disabilities upon the members of a particular sex because of their sex would seem to violate

17. It is true, of course, that when viewed in the abstract, women do not constitute a small and powerless minority. Nevertheless, in part because of past discrimination, women are vastly underrepresented in this Nation's decisionmaking councils. There has never been a female President, nor a female member of this Court. Not a single woman presently sits in the United States Senate, and only 14 women hold seats in the House of Representatives. And, as appellants point out, this underrepresentation is present throughout all levels of our State and Federal Government.

"the basic concept of our system that legal burdens should bear some relationship to individual responsibility. . . ." *Weber v. Aetna Casualty & Surety Co.*, 406 U.S. 164, 175 (1972). And what differentiates sex from such non-suspect statuses as intelligence or physical disability, and aligns it with the recognized suspect criteria, is that the sex characteristic frequently bears no relation to ability to perform or contribute to society. As a result, statutory distinctions between the sexes often have the effect of invidiously relegating the entire class of females to inferior legal status without regard to the actual capabilities of its individual members.

We might also note that, over the past decade, Congress has itself manifested an increasing sensitivity to sex-based classifications. In Tit. VII of the Civil Rights Act of 1964, for example, Congress expressly declared that no employer, labor union, or other organization subject to the provisions of the Act shall discriminate against any individual on the basis of "race, color, religion, *sex*, or national origin." Similarly, the Equal Pay Act of 1963 provides that no employer covered by the Act "shall discriminate . . . between employees on the basis of sex." And § 1 of the Equal Rights Amendment, passed by Congress on March 22, 1972, and submitted to the legislatures of the States for ratification, declares that "[e]quality of rights under the law shall not be denied or abridged by the United States or by any State on account of sex." Thus, Congress itself has concluded that classifications based upon sex are inherently invidious, and this conclusion of a coequal branch of Government is not without significance to the question presently under consideration.

With these considerations in mind, we can only conclude that classifications based upon sex, like classifications based upon race, alienage, or national origin, are inherently suspect, and must therefore be subjected to strict judicial scrutiny. Applying the analysis mandated by that stricter standard of review, it is clear that the statutory scheme now before us is constitutionally invalid.

III

The sole basis of the classification established in the challenged statutes is the sex of the individuals involved. Thus, under 37 U.S.C. §§ 401, 403, and 10 U.S.C. §§ 2072, 2076, a female member of the uniformed services seeking to obtain housing and medical benefits for her spouse must prove his dependency in fact, whereas no such burden is imposed upon male members. In addition, the statutes operate so as to deny benefits to a female member, such as appellant Sharron Frontiero, who provides less than one-half of her spouse's support, while at the same time granting such benefits to a male member who likewise provides less than one-half of his spouse's support. Thus, to this extent at least, it may fairly be said that these statutes command "dissimilar treatment for men and women who are . . . similarly situated." *Reed v. Reed*, 404 U.S., at 77.

Moreover, the Government concedes that the differential treatment accorded men and women under these statutes serves no purpose other than mere "administrative convenience." In essence, the Government maintains that, as an empirical matter, wives in our society frequently are dependent upon their husbands, while husbands rarely are dependent upon their wives. Thus, the Government argues that Congress might reasonably have concluded that it would be both cheaper and easier simply conclusively to presume that wives of male members are financially dependent upon their husbands, while burdening female members with the task of establishing dependency in fact.[22]

The Government offers no concrete evidence, however, tending to support its view that such differential treatment in fact saves the Government any money. In order to satisfy the demands of strict judicial scrutiny, the Government must demonstrate, for example, that it is actually cheaper to grant increased benefits with respect to *all* male members, than it is to determine which male members are in fact entitled to such benefits and to grant increased benefits only to those members whose wives actually meet the dependency requirement. Here, however, there is substantial evidence that, if put to the test, many of the wives of male members would fail to qualify for benefits.[23] And in light of the fact that the dependency determination with respect to the husbands of female members is presently made solely on the basis of affidavits rather than through the more costly hearing process, the Government's explanation of the statutory scheme is, to say the least, questionable.

In any case, our prior decisions make clear that, although efficacious administration of governmental programs is not without some importance, "the Constitution recognizes higher values than speed and efficiency." And when we enter the realm of "strict judicial scrutiny," there can be no doubt that "administrative convenience" is not a shibboleth, the mere recitation of which dictates constitutionality. On the contrary, any statutory scheme which draws a sharp line between the sexes, *solely* for the purpose of achieving administrative convenience, necessarily commands "dissimilar treatment for men and women who are . . . similarly situated," and therefore involves the "very kind of arbitrary legislative choice forbidden by the [Constitution] . . . ." *Reed v. Reed*, 404 U.S., at 77. We therefore conclude that, by according differential treatment to male and female members of the uniformed services for the sole purpose of achieving administrative convenience, the challenged statutes violate the Due Process Clause of the Fifth Amendment insofar as they require a female member to prove the dependency of her husband.

---

22. It should be noted that these statutes are not in any sense designed to rectify the effects of past discrimination against women. On the contrary, these statutes seize upon a group—women—who have historically suffered discrimination in employment, and rely on the effects of this past discrimination as a justification for heaping on additional economic disadvantages.

23. In 1971, 43% of all women over the age of 16 were in the labor force, and 18% of all women worked full time 12 months per year. Moreover, 41.5% of all married women are employed. It is also noteworthy that, while the median income of a male member of the armed forces is approximately $3,686, the median income for all women over the age of 14, including those who are not employed, is approximately $2,237. Applying the statutory definition of "dependency" to these statistics, it appears that in the "median" family, the wife of a male member must have personal expenses of approximately $4,474, or about 75% of the total family income, in order to qualify as a "dependent."

Reversed.

Mr. Justice Stewart concurs in the judgment, agreeing that the statutes before us work an invidious discrimination in violation of the Constitution. *Reed v. Reed*, 404 U.S. 71.

Mr. Justice Rehnquist dissents for the reasons stated by Judge Rives in his opinion for the District Court, *Frontiero v. Laird*, 341 F.Supp. 201 (1972).

Mr. Justice Powell, with whom The Chief Justice and Mr. Justice Blackmun join, concurring in the judgment.

I agree that the challenged statutes constitute an unconstitutional discrimination against servicewomen in violation of the Due Process Clause of the Fifth Amendment, but I cannot join the opinion of Mr. Justice Brennan, which would hold that all classifications based upon sex, "like classifications based upon race, alienage, and national origin," are "inherently suspect and must therefore be subjected to close judicial scrutiny." It is unnecessary for the Court in this case to characterize sex as a suspect classification, with all of the far-reaching implications of such a holding. *Reed v. Reed*, 404 U.S. 71 (1971), which abundantly supports our decision today, did not add sex to the narrowly limited group of classifications which are inherently suspect. In my view, we can and should decide this case on the authority of *Reed* and reserve for the future any expansion of its rationale.

There is another, and I find compelling, reason for deferring a general categorizing of sex classifications as invoking the strictest test of judicial scrutiny. The Equal Rights Amendment, which if adopted will resolve the substance of this precise question, has been approved by the Congress and submitted for ratification by the States. If this Amendment is duly adopted, it will represent the will of the people accomplished in the manner prescribed by the Constitution. By acting prematurely and unnecessarily, as I view it, the Court has assumed a decisional responsibility at the very time when state legislatures, functioning within the traditional democratic process, are debating the proposed Amendment. It seems to me that this reaching out to pre-empt by judicial action a major political decision which is currently in process of resolution does not reflect appropriate respect for duly prescribed legislative processes.

There are times when this Court, under our system, cannot avoid a constitutional decision on issues which normally should be resolved by the elected representatives of the people. But democratic institutions are weakened, and confidence in the restraint of the Court is impaired, when we appear unnecessarily to decide sensitive issues of broad social and political importance at the very time they are under consideration within the prescribed constitutional processes.

Notes and Questions

1. In holding that some form of heightened, and ultimately, strict scrutiny, applies to sex-based classifications, the *Frontiero* plurality relies in part on its earlier decision in *Reed*. How exactly does *Reed* stand for the proposition that heightened scrutiny

applies? And how does such a holding square with earlier decisions such as *Goesaert* and *Hoyt*?

2. The *Frontiero* plurality identifies a number of characteristics about sex that warrant applying strict scrutiny to laws that discriminate on the basis of sex. What, exactly, are those factors, and how did the Court come up with that list of factors? Moreover, are the factors characteristics about *women*, or about *sex* generally? In other words, are all of the factors equally relevant when thinking about discrimination against men *and* women, or are some of them relevant only to discrimination against women?

3. One of the factors cited by the *Frontiero* plurality is political powerlessness, while another factor cited by the plurality is the fact that Congress has legislated to combat the sort of discrimination at issue. Are not those two factors in tension with one another? Or might the latter factor—at least where Congress (as contrasted with a state legislative body) is involved—be viewed as a pertinent finding pursuant to Section 5 of the Fourteenth Amendment under the logic of *Katzenbach v. Morgan*?

4. Because only a plurality of the *Frontiero* Court endorsed strict scrutiny, the actual level of scrutiny to apply to sex-based classifications remained unclear post-*Frontiero*. In cases decided shortly after *Frontiero*, the Court avoided making a definitive ruling regarding the level of scrutiny applicable to such classifications, but two general principles emerged.

First, the Court would generally strike down sex-based classifications that reflected archaic gender stereotypes. Thus, for example, in *Stanton v. Stanton*, 421 U.S. 7 (1975), the Court struck down a statute under which women reach the age of majority at 18 but men at age 21 for child support purposes. According to the Court, the law, which was based on the notion that males are usually breadwinners and so they need support through age 21 to go to college, was based on outmoded stereotypes about women's roles. Similarly, in *Weinberger v. Wiesenfeld*, 420 U.S. 635 (1975), the Court struck down a Social Security provision under which the surviving widow and minor children received benefits based on earnings of a deceased husband/father, but under which only minor children received benefits if a mother/wife died. According to the Court, the law was invalid because based on an archaic stereotype that only wages of the male, but not the female, are vital to supporting family.

In contrast, the Court would generally uphold sex-based remedial laws designed to help women overcome structural barriers. Thus, for example, in *Schlesinger v. Ballard*, 419 U.S. 498 (1975), the Court upheld a statute under which female soldiers had a longer period in which to attain promotion or be discharged from the military than male officers. Reasoning that because other military regulations—the constitutionality of which were not at issue in the case—prohibited women from serving in certain types of positions, females were generally unable to compile a record for promotion as quickly as men, and this preference allowed them time to overcome those structural disadvantages. Similarly, in *Kahn v. Shevin*, 416 U.S. 351 (1974), the Court upheld a state statute giving widows but not widowers a small property tax exemption. The *Kahn* Court reasoned that whether from overt discrimination or from the socialization process, women faced more difficult barriers in the job market than widowers, thus justifying the exemption.

D. Intermediate Scrutiny

Craig v. Boren

429 U.S. 190 (1976)

Mr. Justice Brennan delivered the opinion of the Court.

The interaction of two sections of an Oklahoma statute prohibits the sale of "nonintoxicating" 3.2% beer to males under the age of 21 and to females under the age of 18. The question to be decided is whether such a gender-based differential constitutes a denial to males 18-20 years of age of the equal protection of the laws in violation of the Fourteenth Amendment....

Analysis may appropriately begin with the reminder that *Reed* emphasized that statutory classifications that distinguish between males and females are "subject to scrutiny under the Equal Protection Clause." 404 U.S., at 75. To withstand constitutional challenge, previous cases establish that classifications by gender must serve important governmental objectives and must be substantially related to achievement of those objectives. Thus, in *Reed*, the objectives of "reducing the workload on probate courts," *id.*, at 76, and "avoiding intrafamily controversy," *id.*, at 77, were deemed of insufficient importance to sustain use of an overt gender criterion in the appointment of administrators of intestate decedents' estates. Decisions following *Reed* similarly have rejected administrative ease and convenience as sufficiently important objectives to justify gender-based classifications. And only two Terms ago, *Stanton v. Stanton*, 421 U.S. 7 (1975), expressly stating that *Reed v. Reed* was "controlling," 421 U.S., at 13, held that *Reed* required invalidation of a Utah differential age-of-majority statute, notwithstanding the statute's coincidence with and furtherance of the State's purpose of fostering "old notions" of role typing and preparing boys for their expected performance in the economic and political worlds.

Reed v. Reed has also provided the underpinning for decisions that have invalidated statutes employing gender as an inaccurate proxy for other, more germane bases of classification. Hence, "archaic and overbroad" generalizations, *Schlesinger v. Ballard*, *supra*, 419 U.S., at 508, concerning the financial position of servicewomen, *Frontiero v. Richardson*, *supra*, 411 U.S., at 689 n. 23, and working women, *Weinberger v. Wiesenfeld*, 420 U.S. 636, 643 (1975), could not justify use of a gender line in determining eligibility for certain governmental entitlements. Similarly, increasingly outdated misconceptions concerning the role of females in the home rather than in the "marketplace and world of ideas" were rejected as loose-fitting characterizations incapable of supporting state statutory schemes that were premised upon their accuracy. *Stanton v. Stanton*, *supra*; *Taylor v. Louisiana*, 419 U.S. 522, 535 n. 17

(1975). In light of the weak congruence between gender and the characteristic or trait that gender purported to represent, it was necessary that the legislatures choose either to realign their substantive laws in a gender-neutral fashion, or to adopt procedures for identifying those instances where the sex-centered generalization actually comported with fact.

We accept for purposes of discussion the District Court's identification of the objective underlying [the Oklahoma statute] as the enhancement of traffic safety.[7] Clearly, the protection of public health and safety represents an important function of state and local governments. However, appellees' statistics in our view cannot support the conclusion that the gender-based distinction closely serves to achieve that objective and therefore the distinction cannot under *Reed* withstand equal protection challenge.

The appellees introduced a variety of statistical surveys. First, an analysis of arrest statistics for 1973 demonstrated that 18-20-year-old male arrests for "driving under the influence" and "drunkenness" substantially exceeded female arrests for that same age period. Similarly, youths aged 17-21 were found to be overrepresented among those killed or injured in traffic accidents, with males again numerically exceeding females in this regard. Third, a random roadside survey in Oklahoma City revealed that young males were more inclined to drive and drink beer than were their female counterparts. Fourth, Federal Bureau of Investigation nationwide statistics exhibited a notable increase in arrests for "driving under the influence." Finally, statistical evidence gathered in other jurisdictions, particularly Minnesota and Michigan, was offered to corroborate Oklahoma's experience by indicating the pervasiveness of youthful participation in motor vehicle accidents following the imbibing of alcohol. . . .

Even were this statistical evidence accepted as accurate, it nevertheless offers only a weak answer to the equal protection question presented here. The most focused and relevant of the statistical surveys, arrests of 18-20-year-olds for alcohol-related driving offenses, exemplifies the ultimate unpersuasiveness of this evidentiary record. Viewed in terms of the correlation between sex and the actual activity that Oklahoma seeks to regulate—driving while under the influence of alcohol—the statistics broadly establish that .18% of females and 2% of males in that age group were arrested for that offense. While such a disparity is not trivial in a statistical sense, it hardly can form the basis for employment of a gender line as a classifying device. Certainly if maleness is to serve as a proxy for drinking and driving, a correlation

---

7. That this was the true purpose is not at all self-evident. The purpose is not apparent from the face of the statute and the Oklahoma Legislature does not preserve statutory history materials capable of clarifying the objectives served by its legislative enactments. . . . For this appeal we find adequate the appellee's representation of legislative purpose, leaving for another day consideration of whether the statement of the State's Assistant Attorney General should suffice to inform this Court of the legislature's objectives, or whether the Court must determine if the litigant simply is selecting a convenient, but false, *post hoc* rationalization.

of 2% must be considered an unduly tenuous "fit." Indeed, prior cases have consistently rejected the use of sex as a decisionmaking factor even though the statutes in question certainly rested on far more predictive empirical relationships than this.[13]

Moreover, the statistics exhibit a variety of other shortcomings that seriously impugn their value to equal protection analysis. Setting aside the obvious methodological problems, the surveys do not adequately justify the salient features of Oklahoma's gender-based traffic-safety law. None purports to measure the use and dangerousness of 3.2% beer as opposed to alcohol generally, a detail that is of particular importance since, in light of its low alcohol level, Oklahoma apparently considers the 3.2% beverage to be "nonintoxicating." Moreover, many of the studies, while graphically documenting the unfortunate increase in driving while under the influence of alcohol, make no effort to relate their findings to age-sex differentials as involved here. Indeed, the only survey that explicitly centered its attention upon young drivers and their use of beer—albeit apparently not of the diluted 3.2% variety—reached results that hardly can be viewed as impressive in justifying either a gender or age classification.

There is no reason to belabor this line of analysis. It is unrealistic to expect either members of the judiciary or state officials to be well versed in the rigors of experimental or statistical technique. But this merely illustrates that proving broad sociological propositions by statistics is a dubious business, and one that inevitably is in tension with the normative philosophy that underlies the Equal Protection Clause. Suffice to say that the showing offered by the appellees does not satisfy us that sex represents a legitimate, accurate proxy for the regulation of drinking and driving. In fact, when it is further recognized that Oklahoma's statute prohibits only the selling of 3.2% beer to young males and not their drinking the beverage once acquired (even after purchase by their 18-20-year-old female companions), the relationship between gender and traffic safety becomes far too tenuous to satisfy *Reed*'s requirement that the gender-based difference be substantially related to achievement of the statutory objective. . . .

We conclude that the gender-based differential contained in [the Oklahoma statute] constitutes a denial of the equal protection of the laws to males aged 18-20[23] and reverse the judgment of the District Court. . . .

Mr. Justice Powell, concurring.

---

13. For example, we can conjecture that in *Reed*, Idaho's apparent premise that women lacked experience in formal business matters (particularly compared to men) would have proved to be accurate in substantially more than 2% of all cases. And in both *Frontiero* and *Wiesenfeld*, we expressly found appellees' empirical defense of mandatory dependency tests for men but not women to be unsatisfactory, even though we recognized that husbands are still far less likely to be dependent on their wives than vice versa. See, *e. g.*, 411 U.S., at 688-690.

23. Insofar as *Goesaert v. Cleary*, 335 U.S. 464 (1948), may be inconsistent, that decision is disapproved. . . .

I join the opinion of the Court as I am in general agreement with it. I do have reservations as to some of the discussion concerning the appropriate standard for equal protection analysis and the relevance of the statistical evidence. Accordingly, I add this concurring statement.

With respect to the equal protection standard, I agree that *Reed v. Reed*, 404 U.S. 71 (1971), is the most relevant precedent. But I find it unnecessary, in deciding this case, to read that decision as broadly as some of the Court's language may imply. *Reed* and subsequent cases involving gender-based classifications make clear that the Court subjects such classifications to a more critical examination than is normally applied when "fundamental" constitutional rights and "suspect classes" are not present.*

I view this as a relatively easy case. No one questions the legitimacy or importance of the asserted governmental objective: the promotion of highway safety. The decision of the case turns on whether the state legislature, by the classification it has chosen, had adopted a means that bears a "'fair and substantial relation'" to this objective. *Id.*, at 76, quoting *Royster Guano Co. v. Virginia*, 253 U.S. 412, 415 (1920).

It seems to me that the statistics offered by appellees and relied upon by the District Court do tend generally to support the view that young men drive more, possibly are inclined to drink more, and—for various reasons—are involved in more accidents than young women. Even so, I am not persuaded that these facts and the inferences fairly drawn from them justify this classification based on a three-year age differential between the sexes, and especially one that it so easily circumvented as to be virtually meaningless. Putting it differently, this gender-based classification does not bear a fair and substantial relation to the object of the legislation.

Mr. Justice Stevens, concurring.

There is only one Equal Protection Clause. It requires every State to govern impartially. It does not direct the courts to apply one standard of review in some cases and a different standard in other cases. Whatever criticism may be leveled at a judicial opinion implying that there are at least three such standards applies with the same force to a double standard.

I am inclined to believe that what has become known as the two-tiered analysis of equal protection claims does not describe a completely logical method of deciding

---

* As is evident from our opinions, the Court has had difficulty in agreeing upon a standard of equal protection analysis that can be applied consistently to the wide variety of legislative classifications. There are valid reasons for dissatisfaction with the "two-tier" approach that has been prominent in the Court's decisions in the past decade. Although viewed by many as a result-oriented substitute for more critical analysis, that approach—with its narrowly limited "upper-tier"—now has substantial precedential support. As has been true of *Reed* and its progeny, our decision today will be viewed by some as a "middle-tier" approach. While I would not endorse that characterization and would not welcome a further subdividing of equal protection analysis, candor compels the recognition that the relatively deferential "rational basis" standard of review normally applied takes on a sharper focus when we address a gender-based classification. So much is clear from our recent cases. . . .

cases, but rather is a method the Court has employed to explain decisions that actually apply a single standard in a reasonably consistent fashion. I also suspect that a careful explanation of the reasons motivating particular decisions may contribute more to an identification of that standard than an attempt to articulate it in all-encompassing terms. It may therefore be appropriate for me to state the principal reasons which persuaded me to join the Court's opinion.

In this case, the classification is not as obnoxious as some the Court has condemned, nor as inoffensive as some the Court has accepted. It is objectionable because it is based on an accident of birth, because it is a mere remnant of the now almost universally rejected tradition of discriminating against males in this age bracket, and because, to the extent it reflects any physical difference between males and females, it is actually perverse. The question then is whether the traffic safety justification put forward by the State is sufficient to make an otherwise offensive classification acceptable.

The classification is not totally irrational. For the evidence does indicate that there are more males than females in this age bracket who drive and also more who drink. Nevertheless, there are several reasons why I regard the justification as unacceptable. It is difficult to believe that the statute was actually intended to cope with the problem of traffic safety, since it has only a minimal effect on access to a not very intoxicating beverage and does not prohibit its consumption. Moreover, the empirical data submitted by the State accentuate the unfairness of treating all 18-21-year-old males as inferior to their female counterparts. The legislation imposes a restraint on 100% of the males in the class allegedly because about 2% of them have probably violated one or more laws relating to the consumption of alcoholic beverages. It is unlikely that this law will have a significant deterrent effect either on that 2% or on the law-abiding 98%. But even assuming some such slight benefit, it does not seem to me that an insult to all of the young men of the State can be justified by visiting the sins of the 2% on the 98%.

Mr. Justice Rehnquist, dissenting.

The Court's disposition of this case is objectionable on two grounds. First is its conclusion that *men* challenging a gender-based statute which treats them less favorably than women may invoke a more stringent standard of judicial review than pertains to most other types of classifications. Second is the Court's enunciation of this standard, without citation to any source, as being that "classifications by gender must serve *important* governmental objectives and must be *substantially* related to achievement of those objectives." The only redeeming feature of the Court's opinion, to my mind, is that it apparently signals a retreat by those who joined the plurality opinion in *Frontiero v. Richardson*, 411 U.S. 677 (1973), from their view that sex is a "suspect" classification for purposes of equal protection analysis. . . .

In *Frontiero v. Richardson, supra*, the opinion for the plurality sets forth the reasons of four Justices for concluding that sex should be regarded as a suspect classification for purposes of equal protection analysis. These reasons center on our Nation's "long and unfortunate history of sex discrimination," 411 U.S., at 684, which has been reflected in a whole range of restrictions on the legal rights of women, not the least of which have concerned the ownership of property and participation in the electoral process. Noting that the pervasive and persistent nature of the discrimination experienced by women is in part the result of their ready identifiability, the plurality rested its invocation of strict scrutiny largely upon the fact that "statutory distinctions between the sexes often have the effect of invidiously relegating the entire class of females to inferior legal status without regard to the actual capabilities of its individual members." *Id.*, at 686-687.

Subsequent to *Frontiero*, the Court has declined to hold that sex is a suspect class, and no such holding is imported by the Court's resolution of this case. However, the Court's application here of an elevated or "intermediate" level scrutiny, like that invoked in cases dealing with discrimination against females, raises the question of why the statute here should be treated any differently from countless legislative classifications unrelated to sex which have been upheld under a minimum rationality standard.

Most obviously unavailable to support any kind of special scrutiny in this case, is a history or pattern of past discrimination, such as was relied on by the plurality in *Frontiero* to support its invocation of strict scrutiny. There is no suggestion in the Court's opinion that males in this age group are in any way peculiarly disadvantaged, subject to systematic discriminatory treatment, or otherwise in need of special solicitude from the courts.

The Court does not discuss the nature of the right involved, and there is no reason to believe that it sees the purchase of 3.2% beer as implicating any important interest, let alone one that is "fundamental" in the constitutional sense of invoking strict scrutiny. Indeed, the Court's accurate observation that the statute affects the selling but not the drinking of 3.2% beer, further emphasizes the limited effect that it has on even those persons in the age group involved. There is, in sum, nothing about the statutory classification involved here to suggest that it affects an interest, or works against a group, which can claim under the Equal Protection Clause that it is entitled to special judicial protection.

It is true that a number of our opinions contain broadly phrased dicta implying that the same test should be applied to all classifications based on sex, whether affecting females or males. *E. g., Frontiero v. Richardson, supra*, 411 U.S., at 688; *Reed v. Reed*, 404 U.S. 71, 76 (1971). However, before today, no decision of this Court has applied an elevated level of scrutiny to invalidate a statutory discrimination harmful to males, except where the statute impaired an important personal interest protected by the Constitution. . . .

The Court's conclusion that a law which treats males less favorably than females "must serve important governmental objectives and must be substantially related to achievement of those objectives" apparently comes out of thin air. The Equal

Protection Clause contains no such language, and none of our previous cases adopt that standard. I would think we have had enough difficulty with the two standards of review which our cases have recognized—the norm of "rational basis," and the "compelling state interest" required where a "suspect classification" is involved—so as to counsel weightily against the insertion of still another "standard" between those two. How is this Court to divine what objectives are important? How is it to determine whether a particular law is "substantially" related to the achievement of such objective, rather than related in some other way to its achievement? Both of the phrases used are so diaphanous and elastic as to invite subjective judicial preferences or prejudices relating to particular types of legislation, masquerading as judgments whether such legislation is directed at "important" objectives or, whether the relationship to those objectives is "substantial" enough. . . .

[The concurring opinions of Justices Blackmun and Stewart and the dissenting opinion of Chief Justice Burger are omitted.]

Notes and Questions

1. How, exactly, does the *Craig* Court characterize its prior decisions as standing for the proposition that intermediate scrutiny applies to sex-based classifications? Is Justice Rehnquist correct to accuse the majority of making it up out of thin air?

2. How does intermediate scrutiny differ from the two previously established standards, strict scrutiny and rational basis review?

3. Under intermediate scrutiny, must the Court identify the *real* governmental interest behind the law, or is it sufficient to hypothesize a rationale post-hoc? Does the *Craig* Court opine on that question?

4. Setting precedent to one side, are there sound reasons why discrimination on the basis of sex should be subject to a lower level of scrutiny than discrimination on the basis of race?

5. Justice Rehnquist criticizes the majority for applying heightened scrutiny in this case because the discrimination is against *men*, not women. Does he not have a fair point? After all, two of the factors cited by the *Frontiero* Court were political powerlessness and a history of discrimination. Although women have faced those, men have not, have they? Presumably, Justice Rehnquist would thus agree that strict scrutiny should not apply to laws that discriminate against *whites*. Reconsider Justice Rehnquist's opinion when you read Chapter 17, which includes the Court's race-based affirmative action cases, many of which were decided during Justice Rehnquist's tenure as Chief Justice.

On the other hand, when sex-based classifications are involved, is it always clear whether the law at issue is discriminating against men or women? Consider, for example, the law at issue in *Frontiero*. Is the government in that case discriminating against servicemember Sharon Frontiero because she is a female, or against her husband Joseph Frontiero because he is a male? Similarly, in *Loving*, was the law at issue discriminating against Richard Loving because he was white, or Mildred Loving because she was black? Do cases such as *Frontiero* and *Loving* support focusing on the general *classification* at play (*i.e.*, race or sex) rather than the specific *class* impacted (*i.e.*, African Americans or women)? Which approach would be most consistent with the Court's nineteenth century decisions interpreting the Reconstruction Amendments?

6. In *Craig*, the Court remains splintered both on whether or not to apply heightened scrutiny to sex-based classifications, and if so, on what level of heightened scrutiny to apply. In general, the Court's post-*Craig* decisions continued to distinguish between laws that were based on archaic stereotypes regarding the differences between men and women, and those that were based on real differences between the sexes. However, the Justices often disagreed on whether something reflected an archaic stereotype or a real difference.

For example, in *Caban v. Mohammed*, 441 U.S. 380 (1979), the Court considered the constitutionality of a state law that allowed an unwed mother to block adoption of her child by withholding consent but that denied unwed fathers that right. The majority declared the law unconstitutional, contending that it was grounded in an overbroad stereotypical generalization that unwed mothers are closer than unwed fathers to their newborn children. But the dissent contended that the fact that the unwed mother physically bore and gave birth to the child constituted a real difference between unwed mothers and unwed fathers that justified differential treatment.

Similarly, in *Michael M. v. Superior Court of Sonoma County*, 450 U.S. 464 (1981), the Court considered the constitutionality of a state statutory rape law under which if an underage male and an underage female had sex with one another, only the male would be subject to criminal prosecution. The majority upheld the law, reasoning that the risk of pregnancy was a real difference between underage men and women justifying the absence of criminal punishment for the female, because avoiding pregnancy was a sufficient deterrent for her to refrain from engaging in underage sex. However, the dissent contended that the law was based on archaic stereotypes about protecting the virtue and chastity of young women.

E. Intermediate Scrutiny Plus?

Up until this point, all of the Court's decisions regarding sex-based discrimination have been rendered by all-male Courts. In 1981, Sandra Day O'Connor was appointed as the first female Justice of the U.S. Supreme Court. Twelve years later, in 1993, Ruth Bader Ginsburg—the attorney who argued *Frontiero*—joined Justice O'Connor as the second female on the Court. The next two major decisions involving sex-based classifications were authored by those two Justices. Each decision has elements that appear to nudge the level of scrutiny for such classifications closer to strict scrutiny.

Mississippi University for Women v. Hogan

458 U.S. 718 (1982)

Justice O'Connor delivered the opinion of the Court.

This case presents the narrow issue of whether a state statute that excludes males from enrolling in a state-supported professional nursing school violates the Equal Protection Clause of the Fourteenth Amendment.

I

The facts are not in dispute. In 1884, the Mississippi Legislature created the Mississippi Industrial Institute and College for the Education of White Girls of the State of Mississippi, now the oldest state-supported all-female college in the United States. The school, known today as Mississippi University for Women (MUW), has from its inception limited its enrollment to women.[1]

In 1971, MUW established a School of Nursing, initially offering a 2-year associate degree. Three years later, the school instituted a 4-year baccalaureate program in nursing and today also offers a graduate program. The School of Nursing has its own faculty and administrative officers and establishes its own criteria for admission.

Respondent, Joe Hogan, is a registered nurse but does not hold a baccalaureate degree in nursing. Since 1974, he has worked as a nursing supervisor in a medical center in Columbus, the city in which MUW is located. In 1979, Hogan applied for admission to the MUW School of Nursing's baccalaureate program. Although he was otherwise qualified, he was denied admission to the School of Nursing solely because of his sex. School officials informed him that he could audit the courses in which he was interested, but could not enroll for credit. . . .

II

We begin our analysis aided by several firmly established principles. Because the challenged policy expressly discriminates among applicants on the basis of gender, it is subject to scrutiny under the Equal Protection Clause of the Fourteenth

1. . . . . Mississippi maintains no other single-sex public university or college. Thus, we are not faced with the question of whether States can provide "separate but equal" undergraduate institutions for males and females.

Amendment. *Reed v. Reed*, 404 U.S. 71, 75 (1971). That this statutory policy discriminates against males rather than against females does not exempt it from scrutiny or reduce the standard of review. *Caban v. Mohammed*, 441 U.S. 380, 394 (1979); *Orr v. Orr*, 440 U.S. 268, 279 (1979). Our decisions also establish that the party seeking to uphold a statute that classifies individuals on the basis of their gender must carry the burden of showing an "exceedingly persuasive justification" for the classification. *Kirchberg v. Feenstra*, 450 U.S. 455, 461 (1981); *Personnel Administrator of Mass. v. Feeney*, 442 U.S. 256, 273 (1979). The burden is met only by showing at least that the classification serves "important governmental objectives and that the discriminatory means employed" are "substantially related to the achievement of those objectives." *Wengler v. Druggists Mutual Ins. Co.*, 446 U.S. 142, 150 (1980).[9]

Although the test for determining the validity of a gender-based classification is straightforward, it must be applied free of fixed notions concerning the roles and abilities of males and females. Care must be taken in ascertaining whether the statutory objective itself reflects archaic and stereotypic notions. Thus, if the statutory objective is to exclude or "protect" members of one gender because they are presumed to suffer from an inherent handicap or to be innately inferior, the objective itself is illegitimate. See *Frontiero v. Richardson*, 411 U.S. 677, 684–685 (1973) (plurality opinion).

If the State's objective is legitimate and important, we next determine whether the requisite direct, substantial relationship between objective and means is present. The purpose of requiring that close relationship is to assure that the validity of a classification is determined through reasoned analysis rather than through the mechanical application of traditional, often inaccurate, assumptions about the proper roles of men and women. The need for the requirement is amply revealed by reference to the broad range of statutes already invalidated by this Court, statutes that relied upon the simplistic, outdated assumption that gender could be used as a "proxy for other, more germane bases of classification," *Craig v. Boren*, 429 U.S. 190, 198 (1976), to establish a link between objective and classification. . . .

III

A

The State's primary justification for maintaining the single-sex admissions policy of MUW's School of Nursing is that it compensates for discrimination against women and, therefore, constitutes educational affirmative action. As applied to the School of Nursing, we find the State's argument unpersuasive.

In limited circumstances, a gender-based classification favoring one sex can be justified if it intentionally and directly assists members of the sex that is disproportionately burdened. See *Schlesinger v. Ballard*, 419 U.S. 498 (1975). However,

9. . . . . Because we conclude that the challenged statutory classification is not substantially related to an important objective, we need not decide whether classifications based upon gender are inherently suspect.

we consistently have emphasized that "the mere recitation of a benign, compensatory purpose is not an automatic shield which protects against any inquiry into the actual purposes underlying a statutory scheme." *Weinberger v. Wiesenfeld*, 420 U.S. 636, 648 (1975) . . . .

It is readily apparent that a State can evoke a compensatory purpose to justify an otherwise discriminatory classification only if members of the gender benefited by the classification actually suffer a disadvantage related to the classification. We considered such a situation in *Califano v. Webster*, 430 U.S. 313 (1977), which involved a challenge to a statutory classification that allowed women to eliminate more low-earning years than men for purposes of computing Social Security retirement benefits. Although the effect of the classification was to allow women higher monthly benefits than were available to men with the same earning history, we upheld the statutory scheme, noting that it took into account that women "as such have been unfairly hindered from earning as much as men" and "work[ed] directly to remedy" the resulting economic disparity. *Id.*, at 318.

A similar pattern of discrimination against women influenced our decision in *Schlesinger v. Ballard, supra*. There, we considered a federal statute that granted female Naval officers a 13-year tenure of commissioned service before mandatory discharge, but accorded male officers only a 9-year tenure. We recognized that, because women were barred from combat duty, they had had fewer opportunities for promotion than had their male counterparts. By allowing women an additional four years to reach a particular rank before subjecting them to mandatory discharge, the statute directly compensated for other statutory barriers to advancement.

In sharp contrast, Mississippi has made no showing that women lacked opportunities to obtain training in the field of nursing or to attain positions of leadership in that field when the MUW School of Nursing opened its door or that women currently are deprived of such opportunities. In fact, in 1970, the year before the School of Nursing's first class enrolled, women earned 94 percent of the nursing baccalaureate degrees conferred in Mississippi and 98.6 percent of the degrees earned nationwide. . . .

Rather than compensate for discriminatory barriers faced by women, MUW's policy of excluding males from admission to the School of Nursing tends to perpetuate the stereotyped view of nursing as an exclusively woman's job. By assuring that Mississippi allots more openings in its state-supported nursing schools to women than it does to men, MUW's admissions policy lends credibility to the old view that women, not men, should become nurses, and makes the assumption that nursing is a field for women a self-fulfilling prophecy. Thus, we conclude that, although the State recited a "benign, compensatory purpose," it failed to establish that the alleged objective is the actual purpose underlying the discriminatory classification.[16]

16. Even were we to assume that discrimination against women affects their opportunity to obtain an education or to obtain leadership roles in nursing, the challenged policy nonetheless

The policy is invalid also because it fails the second part of the equal protection test, for the State has made no showing that the gender-based classification is substantially and directly related to its proposed compensatory objective. To the contrary, MUW's policy of permitting men to attend classes as auditors fatally undermines its claim that women, at least those in the School of Nursing, are adversely affected by the presence of men.

MUW permits men who audit to participate fully in classes. Additionally, both men and women take part in continuing education courses offered by the School of Nursing, in which regular nursing students also can enroll. The uncontroverted record reveals that admitting men to nursing classes does not affect teaching style, that the presence of men in the classroom would not affect the performance of the female nursing students, and that men in coeducational nursing schools do not dominate the classroom. In sum, the record in this case is flatly inconsistent with the claim that excluding men from the School of Nursing is necessary to reach any of MUW's educational goals.

Thus, considering both the asserted interest and the relationship between the interest and the methods used by the State, we conclude that the State has fallen far short of establishing the "exceedingly persuasive justification" needed to sustain the gender-based classification. . . .

United States v. Virginia

518 U.S. 515 (1996)

Justice Ginsburg delivered the opinion of the Court.

Virginia's public institutions of higher learning include an incomparable military college, Virginia Military Institute (VMI). The United States maintains that the Constitution's equal protection guarantee precludes Virginia from reserving exclusively to men the unique educational opportunities VMI affords. We agree.

I

Founded in 1839, VMI is today the sole single-sex school among Virginia's 15 public institutions of higher learning. VMI's distinctive mission is to produce "citizen-soldiers," men prepared for leadership in civilian life and in military service. VMI pursues this mission through pervasive training of a kind not available anywhere else in Virginia. Assigning prime place to character development, VMI uses an "adversative method" modeled on English public schools and once characteristic of military instruction. VMI constantly endeavors to instill physical and mental discipline in its cadets and impart to them a strong moral code. The school's graduates leave VMI with heightened comprehension of their capacity to deal with duress and stress, and a large sense of accomplishment for completing the hazardous course.

---

would be invalid, for the State has failed to establish that the legislature intended the single-sex policy to compensate for any perceived discrimination. . . .

VMI has notably succeeded in its mission to produce leaders; among its alumni are military generals, Members of Congress, and business executives. The school's alumni overwhelmingly perceive that their VMI training helped them to realize their personal goals. VMI's endowment reflects the loyalty of its graduates; VMI has the largest per-student endowment of all public undergraduate institutions in the Nation.

Neither the goal of producing citizen-soldiers nor VMI's implementing methodology is inherently unsuitable to women. And the school's impressive record in producing leaders has made admission desirable to some women. Nevertheless, Virginia has elected to preserve exclusively for men the advantages and opportunities a VMI education affords. . . .

II

. . . .

B

In 1990, prompted by a complaint filed with the Attorney General by a female high-school student seeking admission to VMI, the United States sued the Commonwealth of Virginia and VMI, alleging that VMI's exclusively male admission policy violated the Equal Protection Clause of the Fourteenth Amendment. . . .

The District Court ruled in favor of VMI, however, and rejected the equal protection challenge pressed by the United States. . . .

The Court of Appeals for the Fourth Circuit disagreed and vacated the District Court's judgment. . . .

C

In response to the Fourth Circuit's ruling, Virginia proposed a parallel program for women: Virginia Women's Institute for Leadership (VWIL). The 4-year, state-sponsored undergraduate program would be located at Mary Baldwin College, a private liberal arts school for women, and would be open, initially, to about 25 to 30 students. Although VWIL would share VMI's mission—to produce "citizen-soldiers"—the VWIL program would differ, as does Mary Baldwin College, from VMI in academic offerings, methods of education, and financial resources. . . .

IV

We note, once again, the core instruction of this Court's pathmarking decisions in *J.E.B. v. Alabama ex rel. T. B.*, 511 U.S. 127, 136-137, and n. 6 (1994), and *Mississippi Univ. for Women*, 458 U.S., at 724: Parties who seek to defend gender-based government action must demonstrate an "exceedingly persuasive justification" for that action. . . .

Without equating gender classifications, for all purposes, to classifications based on race or national origin,[6] the Court, in post-*Reed* decisions, has carefully inspected official action that closes a door or denies opportunity to women (or to men). To

6. The Court has thus far reserved most stringent judicial scrutiny for classifications based on race or national origin. . . .

summarize the Court's current directions for cases of official classification based on gender: Focusing on the differential treatment for denial of opportunity for which relief is sought, the reviewing court must determine whether the proffered justification is "exceedingly persuasive." The burden of justification is demanding and it rests entirely on the State. See *Mississippi Univ. for Women,* 458 U.S., at 724. The State must show "at least that the [challenged] classification serves 'important governmental objectives and that the discriminatory means employed' are 'substantially related to the achievement of those objectives.'" *Ibid.* The justification must be genuine, not hypothesized or invented *post hoc* in response to litigation. And it must not rely on overbroad generalizations about the different talents, capacities, or preferences of males and females.

The heightened review standard our precedent establishes does not make sex a proscribed classification. Supposed "inherent differences" are no longer accepted as a ground for race or national origin classifications. See *Loving v. Virginia,* 388 U.S. 1 (1967). Physical differences between men and women, however, are enduring: "[T]he two sexes are not fungible; a community made up exclusively of one [sex] is different from a community composed of both." *Ballard v. United States,* 329 U.S. 187, 193 (1946).

"Inherent differences" between men and women, we have come to appreciate, remain cause for celebration, but not for denigration of the members of either sex or for artificial constraints on an individual's opportunity. Sex classifications may be used to compensate women "for particular economic disabilities [they have] suffered," *Califano v. Webster,* 430 U.S. 313, 320 (1977) *(per curiam),* to "promot[e] equal employment opportunity," see *California Fed. Sav. & Loan Assn. v. Guerra,* 479 U.S. 272, 289 (1987), to advance full development of the talent and capacities of our Nation's people.[7] But such classifications may not be used, as they once were, see *Goesaert,* 335 U.S., at 467, to create or perpetuate the legal, social, and economic inferiority of women. . . .

V

. . . .

Virginia . . . asserts two justifications in defense of VMI's exclusion of women. First, the Commonwealth contends, "single-sex education provides important

7. Several *amici* have urged that diversity in educational opportunities is an altogether appropriate governmental pursuit and that single-sex schools can contribute importantly to such diversity. Indeed, it is the mission of some single-sex schools "to dissipate, rather than perpetuate, traditional gender classifications." We do not question the Commonwealth's prerogative evenhandedly to support diverse educational opportunities. We address specifically and only an educational opportunity recognized by the District Court and the Court of Appeals as "unique," an opportunity available only at Virginia's premier military institute, the Commonwealth's sole single-sex public university or college. Cf. *Mississippi Univ. for Women v. Hogan,* 458 U.S. 718, 720, n. 1 (1982) ("Mississippi maintains no other single-sex public university or college. Thus, we are not faced with the question of whether States can provide 'separate but equal' undergraduate institutions for males and females.").

educational benefits,", and the option of single-sex education contributes to "diversity in educational approaches." Second, the Commonwealth argues, "the unique VMI method of character development and leadership training," the school's adversative approach, would have to be modified were VMI to admit women. We consider these two justifications in turn.

A

Single-sex education affords pedagogical benefits to at least some students, Virginia emphasizes, and that reality is uncontested in this litigation. Similarly, it is not disputed that diversity among public educational institutions can serve the public good. But Virginia has not shown that VMI was established, or has been maintained, with a view to diversifying, by its categorical exclusion of women, educational opportunities within the Commonwealth. In cases of this genre, our precedent instructs that "benign" justifications proffered in defense of categorical exclusions will not be accepted automatically; a tenable justification must describe actual state purposes, not rationalizations for actions in fact differently grounded. See *Wiesenfeld,* 420 U.S., at 648, and n. 16 ("mere recitation of a benign [or] compensatory purpose" does not block "inquiry into the actual purposes" of government-maintained gender-based classifications); *Goldfarb,* 430 U.S., at 212-213 (rejecting government-proffered purposes after "inquiry into the actual purposes").

Mississippi Univ. for Women is immediately in point. There the State asserted, in justification of its exclusion of men from a nursing school, that it was engaging in "educational affirmative action" by "compensat[ing] for discrimination against women." 458 U.S., at 727. Undertaking a "searching analysis," *id.,* at 728 the Court found no close resemblance between "the alleged objective" and "the actual purpose underlying the discriminatory classification," *id.,* at 730. Pursuing a similar inquiry here, we reach the same conclusion.

Neither recent nor distant history bears out Virginia's alleged pursuit of diversity through single-sex educational options. In 1839, when the Commonwealth established VMI, a range of educational opportunities for men and women was scarcely contemplated. Higher education at the time was considered dangerous for women. . . . VMI was not at all novel in this respect: In admitting no women, VMI followed the lead of the Commonwealth's flagship school, the University of Virginia, founded in 1819 . . . .

Virginia eventually provided for several women's seminaries and colleges. . . .

Debate concerning women's admission as undergraduates at the main university continued well past the century's midpoint. Familiar arguments were rehearsed. If women were admitted, it was feared, they "would encroach on the rights of men; there would be new problems of government, perhaps scandals; the old honor system would have to be changed; standards would be lowered to those of other coeducational schools; and the glorious reputation of the university, as a school for men, would be trailed in the dust."

Ultimately, in 1970, "the most prestigious institution of higher education in Virginia," the University of Virginia, introduced coeducation and, in 1972, began to admit women on an equal basis with men. . . .

Virginia describes the current absence of public single-sex higher education for women as "an historical anomaly." But the historical record indicates action more deliberate than anomalous: First, protection of women against higher education; next, schools for women far from equal in resources and stature to schools for men; finally, conversion of the separate schools to coeducation. . . .

Our 1982 decision in *Mississippi Univ. for Women* prompted VMI to reexamine its male-only admission policy. Virginia relies on that reexamination as a legitimate basis for maintaining VMI's single-sex character. A Mission Study Committee, appointed by the VMI Board of Visitors, studied the problem from October 1983 until May 1986, and in that month counseled against "change of VMI status as a single-sex college." Whatever internal purpose the Mission Study Committee served—and however well meaning the framers of the report—we can hardly extract from that effort any Commonwealth policy evenhandedly to advance diverse educational options. . . .

In sum, we find no persuasive evidence in this record that VMI's male-only admission policy "is in furtherance of a state policy of 'diversity.'" . . . .

B

Virginia next argues that VMI's adversative method of training provides educational benefits that cannot be made available, unmodified, to women. Alterations to accommodate women would necessarily be "radical," so "drastic," Virginia asserts, as to transform, indeed "destroy," VMI's program. Neither sex would be favored by the transformation, Virginia maintains: Men would be deprived of the unique opportunity currently available to them; women would not gain that opportunity because their participation would "eliminat[e] the very aspects of [the] program that distinguish [VMI] from . . . other institutions of higher education in Virginia."

The District Court forecast from expert witness testimony, and the Court of Appeals accepted, that coeducation would materially affect "at least these three aspects of VMI's program-physical training, the absence of privacy, and the adversative approach." And it is uncontested that women's admission would require accommodations, primarily in arranging housing assignments and physical training programs for female cadets. It is also undisputed, however, that "the VMI methodology could be used to educate women." The District Court even allowed that some women may prefer it to the methodology a women's college might pursue. "[S]ome women, at least, would want to attend [VMI] if they had the opportunity," the District Court recognized, and "some women," the expert testimony established, "are capable of all of the individual activities required of VMI cadets." The parties, furthermore, agree that "*some* women can meet the physical standards

[VMI] now impose[s] on men." In sum, as the Court of Appeals stated, "neither the goal of producing citizen soldiers," VMI's *raison d'être,* "nor VMI's implementing methodology is inherently unsuitable to women."

In support of its initial judgment for Virginia, a judgment rejecting all equal protection objections presented by the United States, the District Court made "findings" on "gender-based developmental differences." These "findings" restate the opinions of Virginia's expert witnesses, opinions about typically male or typically female "tendencies." For example, "[m]ales tend to need an atmosphere of adversativeness," while "[f]emales tend to thrive in a cooperative atmosphere." . . . .

The United States does not challenge any expert witness estimation on average capacities or preferences of men and women. Instead, the United States emphasizes that time and again since this Court's turning point decision in *Reed v. Reed,* 404 U.S. 71 (1971), we have cautioned reviewing courts to take a "hard look" at generalizations or "tendencies" of the kind pressed by Virginia, and relied upon by the District Court. State actors controlling gates to opportunity, we have instructed, may not exclude qualified individuals based on "fixed notions concerning the roles and abilities of males and females." *Mississippi Univ. for Women,* 458 U.S., at 725.

It may be assumed, for purposes of this decision, that most women would not choose VMI's adversative method. . . . The issue, however, is not whether "women—or men—should be forced to attend VMI"; rather, the question is whether the Commonwealth can constitutionally deny to women who have the will and capacity, the training and attendant opportunities that VMI uniquely affords.

The notion that admission of women would downgrade VMI's stature, destroy the adversative system and, with it, even the school, is a judgment hardly proved, a prediction hardly different from other "self-fulfilling prophec[ies]," see *Mississippi Univ. for Women,* 458 U.S., at 730, once routinely used to deny rights or opportunities. When women first sought admission to the bar and access to legal education, concerns of the same order were expressed. . . .

Medical faculties similarly resisted men and women as partners in the study of medicine. . . .

Women's successful entry into the federal military academies, and their participation in the Nation's military forces, indicate that Virginia's fears for the future of VMI may not be solidly grounded. The Commonwealth's justification for excluding all women from "citizen-soldier" training for which some are qualified, in any event, cannot rank as "exceedingly persuasive," as we have explained and applied that standard. . . .

VI

In the second phase of the litigation, Virginia presented its remedial plan—maintain VMI as a male-only college and create VWIL as a separate program for women. . . .

A

. . . .

Having violated the Constitution's equal protection requirement, Virginia was obliged to show that its remedial proposal "directly address[ed] and relate[d] to" the violation, see *Milliken,* 433 U.S., at 282, *i.e.,* the equal protection denied to women ready, willing, and able to benefit from educational opportunities of the kind VMI offers. Virginia described VWIL as a "parallel program," and asserted that VWIL shares VMI's mission of producing "citizen-soldiers" and VMI's goals of providing "education, military training, mental and physical discipline, character . . . and leadership development." If the VWIL program could not "eliminate the discriminatory effects of the past," could it at least "bar like discrimination in the future"? A comparison of the programs said to be "parallel" informs our answer. . . .

VWIL affords women no opportunity to experience the rigorous military training for which VMI is famed. Instead, the VWIL program "deemphasize[s]" military education, 44 F.3d, at 1234, and uses a "cooperative method" of education "which reinforces self-esteem."

VWIL students participate in ROTC and a "largely ceremonial" Virginia Corps of Cadets, but Virginia deliberately did not make VWIL a military institute. The VWIL House is not a military-style residence and VWIL students need not live together throughout the 4-year program, eat meals together, or wear uniforms during the schoolday. VWIL students thus do not experience the "barracks" life "crucial to the VMI experience," the spartan living arrangements designed to foster an "egalitarian ethic." . . . .

VWIL students receive their "leadership training" in seminars, externships, and speaker series, episodes and encounters lacking the "[p]hysical rigor, mental stress, . . . minute regulation of behavior, and indoctrination in desirable values" made hallmarks of VMI's citizen-soldier training. Kept away from the pressures, hazards, and psychological bonding characteristic of VMI's adversative training, VWIL students will not know the "feeling of tremendous accomplishment" commonly experienced by VMI's successful cadets. . . .

Virginia maintains that these methodological differences are "justified pedagogically," based on "important differences between men and women in learning and developmental needs," "psychological and sociological differences" Virginia describes as "real" and "not stereotypes." . . . .

As earlier stated, generalizations about "the way women are," estimates of what is appropriate for *most women,* no longer justify denying opportunity to women whose talent and capacity place them outside the average description. . . .

In contrast to the generalizations about women on which Virginia rests, we note again these dispositive realities: VMI's "implementing methodology" is not "inherently unsuitable to women"; "some women . . . do well under [the] adversative model"; "some women, at least, would want to attend [VMI] if they had the opportunity"; "some women are capable of all of the individual activities required of VMI cadets," and "can meet the physical standards [VMI] now impose[s] on men." It is on behalf of these women that the United States has instituted this suit, and it is for them that a remedy must be crafted. . . .

B

In myriad respects other than military training, VWIL does not qualify as VMI's equal. VWIL's student body, faculty, course offerings, and facilities hardly match VMI's. Nor can the VWIL graduate anticipate the benefits associated with VMI's 157-year history, the school's prestige, and its influential alumni network. . . .

Virginia's VWIL solution is reminiscent of the remedy Texas proposed 50 years ago, in response to a state trial court's 1946 ruling that, given the equal protection guarantee, African-Americans could not be denied a legal education at a state facility. See *Sweatt v. Painter,* 339 U.S. 629 (1950). Reluctant to admit African-Americans to its flagship University of Texas Law School, the State set up a separate school for Heman Sweatt and other black law students. *Id.,* at 632. As originally opened, the new school had no independent faculty or library, and it lacked accreditation. *Id.,* at 633 . . . .

Before this Court considered the case, the new school had gained "a faculty of five full-time professors; a student body of 23; a library of some 16,500 volumes serviced by a full-time staff; a practice court and legal aid association; and one alumnus who ha[d] become a member of the Texas Bar." *Id.,* at 633. This Court contrasted resources at the new school with those at the school from which Sweatt had been excluded. The University of Texas Law School had a full-time faculty of 16, a student body of 850, a library containing over 65,000 volumes, scholarship funds, a law review, and moot court facilities. *Id.,* at 632-633.

More important than the tangible features, the Court emphasized, are "those qualities which are incapable of objective measurement but which make for greatness" in a school, including "reputation of the faculty, experience of the administration, position and influence of the alumni, standing in the community, traditions and prestige." *Id.,* at 634. Facing the marked differences reported in the *Sweatt* opinion, the Court unanimously ruled that Texas had not shown "substantial equality in the [separate] educational opportunities" the State offered. *Id.,* at 633. Accordingly, the Court held, the Equal Protection Clause required Texas to admit African-Americans to the University of Texas Law School. *Id.,* at 636. In line with *Sweatt,* we rule here that Virginia has not shown substantial equality in the separate educational opportunities the Commonwealth supports at VWIL and VMI. . . .

Justice Scalia, dissenting. . . .

I have no problem with a system of abstract tests such as rational basis, intermediate, and strict scrutiny (though I think we can do better than applying strict scrutiny and intermediate scrutiny whenever we feel like it). Such formulas are essential to evaluating whether the new restrictions that a changing society constantly imposes upon private conduct comport with that "equal protection" our society has always accorded in the past. But in my view the function of this Court is to *preserve* our society's values regarding (among other things) equal protection, not to *revise* them; to prevent backsliding from the degree of restriction the Constitution imposed upon democratic government, not to prescribe, on our own authority, progressively higher degrees. For that reason it is my view that, whatever abstract tests we may choose to devise, they cannot supersede—and indeed ought to be crafted *so as to reflect*—those constant and unbroken national traditions that embody the people's understanding of ambiguous constitutional texts. . . .

To reject the Court's disposition today, however, it is not necessary to accept my view that the Court's made-up tests cannot displace longstanding national traditions as the primary determinant of what the Constitution means. It is only necessary to apply honestly the test the Court has been applying to sex-based classifications for the past two decades. It is well settled, as Justice O'CONNOR stated some time ago for a unanimous Court, that we evaluate a statutory classification based on sex under a standard that lies "[b]etween th[e] extremes of rational basis review and strict scrutiny." *Clark v. Jeter,* 486 U.S., at 461. We have denominated this standard "intermediate scrutiny" and under it have inquired whether the statutory classification is "substantially related to an important governmental objective." *Ibid* . . . .

Notwithstanding our above-described precedents and their "'firmly established principles,'" the United States urged us to hold in this litigation "that strict scrutiny is the correct constitutional standard for evaluating classifications that deny opportunities to individuals based on their sex." The Court, while making no reference to the Government's argument, effectively accepts it.

Although the Court in two places recites the test as stated in *Hogan,* see *ante,* at 2271, 2275, which asks whether the State has demonstrated "that the classification serves important governmental objectives and that the discriminatory means employed are substantially related to the achievement of those objectives," 458 U.S., at 724, the Court never answers the question presented in anything resembling that form. When it engages in analysis, the Court instead prefers the phrase "exceedingly persuasive justification" from *Hogan* . . . .

Only the amorphous "exceedingly persuasive justification" phrase, and not the standard elaboration of intermediate scrutiny, can be made to yield this conclusion that VMI's single-sex composition is unconstitutional because there exist several women (or, one would have to conclude under the Court's reasoning, a single woman) willing and able to undertake VMI's program. Intermediate scrutiny has never required a least-restrictive-means analysis, but only a "substantial relation" between the classification and the state interests that it serves. . . .

Not content to execute a *de facto* abandonment of the intermediate scrutiny that has been our standard for sex-based classifications for some two decades, the Court purports to reserve the question whether, even in principle, a higher standard (*i.e.,* strict scrutiny) should apply. "The Court has," it says, "*thus far* reserved most stringent judicial scrutiny for classifications based on race or national origin . . . ," *ante,* at 2275, n. 6 (emphasis added); and it describes our earlier cases as having done no more than decline to "equat[e] gender classifications, *for all purposes*, to classifications based on race or national origin," *ante*, at 2275 (emphasis added) . . . .

The Court's intimations are particularly out of place because it is perfectly clear that, if the question of the applicable standard of review for sex-based classifications were to be regarded as an appropriate subject for reconsideration, the stronger argument would be not for elevating the standard to strict scrutiny, but for reducing it to rational-basis review. The latter certainly has a firmer foundation in our past jurisprudence: Whereas no majority of the Court has ever applied strict scrutiny in a case involving sex-based classifications, we routinely applied rational-basis review until the 1970's, see, *e.g., Hoyt v. Florida*, 368 U.S. 57 (1961); *Goesaert v. Cleary*, 335 U.S. 464 (1948). And of course normal, rational-basis review of sex-based classifications would be much more in accord with the genesis of heightened standards of judicial review, the famous footnote in *United States v. Carolene Products Co.*, 304 U.S. 144 (1938) . . .

It is hard to consider women a "discrete and insular minorit[y]" unable to employ the "political processes ordinarily to be relied upon," when they constitute a majority of the electorate. And the suggestion that they are incapable of exerting that political power smacks of the same paternalism that the Court so roundly condemns. Moreover, a long list of legislation proves the proposition false. . . .

[The concurring opinion of Chief Justice Rehnquist is omitted].

Notes and Questions

1. Both the *Hogan* and *Virginia* majorities use the phrase "exceedingly persuasive justification." Is this a new element to the level of scrutiny applicable to sex-based classifications, or is it merely a way of describing the standard previously established?

2. Do the *Hogan* and *Virginia* majorities leave open the possibility that strict scrutiny would be applicable to sex-based classifications? Do they *de facto* apply strict scrutiny? After *Virginia*, what exactly distinguishes the tailoring required for intermediate scrutiny and that required for strict scrutiny?

3. Do the *Hogan* and *Virginia* cases address the question whether the government's justification for the law must be the actual motivation for the law, or whether *post-hoc* rationalization will suffice?

4. Do the *Hogan* and *Virginia* cases close the door to single-sex education in all circumstances?

5. The *Virginia* majority acknowledges that there are "inherent differences" between men and women that may at times justify differential treatment. What, exactly, are those "inherent differences?" Moreover, are they differences that justify a preference for males or females?

6. In his dissent, Justice Scalia suggests that even if women were politically powerless at the time of *Frontiero*, they are no longer so at the time of *Virginia*. Assuming this to be factually accurate, and to the extent that the factual finding of political

powerlessness justifies heightened scrutiny in the first instance, should subsequent changes in a class's relative political power result in the Court reconsidering the appropriate level of judicial scrutiny to apply to laws targeting that class? As you read subsequent chapters, consider whether the Court ever explicitly does so, or in the alternative, whether it makes other adjustments to its equal protection jurisprudence to account for those changes in political power.

7. Of what significance is it that *Hogan* and *Virginia* were authored by the Court's first two female Justices? Does that suggest that these two Justices are enshrining their personal political perspectives into constitutional doctrine? Or is their presence on the Court causing their male colleagues on the Court to consider the constitutional claims in a more objective fashion than they did in earlier cases?

F. Intermediate Scrutiny Minus?

The Court's decisions thus far reflect a lack of consensus regarding the precise contours of the scrutiny applicable to sex-based classifications. In this next case, arising in the context of immigration, a narrow majority upholds a sex-based classification against a vigorous dissent by Justice O'Connor. As you read the majority and dissenting opinions, try to assess which one is more consistent with the Court's decisions through *Virginia*.

Nguyen v. Immigration and Naturalization Service

533 U.S. 53 (2001)

JUSTICE KENNEDY delivered the opinion of the Court. . . .

Title 8 U.S.C. § 1409 governs the acquisition of United States citizenship by persons born to one United States citizen parent and one noncitizen parent when the parents are unmarried and the child is born outside of the United States or its possessions. The statute imposes different requirements for the child's acquisition of citizenship depending upon whether the citizen parent is the mother or the father. The question before us is whether the statutory distinction is consistent with the equal protection guarantee embedded in the Due Process Clause of the Fifth Amendment. . . .

[Under the statutory scheme at issue in this case, if the citizen parent is the mother, § 1409(c) provides that the child acquires U.S. citizenship at birth if, prior to the birth, the mother had been physically present in the United States or its possessions for a continuous one-year period. If the citizen parent is the father, the child only acquires citizenship if a variety of requirements set forth in § 1409(a) are satisfied. Among these are a requirement that a blood relationship between the child and the father be established by clear and convincing evidence (§ 1409(a)(1)), as well as a requirement that—before the child reaches 18 years of age—the father takes certain steps to formally establish the parent-child relationship (§ 1409(a)(4).]

III

For a gender-based classification to withstand equal protection scrutiny, it must be established "'at least that the [challenged] classification serves "important governmental objectives and that the discriminatory means employed" are "substantially related to the achievement of those objectives."'" *United States v. Virginia,* 518 U.S. 515, 533 (1996) (quoting *Mississippi Univ. for Women v. Hogan,* 458 U.S. 718, 724 (1982), in turn quoting *Wengler v. Druggists Mut. Ins. Co.,* 446 U.S. 142, 150 (1980)). For reasons to follow, we conclude § 1409 satisfies this standard. Given that determination, we need not decide whether some lesser degree of scrutiny pertains because the statute implicates Congress' immigration and naturalization power. . . .

. . . § 1409(a)(4) requires certain conduct to occur before the child of a citizen father, born out of wedlock and abroad, reaches 18 years of age. . . .

. . . § 1409(a)(4) requires one of three affirmative steps to be taken if the citizen parent is the father, but not if the citizen parent is the mother: legitimation; a declaration of paternity under oath by the father; or a court order of paternity. Congress' decision to impose requirements on unmarried fathers that differ from those on unmarried mothers is based on the significant difference between their respective relationships to the potential citizen at the time of birth. Specifically, the imposition of the requirement for a paternal relationship, but not a maternal one, is justified by two important governmental objectives. We discuss each in turn.

A

The first governmental interest to be served is the importance of assuring that a biological parent-child relationship exists. In the case of the mother, the relation is verifiable from the birth itself. The mother's status is documented in most instances by the birth certificate or hospital records and the witnesses who attest to her having given birth.

In the case of the father, the uncontestable fact is that he need not be present at the birth. If he is present, furthermore, that circumstance is not incontrovertible proof of fatherhood. Fathers and mothers are not similarly situated with regard to the proof of biological parenthood. The imposition of a different set of rules for making that legal determination with respect to fathers and mothers is neither surprising nor troublesome from a constitutional perspective. Section 1409(a)(4)'s provision of three options for a father seeking to establish paternity—legitimation, paternity oath, and court order of paternity—is designed to ensure an acceptable documentation of paternity . . .

Petitioners argue that the requirement of § 1409(a)(1), that a father provide clear and convincing evidence of parentage, is sufficient to achieve the end of establishing paternity, given the sophistication of modern DNA tests. Section 1409(a)(1) does not actually mandate a DNA test, however. The Constitution, moreover, does not require that Congress elect one particular mechanism from among many possible methods of establishing paternity, even if that mechanism arguably might be the most scientifically advanced method. With respect to DNA testing, the expense, reliability, and availability of such testing in various parts of the world may have been of particular concern to Congress. The requirement of § 1409(a)(4) represents a reasonable conclusion by the legislature that the satisfaction of one of several alternatives will suffice to establish the blood link between father and child required as a predicate to the child's acquisition of citizenship. Given the proof of motherhood that is inherent in birth itself, it is unremarkable that Congress did not require the same affirmative steps of mothers.

Finally, to require Congress to speak without reference to the gender of the parent with regard to its objective of ensuring a blood tie between parent and child would be to insist on a hollow neutrality. . . . Given that the mother is always present at birth, but that the father need not be, the facially neutral rule would sometimes require fathers to take additional affirmative steps which would not be required of mothers, whose names will appear on the birth certificate as a result of their presence at the birth, and who will have the benefit of witnesses to the birth to call upon. The issue is not the use of gender specific terms instead of neutral ones. Just as neutral terms can mask discrimination that is unlawful, gender specific terms can mark a permissible distinction. The equal protection question is whether the distinction is lawful. Here, the use of gender specific terms takes into account a biological difference between the parents. The differential treatment is inherent in a sensible statutory scheme, given the unique relationship of the mother to the event of birth.

B

1

The second important governmental interest furthered in a substantial manner by § 1409(a)(4) is the determination to ensure that the child and the citizen parent have some demonstrated opportunity or potential to develop not just a relationship that is recognized, as a formal matter, by the law, but one that consists of the real, everyday ties that provide a connection between child and citizen parent and, in turn, the United States. In the case of a citizen mother and a child born overseas, the opportunity for a meaningful relationship between citizen parent and child inheres in the very event of birth, an event so often critical to our constitutional and statutory understandings of citizenship. The mother knows that the child is in being and is hers and has an initial point of contact with him. There is at least an opportunity for mother and child to develop a real, meaningful relationship.

The same opportunity does not result from the event of birth, as a matter of biological inevitability, in the case of the unwed father. Given the 9-month interval between conception and birth, it is not always certain that a father will know that a child was conceived, nor is it always clear that even the mother will be sure of the father's identity. This fact takes on particular significance in the case of a child born overseas and out of wedlock. One concern in this context has always been with young people, men for the most part, who are on duty with the Armed Forces in foreign countries. . . .

When we turn to the conditions which prevail today, we find that the passage of time has produced additional and even more substantial grounds to justify the statutory distinction. The ease of travel and the willingness of Americans to visit foreign countries have resulted in numbers of trips abroad that must be of real concern when we contemplate the prospect of accepting petitioners' argument, which would mandate, contrary to Congress' wishes, citizenship by male parentage subject to no condition save the father's previous length of residence in this country. . . .

Principles of equal protection do not require Congress to ignore this reality. To the contrary, these facts demonstrate the critical importance of the Government's interest in ensuring some opportunity for a tie between citizen father and foreign born child which is a reasonable substitute for the opportunity manifest between mother and child at the time of birth. Indeed, especially in light of the number of Americans who take short sojourns abroad, the prospect that a father might not even know of the conception is a realistic possibility. Even if a father knows of the fact of conception, moreover, it does not follow that he will be present at the birth of the child. Thus, unlike the case of the mother, there is no assurance that the father and his biological child will ever meet. Without an initial point of contact with the child by a father who knows the child is his own, there is no opportunity for father and child to begin a relationship. Section 1409 takes the unremarkable step of ensuring that such an opportunity, inherent in the event of birth as to the mother-child relationship, exists between father and child before citizenship is conferred upon the latter.

The importance of the governmental interest at issue here is too profound to be satisfied merely by conducting a DNA test. The fact of paternity can be established even without the father's knowledge, not to say his presence. Paternity can be established by taking DNA samples even from a few strands of hair, years after the birth. Yet scientific proof of biological paternity does nothing, by itself, to ensure contact between father and child during the child's minority.

Congress is well within its authority in refusing, absent proof of at least the opportunity for the development of a relationship between citizen parent and child, to commit this country to embracing a child as a citizen entitled as of birth to the full protection of the United States, to the absolute right to enter its borders, and to full participation in the political process. If citizenship is to be conferred by the unwitting means petitioners urge, so that its acquisition abroad bears little relation to the realities of the child's own ties and allegiances, it is for Congress, not this Court, to make that determination. Congress has not taken that path but has instead chosen, by means of § 1409, to ensure in the case of father and child the opportunity for a relationship to develop, an opportunity which the event of birth itself provides for the mother and child. It should be unobjectionable for Congress to require some evidence of a minimal opportunity for the development of a relationship with the child in terms the male can fulfill. . . .

Petitioners and their *amici* argue in addition that, rather than fulfilling an important governmental interest, § 1409 merely embodies a gender-based stereotype. Although the above discussion should illustrate that, contrary to petitioners' assertions, § 1409 addresses an undeniable difference in the circumstance of the parents at the time a child is born, it should be noted, furthermore, that the difference does not result from some stereotype, defined as a frame of mind resulting from irrational or uncritical analysis. There is nothing irrational or improper in the recognition that at the moment of birth-a critical event in the statutory scheme and in the whole tradition of citizenship law-the mother's knowledge of the child and the fact of parenthood have been established in a way not guaranteed in the case of the unwed father. This is not a stereotype. See *Virginia,* 518 U.S., at 533 ("The heightened review standard our precedent establishes does not make sex a proscribed classification. . . . Physical differences between men and women . . . are enduring").

2

Having concluded that facilitation of a relationship between parent and child is an important governmental interest, the question remains whether the means Congress chose to further its objective—the imposition of certain additional requirements upon an unwed father—substantially relate to that end. Under this test, the means Congress adopted must be sustained.

First, it should be unsurprising that Congress decided to require that an opportunity for a parent-child relationship occur during the formative years of the child's minority. In furtherance of the desire to ensure some tie between this country and one who seeks citizenship, various other statutory provisions concerning citizenship and naturalization require some act linking the child to the United States to occur before the child reaches 18 years of age.

Second, petitioners argue that § 1409(a)(4) is not effective. In particular, petitioners assert that, although a mother will know of her child's birth, "knowledge that one is a parent, no matter how it is acquired, does not guarantee a relationship with one's child." They thus maintain that the imposition of the additional requirements of § 1409(a)(4) only on the children of citizen fathers must reflect a stereotype that women are more likely than men to actually establish a relationship with their children.

This line of argument misconceives the nature of both the governmental interest at issue and the manner in which we examine statutes alleged to violate equal protection. As to the former, Congress would of course be entitled to advance the interest of ensuring an actual, meaningful relationship in every case before citizenship is conferred. Or Congress could excuse compliance with the formal requirements when an actual father-child relationship is proved. It did neither here, perhaps because of the subjectivity, intrusiveness, and difficulties of proof that might attend an inquiry into any particular bond or tie. Instead, Congress enacted an easily administered scheme to promote the different but still substantial interest of ensuring at least an opportunity for a parent-child relationship to develop. Petitioners' argument confuses the means and ends of the equal protection inquiry; § 1409(a)(4) should not be invalidated because Congress elected to advance an interest that is less demanding to satisfy than some other alternative.

Even if one conceives of the interest Congress pursues as the establishment of a real, practical relationship of considerable substance between parent and child in every case, as opposed simply to ensuring the potential for the relationship to begin, petitioners' misconception of the nature of the equal protection inquiry is fatal to their argument. A statute meets the equal protection standard we here apply so long as it is "'substantially related to the achievement of'" the governmental objective in question. *Virginia, supra,* at 533 (quoting *Hogan,* 458 U.S., at 724, in turn quoting *Wengler,* 446 U.S., at 150). It is almost axiomatic that a policy which seeks to foster the opportunity for meaningful parent-child bonds to develop has a close and substantial bearing on the governmental interest in the actual formation of that bond. None of our gender-based classification equal protection cases have required that the statute under consideration must be capable of achieving its ultimate objective in every instance.

In this difficult context of conferring citizenship on vast numbers of persons, the means adopted by Congress are in substantial furtherance of important governmental objectives. The fit between the means and the important end is "exceedingly persuasive." We have explained that an "exceedingly persuasive justification" is established "by showing at least that the classification serves 'important governmental objectives and that the discriminatory means employed' are 'substantially related to the achievement of those objectives.'" *Hogan, supra,* at 724. Section 1409 meets this standard. . . .

Justice O'Connor, with whom Justice Souter, Justice Ginsburg, and Justice Breyer join, dissenting.

In a long line of cases spanning nearly three decades, this Court has applied heightened scrutiny to legislative classifications based on sex. The Court today confronts another statute that classifies individuals on the basis of their sex. While the Court invokes heightened scrutiny, the manner in which it explains and applies this standard is a stranger to our precedents. . . .

II

The Court recites the governing substantive standard for heightened scrutiny of sex-based classifications, but departs from the guidance of our precedents concerning such classifications in several ways. . . .

For example, the majority hypothesizes about the interests served by the statute and fails adequately to inquire into the actual purposes of § 1409(a)(4). The Court also does not always explain adequately the importance of the interests that it claims to be served by the provision. The majority also fails carefully to consider whether the sex-based classification is being used impermissibly "as a 'proxy for other, more germane bases of classification,'" *Mississippi Univ. for Women,* 458 U.S., at 726 (quoting *Craig,* 429 U.S., at 198), and instead casually dismisses the relevance of available sex-neutral alternatives. And, contrary to the majority's conclusion, the fit between the means and ends of § 1409(a)(4) is far too attenuated for the provision to survive heightened scrutiny. In all, the majority opinion represents far less than the rigorous application of heightened scrutiny that our precedents require.

A

According to the Court, "[t]he first governmental interest to be served is the importance of assuring that a biological parent-child relationship exists." The majority does not elaborate on the importance of this interest, which presumably lies in preventing fraudulent conveyances of citizenship. Nor does the majority demonstrate that this is one of the actual purposes of § 1409(a)(4) . . . .

The gravest defect in the Court's reliance on this interest, however, is the insufficiency of the fit between § 1409(a)(4)'s discriminatory means and the asserted end. . . . It is difficult to see what § 1409(a)(4) accomplishes in furtherance of "assuring that a biological parent-child relationship exists" that § 1409(a)(1) does not achieve on its own. . . .

It is also difficult to see how § 1409(a)(4)'s limitation of the time allowed for obtaining proof of paternity substantially furthers the assurance of a blood relationship. Modern DNA testing, in addition to providing accuracy unmatched by other methods of establishing a biological link, essentially negates the evidentiary significance of the passage of time. . . .

Because § 1409(a)(4) adds little to the work that § 1409(a)(1) does on its own, it is difficult to say that § 1409(a)(4) "substantially furthers" an important governmental interest.

The majority concedes that Congress could achieve the goal of assuring a biological parent-child relationship in a sex-neutral fashion, but then, in a surprising turn, dismisses the availability of sex-neutral alternatives as irrelevant. . . . Indeed, whether one conceives the majority's asserted interest as assuring the existence of a biological parent-child relationship, or as ensuring acceptable documentation of that relationship, a number of sex-neutral arrangements . . . would better serve that end. As the majority seems implicitly to acknowledge at one point, a mother will not always have formal legal documentation of birth because a birth certificate may not issue or may subsequently be lost. Conversely, a father's name may well appear on a birth certificate. While it is doubtless true that a mother's blood relation to a child is uniquely "verifiable from the birth itself" to those present at birth, the majority has not shown that a mother's birth relation is uniquely verifiable *by the INS*, much less that any greater verifiability warrants a sex-based, rather than a sex-neutral, statute. . . .

If rational basis scrutiny were appropriate in this case, then the claim that "[t]he Constitution . . . does not require that Congress elect one particular mechanism from among many possible methods of establishing paternity" would have much greater force. So too would the claim that "[t]he requirement of § 1409(a)(4) represents a reasonable conclusion. . . ." But fidelity to the Constitution's pledge of equal protection demands more when a facially sex-based classification is at issue. . . .

B

The Court states that "[t]he second important governmental interest furthered in a substantial manner by § 1409(a)(4) is the determination to ensure that the child and the citizen parent have some demonstrated opportunity or potential to develop not just a relationship that is recognized, as a formal matter, by the law, but one that consists of the real, everyday ties that provide a connection between child and citizen parent and, in turn, the United States." The Court again fails to demonstrate that this was Congress' actual purpose in enacting § 1409(a)(4). The majority's focus on "some demonstrated opportunity or potential to develop . . . real, everyday ties" in fact appears to be the type of hypothesized rationale that is insufficient under heightened scrutiny. . . .

Assuming, as the majority does, that Congress was actually concerned about ensuring a "demonstrated opportunity" for a relationship, it is questionable whether such an opportunity qualifies as an "important" governmental interest apart from the existence of an actual relationship. By focusing on "opportunity" rather than reality, the majority presumably improves the chances of a sufficient means-end fit. But in doing so, it dilutes significantly the weight of the interest. It is difficult to see how, in this citizenship-conferral context, anyone profits from a "demonstrated opportunity" for a relationship in the absence of the fruition of an actual tie. . . .

Accepting for the moment the majority's focus on "opportunity," the attempt to justify § 1409(a)(4) in these terms is still deficient. Even if it is important "to require that an opportunity for a parent-child relationship occur during the formative years of the child's minority," it is difficult to see how the requirement that *proof* of such opportunity be obtained before the child turns 18 substantially furthers the asserted interest . . .

Moreover, available sex-neutral alternatives would at least replicate, and could easily exceed, whatever fit there is between § 1409(a)(4)'s discriminatory means and the majority's asserted end. . . . Congress could simply substitute for § 1409(a)(4) a requirement that the parent be present at birth or have knowledge of birth. Congress could at least allow proof of such presence or knowledge to be one way of demonstrating an opportunity for a relationship. Under the present law, the statute on its face accords different treatment to a mother who is by nature present at birth and a father who is by choice present at birth even though those two individuals are similarly situated with respect to the "opportunity" for a relationship. The mother can transmit her citizenship at birth, but the father cannot do so in the absence of at least one other affirmative act. . . .

Indeed, the idea that a mother's presence at birth supplies adequate assurance of an opportunity to develop a relationship while a father's presence at birth does not would appear to rest only on an overbroad sex-based generalization. A mother may not have an opportunity for a relationship if the child is removed from his or her mother on account of alleged abuse or neglect, or if the child and mother are separated by tragedy, such as disaster or war, of the sort apparently present in this case. There is no reason, other than stereotype, to say that fathers who are present at birth lack an opportunity for a relationship on similar terms. . . .

The Court admits that "Congress could excuse compliance with the formal requirements when an actual father-child relationship is proved," but speculates that Congress did not do so "perhaps because of the subjectivity, intrusiveness, and difficulties of proof that might attend an inquiry into any particular bond or tie." We have repeatedly rejected efforts to justify sex-based classifications on the ground of administrative convenience. There is no reason to think that this is a case where administrative convenience concerns are so powerful that they would justify the sex-based discrimination, especially where the use of sex as a proxy is so ill fit to the purported ends as it is here. . . .

The claim that § 1409(a)(4) substantially relates to the achievement of the goal of a "real, practical relationship" thus finds support not in biological differences but instead in a stereotype—*i.e.*, "the generalization that mothers are significantly more likely than fathers . . . to develop caring relationships with their children." *Miller, supra*, at 482-483 (BREYER, J., dissenting). Such a claim relies on "the very stereotype the law condemns," *J.E.B.*, 511 U.S., at 138 (internal quotation marks omitted), "lends credibility" to the generalization, *Mississippi Univ. for Women*, 458 U.S., at 730, and helps to convert that "assumption" into "a self-fulfilling prophecy," *ibid* . . . .

In denying petitioner's claim that § 1409(a)(4) rests on stereotypes, the majority articulates a misshapen notion of "stereotype" and its significance in our equal protection jurisprudence. The majority asserts that a "stereotype" is "defined as a frame of mind resulting from irrational or uncritical analysis." This Court has long recognized, however, that an impermissible stereotype may enjoy empirical support and thus be in a sense "rational." . . . .

Nor do stereotypes consist only of those overbroad generalizations that the reviewing court considers to "show disrespect" for a class. The hallmark of a stereotypical sex-based classification under this Court's precedents is not whether the classification is insulting, but whether it "relie[s] upon the simplistic, outdated assumption that gender could be used as a 'proxy for other, more germane bases of classification.'" *Mississippi Univ. for Women, supra,* at 726 (quoting *Craig, supra,* at 198) . . . .

No one should mistake the majority's analysis for a careful application of this Court's equal protection jurisprudence concerning sex-based classifications. Today's decision instead represents a deviation from a line of cases in which we have vigilantly applied heightened scrutiny to such classifications to determine whether a constitutional violation has occurred. I trust that the depth and vitality of these precedents will ensure that today's error remains an aberration. I respectfully dissent.

[The concurring opinion of Justice Scalia is omitted.]

Notes and Questions

1. The statute at issue in *Nguyen* discriminates against both parents and their children in ways that can be classified as discrimination on the basis of the sex of the parents; illegitimacy of the child; or the alien status of the child and one parent. As you will see in the next chapter, discrimination on the basis of alienage is subjected to a lower level of scrutiny when it is undertaken by the federal government. Accordingly, litigating this case on behalf of the parents made the most sense in this case. Moreover, even if the parents opt not to challenge the statute, the Court has held that the child has standing to raise their parent's sex-based constitutional claim in challenging such a law. *See Sessions v. Morales-Santana*, 137 S. Ct. 1678 (2017). In this regard, it is similar to the ability of the distributors of contraceptives in *Griswold* to raise the constitutional claims of the married couple seeking the contraceptives.

2. In his majority opinion, Justice Kennedy asserts that, as a matter of biological differences between men and women, we know with certainty who the mother is due to her necessary presence at birth. Given modern day assisted reproductive technologies, is that always an accurate statement? Does it turn on what we mean by the word "mother"? Or is the Court's willingness to overlook that possibility consistent with the difference between intermediate and strict scrutiny?

3. In her dissent, Justice O'Connor identifies several ways in which she believes the majority's opinion is inconsistent with precedent. How, if at all, does the majority address those criticisms?

4. Might *Nguyen*, like cases such as *Korematsu* and *Hirayabashi*, be explained as areas of the law in which the Court applies its equal protection scrutiny with less vigor because they arise in a context in which the U.S. Constitution has been interpreted to give extraordinary deference to the executive, in these cases, immigration and war powers, respectively? The majority acknowledges the possibility of such a relaxed version of intermediate scrutiny given the context in which it arises, but

contends that it need not address that argument since the law satisfies ordinary intermediate scrutiny. Do Justice O'Connor's criticisms suggest that the majority is *de facto* applying a relaxed form of scrutiny?

5. Sixteen years after its decision in *Nguyen*, the Court struck down another provision of the same statutory scheme that discriminated between males and females. At issue in *Sessions v. Morales-Santana*, 137 S. Ct. 1678 (2017), was the physical presence requirement of Section 1401(a)(7). Under that provision, if the U.S. citizen parent is an unwed female, the mother must have been physically present in the U.S. for at least one year prior to the child's birth, but if the U.S. citizen parent is an unwed male, the father must have been physically present in the U.S. for at least *five* years prior to the child's birth. Without overruling *Nguyen*, the *Sessions* Court, in an opinion written by Justice Ginsburg, declared this distinction between men and women unconstitutional. The Court's opinion in *Sessions* was written in terms consistent with *Hogan*, *Virginia*, and Justice O'Connor's dissent in *Nguyen*, describing the law at issue as based on archaic stereotypes about men and women and demanding that it be supported by real rationales rather than post-hoc ones.

6. The cases that you have examined in this chapter have used the phrases sex and gender somewhat interchangeably, and have declared unconstitutional laws based on archaic stereotypes about men and women. Can these cases be used to challenge laws that discriminate on the basis of sexual orientation or gender identity, in other words, to challenge laws that discriminate against gay and transgender persons?

Consider first a law that discriminates against gays and lesbians, such as a law that prohibits same-sex marriage. Drawing an analogy to *Loving*, is that not discrimination on the basis of sex, just as *Loving* involved discrimination on the basis of race? Consider in this regard Person A, a male, who both Person B, a male, and Person C, a female, have an interest in marrying. The law will let Person C marry Person A, but will not let Person B marry Person A. The law is thus discriminating as between Persons B and C, and solely because they are of different sexes. Should such a law for that reason be subject to intermediate scrutiny?

Another way to think about such a law is that it is based on archaic stereotypes about men and women. Under that archaic stereotype, men should be attracted to women, and vice-versa. The law is thus punishing those men and women who do not conform to that stereotype.

Similar arguments can be made about laws that discriminate against transgender persons. When the law discriminates against a person because of their transgender status—such as a ban on service in the military by transgender persons—the law is characterizing the person as being one gender and punishing them for presenting in a manner stereotypically associated with the other gender.

Characterizing such laws as sex-based classifications has the advantage of getting automatic application of intermediate scrutiny. Alternatively, one could invoke the *Frontiero* factors in an effort to have sexual orientation and gender identity recognized as independent categories subject to heightened scrutiny. As you read the cases in the next chapter and in Chapter 18, consider the likelihood of success in pursuing that alternative route.

A recent U.S. Supreme Court decision interpreting a federal statute, Title VII—which prohibits employment discrimination on a variety of bases, including "sex"—provides a powerful argument for extending the Court's sex-based equal protection jurisprudence to cases involving discrimination on the bases of sexual orientation or gender identity. In *Bostock v. Clayton County*, 590 U.S. ____ (2020), the U.S. Supreme Court, in a 6–3 decision penned by Justice Gorsuch, held that the term "sex" as used in Title VII necessarily encompasses discrimination on the bases of sexual orientation or gender identity:

> [I]t is impossible to discriminate against a person for being homosexual or transgender without discriminating against that individual based on sex. Consider, for example, an employer with two employees, both of whom are attracted to men. The two individuals are, to the employer's mind, materially identical in all respects, except that one is a man and the other a woman. If the employer fires the male employee for no reason other than the fact he is attracted to men, the employer discriminates against him for traits or actions it tolerates in his female colleague. Put differently, the employer intentionally singles out an employee to fire based in part on the employee's sex, and the affected employee's sex is a but-for cause of his discharge. Or take an employer who fires a transgender person who was identified as a male at birth but who now identifies as a female. If the employer retains an otherwise identical employee who was identified as female at birth, the employer intentionally penalizes a person identified as male at birth for traits or actions that it tolerates in an employee identified as female at birth. Again, the individual employee's sex plays an unmistakable and impermissible role in the discharge decision.

Id. at ____, slip op. at 9–10. In a dissenting opinion, Justice Alito warned that the decision could well have consequences for the Court's equal protection jurisprudence:

> [D]espite the important differences between the Fourteenth Amendment and Title VII, the Court's decision may exert a gravitational pull in constitutional cases. Under our precedents, the Equal Protection Clause prohibits sex-based discrimination unless a "heightened" standard of review is met. By equating discrimination because of sexual orientation or gender identity with discrimination because of sex, the Court's decision will be cited as a ground for subjecting all three forms of discrimination to the same exacting standard of review.
>
> Under this logic, today's decision may have effects that extend well beyond the domain of federal anti-discrimination statutes. This potential is

illustrated by pending and recent lower court cases in which transgender individuals have challenged a variety of federal, state, and local laws and policies on constitutional grounds.

Id. at ____, slip op. at 53 (Alito, J., dissenting).

Chapter 13

Other Classifications and the Equal Protection Clause

At the same time that the Court's sex-based equal protection jurisprudence was beginning to apply some form of heightened scrutiny, the Court was considering other classifications that, like race, national origin, or sex, might merit some form of heighted scrutiny. In the cases that follow, the Court considers whether heightened scrutiny is appropriate for laws that discriminate on the basis of alienage (such as discrimination against non-citizens); legitimacy (such as discrimination against those born out-of-wedlock); wealth; age; and intellectual disability.

Many of the cases excerpted below build off of the list of factors identified by the plurality in *Frontiero*. As you read these cases, try to identify the extent to which they incorporate those factors into a majority opinion and the extent to which they add to or subtract from *Frontiero*'s list of relevant considerations. Of the various factors endorsed by the Court, are some accorded more weight than others? Are any of the factors necessary to a finding of heightened scrutiny? Are any sufficient, standing alone, to justify application of heightened scrutiny?

A. Nonmarital Children

For much of U.S. history, the law—especially laws regarding inheritance rights, standing to bring wrongful death actions, and laws providing governmental benefits for children—have drawn distinctions between those children born within wedlock and those born out-of-wedlock, with the latter class disfavored or completely excluded.

Does discrimination on this basis share any characteristics with discrimination on the basis of sex or race such that heightened scrutiny is warranted? In a series of cases decided in tandem with the court's sex-based equal protection cases, the Court began to strike down such laws. As with its sex-based equal protection jurisprudence, however, it took the Court some time to firmly settle on a definitive standard.

Levy v. Louisiana

391 U.S. 68 (1968)

MR. JUSTICE DOUGLAS delivered the opinion of the Court.

Appellant sued on behalf of five illegitimate children to recover, under a Louisiana statute for two kinds of damages as a result of the wrongful death of their mother: (1) the damages to them for the loss of their mother; and (2) those based on the survival of a cause of action which the mother had at the time of her death for pain and suffering....

The Louisiana District Court dismissed the suit. The Court of Appeal affirmed, holding that "child" in Article 2315 means "legitimate child," the denial to illegitimate children of "the right to recover" being "based on morals and general welfare because it discourages bringing children into the world out of wedlock." 192 So.2d 193, 195....

While a State has broad power when it comes to making classifications, it may not draw a line which constitutes an invidious discrimination against a particular class. Though the test has been variously stated, the end result is whether the line drawn is a rational one.

In applying the Equal Protection Clause to social and economic legislation, we give great latitude to the legislature in making classifications. *Williamson v. Lee Optical*, 348 U.S. 483, 489. Even so, would a corporation, which is a "person," for certain purposes, within the meaning of the Equal Protection Clause be required to forgo recovery for wrongs done its interests because its incorporators were all bastards? However that might be, we have been extremely sensitive when it comes to basic civil rights (*Skinner v. Oklahoma, supra*, 316 U.S., at 541; *Harper v. Virginia State Board of Elections*, 383 U.S. 663, 669-670) and have not hesitated to strike down an invidious classification even though it had history and tradition on its side. (*Brown v. Board of Education*, 347 U.S. 483; *Harper v. Virginia State Board of Elections, supra*, 383 U.S. at 669). The rights asserted here involve the intimate, familial relationship between a child and his own mother. When the child's claim of damage for loss of his mother is in issue, why, in terms of "equal protection," should the tortfeasors go free merely because the child is illegitimate? Why should the illegitimate child be denied rights merely because of his birth out of wedlock? He certainly is subject to all the responsibilities of a citizen, including the payment of taxes and conscription under the Selective Service Act. How under our constitutional regime can he be denied correlative rights which other citizens enjoy?

Legitimacy or illegitimacy of birth has no relation to the nature of the wrong allegedly inflicted on the mother. These children, though illegitimate, were dependent on her; she cared for them and nurtured them; they were indeed hers in the biological and in the spiritual sense; in her death they suffered wrong in the sense that any dependent would.

We conclude that it is invidious to discriminate against them when no action, conduct, or demeanor of theirs is possibly relevant to the harm that was done the mother.

Mr. Justice Harlan, whom Mr. Justice Black and Mr. Justice Stewart join, dissenting....

The Court today, for some reason which I am at a loss to understand, rules that the State must base its arbitrary definition of the plaintiff class on biological rather than legal relationships. Exactly how this makes the Louisiana scheme even marginally more "rational" is not clear, for neither a biological relationship nor legal acknowledgment is indicative of the love or economic dependence that may exist between two persons.... The rights at issue here stem from the existence of a family relationship, and the State has decided only that it will not recognize the family relationship unless the formalities of marriage, or of the acknowledgment of children by the parent in question, have been complied with.

There is obvious justification for this decision. If it be conceded, as I assume it is, that the State has power to provide that people who choose to live together should go through the formalities of marriage and, in default, that people who bear children should acknowledge them, it is logical to enforce these requirements by declaring that the general class of rights that are dependent upon family relationships shall be accorded only when the formalities as well as the biology of those relationships are present. Moreover, and for many of the same reasons why a State is empowered to require formalities in the first place, a State may choose to simplify a particular proceeding by reliance on formal papers rather than a contest of proof. That suits for wrongful death, actions to determine the heirs of intestates, and the like, must as a constitutional matter deal with every claim of biological paternity or maternity on its merits is an exceedingly odd proposition.

The Equal Protection Clause states a complex and difficult principle. Certain classifications are "inherently suspect," which I take to mean that any reliance upon them in differentiating legal rights requires very strong affirmative justification. The difference between a child who has been formally acknowledged and one who has not is hardly one of these. Other classifications are impermissible because they bear no intelligible proper relation to the consequences that are made to flow from them. This does not mean that any classification this Court thinks could be better drawn is unconstitutional....

Weber v. Aetna Casualty & Surety Co.

406 U.S. 164 (1972)

Mr. Justice Powell delivered the opinion of the Court....

For purposes of recovery under workmen's compensation, Louisiana law defines children to include "only legitimate children, stepchildren, posthumous children, adopted children, and illegitimate children acknowledged under the provisions of

Civil Code Articles 203, 204, and 205." Thus, legitimate children and acknowledged illegitimates may recover on an equal basis. Unacknowledged illegitimate children, however, are relegated to the lesser status of "other dependents" under § 1232(8) of the workmen's compensation statute and may recover *only* if there are not enough surviving dependents in the preceding classifications to exhaust the maximum allowable benefits. . . .

Here, as in *Levy*, there is impermissible discrimination. An unacknowledged illegitimate child may suffer as much from the loss of a parent as a child born within wedlock or an illegitimate later acknowledged. So far as this record shows, the dependency and natural affinity of the unacknowledged illegitimate children for their father were as great as those of the four legitimate children whom Louisiana law has allowed to recover. The legitimate children and the illegitimate children all lived in the home of the deceased and were equally dependent upon him for maintenance and support. . . .

Having determined that *Levy* is the applicable precedent we briefly reaffirm here the reasoning which produced that result. The tests to determine the validity of state statutes under the Equal Protection Clause have been variously expressed, but this Court requires, at a minimum, that a statutory classification bear some rational relationship to a legitimate state purpose. Though the latitude given state economic and social regulation is necessarily broad, when state statutory classifications approach sensitive and fundamental personal rights, this Court exercises a stricter scrutiny, *Brown v. Board of Education*, 347 U.S. 483 (1954); *Harper v. Virginia State Board of Elections*, 383 U.S. 663 (1966). The essential inquiry in all the foregoing cases is, however, inevitably a dual one: What legitimate state interest does the classification promote? What fundamental personal rights might the classification endanger?

The Louisiana Supreme Court emphasized strongly the State's interest in protecting "legitimate family relationships," and the regulation and protection of the family unit have indeed been a venerable state concern. We do not question the importance of that interest; what we do question is how the challenged statute will promote it. As was said in *Glona*:

> "[W]e see no possible rational basis . . . for assuming that if the natural mother is allowed recovery for the wrongful death of her illegitimate child, the cause of illegitimacy will be served. It would, indeed, be farfetched to assume that women have illegitimate children so that they can be compensated in damages for their death."

Nor can it be thought here that persons will shun illicit relations because the offspring may not one day reap the benefits of workmen's compensation.

It may perhaps be said that statutory distinctions between the legitimate and illegitimate reflect closer family relationships in that the illegitimate is more often not under care in the home of the father nor even supported by him. The illegitimate, so this argument runs, may thus be made less eligible for the statutory recoveries and inheritances reserved for those more likely to be within the ambit of familial care and affection. Whatever the merits elsewhere of this contention, it is not compelling in a statutory compensation scheme where dependency on the deceased is a prerequisite to anyone's recovery, and where the acknowledgment so necessary to equal recovery rights may be unlikely to occur or legally impossible to effectuate even where the illegitimate child may be nourished and loved.

Finally, we are mindful that States have frequently drawn arbitrary lines in workmen's compensation and wrongful death statutes to facilitate potentially difficult problems of proof. Nothing in our decision would impose on state court systems a greater burden in this regard. By limiting recovery to dependents of the deceased, Louisiana substantially lessens the possible problems of locating illegitimate children and of determining uncertain claims of parenthood. . . .

The state interest in legitimate family relationships is not served by the statute; the state interest in minimizing problems of proof is not significantly disturbed by our decision. The inferior classification of dependent unacknowledged illegitimates bears, in this instance, no significant relationship to those recognized purposes of recovery which workmen's compensation statutes commendably serve.

The status of illegitimacy has expressed through the ages society's condemnation of irresponsible liaisons beyond the bonds of marriage. But visiting this condemnation on the head of an infant is illogical and unjust. Moreover, imposing disabilities on the illegitimate child is contrary to the basic concept of our system that legal burdens should bear some relationship to individual responsibility or wrongdoing. Obviously, no child is responsible for his birth and penalizing the illegitimate child is an ineffectual—as well as an unjust—way of deterring the parent. Courts are powerless to prevent the social opprobrium suffered by these hapless children, but the Equal Protection Clause does enable us to strike down discriminatory laws relating to status of birth where—as in this case—the classification is justified by no legitimate state interest, compelling or otherwise. . . .

Clark v. Jeter

486 U.S. 456 (1988)

JUSTICE O'CONNOR delivered the opinion of the Court.

Under Pennsylvania law, an illegitimate child must prove paternity before seeking support from his or her father, and a suit to establish paternity ordinarily must be brought within six years of an illegitimate child's birth. By contrast, a legitimate child may seek support from his or her parents at any time. . . .

In considering whether state legislation violates the Equal Protection Clause of the Fourteenth Amendment, U.S. Const., Amdt. 14, § 1, we apply different levels of scrutiny to different types of classifications. At a minimum, a statutory classification must be rationally related to a legitimate governmental purpose. Classifications based on race or national origin, *e.g., Loving v. Virginia,* 388 U.S. 1, 11 (1967), and classifications affecting fundamental rights, *e.g., Harper v. Virginia Bd. of Elections,* 383 U.S. 663, 672 (1966), are given the most exacting scrutiny. Between these extremes of rational basis review and strict scrutiny lies a level of intermediate scrutiny, which generally has been applied to discriminatory classifications based on sex or illegitimacy.

To withstand intermediate scrutiny, a statutory classification must be substantially related to an important governmental objective. Consequently we have invalidated classifications that burden illegitimate children for the sake of punishing the illicit relations of their parents, because "visiting this condemnation on the head of an infant is illogical and unjust." *Weber v. Aetna Casualty & Surety Co.*, 406 U.S. 164, 175 (1972) . . . .

[The Court proceeds to conclude that the statute at issue does not satisfy intermediate scrutiny.]

Notes and Questions

1. What level of scrutiny do the *Levy* and *Weber* Courts purport to be applying? The word "rational" appears at several places throughout the opinions. However, occasionally words such as "compelling" and "significant relationship," and hints that a fundamental right might be at stake, are sprinkled throughout the opinions.

2. In *Glona v. American Guarantee & Liability Ins. Co.*, 391 U.S. 73 (1968)—quoted in *Weber*—the Court extends its holding in *Levy* to a law that discriminates against a woman who gives birth to an out-of-wedlock child by denying her the right to bring an action for the wrongful death of that child. Does the rationale of *Levy* extend to that scenario? Although the out-of-wedlock child can be said to be "blameless," can the same be said of their parents?

Moreover, how is *Glona* consistent with the Court's subsequent decision in *Parham v. Hughes*, 441 U.S. 347 (1979), in which the Court upheld a law denying fathers the right to bring wrongful death actions for the death of out-of-wedlock children they had not legitimized while allowing the mothers of those children to bring such claims? Is *Parham* more appropriately viewed as a case about discrimination on the basis of legitimacy, or discrimination on the basis of sex? If the latter, is the distinction between the outcomes in *Glona* and *Parham* nonetheless still objectionable?

3. How does the *Clark* Court derive intermediate scrutiny from its prior decisions? Is the *Clark* Court, like the *Craig* Court, pulling that out of thin air?

4. This line of cases does not directly cite to any of the factors identified by the *Frontiero* plurality. Are some of those factors nonetheless at least tacitly addressed in the opinions? If one were to apply the *Frontiero* factors to legitimacy explicitly, how would they stack up?

5. Why did the Court in its sex and legitimacy cases follow the path of first applying a more stringent form of rational basis review and only later re-characterizing its earlier decisions as applying something more stringent? One possibility is that the Court was leaving itself room to retreat back to traditional rational basis scrutiny in the event that it discovered unintended consequences of applying heightened scrutiny to those classifications. For an alternative explanation, see Evan Gerstmann, The Constitutional Underclass: Gays, Lesbians, and the Failure of Class-Based Equal Protection 40-54 (Univ. of Chicago Press 1999) (contending that the Court recharacterized these two lines of cases to prevent the possibility of the rational

basis test being interpreted to have more teeth across the board when run-of-the-mill equal protection claims are involved).

B. Citizenship

In cases such as *Yick Wo* and *Korematsu*, the Court held that discrimination on the basis of national origin is subject to strict scrutiny. A form of discrimination that is distinct—but that can sometimes overlap with—national origin discrimination is discrimination on the basis of one's status as a noncitizen.*

The government is said to be discriminating purely on the basis of national origin if it discriminates against people because of where they (or their ancestors) are from, without regard to their citizenship. Thus, for example, in *Korematsu*, the U.S. government was discriminating against those of Japanese descent, without regard to whether they were U.S. citizens or not. In contrast, the government is said to be discriminating purely on the basis of alienage when it discriminates against someone because they are a non-citizen of the United States. A law discriminating against all non-citizens, without regard to their initial country of origin, would be an example of such a law. A more targeted discriminatory law can raise overlapping claims of national origin and alienage discrimination, such as a law that discriminates only against those non-citizens that originate from China.

The materials that follow explore the question whether discrimination on the basis of citizenship warrants heightened equal protection scrutiny. As you read the materials that follow, consider the following questions:

- Are noncitizens even covered by the equal protection guarantee, or does that guarantee apply only to U.S. citizens?
- Are there sound theoretical and doctrinal reasons for applying heightened scrutiny to classifications based on citizenship?
- Is the level of scrutiny for discrimination on the basis of citizenship always the same, or does it vary depending upon context? Specifically, does it vary depending upon whether the federal government or lower levels of government are engaged in the discriminatory conduct? The subject matter of the discriminatory law? The legal status of the noncitizens targeted by the law?

Graham v. Richardson

403 U.S. 365 (1971)

Mr. Justice Blackmun delivered the opinion of the Court. . . .

The issue here is whether the Equal Protection Clause of the Fourteenth Amendment prevents a State from conditioning welfare benefits either (a) upon the beneficiary's

* Although the cases in this section use the term "alien," the Court's more recent decisions use the term "noncitizen." *See, e.g.*, *Nasrallah v. Barr*, 140 S. Ct. 1683, 1689 n. 2 (2020).

possession of United States citizenship, or (b) if the beneficiary is an alien, upon his having resided in this country for a specified number of years. . . .

The appellants argue initially that the States, consistent with the Equal Protection Clause, may favor United States citizens over aliens in the distribution of welfare benefits. It is said that this distinction involves no "invidious discrimination" . . . for the State is not discriminating with respect to race or nationality.

The Fourteenth Amendment provides, "[N]or shall any State deprive any person of life, liberty, or property, without due process of law; nor deny to any person within its jurisdiction the equal protection of the laws." It has long been settled, and it is not disputed here, that the term "person" in this context encompasses lawfully admitted resident aliens as well as citizens of the United States and entitles both citizens and aliens to the equal protection of the laws of the State in which they reside. *Yick Wo v. Hopkins*, 118 U.S. 356 (1886); *Truax v. Raich*, 239 U.S. 33, 39 (1915); *Takahashi v. Fish & Game Comm'n*, 334 U.S., at 420. Nor is it disputed that the Arizona and Pennsylvania statutes in question create two classes of needy persons, indistinguishable except with respect to whether they are or are not citizens of this country. . . .

Under traditional equal protection principles, a State retains broad discretion to classify as long as its classification has a reasonable basis. This is so in "the area of economics and social welfare." *Dandridge v. Williams*, 397 U.S. 471, 485 (1970). But the Court's decisions have established that classifications based on alienage, like those based on nationality or race, are inherently suspect and subject to close judicial scrutiny. Aliens as a class are a prime example of a "discrete and insular" minority (see *United States v. Carolene Products Co.*, 304 U.S. 144, 152-153, n. 4 (1938)) for whom such heightened judicial solicitude is appropriate. Accordingly, it was said in *Takahashi*, 334 U.S., at 420, that "the power of a state to apply its laws exclusively to its alien inhabitants as a class is confined within narrow limits."

Arizona and Pennsylvania seek to justify their restrictions on the eligibility of aliens for public assistance solely on the basis of a State's 'special public interest' in favoring its own citizens over aliens in the distribution of limited resources such as welfare benefits. . . .

[W]e conclude that a State's desire to preserve limited welfare benefits for its own citizens is inadequate to justify Pennsylvania's making noncitizens ineligible for public assistance, and Arizona's restricting benefits to citizens and longtime resident aliens. . . . [A]s the Court recognized in *Shapiro*:

> "[A] State has a valid interest in preserving the fiscal integrity of its programs. It may legitimately attempt to limit its expenditures, whether for public assistance, public education, or any other program. But a State may not accomplish such a purpose by invidious distinctions between classes of its citizens. . . . The saving of welfare costs cannot justify an otherwise invidious classification." 394 U.S., at 633.

Since an alien as well as a citizen is a "person" for equal protection purposes, a concern for fiscal integrity is no more compelling a justification for the questioned classification in these cases than it was in *Shapiro*. . . .

Mathews v. Diaz

426 U.S. 67 (1976)

Mr. Justice Stevens delivered the opinion of the Court.

The question presented by the Secretary's appeal is whether Congress may condition an alien's eligibility for participation in a federal medical insurance program on continuous residence in the United States for a five-year period and admission for permanent residence. . . .

Each of the appellees is a resident alien who was lawfully admitted to the United States less than five years ago. . . .

There are literally millions of aliens within the jurisdiction of the United States. The Fifth Amendment, as well as the Fourteenth Amendment, protects every one of these persons from deprivation of life, liberty, or property without due process of law. Even one whose presence in this country is unlawful, involuntary, or transitory is entitled to that constitutional protection.

The fact that all persons, aliens and citizens alike, are protected by the Due Process Clause does not lead to the further conclusion that all aliens are entitled to enjoy all the advantages of citizenship or, indeed, to the conclusion that all aliens must be placed in a single homogeneous legal classification. For a host of constitutional and statutory provisions rest on the premise that a legitimate distinction between citizens and aliens may justify attributes and benefits for one class not accorded to the other;[12] and the class of aliens is itself a heterogeneous multitude of persons with a wide-ranging variety of ties to this country.

In the exercise of its broad power over naturalization and immigration, Congress regularly makes rules that would be unacceptable if applied to citizens. The exclusion of aliens and the reservation of the power to deport have no permissible counterpart in the Federal Government's power to regulate the conduct of its own citizenry. The fact that an Act of Congress treats aliens differently from citizens does not in itself imply that such disparate treatment is "invidious."

In particular, the fact that Congress has provided some welfare benefits for citizens does not require it to provide like benefits for *all aliens*. Neither the overnight visitor, the unfriendly agent of a hostile foreign power, the resident diplomat, nor the

12. The Constitution protects the privileges and immunities only of citizens, Amdt. 14, s 1; see Art. IV, s 2, cl. 1, and the right to vote only of citizens. Amdts. 15, 19, 24, 26. It requires that Representatives have been citizens for seven years, Art. I, s 2, cl. 2, and Senators citizens for nine, Art. I, s 3, cl. 3, and that the President be a "natural born Citizen." Art. II, s 1, cl. 5 . . . .

illegal entrant, can advance even a colorable constitutional claim to a share in the bounty that a conscientious sovereign makes available to its own citizens and *some* of its guests....

For reasons long recognized as valid, the responsibility for regulating the relationship between the United States and our alien visitors has been committed to the political branches of the Federal Government. Since decisions in these matters may implicate our relations with foreign powers, and since a wide variety of classifications must be defined in the light of changing political and economic circumstances, such decisions are frequently of a character more appropriate to either the Legislature or the Executive than to the Judiciary.... Any rule of constitutional law that would inhibit the flexibility of the political branches of government to respond to changing world conditions should be adopted only with the greatest caution. The reasons that preclude judicial review of political questions also dictate a narrow standard of review of decisions made by the Congress or the President in the area of immigration and naturalization.

Since it is obvious that Congress has no constitutional duty to provide *all aliens* with the welfare benefits provided to citizens, the party challenging the constitutionality of the particular line Congress has drawn has the burden of advancing principled reasoning that will at once invalidate that line and yet tolerate a different line separating some aliens from others. In this case the appellees have challenged two requirements first, that the alien be admitted as a permanent resident, and, second, that his residence be of a duration of at least five years.... [I]t is unquestionably reasonable for Congress to make an alien's eligibility depend on both the character and the duration of his residence. Since neither requirement is wholly irrational, this case essentially involves nothing more than a claim that it would have been more reasonable for Congress to select somewhat different requirements of the same kind....

Graham v. Richardson, 403 U.S. 365, provides the strongest support for appellees' position. That case holds that state statutes that deny welfare benefits to resident aliens, or to aliens not meeting a requirement of durational residence within the United States, violate the Equal Protection Clause of the Fourteenth Amendment....The equal protection analysis ... involves significantly different considerations because it concerns the relationship between aliens and the States rather than between aliens and the Federal Government.

Insofar as state welfare policy is concerned,[24] there is little, if any, basis for treating persons who are citizens of another State differently from persons who are citizens of another country. Both groups are noncitizens as far as the State's interests in administering its welfare programs are concerned. Thus, a division by a State of the

24. We have left open the question whether a State may prohibit aliens from holding elective or important nonelective positions or whether a State may, in some circumstances, consider the alien status of an applicant or employee in making an individualized employment decision.

category of persons who are not citizens of that State into subcategories of United States citizens and aliens has no apparent justification, whereas, a comparable classification by the Federal Government is a routine and normally legitimate part of its business. Furthermore, whereas the Constitution inhibits every State's power to restrict travel across its own borders, Congress is explicitly empowered to exercise that type of control over travel across the borders of the United States.

. . . .Contrary to appellees' characterization, it is not "political hypocrisy" to recognize that the Fourteenth Amendment's limits on state powers are substantially different from the constitutional provisions applicable to the federal power over immigration and naturalization. . . .

Ambach v. Norwick

441 U.S. 68 (1979)

Mr. Justice Powell delivered the opinion of the Court.

This case presents the question whether a State, consistently with the Equal Protection Clause of the Fourteenth Amendment, may refuse to employ as elementary and secondary school teachers aliens who are eligible for United States citizenship but who refuse to seek naturalization. . . .

The decisions of this Court regarding the permissibility of statutory classifications involving aliens have not formed an unwavering line over the years. State regulation of the employment of aliens long has been subject to constitutional constraints. . . .At the same time, however, the Court also has recognized a greater degree of latitude for the States when aliens were sought to be excluded from public employment. . . .

In *Sugarman*, we recognized that a State could, "in an appropriately defined class of positions, require citizenship as a qualification for office." We went on to observe:

> "Such power inheres in the State by virtue of its obligation, already noted above, 'to preserve the basic conception of a political community.' . . . And this power and responsibility of the State applies, not only to the qualifications of voters, but also to persons holding state elective or important nonelective executive, legislative, and judicial positions, for officers who participate directly in the formulation, execution, or review of broad public policy perform functions that go to the heart of representative government." 413 U.S., at 647.

The exclusion of aliens from such governmental positions would not invite as demanding scrutiny from this Court.

Applying the rational-basis standard, we held last Term that New York could exclude aliens from the ranks of its police force. *Foley v. Connelie*, 435 U.S. 291 (1978). Because the police function fulfilled "a most fundamental obligation of government to its constituency" and by necessity cloaked policemen with substantial discretionary powers, we view the police force as being one of those appropriately defined classes of positions for which a citizenship requirement could be imposed.

Accordingly, the State was required to justify its classification only "by a showing of some rational relationship between the interest sought to be protected and the limiting classification."

The rule for governmental functions, which is an exception to the general standard applicable to classifications based on alienage, rests on important principles inherent in the Constitution. The distinction between citizens and aliens, though ordinarily irrelevant to private activity, is fundamental to the definition and government of a State. The Constitution itself refers to the distinction no less than 11 times, indicating that the status of citizenship was meant to have significance in the structure of our government. The assumption of that status, whether by birth or naturalization, denotes an association with the polity which, in a democratic republic, exercises the powers of governance. The form of this association is important: an oath of allegiance or similar ceremony cannot substitute for the unequivocal legal bond citizenship represents. It is because of this special significance of citizenship that governmental entities, when exercising the functions of government, have wider latitude in limiting the participation of noncitizens.

In determining whether, for purposes of equal protection analysis, teaching in public schools constitutes a governmental function, we look to the role of public education and to the degree of responsibility and discretion teachers possess in fulfilling that role. Each of these considerations supports the conclusion that public school teachers may be regarded as performing a task "that go[es] to the heart of representative government." *Sugarman v. Dougall, supra*, 413 U.S., at 647.

Public education, like the police function, "fulfills a most fundamental obligation of government to its constituency." *Foley, supra*, 435 U.S., at 297. The importance of public schools in the preparation of individuals for participation as citizens, and in the preservation of the values on which our society rests, long has been recognized by our decisions. . . .

Other authorities have perceived public schools as an "assimilative force" by which diverse and conflicting elements in our society are brought together on a broad but common ground. These perceptions of the public schools as inculcating fundamental values necessary to the maintenance of a democratic political system have been confirmed by the observations of social scientists.

Within the public school system, teachers play a critical part in developing students' attitude toward government and understanding of the role of citizens in our society. Alone among employees of the system, teachers are in direct, day-to-day contact with students both in the classrooms and in the other varied activities of a modern school. In shaping the students' experience to achieve educational goals, teachers by necessity have wide discretion over the way the course material is communicated to students. They are responsible for presenting and explaining the subject matter in a way that is both comprehensible and inspiring. No amount of standardization of teaching materials or lesson plans can eliminate the personal qualities a teacher brings to bear in achieving these goals. Further, a teacher serves as a role model for his students, exerting a subtle but important influence over their perceptions and values. Thus, through both the presentation of course materials and the example he sets, a teacher has an opportunity to influence the attitudes of students toward government, the political process, and a citizen's social responsibilities. This influence is crucial to the continued good health of a democracy. . . .

As the legitimacy of the State's interest in furthering the educational goals outlined above is undoubted, it remains only to consider whether § 3001(3) bears a rational relationship to this interest. The restriction is carefully framed to serve its purpose, as it bars from teaching only those aliens who have demonstrated their unwillingness to obtain United States citizenship. Appellees, and aliens similarly situated, in effect have chosen to classify themselves. They prefer to retain citizenship in a foreign country with the obligations it entails of primary duty and loyalty. They have rejected the open invitation extended to qualify for eligibility to teach by applying for citizenship in this country. The people of New York, acting through their elected representatives, have made a judgment that citizenship should be a qualification for teaching the young of the State in the public schools, and § 3001(3) furthers that judgment.

[The dissenting opinion of Justice Blackmun is omitted.]

Plyler v. Doe

457 U.S. 202 (1982)

Justice Brennan delivered the opinion of the Court.

The question presented by these cases is whether, consistent with the Equal Protection Clause of the Fourteenth Amendment, Texas may deny to undocumented school-age children the free public education that it provides to children who are citizens of the United States or legally admitted aliens. . . .

The Fourteenth Amendment provides that "[n]o State shall . . . deprive any person of life, liberty, or property, without due process of law; nor deny to *any person within its jurisdiction* the equal protection of the laws." (Emphasis added.) Appellants argue at the outset that undocumented aliens, because of their immigration status, are not "persons within the jurisdiction" of the State of Texas, and that they therefore have no right to the equal protection of Texas law. We reject this argument. Whatever his status under the immigration laws, an alien is surely a "person" in any ordinary sense of that term. Aliens, even aliens whose presence in this country is unlawful, have long been recognized as "persons" guaranteed due process of law by the Fifth and Fourteenth Amendments. . . .

In applying the Equal Protection Clause to most forms of state action, we . . . seek only the assurance that the classification at issue bears some fair relationship to a legitimate public purpose.

But we would not be faithful to our obligations under the Fourteenth Amendment if we applied so deferential a standard to every classification. The Equal Protection

Clause was intended as a restriction on state legislative action inconsistent with elemental constitutional premises. Thus we have treated as presumptively invidious those classifications that disadvantage a "suspect class," or that impinge upon the exercise of a "fundamental right." With respect to such classifications, it is appropriate to enforce the mandate of equal protection by requiring the State to demonstrate that its classification has been precisely tailored to serve a compelling governmental interest. In addition, we have recognized that certain forms of legislative classification, while not facially invidious, nonetheless give rise to recurring constitutional difficulties; in these limited circumstances we have sought the assurance that the classification reflects a reasoned judgment consistent with the ideal of equal protection by inquiring whether it may fairly be viewed as furthering a substantial interest of the State.[16] We turn to a consideration of the standard appropriate for the evaluation of § 21.031.

Sheer incapability or lax enforcement of the laws barring entry into this country, coupled with the failure to establish an effective bar to the employment of undocumented aliens, has resulted in the creation of a substantial "shadow population" of illegal migrants-numbering in the millions-within our borders. This situation raises the specter of a permanent caste of undocumented resident aliens, encouraged by some to remain here as a source of cheap labor, but nevertheless denied the benefits that our society makes available to citizens and lawful residents. The existence of such an underclass presents most difficult problems for a Nation that prides itself on adherence to principles of equality under law.[19]

The children who are plaintiffs in these cases are special members of this underclass. Persuasive arguments support the view that a State may withhold its beneficence from those whose very presence within the United States is the product of their own unlawful conduct. These arguments do not apply with the same force to classifications imposing disabilities on the minor *children* of such illegal entrants. At the least, those who elect to enter our territory by stealth and in violation of our law should be prepared to bear the consequences, including, but not limited to, deportation. But the children of those illegal entrants are not comparably situated.

---

16. This technique of "intermediate" scrutiny permits us to evaluate the rationality of the legislative judgment with reference to well-settled constitutional principles. . . .

19. We reject the claim that "illegal aliens" are a "suspect class." No case in which we have attempted to define a suspect class has addressed the status of persons unlawfully in our country. Unlike most of the classifications that we have recognized as suspect, entry into this class, by virtue of entry into this country, is the product of voluntary action. Indeed, entry into the class is itself a crime. In addition, it could hardly be suggested that undocumented status is a "constitutional irrelevancy." With respect to the actions of the Federal Government, alienage classifications may be intimately related to the conduct of foreign policy, to the federal prerogative to control access to the United States, and to the plenary federal power to determine who has sufficiently manifested his allegiance to become a citizen of the Nation. No State may independently exercise a like power. But if the Federal Government has by uniform rule prescribed what it believes to be appropriate standards for the treatment of an alien subclass, the States may, of course, follow the federal direction. See *DeCanas v. Bica*, 424 U.S. 351 (1976).

Their "parents have the ability to conform their conduct to societal norms," and presumably the ability to remove themselves from the State's jurisdiction; but the children who are plaintiffs in these cases "can affect neither their parents' conduct nor their own status." *Trimble v. Gordon*, 430 U.S. 762, 770 (1977). Even if the State found it expedient to control the conduct of adults by acting against their children, legislation directing the onus of a parent's misconduct against his children does not comport with fundamental conceptions of justice.

> "[V]isiting . . . condemnation on the head of an infant is illogical and unjust. Moreover, imposing disabilities on the . . . child is contrary to the basic concept of our system that legal burdens should bear some relationship to individual responsibility or wrongdoing. Obviously, no child is responsible for his birth and penalizing the . . . child is an ineffectual—as well as unjust—way of deterring the parent." *Weber v. Aetna Casualty & Surety Co.*, 406 U.S. 164, 175 (1972).

Of course, undocumented status is not irrelevant to any proper legislative goal. Nor is undocumented status an absolutely immutable characteristic since it is the product of conscious, indeed unlawful, action. But § 21.031 is directed against children, and imposes its discriminatory burden on the basis of a legal characteristic over which children can have little control. It is thus difficult to conceive of a rational justification for penalizing these children for their presence within the United States. Yet that appears to be precisely the effect of § 21.031.

Public education is not a "right" granted to individuals by the Constitution. *San Antonio Independent School Dist. v. Rodriguez*, 411 U.S. 1, 35 (1973). But neither is it merely some governmental "benefit" indistinguishable from other forms of social welfare legislation. Both the importance of education in maintaining our basic institutions, and the lasting impact of its deprivation on the life of the child, mark the distinction. . . .

In addition to the pivotal role of education in sustaining our political and cultural heritage, denial of education to some isolated group of children poses an affront to one of the goals of the Equal Protection Clause: the abolition of governmental barriers presenting unreasonable obstacles to advancement on the basis of individual merit. . . .

These well-settled principles allow us to determine the proper level of deference to be afforded § 21.031. Undocumented aliens cannot be treated as a suspect class because their presence in this country in violation of federal law is not a "constitutional irrelevancy." Nor is education a fundamental right; a State need not justify by compelling necessity every variation in the manner in which education is provided to its population. But more is involved in these cases than the abstract question whether § 21.031 discriminates against a suspect class, or whether education is a fundamental right. Section 21.031 imposes a lifetime hardship on a discrete class of children not accountable for their disabling status. The stigma of illiteracy will mark them for the rest of their lives. By denying these children a basic education, we deny them the ability to live within the structure of our civic institutions, and foreclose any realistic possibility that they will contribute in even the smallest way to the progress of our Nation. In determining the rationality of § 21.031, we may appropriately take into account its costs to the Nation and to the innocent children who are its victims. In light of these countervailing costs, the discrimination contained in § 21.031 can hardly be considered rational unless it furthers some substantial goal of the State. . . .

[The Court proceeds to consider and reject a variety of rationales for the law, none of which it deems to be either sufficiently strong or sufficiently tailored to overcome the applicable level of judicial scrutiny.]

[The concurring opinions of Justices Marshall, Blackmun, and Powell, and the dissenting opinion of Chief Justice Burger, are omitted.]

Notes and Questions

1. Quoting footnote 4 of *Carolene Products*, the *Graham* Court identifies aliens as "a prime example of a 'discrete and insular' minority." What do the terms "discrete" and "insular" mean? Do you agree that noncitizens as a class exemplify those qualities?

2. Since *Frontiero* was decided after *Graham*, the *Graham* Court naturally did not consider the various factors identified in *Frontiero*. Had it done so, how would those factors stack up in the case of citizenship status?

3. Can the difference between the level of scrutiny applicable to the federal government on the one hand and lower levels of the government on the other be attributed to the fact that the Equal Protection Clause does not in terms apply directly to the federal government, and is instead derived from the Fifth Amendment's Due Process Clause? Is that consistent with the Court's decisions with respect to race and sex? Might it instead be explained by the fact that such cases involve immigration, and are thus subject to a more relaxed form of scrutiny under the logic of cases such as *Nguyen*?

4. Footnote 19 of the *Plyler* decision refers to the "uniform federal rule" doctrine. Under *Mathews*, discrimination by the federal government is subject only to rational basis review. If states discriminate on the basis of citizenship pursuant to a uniform federal mandate, the relaxed level of scrutiny applicable to the direct actions of the federal government are also applicable to the actions of a state acting pursuant to a federal mandate.

5. What level of scrutiny does *Plyler* hold applicable to those noncitizens present in the United States unlawfully? Does the answer to that question turn on whether an adult or a minor is involved, and if so, why?

6. To what extent is the heightened standard of review applied in *Plyler* related to the importance of the right at stake, to wit, education? Stated somewhat differently, would the Court have been as likely to declare the law unconstitutional if it targeted something less weighty than education?

C. Wealth

In a number of the Court's decisions from the 1960s involving fundamental rights, such as the right to vote, there was a strong inference in the Court's opinions that the laws were independently unconstitutional because they discriminated on the basis of wealth. Thus, in *Harper v. Virginia Bd. of Elections*, the Court, in striking down a poll tax, stated that "[l]ines drawn on the basis of wealth or property, like those of race, are traditionally disfavored." In the case that follows, the Court directly addresses that question.

San Antonio Independent School District v. Rodriguez

411 U.S. 1 (1973)

Mr. Justice Powell delivered the opinion of the Court.

[At issue in this case is the constitutionality of Texas's dual system of funding elementary and secondary education, under which part of the funding is distributed by the state and part of it is based on local property tax levies. Under the system, significant interdistrict disparities in funding exist due to differences in the property tax base in richer and poorer districts.]

The District Court held that the Texas system discriminates on the basis of wealth in the manner in which education is provided for its people. Finding that wealth is a "suspect" classification . . . the District Court held that the Texas system could be sustained only if the State could show that it was premised upon some compelling state interest. . . .

Texas virtually concedes that its historically rooted dual system of financing education could not withstanding the strict judicial scrutiny that this Court has found appropriate in reviewing legislative judgments that interfere with fundamental constitutional rights or that involve suspect classifications. . . .

This, then, establishes the framework for our analysis. We must decide, first, whether the Texas system of financing public education operates to the disadvantage of some suspect class or impinges upon a fundamental right explicitly or implicitly protected by the Constitution, thereby requiring strict judicial scrutiny. If so, the judgment of the District Court should be affirmed. If not, the Texas scheme must still be examined to determine whether it rationally furthers some legitimate, articulated state purpose and therefore does not constitute an invidious discrimination in violation of the Equal Protection Clause of the Fourteenth Amendment.

The District Court's opinion does not reflect the novelty and complexity of the constitutional questions posed by appellees' challenge to Texas' system of school financing. In concluding that strict judicial scrutiny was required, that court relied on decisions dealing with the rights of indigents to equal treatment in the criminal trial and appellate processes, and on cases disapproving wealth restrictions on the right to vote. Those cases, the District Court concluded, established wealth as a suspect classification. Finding that the local property tax system discriminated on the basis of wealth, it regarded those precedents as controlling. It then reasoned, based on decisions of this Court affirming the undeniable importance of education, that there is a fundamental right to education and that, absent some compelling state justification, the Texas system could not stand.

We are unable to agree that this case, which in significant aspects is *sui generis*, may be so neatly fitted into the conventional mosaic of constitutional analysis under the Equal Protection Clause. Indeed, for the several reasons that follow, we find neither the suspect-classification not the fundamental-interest analysis persuasive.

The wealth discrimination discovered by the District Court in this case, and by several other courts that have recently struck down school-financing laws in other States, is quite unlike any of the forms of wealth discrimination heretofore reviewed by this Court. Rather than focusing on the unique features of the alleged discrimination, the courts in these cases have virtually assumed their findings of a suspect classification through a simplistic process of analysis: since, under the traditional systems of financing public schools, some poorer people receive less expensive educations than other more affluent people, these systems discriminate on the basis of wealth. This approach largely ignores the hard threshold questions, including whether it makes a difference for purposes of consideration under the Constitution that the class of disadvantaged "poor" cannot be identified or defined in customary equal protection terms, and whether the relative—rather than absolute—nature of the asserted deprivation is of significant consequence....

The case comes to us with no definitive description of the classifying facts or delineation of the disfavored class. Examination of the District Court's opinion and of appellees' complaint, briefs, and contentions at oral argument suggests, however, at least three ways in which the discrimination claimed here might be described. The Texas system of school financing might be regarded as discriminating (1) against "poor" persons whose incomes fall below some identifiable level of poverty or who might be characterized as functionally "indigent," or (2) against those who are relatively poorer than others, or (3) against all those who, irrespective of their personal incomes, happen to reside in relatively poorer school districts. Our task must be to ascertain whether, in fact, the Texas system has been shown to discriminate on any of these possible bases and, if so, whether the resulting classification may be regarded as suspect.

The precedents of this Court provide the proper starting point. The individuals, or groups of individuals, who constituted the class discriminated against in our prior cases shared two distinguishing characteristics: because of their impecunity they were completely unable to pay for some desired benefit, and as a consequence, they sustained an absolute deprivation of a meaningful opportunity to enjoy that benefit....

Only appellees' first possible basis for describing the class disadvantaged by the Texas school-financing system—discrimination against a class of defineably "poor" persons—might arguably meet the criteria established in these prior cases. Even a cursory examination, however, demonstrates that neither of the two distinguishing characteristics of wealth classifications can be found here. First, in support of their charge that the system discriminates against the "poor," appellees have made no effort to demonstrate that it operates to the peculiar disadvantage of any class fairly definable as indigent, or as composed of persons whose incomes are beneath any designated poverty level. Indeed, there is reason to believe that the poorest families are not necessarily clustered in the poorest property districts. . . .

Second, neither appellees nor the District Court addressed the fact that, unlike each of the foregoing cases, lack of personal resources has not occasioned an absolute deprivation of the desired benefit. The argument here is not that the children in districts having relatively low assessable property values are receiving no public education; rather, it is that they are receiving a poorer quality education than that available to children in districts having more assessable wealth. Apart from the unsettled and disputed question whether the quality of education may be determined by the amount of money expended for it, a sufficient answer to appellees' argument is that, at least where wealth is involved, the Equal Protection Clause does not require absolute equality or precisely equal advantages. Nor indeed, in view of the infinite variables affecting the educational process, can any system assure equal quality of education except in the most relative sense. . . .

For these two reasons — the absence of any evidence that the financing system discriminates against any definable category of "poor" people or that it results in the absolute deprivation of education — the disadvantaged class is not susceptible of identification in traditional terms.[60]

As suggested above, appellees and the District Court may have embraced a second or third approach, the second of which might be characterized as a theory of relative or comparative discrimination based on family income. Appellees sought to prove that a direct correlation exists between the wealth of families within each district and the expenditures therein for education. That is, along a continuum, the poorer the family the lower the dollar amount of education received by the family's children. . . .

If, in fact, these correlations could be sustained, then it might be argued that expenditures on education — equated by appellees to the quality of education — are dependent on personal wealth. Appellees' comparative-discrimination theory

---

60. An educational financing system might be hypothesized, however, in which the analogy to the wealth discrimination cases would be considerably closer. If elementary and secondary education were made available by the State only to those able to pay a tuition assessed against each pupil, there would be a clearly defined class of "poor" people — definable in terms of their inability to pay the prescribed sum — who would be absolutely precluded from receiving an education. That case would present a far more compelling set of circumstances for judicial assistance than the case before us today. After all, Texas has undertaken to do a good deal more than provide an education to those who can afford it. It has provided what it considers to be an adequate base education for all children and has attempted, though imperfectly, to ameliorate by state funding and by the local assessment program the disparities in local tax resources.

would still face serious unanswered questions, including whether a bare positive correlation or some higher degree of correlation is necessary to provide a basis for concluding that the financing system is designed to operate to the peculiar disadvantage of the comparatively poor, and whether a class of this size and diversity could ever claim the special protection accorded "suspect" classes. These questions need not be addressed in this case, however, since appellees' proof fails to support their allegations or the District Court's conclusions. . . .

This brings us, then, to the third way in which the classification scheme might be defined—district wealth discrimination. Since the only correlation indicated by the evidence is between district property wealth and expenditures, it may be argued that discrimination might be found without regard to the individual income characteristics of district residents. Assuming a perfect correlation between district property wealth and expenditures from top to bottom, the disadvantaged class might be viewed as encompassing every child in every district except the district that has the most assessable wealth and spends the most on education. Alternatively . . . the class might be defined more restrictively to include children in districts with assessable property which falls below the statewide average, or median, or below some other artificially defined level.

However described, it is clear that appellees' suit asks this Court to extend its most exacting scrutiny to review a system that allegedly discriminates against a large, diverse, and amorphous class, unified only by the common factor of residence in districts that happen to have less taxable wealth than other districts. The system of alleged discrimination and the class it defines have none of the traditional indicia of suspectness: the class is not saddled with such disabilities, or subjected to such a history of purposeful unequal treatment, or relegated to such a position of political powerlessness as to command extraordinary protection from the majoritarian political process.

We thus conclude that the Texas system does not operate to the peculiar disadvantage of any suspect class. . . .

[The concurring opinion of Justice Stewart and the dissenting opinions of Justices Brennan, White, and Marshall are omitted.]

Notes and Questions

1. According to the *Rodriguez* Court, it is not clear that, as a constitutional matter, this law discriminates against poor people. It is certainly the case that the law has a disparate impact on poor people. Does the decision thus stand for the proposition that disparate impact, standing alone, is not sufficient to make out an equal protection claim? Is that consistent with the Court's earlier decisions? How would the *Rodriguez* Court assess a law that explicitly divided people up between schools of varying funding based on each family's income or asset levels? A law that assessed a flat tuition rate to attend public schools?

2. Even assuming wealth discrimination is at play, the *Rodriguez* Court determines that heightened scrutiny is not warranted. What factors does it take into account in making that determination, and how does that compare with the plurality's approach in *Frontiero*?

D. Age

Massachusetts Board of Retirement v. Murgia

427 U.S. 307 (1976)

Per Curiam.

This case presents the question whether the provision of Mass. Gen. Laws Ann. c. 32, § 26(3)(a) (1969), that a uniformed state police officer "shall be retired . . . upon his attaining age fifty," denies appellee police officer equal protection of the laws in violation of the Fourteenth Amendment. . . .

We need state only briefly our reasons for agreeing that strict scrutiny is not the proper test for determining whether the mandatory retirement provision denies appellee equal protection. *San Antonio School District v. Rodriguez*, 411 U.S. 1, 16 (1973), reaffirmed that equal protection analysis requires strict scrutiny of a legislative classification only when the classification impermissibly interferes with the exercise of a fundamental right or operates to the peculiar disadvantage of a suspect class. Mandatory retirement at age 50 under the Massachusetts statute involves neither situation.

This Court's decisions give no support to the proposition that a right of governmental employment *per se* is fundamental. . . .

Nor does the class of uniformed state police officers over 50 constitute a suspect class for purposes of equal protection analysis. *Rodriguez* observed that a suspect class is one "saddled with such disabilities, or subjected to such a history of purposeful unequal treatment, or relegated to such a position of political powerlessness as to command extraordinary protection from the majoritarian political process." While the treatment of the aged in this Nation has not been wholly free of discrimination, such persons, unlike, say, those who have been discriminated against on the basis of race or national origin, have not experienced a "history of purposeful unequal treatment" or been subjected to unique disabilities on the basis of stereotyped characteristics not truly indicative of their abilities. The class subject to the compulsory retirement feature of the Massachusetts statute consists of uniformed state police officers over the age of 50. It cannot be said to discriminate only against the elderly. Rather, it draws the line at a certain age in middle life. But even old age does not define a "discrete and insular" group, *United States v. Carolene Products Co.*, 304 U.S. 144, 152-153, n. 4 (1938), in need of "extraordinary protection from the majoritarian political process." Instead, it marks a stage that each of us will reach if we live out our normal span. Even if the statute could be said to impose a penalty upon a class defined as the aged, it would not impose a distinction sufficiently akin to those classifications that we have found suspect to call for strict judicial scrutiny.

Under the circumstances, it is unnecessary to subject the State's resolution of competing interests in this case to the degree of critical examination that our cases under the Equal Protection Clause recently have characterized as "strict judicial scrutiny."

We turn then to examine this state classification under the rational-basis standard. This inquiry employs a relatively relaxed standard reflecting the Court's awareness that the drawing of lines that create distinctions is peculiarly a legislative task and an unavoidable one. Perfection in making the necessary classifications is neither possible nor necessary. Such action by a legislature is presumed to be valid.

In this case, the Massachusetts statute clearly meets the requirements of the Equal Protection Clause, for the State's classification rationally furthers the purpose identified by the State: Through mandatory retirement at age 50, the legislature seeks to protect the public by assuring physical preparedness of its uniformed police. Since physical ability generally declines with age, mandatory retirement at 50 serves to remove from police service those whose fitness for uniformed work presumptively has diminished with age. This clearly is rationally related to the State's objective. There is no indication that § 26(3)(a) has the effect of excluding from service so few officers who are in fact unqualified as to render age 50 a criterion wholly unrelated to the objective of the statute.

That the State chooses not to determine fitness more precisely through individualized testing after age 50 is not to say that the objective of assuring physical fitness is not rationally furthered by a maximum-age limitation. It is only to say that with regard to the interest of all concerned, the State perhaps has not chosen the best means to accomplish this purpose. But where rationality is the test, a State "does not violate the Equal Protection Clause merely because the classifications made by its laws are imperfect." *Dandridge v. Williams*, 397 U.S., at 485.

We do not make light of the substantial economic and psychological effects premature and compulsory retirement can have on an individual; nor do we denigrate the ability of elderly citizens to continue to contribute to society. The problems of retirement have been well documented and are beyond serious dispute. But "(w)e do not decide today that the (Massachusetts statute) is wise, that it best fulfills the relevant social and economic objectives that (Massachusetts) might ideally espouse, or that a more just and humane system could not be devised." *Id.*, at 487. We decide only that the system enacted by the Massachusetts Legislature does not deny appellee equal protection of the laws.

The judgment is reversed.

[The dissenting opinion of Justice Marshall is omitted.]

Notes and Questions

1. According to the *Murgia* Court, what distinguishes old age from other types of classes for which the Court has deemed heightened scrutiny to be appropriate? Is it

that all of us will eventually become members of the class of elderly persons, while not all of us will eventually be women, African Americans, non-citizens, and the like?

2. The *Murgia* Court refers to some, but not all, of the *Frontiero* factors. How do the other *Frontiero* factors stack up in determining whether to accord heightened scrutiny to laws that discriminate on the basis of age?

3. *Murgia* involves discrimination against the elderly. Are there reasons to conclude that discrimination against *young* persons should be scrutinized more carefully? *See Hutchins v. District of Columbia*, 188 F.3d 537, 556 n.4 (1999) (leaving open the possibility that "laws that target the young rather than the elderly would warrant a different result under the political process theories on which the Court has relied in this area.").

E. Intellectual Disability*

City of Cleburne v. Cleburne Living Center, Inc.

473 U.S. 432 (1985)

Justice White delivered the opinion of the Court. . . .

[At issue in this case is the constitutionality of a city ordinance that required a special use permit, renewably annually, for constructing group homes for intellectually disabled persons, although such a permit was not required for other types of uses that arguably had a similar neighborhood impact. The Court of Appeals held that intermediate scrutiny was applicable to laws that discriminate against the intellectually disabled, and declared the ordinance unconstitutional as applied.]

[W]e conclude for several reasons that the Court of Appeals erred in holding mental retardation a quasi-suspect classification calling for a more exacting standard of judicial review than is normally accorded economic and social legislation. First, it is undeniable, and it is not argued otherwise here, that those who are mentally retarded have a reduced ability to cope with and function in the everyday world. Nor are they all cut from the same pattern: as the testimony in this record indicates, they range from those whose disability is not immediately evident to those who must be constantly cared for. They are thus different, immutably so, in relevant respects, and the States' interest in dealing with and providing for them is plainly a legitimate one.[10] How this large and diversified group is to be treated under the law

---

* Although the case in this section uses the phrase "mentally retarded," the Court has since held that it is more appropriate to use the term "intellectual disability." See *Brumfield v. Cain*, 576 U.S. 305, 308 n. 1 (2015).

10. As Dean Ely has observed:

"Surely one has to feel sorry for a person disabled by something he or she can't do anything about, but I'm not aware of any reason to suppose that elected officials are unusually unlikely to share that feeling. Moreover, classifications based on physical disability and intelligence are typically accepted as legitimate, even by judges and commentators who assert that immutability is relevant. The explanation, when one is given, is that *those*

is a difficult and often a technical matter, very much a task for legislators guided by qualified professionals and not by the perhaps ill-informed opinions of the judiciary. Heightened scrutiny inevitably involves substantive judgments about legislative decisions, and we doubt that the predicate for such judicial oversight is present where the classification deals with mental retardation.

Second, the distinctive legislative response, both national and state, to the plight of those who are mentally retarded demonstrates not only that they have unique problems, but also that the lawmakers have been addressing their difficulties in a manner that belies a continuing antipathy or prejudice and a corresponding need for more intrusive oversight by the judiciary. Thus, the Federal Government has not only outlawed discrimination against the mentally retarded in federally funded programs, but it has also provided the retarded with the right to receive "appropriate treatment, services, and habilitation" in a setting that is "least restrictive of [their] personal liberty." In addition, the Government has conditioned federal education funds on a State's assurance that retarded children will enjoy an education that, "to the maximum extent appropriate," is integrated with that of nonmentally retarded children. The Government has also facilitated the hiring of the mentally retarded into the federal civil service by exempting them from the requirement of competitive examination. The State of Texas has similarly enacted legislation that acknowledges the special status of the mentally retarded by conferring certain rights upon them, such as "the right to live in the least restrictive setting appropriate to [their] individual needs and abilities," including "the right to live . . . in a group home."

Such legislation thus singling out the retarded for special treatment reflects the real and undeniable differences between the retarded and others. That a civilized and decent society expects and approves such legislation indicates that governmental consideration of those differences in the vast majority of situations is not only legitimate but also desirable. It may be, as CLC contends, that legislation designed to benefit, rather than disadvantage, the retarded would generally withstand examination under a test of heightened scrutiny. The relevant inquiry, however, is whether heightened scrutiny is constitutionally mandated in the first instance. Even assuming that many of these laws could be shown to be substantially related to an important governmental purpose, merely requiring the legislature to justify its efforts in these terms may lead it to refrain from acting at all. Much recent legislation intended to benefit the retarded also assumes the need for measures that might be perceived to disadvantage them. The Education of the Handicapped Act, for example, requires an "appropriate" education, not one that is equal in all respects to the education of nonretarded children; clearly, admission to a class that exceeded the abilities of a retarded child would not be appropriate. Similarly, the Developmental Disabilities

---

characteristics (unlike the one the commentator is trying to render suspect) are often relevant to legitimate purposes. At that point there's not much left of the immutability theory, is there?" J. Ely, Democracy and Distrust 150 (1980) (footnote omitted). See also *id.*, at 154-155.

Assistance Act and the Texas Act give the retarded the right to live only in the "least restrictive setting" appropriate to their abilities, implicitly assuming the need for at least some restrictions that would not be imposed on others. Especially given the wide variation in the abilities and needs of the retarded themselves, governmental bodies must have a certain amount of flexibility and freedom from judicial oversight in shaping and limiting their remedial efforts.

Third, the legislative response, which could hardly have occurred and survived without public support, negates any claim that the mentally retarded are politically powerless in the sense that they have no ability to attract the attention of the lawmakers. Any minority can be said to be powerless to assert direct control over the legislature, but if that were a criterion for higher level scrutiny by the courts, much economic and social legislation would now be suspect.

Fourth, if the large and amorphous class of the mentally retarded were deemed quasi-suspect for the reasons given by the Court of Appeals, it would be difficult to find a principled way to distinguish a variety of other groups who have perhaps immutable disabilities setting them off from others, who cannot themselves mandate the desired legislative responses, and who can claim some degree of prejudice from at least part of the public at large. One need mention in this respect only the aging, the disabled, the mentally ill, and the infirm. We are reluctant to set out on that course, and we decline to do so.

Doubtless, there have been and there will continue to be instances of discrimination against the retarded that are in fact invidious, and that are properly subject to judicial correction under constitutional norms. But the appropriate method of reaching such instances is not to create a new quasi-suspect classification and subject all governmental action based on that classification to more searching evaluation. Rather, we should look to the likelihood that governmental action premised on a particular classification is valid as a general matter, not merely to the specifics of the case before us. Because mental retardation is a characteristic that the government may legitimately take into account in a wide range of decisions, and because both State and Federal Governments have recently committed themselves to assisting the retarded, we will not presume that any given legislative action, even one that disadvantages retarded individuals, is rooted in considerations that the Constitution will not tolerate. . . .

[The concurring opinion of Justice Stevens, and the opinion of Justice Marshall, concurring in the judgment in part and dissenting in part, are omitted.]

Notes and Questions

1. What distinguishes intellectual disability from characteristics such as sex or race? They are all similar in that they are immutable characteristics; there has been a history of discriminating against people on those bases; and the targeted groups have minimal political power. Is the key difference that differences in intellectual disability are relevant in a way that differences in race and sex are not? Does

that suggest that some of the *Frontiero* factors are more relevant and decisive than others?

2. One reason the *Cleburne* Court concludes that it should not apply heightened scrutiny to laws that discriminate *against* the intellectually disabled is that the Court would then be required to apply heightened scrutiny to laws that discriminate *in favor* of the intellectual disabled. Is it that necessarily the case? Is it the logical implication of cases such as *Craig*? Keep this statement in mind when you read the Court's affirmative action cases in Chapter 17.

3. One year after its decision in *Cleburne*, the Court in *Lyng v. Castillo*, 477 U.S. 635 (1986) reorganized the factors in a way that presented some of them in the disjunctive, thus making it clear that not all of the factors need to point in a given direction in order for the Court to apply heightened scrutiny. The *Lyng* Court thus identified the three relevant inquiries in deciding whether to accord a group heightened scrutiny as (1) whether the group has suffered a history of discrimination; (2) whether the group exhibits "obvious, immutable, *or* distinguishing characteristics that define them as a discrete group"; and (3) whether they are either a minority *or* politically powerless.

F. Fleeting Rational Basis Plus Review

Chapter 4 examined the Court's decisions in *Lee Optical*, *Railway Express*, and *Beach Communications*, which together epitomize the traditional form of rational basis review in equal protection jurisprudence. As those cases demonstrated, the standard is extraordinarily deferential, and is tantamount to no review at all. Indeed, the moment you see one of those cases cited in a U.S. Supreme Court or lower court opinion, you typically need not read any further, as the outcome is all but certain.

However, in both Chapter 12 and earlier in this chapter, you saw that the Court's decisions regarding sex and legitimacy discrimination exemplified another version of rational basis review, referred to herein as "transitional rational basis plus" review. Under this form of review the Court purports to apply rational basis review—often using that standard's jargon—but in fact applies something more robust. In a subsequent opinion, the Court re-characterizes the earlier case as in fact applying a higher level of scrutiny, such as intermediate.

The cases that follow exemplify a third form of rational basis review. Referred to herein as "fleeting rational basis plus review," this form of review is similar to transitional rational basis plus review in that it is more robust than traditional rational basis review, and often results in the law at issue being declared unconstitutional. Indeed, when you see a Court cite the decisions below, it is almost certain that the remainder of the opinion will declare the law at issue unconstitutional. However, it differs from "transitional rational basis plus" review in that it does not signal a permanent transition to a higher level of scrutiny for the class impacted by the law. Rather, there is something situation specific to the case itself that causes the Court to take a closer look. While the Court itself has never formally acknowledged this as a different level of scrutiny, individual Justices, lower court judges, and scholars have.

As you read the cases that follow, see if you can identify both what it is that triggers fleeting rational basis review, and how exactly it differs from traditional rational basis review.

United States Dep't of Agriculture v. Moreno

413 U.S. 528 (1973)

MR. JUSTICE BRENNAN delivered the opinion of the Court.

This case requires us to consider the constitutionality of § 3(e) of the Food Stamp Act of 1964, which, with certain exceptions, excludes from participation in the food stamp program any household containing an individual who is unrelated to any other member of the household. In practical effect, § 3(e) creates two classes of persons for food stamp purposes: one class is composed of those individuals who live in households all of whose members are related to one another, and the other class consists of those individuals who live in households containing one or more members who are unrelated to the rest. The latter class of persons is denied federal food assistance....

Appellees in this case consist of several groups of individuals who allege that, although they satisfy the income eligibility requirements for federal food assistance, they have nevertheless been excluded from the program solely because the persons in each group are not "all related to each other." ....

Under traditional equal protection analysis, a legislative classification must be sustained, if the classification itself is rationally related to a legitimate governmental interest. The purposes of the Food Stamp Act were expressly set forth in the congressional "declaration of policy":

> "It is hereby declared to be the policy of Congress ... to safeguard the health and well-being of the Nation's population and raise levels of nutrition among low-income households. The Congress hereby finds that the limited food purchasing power of low-income households contributes to hunger and malnutrition among members of such households. The Congress further finds that increased utilization of food in establishing and maintaining adequate national levels of nutrition will promote the distribution in a beneficial manner of our agricultural abundances and will strengthen our agricultural economy, as well as result in more orderly marketing and distribution of food. To alleviate such hunger and malnutrition, a food stamp program is herein authorized which will permit low-income households to purchase a nutritionally adequate diet through normal channels of trade."

The challenged statutory classification (households of related persons versus households containing one or more unrelated persons) is clearly irrelevant to the stated purposes of the Act. As the District Court recognized, "[t]he relationships among persons constituting one economic unit and sharing cooking facilities have nothing to do with their abilities to stimulate the agricultural economy by purchasing farm surpluses, or with their personal nutritional requirements."

Thus, if it is to be sustained, the challenged classification must rationally further some legitimate governmental interest other than those specifically stated in the congressional "declaration of policy." Regrettably, there is little legislative history to illuminate the purposes of the 1971 amendment of § 3(e). The legislative history that does exist, however, indicates that that amendment was intended to prevent so-called "hippies" and "hippie communes" from participating in the food stamp program. The challenged classification clearly cannot be sustained by reference to this congressional purpose. For if the constitutional conception of "equal protection of the laws" means anything, it must at the very least mean that a bare congressional desire to harm a politically unpopular group cannot constitute a *legitimate* governmental interest. As a result, "[a] purpose to discriminate against hippies cannot, in and of itself and without reference to (some independent) considerations in the public interest, justify the 1971 amendment."

Although apparently conceding this point, the Government maintains that the challenged classification should nevertheless be upheld as rationally related to the clearly legitimate governmental interest in minimizing fraud in the administration of the food stamp program.[7] In essence, the Government contends that, in adopting the 1971 amendment, Congress might rationally have thought (1) that households with one or more unrelated members are more likely than "fully related" households to contain individuals who abuse the program by fraudulently failing to report sources of income or by voluntarily remaining poor; and (2) that such households are "relatively unstable," thereby increasing the difficulty of detecting such abuses. But even if we were to accept as rational the Government's wholly unsubstantiated assumptions concerning the differences between "related" and "unrelated" households we still could not agree with the Government's conclusion that the denial of essential federal food assistance to *all* otherwise eligible households containing unrelated members constitutes a rational effort to deal with these concerns.

---

7. The Government initially argued to the District Court that the challenged classification might be justified as a means to foster "morality." In rejecting that contention, the District Court noted that "interpreting the amendment as an attempt to regulate morality would raise serious constitutional questions." Indeed, citing this Court's decisions in *Griswold v. Connecticut*, 381 U.S. 479 (1965), *Stanley v. Georgia*, 394 U.S. 557 (1969), and *Eisenstadt v. Baird*, 405 U.S. 438 (1972), the District Court observed that it was doubtful at best, whether Congress, "in the name of morality," could "infringe the rights to privacy and freedom of association *in the home*." Moreover, the court also pointed out that the classification established in § 3(e) was not rationally related "to prevailing notions of morality, since it in terms disqualifies all households of unrelated individuals, without reference to whether a particular group contains both sexes." The Government itself has now abandoned the "morality" argument.

At the outset, it is important to note that the Food Stamp Act itself contains provisions, wholly independent of § 3(e), aimed specifically at the problems of fraud and of the voluntarily poor. For example, with certain exceptions, § 5(c) of the Act renders ineligible for assistance any household containing "an able-bodied adult person between the ages of eighteen and sixty-five" who fails to register for, and accept, offered employment. Similarly, § 14(b) and (c) specifically impose strict criminal penalties upon any individual who obtains or uses food stamps fraudulently. The existence of these provisions necessarily casts considerable doubt upon the proposition that the 1971 amendment could rationally have been intended to prevent those very same abuses. See *Eisenstadt v. Baird*, 405 U.S. 438, 452 (1972).

Moreover, in practical effect, the challenged classification simply does not operate so as rationally to further the prevention of fraud. As previously noted, § 3(e) defines an eligible "household" as "a group of related individuals ... [1] living as one economic unit [2] sharing common cooking facilities [and 3] for whom food is customarily purchased in common." Thus, two *unrelated* persons living together and meeting all three of these conditions would constitute a single household ineligible for assistance. If financially feasible, however, these same two individuals can legally avoid the "unrelated person" exclusion simply by altering their living arrangements so as to eliminate any one of the three conditions. By so doing, they effectively create two separate "households" both of which are eligible for assistance. Indeed, as the California Director of Social Welfare has explained:

> "The 'related household' limitations will eliminate many households from eligibility in the Food Stamp Program. It is my understanding that the Congressional intent of the new regulations are specifically aimed at the 'hippies' and 'hippie communes.' Most people in this category can and will alter their living arrangements in order to remain eligible for food stamps. However, the AFDC mothers who try to raise their standard of living by sharing housing will be affected. They will not be able to utilize the altered living patterns in order to continue to be eligible without giving up their advantage of shared housing costs."

Thus, in practical operation, the 1971 amendment excludes from participation in the food stamp program, *not* those persons who are "likely to abuse the program," but, rather, *only* those persons who are so desperately in need of aid that they cannot even afford to alter their living arrangements so as to retain their eligibility. Traditional equal protection analysis does not require that every classification be drawn with precise "'mathematical nicety.'" *Dandridge v. Williams*, 397 U.S., at 485. But the classification here in issue is not only "imprecise", it is wholly without any rational basis. The judgment of the District Court holding the "unrelated person" provision invalid under the Due Process Clause of the Fifth Amendment is therefore affirmed.

Mr. Justice Douglas, concurring....

The test of equal protection is whether the legislative line that is drawn bears "some rational relationship to a legitimate" governmental purpose....

But for the constitutional aspects of the problem, the "unrelated" person provision of the Act might well be sustained as a means to prevent fraud. Fraud is a concern of the Act. Able-bodied persons must register and accept work or lose their food stamp rights. I could not say that this "unrelated" person provision has no "rational" relation to control of fraud. We deal here, however, with the right of association, protected by the First Amendment. People who are desperately poor but unrelated come together and join hands with the aim better to combat the crises of poverty. The need of those living together better to meet those crises is denied, while the need of households made up of relatives that is no more acute is serviced. . . .

Dandridge v. Williams, 397 U.S. 471, is not opposed. It sustained a Maryland grant of welfare, against the claim of violation of equal protection, which placed an upper limit on the monthly amount any single family could receive. The claimants had large families so that their standard of need exceeded the actual grants. Their claim was that the grants of aid considered in light of the size of their families created an invidious discrimination against them and in favor of small needy families. The claim was rejected on the basis that state economic or social legislation had long been judged by a less strict standard than comes into play when constitutionally protected rights are involved. Laws touching social and economic matters can pass muster under the Equal Protection Clause though they are imperfect, the test being whether the classification has some "reasonable basis." *Dandridge* held that "the Fourteenth Amendment gives the federal courts no power to impose upon the States their views of what constitutes wise economic or social policy." But for the First Amendment aspect of the case, Dandridge would control here.

Dandridge, however, did not reach classifications touching on associational rights that lie in the penumbra of the First Amendment. Since the "unrelated" person provision is not directed to the maintenance of the family as a unit but treats impoverished households composed of relatives more favorably than impoverished households having a single unrelated person, it draws a line that can be sustained only on a showing of a "compelling" governmental interest. . . .

Mr. Justice Rehnquist, with whom The Chief Justice concurs, dissenting. . . .

The Court's opinion would make a very persuasive congressional committee report arguing against the adoption of the limitation in question. Undoubtedly, Congress attacked the problem with a rather blunt instrument and, just as undoubtedly, persuasive arguments may be made that what we conceive to be its purpose will not be significantly advanced by the enactment of the limitation. But questions such as this are for Congress, rather than for this Court; our role is limited to the determination of whether there is any rational basis on which Congress could decide that public funds made available under the food stamp program should not go to a household containing an individual who is unrelated to any other member of the household.

I do not believe that asserted congressional concern with the fraudulent use of food stamps is, when interpreted in the light most favorable to sustaining the limitation, quite as irrational as the Court seems to believe. A basic unit which Congress has chosen for determination of availability for food stamps is the "household," a determination which is not criticized by the Court. By the limitation here challenged, it has singled out households which contain unrelated persons and made such households ineligible. I do not think it is unreasonable for Congress to conclude that the basic unit which it was willing to support with federal funding through food stamps is some variation on the family as we know it—a household consisting of related individuals. This unit provides a guarantee which is not provided by households containing unrelated individuals that the household exists for some purpose other than to collect federal food stamps.

Admittedly, as the Court points out, the limitation will make ineligible many households which have not been formed for the purpose of collecting federal food stamps, and will at the same time not wholly deny food stamps to those households which may have been formed in large part to take advantage of the program. But, as the Court concedes, "[t]raditional equal protection analysis does not require that every classification be drawn with precise 'mathematical nicety" . . . .

The limitation which Congress enacted could, in the judgment of reasonable men, conceivably deny food stamps to members of households which have been formed solely for the purpose of taking advantage of the food stamp program. Since the food stamp program is not intended to be a subsidy for every individual who desires low-cost food, this was a permissible congressional decision quite consistent with the underlying policy of the Act. The fact that the limitation will have unfortunate and perhaps unintended consequences beyond this does not make it unconstitutional.

City of Cleburne v. Cleburne Living Center, Inc.

473 U.S. 432 (1985)

Justice White delivered the opinion of the Court.

[At issue in this case is the constitutionality of a city ordinance that required a special use permit, renewably annually, for constructing group homes for intellectually disabled persons, although such a permit was not required for other types of uses that arguably had a similar neighborhood impact. In an earlier portion of this opinion, excerpted above, the Court rejected a claim that discrimination on the basis of intellectual disability is subject to heightened scrutiny. In the excerpt that follows, the Court proceeded to apply what it characterized as rational basis review to the claim.]

Our refusal to recognize the retarded as a quasi-suspect class does not leave them entirely unprotected from invidious discrimination. To withstand equal protection review, legislation that distinguishes between the mentally retarded and others must be rationally related to a legitimate governmental purpose. This standard, we believe, affords government the latitude necessary both to pursue policies designed to assist the retarded in realizing their full potential, and to freely and efficiently engage in activities that burden the retarded in what is essentially an incidental manner. The State may not rely on a classification whose relationship to an asserted goal is so attenuated as to render the distinction arbitrary or irrational. See *Zobel v. Williams,* 457 U.S. 55, 61–63 (1982); *United States Dept. of Agriculture v. Moreno,* 413 U.S. 528, 535 (1973). Furthermore, some objectives—such as "a bare . . . desire to harm a politically unpopular group," *id.,* at 534—are not legitimate state interests. Beyond that, the mentally retarded, like others, have and retain their substantive constitutional rights in addition to the right to be treated equally by the law.

We turn to the issue of the validity of the zoning ordinance insofar as it requires a special use permit for homes for the mentally retarded. We inquire first whether requiring a special use permit for the Featherston home in the circumstances here deprives respondents of the equal protection of the laws. If it does, there will be no occasion to decide whether the special use permit provision is facially invalid where the mentally retarded are involved, or to put it another way, whether the city may never insist on a special use permit for a home for the mentally retarded in an R–3 zone. This is the preferred course of adjudication since it enables courts to avoid making unnecessarily broad constitutional judgments.

The constitutional issue is clearly posed. The city does not require a special use permit in an R–3 zone for apartment houses, multiple dwellings, boarding and lodging houses, fraternity or sorority houses, dormitories, apartment hotels, hospitals, sanitariums, nursing homes for convalescents or the aged (other than for the insane or feebleminded or alcoholics or drug addicts), private clubs or fraternal orders, and other specified uses. It does, however, insist on a special permit for the Featherston home, and it does so, as the District Court found, because it would be a facility for the mentally retarded. May the city require the permit for this facility when other care and multiple-dwelling facilities are freely permitted?

It is true, as already pointed out, that the mentally retarded as a group are indeed different from others not sharing their misfortune, and in this respect they may be different from those who would occupy other facilities that would be permitted in an R–3 zone without a special permit. But this difference is largely irrelevant unless the Featherston home and those who would occupy it would threaten legitimate interests of the city in a way that other permitted uses such as boarding houses and hospitals would not. Because in our view the record does not reveal any rational basis for believing that the Featherston home would pose any special threat to the city's legitimate interests, we affirm the judgment below insofar as it holds the ordinance invalid as applied in this case.

The District Court found that the City Council's insistence on the permit rested on several factors. First, the Council was concerned with the negative attitude of the majority of property owners located within 200 feet of the Featherston facility, as well as with the fears of elderly residents of the neighborhood. But mere negative attitudes, or fear, unsubstantiated by factors which are properly cognizable in a zoning proceeding, are not permissible bases for treating a home for the mentally retarded differently from apartment houses, multiple dwellings, and the like. It is plain that the electorate as a whole, whether by referendum or otherwise, could not order city action violative of the Equal Protection Clause, and the City may not avoid the strictures of that Clause by deferring to the wishes or objections of some fraction of the body politic. "Private biases may be outside the reach of the law, but the law cannot, directly or indirectly, give them effect." *Palmore v. Sidoti,* 466 U.S. 429, 433 (1984).

Second, the Council had two objections to the location of the facility. It was concerned that the facility was across the street from a junior high school, and it feared that the students might harass the occupants of the Featherston home. But the school itself is attended by about 30 mentally retarded students, and denying a permit based on such vague, undifferentiated fears is again permitting some portion of the community to validate what would otherwise be an equal protection violation. The other objection to the home's location was that it was located on "a five hundred year flood plain." This concern with the possibility of a flood, however, can hardly be based on a distinction between the Featherston home and, for example, nursing homes, homes for convalescents or the aged, or sanitariums or hospitals, any of which could be located on the Featherston site without obtaining a special use permit. The same may be said of another concern of the Council—doubts about the legal responsibility for actions which the mentally retarded might take. If there is no concern about legal responsibility with respect to other uses that would be permitted in the area, such as boarding and fraternity houses, it is difficult to believe that the groups of mildly or moderately mentally retarded individuals who would live at 201 Featherston would present any different or special hazard.

Fourth, the Council was concerned with the size of the home and the number of people that would occupy it. The District Court found, and the Court of Appeals repeated, that "[i]f the potential residents of the Featherston Street home were not mentally retarded, but the home was the same in all other respects, its use would be permitted under the city's zoning ordinance." Given this finding, there would be no restrictions on the number of people who could occupy this home as a boarding house, nursing home, family dwelling, fraternity house, or dormitory. The question is whether it is rational to treat the mentally retarded differently. It is true that they suffer disability not shared by others; but why this difference warrants a density regulation that others need not observe is not at all apparent. At least this record does not clarify how, in this connection, the characteristics of the intended occupants of the Featherston home rationally justify denying to those occupants what would be permitted to groups occupying the same site for different purposes. Those who would live in the Featherston home are the type of individuals who, with supporting staff, satisfy federal and state standards for group housing in the community; and there is no dispute that the home would meet the federal square-footage-per-resident requirement for facilities of this type. In the words of the Court of Appeals, "[t]he City never justifies its apparent view that other people can live under such 'crowded' conditions when mentally retarded persons cannot."

In the courts below the city also urged that the ordinance is aimed at avoiding concentration of population and at lessening congestion of the streets. These concerns obviously fail to explain why apartment houses, fraternity and sorority houses, hospitals and the like, may freely locate in the area without a permit. So, too, the expressed worry about fire hazards, the serenity of the neighborhood, and the avoidance of danger to other residents fail rationally to justify singling out a home such as 201 Featherston for the special use permit, yet imposing no such restrictions on the many other uses freely permitted in the neighborhood.

The short of it is that requiring the permit in this case appears to us to rest on an irrational prejudice against the mentally retarded, including those who would occupy the Featherston facility and who would live under the closely supervised and highly regulated conditions expressly provided for by state and federal law.

The judgment of the Court of Appeals is affirmed insofar as it invalidates the zoning ordinance as applied to the Featherston home. The judgment is otherwise vacated, and the case is remanded.

Justice Stevens, with whom The Chief Justice joins, concurring.

The Court of Appeals disposed of this case as if a critical question to be decided were which of three clearly defined standards of equal protection review should be applied to a legislative classification discriminating against the mentally retarded. In fact, our cases have not delineated three—or even one or two—such well-defined standards. Rather, our cases reflect a continuum of judgmental responses to differing classifications which have been explained in opinions by terms ranging from "strict scrutiny" at one extreme to "rational basis" at the other. I have never been persuaded that these so-called "standards" adequately explain the decisional process. Cases involving classifications based on alienage, illegal residency, illegitimacy, gender, age, or—as in this case—mental retardation, do not fit well into sharply defined classifications.

"I am inclined to believe that what has become known as the [tiered] analysis of equal protection claims does not describe a completely logical method of deciding cases, but rather is a method the Court has employed to explain decisions that actually apply a single standard in a reasonably consistent fashion." *Craig v. Boren*, 429 U.S. 190, 212 (1976) (STEVENS, J., concurring). In my own approach to these cases, I have always asked myself whether I could find a "rational basis" for the classification at issue. The term "rational," of course, includes a requirement that an impartial lawmaker could logically believe that the classification would serve a legitimate public purpose that transcends the harm to the members of the disadvantaged class. Thus, the word "rational"—for me at least—includes elements of legitimacy and neutrality that must always characterize the performance of the sovereign's duty to govern impartially.

The rational-basis test, properly understood, adequately explains why a law that deprives a person of the right to vote because his skin has a different pigmentation than that of other voters violates the Equal Protection Clause. It would be utterly irrational to limit the franchise on the basis of height or weight; it is equally invalid to limit it on the basis of skin color. None of these attributes has any bearing at all on the citizen's willingness or ability to exercise that civil right. We do not need to apply a special standard, or to apply "strict scrutiny," or even "heightened scrutiny," to decide such cases.

In every equal protection case, we have to ask certain basic questions. What class is harmed by the legislation, and has it been subjected to a "tradition of disfavor" by our laws? What is the public purpose that is being served by the law? What is the characteristic of the disadvantaged class that justifies the disparate treatment? In most cases the answer to these questions will tell us whether the statute has a "rational basis." The answers will result in the virtually automatic invalidation of racial classifications and in the validation of most economic classifications, but they will provide differing results in cases involving classifications based on alienage, gender, or illegitimacy. But that is not because we apply an "intermediate standard of review" in these cases; rather it is because the characteristics of these groups are sometimes relevant and sometimes irrelevant to a valid public purpose, or, more specifically, to the purpose that the challenged laws purportedly intended to serve.

Every law that places the mentally retarded in a special class is not presumptively irrational. The differences between mentally retarded persons and those with greater mental capacity are obviously relevant to certain legislative decisions. An impartial lawmaker—indeed, even a member of a class of persons defined as mentally retarded—could rationally vote in favor of a law providing funds for special education and special treatment for the mentally retarded. A mentally retarded person could also recognize that he is a member of a class that might need special supervision in some situations, both to protect himself and to protect others. Restrictions on his right to drive cars or to operate hazardous equipment might well seem rational even though they deprived him of employment opportunities and the kind of freedom of travel enjoyed by other citizens. "That a civilized and decent society expects and approves such legislation indicates that governmental consideration of those differences in the vast majority of situations is not only legitimate but also desirable."

Even so, the Court of Appeals correctly observed that through ignorance and prejudice the mentally retarded "have been subjected to a history of unfair and often grotesque mistreatment." The discrimination against the mentally retarded that is at issue in this case is the city's decision to require an annual special use permit before property in an apartment house district may be used as a group home for persons who are mildly retarded. The record convinces me that this permit was required because of the irrational fears of neighboring property owners, rather than for the protection of the mentally retarded persons who would reside in respondent's home.

Although the city argued in the Court of Appeals that legitimate interests of the neighbors justified the restriction, the court unambiguously rejected that argument. In this Court, the city has argued that the discrimination was really motivated by a desire to protect the mentally retarded from the hazards presented by the neighborhood. Zoning ordinances are not usually justified on any such basis, and in this case, for the reasons explained by the Court, I find that justification wholly unconvincing. I cannot believe that a rational member of this disadvantaged class could ever approve of the discriminatory application of the city's ordinance in this case.

Accordingly, I join the opinion of the Court.

JUSTICE MARSHALL, with whom JUSTICE BRENNAN and JUSTICE BLACKMUN join, concurring in the judgment in part and dissenting in part. . . .

At the outset, two curious and paradoxical aspects of the Court's opinion must be noted. First, because the Court invalidates Cleburne's zoning ordinance on rational-basis grounds, the Court's wide-ranging discussion of heightened scrutiny is wholly superfluous to the decision of this case. . . .

Second, the Court's heightened-scrutiny discussion is even more puzzling given that Cleburne's ordinance is invalidated only after being subjected to precisely the sort of probing inquiry associated with heightened scrutiny. To be sure, the Court does not label its handiwork heightened scrutiny, and perhaps the method employed must hereafter be called "second order" rational-basis review rather than "heightened scrutiny." But however labeled, the rational basis test invoked today is most assuredly not the rational-basis test of *Williamson v. Lee Optical of Oklahoma, Inc.,* 348 U.S. 483 (1955), *Allied Stores of Ohio, Inc. v. Bowers,* 358 U.S. 522 (1959), and their progeny.

The Court, for example, concludes that legitimate concerns for fire hazards or the serenity of the neighborhood do not justify singling out respondents to bear the burdens of these concerns, for analogous permitted uses appear to pose similar threats. Yet under the traditional and most minimal version of the rational-basis test, "reform may take one step at a time, addressing itself to the phase of the problem which seems most acute to the legislative mind." *Williamson v. Lee Optical of Oklahoma, Inc., supra,* 348 U.S., at 489. The "record" is said not to support the ordinance's classifications, but under the traditional standard we do not sift through the record to determine whether policy decisions are squarely supported by a firm factual foundation. Finally, the Court further finds it "difficult to believe" that the retarded present different or special hazards inapplicable to other groups. In normal circumstances, the burden is not on the legislature to convince the Court that the lines it has drawn are sensible; legislation is presumptively constitutional, and a State "is not required to resort to close distinctions or to maintain a precise, scientific uniformity with reference" to its goals.

I share the Court's criticisms of the overly broad lines that Cleburne's zoning ordinance has drawn. But if the ordinance is to be invalidated for its imprecise classifications, it must be pursuant to more powerful scrutiny than the minimal rational-basis test used to review classifications affecting only economic and commercial matters. The same imprecision in a similar ordinance that required opticians but not optometrists to be licensed to practice, see *Williamson v. Lee Optical of Oklahoma, Inc.,* or that excluded new but not old businesses from parts of a community, see *New Orleans v. Dukes,* would hardly be fatal to the statutory scheme.

The refusal to acknowledge that something more than minimum rationality review is at work here is, in my view, unfortunate in at least two respects.[4] The suggestion that the traditional rational-basis test allows this sort of searching inquiry creates precedent for this Court and lower courts to subject economic and commercial classifications to similar and searching "ordinary" rational-basis review—a small and regrettable step back toward the days of *Lochner v. New York*, 198 U.S. 45 (1905). Moreover, by failing to articulate the factors that justify today's "second order" rational-basis review, the Court provides no principled foundation for determining when more searching inquiry is to be invoked. Lower courts are thus left in the dark on this important question, and this Court remains unaccountable for its decisions employing, or refusing to employ, particularly searching scrutiny. Candor requires me to acknowledge the particular factors that justify invalidating Cleburne's zoning ordinance under the careful scrutiny it today receives. . . .

Notes and Questions

1. As indicated above, what sets cases like *Moreno* and *Cleburne* apart from the transitional rational basis plus review cases is that the Court never proceeds to "upgrade" the level of scrutiny for the impacted class. Thus, for example, in no subsequent case has the Court declared discrimination against "hippies" or the intellectually disabled to be subject to intermediate or strict scrutiny.

2. In each of these two cases, what key fact or set of facts triggered the Court's decision to apply a more robust form of rational basis scrutiny?

3. In what ways does fleeting rational basis plus review differ from traditional rational basis review? In considering the answer to this question, re-read *Beach Communications* and identify the hallmarks of traditional rational basis review delineated therein. Compare this list with what the Court did in the *Moreno* and *Cleburne* cases.

4. What do you make of Justice Stevens's suggested approach and his general rejection of tiered scrutiny in his separate opinion in *Cleburne*? As you read later decisions by the Court, consider whether some of them can be explained in the way Justice Stevens suggests.

5. Do you agree with Justice Marshall's criticisms of fleeting rational basis review that he sets forth in his separate opinion in *Cleburne*? Why do you suppose the Court engages in this stealth form of review?

---

4. The two cases the Court cites in its rational-basis discussion, *Zobel v. Williams*, 457 U.S. 55 (1982), and *United States Dept. of Agriculture v. Moreno*, 413 U.S. 528 (1973), expose the special nature of the rational-basis test employed today. As two of only a handful of modern equal protection cases striking down legislation under what purports to be a rational-basis standard, these cases must be and generally have been viewed as intermediate review decisions masquerading in rational-basis language.

6. References to morality and moral disapproval are alluded to in many of the Court's Due Process and Equal Protection decisions issued in the 1970s, including *Eisenstadt*, *Roe*, and *Moreno*. Do the Court's decisions leave open the possibility that concerns about morality, or moral disapproval of a particular group of persons (or conduct associated with that group of persons) can ever be a valid governmental interest? Is moral disapproval of a group (or its conduct) synonymous with a "bare . . . desire to harm" that group? Are there reasons why moral disapproval might be deemed a valid governmental interest when a law is challenged on due process grounds but not when it is challenged on equal protection grounds? If so, why?

Chapter 14

The Concept of "State Action" Revisited

A. The Concept Narrowed

Recall that in *The Civil Rights Cases*, the Court made clear that the Fourteenth Amendment applied only when "state action" was involved. Moreover, the majority in that case took a relatively narrow view of what constituted state action, with Justice Harlan's dissent arguing for a much more expansive definition of the phrase.

Recall as well from Chapter 7 that the Court's decisions recognized three broad categories in which the Court would treat conduct by seemingly private actors as state action. First, as evidenced by cases such as *Marsh* and the White Primary Cases, when a private actor was performing a traditional governmental function, such as running a municipal government or holding elections. Second, as in *Burton*, when the private actor had entered into a symbiotic relationship with the state. And third, as in *Shelley*, *Anderson*, and *Reitman*, when the government was encouraging, enforcing or facilitating a private actor's conduct.

More generally, however, the Court's decisions between the 1940s and the 1960s took an increasingly expansive view of what constituted sufficient "state action" to make conduct subject to the strictures of the Fourteenth Amendment. Indeed, the trajectory of the Court's state action decisions through the 1960s was such that one could anticipate the Court eventually arriving at a definition of "state action" more consistent with Justice Harlan's dissent in *The Civil Rights Cases* than the definition espoused by the majority in that case. However, between 1969 and 1971, Republican President Richard Nixon was able to appoint four new Justices to the Court who together took the Court in a different ideological direction. The next two cases represent a clear break from the trajectory of their predecessors.

Moose Lodge No. 107 v. Irvis

407 U.S. 163 (1972)

MR. JUSTICE REHNQUIST delivered the opinion of the Court.

Appellee Irvis, a Negro (hereafter appellee), was refused service by appellant Moose Lodge, a local branch of the national fraternal organization located in Harrisburg, Pennsylvania. Appellee then brought this action under 42 U.S.C. § 1983 for injunctive relief in the United States District Court for the Middle District of Pennsylvania.

He claimed that because the Pennsylvania liquor board had issued appellant Moose Lodge a private club license that authorized the sale of alcoholic beverages on its premises, the refusal of service to him was "state action" for the purposes of the Equal Protection Clause of the Fourteenth Amendment. . . .

The District Court in its opinion found that "a Caucasian member in good standing brought plaintiff, a Negro, to the Lodge's dining room and bar as his guest and requested service of food and beverages. The Lodge through its employees refused service to plaintiff solely because he is a Negro." It is undisputed that each local Moose Lodge is bound by the constitution and general bylaws of the Supreme Lodge, the latter of which contain a provision limiting membership in the lodges to white male Caucasians. The District Court in this connection found that "[t]he lodges accordingly maintain a policy and practice of restricting membership to the Caucasian race and permitting members to bring only Caucasian guests on lodge premises, particularly to the dining room and bar." . . . .

Moose Lodge is a private club in the ordinary meaning of that term. It is a local chapter of a national fraternal organization having well-defined requirements for membership. It conducts all of its activities in a building that is owned by it. It is not publicly funded. Only members and guests are permitted in any lodge of the order; one may become a guest only by invitation of a member or upon invitation of the house committee.

Appellee, while conceding the right of private clubs to choose members upon a discriminatory basis, asserts that the licensing of Moose Lodge to serve liquor by the Pennsylvania Liquor Control Board amounts to such state involvement with the club's activities as to make its discriminatory practices forbidden by the Equal Protection Clause of the Fourteenth Amendment. The relief sought and obtained by appellee in the District Court was an injunction forbidding the licensing by the liquor authority of Moose Lodge until it ceased its discriminatory practices. We conclude that Moose Lodge's refusal to serve food and beverages to a guest by reason of the fact that he was a Negro does not, under the circumstances here presented, violate the Fourteenth Amendment.

In 1883, this Court in *The Civil Rights Cases*, 109 U.S. 3, set forth the essential dichotomy between discriminatory action by the State, which is prohibited by the Equal Protection Clause, and private conduct, "however discriminatory or wrongful," against which that clause "erects no shield," *Shelley v. Kraemer*, 334 U.S. 1, 13 (1948). That dichotomy has been subsequently reaffirmed in *Shelley v. Kraemer, supra*, and in *Burton v. Wilmington Parking Authority*, 365 U.S. 715 (1961).

While the principle is easily stated, the question of whether particular discriminatory conduct is private, on the one hand, or amounts to "state action," on the other hand, frequently admits of no easy answer. "Only by sifting facts and weighing circumstances can the nonobvious involvement of the State in private conduct be attributed its true significance." *Burton v. Wilmington Parking Authority, supra*, at 722.

Our cases make clear that the impetus for the forbidden discrimination need not originate with the State if it is state action that enforces privately originated discrimination. *Shelley v. Kraemer, supra.* The Court held in *Burton v. Wilmington Parking Authority, supra*, that a private restaurant owner who refused service because of a customer's race violated the Fourteenth Amendment, where the restaurant was located in a building owned by a state-created parking authority and leased from the authority. The Court, after a comprehensive review of the relationship between the lessee and the parking authority concluded that the latter had "so far insinuated itself into a position of interdependence with Eagle (the restaurant owner) that it must be recognized as a joint participant in the challenged activity, which, on that account, cannot be considered to have been so 'purely private' as to fall without the scope of the Fourteenth Amendment." 365 U.S., at 725.

The Court has never held, of course, that discrimination by an otherwise private entity would be violative of the Equal Protection Clause if the private entity receives any sort of benefit or service at all from the State, or if it is subject to state regulation in any degree whatever. Since state-furnished services include such necessities of life as electricity, water, and police and fire protection, such a holding would utterly emasculate the distinction between private as distinguished from state conduct set forth in *The Civil Rights Cases, supra*, and adhered to in subsequent decisions. Our holdings indicate that where the impetus for the discrimination is private, the State must have "significantly involved itself with invidious discriminations," *Reitman v. Mulkey*, 387 U.S. 369, 380 (1967), in order for the discriminatory action to fall within the ambit of the constitutional prohibition. . . .

Here there is nothing approaching the symbiotic relationship between lessor and lessee that was present in *Burton*, where the private lessee obtained the benefit of locating in a building owned by the state-created parking authority, and the parking authority was enabled to carry out its primary public purpose of furnishing parking space by advantageously leasing portions of the building constructed for that purpose to commercial lessees such as the owner of the Eagle Restaurant. Unlike *Burton*, the Moose Lodge building is located on land owned by it, not by any public authority. Far from apparently holding itself out as a place of public accommodation, Moose Lodge quite ostentatiously proclaims the fact that it is not open to the public at large. Nor is it located and operated in such surroundings that although private in name, it discharges a function or performs a service that would otherwise in all likelihood be performed by the State. In short, while Eagle was a public restaurant in a public building, Moose Lodge is a private social club in a private building.

With the exception hereafter noted, the Pennsylvania Liquor Control Board plays absolutely no part in establishing or enforcing the membership or guest policies of the club that it licenses to serve liquor. There is no suggestion in this record that Pennsylvania law, either as written or as applied, discriminates against minority groups either in their right to apply for club licenses themselves or in their right to purchase and be served liquor in places of public accommodation. The only effect that the state licensing of Moose Lodge to serve liquor can be said to have on the right of any other Pennsylvanian to buy or be served liquor on premises other than those of Moose Lodge is that for some purposes club licenses are counted in the maximum number of licenses that may be issued in a given municipality. Basically each municipality has a quota of one retail license for each 1,500 inhabitants. Licenses issued to hotels, municipal golf courses, and airport restaurants are not counted in this quota, nor are club licenses until the maximum number of retail licenses is reached. Beyond that point, neither additional retail licenses nor additional club licenses may be issued so long as the number of issued and outstanding retail licenses remains at or above the statutory maximum.

The District Court was at pains to point out in its opinion what it considered to be the "pervasive" nature of the regulation of private clubs by the Pennsylvania Liquor Control Board. As that court noted, an applicant for a club license must make such physical alterations in its premises as the board may require, must file a list of the names and addresses of its members and employees, and must keep extensive financial records. The board is granted the right to inspect the licensed premises at any time when patrons, guests, or members are present.

However detailed this type of regulation may be in some particulars, it cannot be said to in any way foster or encourage racial discrimination. Nor can it be said to make the State in any realistic sense a partner or even a joint venturer in the club's enterprise. The limited effect of the prohibition against obtaining additional club licenses when the maximum number of retail licenses allotted to a municipality has been issued, when considered together with the availability of liquor from hotel, restaurant, and retail licensees, falls far short of conferring upon club licensees a monopoly in the dispensing of liquor in any given municipality or in the State as a whole. We therefore hold that, with the exception hereafter noted, the operation of the regulatory scheme enforced by the Pennsylvania Liquor Control Board does not sufficiently implicate the State in the discriminatory guest policies of Moose Lodge to make the latter "state action" within the ambit of the Equal Protection Clause of the Fourteenth Amendment.

The District Court found that the regulations of the Liquor Control Board adopted pursuant to statute affirmatively require that "[e]very club licensee shall adhere to all of the provisions of its Constitution and By-Laws." ....

The effect of this particular regulation on Moose Lodge under the provisions of the constitution placed in the record in the court below would be to place state sanctions behind its discriminatory membership rules, but not behind its guest practices, which were not embodied in the constitution of the lodge.... Appellee stated upon oral argument, though, and Moose Lodge conceded in its brief that the bylaws of the Supreme Lodge have been altered since the lower court decision to make applicable to guests the same sort of racial restrictions as are presently applicable to members.

Even though the Liquor Control Board regulation in question is neutral in its terms, the result of its application in a case where the constitution and bylaws of a club required racial discrimination would be to invoke the sanctions of the State to enforce a concededly discriminatory private rule.... *Shelley v. Kraemer*, 334 U.S. 1 (1948), makes it clear that the application of state sanctions to enforce such a rule would violate the Fourteenth Amendment....

Appellee was entitled to a decree enjoining the enforcement of § 113.09 of the regulations promulgated by the Pennsylvania Liquor Control Board insofar as that regulation requires compliance by Moose Lodge with provisions of its constitution and bylaws containing racially discriminatory provisions. He was entitled to no more....

MR. JUSTICE DOUGLAS, with whom MR. JUSTICE MARSHALL joins, dissenting....

Liquor licenses in Pennsylvania, unlike driver's licenses, or marriage licenses, are not freely available to those who meet racially neutral qualifications. There is a complex quota system, which the majority accurately describes. *Ante*, at 1973. What the majority neglects to say is that the quota for Harrisburg, where Moose Lodge No. 107 is located, has been full for many years. No more club licenses may be issued in that city.

This state-enforced scarcity of licenses restricts the ability of blacks to obtain liquor, for liquor is commercially available *only* at private clubs for a significant portion of each week. Access by blacks to places that serve liquor is further limited by the fact that the state quota is filled. A group desiring to form a nondiscriminatory club which would serve blacks must purchase a license held by an existing club, which can exact a monopoly price for the transfer. The availability of such a license is speculative at best, however, for, as Moose Lodge itself concedes, without a liquor license a fraternal organization would be hard pressed to survive.

Thus, the State of Pennsylvania is putting the weight of its liquor license, concededly a valued and important adjunct to a private club, behind racial discrimination....

MR. JUSTICE BRENNAN, with whom MR. JUSTICE MARSHALL joins, dissenting.

When Moose Lodge obtained its liquor license, the State of Pennsylvania became an active participant in the operation of the Lodge bar. Liquor licensing laws are only incidentally revenue measures; they are primarily pervasive regulatory schemes under which the State dictates and continually supervises virtually every detail of the operation of the licensee's business. Very few, if any, other licensed businesses experience such complete state involvement. Yet the Court holds that such involvement does not constitute "state action" making the Lodge's refusal to serve a guest liquor solely because of his race a violation of the Fourteenth Amendment. The vital flaw in the Court's reasoning is its complete disregard of the fundamental value underlying the "state action" concept. That value is discussed in my separate opinion in *Adickes v. S.H. Kress & Co.*, 398 U.S. 144, 190-191:

> "The state-action doctrine reflects the profound judgment that denials of equal treatment, and particularly denials on account of race or color, are singularly grave when government has or shares responsibility for them.

> Government is the social organ to which all in our society look for the promotion of liberty, justice, fair and equal treatment, and the setting of worthy norms and goals for social conduct. Therefore something is uniquely amiss in a society where the government, the authoritative oracle of community values, involves itself in racial discrimination. Accordingly, . . . the cases that have come before us [in which] this Court has condemned significant state involvement in racial discrimination, however subtle and indirect it may have been and whatever form it may have taken [,] . . . represent vigilant fidelity to the constitutional principle that no State shall in any significant way lend its authority to the sordid business of racial discrimination."

Plainly, the State of Pennsylvania's liquor regulations intertwine the State with the operation of the Lodge bar in a "significant way [and] lend [the State's] authority to the sordid business of racial discrimination." . . . .

Jackson v. Metropolitan Edison Co.

419 U.S. 345 (1974)

MR. JUSTICE REHNQUIST delivered the opinion of the Court.

Respondent Metropolitan Edison Co. is a privately owned and operated Pennsylvania corporation which holds a certificate of public convenience issued by the Pennsylvania Public Utility Commission empowering it to deliver electricity to a service area which includes the city of York, Pa. As a condition of holding its certificate, it is subject to extensive regulation by the Commission. Under a provision of its general tariff filed with the Commission, it has the right to discontinue service to any customer on reasonable notice of nonpayment of bills.

[A resident of York whose electricity service was disconnected by Metropolitan Edison filed suit, claiming that the failure to provide adequate notice, a hearing, and an opportunity to pay any amounts found due violated the Fourteenth Amendment's guarantee of due process of law.]

The Due Process Clause of the Fourteenth Amendment provides: "[N]or shall any State deprive any person of life, liberty, or property, without due process of law.' In 1883, this Court in *The Civil Rights Cases*, 109 U.S. 3, affirmed the essential dichotomy set forth in that Amendment between deprivation by the State, subject to scrutiny under its provisions, and private conduct, "however discriminatory or wrongful," against which the Fourteenth Amendment offers no shield. *Shelley v. Kraemer*, 335 U.S. 1 (1948).

We have reiterated that distinction on more than one occasion since then. See, *e.g.*, *Evans v. Abney*, 396 U.S. 435, 445 (1970); *Moose Lodge No. 107 v. Irvis*, 407 U.S. 163, 171–179 (1972). While the principle that private action is immune from the restrictions of the Fourteenth Amendment is well established and easily stated, the question whether particular conduct is "private," on the one hand, or "state action," on the other, frequently admits of no easy answer. *Burton v. Wilmington Parking Authority*, 365 U.S. 715, 723 (1961); *Moose Lodge No. 107 v. Irvis*, supra, 407 U.S. at 172.

Here the action complained of was taken by a utility company which is privately owned and operated, but which in many particulars of its business is subject to extensive state regulation. The mere fact that a business is subject to state regulation does not by itself convert its action into that of the State for purposes of the Fourteenth Amendment. 407 U.S., at 176-177. Nor does the fact that the regulation is extensive and detailed, as in the case of most public utilities, do so. It may well be that acts of a heavily regulated utility with at least something of a governmentally protected monopoly will more readily be found to be "state" acts than will the acts of an entity lacking these characteristics. But the inquiry must be whether there is a sufficiently close nexus between the State and the challenged action of the regulated entity so that the action of the latter may be fairly treated as that of the State itself. *Moose Lodge No. 107, supra*, 407 U.S. at 176. The true nature of the State's involvement may not be immediately obvious, and detailed inquiry may be required in order to determine whether the test is met. *Burton v. Wilmington Parking Authority, supra.*

Petitioner advances a series of contentions which, in her view, lead to the conclusion that this case should fall on the *Burton* side of the line drawn in *The Civil Rights Cases, supra*, rather than on the *Moose Lodge* side of that line. We find none of them persuasive.

Petitioner first argues that "state action" is present because of the monopoly status allegedly conferred upon Metropolitan by the State of Pennsylvania.... [A]lthough certain monopoly aspects were presented in *Moose Lodge No. 107, supra*, we found that the Lodge's action was not subject to the provisions of the Fourteenth Amendment....

Petitioner next urges that state action is present because respondent provides an essential public service required to be supplied on a reasonably continuous basis by Pa. Stat. Ann., Tit. 66, § 1171 (1959), and hence performs a "public function." We have, of course, found state action present in the exercise by a private entity of powers traditionally exclusively reserved to the State. See, *e.g., Nixon v. Condon*, 286 U.S. 73 (1932) (election); *Terry v. Adams*, 345 U.S. 461 (1953) (election); *Marsh v. Alabama*, 326 U.S. 501 (1946) (company town); *Evans v. Newton*, 382 U.S. 296 (1966) (municipal park). If we were dealing with the exercise by Metropolitan of some power delegated to it by the State which is traditionally associated with sovereignty, such as eminent domain, our case would be quite a different one. But while the Pennsylvania statute imposes an obligation to furnish service on regulated utilities, it imposes no such obligation on the State. The Pennsylvania courts have rejected the contention that the furnishing of utility services is either a state function or a municipal duty....

We also find absent in the instant case the symbiotic relationship presented in *Burton v. Wilmington Parking Authority*, 365 U.S. 715 (1961). There where a private lessee, who practiced racial discrimination, leased space for a restaurant from a state parking authority in a publicly owned building, the Court held that the State had so far insinuated itself into a position of interdependence with the restaurant that it was a joint participant in the enterprise. *Id.*, at 725. We cautioned, however, that while "a multitude of relationships might appear to some to fall within the Amendment's embrace," differences in circumstances beget differences in law, limiting the actual holding to lessees of public property. *Id.*, at 726.

Metropolitan is a privately owned corporation, and it does not lease its facilities from the State of Pennsylvania. It alone is responsible for the provision of power to its customers. In common with all corporations of the State it pays taxes to the State, and it is subject to a form of extensive regulation by the State in a way that most other business enterprises are not. But this was likewise true of the appellant club in *Moose Lodge No. 107 v. Irvis*, *supra*, where we said:

> "However detailed this type of regulation may be in some particulars, it cannot be said to in any way foster or encourage racial discrimination. Nor can it be said to make the State in any realistic sense a partner or even a joint venturer in the club's enterprise." 407 U.S., at 176-177.

All of petitioner's arguments taken together show no more than that Metropolitan was a heavily regulated, privately owned utility, enjoying at least a partial monopoly in the providing of electrical service within its territory, and that it elected to terminate service to petitioner in a manner which the Pennsylvania Public Utility Commission found permissible under state law. Under our decision this is not sufficient to connect the State of Pennsylvania with respondent's action so as to make the latter's conduct attributable to the State for purposes of the Fourteenth Amendment. . . .

[The dissenting opinions of Justices Douglas, Brennan, and Marshall are omitted.]

Notes and Questions

1. The *Moose Lodge* and *Jackson* Courts go to great efforts to distinguish *Burton*. How persuasive is the effort? Is it necessary to distinguish *Burton* in order to maintain some jurisprudential line between state and private action? Or are there ways to find state action in these two cases while still maintaining a distinction between state and private action?

2. The *Jackson* Court characterizes *Marsh* and the White Primary Cases as cases in which a private actor was deemed to be engaged in state action because they were exercising powers traditionally reserved to the state, such as operating a municipality or running an election. How does the *Jackson* Court determine the types of activities that are "traditionally" reserved to the state?

3. In both *Moose Lodge* and *Jackson*, the government has, in effect, given monopoly power to private actors who are engaging in what would be unconstitutional conduct if carried out directly by the government. Why, in the Court's view, is that not sufficient to constitute state action?

B. The Modern Approach

The following case provides a modern summary of the Court's state action decisions and applies them in a case in which a private litigant in a civil case is accused of exercising peremptory challenges in a racially discriminatory manner.

Edmonson v. Leesville Concrete Company, Inc.

500 U.S. 614 (1991)

JUSTICE KENNEDY delivered the opinion of the Court.

We must decide in the case before us whether a private litigant in a civil case may use peremptory challenges to exclude jurors on account of their race. . . .

Thaddeus Donald Edmonson, a construction worker, was injured in a jobsite accident at Fort Polk, Louisiana, a federal enclave. Edmonson sued Leesville Concrete Company for negligence in the United States District Court for the Western District of Louisiana. . . .

During *voir dire,* Leesville used two of its three peremptory challenges authorized by statute to remove black persons from the prospective jury. Citing our decision in *Batson v. Kentucky,* 476 U.S. 79 (1986), Edmonson, who is himself black, requested that the District Court require Leesville to articulate a race-neutral explanation for striking the two jurors. The District Court denied the request on the ground that *Batson* does not apply in civil proceedings. . . .

The Constitution's protections of individual liberty and equal protection apply in general only to action by the government. Racial discrimination, though invidious in all contexts, violates the Constitution only when it may be attributed to state action. *Moose Lodge No. 107 v. Irvis,* 407 U.S. 163, 172 (1972) . . . .

The Constitution structures the National Government, confines its actions, and, in regard to certain individual liberties and other specified matters, confines the actions of the States. With a few exceptions, such as the provisions of the Thirteenth Amendment, constitutional guarantees of individual liberty and equal protection do not apply to the actions of private entities. This fundamental limitation on the scope of constitutional guarantees "preserves an area of individual freedom by limiting the reach of federal law" and "avoids imposing on the State, its agencies or officials, responsibility for conduct for which they cannot fairly be blamed." *Lugar v. Edmondson Oil Co.,* 457 U.S. 922, 936–937 (1982). One great object of the Constitution is to permit citizens to structure their private relations as they choose subject only to the constraints of statutory or decisional law.

To implement these principles, courts must consider from time to time where the governmental sphere ends and the private sphere begins. Although the conduct of private parties lies beyond the Constitution's scope in most instances, governmental authority may dominate an activity to such an extent that its participants must be deemed to act with the authority of the government and, as a result, be subject to constitutional constraints. This is the jurisprudence of state action, which explores the "essential dichotomy" between the private sphere and the public sphere, with all its attendant constitutional obligations. *Moose Lodge, supra,* 407 U.S., at 172.

We begin our discussion within the framework for state-action analysis set forth in *Lugar, supra,* 457 U.S., at 937. There we considered the state-action question in the context of a due process challenge to a State's procedure allowing private parties to obtain prejudgment attachments. We asked first whether the claimed constitutional deprivation resulted from the exercise of a right or privilege having its source in state authority; and second, whether the private party charged with the deprivation could be described in all fairness as a state actor.

There can be no question that the first part of the *Lugar* inquiry is satisfied here. By their very nature, peremptory challenges have no significance outside a court of law. Their sole purpose is to permit litigants to assist the government in the selection of an impartial trier of fact. While we have recognized the value of peremptory challenges in this regard, particularly in the criminal context, there is no constitutional obligation to allow them. Peremptory challenges are permitted only when the government, by statute or decisional law, deems it appropriate to allow parties to exclude a given number of persons who otherwise would satisfy the requirements for service on the petit jury. . . .

Today in most jurisdictions, statutes or rules make a limited number of peremptory challenges available to parties in both civil and criminal proceedings. In the case before us, the challenges were exercised under a federal statute. . . .

Without this authorization, granted by an Act of Congress itself, Leesville would not have been able to engage in the alleged discriminatory acts.

Given that the statutory authorization for the challenges exercised in this case is clear, the remainder of our state-action analysis centers around the second part of the *Lugar* test, whether a private litigant in all fairness must be deemed a government actor in the use of peremptory challenges. Although we have recognized that this aspect of the analysis is often a factbound inquiry, our cases disclose certain principles of general application. Our precedents establish that, in determining whether a particular action or course of conduct is governmental in character, it is relevant to examine the following: the extent to which the actor relies on governmental assistance and benefits, see *Tulsa Professional Collection Services, Inc. v. Pope,* 485 U.S. 478 (1988); *Burton v. Wilmington Parking Authority,* 365 U.S. 715 (1961); whether the actor is performing a traditional governmental function, see *Terry v. Adams,* 345 U.S. 461 (1953); *Marsh v. Alabama,* 326 U.S. 501 (1946); cf. *San Francisco Arts & Athletics, Inc. v. United States Olympic Comm.,* 483 U.S. 522, 544–545 (1987); and whether the injury caused is aggravated in a unique way by the incidents of governmental authority, see *Shelley v. Kraemer,* 334 U.S. 1 (1948). Based on our application of these three principles to the circumstances here, we hold that the exercise of peremptory challenges by the defendant in the District Court was pursuant to a course of state action.

Although private use of state-sanctioned private remedies or procedures does not rise, by itself, to the level of state action, *Tulsa Professional,* 485 U.S., at 485, our cases have found state action when private parties make extensive use of state procedures with "the overt, significant assistance of state officials." *Id.*, at 486. It cannot be disputed that, without the overt, significant participation of the government, the peremptory challenge system, as well as the jury trial system of which it is a part, simply could not exist. . . .

[A] private party could not exercise its peremptory challenges absent the overt, significant assistance of the court. The government summons jurors, constrains their freedom of movement, and subjects them to public scrutiny and examination. The party who exercises a challenge invokes the formal authority of the court, which must discharge the prospective juror, thus effecting the "final and practical denial" of the excluded individual's opportunity to serve on the petit jury. *Virginia v. Rives,* 100 U.S. 313, 322 (1880). Without the direct and indispensable participation of the judge, who beyond all question is a state actor, the peremptory challenge system would serve no purpose. By enforcing a discriminatory peremptory challenge, the court "has not only made itself a party to the [biased act], but has elected to place its power, property and prestige behind the [alleged] discrimination." *Burton v. Wilmington Parking Authority,* 365 U.S., at 725. In so doing, the government has "create[d] the legal framework governing the [challenged] conduct," *National Collegiate Athletic Assn.,* 488 U.S., at 192, and in a significant way has involved itself with invidious discrimination.

In determining Leesville's state-actor status, we next consider whether the action in question involves the performance of a traditional function of the government. A traditional function of government is evident here. The peremptory challenge is used in selecting an entity that is a quintessential governmental body, having no attributes of a private actor. The jury exercises the power of the court and of the government that confers the court's jurisdiction. . . .

If a government confers on a private body the power to choose the government's employees or officials, the private body will be bound by the constitutional mandate of race neutrality. At least a plurality of the Court recognized this principle in *Terry v. Adams,* 345 U.S. 461 (1953). There we found state action in a scheme in which a private organization known as the Jaybird Democratic Association conducted whites-only elections to select candidates to run in the Democratic primary elections in Ford Bend County, Texas. The Jaybird candidate was certain to win the Democratic primary and the Democratic candidate was certain to win the general election. Justice Clark's concurring opinion drew from *Smith v. Allwright,* 321 U.S. 649, 664 (1944), the principle that "any 'part of the machinery for choosing officials' becomes subject to the Constitution's constraints." *Terry, supra,* 345 U.S., at 481. The concurring opinion concluded:

> "[W]hen a state structures its electoral apparatus in a form which devolves upon a political organization the uncontested choice of public officials, that organization itself, in whatever disguise, takes on those attributes of government which draw the Constitution's safeguards into play." 345 U.S., at 484.

The principle that the selection of state officials, other than through election by all qualified voters, may constitute state action applies with even greater force in the context of jury selection through the use of peremptory challenges. Though the motive of a peremptory challenge may be to protect a private interest, the objective of jury selection proceedings is to determine representation on a governmental body. Were it not for peremptory challenges, there would be no question that the entire process of determining who will serve on the jury constitutes state action. The fact that the government delegates some portion of this power to private litigants does not change the governmental character of the power exercised. The delegation of authority that in *Terry* occurred without the aid of legislation occurs here through explicit statutory authorization. . . .

Finally, we note that the injury caused by the discrimination is made more severe because the government permits it to occur within the courthouse itself. Few places are a more real expression of the constitutional authority of the government than a courtroom, where the law itself unfolds. Within the courtroom, the government invokes its laws to determine the rights of those who stand before it. In full view of the public, litigants press their cases, witnesses give testimony, juries render verdicts, and judges act with the utmost care to ensure that justice is done.

Race discrimination within the courtroom raises serious questions as to the fairness of the proceedings conducted there. Racial bias mars the integrity of the judicial system and prevents the idea of democratic government from becoming a reality. . . . To permit racial exclusion in this official forum compounds the racial insult inherent in judging a citizen by the color of his or her skin. . . .

[The dissenting opinions of Justices O'Connor and Scalia are omitted.]

Problem 14-A: Scholarships for Law Students

A public law school's career services office (hereinafter, "office") regularly notifies students of external scholarship opportunities. Recently, the office notified enrolled students via email about two scholarship opportunities. The first scholarship, sponsored by the Latina/o Lawyers Association (hereinafter, "LLA")—a private, non-profit organization—provides a $10,000 scholarship for "a second-year student with an outstanding academic record who is of Latina/o origin." The second scholarship, sponsored by the Minority Lawyers Association (hereinafter "MLA")—a private, non-profit organization—provides a $5,000 scholarship for "a second-year student who both contributes to the racial diversity of the law school and who plans to pursue a career in the field of civil rights." Interested students submit their applications to the office. The applications for the MLA scholarship are collected by the office and are forwarded in a single envelope to MLA to assess as it sees fit. The applications for LLA are—at LLA's request—screened by a small committee of faculty and ranked based on the applicant's academic record, and those rankings along with the applications themselves are forwarded to LLA.

Doris Williams, a white student who is enrolled at the law school, has hired you to bring a lawsuit on the ground that the scheme for awarding the LLA and MLA scholarships described above violates the Equal Protection Clause.

Does the Equal Protection Clause apply to the challenged conduct?

Problem 14-B: Judicial Haircuts, Part I

A state courthouse contains not only several courtrooms, but also a variety of small businesses that cater to courthouse employees and members of the public. The state leases space to ten different businesses, including restaurants, convenience stores, and other service providers. The state charges each business a fixed amount of rent and does not share in the profits of the lessees.

One such business is a hair salon that goes by the name "Judicial Haircuts." The salon's logo—which appears on both its door and on a large sign above the door—depicts the scales of justice. The walls inside the hair salon are covered with photos of virtually every judge who works in the state courthouse, depicting each judge sitting in one of the salon's chairs receiving a haircut (the salon has a policy of providing free haircuts to all of the judges). A sign next to the salon's entrance lists prices for its services. In relevant part, the sign reads as follows:

Basic Men's Haircut	**$20**
Basic Women's Haircut	**$40**

A female juror is told by one of her fellow male jurors that there is a great salon in the courthouse that gives haircuts for twenty dollars. She goes to the salon to get a haircut during a long break in the case she is sitting on. She asks about the "twenty dollar haircut" but she is told that her haircut will be forty dollars. The price difference for women, she is told, reflects the fact that women generally have longer hair and more complex styling requests.

The juror grudgingly pays the higher price, and subsequently hires a lawyer to represent her in suing the salon. The attorney files suit against Judicial Haircuts in a federal district court, contending that their pricing scheme constitutes sex discrimination in violation of the Equal Protection Clause.

Does the Equal Protection Clause apply to the challenged conduct? Assuming that it does—and based on the materials from Chapter 12—will the challenged conduct likely be deemed unconstitutional?

Notes and Questions

1. The *Edmonson* Court identifies three factors that are relevant in applying what it characterizes as the second step in the *Lugar* test, and finds that all three point in

the direction of finding state action. What if only one or two of the factors pointed in that direction?

2. In general, the Court's modern decisions are likely to find state action in one of three circumstances: when private actors are performing public functions traditionally performed by the state (*Edmonson*); when the government actively encourages or facilitates private conduct that would be unconstitutional if performed by the government directly (*Anderson*); or where the government entangles itself with a private actor, and the private actor engages in conduct that would be unconstitutional if performed directly by the government (*Burton*).

3. Do appearances seem to play a prominent role in deciding whether state action exists? To what extent do *Shelley*, *Burton*, and *Edmonson* take into account likely public perception of who is engaged in the discriminatory conduct in determining whether state action exists?

4. Does the underlying constitutional claim seem to influence the Court's findings? If you were to survey the Court's state action decisions, you would find that the Court has been most likely to find state action where race-based equal protection claims are made. Why would that be so?

Chapter 15

The Rise of the Discriminatory Purpose Requirement

There are three different ways in which a law can be said to be discriminating against a class of persons. First, a law can be discriminatory on its face, for example, a statute that prohibits African-Americans from serving on juries. There is no question that such laws are unconstitutional unless they pass heightened scrutiny, as cases such as *Strauder* have demonstrated. With the passage of time and knowledge of the constitutional ramifications of enacting such laws, this category of discriminatory laws is extremely rare today, at least for classifications such as race or sex for which heightened scrutiny applies.

Second, a law might be facially neutral, but administered in a discriminatory way. For example, a state might have a literacy test that in terms is applicable to all voters, but they might enforce it more strictly against African Americans. As *Yick Wo* makes clear, such laws, like facially discriminatory laws, are also unconstitutional unless they pass heightened scrutiny. The challenge of making out such a claim is that the discriminatory administration is typically covert and thus difficult to prove.

Third, a law might be facially neutral, and although there is no clear evidence of discriminatory administration, it is clear that the law has a discriminatory effect on a given class. For example, a public university might use an admissions test on which African Americans statistically perform worse than others. Such a claim is easier to prove than a claim based on discriminatory administration, for one need only look to the laws objectively verifiable impact on a given class. However, it is not entirely clear from the cases we have examined thus far whether discriminatory effects against a given class, standing alone, suffice to make out a constitutional claim. Three of the cases that we have examined so far—*Neal v. Delaware*, *Yick Wo*, and *Gomillion*—arguably provide support for establishing a claim in such circumstances, at least where the effects are extreme.

Part A explores the general question whether proof of discriminatory purpose is necessarily required when equal protection claims are brought, or instead if discriminatory effects, standing alone, can ever suffice to make out such a claim. Part B explores what, exactly, it means to be facially neutral in the equal protection context. Part C considers the question whether proof of discriminatory purpose is required when other provisions of the Reconstruction Amendments are at play, including the Due Process Clause, the Thirteenth and Fifteenth Amendments, and the enforcement provisions of all three Reconstruction Amendments.

A. Discriminatory Purpose and the Equal Protection Clause

Washington v. Davis

426 U.S. 229 (1976)

MR. JUSTICE WHITE delivered the opinion of the Court.

This case involves the validity of a qualifying test administered to applicants for positions as police officers in the District of Columbia Metropolitan Police Department. . . .

This action began on April 10, 1970, when two Negro police officers filed suit against the then Commissioner of the District of Columbia, the Chief of the District's Metropolitan Police Department, and the Commissioners of the United States Civil Service Commission. . . . The respondents Harley and Sellers were permitted to intervene, their amended complaint asserting that their applications to become officers in the Department had been rejected, and that the Department's recruiting procedures discriminated on the basis of race against black applicants by a series of practices including, but not limited to, a written personnel test which excluded a disproportionately high number of Negro applicants. These practices were asserted to violate respondents' rights "under the due process clause of the Fifth Amendment to the United States Constitution" . . . .

The validity of Test 21 was the sole issue before the court on the motions for summary judgment. The District Court noted that there was no claim of "an intentional discrimination or purposeful discriminatory acts" but only a claim that Test 21 bore no relationship to job performance and "has a highly discriminatory impact in screening out black candidates." . . . .

The Court of Appeals . . . announced that it would be guided by *Griggs v. Duke Power Co.*, 401 U.S. 424 (1971), a case involving the interpretation and application of Title VII of the Civil Rights Act of 1964, and held that the statutory standards elucidated in that case were to govern the due process question tendered in this one. The court went on to declare that lack of discriminatory intent in designing and administering Test 21 was irrelevant; the critical fact was rather that a far greater proportion of blacks—four times as many—failed the test than did whites. This disproportionate impact, standing alone and without regard to whether it indicated a discriminatory purpose, was held sufficient to establish a constitutional violation, absent proof by petitioners that the test was an adequate measure of job performance in addition to being an indicator of probable success in the training program, a burden which the court ruled petitioners had failed to discharge. . . .

As the Court of Appeals understood Title VII,[10] employees or applicants proceeding under it need not concern themselves with the employer's possibly discriminatory purpose but instead may focus solely on the racially differential impact of the challenged hiring or promotion practices. This is not the constitutional rule. We have never held that the constitutional standard for adjudicating claims of invidious racial discrimination is identical to the standards applicable under Title VII, and we decline to do so today.

The central purpose of the Equal Protection Clause of the Fourteenth Amendment is the prevention of official conduct discriminating on the basis of race. It is also true that the Due Process Clause of the Fifth Amendment contains an equal protection component prohibiting the United States from invidiously discriminating between individuals or groups. *Bolling v. Sharpe*, 347 U.S. 497 (1954). But our cases have not embraced the proposition that a law or other official act, without regard to whether it reflects a racially discriminatory purpose, is unconstitutional *solely* because it has a racially disproportionate impact.

Almost 100 years ago, *Strauder v. West Virginia*, 100 U.S. 303 (1880), established that the exclusion of Negroes from grand and petit juries in criminal proceedings violated the Equal Protection Clause, but the fact that a particular jury or a series of juries does not statistically reflect the racial composition of the community does not in itself make out an invidious discrimination forbidden by the Clause. "A purpose to discriminate must be present which may be proven by systematic exclusion of eligible jurymen of the proscribed race or by unequal application of the law to such an extent as to show intentional discrimination." *Akins v. Texas*, 325 U.S. 398, 403–404 (1945). A defendant in a criminal case is entitled "to require that the State not deliberately and systematically deny to members of his race the right to participate as jurors in the administration of justice." *Alexander v. Louisiana*, 405 U.S. 625, 628-629.

The rule is the same in other contexts. *Wright v. Rockefeller*, 376 U.S. 52 (1964), upheld a New York congressional apportionment statute against claims that district lines had been racially gerrymandered. The challenged districts were made up predominantly of whites or of minority races, and their boundaries were irregularly drawn. The challengers did not prevail because they failed to prove that the New York Legislature "was either motivated by racial considerations or in fact drew the districts on racial lines"; the plaintiffs had not shown that the statute "was the product of a state contrivance to segregate on the basis of race or place of origin." The dissenters were in agreement that the issue was whether the "boundaries . . . were purposefully drawn on racial lines."

The school desegregation cases have also adhered to the basic equal protection principle that the invidious quality of a law claimed to be racially discriminatory

10. Although Title VII standards have dominated this case, the statute was not applicable to federal employees when the complaint was filed. . . .

must ultimately be traced to a racially discriminatory purpose. That there are both predominantly black and predominantly white schools in a community is not alone violative of the Equal Protection Clause. The essential element of *de jure* segregation is "a current condition of segregation resulting from intentional state action. *Keyes v. School Dist. No. 1*, 413 U.S. 189, 205 (1973). The differentiating factor between *de jure* segregation and so-called *de facto* segregation . . . is *purpose* or *intent* to segregate." *Id.*, at 208 . . . .

This is not to say that the necessary discriminatory racial purpose must be express or appear on the face of the statute, or that a law's disproportionate impact is irrelevant in cases involving Constitution-based claims of racial discrimination. A statute, otherwise neutral on its face, must not be applied so as invidiously to discriminate on the basis of race. *Yick Wo v. Hopkins*, 118 U.S. 356 (1886). It is also clear from the cases dealing with racial discrimination in the selection of juries that the systematic exclusion of Negroes is itself such an "unequal application of the law . . . as to show intentional discrimination." *Akins v. Texas*, *supra*, 325 U.S., at 404. A prima facie case of discriminatory purpose may be proved as well by the absence of Negroes on a particular jury combined with the failure of the jury commissioners to be informed of eligible Negro jurors in a community, *Hill v. Texas*, 316 U.S. 400, 404 (1942), or with racially non-neutral selection procedures, *Alexander v. Louisiana*, *supra*. With a prima facie case made out, "the burden of proof shifts to the State to rebut the presumption of unconstitutional action by showing that permissible racially neutral selection criteria and procedures have produced the monochromatic result." *Alexander*, *supra*, 405 U.S., at 632.

Necessarily, an invidious discriminatory purpose may often be inferred from the totality of the relevant facts, including the fact, if it is true, that the law bears more heavily on one race than another. It is also not infrequently true that the discriminatory impact—in the jury cases for example, the total or seriously disproportionate exclusion of Negroes from jury venires—may for all practical purposes demonstrate unconstitutionality because in various circumstances the discrimination is very difficult to explain on nonracial grounds. Nevertheless, we have not held that a law, neutral on its face and serving ends otherwise within the power of government to pursue, is invalid under the Equal Protection Clause simply because it may affect a greater proportion of one race than of another. Disproportionate impact is not irrelevant, but it is not the sole touchstone of an invidious racial discrimination forbidden by the Constitution. Standing alone, it does not trigger the rule, *McLaughlin v. Florida*, 379 U.S. 184 (1964), that racial classifications are to be subjected to the strictest scrutiny and are justifiable only by the weightiest of considerations. . . .

As an initial matter, we have difficulty understanding how a law establishing a racially neutral qualification for employment is nevertheless racially discriminatory and denies "any person . . . equal protection of the laws" simply because a greater proportion of Negroes fail to qualify than members of other racial or ethnic groups. Had respondents, along with all others who had failed Test 21, whether white or black, brought an action claiming that the test denied each of them equal protection of the laws as compared with those who had passed with high enough scores to qualify them as police recruits, it is most unlikely that their challenge would have been sustained. Test 21, which is administered generally to prospective Government employees, concededly seeks to ascertain whether those who take it have acquired a particular level of verbal skill; and it is untenable that the Constitution prevents the Government from seeking modestly to upgrade the communicative abilities of its employees rather than to be satisfied with some lower level of competence, particularly where the job requires special ability to communicate orally and in writing. Respondents, as Negroes, could no more successfully claim that the test denied them equal protection than could white applicants who also failed. The conclusion would not be different in the face of proof that more Negroes than whites had been disqualified by Test 21. That other Negroes also failed to score well would, alone, not demonstrate that respondents individually were being denied equal protection of the laws by the application of an otherwise valid qualifying test being administered to prospective police recruits.

Nor on the facts of the case before us would the disproportionate impact of Test 21 warrant the conclusion that it is a purposeful device to discriminate against Negroes and hence an infringement of the constitutional rights of respondents as well as other black applicants. As we have said, the test is neutral on its face and rationally may be said to serve a purpose the Government is constitutionally empowered to pursue. Even agreeing with the District Court that the differential racial effect of Test 21 called for further inquiry, we think the District Court correctly held that the affirmative efforts of the Metropolitan Police Department to recruit black officers, the changing racial composition of the recruit classes and of the force in general, and the relationship of the test to the training program negated any inference that the Department discriminated on the basis of race or that "a police officer qualifies on the color of his skin rather than ability." 348 F.Supp., at 18.

Under Title VII, Congress provided that when hiring and promotion practices disqualifying substantially disproportionate numbers of blacks are challenged, discriminatory purpose need not be proved, and that it is an insufficient response to demonstrate some rational basis for the challenged practices. It is necessary, in addition, that they be "validated" in terms of job performance in any one of several ways, perhaps by ascertaining the minimum skill, ability, or potential necessary for the position at issue and determining whether the qualifying tests are appropriate for the selection of qualified applicants for the job in question. However this process proceeds, it involves a more probing judicial review of, and less deference to, the seemingly reasonable acts of administrators and executives than is appropriate under the Constitution where special racial impact, without discriminatory purpose, is claimed. We are not disposed to adopt this more rigorous standard for the purposes of applying the Fifth and the Fourteenth Amendments in cases such as this.

A rule that a statute designed to serve neutral ends is nevertheless invalid, absent compelling justification, if in practice it benefits or burdens one race more than another would be far-reaching and would raise serious questions about, and perhaps invalidate, a whole range of tax, welfare, public service, regulatory, and licensing statutes that may be more burdensome to the poor and to the average black than to the more affluent white.

Given that rule, such consequences would perhaps be likely to follow. However, in our view, extension of the rule beyond those areas where it is already applicable by reason of statute, such as in the field of public employment, should await legislative prescription....

Mr. Justice Stevens, concurring.

The requirement of purposeful discrimination is a common thread running through the cases summarized in Part II. These cases include criminal convictions which were set aside because blacks were excluded from the grand jury, a reapportionment case in which political boundaries were obviously influenced to some extent by racial considerations, a school desegregation case, and a case involving the unequal administration of an ordinance purporting to prohibit the operation of laundries in frame buildings. Although it may be proper to use the same language to describe the constitutional claim in each of these contexts, the burden of proving a prima facie case may well involve differing evidentiary considerations. The extent of deference that one pays to the trial court's determination of the factual issue, and indeed, the extent to which one characterizes the intent issue as a question of fact or a question of law, will vary in different contexts.

Frequently the most probative evidence of intent will be objective evidence of what actually happened rather than evidence describing the subjective state of mind of the actor. For normally the actor is presumed to have intended the natural consequences of his deeds. This is particularly true in the case of governmental action which is frequently the product of compromise, of collective decisionmaking, and of mixed motivation. It is unrealistic, on the one hand, to require the victim of alleged discrimination to uncover the actual subjective intent of the decisionmaker or, conversely, to invalidate otherwise legitimate action simply because an improper motive affected the deliberation of a participant in the decisional process. A law conscripting clerics should not be invalidated because an atheist voted for it.

My point in making this observation is to suggest that the line between discriminatory purpose and discriminatory impact is not nearly as bright, and perhaps not quite as critical, as the reader of the Court's opinion might assume. I agree, of course, that a constitutional issue does not arise every time some disproportionate impact is shown. On the other hand, when the disproportion is as dramatic as in *Gomillion v. Lightfoot*, 364 U.S. 339 or *Yick Wo v. Hopkins*, 118 U.S. 356 (1886), it really does not matter whether the standard is phrased in terms of purpose or effect. Therefore, although I accept the statement of the general rule in the Court's opinion, I am not yet prepared to indicate how that standard should be applied in the many cases which have formulated the governing standard in different language....

[The dissenting opinion of Justice Brennan is omitted.]

Notes and Questions

1. How does the *Davis* Court characterize the Court's prior decision in *Yick Wo*? Is that the only way to characterize its holding?

2. The *Davis* Court holds that discriminatory effects, standing alone, do not suffice to make out a constitutional claim. What are its rationales for so holding? Does the *Davis* Court deem discriminatory effects to be irrelevant? If not, what role do they play?

3. In his separate opinion, Justice Stevens writes that in cases with extreme discriminatory effects—such as *Yick Wo* and *Gomillion*—that "it really does not matter whether the standard is phrased in terms of purpose or effect." What does he mean by that?

Village of Arlington Heights v. Metropolitan Housing Development Corp.

429 U.S. 252 (1977)

Mr. Justice Powell delivered the opinion of the Court.

In 1971 respondent Metropolitan Housing Development Corporation (MHDC) applied to petitioner, the Village of Arlington Heights, Ill., for the rezoning of a 15-acre parcel from single-family to multiple-family classification. Using federal financial assistance, MHDC planned to build 190 clustered townhouse units for low- and moderate-income tenants. The Village denied the rezoning request. MHDC, joined by other plaintiffs who are also respondents here, brought suit in the United States District Court for the Northern District of Illinois. They alleged that the denial was racially discriminatory and that it violated, *inter alia*, the Fourteenth Amendment.... Following a bench trial, the District Court entered judgment for the Village, and respondents appealed. The Court of Appeals for the Seventh Circuit reversed, finding that the "ultimate effect" of the denial was racially discriminatory, and that the refusal to rezone therefore violated the Fourteenth Amendment....

Our decision last Term in *Washington v. Davis*, 426 U.S. 229 (1976), made it clear that official action will not be held unconstitutional solely because it results in a racially disproportionate impact. "Disproportionate impact is not irrelevant, but it is not the sole touchstone of an invidious racial discrimination." Proof of racially discriminatory intent or purpose is required to show a violation of the Equal Protection Clause....

Davis does not require a plaintiff to prove that the challenged action rested solely on racially discriminatory purposes. Rarely can it be said that a legislature or administrative body operating under a broad mandate made a decision motivated solely by a single concern, or even that a particular purpose was the "dominant" or "primary" one. In fact, it is because legislators and administrators are properly concerned with balancing numerous competing considerations that courts refrain from reviewing the merits of their decisions, absent a showing of arbitrariness or irrationality. But racial discrimination is not just another competing consideration. When there is a proof that a discriminatory purpose has been a motivating factor in the decision, this judicial deference is no longer justified.

Determining whether invidious discriminatory purpose was a motivating factor demands a sensitive inquiry into such circumstantial and direct evidence of intent as may be available. The impact of the official action—whether it "bears more heavily on one race than another," *Washington v. Davis*, *supra*, 426 U.S., at 242—may provide an important starting point. Sometimes a clear pattern, unexplainable on grounds other than race, emerges from the effect of the state action even when the governing legislation appears neutral on its face. *Yick Wo v. Hopkins*, 118 U.S. 356 (1886); *Guinn v. United States*, 238 U.S. 347 (1915); *Lane v. Wilson*, 307 U.S. 268 (1939); *Gomillion v. Lightfoot*, 364 U.S. 339 (1960). The evidentiary inquiry is then relatively easy.[13] But such cases are rare. Absent a pattern as stark as that in *Gomillion* or *Yick Wo*, impact alone is not determinative, and the Court must look to other evidence.

The historical background of the decision is one evidentiary source, particularly if it reveals a series of official actions taken for invidious purposes. The specific sequence of events leading up the challenged decision also may shed some light on the decisionmaker's purposes. For example, if the property involved here always had been zoned R-5 but suddenly was changed to R-3 when the town learned of MHDC's plans to erect integrated housing, we would have a far different case. Departures from the normal procedural sequence also might afford evidence that improper purposes are playing a role. Substantive departures too may be relevant, particularly if the factors usually considered important by the decisionmaker strongly favor a decision contrary to the one reached.

The legislative or administrative history may be highly relevant, especially where there are contemporary statements by members of the decisionmaking body, minutes of its meetings, or reports. In some extraordinary instances the members might be called to the stand at trial to testify concerning the purpose of the official action, although even then such testimony frequently will be barred by privilege.

The foregoing summary identifies, without purporting to be exhaustive, subjects of proper inquiry in determining whether racially discriminatory intent existed....

[The Court reviews the factual record and determines that there is no proof of a racially discriminatory intent.]

In sum, the evidence does not warrant overturning the concurrent findings of both courts below. Respondents simply failed to carry their burden of proving that

---

13. Several of our jury-selection cases fall into this category. Because of the nature of the jury-selection task, however, we have permitted a finding of constitutional violation even when the statistical pattern does not approach the extremes of *Yick Wo* or *Gomillion*.

discriminatory purpose was a motivating factor in the Village's decision.[21] This conclusion ends the constitutional inquiry. The court of Appeals' further finding that the Village's decision carried a discriminatory "ultimate effect" is without independent constitutional significance. . . .

[The opinion of Justice Marshall, concurring in part and dissenting in part, and the dissenting opinion of Justice White, are omitted.]

Notes and Questions

1. According to *Arlington Heights*, one can make out a race-based equal protection claim even when race was not the sole or dominant motivation for the challenged action; it is enough that race is a motivating factor. Does proof that it was a motivating factor result in a victory for the challenger, or does *Arlington Heights* provide a way for the government to nonetheless defend such a law?

2. Does *Arlington Heights* acknowledge *any* situations in which proof of discriminatory effects, standing alone, is sufficient to make out a claim? If so, do those effects *always* have to be extreme?

3. To the extent that proof of discriminatory intent is required, how does the *Arlington Heights* Court suggest a litigant prove that intent? How easy will it likely be to do so in practice?

Personnel Administrator of Massachusetts v. Feeney

442 U.S. 256 (1979)

MR. JUSTICE STEWART delivered the opinion of the Court.

This case presents a challenge to the constitutionality of the Massachusetts veterans' preference statute, Mass. Gen. Laws Ann., ch. 31, § 23, on the ground that it discriminates against women in violation of the Equal Protection Clause of the Fourteenth Amendment. Under ch. 31, § 23, all veterans who qualify for state civil service positions must be considered for appointment ahead of any qualifying nonveterans. The preference operates overwhelmingly to the advantage of males.

The appellee Helen B. Feeney is not a veteran. She brought this action . . . alleging that the absolute preference formula established in ch. 31, § 23, inevitably operates to exclude women from consideration for the best Massachusetts civil service jobs and thus unconstitutionally denies them the equal protection of the laws. . . .

---

21. Proof that the decision by the Village was motivated in part by a racially discriminatory purpose would not necessarily have required invalidation of the challenged decision. Such proof would, however, have shifted to the Village the burden of establishing that the same decision would have resulted even had the impermissible purpose not been considered. If this were established, the complaining party in a case of this kind no longer fairly could attribute the injury complained of to improper consideration of a discriminatory purpose. In such circumstances, there would be no justification for judicial interference with the challenged decision. But in this case respondents failed to make the required threshold showing.

The appellee has lived in Dracut, Mass., most of her life. She entered the work force in 1948, and for the next 14 years worked at a variety of jobs in the private sector. She first entered the state civil service system in 1963, having competed successfully for a position as Senior Clerk Stenographer in the Massachusetts Civil Defense Agency. There she worked for four years. In 1967, she was promoted to the position of Federal Funds and Personnel Coordinator in the same agency. The agency, and with it her job, was eliminated in 1975.

During her 12-year tenure as a public employee, Ms. Feeney took and passed a number of open competitive civil service examinations. On several she did quite well, receiving in 1971 the second highest score on an examination for a job with the Board of Dental Examiners, and in 1973 the third highest on a test for an Administrative Assistant position with a mental health center. Her high scores, however, did not win her a place on the certified eligible list. Because of the veterans' preference, she was ranked sixth behind five male veterans on the Dental Examiner list. She was not certified, and a lower scoring veteran was eventually appointed. On the 1973 examination, she was placed in a position on the list behind 12 male veterans, 11 of whom had lower scores. Following the other examinations that she took, her name was similarly ranked below those of veterans who had achieved passing grades.

Ms. Feeney's interest in securing a better job in state government did not wane. Having been consistently eclipsed by veterans, however, she eventually concluded that further competition for civil service positions of interest to veterans would be futile. In 1975, shortly after her civil defense job was abolished, she commenced this litigation. . . .

When this litigation was commenced . . . over 98% of the veterans in Massachusetts were male; only 1.8% were female. And over one-quarter of the Massachusetts population were veterans. During the decade between 1963 and 1973 when the appellee was actively participating in the State's merit selection system, 47,005 new permanent appointments were made in the classified official service. Forty-three percent of those hired were women, and 57% were men. Of the women appointed, 1.8% were veterans, while 54% of the men had veteran status. A large unspecified percentage of the female appointees were serving in lower paying positions for which males traditionally had not applied. On each of 50 sample eligible lists that are part of the record in this case, one or more women who would have been certified as eligible for appointment on the basis of test results were displaced by veterans whose test scores were lower.

At the outset of this litigation appellants conceded that for "many of the permanent positions for which males and females have competed" the veterans' preference has "resulted in a substantially greater proportion of female eligibles than male eligibles" not being certified for consideration. The impact of the veterans' preference law upon the public employment opportunities of women has thus been severe. This impact lies at the heart of the appellee's federal constitutional claim. . . .

The cases of *Washington v. Davis, supra,* and *Arlington Heights v. Metropolitan Housing Dev. Corp., supra,* recognize that when a neutral law has a disparate impact upon a group that has historically been the victim of discrimination, an unconstitutional purpose may still be at work. But those cases signaled no departure from the settled rule that the Fourteenth Amendment guarantees equal laws, not equal results. *Davis* upheld a job-related employment test that white people passed in proportionately greater numbers than Negroes, for there had been no showing that racial discrimination entered into the establishment or formulation of the test. *Arlington Heights* upheld a zoning board decision that tended to perpetuate racially segregated housing patterns, since, apart from its effect, the board's decision was shown to be nothing more than an application of a constitutionally neutral zoning policy. Those principles apply with equal force to a case involving alleged gender discrimination.

When a statute gender-neutral on its face is challenged on the ground that its effects upon women are disproportionably adverse, a twofold inquiry is thus appropriate. The first question is whether the statutory classification is indeed neutral in the sense that it is not gender-based. If the classification itself, covert of overt, is not based upon gender, the second question is whether the adverse effect reflects invidious gender-based discrimination. See *Arlington Heights v. Metropolitan Housing Dev. Corp., supra.* In this second inquiry, impact provides an "important starting point," 429 U.S., at 266, but purposeful discrimination is "the condition that offends the Constitution." *Swann v. Charlotte-Mecklenburg Board of Education,* 402 U.S. 1, 16 . . . .

The question whether ch. 31, § 23, establishes a classification that is overtly or covertly based upon gender must first be considered. The appellee has conceded that ch. 31, § 23, is neutral on its face. She has also acknowledged that state hiring preferences for veterans are not *per se* invalid, for she has limited her challenge to the absolute lifetime preference that Massachusetts provides to veterans. The District Court made two central findings that are relevant here: first, that ch. 31, § 23, serves legitimate and worthy purposes; second, that the absolute preference was not established for the purpose of discriminating against women. The appellee has thus acknowledged and the District Court has thus found that the distinction between veterans and nonveterans drawn by ch. 31, § 23, is not a pretext for gender discrimination. The appellee's concession and the District Court's finding are clearly correct.

If the impact of this statute could not be plausibly explained on a neutral ground, impact itself would signal that the real classification made by the law was in fact not neutral. See *Washington v. Davis,* 426 U.S., at 242; *Arlington Heights v. Metropolitan Housing Dev. Corp., supra,* 429 U.S., at 266. But there can be but one answer to the question whether this veteran preference excludes significant numbers of women from preferred state jobs because they are women or because they are nonveterans. Apart from the facts that the definition of "veterans" in the statute has always been neutral as to gender and that Massachusetts has consistently defined veteran status in a way that has been inclusive of women who have served in the military, this is not a law that can plausibly be explained only as a gender-based classification. Indeed, it is not a law that can rationally be explained on that ground. Veteran status is not uniquely male. Although few women benefit from the preference the nonveteran class is not substantially all female. To the contrary, significant numbers of nonveterans are men, and all nonveterans—male as well as female—are placed at a disadvantage. Too many men are affected by ch. 31, § 23, to permit the inference that the statute is but a pretext for preferring men over women.

Moreover, as the District Court implicitly found, the purposes of the statute provide the surest explanation for its impact. Just as there are cases in which impact alone can unmask an invidious classification, cf. *Yick Wo v. Hopkins,* 118 U.S. 356, there are others, in which—notwithstanding impact—the legitimate noninvidious purposes of a law cannot be missed. This is one. The distinction made by ch. 31, § 23, is, as it seems to be, quite simply between veterans and nonveterans, not between men and women.

The dispositive question, then, is whether the appellee has shown that a gender-based discriminatory purpose has, at least in some measure, shaped the Massachusetts veterans' preference legislation. . . .

The appellee's ultimate argument rests upon the presumption, common to the criminal and civil law, that a person intends the natural and foreseeable consequences of his voluntary actions. . . .

The decision to grant a preference to veterans was of course "intentional." So, necessarily, did an adverse impact upon nonveterans follow from that decision. And it cannot seriously be argued that the Legislature of Massachusetts could have been unaware that most veterans are men. It would thus be disingenuous to say that the adverse consequences of this legislation for women were unintended, in the sense that they were not volitional or in the sense that they were not foreseeable.

"Discriminatory purpose," however, implies more than intent as volition or intent as awareness of consequences. It implies that the decisionmaker, in this case a state legislature, selected or reaffirmed a particular course of action at least in part "because of," not merely "in spite of," its adverse effects upon an identifiable group.[25] Yet, nothing in the record demonstrates that this preference for veterans was originally devised or subsequently re-enacted because it would accomplish the collateral goal of keeping women in a stereotypic and predefined place in the Massachusetts Civil Service. . . .

---

25. This is not to say that the inevitability or foreseeability of consequences of a neutral rule has no bearing upon the existence of discriminatory intent. Certainly, when the adverse consequences of a law upon an identifiable group are as inevitable as the gender-based consequences of ch. 31, § 23, a strong inference that the adverse effects were desired can reasonably be drawn. But in this inquiry-made as it is under the Constitution-an inference is a working tool, not a synonym for proof. When, as here, the impact is essentially an unavoidable consequence of a legislative policy that has in itself always been deemed to be legitimate, and when, as here, the statutory history and all of the available evidence affirmatively demonstrate the opposite, the inference simply fails to ripen into proof.

MR. JUSTICE STEVENS, with whom MR. JUSTICE WHITE joins, concurring.

While I concur in the Court's opinion, I confess that I am not at all sure that there is any difference between the two questions posed. If a classification is not overtly based on gender, I am inclined to believe the question whether it is covertly gender based is the same as the question whether its adverse effects reflect invidious gender-based discrimination. However the question is phrased, for me the answer is largely provided by the fact that the number of males disadvantaged by Massachusetts' veterans' preference (1,867,000) is sufficiently large—and sufficiently close to the number of disadvantaged females (2,954,000)—to refute the claim that the rule was intended to benefit males as a class over females as a class.

[The dissenting opinion of Justice Marshall is omitted.]

Notes and Questions

1. The *Feeney* Court holds that awareness of the discriminatory consequences of a given action, standing alone, does not suffice to prove discriminatory purpose. Rather, there must be proof that the action was undertaken *because of*, not in spite of, its adverse effects on a given class. Why does it so hold?

2. What distinguishes a case like this from cases like *Yick Wo* and *Gomillion*? Does this case not involve an extreme discriminatory effect against women? Or is it enough that, despite the percentages, some quantity of women do still benefit from this preference, and a large number of men (the many who are not veterans) are also negatively impacted by the law?

3. Consider a variant of the facts of *Yick Wo*. Suppose that after a fire at a Chinese-owned laundry facility located in a wooden building, the San Francisco Board of Supervisors adopted a simple ordinance that, without exception, banned laundries in wooden buildings, based on a finding that such buildings were more prone to fires than brick or stone ones. Suppose further that, due to differences in wealth and the cost of different types of building materials, nearly all Chinese-owned laundries in the city were located in wooden buildings while nearly all non-Chinese laundries were located in brick or stone buildings. Would such a law violate the Equal Protection Clause? How, if at all, would your answer be impacted by the fact that the ownership statistics were brought to the attention of the Board of Supervisors prior to their vote on the ordinance?

Hunter v. Underwood

471 U.S. 222 (1985)

JUSTICE REHNQUIST delivered the opinion of the Court.

We are required in this case to decide the constitutionality of Art. VIII, § 182, of the Alabama Constitution of 1901, which provides for the disenfranchisement of persons convicted of, among other offenses, "any crime . . . involving moral turpitude."

Appellees Carmen Edwards, a black, and Victor Underwood, a white, have been blocked from the voter rolls pursuant to § 182 by the Boards of Registrars for Montgomery and Jefferson Counties, respectively, because they each have been convicted of presenting a worthless check. In determining that the misdemeanor of presenting a worthless check is a crime involving moral turpitude, the Registrars relied on opinions of the Alabama Attorney General.

Edwards and Underwood sued the Montgomery and Jefferson Boards of Registrars. . . . The case proceeded to trial on two causes of action, including a claim that the misdemeanors encompassed within § 182 were intentionally adopted to disenfranchise blacks on account of their race and that their inclusion in § 182 has had the intended effect. For the purposes of this claim, the District Court treated appellee Edwards as the representative of a subclass of black members of the plaintiff class. . . .

Presented with a neutral state law that produces disproportionate effects along racial lines, the Court of Appeals was correct in applying the approach of *Arlington Heights* to determine whether the law violates the Equal Protection Clause of the Fourteenth Amendment. . . .

Once racial discrimination is shown to have been a "substantial" or "motivating" factor behind enactment of the law, the burden shifts to the law's defenders to demonstrate that the law would have been enacted without this factor. See *Mt. Healthy*, 429 U.S., at 287.

Proving the motivation behind official action is often a problematic undertaking. See *Rogers v. Lodge*, 458 U.S. 613 (1982). When we move from an examination of a board of county commissioners such as was involved in *Rogers* to a body the size of the Alabama Constitutional Convention of 1901, the difficulties in determining the actual motivations of the various legislators that produced a given decision increase. With respect to Congress, the Court said in *United States v. O'Brien*, 391 U.S. 367, 383–384 (1968):

> "Inquiries into congressional motives or purposes are a hazardous matter. When the issue is simply the interpretation of legislation, the Court will look to statements by legislators for guidance as to the purpose of the legislature, because the benefit to sound decision-making in this circumstance is thought sufficient to risk the possibility of misreading Congress' purpose. It is entirely a different matter when we are asked to void a statute that is, under well-settled criteria, constitutional on its face, on the basis of what fewer than a handful of Congressmen said about it. What motivates one legislator to make a speech about a statute is not necessarily what motivates scores of others to enact it, and the stakes are sufficiently high for us to eschew guesswork."

But the sort of difficulties of which the Court spoke in *O'Brien* do not obtain in this case. Although understandably no "eyewitnesses" to the 1901 proceedings testified, testimony and opinions of historians were offered and received without objection.

These showed that the Alabama Constitutional Convention of 1901 was part of a movement that swept the post-Reconstruction South to disenfranchise blacks. The delegates to the all-white convention were not secretive about their purpose. . . .

In their brief to this Court, appellants maintain on the basis of their expert's testimony that the real purpose behind § 182 was to disenfranchise poor whites as well as blacks. . . .

Even were we to accept this explanation as correct, it hardly saves § 182 from invalidity. The explanation concedes both that discrimination against blacks, as well as against poor whites, was a motivating factor for the provision and that § 182 certainly would not have been adopted by the convention or ratified by the electorate in the absence of the racially discriminatory motivation. . . .

Whether or not intentional disenfranchisement of poor whites would qualify as a "permissible motive" . . . it is clear that where both impermissible racial motivation and racially discriminatory impact are demonstrated, *Arlington Heights* and *Mt. Healthy* supply the proper analysis. . . .

At oral argument in this Court, the appellants' counsel suggested that, regardless of the original purpose of § 182, events occurring in the succeeding 80 years had legitimated the provision. Some of the more blatantly discriminatory selections, such as assault and battery on the wife and miscegenation, have been struck down by the courts, and appellants contend that the remaining crimes—felonies and moral turpitude misdemeanors—are acceptable bases for denying the franchise. Without deciding whether § 182 would be valid if enacted today without any impermissible motivation, we simply observe that its original enactment was motivated by a desire to discriminate against blacks on account of race and the section continues to this day to have that effect. As such, it violates equal protection under *Arlington Heights* . . . .

Abbott v. Perez

138 S.Ct. 2305 (2018)

Justice Alito delivered the opinion of the Court.

Before us for review are orders of a three-judge court in the Western District of Texas effectively directing the State not to conduct this year's elections using districting plans that the court itself adopted some years earlier. The court developed those plans for use in the 2012 elections pursuant to our directions in *Perry v. Perez*, 565 U.S. 388 (2012) (*per curiam*). We instructed the three-judge court to start with the plans adopted by the Texas Legislature in 2011 but to make adjustments as required by the Constitution and the Voting Rights Act. After those plans were used in 2012, the Texas Legislature enacted them (with only minor modifications) in 2013, and the plans were used again in both 2014 and 2016.

Last year, however, the three-judge court reversed its prior analysis and held that some of the districts in those plans are unlawful. After reviewing the repealed 2011 plans, which had never been used, the court found that they were tainted by discriminatory intent and that the 2013 Legislature had not "cured" that "taint."

We now hold that the three-judge court committed a fundamental legal error. It was the challengers' burden to show that the 2013 Legislature acted with discriminatory intent when it enacted plans that the court itself had produced. The 2013 Legislature was not obligated to show that it had "cured" the unlawful intent that the court attributed to the 2011 Legislature. Thus, the essential pillar of the three-judge court's reasoning was critically flawed. . . .

Whenever a challenger claims that a state law was enacted with discriminatory intent, the burden of proof lies with the challenger, not the State. . . .

The allocation of the burden of proof and the presumption of legislative good faith are not changed by a finding of past discrimination. "[P]ast discrimination cannot, in the manner of original sin, condemn governmental action that is not itself unlawful." *Mobile*, 446 U.S., at 74 (plurality opinion). The "ultimate question remains whether a discriminatory intent has been proved in a given case." *Ibid.* The "historical background" of a legislative enactment is "one evidentiary source" relevant to the question of intent. *Arlington Heights v. Metropolitan Housing Development Corp.*, 429 U.S. 252, 267 (1977). But we have never suggested that past discrimination flips the evidentiary burden on its head.

Neither the District Court nor appellees have pointed to any authority that would justify shifting the burden. The appellees rely primarily on *Hunter v. Underwood*, 471 U.S. 222 (1985), but that case addressed a very different situation. *Hunter* involved an equal protection challenge to an article of the Alabama Constitution adopted in 1901 at a constitutional convention avowedly dedicated to the establishment of white supremacy. *Id.*, at 228–230. The article disenfranchised anyone convicted of any crime on a long list that included many minor offenses. *Id.*, at 226–227. The court below found that the article had been adopted with discriminatory intent, and this Court accepted that conclusion. *Id.*, at 229. The article was never repealed, but over the years, the list of disqualifying offenses had been pruned, and the State argued that what remained was facially constitutional. *Id.*, at 232–233. This Court rejected that argument because the amendments did not alter the intent with which the article, including the parts that remained, had been adopted. *Id.*, at 233. But the Court specifically declined to address the question whether the then-existing version would have been valid if "[re]enacted today." *Ibid.*

In these cases, we do not confront a situation like the one in *Hunter*. Nor is this a case in which a law originally enacted with discriminatory intent is later reenacted by a different legislature. The 2013 Texas Legislature did not reenact the plan previously passed by its 2011 predecessor. Nor did it use criteria that arguably carried forward the effects of any discriminatory intent on the part of the 2011 Legislature. Instead, it enacted, with only very small changes, plans that had been developed by the Texas court pursuant to instructions from this Court "not to incorporate . . . any legal defects." *Perry*, 565 U.S., at 394.

Under these circumstances, there can be no doubt about what matters: It is the intent of the 2013 Legislature. And it was the plaintiffs' burden to overcome the presumption of legislative good faith and show that the 2013 Legislature acted with invidious intent....

In holding that the District Court disregarded the presumption of legislative good faith and improperly reversed the burden of proof, we do not suggest either that the intent of the 2011 Legislature is irrelevant or that the plans enacted in 2013 are unassailable because they were previously adopted on an interim basis by the Texas court. Rather, both the intent of the 2011 Legislature and the court's adoption of the interim plans are relevant to the extent that they naturally give rise to—or tend to refute—inferences regarding the intent of the 2013 Legislature. They must be weighed together with any other direct and circumstantial evidence of that Legislature's intent. But when all the relevant evidence in the record is taken into account, it is plainly insufficient to prove that the 2013 Legislature acted in bad faith and engaged in intentional discrimination. There is thus no need for any further prolongation of this already protracted litigation.

The only direct evidence brought to our attention suggests that the 2013 Legislature's intent was legitimate. It wanted to bring the litigation about the State's districting plans to an end as expeditiously as possible. The attorney general advised the Legislature that the best way to do this was to adopt the interim, court-issued plans. The sponsor of the 2013 plans voiced the same objective, and the Legislature then adopted the court-approved plans.

On its face, this explanation of the Legislature's intent is entirely reasonable and certainly legitimate. The Legislature had reason to know that any new plans it devised were likely to be attacked by one group of plaintiffs or another. (The plaintiffs' conflicting positions with regard to some of the districts in the plans now before us bear this out.) Litigating districting cases is expensive and time consuming, and until the districts to be used in the next election are firmly established, a degree of uncertainty clouds the electoral process. Wishing to minimize these effects is understandable and proper....

Not only does the direct evidence suggest that the 2013 Legislature lacked discriminatory intent, but the circumstantial evidence points overwhelmingly to the same conclusion. Consider the situation when the Legislature adopted the court-approved interim plans. First, the Texas court had adopted those plans, and no one would claim that the court acted with invidious intent when it did so. Second, the Texas court approved those plans only after reviewing them and modifying them as required to comply with our instructions. Not one of the judges on that court expressed the view that the plans were unlawful. Third, we had directed the Texas court to make changes in response to any claims under the Equal Protection Clause and § 2 of the Voting Rights Act if those claims were merely likely to prevail. *Perry*, 565 U.S., at 394. And the Texas court was told to accommodate any claim under § 5 of the VRA unless it was "insubstantial." *Id.*, at 395. Fourth, the Texas court had made a careful analysis of all the claims, had provided a detailed examination of individual districts, and had modified many districts. Its work was anything but slapdash. All these facts gave the Legislature good reason to believe that the court-approved interim plans were legally sound.

Is there any evidence from which a contrary inference can reasonably be drawn? Appellees stress the preliminary nature of the Texas court's approval of the interim plans, and as we have said, that fact is relevant. But in light of our instructions to the Texas court and the care with which the interim plans were developed, the court's approval still gave the Legislature a sound basis for thinking that the interim plans satisfied all legal requirements. . . .

[The concurring opinion of Justice Thomas, and the dissenting opinion of Justice Sotomayor, are omitted.]

Notes and Questions

1. *Hunter* is a rare example of a case in which there is a "smoking gun" proving the discriminatory intent behind a facially neutral law. How likely is it, particularly where modern legislators are involved, that it would be as easy to find such evidence? Moreover, given how narrowly *Abbott* construes *Hunter*, how likely is it that a litigant is going to succeed in proving discriminatory purpose sufficiently to make out an equal protection claim?

B. What Constitutes Facial Neutrality?

In the last several decades, legislators have enacted laws that negatively impact the rights of gays, lesbians, and bisexuals, including bans on same-sex marriage, adoption, and sexual intimacy. Although we have not yet considered whether discrimination on the basis of sexual orientation warrants heightened scrutiny, assume for the moment that it does. Are laws banning same-sex marriage, adoption, and sexual intimacy facially discriminatory against gays, lesbians, and bisexuals? After all, the laws nowhere state that "gay" people cannot get married, or that "lesbians" cannot have sex or adopt children. Rather, it bans certain activities involving two people of the same sex. Theoretically, two heterosexuals might seek to enter into a same-sex marriage or to adopt children together. Similarly, a gay man and a lesbian might theoretically seek to enter into an opposite-sex marriage or to adopt children together.

Lest you think this seems far-fetched, consider a few examples of court decisions relying on *Davis* and its progeny to conclude that such laws are facially neutral. In *Baehr v. Lewin*, 852 P.2d 44 (1993), the Hawaii Supreme Court rejected an argument that Hawaii's ban on same-sex marriage facially discriminated against gays and lesbians:

> "Homosexual" and "same-sex" marriages are not synonymous; by the same token, a "heterosexual" same-sex marriage is, in theory, not oxymoronic Parties to "a union between a man and a woman" may or may not be

> homosexuals. Parties to a same-sex marriage could theoretically be either homosexuals or heterosexuals.

Id. at 51 n.11. Perhaps an even more extreme example is the Texas Court of Appeals' conclusion in *Lawrence v. State*, 41 S.W.3d 349 (2001) that the state's prohibition on same-sex sexual intimacy did not facially discriminate on the basis of sexual orientation:

> On its face, the statute makes no classification on the basis of sexual orientation; rather, the statute is expressly directed at conduct. While homosexuals may be disproportionately affected by the statute, we cannot assume homosexual conduct is limited only to those possessing a homosexual 'orientation.' Persons having a predominately heterosexual inclination may sometimes engage in homosexual conduct.

Do these decisions from the Hawaii and Texas high courts seem doctrinally sound? As you read the two U.S. Supreme Court decisions that follow, consider the following question: how close can you get to a trait associated with a class without being said to be facially discriminating against that class? Stated somewhat differently, under what circumstances should facially discriminating against a given trait be treated as a proxy for facially discriminating against a class associated with that trait?

Geduldig v. Aiello

417 U.S. 484 (1974)

Mr. Justice Stewart delivered the opinion of the Court.

For almost 30 years California has administered a disability insurance system that pays benefits to persons in private employment who are temporarily unable to work because of disability not covered by workmen's compensation. The appellees brought this action to challenge the constitutionality of a provision of the California program that, in defining "disability," excludes from coverage certain disabilities resulting from pregnancy....

In return for his one-percent contribution to the Disability Fund, the individual employee is insured against the risk of disability stemming from a substantial number of "mental or physical illness[es] and mental or physical injur[ies]." It is not every disabling condition, however, that triggers the obligation to pay benefits under the program.... [F]or example, any disability of less than eight days' duration is not compensable, except when the employee is hospitalized. Conversely, no benefits are payable for any single disability beyond 26 weeks. Further, disability is not compensable if it results from the individual's court commitment as a dipsomaniac, drug addict, or sexual psychopath. Finally, § 2626 of the Unemployment Insurance Code excludes from coverage certain disabilities that are attributable to pregnancy. It is this provision that is at issue in the present case....

Appellees are four women who have paid sufficient amounts into the Disability Fund to be eligible for benefits under the program. Each of the appellees became pregnant and suffered employment disability as a result of her pregnancy. With respect to three of the appellees, Carolyn Aiello, Augustina Armendariz, and Elizabeth Johnson, the disabilities were attributable to abnormal complications encountered during their pregnancies. The fourth, Jacqueline Jaramillo, experienced a normal pregnancy, which was the sole cause of her disability.

The District Court, finding "that the exclusion of pregnancy-related disabilities is not based upon a classification having a rational and substantial relationship to a legitimate state purpose," held that the exclusion was unconstitutional under the Equal Protection Clause. . . .

It is clear that California intended to establish this benefit system as an insurance program that was to function essentially in accordance with insurance concepts. Since the program was instituted in 1946, it has been totally self-supporting, never drawing on general state revenues to finance disability or hospital benefits. The Disability Fund is wholly supported by the one percent of wages annually contributed by participating employees. . . .

Over the years California has demonstrated a strong commitment not to increase the contribution rate above the one-percent level. The State has sought to provide the broadest possible disability protection that would be affordable by all employees, including those with very low incomes. Because any larger percentage or any flat dollar-amount rate of contribution would impose an increasingly regressive levy bearing most heavily upon those with the lowest incomes, the State has resisted any attempt to change the required contribution from the one-percent level. The program is thus structured, in terms of the level of benefits and the risks insured, to maintain the solvency of the Disability Fund at a one-percent annual level of contribution.

In ordering the State to pay benefits for disability accompanying normal pregnancy and delivery, the District Court acknowledged the State's contention "that coverage of these disabilities is so extraordinarily expensive that it would be impossible to maintain a program supported by employee contributions if these disabilities are included." There is considerable disagreement between the parties with respect to how great the increased costs would actually be, but they would clearly be substantial. For purposes of analysis the District Court accepted the State's estimate, which was in excess of $100 million annually, and stated: "[I]t is clear that including these disabilities would not destroy the program The increased costs could be accommodated quite easily by making reasonable changes in the contribution rate, the maximum benefits allowable, and the other variables affecting the solvency of the program." *Ibid.*

Each of these "variables"—the benefit level deemed appropriate to compensate employee disability, the risks selected to be insured under the program, and the contribution rate chosen to maintain the solvency of the program and at the same time to permit low-income employees to participate with minimal personal sacrifice—represents a policy determination by the State. The essential issue in this case is whether the Equal Protection Clause requires such policies to be sacrificed or compromised in order to finance the payment of benefits to those whose disability is attributable to normal pregnancy and delivery.

We cannot agree that the exclusion of this disability from coverage amounts to invidious discrimination under the Equal Protection Clause. California does not discriminate with respect to the persons or groups which are eligible for disability insurance protection under the program. The classification challenged in this case relates to the asserted underinclusiveness of the set of risks that the State has selected to insure. Although California has created a program to insure most risks of employment disability, it has not chosen to insure all such risks, and this decision is reflected in the level of annual contributions exacted from participating employees. This Court has held that, consistently with the Equal Protection Clause, a State "may take one step at a time, addressing itself to the phase of the problem which seems most acute to the legislative mind. . . . The legislature may select one phase of one field and apply a remedy there, neglecting the others. . . ." *Williamson v. Lee Optical of Oklahoma Inc.*, 348 U.S. 483, 489 (1955); *Jefferson v. Hackney*, 406 U.S. 535 (1972). Particularly with respect to social welfare programs, so long as the line drawn by the State is rationally supportable, the courts will not interpose their judgment as to the appropriate stopping point. "[T]he Equal Protection Clause does not require that a State must choose between attacking every aspect of a problem or not attacking the problem at all." Dandridge v. Williams, 397 U.S. 471, 486–487 (1970) . . . .

It is evident that a totally comprehensive program would be substantially more costly than the present program and would inevitably require state subsidy, a higher rate of employee contribution, a lower scale of benefits for those suffering insured disabilities, or some combination of these measures. There is nothing in the Constitution, however, that requires the State to subordinate or compromise its legitimate interests solely to create a more comprehensive social insurance program than it already has.

The State has a legitimate interest in maintaining the self-supporting nature of its insurance program. Similarly, it has an interest in distributing the available resources in such a way as to keep benefit payments at an adequate level for disabilities that are covered, rather than to cover all disabilities inadequately. Finally, California has a legitimate concern in maintaining the contribution rate at a level that will not unduly burden participating employees, particularly low-income employees who may be most in need of the disability insurance.

These policies provide an objective and wholly noninvidious basis for the State's decision not to create a more comprehensive insurance program than it has. There is no evidence in the record that the selection of the risks insured by the program worked to discriminate against any definable group or class in terms of the aggregate risk protection derived by that group or class from the program.[20] There is no

---

20. The dissenting opinion to the contrary, this case is thus a far cry from cases like *Reed v. Reed*, 404 U.S. 71 (1971), and *Frontiero v. Richardson*, 411 U.S. 677 (1973), involving discrimination based

risk from which men are protected and women are not. Likewise, there is no risk from which women are protected and men are not. . . .

Mr. Justice Brennan, with whom Mr. Justice Douglas and Mr. Justice Marshall join, dissenting. . . .

Despite the Code's broad goals and scope of coverage, compensation is denied for disabilities suffered in connection with a "normal" pregnancy—disabilities suffered only by women. Disabilities caused by pregnancy, however, like other physically disabling conditions covered by the Code, require medical care, often include hospitalization, anesthesia and surgical procedures, and may involve genuine risk to life. Moreover, the economic effects caused by pregnancy-related disabilities are functionally indistinguishable from the effects caused by any other disability: wages are lost due to a physical inability to work, and medical expenses are incurred for the delivery of the child and for postpartum care. In my view, by singling out for less favorable treatment a gender-linked disability peculiar to women, the State has created a double standard for disability compensation: a limitation is imposed upon the disabilities for which women workers may recover, while men receive full compensation for all disabilities suffered, including those that affect only or primarily their sex, such as prostatectomies, circumcision, hemophilia, and gout. In effect, one set of rules is applied to females and another to males. Such dissimilar treatment of men and women, on the basis of physical characteristics inextricably linked to one sex, inevitably constitutes sex discrimination. . . .

In the past, when a legislative classification has turned on gender, the Court has justifiably applied a standard of judicial scrutiny more strict than that generally accorded economic or social welfare programs. Yet, by its decision today, the Court appears willing to abandon that higher standard of review without satisfactorily explaining what differentiates the gender-based classification employed in this case from those found unconstitutional in *Reed* and *Frontiero*. The Court's decision threatens to return men and women to a time when 'traditional' equal protection

---

upon gender as such. The California insurance program does not exclude anyone from benefit eligibility because of gender but merely removes one physical condition—pregnancy—from the list of compensable disabilities. While it is true that only women can become pregnant it does not follow that every legislative classification concerning pregnancy is a sex-based classification like those considered in *Reed*, *supra*, and *Frontiero*, *supra*. Normal pregnancy is an objectively identifiable physical condition with unique characteristics. Absent a showing that distinctions involving pregnancy are mere pretexts designed to effect an invidious discrimination against the members of one sex or the other, lawmakers are constitutionally free to include or exclude pregnancy from the coverage of legislation such as this on any reasonable basis, just as with respect to any other physical condition.

The lack of identity between the excluded disability and gender as such under this insurance program becomes clear upon the most cursory analysis. The program divides potential recipients into two groups—pregnant women and nonpregnant persons. While the first group is exclusively female, the second includes members of both sexes. The fiscal and actuarial benefits of the program thus accrue to members of both sexes.

analysis sustained legislative classifications that treated differently members of a particular sex solely because of their sex. . . .

Notes and Questions

1. Recall from Chapter 12 that one reason the Court's equal protection jurisprudence applies intermediate rather than strict scrutiny to sex-based classifications is because there exist real differences between the sexes. One of the few real differences identified by that line of cases is a woman's capacity to get pregnant. If that is so, how is it that the *Geduldig* Court decouples sex and pregnancy? Keep in mind that this case is decided in 1974, and so the Court's reasons for doing so are likely not based on an enlightened view of gender fluidity! For a critique of the opinion, *see Coleman v. Court of Appeals of Md.*, 566 U.S. 30, 54-61 & n.6 (2012) (Ginsburg, J., dissenting) (describing the case as embodying an "Alice-in-Wonderland view of pregnancy as a sex-neutral phenomenon.").

2. The same day that the Court issued its decision in *Geduldig*, it also issued an opinion in *Morton v. Mancari*, 417 U.S. 535 (1974). In *Morton*, the Court rejected an equal protection challenge to a federal law giving an employment preference at the Bureau of Indian Affairs to "Indians." To qualify for the preference, an individual was required to be "one-fourth or more degree Indian blood and be a member of a Federally-recognized tribe." The Court held that only rational basis review, not strict scrutiny, was applicable because the preference was not racial in nature:

> The preference is not directed towards a "racial" group consisting of "Indians"; instead, it applies only to members of "federally recognized" tribes. This operates to exclude many individuals who are racially to be classified as "Indians." In this sense, the preference is political rather than racial in nature.

Do you agree? It may be the case that being racially Indian is not a sufficient condition for receiving the employment preference, but the additional requirement that the person be at least "one-fourth or more degree Indian blood" certainly makes it a necessary one, does it not?

3. If the laws at issue in *Geduldig* and *Morton* are not a perfect proxy for sex and race, respectively, is that because the laws operate in such a way that they do not result in one sex or race *always* benefiting and the other *always* losing? For example, *Geduldig* makes much of the fact that although only women can become pregnant, there are plenty of non-pregnant women who, together with men, reap the actuarial benefits of this program. Similarly, *Morton* makes much of the fact that not all racial Indians benefit from the program, and thus that both racial Indians and individuals of other races are denied the benefits of the law.

4. One consequence of *Geduldig* has been that it has made it easier for governments to extend certain benefits *exclusively* to pregnant persons. Because *Geduldig* holds that such preferences are not sex-based in nature, they are subject only to rational basis review.

5. Suppose that a law or government regulation drew a distinction based not on *actual* pregnancy, but rather on physical *capacity* to become pregnant? Would such a law be distinguishable from that at issue in *Geduldig*?

Hernandez v. New York

500 U.S. 352 (1991)

JUSTICE KENNEDY announced the judgment of the Court and delivered an opinion in which THE CHIEF JUSTICE, JUSTICE WHITE and JUSTICE SOUTER join.

Petitioner Dionisio Hernandez asks us to review the New York state courts' rejection of his claim that the prosecutor in his criminal trial exercised peremptory challenges to exclude Latinos from the jury by reason of their ethnicity. If true, the prosecutor's discriminatory use of peremptory strikes would violate the Equal Protection Clause as interpreted by our decision in *Batson v. Kentucky,* 476 U.S. 79 (1986). We must determine whether the prosecutor offered a race-neutral basis for challenging Latino potential jurors and, if so, whether the state courts' decision to accept the prosecutor's explanation should be sustained. . . .

After 63 potential jurors had been questioned and 9 had been empaneled, defense counsel objected that the prosecutor had used four peremptory challenges to exclude Latino potential jurors. Two of the Latino venirepersons challenged by the prosecutor had brothers who had been convicted of crimes, and the brother of one of those potential jurors was being prosecuted by the same District Attorney's office for a probation violation. Petitioner does not press his *Batson* claim with respect to those prospective jurors, and we concentrate on the other two excluded individuals.

After petitioner raised his *Batson* objection, the prosecutor did not wait for a ruling on whether petitioner had established a *prima facie* case of racial discrimination. Instead, the prosecutor volunteered his reasons for striking the jurors in question. He explained:

> "Your honor, my reason for rejecting the—these two jurors—I'm not certain as to whether they're Hispanics. I didn't notice how many Hispanics had been called to the panel, but my reason for rejecting these two is I feel very uncertain that they would be able to listen and follow the interpreter."

After an interruption by defense counsel, the prosecutor continued:

> "We talked to them for a long time; the Court talked to them, I talked to them. I believe that in their heart they will try to follow it, but I felt there was a great deal of uncertainty as to whether they could accept the interpreter as the final arbiter of what was said by each of the witnesses, especially where there were going to be Spanish-speaking witnesses, and I didn't feel, when I asked them whether or not they could accept the interpreter's translation of it, I didn't feel that they could. They each looked away from me and said with some hesitancy that they would try, not that they could, but that they would try to follow the interpreter, and I feel that in a case

> where the interpreter will be for the main witnesses, they would have an undue impact upon the jury."

. . . .

Petitioner argues that Spanish-language ability bears a close relation to ethnicity, and that, as a consequence, it violates the Equal Protection Clause to exercise a peremptory challenge on the ground that a Latino potential juror speaks Spanish. He points to the high correlation between Spanish-language ability and ethnicity in New York, where the case was tried. We need not address that argument here, for the prosecutor did not rely on language ability without more, but explained that the specific responses and the demeanor of the two individuals during *voir dire* caused him to doubt their ability to defer to the official translation of Spanish-language testimony.

The prosecutor here offered a race-neutral basis for these peremptory strikes. As explained by the prosecutor, the challenges rested neither on the intention to exclude Latino or bilingual jurors, nor on stereotypical assumptions about Latinos or bilinguals. The prosecutor's articulated basis for these challenges divided potential jurors into two classes: those whose conduct during *voir dire* would persuade him they might have difficulty in accepting the translator's rendition of Spanish-language testimony and those potential jurors who gave no such reason for doubt. Each category would include both Latinos and non-Latinos. While the prosecutor's criterion might well result in the disproportionate removal of prospective Latino jurors, that disproportionate impact does not turn the prosecutor's actions into a *per se* violation of the Equal Protection Clause.

Petitioner contends that despite the prosecutor's focus on the individual responses of these jurors, his reason for the peremptory strikes has the effect of a pure, language-based reason because "[a]ny honest bilingual juror would have answered the prosecutor in the exact same way." Petitioner asserts that a bilingual juror would hesitate in answering questions like those asked by the judge and prosecutor due to the difficulty of ignoring the actual Spanish-language testimony. In his view, no more can be expected than a commitment by a prospective juror to try to follow the interpreter's translation.

But even if we knew that a high percentage of bilingual jurors would hesitate in answering questions like these and, as a consequence, would be excluded under the prosecutor's criterion, that fact alone would not cause the criterion to fail the race-neutrality test. As will be discussed below, disparate impact should be given appropriate weight in determining whether the prosecutor acted with a forbidden intent, but it will not be conclusive in the preliminary race-neutrality step of the *Batson* inquiry. An argument relating to the impact of a classification does not alone show its purpose. See *Personnel Administrator of Mass. v. Feeney, supra,* 442 U.S., at 279. Equal protection analysis turns on the intended consequences of government classifications. Unless the government actor adopted a criterion with the intent of causing the impact asserted, that impact itself does not violate the principle of race neutrality. Nothing in the prosecutor's explanation shows that he chose to exclude jurors who hesitated in answering questions about following the interpreter *because* he wanted to prevent bilingual Latinos from serving on the jury. . . .

Once the prosecutor offers a race-neutral basis for his exercise of peremptory challenges, "[t]he trial court then [has] the duty to determine if the defendant has established purposeful discrimination." While the disproportionate impact on Latinos resulting from the prosecutor's criterion for excluding these jurors does not answer the race-neutrality inquiry, it does have relevance to the trial court's decision on this question. "[A]n invidious discriminatory purpose may often be inferred from the totality of the relevant facts, including the fact, if it is true, that the [classification] bears more heavily on one race than another." *Washington v. Davis*, 426 U.S., at 242. If a prosecutor articulates a basis for a peremptory challenge that results in the disproportionate exclusion of members of a certain race, the trial judge may consider that fact as evidence that the prosecutor's stated reason constitutes a pretext for racial discrimination.

In the context of this trial, the prosecutor's frank admission that his ground for excusing these jurors related to their ability to speak and understand Spanish raised a plausible, though not a necessary, inference that language might be a pretext for what in fact were race-based peremptory challenges. This was not a case where by some rare coincidence a juror happened to speak the same language as a key witness, in a community where few others spoke that tongue. If it were, the explanation that the juror could have undue influence on jury deliberations might be accepted without concern that a racial generalization had come into play. But this trial took place in a community with a substantial Latino population, and petitioner and other interested parties were members of that ethnic group. It would be common knowledge in the locality that a significant percentage of the Latino population speaks fluent Spanish, and that many consider it their preferred language, the one chosen for personal communication, the one selected for speaking with the most precision and power, the one used to define the self.

The trial judge can consider these and other factors when deciding whether a prosecutor intended to discriminate. For example, though petitioner did not suggest the alternative to the trial court here, Spanish-speaking jurors could be permitted to advise the judge in a discreet way of any concerns with the translation during the course of trial. A prosecutor's persistence in the desire to exclude Spanish-speaking jurors despite this measure could be taken into account in determining whether to accept a race-neutral explanation for the challenge.

The trial judge in this case chose to believe the prosecutor's race-neutral explanation for striking the two jurors in question, rejecting petitioner's assertion that the reasons were pretextual. In *Batson*, we explained that the trial court's decision on the ultimate question of discriminatory intent represents a finding of fact of the sort accorded great deference on appeal. . . .

We discern no clear error in the state trial court's determination that the prosecutor did not discriminate on the basis of the ethnicity of Latino jurors. . . .

Language permits an individual to express both a personal identity and membership in a community, and those who share a common language may interact in ways more intimate than those without this bond. Bilinguals, in a sense, inhabit two communities, and serve to bring them closer. Indeed, some scholarly comment suggests that people proficient in two languages may not at times think in one language to the exclusion of the other. The analogy is that of a high-hurdler, who combines the ability to sprint and to jump to accomplish a third feat with characteristics of its own, rather than two separate functions. This is not to say that the cognitive processes and reactions of those who speak two languages are susceptible of easy generalization, for even the term "bilingual" does not describe a uniform category. It is a simple word for a more complex phenomenon with many distinct categories and subdivisions.

Our decision today does not imply that exclusion of bilinguals from jury service is wise, or even that it is constitutional in all cases. It is a harsh paradox that one may become proficient enough in English to participate in trial, see, *e.g.,* 28 U.S.C. §§ 1865(b)(2), (3) (English-language ability required for federal jury service), only to encounter disqualification because he knows a second language as well. As the Court observed in a somewhat related context: "Mere knowledge of [a foreign] language cannot reasonably be regarded as harmful. Heretofore it has been commonly looked upon as helpful and desirable." *Meyer v. Nebraska,* 262 U.S. 390, 400 (1923).

Just as shared language can serve to foster community, language differences can be a source of division. Language elicits a response from others, ranging from admiration and respect, to distance and alienation, to ridicule and scorn. Reactions of the latter type all too often result from or initiate racial hostility. In holding that a race-neutral reason for a peremptory challenge means a reason other than race, we do not resolve the more difficult question of the breadth with which the concept of race should be defined for equal protection purposes. We would face a quite different case if the prosecutor had justified his peremptory challenges with the explanation that he did not want Spanish-speaking jurors. It may well be, for certain ethnic groups and in some communities, that proficiency in a particular language, like skin color, should be treated as a surrogate for race under an equal protection analysis. Cf. *Yu Cong Eng v. Trinidad,* 271 U.S. 500 (1926) (law prohibiting keeping business records in other than specified languages violated equal protection rights of Chinese businessmen); *Meyer v. Nebraska, supra* (striking down law prohibiting grade schools from teaching languages other than English). And, as we make clear, a policy of striking all who speak a given language, without regard to the particular circumstances of the trial or the individual responses of the jurors, may be found by the trial judge to be a pretext for racial discrimination. But that case is not before us....

Justice O'Connor, with whom Justice Scalia joins, concurring in the judgment.

I agree with the plurality that we review for clear error the trial court's finding as to discriminatory intent, and agree with its analysis of this issue. I agree also that the finding of no discriminatory intent was not clearly erroneous in this case. I write separately because I believe that the plurality opinion goes further than it needs to in assessing the constitutionality of the prosecutor's asserted justification for his peremptory strikes. . . .

An unwavering line of cases from this Court holds that a violation of the Equal Protection Clause requires state action motivated by discriminatory intent; the disproportionate effects of state action are not sufficient to establish such a violation. . . .

We have recognized the discriminatory intent requirement explicitly in the context of jury selection. . . .

Consistent with our established equal protection jurisprudence, a peremptory strike will constitute a *Batson* violation only if the prosecutor struck a juror *because of the juror's race* . . . . *Batson*'s requirement of a race-neutral explanation means an explanation other than race. . . .

In this case, the prosecutor's asserted justification for striking certain Hispanic jurors was his uncertainty about the jurors' ability to accept the official translation of trial testimony. If this truly was the purpose of the strikes, they were not strikes because of race, and therefore did not violate the Equal Protection Clause under *Batson*. They may have acted like strikes based on race, but they were *not* based on race. No matter how closely tied or significantly correlated to race the explanation for a peremptory strike may be, the strike does not implicate the Equal Protection Clause unless it is based on race. That is the distinction between disproportionate effect, which is not sufficient to constitute an equal protection violation, and intentional discrimination, which is.

Disproportionate effect may, of course, constitute evidence of intentional discrimination. The trial court may, because of such effect, disbelieve the prosecutor and find that the asserted justification is merely a pretext for intentional race-based discrimination. But if, as in this case, the trial court believes the prosecutor's nonracial justification, and that finding is not clearly erroneous, that is the end of the matter. *Batson* does not require that a prosecutor justify a jury strike at the level of a for-cause challenge. It also does not require that the justification be unrelated to race. *Batson* requires only that the prosecutor's reason for striking a juror not *be* the juror's race.

[The dissenting opinions of Justices Blackmun and Stevens are omitted]

Problem 15-A: Parental Leave Policy

A public university has a policy regarding paid parental leave for faculty members that provides as follows:

> Any woman who gives birth while holding a faculty appointment at the University is covered under the University's sick leave policy. She is eligible for up to 90 days leave with salary continued during that period for which she would normally be on the payroll. Sick leave coverage begins from the date of childbirth or from an earlier date if recommended by a health care provider. As with other medical leaves,

> the faculty member must present written certification from a health care provider that she cannot work as a result of the pregnancy, childbirth, and/or recovery. Paid sick leave is not available for adoptive mothers.

An attorney representing a group of male faculty members at the university who recently became parents but who are not eligible for paid parental leave under the university's policy files a legal challenge in federal district court, contending that the policy violates the Equal Protection Clause. The attorney characterizes the policy as designed to give new parents "bonding time" with their children, and contends that her clients are being discriminated against through the denial of such "bonding time." The attorney further contends that, in reality, doctors routinely provide the written certification for pregnant women without regard to actual ability to work as a result of pregnancy, that many of the faculty members receiving paid leave under the policy are thus not, in fact, sick, and that the university was aware of this when they enacted the policy.

The plaintiffs' attorney contends that the statute should be subjected to intermediate scrutiny, but the university's attorney contends that it should be subjected only to rational basis scrutiny.

What are the arguments in favor of the plaintiffs' and the university's positions with respect to the level of scrutiny? Assuming that intermediate scrutiny applies—and based on the materials from Chapter 12—is it likely to be upheld? What result if rational basis review applies? In framing the legal challenge, what sorts of information would the attorney for the plaintiffs likely request from the university pursuant to a public records request, and how would that information impact the viability of the plaintiffs' claim?

Problem 15-B: Judicial Haircuts, Part II

Assume the same facts as in Problem 14-B. Assume further that the sign next to the salon's entrance that lists prices for its services includes the following surcharges:

Hair Color	**$40 extra**
Highlights	**$55 extra**
French Braids	**$20 extra**
"Afro" Style Hair	**$25 extra**

An African-American juror with "Afro" style hair who paid the surcharge for such hair hires an attorney to sue Judicial Haircuts in a federal district court. In the complaint, the juror's attorney contends that the pricing scheme constitutes race discrimination in violation of the Equal Protection Clause. In support of the claim, the attorney notes in the complaint that approximately 99.8 percent of people with "Afro" hairstyles in the United

> States are African American. As a result, the attorney contends that strict scrutiny applies and that the law cannot survive that level of scrutiny.
>
> In response, Judicial Haircuts contends that: (a) it is not subject to the Equal Protection Clause; (b) even assuming that it is, only rational basis review applies; and (c) the price difference is justified by the additional complexities associated with styling hair in that fashion, and is no different than surcharges for French braids, highlights, or hair color.
>
> The trial judge rejects the contention that Judicial Haircuts is not subject to the Equal Protection Clause, but schedules a hearing to address the appropriate level of scrutiny.
>
> ***What are the arguments in favor of the juror's and Judicial Haircut's positions with respect to the level of scrutiny? Assuming that strict scrutiny applies—and based on the materials from Chapter 5—is it likely to be upheld? What result if rational basis review applies?***

Notes and Questions

1. The *Hernandez* Court refers to the *Batson* procedure. Recall that *Arlington Heights* acknowledged that under its precedents, if a pattern of striking jurors of a specific race arises, that can result in a finding of an equal protection violation, even if the pattern is not nearly as stark as that in the *Yick Wo* and *Gomillion* cases. However, under *Batson*, the pattern itself does not result in an automatic finding of a constitutional violation; rather, the pattern gives rise to an inference of racial discrimination, and the burden of proof shifts to the party striking jurors to state a neutral reason for having done so.

2. Is there language in *Hernandez* that would lend support for striking down the hypothetical law described at the end of the previous section that drew a distinction based on capacity to become pregnant on the ground that it was a proxy for sex? That would lend support for striking down the laws targeting same-sex marriage, adoption, and sexual intimacy described at the start of this section on the ground that they were a proxy for sexual orientation?

3. Justice Scalia joined Justice O'Connor's separate opinion in *Hernandez*, which rejected the idea of language as a proxy for ethnicity. Justice Scalia's position in *Hernandez*, however, seems inconsistent with his position in *Bray v. Alexandria Women's Health Clinic*, 506 U.S. 263, 270 (1993), in which he wrote the following:

> Some activities may be such an irrational object of disfavor that, if they are targeted, and if they also happen to be engaged in exclusively or predominantly by a particular class of people, an intent to disfavor that class can readily be presumed. A tax on wearing yarmulkes is a tax on Jews.

Are the two positions reconcilable?

4. Reconsider the laws at issue in *Griswold* and *Eisenstadt* banning contraceptive devices used to prevent conception but allowing their use to prevent disease

transmission. Suppose that a challenge to those laws was brought *after* heightened equal protection scrutiny was established for sex-based classifications. Are such laws facially neutral so far as sex is concerned? If so, is there nonetheless an argument under the cases that you have read in this Chapter that a viable equal protection claim could be brought against such laws?

C. Discriminatory Purpose Outside of Equal Protection Claims

The cases that you have examined thus far have involved exclusively class-based equal protection claims. Does the requirement that there be proof of a discriminatory purpose apply to claims grounded in the Thirteenth or Fifteenth Amendments? How about fundamental rights claims grounded in either the Equal Protection or Due Process Clauses? Laws enacted pursuant to Congress's power to enforce the Reconstruction Amendments? If it is not applicable to one or more of those types of claims, what is the basis for drawing a distinction? Is it based on the text of the various Amendments? Their scope? Policy considerations? The cases that follow explore the answers to these questions.

City of Mobile v. Bolden

446 U.S. 55 (1980)

Mr. Justice Stewart announced the judgment of the Court and delivered an opinion, in which The Chief Justice, Mr. Justice Powell, and Mr. Justice Rehnquist joined.

The city of Mobile, Ala., has since 1911 been governed by a City Commission consisting of three members elected by the voters of the city at large. The question in this case is whether this at-large system of municipal elections violates the rights of Mobile's Negro voters in contravention of federal statutory or constitutional law. . . .

The complaint alleged that the practice of electing the City Commissioners at large unfairly diluted the voting strength of Negroes in violation of . . . the Fifteenth Amendment. . . .

The Court's early decisions under the Fifteenth Amendment established that it imposes but one limitation on the powers of the States. It forbids them to discriminate against Negroes in matters having to do with voting. . . .

Our decisions, moreover, have made clear that action by a State that is racially neutral on its face violates the Fifteenth Amendment only if motivated by a discriminatory purpose. In *Guinn v. United States*, 238 U.S. 347, this Court struck down a "grandfather" clause in a state constitution exempting from the requirement that voters be literate any person or the descendants of any person who had been entitled to vote before January 1, 1866. It was asserted by way of defense that the provision was immune from successful challenge, since a law could not be found unconstitutional either "by attributing to the legislative authority an occult motive," or "because of conclusions concerning its operation in practical execution and resulting discrimination arising . . . from inequalities naturally inhering in those who must come within the standard in order to enjoy the right to vote." *Id.*, at 359. Despite this argument, the Court did not hesitate to hold the grandfather clause unconstitutional, because it was not "possible to discover any basis in reason for the standard thus fixed other than the purpose" to circumvent the Fifteenth Amendment. *Id.*, at 365.

The Court's more recent decisions confirm the principle that racially discriminatory motivation is a necessary ingredient of a Fifteenth Amendment violation. In *Gomillion v. Lightfoot*, 364 U.S. 339, the Court held that allegations of a racially motivated gerrymander of municipal boundaries stated a claim under the Fifteenth Amendment. The constitutional infirmity of the state law in that case, according to the allegations of the complaint, was that in drawing the municipal boundaries the legislature was "solely concerned with segregating white and colored voters by fencing Negro citizens out of town so as to deprive them of their pre-existing municipal vote." *Id.*, at 341. The Court made clear that in the absence of such an invidious purpose, a State is constitutionally free to redraw political boundaries in any manner it chooses. *Id.*, at 347.[10]

In *Wright v. Rockefeller*, 376 U.S. 52, the Court upheld by like reasoning a state congressional reapportionment statute against claims that district lines had been racially gerrymandered, because the plaintiffs failed to prove that the legislature "was either motivated by racial considerations or in fact drew the districts on racial lines"; or that the statute "was the product of a state contrivance to segregate on the basis of race or place of origin." *Id.*, at 56, 58.

---

10. The Court has repeatedly cited *Gomillion v. Lightfoot*, for the principle that an invidious *purpose* must be adduced to support a claim of unconstitutionality. See *Personnel Administrator of Mass. v. Feeney*, 442 U.S. 256, 272; *Arlington Heights v. Metropolitan Housing Dev. Corp.*, 429 U.S. 252, 265, 266; *Washington v. Davis*, 426 U.S. 229, 240.

While other of the Court's Fifteenth Amendment decisions have dealt with different issues, none has questioned the necessity of showing purposeful discrimination in order to show a Fifteenth Amendment violation. . . .

Mr. Justice Marshall, dissenting. . . .

The plurality concludes that our prior decisions establish the principle that proof of discriminatory intent is a necessary element of a Fifteenth Amendment claim. . . . In my view, our Fifteenth Amendment jurisprudence on the necessity of proof of discriminatory purpose is no less unsettled than was our approach to the importance of such proof in Fourteenth Amendment racial discrimination cases prior to *Washington v. Davis*, 426 U.S. 229 (1976). What is called for in the present cases is a fresh consideration—similar to our inquiry in *Washington v. Davis, supra*, with regard to Fourteenth Amendment discrimination claims—of whether proof of discriminatory purpose is necessary to establish a claim under the Fifteenth Amendment. . . .

The Court in *Washington v. Davis* required a showing of discriminatory purpose to support racial discrimination claims largely because it feared that a standard based solely on disproportionate impact would unduly interfere with the far ranging governmental distribution of constitutional gratuities. Underlying the Court's decision was a determination that, since the Constitution does not entitle any person to such governmental benefits, courts should accord discretion to those officials who decide how the government shall allocate its scarce resources. If the plaintiff proved only that governmental distribution of constitutional gratuities had a disproportionate effect on a racial minority, the Court was willing to presume that the officials who approved the allocation scheme either had made an honest error or had foreseen that the decision would have a discriminatory impact and had found persuasive, legitimate reasons for imposing it nonetheless. These assumptions about the good faith of officials allowed the Court to conclude that, standing alone, a showing that a governmental policy had a racially discriminatory impact did not indicate that the affected minority had suffered the stigma, frustration, and unjust treatment prohibited under the suspect-classification branch of our equal protection jurisprudence.

Such judicial deference to official decisionmaking has no place under the Fifteenth Amendment. Section 1 of that Amendment differs from the Fourteenth Amendment's prohibition on racial discrimination in two crucial respects: it explicitly recognizes the right to vote free of hindrances related to race, and it sweeps no further. In my view, these distinctions justify the conclusion that proof of racially discriminatory impact should be sufficient to support a claim under the Fifteenth Amendment. The right to vote is of such fundamental importance in the constitutional scheme that the Fifteenth Amendment's command that it shall not be "abridged" on account of race must be interpreted as providing that the votes of citizens of all races shall be of substantially equal weight. Furthermore, a disproportionate-impact test under the Fifteenth Amendment would not lead to constant judicial intrusion into the process of official decisionmaking. Rather, the standard would reach only those decisions having a discriminatory effect upon the minority's vote.

The Fifteenth Amendment cannot tolerate that kind of decision, even if made in good faith, because the Amendment grants racial minorities the full enjoyment of the right to vote, not simply protection against the unfairness of intentional vote dilution along racial lines.

In addition, it is beyond dispute that a standard based solely upon the motives of official decision-makers creates significant problems of proof for plaintiffs and forces the inquiring court to undertake an unguided, tortious look into the minds of officials in the hope of guessing why certain policies were adopted and others rejected. An approach based on motivation creates the risk that officials will be able to adopt policies that are the products of discriminatory intent so long as they sufficiently mask their motives through the use of subtlety and illusion. *Washington v. Davis* is premised on the notion that this risk is insufficient to overcome the deference the judiciary must accord to governmental decisions about the distribution of constitutional gratuities. That risk becomes intolerable, however, when the precious right to vote protected by the Fifteenth Amendment is concerned. . . .

[The concurring opinions of Justices Blackmun and Stevens, and the dissenting opinion of Justices White and Brennan, are omitted.]

City of Memphis v. Greene

451 U.S. 100 (1981)

Justice Stevens delivered the opinion of the Court.

The question presented is whether a decision by the city of Memphis to close the north end of West Drive, a street that traverses a white residential community, violated . . . the Thirteenth Amendment to the United States Constitution. The city's action was challenged by respondents, who resided in a predominantly black area to the north. . . .

Hein Park, a small residential community in Memphis, Tenn., is bounded on three sides by thoroughfares and on the west by the campus of Southwestern University. West Drive is a two-lane street about a half-mile long passing through the center of Hein Park. Its southern terminus is a short distance from an entrance to Overton Park, a large recreation area containing, among other facilities, the municipal zoo. Its northern terminus is at the intersection of Jackson Ave. and Springdale St., two heavily traveled four-lane avenues. West Drive is one of three streets that enter Hein Park from the north; two streets enter from the east.

The closing will have some effect on both through traffic and local traffic. Prior to the closing, a significant volume of traffic southbound on Springdale St. would continue south on West Drive and then—because of the location of Overton Park to the south of Hein Park—make either a right or a left turn to the next through street a few blocks away, before resuming the southerly route to the center of the city. The closing of West Drive will force this traffic to divert to the east or west before entering Hein Park, instead of when it leaves, but the closing will not make the entire route any longer. With respect to local traffic, the street closing will add some distance to the trip from Springdale St. to the entrance to Overton Park and will make access to some homes in Hein Park slightly less convenient.

The area to the north of Hein Park is predominantly black. All of the homes in Hein Park were owned by whites when the decision to close the street was made. . . .

[T]he critical facts established by the record are these: The city's decision to close West Drive was motivated by its interest in protecting the safety and tranquility of a residential neighborhood. The procedures followed in making the decision were fair and were not affected by any racial or other impermissible factors. The city has conferred a benefit on certain white property owners but there is no reason to believe that it would refuse to confer a comparable benefit on black property owners. The closing has not affected the value of property owned by black citizens, but it has caused some slight inconvenience to black motorists.

Under the Court's recent decisions in *Washington v. Davis*, 426 U.S. 229 and *Arlington Heights v. Metropolitan Housing Dev. Corp.*, 429 U.S. 252, the absence of proof of discriminatory intent forecloses any claim that the official action challenged in this case violates the Equal Protection Clause of the Fourteenth Amendment. Petitioners ask us to hold that respondents' claims under . . . the Thirteenth Amendment are likewise barred by the absence of proof of discriminatory purpose. We note initially that the coverage of . . . the Thirteenth Amendment is significantly different from the coverage of the Fourteenth Amendment. The prohibitions of the latter apply only to official action. . . . We have squarely decided, however, that § 1982 is directly applicable to private parties, *Jones v. Alfred H. Mayer Co.*, 392 U.S. 409; cf. *Runyon v. McCrary*, 427 U.S. 160, 170-174; and it has long been settled that the Thirteenth Amendment "is not a mere prohibition of State laws establishing or upholding slavery, but an absolute declaration that slavery or involuntary servitude shall not exist in any part of the United States." *Civil Rights Cases*, 109 U.S. 3, 20. Thus, although respondents challenge official action in this case, the provisions of the law on which the challenge is based cover certain private action as well. Rather than confront prematurely the rather general question whether either § 1982 or the Thirteenth Amendment requires proof of a specific unlawful purpose, we first consider the extent to which either provision applies at all to this street closing case. . . .

In this case respondents challenge the conferring of a benefit upon white citizens by a measure that places a burden on black citizens as an unconstitutional "badge of slavery." . . . .

In *Jones*, the Court left open the question whether § 1 of the Amendment by its own terms did anything more than abolish slavery. It is also appropriate today to leave that question open because a review of the justification for the official action challenged in this case demonstrates that its disparate impact on black citizens could not, in any event, be fairly characterized as a badge or incident of slavery.

We begin our examination of respondents' Thirteenth Amendment argument by reiterating the conclusion that the record discloses no racially discriminatory motive on the part of the City Council. Instead, the record demonstrates that the interests that did motivate the Council are legitimate. Proper management of the flow of vehicular traffic within a city requires the accommodation of a variety of conflicting interests: the motorist's interest in unhindered access to his destination, the city's interest in the efficient provision of municipal services, the commercial interest in adequate parking, the residents' interest in relative quiet, and the pedestrians' interest in safety. Local governments necessarily exercise wide discretion in making the policy decisions that accommodate these interests.

In this case the city favored the interests of safety and tranquility. . . .

The interests motivating the city's action are thus sufficient to justify an adverse impact on motorists who are somewhat inconvenienced by the street closing. That inconvenience cannot be equated to an actual restraint on the liberty of black citizens that is in any sense comparable to the odious practice the Thirteenth Amendment was designed to eradicate. The argument that the closing violates the Amendment must therefore rest, not on the actual consequences of the closing, but rather on the symbolic significance of the fact that most of the drivers who will be inconvenienced by the action are black. . . .

Almost any traffic regulation—whether it be a temporary detour during construction, a speed limit, a one-way street, or a no-parking sign—may have a differential impact on residents of adjacent or nearby neighborhoods. Because urban neighborhoods are so frequently characterized by a common ethnic or racial heritage, a regulation's adverse impact on a particular neighborhood will often have a disparate effect on an identifiable ethnic or racial group. To regard an inevitable consequence of that kind as a form of stigma so severe as to violate the Thirteenth Amendment would trivialize the great purpose of that charter of freedom. Proper respect for the dignity of the residents of any neighborhood requires that they accept the same burdens as well as the same benefits of citizenship regardless of their racial or ethnic origin.

This case does not disclose a violation of any of the enabling legislation enacted by Congress pursuant to § 2 of the Thirteenth Amendment. To decide the narrow constitutional question presented by this record we need not speculate about the sort of impact on a racial group that might be prohibited by the Amendment itself. . . .

[The concurring opinion of Justice White and the dissenting opinion of Justice Marshall are omitted.]

Notes and Questions

1. In *City of Mobile*, only the four Justices in the plurality expressly reached the question whether the self-executing section of the Fifteenth Amendment—Section 1—requires a showing of discriminatory intent. However, the plurality's reasoning was subsequently endorsed by a Court majority in *Reno v. Bossier Parish School Board*, 520 U.S. 471, 481–82 (1997). The same day that the Court decided *City of Mobile*, the Court in *City of Rome v. United States*, 446 U.S. 156 (1980), addressed the constitutionality of Section 5 of the Voting Rights Act, which the Court interpreted as encompassing not only voting practices that have a discriminatory purpose, but

also those that have a discriminatory effect. Ironically, in *City of Rome*, a six-Justice majority concluded that Congress, legislating pursuant to its power under Section 2 of the Fifteenth Amendment, could reach conduct that has only a discriminatory effect:

> The appellants contend that the Act is unconstitutional because it exceeds Congress' power to enforce that Amendment. They claim that § 1 of the Amendment prohibits only purposeful racial discrimination in voting, and that in enforcing that provision pursuant to § 2, Congress may not prohibit voting practices lacking discriminatory intent even if they are discriminatory in effect. We hold that, even if § 1 of the Amendment prohibits only purposeful discrimination, the prior decisions of this Court foreclose any argument that Congress may not, pursuant to § 2, outlaw voting practices that are discriminatory in effect.
>
> The appellants are asking us to do nothing less than overrule our decision in *South Carolina v. Katzenbach*, 383 U.S. 301 (1966), in which we upheld the constitutionality of the Act....
>
> Congress' authority under § 2 of the Fifteenth Amendment, we held, was no less broad than its authority under the Necessary and Proper Clause, see *McCulloch v. Maryland*, 4 Wheat. 316, 421 (1819) ....
>
> Applying this standard, the Court held that the coverage formula of § 4(b), the ban on the use of literacy tests and related devices, the requirement that new voting rules must be precleared and must lack both discriminatory purpose and effect, and the use of federal examiners were all appropriate methods for Congress to use to enforce the Fifteenth Amendment.
>
> The Court's treatment in *South Carolina v. Katzenbach* of the Act's ban on literacy tests demonstrates that, under the Fifteenth Amendment, Congress may prohibit voting practices that have only a discriminatory effect. The Court had earlier held in *Lassiter v. Northampton County Board of Elections*, 360 U.S. 45 (1959), that the use of a literacy test that was fair on its face and was not employed in a discriminatory fashion did not violate § 1 of the Fifteenth Amendment. In upholding the Act's *per se* ban on such tests in *South Carolina v. Katzenbach*, the Court found no reason to overrule *Lassiter*. Instead, the Court recognized that the prohibition was an appropriate method of enforcing the Fifteenth Amendment because for many years most of the covered jurisdictions had imposed such tests to effect voting discrimination and the continued use of even nondiscriminatory, fairly administered literacy tests would "freeze the effect" of past discrimination by allowing white illiterates to remain on the voting rolls while excluding illiterate Negroes. *South Carolina v. Katzenbach, supra*, at 334. This holding makes clear that Congress may, under the authority of § 2 of the Fifteenth Amendment, prohibit state action that, though in itself not violative of § 1, perpetuates the effects of past discrimination....

City of Rome, 446 U.S., at 173-76. What justifies interpreting direct suits pursuant to Section 1 of the Fifteenth Amendment to require proof of discriminatory purpose, but not those brought pursuant to legislation promulgated by Congress pursuant to Section 2 of the Fifteenth Amendment? Is this related to the deferential standard of review of congressional legislation enacted pursuant to its enforcement powers, examined in Chapter 9? Should the same principle apply to laws enacted pursuant to Section 2 of the Thirteenth Amendment or Section 5 of the Fourteenth Amendment? Keep these questions in mind when you revisit Congress's power to enforce the Reconstruction Amendments in Chapter 21.

2. Are you persuaded by Justice Marshall's efforts in *City of Mobile* to distinguish the Fourteenth Amendment from the Fifteenth Amendment? Would those same rationales also justify treating the Thirteenth Amendment differently? Should those arguments apply not only to the question whether the discriminatory purpose requirement is applicable, but also to the scope of Congress's enforcement powers? Keep these questions in mind as well when you revisit Congress's power to enforce the Reconstruction Amendments in Chapter 21.

3. Reconsider the Court's decisions recognizing fundamental rights under both the Equal Protection and Due Process Clauses. Did those cases focus on the question whether the law at issue was purposefully targeted at the right at issue? Given the nature of fundamental rights, should it really matter whether the government acted with a discriminatory purpose or not? Or is the nature of those rights such that mere infringement results in a constitutional injury, without regard to the intent of the governmental actors involved? You will revisit the Court's fundamental rights cases in Chapters 16, 18, and 19. When you read those cases, keep an eye out for references to the presence or absence of a discriminatory purpose.

Chapter 16

Refining "Fundamental Rights" Under the Equal Protection and Due Process Clauses

As you saw in Chapters 8 and 11, the Court's decisions between the 1940s and the early 1970s recognized and enforced a number of so-called fundamental rights, some pursuant to the Equal Protection Clause and others pursuant to the Due Process Clause. This Chapter examines the Court's fundamental rights decisions from 1973 through 2000, a period of time when the Court's ideology shifted in a rightward direction, but was tempered by a number of moderate Justices, including Justices Kennedy, O'Connor, and Souter.

The first four parts of this chapter examines the Court's decisions during this period in a number of discrete areas in which a fundamental right is claimed, including education, marriage, parental and familial rights, and sexual intimacy. As you read these cases, consider the extent to which the Court is relying on the Due Process Clause, the Equal Protection Clause, or both. Moreover, see if you can identify the methodology used by the Court in determining the existence and scope of rights derived from each constitutional clause. The final part of this chapter examines three cases that, while addressing discrete substantive rights, focus more explicitly on general fundamental rights methodological questions.

A. Education

If you re-read the Court's decision in *Brown*, you will see that there is some ambiguity as to whether or not the Court's equal protection holding was class based, rights based, or an amalgam of the two. On the one hand, the Court focused on the nature of the classification, asking whether "segregation . . . solely on the basis of race . . . deprive[s] the children of the minority group of equal educational opportunities," suggesting a class-based decision. On the other hand, the Court focused on the importance of the right at issue, writing that "[t]oday, education is perhaps the most important function of state and local governments, and concluding that "in the field of public education the doctrine of 'separate but equal' has no place," suggesting a rights based focus.

In Chapter 13, you read an excerpt from the Court's decision in *Rodriguez*, which involved a constitutional challenge to Texas's scheme for funding public education. In that excerpt, the Court rejected a claim that the statute involved a wealth-based classification subject to heightened scrutiny under the Equal Protection Clause. In that decision, the Court also considered a claim that education is a fundamental right protected by the Equal Protection Clause, and that Texas's funding scheme infringed upon that right.

San Antonio Independent School District v. Rodriguez

411 U.S. 1 (1973)

Mr. Justice Powell delivered the opinion of the Court. . . .

[I]n recognition of the fact that this Court has never heretofore held that wealth discrimination alone provides an adequate basis for invoking strict scrutiny, appellees have not relied solely on this contention. They also assert that the State's system impermissibly interferes with the exercise of a "fundamental" right and that accordingly the prior decisions of this Court require the application of the strict standard of judicial review. *Graham v. Richardson*, 403 U.S. 365, 375–376 (1971); *Kramer v. Union Free School District*, 395 U.S. 621 (1969); *Shapiro v. Thompson*, 394 U.S. 618 (1969). It is this question—whether education is a fundamental right, in the sense that it is among the rights and liberties protected by the Constitution—which has so consumed the attention of courts and commentators in recent years.

In *Brown v. Board of Education*, 347 U.S. 483 (1954), a unanimous Court recognized that "education is perhaps the most important function of state and local governments." *Id.*, at 493. What was said there in the context of racial discrimination has lost none of its vitality with the passage of time:

> "Compulsory school attendance laws and the great expenditures for education both demonstrate our recognition of the importance of education to our democratic society. It is required in the performance of our most basic public responsibilities, even service in the armed forces. It is the very foundation of good citizenship. Today it is a principal instrument in awakening the child to cultural values, in preparing him for later professional training, and in helping him to adjust normally to his environment. In these days, it is doubtful that any child may reasonably be expected to succeed in life if he is denied the opportunity of an education. Such an opportunity, where the state has undertaken to provide it, is a right which must be made available to all on equal terms."

This theme, expressing an abiding respect for the vital role of education in a free society, may be found in numerous opinions of Justices of this Court writing both before and after *Brown* was decided.

Nothing this Court holds today in any way detracts from our historic dedication to public education. . . . But the importance of a service performed by the State does not determine whether it must be regarded as fundamental for purposes of examination under the Equal Protection Clause. Mr. Justice Harlan, dissenting from the Court's application of strict scrutiny to a law impinging upon the right of interstate travel, admonished that "[v]irtually every state statute affects important rights." *Shapiro v. Thompson*, 394 U.S., at 655, 661. In his view, if the degree of judicial scrutiny of state legislation fluctuated, depending on a majority's view of the importance of the interest affected, we would have gone "far toward making this Court a 'super-legislature.'" *Ibid.* We would, indeed, then be assuming a legislative role and one for which the Court lacks both authority and competence. But MR. JUSTICE STEWART's response in *Shapiro* to Mr. Justice Harlan's concern correctly articulates the limits of the fundamental-rights rationale employed in the Court's equal protection decisions:

> "The Court today does *not* 'pick out particular human activities, characterize them as "fundamental," and give them added protection. . . .' To the contrary, the Court simply recognizes, as it must, an established constitutional right, and gives to that right no less protection than the Constitution itself demands." *Id.*, at 642

MR. JUSTICE STEWART's statement serves to underline what the opinion of the Court in *Shapiro* makes clear. In subjecting to strict judicial scrutiny state welfare eligibility statutes that imposed a one-year durational residency requirement as a precondition to receiving AFDC benefits, the Court explained:

> "[I]n moving from State to State . . . appellees were exercising a constitutional right, and any classification which serves to penalize the exercise of that right, unless shown to be necessary to promote a *compelling* governmental interest, is unconstitutional." *Id.*, at 634.

The right to interstate travel had long been recognized as a right of constitutional significance, and the Court's decision, therefore, did not require an ad hoc determination as to the social or economic importance of that right. . . .

The lesson of these cases in addressing the question now before the Court is plain. It is not the province of this Court to create substantive constitutional rights in the name of guaranteeing equal protection of the laws. Thus, the key to discovering whether education is "fundamental" is not to be found in comparisons of the relative societal significance of education as opposed to subsistence or housing. Nor is it to be found by weighing whether education is as important as the right to travel. Rather, the answer lies in assessing whether there is a right to education explicitly or implicitly guaranteed by the Constitution.

Education, of course, is not among the rights afforded explicit protection under our Federal Constitution. Nor do we find any basis for saying it is implicitly so protected. As we have said, the undisputed importance of education will not alone cause this Court to depart from the usual standard for reviewing a State's social and economic legislation. It is appellees' contention, however, that education is distinguishable from other services and benefits provided by the State because it bears a peculiarly close relationship to other rights and liberties accorded protection under the Constitution. Specifically, they insist that education is itself a fundamental personal right because it is essential to the effective exercise of First Amendment freedoms and to intelligent utilization of the right to vote. In asserting a nexus between speech and education, appellees urge that the right to speak is meaningless unless the speaker is capable of articulating his thoughts intelligently and persuasively. The "marketplace of ideas" is an empty forum for those lacking basic communicative tools. Likewise, they argue that the corollary right to receive information becomes little more than a hollow privilege when the recipient has not been taught to read, assimilate, and utilize available knowledge.

A similar line of reasoning is pursued with respect to the right to vote.[78] Exercise of the franchise, it is contended, cannot be divorced from the educational foundation of the voter. The electoral process, if reality is to conform to the democratic ideal, depends on an informed electorate: a voter cannot cast his ballot intelligently unless his reading skills and thought processes have been adequately developed.

We need not dispute any of these propositions. The Court has long afforded zealous protection against unjustifiable governmental interference with the individual's rights to speak and to vote. Yet we have never presumed to possess either the ability or the authority to guarantee to the citizenry the most *effective* speech or the most *informed* electoral choice. That these may be desirable goals of a system of freedom of expression and of a representative form of government is not to be doubted. These are indeed goals to be pursued by a people whose thoughts and beliefs are freed from governmental interference. But they are not values to be implemented by judicial instruction into otherwise legitimate state activities.

Even if it were conceded that some identifiable quantum of education is a constitutionally protected prerequisite to the meaningful exercise of either right, we have no indication that the present levels of educational expenditures in Texas provide an education that falls short. Whatever merit appellees' argument might have if a State's financing system occasioned an absolute denial of educational opportunities to any of its children, that argument provides no basis for finding an interference with fundamental rights where only relative differences in spending levels are involved and where—as is true in the present case—no charge fairly could be made that the system fails to provide each child with an opportunity to acquire the basic minimal skills necessary for the enjoyment of the rights of speech and of full participation in the political process.

Furthermore, the logical limitations on appellees' nexus theory are difficult to perceive. How, for instance, is education to be distinguished from the significant personal interests in the basics of decent food and shelter? Empirical examination

78. Since the right to vote, *per se*, is not a constitutionally protected right, we assume that appellees' references to that right are simply shorthand references to the protected right, implicit in our constitutional system, to participate in state elections on an equal basis with other qualified voters whenever the State has adopted an elective process for determining who will represent any segment of the State's population.

might well buttress an assumption that the ill-fed, ill-clothed, and ill-housed are among the most ineffective participants in the political process, and that they derive the least enjoyment from the benefits of the First Amendment. . . .

We have carefully considered each of the arguments supportive of the District Court's finding that education is a fundamental right or liberty and have found those arguments unpersuasive. In one further respect we find this a particularly inappropriate case in which to subject state action to strict judicial scrutiny. The present case, in another basic sense, is significantly different from any of the cases in which the Court has applied strict scrutiny to state or federal legislation touching upon constitutionally protected rights. Each of our prior cases involved legislation which "deprived," "infringed," or "interfered" with the free exercise of some such fundamental personal right or liberty. . . .

Every step leading to the establishment of the system Texas utilizes today—including the decisions permitting localities to tax and expend locally, and creating and continuously expanding the state aid—was implemented in an effort to extend public education and to improve its quality. Of course, every reform that benefits some more than others may be criticized for what it fails to accomplish. But we think it plain that, in substance, the thrust of the Texas system is affirmative and reformatory and, therefore, should be scrutinized under judicial principles sensitive to the nature of the State's efforts and to the rights reserved to the States under the Constitution. . . .

[The concurring opinion of Justice Stewart and the dissenting opinions of Justices Brennan, White, and Marshall are omitted.]

Notes and Questions

1. *Rodriguez* addresses the question whether education is a fundamental right protected by the Equal Protection Clause. Recall from Chapter 8 that such rights are distinguished by the fact that the government is under no obligation to extend them to people at all, but if they choose to do so, they must extend the right in an even-handed manner. In other words, unlike the rights recognized under the Due Process Clause, which are freestanding rights, the ones recognized under the Equal Protection Clause are qualified.

How does the Court decide in the first instance whether or not a fundamental right is protected by the Equal Protection Clause or the Due Process Clause? Moreover, besides the freestanding versus qualified nature of the rights, are there any other ways in which these rights differ? What about the methodology for deciding whether or not the right exists in the first instance?

2. Does *Rodriguez* explicitly hold that the right to an education is not protected whatsoever by the Equal Protection Clause? Or is there language in the decision that leaves the door open to such a finding? Note that in *Rodriguez*, nobody is denied an education. Rather, some receive more public funding than others. Recall that in *Plyler v. Doe*, 457 U.S. 202 (1982), the law at issue wholly deprived children present unlawfully in the United States of an education. Although the majority in *Plyler* decided the case on class-based equal protection grounds, Justice Blackmun wrote a separate concurring opinion deciding the case on rights-based equal protection grounds. Justice Blackmun distinguished *Rodriguez*, noting that the Court there "reserved judgment on the constitutionality of a state system that "occasioned an absolute denial of educational opportunities to any of its children." *Id.* at 235 (Blackmun, J., concurring). In a groundbreaking opinion, a federal appeals court recently recognized a fundamental right to a basic minimal level of education. In so doing, the court invoked not the Equal Protection Clause at issue in *Rodriguez*, but instead the Due Process Clause. *See Gary B. v. Whitmer*, 957 F.3d 616 (6th Cir. 2020). At the time this book went to press, the case was awaiting *en banc* review.

B. Marriage

Recall that the right to marry was mentioned, by way of dicta, in both the Court's early due process and equal protection fundamental rights decisions. The Court's 1923 decision in *Meyer* spoke of a right "to marry" protected by the Due Process Clause, and the Court's 1942 decision in *Skinner* wrote that "marriage and procreation" are fundamental rights protected by the Equal Protection Clause. In 1967, the Court in *Loving* declared unconstitutional laws prohibiting interracial marriage. While the decision in *Loving* was mostly focused on the race-based classification involved, the Court also concluded that marriage was a fundamental right protected by the Due Process Clause. In so concluding, it relied upon *Skinner*, a case decided on Equal Protection grounds.

The two decisions that follow, as well as cases you will read later in the book, examine the Court's consideration of laws restricting the right to marry on grounds other than race. As you read these cases, consider the following questions:

- To the extent that marriage is a fundamental right, is it one protected by the Equal Protection Clause, the Due Process Clause, or both, and what are the consequences of that determination?
- To what extent is the fundamental right to marry tied to procreation, given that *Skinner* discussed "marriage and procreation" together? What consequences would such a conclusion have for couples that cannot naturally reproduce together, such as same-sex couples?
- What level of scrutiny applies to laws infringing upon the right to marry?
- Is the right at stake the specific right to marry, or merely the right to some form of official government recognition of one's relationship?

Zablocki v. Redhail

434 U.S. 374 (1978)

Mr. Justice Marshall delivered the opinion of the Court.

At issue in this case is the constitutionality of a Wisconsin statute, Wis. Stat. §§ 245.10(1), (4), (5) (1973), which provides that members of a certain class of Wisconsin residents may not marry, within the State or elsewhere, without first obtaining a court order granting permission to marry. The class is defined by the statute to include any "Wisconsin resident having minor issue not in his custody and which he is under obligation to support by any court order or judgment." The statute specifies that court permission cannot be granted unless the marriage applicant submits proof of compliance with the support obligation and, in addition, demonstrates that the children covered by the support order "are not then and are not likely thereafter to become public charges." No marriage license may lawfully be issued in Wisconsin to a person covered by the statute, except upon court order; any marriage entered into without compliance with § 245.10 is declared void; and persons acquiring marriage licenses in violation of the section are subject to criminal penalties....

On the merits, the three-judge panel analyzed the challenged statute under the Equal Protection Clause and concluded that "strict scrutiny" was required because the classification created by the statute infringed upon a fundamental right, the right to marry. The court then proceeded to evaluate the interests advanced by the State to justify the statute, and, finding that the classification was not necessary for the achievement of those interests, the court held the statute invalid and enjoined the county clerks from enforcing it....

In evaluating §§ 245.10(1), (4), (5) under the Equal Protection Clause, "we must first determine what burden of justification the classification created thereby must meet, by looking to the nature of the classification and the individual interests affected." Since our past decisions make clear that the right to marry is of fundamental importance, and since the classification at issue here significantly interferes with the exercise of that right, we believe that "critical examination" of the state interests advanced in support of the classification is required.

The leading decision of this Court on the right to marry is *Loving v. Virginia*, 388 U.S. 1 (1967). In that case, an interracial couple who had been convicted of violating Virginia's miscegenation laws challenged the statutory scheme on both equal protection and due process grounds. The Court's opinion could have rested solely on the ground that the statutes discriminated on the basis of race in violation of the Equal Protection Clause. But the Court went on to hold that the laws arbitrarily deprived the couple of a fundamental liberty protected by the Due Process Clause, the freedom to marry. . . .

Although *Loving* arose in the context of racial discrimination, prior and subsequent decisions of this Court confirm that the right to marry is of fundamental importance for all individuals. Long ago, in *Maynard v. Hill*, 125 U.S. 190 (1888), the Court characterized marriage as "the most important relation in life," and as "the foundation of the family and of society, without which there would be neither civilization nor progress." In *Meyer v. Nebraska*, 262 U.S. 390 (1923), the Court recognized that the right "to marry, establish a home and bring up children" is a central part of the liberty protected by the Due Process Clause, and in *Skinner v. Oklahoma ex rel. Williamson, supra*, 316 U.S. 535 (1942), marriage was described as "fundamental to the very existence and survival of the race."

More recent decisions have established that the right to marry is part of the fundamental "right of privacy" implicit in the Fourteenth Amendment's Due Process Clause. In *Griswold v. Connecticut*, 381 U.S. 479 (1965), the Court observed:

> "We deal with a right of privacy older than the Bill of Rights—older than our political parties, older than our school system. Marriage is a coming together for better or for worse, hopefully enduring, and intimate to the degree of being sacred. It is an association that promotes a way of life, not causes; a harmony in living, not political faiths; a bilateral loyalty, not commercial or social projects. Yet it is an association for as noble a purpose as any involved in our prior decisions."

Cases subsequent to *Griswold* and *Loving* have routinely categorized the decision to marry as among the personal decisions protected by the right of privacy. . . .

It is not surprising that the decision to marry has been placed on the same level of importance as decisions relating to procreation, childbirth, child rearing, and family relationships. As the facts of this case illustrate, it would make little sense to recognize a right of privacy with respect to other matters of family life and not with respect to the decision to enter the relationship that is the foundation of the family in our society. The woman whom appellee desired to marry had a fundamental right to seek an abortion of their expected child, see *Roe v. Wade, supra,* or to bring the child into life to suffer the myriad social, if not economic, disabilities that the status of illegitimacy brings. Surely, a decision to marry and raise the child in a traditional family setting must receive equivalent protection. And, if appellee's right to procreate means anything at all, it must imply some right to enter the only relationship in which the State of Wisconsin allows sexual relations legally to take place.[11]

By reaffirming the fundamental character of the right to marry, we do not mean to suggest that every state regulation which relates in any way to the incidents of or prerequisites for marriage must be subjected to rigorous scrutiny. To the contrary, reasonable regulations that do not significantly interfere with decisions to enter into the marital relationship may legitimately be imposed. The statutory classification at issue here, however, clearly does interfere directly and substantially with the right to marry....

Some of those in the affected class, like appellee, will never be able to obtain the necessary court order, because they either lack the financial means to meet their support obligations or cannot prove that their children will not become public charges. These persons are absolutely prevented from getting married. Many others, able in theory to satisfy the statute's requirements, will be sufficiently burdened by having to do so that they will in effect be coerced into forgoing their right to marry. And even those who can be persuaded to meet the statute's requirements suffer a serious intrusion into their freedom of choice in an area in which we have held such freedom to be fundamental.

When a statutory classification significantly interferes with the exercise of a fundamental right, it cannot be upheld unless it is supported by sufficiently important state interests and is closely tailored to effectuate only those interests. Appellant asserts that two interests are served by the challenged statute: the permission-to-marry proceeding furnishes an opportunity to counsel the applicant as to the necessity of fulfilling his prior support obligations; and the welfare of the out-of-custody children is protected. We may accept for present purposes that these are legitimate and substantial interests, but, since the means selected by the State for achieving these interests unnecessarily impinge on the right to marry, the statute cannot be sustained.

There is evidence that the challenged statute, as originally introduced in the Wisconsin Legislature, was intended merely to establish a mechanism whereby persons with support obligations to children from prior marriages could be counseled before they entered into new marital relationships and incurred further support obligations. Court permission to marry was to be required, but apparently permission was automatically to be granted after counseling was completed. The statute actually enacted, however, does not expressly require or provide for any counseling whatsoever, nor for any automatic granting of permission to marry by the court, and thus it can hardly be justified as a means for ensuring counseling of the persons

11. Wisconsin punishes fornication as a criminal offense:
"Whoever has sexual intercourse with a person not his spouse may be fined not more than $200 or imprisoned not more than 6 months or both." Wis. Stat. § 944.15 (1973).

within its coverage. Even assuming that counseling does take place—a fact as to which there is no evidence in the record—this interest obviously cannot support the withholding of court permission to marry once counseling is completed.

With regard to safeguarding the welfare of the out-of-custody children, appellant's brief does not make clear the connection between the State's interest and the statute's requirements. At argument, appellant's counsel suggested that, since permission to marry cannot be granted unless the applicant shows that he has satisfied his court-determined support obligations to the prior children and that those children will not become public charges, the statute provides incentive for the applicant to make support payments to his children. This "collection device" rationale cannot justify the statute's broad infringement on the right to marry.

First, with respect to individuals who are unable to meet the statutory requirements, the statute merely prevents the applicant from getting married, without delivering any money at all into the hands of the applicant's prior children. More importantly, regardless of the applicant's ability or willingness to meet the statutory requirements, the State already has numerous other means for exacting compliance with support obligations, means that are at least as effective as the instant statute's and yet do not impinge upon the right to marry. Under Wisconsin law, whether the children are from a prior marriage or were born out of wedlock, court-determined support obligations may be enforced directly via wage assignments, civil contempt proceedings, and criminal penalties. And, if the State believes that parents of children out of their custody should be responsible for ensuring that those children do not become public charges, this interest can be achieved by adjusting the criteria used for determining the amounts to be paid under their support orders.

There is also some suggestion that § 245.10 protects the ability of marriage applicants to meet support obligations to prior children by preventing the applicants from incurring new support obligations. But the challenged provisions of § 245.10 are grossly underinclusive with respect to this purpose, since they do not limit in any way new financial commitments by the applicant other than those arising out of the contemplated marriage. The statutory classification is substantially overinclusive as well: Given the possibility that the new spouse will actually better the applicant's financial situation, by contributing income from a job or otherwise, the statute in many cases may prevent affected individuals from improving their ability to satisfy their prior support obligations. And, although it is true that the applicant will incur support obligations to any children born during the contemplated marriage, preventing the marriage may only result in the children being born out of wedlock, as in fact occurred in appellee's case. Since the support obligation is the same whether the child is born in or out of wedlock, the net result of preventing the marriage is simply more illegitimate children.

The statutory classification created by §§ 245.10(1), (4), (5) thus cannot be justified by the interests advanced in support of it. . . .

Mr. Justice Stewart, concurring in the judgment.

I cannot join the opinion of the Court. To hold, as the Court does, that the Wisconsin statute violates the Equal Protection Clause seems to me to misconceive the meaning of that constitutional guarantee. The Equal Protection Clause deals not with substantive rights or freedoms but with invidiously discriminatory classifications....

Like almost any law, the Wisconsin statute now before us affects some people and does not affect others. But to say that it thereby creates "classifications" in the equal protection sense strikes me as little short of fantasy. The problem in this case is not one of discriminatory classifications, but of unwarranted encroachment upon a constitutionally protected freedom. I think that the Wisconsin statute is unconstitutional because it exceeds the bounds of permissible state regulation of marriage, and invades the sphere of liberty protected by the Due Process Clause of the Fourteenth Amendment....

In an opinion of the Court half a century ago, Mr. Justice Holmes described an equal protection claim as "the usual last resort of constitutional arguments." *Buck v. Bell*, 274 U.S. 200, 208. Today equal protection doctrine has become the Court's chief instrument for invalidating state laws. Yet, in a case like this one, the doctrine is no more than substantive due process by another name.

Although the Court purports to examine the bases for legislative classifications and to compare the treatment of legislatively defined groups, it actually erects substantive limitations on what States may do. Thus, the effect of the Court's decision in this case is not to require Wisconsin to draw its legislative classifications with greater precision or to afford similar treatment to similarly situated persons. Rather, the message of the Court's opinion is that Wisconsin may not use its control over marriage to achieve the objectives of the state statute. Such restrictions on basic governmental power are at the heart of substantive due process.

The Court is understandably reluctant to rely on substantive due process. But to embrace the essence of that doctrine under the guise of equal protection serves no purpose but obfuscation....

To conceal this appropriate inquiry invites mechanical or thoughtless application of misfocused doctrine. To bring it into the open forces a healthy and responsible recognition of the nature and purpose of the extreme power we wield when, in invalidating a state law in the name of the Constitution, we invalidate *pro tanto* the process of representative democracy in one of the sovereign States of the Union.

Mr. Justice Powell, concurring in the judgment.

I concur in the judgment of the Court that Wisconsin's restrictions on the exclusive means of creating the marital bond, erected by Wis. Stat. §§ 245.10(1), (4), and (5) (1973), cannot meet applicable constitutional standards. I write separately because the majority's rationale sweeps too broadly in an area which traditionally has been subject to pervasive state regulation. The Court apparently would subject all state regulation which "directly and substantially" interferes with the decision to marry in a traditional family setting to "critical examination" or "compelling state interest" analysis. Presumably, "reasonable regulations that do not significantly interfere with decisions to enter into the marital relationship may legitimately be imposed." The Court does not present, however, any principled means for distinguishing between the two types of regulations. Since state regulation in this area typically takes the form of a prerequisite or barrier to marriage or divorce, the degree of "direct" interference with the decision to marry or to divorce is unlikely to provide either guidance for state legislatures or a basis for judicial oversight.

[I]t is fair to say that there is a right of marital and familial privacy which places some substantive limits on the regulatory power of government. But the Court has yet to hold that all regulation touching upon marriage implicates a "fundamental right" triggering the most exacting judicial scrutiny.

The principal authority cited by the majority is *Loving v. Virginia*, 388 U.S. 1 (1967). Although *Loving* speaks of the "freedom to marry" as "one of the vital personal rights essential to the orderly pursuit of happiness by free men," the Court focused on the miscegenation statute before it.... Thus, *Loving* involved a denial of a "fundamental freedom" on a wholly unsupportable basis—the use of classifications "directly subversive of the principle of equality at the heart of the Fourteenth Amendment...." It does not speak to the level of judicial scrutiny of, or governmental justification for, "supportable" restrictions on the "fundamental freedom" of individuals to marry or divorce.

In my view, analysis must start from the recognition of domestic relations as "an area that has long been regarded as a virtually exclusive province of the States." *Sosna v. Iowa*, 419 U.S. 393, 404 (1975) .... State regulation has included bans on incest, bigamy, and homosexuality, as well as various preconditions to marriage, such as blood tests. Likewise, a showing of fault on the part of one of the partners traditionally has been a prerequisite to the dissolution of an unsuccessful union. A "compelling state purpose" inquiry would cast doubt on the network of restrictions that the States have fashioned to govern marriage and divorce....

Mr. Justice Rehnquist, dissenting.

I substantially agree with my Brother Powell's reasons for rejecting the Court's conclusion that marriage is the sort of "fundamental right" which must invariably trigger the strictest judicial scrutiny. I disagree with his imposition of an "intermediate" standard of review, which leads him to conclude that the statute, though generally valid as an "additional collection mechanism" offends the Constitution by its "failure to make provision for those without the means to comply with child-support obligations." For similar reasons, I disagree with my Brother Stewart's conclusion that the statute is invalid for its failure to exempt those persons who "simply cannot afford to meet the statute's financial requirements." I would view this legislative judgment in the light of the traditional presumption of validity. I think that under the Equal Protection Clause the statute need pass only the "rational basis test," *Dandridge v. Williams*, 397 U.S. 471, 485 (1970), and that under the Due Process Clause it need only be shown that it bears a rational relation to a constitutionally permissible objective. *Williamson v. Lee Optical Co.,* 348 U.S. 483, 491 (1955); *Ferguson v. Skrupa,* 372 U.S. 726, 733 (1963) (Harlan, J., concurring). The statute so viewed is a permissible exercise of the State's power to regulate family life and to assure the support of minor children, despite its possible imprecision in the extreme cases envisioned in the concurring opinions. . . .

[The concurring opinions of Chief Justice Burger and Justice Stevens are omitted.]

Turner v. Safley

482 U.S. 78 (1987)

Justice O'Connor delivered the opinion of the Court.

This case requires us to determine the constitutionality of regulations promulgated by the Missouri Division of Corrections relating to inmate marriages. . . .

The challenged marriage regulation, which was promulgated while this litigation was pending, permits an inmate to marry only with the permission of the superintendent of the prison, and provides that such approval should be given only "when there are compelling reasons to do so." The term "compelling" is not defined, but prison officials testified at trial that generally only a pregnancy or the birth of an illegitimate child would be considered a compelling reason. Prior to the promulgation of this rule, the applicable regulation did not obligate Missouri Division of Corrections officials to assist an inmate who wanted to get married, but it also did not specifically authorize the superintendent of an institution to prohibit inmates from getting married. . . .

The [District] court, relying on *Procunier v. Martinez,* 416 U.S. 396, 413–414 (1974), applied a strict scrutiny standard. It held the marriage regulation to be an unconstitutional infringement upon the fundamental right to marry because it was far more restrictive than was either reasonable or essential for the protection of the State's interests in security and rehabilitation. . . .

The Court of Appeals for the Eighth Circuit affirmed. The Court of Appeals held that the District Court properly used strict scrutiny. . . .

We granted certiorari. . . .

[W]hen a prison regulation impinges on inmates' constitutional rights, the regulation is valid if it is reasonably related to legitimate penological interests. In our view, such a standard is necessary if "prison administrators . . . , and not the courts, [are] to make the difficult judgments concerning institutional operations." *Jones v. North Carolina Prisoners' Union,* 433 U.S., at 128. Subjecting the day-to-day judgments of prison officials to an inflexible strict scrutiny analysis would seriously hamper their ability to anticipate security problems and to adopt innovative solutions to the intractable problems of prison administration. . . .

[S]everal factors are relevant in determining the reasonableness of the regulation at issue. First, there must be a "valid, rational connection" between the prison regulation and the legitimate governmental interest put forward to justify it. . . .

A second factor relevant in determining the reasonableness of a prison restriction . . . is whether there are alternative means of exercising the right that remain open to prison inmates. . . .

A third consideration is the impact accommodation of the asserted constitutional right will have on guards and other inmates, and on the allocation of prison resources generally. . . .

Finally, the absence of ready alternatives is evidence of the reasonableness of a prison regulation. By the same token, the existence of obvious, easy alternatives may be evidence that the regulation is not reasonable, but is an "exaggerated response" to prison concerns. . . .

In support of the marriage regulation, petitioners first suggest that the rule does not deprive prisoners of a constitutionally protected right. They concede that the decision to marry is a fundamental right under *Zablocki v. Redhail,* 434 U.S. 374 (1978), and *Loving v. Virginia,* 388 U.S. 1 (1967), but they imply that a different rule should obtain "in . . . a prison forum." Petitioners then argue that even if the regulation burdens inmates' constitutional rights, the restriction should be tested under a reasonableness standard. They urge that the restriction is reasonably related to legitimate security and rehabilitation concerns.

We disagree with petitioners that *Zablocki* does not apply to prison inmates. It is settled that a prison inmate "retains those [constitutional] rights that are not inconsistent with his status as a prisoner or with the legitimate penological objectives of the corrections system." The right to marry, like many other rights, is subject to substantial restrictions as a result of incarceration. Many important attributes of marriage remain, however, after taking into account the limitations imposed by prison life. First, inmate marriages, like others, are expressions of emotional support and public commitment. These elements are an important and significant aspect of the marital relationship. In addition, many religions recognize marriage as having spiritual significance; for some inmates and their spouses, therefore, the commitment of marriage may be an exercise of religious faith as well as an expression of personal dedication. Third, most inmates eventually will be released by parole or commutation, and therefore most inmate marriages are formed in the expectation that they ultimately will be fully consummated. Finally, marital status often is a precondition to the receipt of government benefits (*e.g.*, Social Security benefits), property rights (*e.g.*, tenancy by the entirety, inheritance rights), and other, less tangible benefits (*e.g.*, legitimation of children born out of wedlock). These incidents of marriage, like the religious and personal aspects of the marriage commitment, are unaffected by the fact of confinement or the pursuit of legitimate corrections goals.

Taken together, we conclude that these remaining elements are sufficient to form a constitutionally protected marital relationship in the prison context. . . .

[The Court proceeds to conclude that the regulations at issue do not satisfy even the relaxed standard of review applicable in prison settings.]

[The opinion of Justice Stevens, concurring in part and dissenting in part, is omitted.]

Notes and Questions

1. On which provision of the Fourteenth Amendment, the Due Process or the Equal Protection Clause, do the *Zablocki* and *Turner* Courts rely? Why might the answer to that question be significant? Consider, for example, a modern U.S. state government that is unhappy with the concept of same-sex marriage and wishes to withdraw altogether from the "marriage business." Would the determination whether marriage is a Due Process or an Equal Protection right matter, and if so, why?

2. What level of scrutiny does the *Zablocki* Court apply? It is clearly more than rational basis review, but is it strict scrutiny? Or some other level of scrutiny?

3. The *Zablocki* Court distinguishes between regulations that "directly and substantially interfere with the right to marry," for which heightened scrutiny is required, and "reasonable regulations that do not significantly interfere with decisions to enter into the marital relationship," which appear to be subject only to rational basis scrutiny. How clear is the line between these two categories of regulations?

4. Recall that *Skinner* appeared to link marriage with procreation. To what extent does *Zablocki* arguably reinforce that link? To what extent does *Turner* arguably sever it?

5. What explains the Court's ambiguity in these cases on the question whether an equal protection or a due process fundamental right is involved? Is it fear of being accused of a return to *Lochner* that has resulted in the search for a textual hook other than the Due Process Clause? Is it Justice Jackson's belief, as articulated in *Railway Express*, that equal protection is the weaker medicine of the two and thus more consistent with democratic ideals? Are the two clauses working in tandem in these cases, perhaps because the right to marry encompasses within it multiple individual rights, some of which are protected by one clause and some by the other?

6. How does the Court frame the right at issue in its marriage cases? Is it done in very narrow terms, such as the right to "interracial marriage" in *Loving*, "prisoner marriage" in *Turner*, and "deadbeat dad marriage" in *Zablocki*? Do they speak more generally in these cases instead of a "right to marry?" Or do they speak even more broadly about a right to "privacy" or "autonomy"? Keep this question in mind as you examine the Court's methodological approach to recognizing and enforcing fundamental rights in the materials that follow.

C. Parental and Familial Rights

Recall from Chapter 3 that, in the midst of the *Lochner* era, the Court struck down two laws that could be characterized as interfering with the rights of parents vis-à-vis their children. The *Meyer* Court, in striking down a law prohibiting the teaching of foreign languages in grade school, spoke generally about the right to "establish a home and bring up children." And the *Pierce* Court, in striking down a law prohibiting children from attending private school between the ages of 8 and 16, characterized the law as interfering with "the liberty of parents and guardians to direct the upbringing and education of children under their control." In a subsequent opinion, the Court in describing the *Meyer* and *Pierce* holdings, wrote that "these decisions have respected the private realm of family life which the state cannot enter." *Prince v. Massachusetts*, 321 U.S. 158, 166 (1944).

The cases that follow consider both the right of the government to interfere with parent-child relationships and also consider the extent to which there is a broader familial right that encompasses other sorts of relationships, such as that between a grandparent and a child.

Moore v. City of East Cleveland, Ohio

431 U.S. 494 (1977)

Mr. Justice Powell announced the judgment of the Court, and delivered an opinion in which Mr. Justice Brennan, Mr. Justice Marshall, and Mr. Justice Blackmun joined.

East Cleveland's housing ordinance, like many throughout the country, limits occupancy of a dwelling unit to members of a single family. § 1351.02. But the ordinance contains an unusual and complicated definitional section that recognizes as a "family" only a few categories of related individuals, § 1341.08. Because her family, living together in her home, fits none of those categories, appellant stands convicted of a criminal offense. The question in this case is whether the ordinance violates the Due Process Clause of the Fourteenth Amendment.

Appellant, Mrs. Inez Moore, lives in her East Cleveland home together with her son, Dale Moore Sr., and her two grandsons, Dale, Jr., and John Moore, Jr. The two boys are first cousins rather than brothers; we are told that John came to live with his grandmother and with the elder and younger Dale Moores after his mother's death.

In early 1973, Mrs. Moore received a notice of violation from the city, stating that John was an "illegal occupant" and directing her to comply with the ordinance. When she failed to remove him from her home, the city filed a criminal charge. Mrs. Moore moved to dismiss, claiming that the ordinance was constitutionally invalid on its face. Her motion was overruled, and upon conviction she was sentenced to five days in jail and a $25 fine. . . .

The city argues that our decision in *Village of Belle Terre v. Boraas*, 416 U.S. 1 (1974), requires us to sustain the ordinance attacked here. Belle Terre, like East Cleveland, imposed limits on the types of groups that could occupy a single dwelling unit. Applying the constitutional standard announced in this Court's leading land-use case, *Euclid v. Ambler Realty Co.*, 272 U.S. 365 (1926), we sustained the Belle Terre ordinance on the ground that it bore a rational relationship to permissible state objectives.

But one overriding factor sets this case apart from *Belle Terre*. The ordinance there affected only *unrelated* individuals. It expressly allowed all who were related by "blood, adoption, or marriage" to live together, and in sustaining the ordinance we were careful to note that it promoted "family needs" and "family values." East Cleveland, in contrast, has chosen to regulate the occupancy of its housing by slicing deeply into the family itself. This is no mere incidental result of the ordinance. On its face it selects certain categories of relatives who may live together and declares that others may not. In particular, it makes a crime of a grandmother's choice to live with her grandson in circumstances like those presented here.

When a city undertakes such intrusive regulation of the family, neither *Belle Terre* nor *Euclid* governs; the usual judicial deference to the legislature is inappropriate. "This Court has long recognized that freedom of personal choice in matters of marriage and family life is one of the liberties protected by the Due Process Clause of the Fourteenth Amendment." A host of cases, tracing their lineage to *Meyer v. Nebraska*, 262 U.S. 390, 399–401 (1923), and *Pierce v. Society of Sisters*, 268 U.S. 510, 534–535 (1925), have consistently acknowledged a "private realm of family life which the state cannot enter." *Prince v. Massachusetts*, 321 U.S. 158, 166 (1944) . . . . Of course, the family is not beyond regulation. But when the government intrudes on choices concerning family living arrangements, this Court must examine carefully the importance of the governmental interests advanced and the extent to which they are served by the challenged regulation. See *Poe v. Ullman*, *supra*, 367 U.S., at 554 (Harlan, J., dissenting).

When thus examined, this ordinance cannot survive. The city seeks to justify it as a means of preventing overcrowding, minimizing traffic and parking congestion, and avoiding an undue financial burden on East Cleveland's school system. Although these are legitimate goals, the ordinance before us serves them marginally, at best. For example, the ordinance permits any family consisting only of husband, wife, and unmarried children to live together, even if the family contains a half dozen licensed drivers, each with his or her own car. At the same time it forbids an adult brother and sister to share a household, even if both faithfully use public transportation. The ordinance would permit a grandmother to live with a single dependent son and children, even if his school-age children number a dozen, yet it forces Mrs. Moore to find another dwelling for her grandson John, simply because of the presence of his uncle and cousin in the same household. We need not labor the point. Section 1341.08 has but a tenuous relation to alleviation of the conditions mentioned by the city.

The city would distinguish the cases based on *Meyer* and *Pierce*. It points out that none of them "gives grandmothers any fundamental rights with respect to grandsons," and suggests that any constitutional right to live together as a family extends only to the nuclear family—essentially a couple and their dependent children.

To be sure, these cases did not expressly consider the family relationship presented here. . . . But unless we close our eyes to the basic reasons why certain rights associated with the family have been accorded shelter under the Fourteenth Amendment's

Due Process Clause, we cannot avoid applying the force and rationale of these precedents to the family choice involved in this case. . . .

Substantive due process has at times been a treacherous field for this Court. There are risks when the judicial branch gives enhanced protection to certain substantive liberties without the guidance of the more specific provisions of the Bill of Rights. As the history of the *Lochner* era demonstrates, there is reason for concern lest the only limits to such judicial intervention become the predilections of those who happen at the time to be Members of this Court. That history counsels caution and restraint. But it does not counsel abandonment, nor does it require what the city urges here: cutting off any protection of family rights at the first convenient, if arbitrary boundary the boundary of the nuclear family.

Appropriate limits on substantive due process come not from drawing arbitrary lines but rather from careful "respect for the teachings of history [and], solid recognition of the basic values that underlie our society". *Griswold v. Connecticut*, 381 U.S., at 501 (Harlan, J., concurring). Our decisions establish that the Constitution protects the sanctity of the family precisely because the institution of the family is deeply rooted in this Nation's history and tradition. It is through the family that we inculcate and pass down many of our most cherished values, moral and cultural.

Ours is by no means a tradition limited to respect for the bonds uniting the members of the nuclear family. The tradition of uncles, aunts, cousins, and especially grandparents sharing a household along with parents and children has roots equally venerable and equally deserving of constitutional recognition. Over the years millions of our citizens have grown up in just such an environment, and most, surely, have profited from it. Even if conditions of modern society have brought about a decline in extended family households, they have not erased the accumulated wisdom of civilization, gained over the centuries and honored throughout our history, that supports a larger conception of the family. Out of choice, necessity, or a sense of family responsibility, it has been common for close relatives to draw together and participate in the duties and the satisfactions of a common home. Decisions concerning child rearing, which *Yoder, Meyer, Pierce* and other cases have recognized as entitled to constitutional protection, long have been shared with grandparents or other relatives who occupy the same household indeed who may take on major responsibility for the rearing of the children. Especially in times of adversity, such as the death of a spouse or economic need, the broader family has tended to come together for mutual sustenance and to maintain or rebuild a secure home life. This is apparently what happened here.

Whether or not such a household is established because of personal tragedy, the choice of relatives in this degree of kinship to live together may not lightly be denied by the State. *Pierce* struck down an Oregon law requiring all children to attend the State's public schools, holding that the Constitution "excludes any general power of the State to standardize its children by forcing them to accept instruction from public teachers only." By the same token the Constitution prevents East Cleveland from standardizing its children and its adults by forcing all to live in certain narrowly defined family patterns.

[The concurring opinions of Justices Brennan and Stevens, and the dissenting opinions of Chief Justice Burger and Justices Stewart and White, are omitted.]

Notes and Questions

1. The *Moore* Court notes that it is not exercising unbridled discretion in interpreting the scope of the Due Process Clause, but rather is constrained by a particular methodology. What, exactly, is the Court relying on to determine that the relationship between a grandparent and a grandchild is entitled to constitutional protection?

2. Suppose what was involved in *Moore* was not the relationship between a grandparent and a grandchild, but instead between two unmarried persons of the same sex living together in an intimate relationship. Would that relationship be equally entitled to constitutional protection against governmental interference? If not, what distinguishes the two situations?

3. Does the right to protection of the grandparent-grandchild relationship come into play only if the child's parents are out of the picture, as in *Moore* itself? In other words, is the grandparent-grandchild relationship in this case derivative of the pre-existing parent-child relationship? If it is instead an independent right, what happens if there is a conflict between the wishes of a parent and the wishes of a grandparent with respect to a given child?

Lehr v. Robertson

463 U.S. 248 (1983)

Justice Stevens delivered the opinion of the Court.

The question presented is whether New York has sufficiently protected an unmarried father's inchoate relationship with a child whom he has never supported and rarely seen in the two years since her birth. The appellant, Jonathan Lehr, claims that the Due Process and Equal Protection Clauses of the Fourteenth Amendment, as interpreted in *Stanley v. Illinois*, 405 U.S. 645 (1972), and *Caban v. Mohammed*, 441 U.S. 380 (1979), give him an absolute right to notice and an opportunity to be heard before the child may be adopted. We disagree.

Jessica M. was born out of wedlock on November 9, 1976. Her mother, Lorraine Robertson, married Richard Robertson eight months after Jessica's birth. On December 21, 1978, when Jessica was over two years old, the Robertsons filed an adoption petition in the Family Court of Ulster County, New York. The court heard their testimony and received a favorable report from the Ulster County Department of Social Services. On March 7, 1979, the court entered an order of adoption. In this proceeding, appellant contends that the adoption order is invalid because he, Jessica's putative father, was not given advance notice of the adoption proceeding.

The State of New York maintains a "putative father registry." A man who files with that registry demonstrates his intent to claim paternity of a child born out of wedlock and is therefore entitled to receive notice of any proceeding to adopt that child. Before entering Jessica's adoption order, the Ulster County Family Court had the putative father registry examined. Although appellant claims to be Jessica's natural father, he had not entered his name in the registry.

In addition to the persons whose names are listed on the putative father registry, New York law requires that notice of an adoption proceeding be given to several other classes of possible fathers of children born out of wedlock—those who have been adjudicated to be the father, those who have been identified as the father on the child's birth certificate, those who live openly with the child and the child's mother and who hold themselves out to be the father, those who have been identified as the father by the mother in a sworn written statement, and those who were married to the child's mother before the child was six months old. Appellant admittedly was not a member of any of those classes. He had lived with appellee prior to Jessica's birth and visited her in the hospital when Jessica was born, but his name does not appear on Jessica's birth certificate. He did not live with appellee or Jessica after Jessica's birth, he has never provided them with any financial support, and he has never offered to marry appellee. Nevertheless, he contends that the following special circumstances gave him a constitutional right to notice and a hearing before Jessica was adopted....

This Court has examined the extent to which a natural father's biological relationship with his illegitimate child receives protection under the Due Process Clause in precisely three cases: *Stanley v. Illinois,* 405 U.S. 645, 92 S.Ct. 1208, 31 L.Ed.2d 551 (1972), *Quilloin v. Walcott*, 434 U.S. 246 (1978), and *Caban v. Mohammed*, 441 U.S. 380 (1979).

Stanley involved the constitutionality of an Illinois statute that conclusively presumed every father of a child born out of wedlock to be an unfit person to have custody of his children. The father in that case had lived with his children all their lives and had lived with their mother for 18 years. There was nothing in the record to indicate that Stanley had been a neglectful father who had not cared for his children. Under the statute, however, the nature of the actual relationship between parent and child was completely irrelevant. Once the mother died, the children were automatically made wards of the state.... [T]he Court held that the Due Process Clause was violated by the automatic destruction of the custodial relationship without giving the father any opportunity to present evidence regarding his fitness as a parent.

Quilloin involved the constitutionality of a Georgia statute that authorized the adoption, over the objection of the natural father, of a child born out of wedlock. The father in that case had never legitimated the child. It was only after the mother had remarried and her new husband had filed an adoption petition that the natural father sought visitation rights and filed a petition for legitimation. The trial court found adoption by the new husband to be in the child's best interests, and we unanimously held that action to be consistent with the Due Process Clause.

Caban involved the conflicting claims of two natural parents who had maintained joint custody of their children from the time of their birth until they were respectively two and four years old. The father challenged the validity of an order authorizing the mother's new husband to adopt the children; he relied on both the Equal Protection Clause and the Due Process Clause. Because this Court upheld his equal protection claim, the majority did not address his due process challenge. The comments on the latter claim by the four dissenting Justices are nevertheless instructive, because they identify the clear distinction between a mere biological relationship and an actual relationship of parental responsibility.

Justice Stewart correctly observed:

> "Even if it be assumed that each married parent after divorce has some substantive due process right to maintain his or her parental relationship, it by no means follows that each unwed parent has any such right. *Parental rights do not spring full-blown from the biological connection between parent and child. They require relationships more enduring.*" (emphasis added).

In a similar vein, the other three dissenters in *Caban* were prepared to "assume that, *if and when one develops,* the relationship between a father and his natural child is entitled to protection against arbitrary state action as a matter of due process." (emphasis added).

The difference between the developed parent-child relationship that was implicated in *Stanley* and *Caban,* and the potential relationship involved in *Quilloin* and this case, is both clear and significant. When an unwed father demonstrates a full commitment to the responsibilities of parenthood by "com[ing] forward to participate in the rearing of his child," *Caban,* 441 U.S., at 392, his interest in personal contact with his child acquires substantial protection under the due process clause. At that point it may be said that he "act[s] as a father toward his children." *Id.,* at 389, n. 7. But the mere existence of a biological link does not merit equivalent constitutional protection. . . .

The significance of the biological connection is that it offers the natural father an opportunity that no other male possesses to develop a relationship with his offspring. If he grasps that opportunity and accepts some measure of responsibility for the child's future, he may enjoy the blessings of the parent-child relationship and make uniquely valuable contributions to the child's development. If he fails to do so, the Federal Constitution will not automatically compel a state to listen to his opinion of where the child's best interests lie.

In this case, we are not assessing the constitutional adequacy of New York's procedures for terminating a developed relationship. Appellant has never had any significant custodial, personal, or financial relationship with Jessica, and he did not seek to establish a legal tie until after she was two years old. We are concerned only with whether New York has adequately protected his opportunity to form such a relationship. . . .

After this Court's decision in *Stanley*, the New York Legislature appointed a special commission to recommend legislation that would accommodate both the interests of biological fathers in their children and the children's interest in prompt and certain adoption procedures. The commission recommended, and the legislature enacted, a statutory adoption scheme that automatically provides notice to seven categories of putative fathers who are likely to have assumed some responsibility for the care of their natural children. If this scheme were likely to omit many responsible fathers, and if qualification for notice were beyond the control of an interested putative father, it might be thought procedurally inadequate. Yet, as all of the New York courts that reviewed this matter observed, the right to receive notice was completely within appellant's control. By mailing a postcard to the putative father registry, he could have guaranteed that he would receive notice of any proceedings to adopt Jessica. The possibility that he may have failed to do so because of his ignorance of the law cannot be a sufficient reason for criticizing the law itself. The New York legislature concluded that a more open-ended notice requirement would merely complicate the adoption process, threaten the privacy interests of unwed mothers, create the risk of unnecessary controversy, and impair the desired finality of adoption decrees. Regardless of whether we would have done likewise if we were legislators instead of judges, we surely cannot characterize the state's conclusion as arbitrary. . . .

Since the New York statutes adequately protected appellant's inchoate interest in establishing a relationship with Jessica, we find no merit in the claim that his constitutional rights were offended because the family court strictly complied with the notice provisions of the statute. . . .

[The dissenting opinion of Justice White is omitted.]

Notes and Questions

1. What is the nature of the due process right recognized in the line of cases leading up to *Lehr*, and why is that right not applicable under the facts of *Lehr* itself?

2. Is there an alternative argument that the law is unconstitutional because it draws a sex-based distinction between the rights of unwed fathers and unwed mothers? In a separate portion of the opinion, the *Lehr* Court rejected such a claim, distinguishing its earlier decision in *Caban* on the ground that there, unlike in *Lehr*, the unwed father and unwed mother were similarly situated in that both had an established and ongoing relationship with the child at issue.

Troxel v. Granville

530 U.S. 57 (2000)

Justice O'Connor announced the judgment of the Court and delivered an opinion, in which The Chief Justice, Justice Ginsburg, and Justice Breyer join.

Section 26.10.160(3) of the Revised Code of Washington permits "[a]ny person" to petition a superior court for visitation rights "at any time," and authorizes that court to grant such visitation rights whenever "visitation may serve the best interest of the child." Petitioners Jenifer and Gary Troxel petitioned a Washington Superior Court for the right to visit their grandchildren, Isabelle and Natalie Troxel. Respondent Tommie Granville, the mother of Isabelle and Natalie, opposed the petition. The case ultimately reached the Washington Supreme Court, which held that § 26.10.160(3) unconstitutionally interferes with the fundamental right of parents to rear their children.

Tommie Granville and Brad Troxel shared a relationship that ended in June 1991. The two never married, but they had two daughters, Isabelle and Natalie. Jenifer and Gary Troxel are Brad's parents, and thus the paternal grandparents of Isabelle and Natalie. After Tommie and Brad separated in 1991, Brad lived with his parents and regularly brought his daughters to his parents' home for weekend visitation. Brad committed suicide in May 1993. Although the Troxels at first continued to see Isabelle and Natalie on a regular basis after their son's death, Tommie Granville informed the Troxels in October 1993 that she wished to limit their visitation with her daughters to one short visit per month.

In December 1993, the Troxels commenced the present action by filing, in the Washington Superior Court for Skagit County, a petition to obtain visitation rights with Isabelle and Natalie. . . . At trial, the Troxels requested two weekends of overnight visitation per month and two weeks of visitation each summer. Granville did not oppose visitation altogether, but instead asked the court to order one day of visitation per month with no overnight stay. In 1995, the Superior Court issued an oral ruling and entered a visitation decree ordering visitation one weekend per month, one week during the summer, and four hours on both of the petitioning grandparents' birthdays. . . .

[The case ultimately made its way to the Washington Supreme Court, which held the statute violated the Due Process Clause of the Fourteenth Amendment.]

The demographic changes of the past century make it difficult to speak of an average American family. The composition of families varies greatly from household to household. While many children may have two married parents and grandparents who visit regularly, many other children are raised in single-parent households. In 1996, children living with only one parent accounted for 28 percent of all children under age 18 in the United States. Understandably, in these single-parent households, persons outside the nuclear family are called upon with increasing frequency to assist in the everyday tasks of child rearing. In many cases, grandparents play an important role. . . .

The nationwide enactment of nonparental visitation statutes is assuredly due, in some part, to the States' recognition of these changing realities of the American family. Because grandparents and other relatives undertake duties of a parental nature in many households, States have sought to ensure the welfare of the children therein by protecting the relationships those children form with such third parties. The States' nonparental visitation statutes are further supported by a recognition, which varies from State to State, that children should have the opportunity to benefit from relationships with statutorily specified persons—for example, their grandparents. The extension of statutory rights in this area to persons other than a child's parents, however, comes with an obvious cost. For example, the State's recognition of an independent third-party interest in a child can place a substantial burden on the traditional parent-child relationship.... [W]e are asked to decide whether § 26.10.160(3), as applied to Tommie Granville and her family, violates the Federal Constitution....

The liberty interest at issue in this case—the interest of parents in the care, custody, and control of their children—is perhaps the oldest of the fundamental liberty interests recognized by this Court. More than 75 years ago, in *Meyer v. Nebraska,* 262 U.S. 390, 399, 401 (1923), we held that the "liberty" protected by the Due Process Clause includes the right of parents to "establish a home and bring up children" and "to control the education of their own." Two years later, in *Pierce v. Society of Sisters,* 268 U.S. 510, 534–535 (1925), we again held that the "liberty of parents and guardians" includes the right "to direct the upbringing and education of children under their control." We explained in *Pierce* that "[t]he child is not the mere creature of the State; those who nurture him and direct his destiny have the right, coupled with the high duty, to recognize and prepare him for additional obligations." *Id.,* at 535. We returned to the subject in *Prince v. Massachusetts,* 321 U.S. 158 (1944), and again confirmed that there is a constitutional dimension to the right of parents to direct the upbringing of their children. "It is cardinal with us that the custody, care and nurture of the child reside first in the parents, whose primary function and freedom include preparation for obligations the state can neither supply nor hinder." *Id.,* at 166.

In subsequent cases also, we have recognized the fundamental right of parents to make decisions concerning the care, custody, and control of their children. In light of this extensive precedent, it cannot now be doubted that the Due Process Clause of the Fourteenth Amendment protects the fundamental right of parents to make decisions concerning the care, custody, and control of their children.

Section 26.10.160(3), as applied to Granville and her family in this case, unconstitutionally infringes on that fundamental parental right. The Washington nonparental visitation statute is breathtakingly broad. According to the statute's text, "*[a]ny person* may petition the court for visitation rights *at any time,*" and the court may grant such visitation rights whenever "visitation may serve *the best interest of the child.*" § 26.10.160(3) (emphases added). That language effectively permits any third party seeking visitation to subject any decision by a parent concerning visitation of the parent's children to state-court review. Once the visitation petition has been filed in court and the matter is placed before a judge, a parent's decision that visitation would not be in the child's best interest is accorded no deference. Section 26.10.160(3) contains no requirement that a court accord the parent's decision any presumption of validity or any weight whatsoever. Instead, the Washington statute places the best-interest determination solely in the hands of the judge. Should the judge disagree with the parent's estimation of the child's best interests, the judge's view necessarily prevails. Thus, in practical effect, in the State of Washington a court can disregard and overturn *any* decision by a fit custodial parent concerning visitation whenever a third party affected by the decision files a visitation petition, based solely on the judge's determination of the child's best interests. The Washington Supreme Court had the opportunity to give § 26.10.160(3) a narrower reading, but it declined to do so.

Turning to the facts of this case, the record reveals that the Superior Court's order was based on precisely the type of mere disagreement we have just described and nothing more. The Superior Court's order was not founded on any special factors that might justify the State's interference with Granville's fundamental right to make decisions concerning the rearing of her two daughters. To be sure, this case involves a visitation petition filed by grandparents soon after the death of their son—the father of Isabelle and Natalie—but the combination of several factors here compels our conclusion that § 26.10.160(3), as applied, exceeded the bounds of the Due Process Clause.

First, the Troxels did not allege, and no court has found, that Granville was an unfit parent. That aspect of the case is important, for there is a presumption that fit parents act in the best interests of their children. . . .

Accordingly, so long as a parent adequately cares for his or her children (*i.e.*, is fit), there will normally be no reason for the State to inject itself into the private realm of the family to further question the ability of that parent to make the best decisions concerning the rearing of that parent's children.

The problem here is not that the Washington Superior Court intervened, but that when it did so, it gave no special weight at all to Granville's determination of her daughters' best interests. More importantly, it appears that the Superior Court applied exactly the opposite presumption. . . .

In effect, the judge placed on Granville, the fit custodial parent, the burden of *disproving* that visitation would be in the best interest of her daughters. . . .

The decisional framework employed by the Superior Court directly contravened the traditional presumption that a fit parent will act in the best interest of his or her child. In that respect, the court's presumption failed to provide any protection for Granville's fundamental constitutional right to make decisions concerning the rearing of her own daughters. In an ideal world, parents might always seek to cultivate the bonds between grandparents and their grandchildren. Needless to say, however, our world is far from perfect, and in it the decision whether such an intergenerational relationship would be beneficial in any specific case is for the parent to make in the first instance. And, if a fit parent's decision of the kind at issue here becomes subject to judicial review, the court must accord at least some special weight to the parent's own determination.

Finally, we note that there is no allegation that Granville ever sought to cut off visitation entirely. Rather, the present dispute originated when Granville informed the Troxels that she would prefer to restrict their visitation with Isabelle and Natalie to one short visit per month and special holidays. In the Superior Court proceedings Granville did not oppose visitation but instead asked that the duration of any visitation order be shorter than that requested by the Troxels. . . . The Superior Court gave no weight to Granville's having assented to visitation even before the filing of any visitation petition or subsequent court intervention. . . . Significantly, many other States expressly provide by statute that courts may not award visitation unless a parent has denied (or unreasonably denied) visitation to the concerned third party.

Considered together with the Superior Court's reasons for awarding visitation to the Troxels, the combination of these factors demonstrates that the visitation order in this case was an unconstitutional infringement on Granville's fundamental right to make decisions concerning the care, custody, and control of her two daughters. The Washington Superior Court failed to accord the determination of Granville, a fit custodial parent, any material weight. . . . As we have explained, the Due Process Clause does not permit a State to infringe on the fundamental right of parents to make child rearing decisions simply because a state judge believes a "better" decision could be made. Neither the Washington nonparental visitation statute generally—which places no limits on either the persons who may petition for visitation or the circumstances in which such a petition may be granted—nor the Superior Court in this specific case required anything more. Accordingly, we hold that § 26.10.160(3), as applied in this case, is unconstitutional.

Because we rest our decision on the sweeping breadth of § 26.10.160(3) and the application of that broad, unlimited power in this case, we do not consider the primary constitutional question passed on by the Washington Supreme Court—whether the Due Process Clause requires all nonparental visitation statutes to include a showing of harm or potential harm to the child as a condition precedent to granting visitation. We do not, and need not, define today the precise scope of the parental due process right in the visitation context. . . . Because much state-court adjudication in this context occurs on a case-by-case basis, we would be hesitant to hold that specific nonparental visitation statutes violate the Due Process Clause as a *per se* matter. . . .

[The concurring opinions of Justices Souter and Thomas, and the dissenting opinions of Justices Stevens, Scalia, and Kennedy, are omitted.]

Notes and Questions

1. Is there a tension between this decision and the Court's decision in *Moore*? Is there a way to reconcile the two decisions?

2. Does the Court's decision leave the door open to upholding a narrower nonparental visitation and custody statute? If so, what changes to the Washington statute would likely have to be made in order for it to pass constitutional muster? In

2018, the Washington legislature enacted a revised non-parental visitation statute designed to address some of the constitutional concerns raised by the *Troxel* Court. *See* Wash. Stat. § 26.11.040. Do you believe that the revised statute would survive a constitutional challenge?

D. Sexual Intimacy

Bowers v. Hardwick

478 U.S. 186 (1986)

Justice White delivered the opinion of the Court.

In August 1982, respondent Hardwick (hereafter respondent) was charged with violating the Georgia statute criminalizing sodomy[1] by committing that act with another adult male in the bedroom of respondent's home. After a preliminary hearing, the District Attorney decided not to present the matter to the grand jury unless further evidence developed.

Respondent then brought suit in the Federal District Court, challenging the constitutionality of the statute insofar as it criminalized consensual sodomy.[2] He asserted that he was a practicing homosexual, that the Georgia sodomy statute, as administered by the defendants, placed him in imminent danger of arrest, and that the statute for several reasons violates the Federal Constitution. The District Court granted the defendants' motion to dismiss for failure to state a claim....

A divided panel of the Court of Appeals for the Eleventh Circuit reversed.... Relying on our decisions in *Griswold v. Connecticut,* 381 U.S. 479 (1965); *Eisenstadt v. Baird,* 405 U.S. 438 (1972); *Stanley v. Georgia,* 394 U.S. 557 (1969); and *Roe v. Wade,* 410 U.S. 113 (1973), the court went on to hold that the Georgia statute violated respondent's fundamental rights because his homosexual activity is

---

1. Georgia Code Ann. § 16–6–2 (1984) provides, in pertinent part, as follows:

"(a) A person commits the offense of sodomy when he performs or submits to any sexual act involving the sex organs of one person and the mouth or anus of another....

"(b) A person convicted of the offense of sodomy shall be punished by imprisonment for not less than one nor more than 20 years...."

2. John and Mary Doe were also plaintiffs in the action. They alleged that they wished to engage in sexual activity proscribed by § 16–6–2 in the privacy of their home, and that they had been "chilled and deterred" from engaging in such activity by both the existence of the statute and Hardwick's arrest. The District Court held, however, that because they had neither sustained, nor were in immediate danger of sustaining, any direct injury from the enforcement of the statute, they did not have proper standing to maintain the action. The Court of Appeals affirmed the District Court's judgment dismissing the Does' claim for lack of standing, and the Does do not challenge that holding in this Court.

The only claim properly before the Court, therefore, is Hardwick's challenge to the Georgia statute as applied to consensual homosexual sodomy. We express no opinion on the constitutionality of the Georgia statute as applied to other acts of sodomy.

a private and intimate association that is beyond the reach of state regulation by reason of the Ninth Amendment and the Due Process Clause of the Fourteenth Amendment....

This case does not require a judgment on whether laws against sodomy between consenting adults in general, or between homosexuals in particular, are wise or desirable. It raises no question about the right or propriety of state legislative decisions to repeal their laws that criminalize homosexual sodomy, or of state-court decisions invalidating those laws on state constitutional grounds. The issue presented is whether the Federal Constitution confers a fundamental right upon homosexuals to engage in sodomy and hence invalidates the laws of the many States that still make such conduct illegal and have done so for a very long time. The case also calls for some judgment about the limits of the Court's role in carrying out its constitutional mandate.

We first register our disagreement with the Court of Appeals and with respondent that the Court's prior cases have construed the Constitution to confer a right of privacy that extends to homosexual sodomy and for all intents and purposes have decided this case. The reach of this line of cases was sketched in *Carey v. Population Services International,* 431 U.S. 678, 685 (1977). *Pierce v. Society of Sisters,* 268 U.S. 510 (1925), and *Meyer v. Nebraska,* 262 U.S. 390 (1923), were described as dealing with child rearing and education; *Prince v. Massachusetts,* 321 U.S. 158 (1944), with family relationships; *Skinner v. Oklahoma ex rel. Williamson,* 316 U.S. 535 (1942), with procreation; *Loving v. Virginia,* 388 U.S. 1 (1967), with marriage; *Griswold v. Connecticut, supra,* and *Eisenstadt v. Baird, supra,* with contraception; and *Roe v. Wade,* 410 U.S. 113 (1973), with abortion. The latter three cases were interpreted as construing the Due Process Clause of the Fourteenth Amendment to confer a fundamental individual right to decide whether or not to beget or bear a child. *Carey v. Population Services International, supra,* 431 U.S., at 688-689.

Accepting the decisions in these cases and the above description of them, we think it evident that none of the rights announced in those cases bears any resemblance to the claimed constitutional right of homosexuals to engage in acts of sodomy that is asserted in this case. No connection between family, marriage, or procreation on the one hand and homosexual activity on the other has been demonstrated, either by the Court of Appeals or by respondent. Moreover, any claim that these cases nevertheless stand for the proposition that any kind of private sexual conduct between consenting adults is constitutionally insulated from state proscription is unsupportable....

Precedent aside, however, respondent would have us announce, as the Court of Appeals did, a fundamental right to engage in homosexual sodomy. This we are quite unwilling to do. It is true that despite the language of the Due Process Clauses of the Fifth and Fourteenth Amendments, which appears to focus only on the processes by which life, liberty, or property is taken, the cases are legion in which those Clauses have been interpreted to have substantive content, subsuming rights that to a great extent are immune from federal or state regulation or proscription. Among such cases are those recognizing rights that have little or no textual support in the constitutional language. *Meyer, Prince,* and *Pierce* fall in this category, as do the privacy cases from *Griswold* to *Carey.*

Striving to assure itself and the public that announcing rights not readily identifiable in the Constitution's text involves much more than the imposition of the Justices' own choice of values on the States and the Federal Government, the Court has sought to identify the nature of the rights qualifying for heightened judicial protection. In *Palko v. Connecticut,* 302 U.S. 319, 325, 326 (1937), it was said that this category includes those fundamental liberties that are "implicit in the concept of ordered liberty," such that "neither liberty nor justice would exist if [they] were sacrificed." A different description of fundamental liberties appeared in *Moore v. East Cleveland,* 431 U.S. 494, 503 (1977) (opinion of POWELL, J..), where they are characterized as those liberties that are "deeply rooted in this Nation's history and tradition." *Id.,* at 503 (POWELL, J.). See also *Griswold v. Connecticut,* 381 U.S., at 506.

It is obvious to us that neither of these formulations would extend a fundamental right to homosexuals to engage in acts of consensual sodomy. Proscriptions against that conduct have ancient roots. Sodomy was a criminal offense at common law and was forbidden by the laws of the original thirteen States when they ratified the Bill of Rights. In 1868, when the Fourteenth Amendment was ratified, all but 5 of the 37 States in the Union had criminal sodomy laws. In fact, until 1961, all 50 States outlawed sodomy, and today, 24 States and the District of Columbia continue to provide criminal penalties for sodomy performed in private and between consenting adults. Against this background, to claim that a right to engage in such conduct is "deeply rooted in this Nation's history and tradition" or "implicit in the concept of ordered liberty" is, at best, facetious.

Nor are we inclined to take a more expansive view of our authority to discover new fundamental rights imbedded in the Due Process Clause. The Court is most vulnerable and comes nearest to illegitimacy when it deals with judge-made constitutional law having little or no cognizable roots in the language or design of the Constitution. That this is so was painfully demonstrated by the face-off between the Executive and the Court in the 1930's, which resulted in the repudiation of much of the substantive gloss that the Court had placed on the Due Process Clauses of the Fifth and Fourteenth Amendments. There should be, therefore, great resistance to expand the substantive reach of those Clauses, particularly if it requires redefining the category of rights deemed to be fundamental. Otherwise, the Judiciary necessarily takes to itself further authority to govern the country without express constitutional authority. The claimed right pressed on us today falls far short of overcoming this resistance.

Respondent, however, asserts that the result should be different where the homosexual conduct occurs in the privacy of the home. He relies on *Stanley v. Georgia,* 394 U.S. 557 (1969), where the Court held that the First Amendment prevents conviction for possessing and reading obscene material in the privacy of one's home: "If the First Amendment means anything, it means that a State has no business telling a man, sitting alone in his house, what books he may read or what films he may watch." *Id.*, at 565.

Stanley did protect conduct that would not have been protected outside the home, and it partially prevented the enforcement of state obscenity laws; but the decision was firmly grounded in the First Amendment. The right pressed upon us here has no similar support in the text of the Constitution, and it does not qualify for recognition under the prevailing principles for construing the Fourteenth Amendment. Its limits are also difficult to discern. Plainly enough, otherwise illegal conduct is not always immunized whenever it occurs in the home. Victimless crimes, such as the possession and use of illegal drugs, do not escape the law where they are committed at home. *Stanley* itself recognized that its holding offered no protection for the possession in the home of drugs, firearms, or stolen goods. And if respondent's submission is limited to the voluntary sexual conduct between consenting adults, it would be difficult, except by fiat, to limit the claimed right to homosexual conduct while leaving exposed to prosecution adultery, incest, and other sexual crimes even though they are committed in the home. We are unwilling to start down that road.

Even if the conduct at issue here is not a fundamental right, respondent asserts that there must be a rational basis for the law and that there is none in this case other than the presumed belief of a majority of the electorate in Georgia that homosexual sodomy is immoral and unacceptable. This is said to be an inadequate rationale to support the law. The law, however, is constantly based on notions of morality, and if all laws representing essentially moral choices are to be invalidated under the Due Process Clause, the courts will be very busy indeed. Even respondent makes no such claim, but insists that majority sentiments about the morality of homosexuality should be declared inadequate. We do not agree, and are unpersuaded that the sodomy laws of some 25 States should be invalidated on this basis.[8] . . . .

CHIEF JUSTICE BURGER, concurring.

I join the Court's opinion, but I write separately to underscore my view that in constitutional terms there is no such thing as a fundamental right to commit homosexual sodomy.

As the Court notes, the proscriptions against sodomy have very "ancient roots." Decisions of individuals relating to homosexual conduct have been subject to state intervention throughout the history of Western civilization. Condemnation of those practices is firmly rooted in Judaeo-Christian moral and ethical standards. Homosexual sodomy was a capital crime under Roman law. During the English Reformation when powers of the ecclesiastical courts were transferred to the King's Courts, the first English statute criminalizing sodomy was passed. Blackstone described "the infamous *crime against nature*" as an offense of "deeper malignity" than rape, a heinous act "the very mention of which is a disgrace to human nature," and "a

8. Respondent does not defend the judgment below based on the Ninth Amendment, the Equal Protection Clause, or the Eighth Amendment.

crime not fit to be named." The common law of England, including its prohibition of sodomy, became the received law of Georgia and the other Colonies. In 1816 the Georgia Legislature passed the statute at issue here, and that statute has been continuously in force in one form or another since that time. To hold that the act of homosexual sodomy is somehow protected as a fundamental right would be to cast aside millennia of moral teaching.

This is essentially not a question of personal "preferences" but rather of the legislative authority of the State. I find nothing in the Constitution depriving a State of the power to enact the statute challenged here.

JUSTICE POWELL, concurring.

I join the opinion of the Court. I agree with the Court that there is no fundamental right—*i.e.,* no substantive right under the Due Process Clause—such as that claimed by respondent Hardwick, and found to exist by the Court of Appeals. This is not to suggest, however, that respondent may not be protected by the Eighth Amendment of the Constitution. The Georgia statute at issue in this case, Ga. Code Ann. § 16–6–2 (1984), authorizes a court to imprison a person for up to 20 years for a single private, consensual act of sodomy. In my view, a prison sentence for such conduct—certainly a sentence of long duration—would create a serious Eighth Amendment issue. Under the Georgia statute a single act of sodomy, even in the private setting of a home, is a felony comparable in terms of the possible sentence imposed to serious felonies such as aggravated battery, § 16–5–24, first-degree arson, § 16–7–60, and robbery, § 16–8–40.

In this case, however, respondent has not been tried, much less convicted and sentenced.[2] Moreover, respondent has not raised the Eighth Amendment issue below. For these reasons this constitutional argument is not before us.

JUSTICE BLACKMUN, with whom JUSTICE BRENNAN, JUSTICE MARSHALL, and JUSTICE STEVENS join, dissenting.

This case is no more about "a fundamental right to engage in homosexual sodomy," as the Court purports to declare, than *Stanley v. Georgia,* 394 U.S. 557 (1969), was about a fundamental right to watch obscene movies, or *Katz v. United States,* 389 U.S. 347 (1967), was about a fundamental right to place interstate bets from a telephone booth. Rather, this case is about "the most comprehensive of rights and the right most valued by civilized men," namely, "the right to be let alone." *Olmstead v. United States,* 277 U.S. 438, 478 (1928) (Brandeis, J., dissenting) . . . .

---

2. It was conceded at oral argument that, prior to the complaint against respondent Hardwick, there had been no reported decision involving prosecution for private homosexual sodomy under this statute for several decades. Moreover, the State has declined to present the criminal charge against Hardwick to a grand jury, and this is a suit for declaratory judgment brought by respondents challenging the validity of the statute. The history of nonenforcement suggests the moribund character today of laws criminalizing this type of private, consensual conduct. . . .

In its haste to reverse the Court of Appeals and hold that the Constitution does not "confe[r] a fundamental right upon homosexuals to engage in sodomy," the Court relegates the actual statute being challenged to a footnote and ignores the procedural posture of the case before it. A fair reading of the statute and of the complaint clearly reveals that the majority has distorted the question this case presents.

First, the Court's almost obsessive focus on homosexual activity is particularly hard to justify in light of the broad language Georgia has used. . . . The sex or status of the persons who engage in the act is irrelevant as a matter of state law. In fact, to the extent I can discern a legislative purpose for Georgia's 1968 enactment of § 16–6–2, that purpose seems to have been to broaden the coverage of the law to reach heterosexual as well as homosexual activity.[1] I therefore see no basis for the Court's decision to treat this case as an "as applied" challenge to § 16–6–2, or for Georgia's attempt, both in its brief and at oral argument, to defend § 16–6–2 solely on the grounds that it prohibits homosexual activity. . . .

"Our cases long have recognized that the Constitution embodies a promise that a certain private sphere of individual liberty will be kept largely beyond the reach of government." *Thornburgh v. American College of Obstetricians & Gynecologists,* 476 U.S. 747, 772 (1986). In construing the right to privacy, the Court has proceeded along two somewhat distinct, albeit complementary, lines. First, it has recognized a privacy interest with reference to certain *decisions* that are properly for the individual to make. *E.g., Roe v. Wade,* 410 U.S. 113 (1973); *Pierce v. Society of Sisters,* 268 U.S. 510 (1925). Second, it has recognized a privacy interest with reference to certain *places* without regard for the particular activities in which the individuals who occupy them are engaged. The case before us implicates both the decisional and the spatial aspects of the right to privacy. . . .

Only the most willful blindness could obscure the fact that sexual intimacy is "a sensitive, key relationship of human existence, central to family life, community welfare, and the development of human personality." The fact that individuals define themselves in a significant way through their intimate sexual relationships with others suggests, in a Nation as diverse as ours, that there may be many "right" ways of conducting those relationships, and that much of the richness of a relationship will come from the freedom an individual has to *choose* the form and nature of these intensely personal bonds. . . .

The behavior for which Hardwick faces prosecution occurred in his own home, a place to which the Fourth Amendment attaches special significance. The Court's

---

1. Until 1968, Georgia defined sodomy as "the carnal knowledge and connection against the order of nature, by man with man, or in the same unnatural manner with woman." Ga. Crim. Code § 26–5901 (1933). In *Thompson v. Aldredge,* 187 Ga. 467 (1939), the Georgia Supreme Court held that § 26–5901 did not prohibit lesbian activity. And in *Riley v. Garrett,* 219 Ga. 345 (1963), the Georgia Supreme Court held that § 26–5901 did not prohibit heterosexual cunnilingus. Georgia passed the act-specific statute currently in force "perhaps in response to the restrictive court decisions such as *Riley,*" Note, The Crimes Against Nature, 16 J.Pub.L. 159, 167, n. 47 (1967).

treatment of this aspect of the case is symptomatic of its overall refusal to consider the broad principles that have informed our treatment of privacy in specific cases. Just as the right to privacy is more than the mere aggregation of a number of entitlements to engage in specific behavior, so too, protecting the physical integrity of the home is more than merely a means of protecting specific activities that often take place there. . . .

The Court's failure to comprehend the magnitude of the liberty interests at stake in this case leads it to slight the question whether petitioner, on behalf of the State, has justified Georgia's infringement on these interests. I believe that neither of the two general justifications for § 16-6-2 that petitioner has advanced warrants dismissing respondent's challenge for failure to state a claim.

First, petitioner asserts that the acts made criminal by the statute may have serious adverse consequences for "the general public health and welfare," such as spreading communicable diseases or fostering other criminal activity. . . . I see no justification for the Court's attempt to equate the private, consensual sexual activity at issue here with the "possession in the home of drugs, firearms, or stolen goods," to which *Stanley* refused to extend its protection. None of the behavior so mentioned in *Stanley* can properly be viewed as "[v]ictimless": drugs and weapons are inherently dangerous, and for property to be "stolen," someone must have been wrongfully deprived of it. Nothing in the record before the Court provides any justification for finding the activity forbidden by § 16–6–2 to be physically dangerous, either to the persons engaged in it or to others.[4]

The core of petitioner's defense of § 16–6–2, however, is that respondent and others who engage in the conduct prohibited by § 16–6–2 interfere with Georgia's exercise of the "'right of the Nation and of the States to maintain a decent society.'" Essentially, petitioner argues, and the Court agrees, that the fact that the acts described in § 16–6–2 "for hundreds of years, if not thousands, have been uniformly condemned as immoral" is a sufficient reason to permit a State to ban them today.

4. Although I do not think it necessary to decide today issues that are not even remotely before us, it does seem to me that a court could find simple, analytically sound distinctions between certain private, consensual sexual conduct, on the one hand, and adultery and incest (the only two vaguely specific "sexual crimes" to which the majority points, *ante,* at 2846), on the other. For example, marriage, in addition to its spiritual aspects, is a civil contract that entitles the contracting parties to a variety of governmentally provided benefits. A State might define the contractual commitment necessary to become eligible for these benefits to include a commitment of fidelity and then punish individuals for breaching that contract. Moreover, a State might conclude that adultery is likely to injure third persons, in particular, spouses and children of persons who engage in extramarital affairs. With respect to incest, a court might well agree with respondent that the nature of familial relationships renders true consent to incestuous activity sufficiently problematical that a blanket prohibition of such activity is warranted. Notably, the Court makes no effort to explain why it has chosen to group private, consensual homosexual activity with adultery and incest rather than with private, consensual heterosexual activity by unmarried persons or, indeed, with oral or anal sex within marriage.

I cannot agree that either the length of time a majority has held its convictions or the passions with which it defends them can withdraw legislation from this Court's scrutiny. See, *e.g., Roe v. Wade*, 410 U.S. 113 (1973); *Loving v. Virginia*, 388 U.S. 1 (1967); *Brown v. Board of Education*, 347 U.S. 483 (1954).[5] . . . .

Nor can § 16–6–2 be justified as a "morally neutral" exercise of Georgia's power to "protect the public environment," *Paris Adult Theatre I*, 413 U.S., at 68-69. Certainly, some private behavior can affect the fabric of society as a whole. Reasonable people may differ about whether particular sexual acts are moral or immoral, but "we have ample evidence for believing that people will not abandon morality, will not think any better of murder, cruelty and dishonesty, merely because some private sexual practice which they abominate is not punished by the law." Petitioner and the Court fail to see the difference between laws that protect public sensibilities and those that enforce private morality. Statutes banning public sexual activity are entirely consistent with protecting the individual's liberty interest in decisions concerning sexual relations: the same recognition that those decisions are intensely private which justifies protecting them from governmental interference can justify protecting individuals from unwilling exposure to the sexual activities of others. But the mere fact that intimate behavior may be punished when it takes place in public cannot dictate how States can regulate intimate behavior that occurs in intimate places.

This case involves no real interference with the rights of others, for the mere knowledge that other individuals do not adhere to one's value system cannot be a legally cognizable interest, let alone an interest that can justify invading the houses, hearts, and minds of citizens who choose to live their lives differently. . . .

Justice Stevens, with whom Justice Brennan and Justice Marshall join, dissenting. . . .

Because the Georgia statute expresses the traditional view that sodomy is an immoral kind of conduct regardless of the identity of the persons who engage in it, I believe that a proper analysis of its constitutionality requires consideration of two questions: First, may a State totally prohibit the described conduct by means of a

5. The parallel between *Loving* and this case is almost uncanny. There, too, the State relied on a religious justification for its law. Compare 388 U.S., at 3, 87 S.Ct., at 1819 (quoting trial court's statement that "Almighty God created the races white, black, yellow, malay and red, and he placed them on separate continents. . . . The fact that he separated the races shows that he did not intend for the races to mix"), with Brief for Petitioner 20-21 (relying on the Old and New Testaments and the writings of St. Thomas Aquinas to show that "traditional Judeo-Christian values proscribe such conduct"). There, too, defenders of the challenged statute relied heavily on the fact that when the Fourteenth Amendment was ratified, most of the States had similar prohibitions. There, too, at the time the case came before the Court, many of the States still had criminal statutes concerning the conduct at issue. Yet the Court held, not only that the invidious racism of Virginia's law violated the Equal Protection Clause, but also that the law deprived the Lovings of due process by denying them the "freedom of choice to marry" that had "long been recognized as one of the vital personal rights essential to the orderly pursuit of happiness by free men."

neutral law applying without exception to all persons subject to its jurisdiction? If not, may the State save the statute by announcing that it will only enforce the law against homosexuals? The two questions merit separate discussion.

Our prior cases make two propositions abundantly clear. First, the fact that the governing majority in a State has traditionally viewed a particular practice as immoral is not a sufficient reason for upholding a law prohibiting the practice; neither history nor tradition could save a law prohibiting miscegenation from constitutional attack.[9] Second, individual decisions by married persons, concerning the intimacies of their physical relationship, even when not intended to produce offspring, are a form of "liberty" protected by the Due Process Clause of the Fourteenth Amendment. *Griswold v. Connecticut,* 381 U.S. 479 (1965). Moreover, this protection extends to intimate choices by unmarried as well as married persons. *Carey v. Population Services International,* 431 U.S. 678 (1977); *Eisenstadt v. Baird,* 405 U.S. 438 (1972) . . . .

Society has every right to encourage its individual members to follow particular traditions in expressing affection for one another and in gratifying their personal desires. It, of course, may prohibit an individual from imposing his will on another to satisfy his own selfish interests. It also may prevent an individual from interfering with, or violating, a legally sanctioned and protected relationship, such as marriage. And it may explain the relative advantages and disadvantages of different forms of intimate expression. But when individual married couples are isolated from observation by others, the way in which they voluntarily choose to conduct their intimate relations is a matter for them—not the State—to decide.[10] The essential "liberty" that animated the development of the law in cases like *Griswold, Eisenstadt,* and *Carey* surely embraces the right to engage in nonreproductive, sexual conduct that others may consider offensive or immoral.

Paradoxical as it may seem, our prior cases thus establish that a State may not prohibit sodomy within "the sacred precincts of marital bedrooms," *Griswold,* 381 U.S., at 485, or, indeed, between unmarried heterosexual adults. *Eisenstadt,* 405 U.S., at 453. In all events, it is perfectly clear that the State of Georgia may not totally prohibit the conduct proscribed by § 16–6–2 of the Georgia Criminal Code.

If the Georgia statute cannot be enforced as it is written—if the conduct it seeks to prohibit is a protected form of liberty for the vast majority of Georgia's citizens—the State must assume the burden of justifying a selective application of its law. Either the persons to whom Georgia seeks to apply its statute do not have the same interest in "liberty" that others have, or there must be a reason why the State may be permitted to apply a generally applicable law to certain persons that it does not apply to others.

9. See *Loving v. Virginia,* 388 U.S. 1 (1967). Interestingly, miscegenation was once treated as a crime similar to sodomy.

10. Indeed, the Georgia Attorney General concedes that Georgia's statute would be unconstitutional if applied to a married couple. Significantly, Georgia passed the current statute three years after the Court's decision in *Griswold.*

The first possibility is plainly unacceptable. Although the meaning of the principle that "all men are created equal" is not always clear, it surely must mean that every free citizen has the same interest in "liberty" that the members of the majority share. From the standpoint of the individual, the homosexual and the heterosexual have the same interest in deciding how he will live his own life, and, more narrowly, how he will conduct himself in his personal and voluntary associations with his companions. State intrusion into the private conduct of either is equally burdensome.

The second possibility is similarly unacceptable. A policy of selective application must be supported by a neutral and legitimate interest—something more substantial than a habitual dislike for, or ignorance about, the disfavored group. Neither the State nor the Court has identified any such interest in this case. The Court has posited as a justification for the Georgia statute "the presumed belief of a majority of the electorate in Georgia that homosexual sodomy is immoral and unacceptable." But the Georgia electorate has expressed no such belief—instead, its representatives enacted a law that presumably reflects the belief that *all sodomy* is immoral and unacceptable. Unless the Court is prepared to conclude that such a law is constitutional, it may not rely on the work product of the Georgia Legislature to support its holding. For the Georgia statute does not single out homosexuals as a separate class meriting special disfavored treatment. . . .

Notes and Questions

1. During deliberations on *Bowers v. Hardwick*, Justice Powell changed his vote, initially voting to strike down the law on Eighth Amendment grounds, but later changing his mind. One of Justice Powell's law clerks at the time was gay, but never disclosed that fact to the Justice. During the clerk's discussions with Justice Powell, the Justice said, "I don't believe I've ever met a homosexual," to which his gay clerk replied, "Certainly you have, but you just don't know that they are." *See* John C. Jeffries, Jr., Justice Lewis F. Powell, Jr. 511–29 (1994). Four years after *Bowers* was decided, Justice Powell publicly stated that he "probably made a mistake" in *Bowers. See id.* at 530. Would the outcome have been different had his clerk come out to him, and if so, *should* it have impacted the outcome?

2. To what extent, do you suppose, was the Court's willingness to uphold the law made easier by the fact that nobody was facing a criminal conviction in this case? At the very least, to what extent did that impact Justice Powell? For an argument that Hardwick did not have standing, and that the lack of actual consequences to him made it easier for the Court to rule against him on his constitutional claim, *see* Donald A. Dripps, Bowers v. Hardwick *and the Law of Standing: Noncases Make Bad Law*, 44 Emory L.J. 1417 (1995).

3. To what extent is the outcome in *Bowers* pre-determined by the way in which Justice White frames both the right identified in its prior cases and the right claimed by Hardwick in this case? To what extent is the framing impacted by the Court's standing determination with respect to John and Mary Doe in footnote 2 of the opinion? Note, in contrast, the way in which Justice Blackmun frames the right claimed

and the right previously recognized. Compare as well the way in which the Court framed the right at issue in earlier fundamental rights cases, such as *Roe*. What are the advantages and disadvantages of each approach?

4. What is the role of history in *Bowers*? How does it compare with the role history played in earlier fundamental rights cases, including *Roe*?

5. Justice White criticizes the *Meyer*, *Prince*, and *Pierce* cases, along with the privacy cases from *Griswold* to *Carey*, as "recognizing rights that have little or no textual support." He leaves out two other cases in the list immediately preceding this criticism: *Loving v. Virginia* and *Skinner v. Oklahoma*. Why are those two cases left off of the list? Is he perhaps re-characterizing those cases, or instead maybe undoing an earlier re-characterization of those cases by the Court?

6. In rejecting a more broadly framed right that encompasses voluntary sexual conduct between consenting adults in the home, Justice White notes that it would be difficult to distinguish homosexual conduct from adultery, incest, and other sexual crimes. How persuasive is this claim? Wouldn't a principle that focused on whether there was harm to others—as suggested by Justice Blackmun in footnote 4 of his dissent—serve to distinguish homosexual conduct from Justice White's list? Indeed, wouldn't such a principle make *Bowers* an easier case than *Roe*, which arguably involved harm to others (i.e., the unborn fetus) in a way that *Bowers* did not?

7. To the extent that the unenumerated right at issue is "privacy," isn't the claim to "privacy" at least as strong, if not stronger, in *Bowers* than it was in *Roe*? To what extent does this turn on the definition of "privacy"?

8. Justice White rather easily concludes that majority sentiments regarding morality suffice to justify the sodomy law. Is this consistent with the Court's earlier decisions in *Eisenstadt*, *Moreno*, and *Roe*, which each quickly dismissed morality-based rationales for the laws at issue in those cases? Perhaps the difference between *Roe* and *Bowers* can be explained by the level of scrutiny (strict versus rational basis), but what about the difference between *Eisenstadt*, *Moreno*, and *Bowers*, all of which purport to apply rational basis? Is it possible that morality can serve as a rational basis in due process but not equal protection challenges? If so, what justifies treating morality differently under each clause?

9. In Justice Blackmun's dissent, he brushes to one side a rationale for criminalizing sodomy raised by the state: preventing the spread of communicable diseases. Is that such an unsound rationale for the law? Might it have been more sound if, say, limited to anal intercourse and supported by scientific evidence indicating increased risks of disease transmission? To what extent was this concern likely on the minds of the Justices, who decided this case in the mid-1980s, at the height of the AIDS crisis in the United States?

10. What do you make of the approach to the question that Justice Stevens takes in his dissent? Is it not akin to the reasoning employed by Justice Brennan in *Eisenstadt*? Under his approach, are due process and equal protection working independently or as a team?

11. As indicated by Justice White in footnote 8 of his opinion for the Court, the opinion does not address the question whether the statute violates the Equal Protection Clause. What would be the Equal Protection Clause claim, given that the statute, in terms, applies equally to sodomy performed between same-sex and opposite-sex couples? Might a claim akin to that made in *Eisenstadt* succeed?

E. General Methodological Questions

The next three cases involve three specific claimed fundamental rights: the right of an unwed biological father vis-à-vis his child; the right to procure an abortion; and the right to physician-assisted suicide. In addition to their specific holdings, these cases are also of great value in understanding the Court's methodological approach to fundamental rights claims. As you read these cases, keep an eye out on how the Justices frame the claimed rights, as well as what they rely on to determine the existence and scope of those rights.

Michael H. v. Gerald D.

491 U.S. 110 (1989)

Justice Scalia announced the judgment of the Court and delivered an opinion, in which The Chief Justice joins, and in all but footnote 6 of which Justice O'Connor and Justice Kennedy join.

Under California law, a child born to a married woman living with her husband is presumed to be a child of the marriage. The presumption of legitimacy may be rebutted only by the husband or wife, and then only in limited circumstances. The instant appeal presents the claim that this presumption infringes upon the due process rights of a man who wishes to establish his paternity of a child born to the wife of another man, and the claim that it infringes upon the constitutional right of the child to maintain a relationship with her natural father.

The facts of this case are, we must hope, extraordinary. On May 9, 1976, in Las Vegas, Nevada, Carole D., an international model, and Gerald D., a top executive in a French oil company, were married. The couple established a home in Playa del Rey, California, in which they resided as husband and wife when one or the other was not out of the country on business. In the summer of 1978, Carole became involved in an adulterous affair with a neighbor, Michael H. In September 1980, she conceived a child, Victoria D., who was born on May 11, 1981. Gerald was listed as father on the birth certificate and has always held Victoria out to the world as his daughter. Soon after delivery of the child, however, Carole informed Michael that she believed he might be the father. . . .

In October 1981, Gerald moved to New York City to pursue his business interests, but Carole chose to remain in California. At the end of that month, Carole and Michael had blood tests of themselves and Victoria, which showed a 98.07% probability that

Michael was Victoria's father. In January 1982, Carole visited Michael in St. Thomas, where his primary business interests were based. There Michael held Victoria out as his child. In March, however, Carole left Michael and returned to California, where she took up residence with yet another man, Scott K. . . .

In November 1982, rebuffed in his attempts to visit Victoria, Michael filed a filiation action in California Superior Court to establish his paternity and right to visitation. In March 1983, the court appointed an attorney and guardian ad litem to represent Victoria's interests. . . .

On October 19, 1984, Gerald, who had intervened in the action, moved for summary judgment on the ground that under Cal.Evid.Code § 621 there were no triable issues of fact as to Victoria's paternity. This law provides that "the issue of a wife cohabiting with her husband, who is not impotent or sterile, is conclusively presumed to be a child of the marriage." The presumption may be rebutted by blood tests, but only if a motion for such tests is made, within two years from the date of the child's birth, either by the husband or, if the natural father has filed an affidavit acknowledging paternity, by the wife.

On January 28, 1985, having found that affidavits submitted by Carole and Gerald sufficed to demonstrate that the two were cohabiting at conception and birth and that Gerald was neither sterile nor impotent, the Superior Court granted Gerald's motion for summary judgment, rejecting Michael's and Victoria's challenges to the constitutionality of § 621 . . . .

Michael contends as a matter of substantive due process that, because he has established a parental relationship with Victoria, protection of Gerald's and Carole's marital union is an insufficient state interest to support termination of that relationship. This argument is, of course, predicated on the assertion that Michael has a constitutionally protected liberty interest in his relationship with Victoria. . . .

In an attempt to limit and guide interpretation of the [Due Process] Clause, we have insisted not merely that the interest denominated as a "liberty" be "fundamental" (a concept that, in isolation, is hard to objectify), but also that it be an interest traditionally protected by our society.[2] As we have put it, the Due Process Clause affords only those protections "so rooted in the traditions and conscience of our people as to be ranked as fundamental." *Snyder v. Massachusetts,* 291 U.S. 97, 105 (1934) (Cardozo, J.). Our cases reflect "continual insistence upon respect for the teachings of history [and] solid recognition of the basic values that underlie our society. . . ." *Griswold v. Connecticut,* 381 U.S. 479, 501 (1965) (Harlan, J., concurring in judgment).

---

2. . . . . The protection need not take the form of an explicit constitutional provision or statutory guarantee, but it must at least exclude (all that is necessary to decide the present case) a societal tradition of enacting laws *denying* the interest. . . . Its purpose is to prevent future generations from lightly casting aside important traditional values—not to enable this Court to invent new ones.

This insistence that the asserted liberty interest be rooted in history and tradition is evident, as elsewhere, in our cases according constitutional protection to certain parental rights. Michael reads the landmark case of *Stanley v. Illinois,* 405 U.S. 645 (1972), and the subsequent cases of *Quilloin v. Walcott,* 434 U.S. 246 (1978), *Caban v. Mohammed,* 441 U.S. 380 (1979), and *Lehr v. Robertson,* 463 U.S. 248 (1983), as establishing that a liberty interest is created by biological fatherhood plus an established parental relationship—factors that exist in the present case as well. We think that distorts the rationale of those cases. As we view them, they rest not upon such isolated factors but upon the historic respect—indeed, sanctity would not be too strong a term—traditionally accorded to the relationships that develop within the unitary family. In *Stanley,* for example, we forbade the destruction of such a family when, upon the death of the mother, the State had sought to remove children from the custody of a father who had lived with and supported them and their mother for 18 years. As Justice Powell stated for the plurality in *Moore v. East Cleveland, supra,* 431 U.S., at 503: "Our decisions establish that the Constitution protects the sanctity of the family precisely because the institution of the family is deeply rooted in this Nation's history and tradition."

Thus, the legal issue in the present case reduces to whether the relationship between persons in the situation of Michael and Victoria has been treated as a protected family unit under the historic practices of our society, or whether on any other basis it has been accorded special protection. We think it impossible to find that it has. In fact, quite to the contrary, our traditions have protected the marital family (Gerald, Carole, and the child they acknowledge to be theirs) against the sort of claim Michael asserts.

The presumption of legitimacy was a fundamental principle of the common law. Traditionally, that presumption could be rebutted only by proof that a husband was incapable of procreation or had had no access to his wife during the relevant period.... The primary policy rationale underlying the common law's severe restrictions on rebuttal of the presumption appears to have been an aversion to declaring children illegitimate, thereby depriving them of rights of inheritance and succession, and likely making them wards of the state. A secondary policy concern was the interest in promoting the "peace and tranquillity of States and families," a goal that is obviously impaired by facilitating suits against husband and wife asserting that their children are illegitimate....

We have found nothing in the older sources, nor in the older cases, addressing specifically the power of the natural father to assert parental rights over a child born into a woman's existing marriage with another man. Since it is Michael's burden to establish that such a power (at least where the natural father has established a relationship with the child) is so deeply embedded within our traditions as to be a fundamental right, the lack of evidence alone might defeat his case. But the evidence shows that even in modern times—when, as we have noted, the rigid protection of the marital family has in other respects been relaxed—the ability of a person in Michael's position to claim paternity has not been generally acknowledged....

Moreover, even if it were clear that one in Michael's position generally possesses, and has generally always possessed, standing to challenge the marital child's legitimacy, that would still not establish Michael's case. As noted earlier, what is at issue here is not entitlement to a state pronouncement that Victoria was begotten by Michael. It is no conceivable denial of constitutional right for a State to decline to declare facts unless some legal consequence hinges upon the requested declaration. What Michael asserts here is a right to have himself declared the natural father *and thereby to obtain parental prerogatives.* What he must establish, therefore, is not that our society has traditionally allowed a natural father in his circumstances to establish paternity, but that it has traditionally accorded such a father parental rights, or at least has not traditionally denied them. Even if the law in all States had always been that the entire world could challenge the marital presumption and obtain a declaration as to who was the natural father, that would not advance Michael's claim. Thus, it is ultimately irrelevant, even for purposes of determining *current* social attitudes towards the alleged substantive right Michael asserts, that the present law in a number of States appears to allow the natural father—including the natural father who has not established a relationship with the child—the theoretical power to rebut the marital presumption. What counts is whether the States in fact award substantive parental rights to the natural father of a child conceived within, and born into, an extant marital union that wishes to embrace the child. We are not aware of a single case, old or new, that has done so. This is not the stuff of which fundamental rights qualifying as liberty interests are made.[6]

---

6. Justice Brennan criticizes our methodology in using historical traditions specifically relating to the rights of an adulterous natural father, rather than inquiring more generally "whether parenthood is an interest that historically has received our attention and protection." There seems to us no basis for the contention that this methodology is "nove[l]." For example, in *Bowers v. Hardwick,* 478 U.S. 186, 106 S.Ct. 2841, 92 L.Ed.2d 140 (1986), we noted that at the time the Fourteenth Amendment was ratified all but 5 of the 37 States had criminal sodomy laws, that all 50 of the States had such laws prior to 1961, and that 24 States and the District of Columbia continued to have them; and we concluded from that record, regarding that very specific aspect of sexual conduct, that "to claim that a right to engage in such conduct is 'deeply rooted in this Nation's history and tradition' or 'implicit in the concept of ordered liberty' is, at best, facetious." *Id.,* at 194. In *Roe v. Wade,* 410 U.S. 113 (1973), we spent about a fifth of our opinion negating the proposition that there was a longstanding tradition of laws proscribing abortion. *Id.,* at 129-141.

We do not understand why, having rejected our focus upon the societal tradition regarding the natural father's rights vis-à-vis a child whose mother is married to another man, Justice Brennan would choose to focus instead upon "parenthood." Why should the relevant category not be even more general—perhaps "family relationships"; or "personal relationships"; or even "emotional attachments in general"? Though the dissent has no basis for the level of generality it would select, we do: We refer to the most specific level at which a relevant tradition protecting, or denying protection to, the asserted right can be identified. If, for example, there were no societal tradition, either way, regarding the rights of the natural father of a child adulterously conceived, we would have to consult, and (if possible) reason from, the traditions regarding natural fathers in general. But there is such a more specific tradition, and it unqualifiedly denies protection to such a parent....

The need, if arbitrary decisionmaking is to be avoided, to adopt the most specific tradition as the point of reference-or at least to announce, as Justice Brennan declines to do, some other

. . . .

We have never had occasion to decide whether a child has a liberty interest, symmetrical with that of her parent, in maintaining her filial relationship. We need not do so here because, even assuming that such a right exists, Victoria's claim must fail. Victoria's due process challenge is, if anything, weaker than Michael's. Her basic claim is not that California has erred in preventing her from establishing that Michael, not Gerald, should stand as her legal father. Rather, she claims a due process right to maintain filial relationships with both Michael and Gerald. This assertion merits little discussion, for, whatever the merits of the guardian ad litem's belief that such an arrangement can be of great psychological benefit to a child, the claim that a State must recognize multiple fatherhood has no support in the history or traditions of this country. Moreover, even if we were to construe Victoria's argument as forwarding the lesser proposition that, whatever her status vis-à-vis Gerald, she has a liberty interest in maintaining a filial relationship with her natural father, Michael, we find that, at best, her claim is the obverse of Michael's and fails for the same reasons. . . .

Justice O'Connor, with whom Justice Kennedy joins, concurring in part.

I concur in all but footnote 6 of Justice SCALIA's opinion. This footnote sketches a mode of historical analysis to be used when identifying liberty interests protected by the Due Process Clause of the Fourteenth Amendment that may be somewhat inconsistent with our past decisions in this area. See *Griswold v. Connecticut,* 381 U.S. 479 (1965); *Eisenstadt v. Baird,* 405 U.S. 438 (1972). On occasion the Court has characterized relevant traditions protecting asserted rights at levels of generality that might not be "the most specific level" available. See *Loving v. Virginia,* 388 U.S. 1, 12 (1967); *Turner v. Safley,* 482 U.S. 78, 94 (1987). I would not foreclose the unanticipated by the prior imposition of a single mode of historical analysis.

Justice Brennan, with whom Justice Marshall and Justice Blackmun join, dissenting. . . .

[O]nly one other Member of the Court fully endorses Justice Scalia's view of the proper method of analyzing questions arising under the Due Process Clause.,,,

The plurality's reworking of our interpretive approach is all the more troubling because it is unnecessary. This is not a case in which we face a "new" kind of interest, one that requires us to consider for the first time whether the Constitution protects it. On the contrary, we confront an interest—that of a parent and child

criterion for selecting among the innumerable relevant traditions that could be consulted—is well enough exemplified by the fact that in the present case Justice Brennan's opinion and Justice O'Connor's opinion, which disapproves this footnote, *both* appeal to tradition, but on the basis of the tradition they select reach opposite results. Although assuredly having the virtue (if it be that) of leaving judges free to decide as they think best when the unanticipated occurs, a rule of law that binds neither by text nor by any particular, identifiable tradition is no rule of law at all. . . .

in their relationship with each other—that was among the first that this Court acknowledged in its cases defining the "liberty" protected by the Constitution, see, *e.g., Meyer v. Nebraska,* 262 U.S. 390, 399 (1923); *Skinner v. Oklahoma,* 316 U.S. 535, 541 (1942); *Prince v. Massachusetts,* 321 U.S. 158, 166 (1944), and I think I am safe in saying that no one doubts the wisdom or validity of those decisions. Where the interest under consideration is a parent-child relationship, we need not ask, over and over again, whether that interest is one that society traditionally protects.

Thus, to describe the issue in this case as whether the relationship existing between Michael and Victoria "has been treated as a protected family unit under the historic practices of our society, or whether on any other basis it has been accorded special protection," is to reinvent the wheel. The better approach—indeed, the one commanded by our prior cases and by common sense—is to ask whether the specific parent-child relationship under consideration is close enough to the interests that we already have protected to be deemed an aspect of "liberty" as well. On the facts before us, therefore, the question is not what "level of generality" should be used to describe the relationship between Michael and Victoria, see *ante,* at 2344, n. 6, but whether the relationship under consideration is sufficiently substantial to qualify as a liberty interest under our prior cases.

On four prior occasions, we have considered whether unwed fathers have a constitutionally protected interest in their relationships with their children. See *Stanley v. Illinois,* 405 U.S. 645 (1972); *Quilloin v. Walcott,* 434 U.S. 246 (1978); *Caban v. Mohammed,* 441 U.S. 380 (1979); and *Lehr v. Robertson,* 463 U.S. 248 (1983). Though different in factual and legal circumstances, these cases have produced a unifying theme: although an unwed father's biological link to his child does not, in and of itself, guarantee him a constitutional stake in his relationship with that child, such a link combined with a substantial parent-child relationship will do so. "When an unwed father demonstrates a full commitment to the responsibilities of parenthood by 'com[ing] forward to participate in the rearing of his child,' . . . his interest in personal contact with his child acquires substantial protection under the Due Process Clause. At that point it may be said that he 'act[s] as a father toward his children.'" *Lehr v. Robertson, supra,* at 261, quoting *Caban v. Mohammed, supra,* 441 U.S., at 392, 389, n. 7. This commitment is why Mr. Stanley and Mr. Caban won; why Mr. Quilloin and Mr. Lehr lost; and why Michael H. should prevail today. Michael H. is almost certainly Victoria D.'s natural father, has lived with her as her father, has contributed to her support, and has from the beginning sought to strengthen and maintain his relationship with her. . . .

[The concurring opinion of Justice Stevens, and the dissenting opinion of Justice White is omitted.]

Notes and Questions

1. Even if, as the *Michael H.* Court holds, no fundamental right is at stake, the law at issue must still pass rational basis review. What rationales are there for a law such as the one at issue in the case?

2. The Justices do not agree on the appropriate way to frame a right for fundamental rights purposes. What are the various ways in which the opinions suggest the right should be framed? Which approach is most consistent with the way in which the Court's earlier fundamental rights cases have framed the rights at stake?

3. In determining whether historically a right, however framed, has been protected, does the *Michael H.* Court require *affirmative* recognition of the right, or does mere non-interference with the challenged right suffice? Why might the distinction be significant?

Planned Parenthood of Southeastern Pennsylvania v. Casey

505 U.S. 833 (1992)

Justice O'Connor, Justice Kennedy, and Justice Souter announced the judgment of the Court and delivered the opinion of the Court with respect to Parts I, II, III, V–A, V–C, and VI, an opinion with respect to Part V–E, in which Justice Stevens joins, and an opinion with respect to Parts IV, V–B, and V–D.

I

Liberty finds no refuge in a jurisprudence of doubt. Yet 19 years after our holding that the Constitution protects a woman's right to terminate her pregnancy in its early stages, *Roe v. Wade,* 410 U.S. 113 (1973), that definition of liberty is still questioned. Joining the respondents as *amicus curiae,* the United States, as it has done in five other cases in the last decade, again asks us to overrule *Roe*. . . .

[The Court describes the Pennsylvania abortion statute being challenged in the case, which contains: (a) an informed consent provision with a 24-hour waiting period; (b) a parental consent provision for minors seeking an abortion (with a judicial bypass option); (c) a spousal notification provision for adult women seeking an abortion; and (d) a provision imposing certain reporting requirements on facilities that provide abortion services.]

After considering the fundamental constitutional questions resolved by *Roe,* principles of institutional integrity, and the rule of *stare decisis,* we are led to conclude this: the essential holding of *Roe v. Wade* should be retained and once again reaffirmed.

It must be stated at the outset and with clarity that *Roe*'s essential holding, the holding we reaffirm, has three parts. First is a recognition of the right of the woman to choose to have an abortion before viability and to obtain it without undue interference from the State. Before viability, the State's interests are not strong enough to support a prohibition of abortion or the imposition of a substantial obstacle to the woman's effective right to elect the procedure. Second is a confirmation of the State's power to restrict abortions after fetal viability, if the law contains exceptions for pregnancies which endanger the woman's life or health. And third is the principle that the State has legitimate interests from the outset of the pregnancy in protecting the health of the woman and the life of the fetus that may become a child. These principles do not contradict one another; and we adhere to each.

II

Constitutional protection of the woman's decision to terminate her pregnancy derives from the Due Process Clause of the Fourteenth Amendment. It declares that no State shall "deprive any person of life, liberty, or property, without due process of law." The controlling word in the cases before us is "liberty." . . . .

It is tempting, as a means of curbing the discretion of federal judges, to suppose that liberty encompasses no more than those rights already guaranteed to the individual against federal interference by the express provisions of the first eight Amendments to the Constitution. But of course this Court has never accepted that view.

It is also tempting, for the same reason, to suppose that the Due Process Clause protects only those practices, defined at the most specific level, that were protected against government interference by other rules of law when the Fourteenth Amendment was ratified. But such a view would be inconsistent with our law. It is a promise of the Constitution that there is a realm of personal liberty which the government may not enter. We have vindicated this principle before. Marriage is mentioned nowhere in the Bill of Rights and interracial marriage was illegal in most States in the 19th century, but the Court was no doubt correct in finding it to be an aspect of liberty protected against state interference by the substantive component of the Due Process Clause in *Loving v. Virginia,* 388 U.S. 1, 12 (1967) . . . .

Neither the Bill of Rights nor the specific practices of States at the time of the adoption of the Fourteenth Amendment marks the outer limits of the substantive sphere of liberty which the Fourteenth Amendment protects. See U.S. Const., Amdt. 9 . . . .

It is settled now, as it was when the Court heard arguments in *Roe v. Wade,* that the Constitution places limits on a State's right to interfere with a person's most basic decisions about family and parenthood, as well as bodily integrity. . . .

Our law affords constitutional protection to personal decisions relating to marriage, procreation, contraception, family relationships, child rearing, and education. Our cases recognize "the right of the *individual,* married or single, to be free from unwarranted governmental intrusion into matters so fundamentally affecting a person as the decision whether to bear or beget a child." *Eisenstadt v. Baird,* 405 U.S., at 453 (emphasis in original). Our precedents "have respected the private realm of family life which the state cannot enter." *Prince v. Massachusetts,* 321 U.S. 158, 166 (1944). These matters, involving the most intimate and personal choices a person may make in a lifetime, choices central to personal dignity and autonomy, are central to the liberty protected by the Fourteenth Amendment. At the heart of liberty is the right to define one's own concept of existence, of meaning, of the universe, and of the mystery of human life. Beliefs about these matters could not define the attributes of personhood were they formed under compulsion of the State.

These considerations begin our analysis of the woman's interest in terminating her pregnancy but cannot end it, for this reason: though the abortion decision may originate within the zone of conscience and belief, it is more than a philosophic exercise. Abortion is a unique act. It is an act fraught with consequences for others:

for the woman who must live with the implications of her decision; for the persons who perform and assist in the procedure; for the spouse, family, and society which must confront the knowledge that these procedures exist, procedures some deem nothing short of an act of violence against innocent human life; and, depending on one's beliefs, for the life or potential life that is aborted. Though abortion is conduct, it does not follow that the State is entitled to proscribe it in all instances. That is because the liberty of the woman is at stake in a sense unique to the human condition and so unique to the law. The mother who carries a child to full term is subject to anxieties, to physical constraints, to pain that only she must bear. That these sacrifices have from the beginning of the human race been endured by woman with a pride that ennobles her in the eyes of others and gives to the infant a bond of love cannot alone be grounds for the State to insist she make the sacrifice. Her suffering is too intimate and personal for the State to insist, without more, upon its own vision of the woman's role, however dominant that vision has been in the course of our history and our culture. The destiny of the woman must be shaped to a large extent on her own conception of her spiritual imperatives and her place in society.

It should be recognized, moreover, that in some critical respects the abortion decision is of the same character as the decision to use contraception, to which *Griswold v. Connecticut, Eisenstadt v. Baird,* and *Carey v. Population Services International* afford constitutional protection. We have no doubt as to the correctness of those decisions. They support the reasoning in *Roe* relating to the woman's liberty because they involve personal decisions concerning not only the meaning of procreation but also human responsibility and respect for it. . . .

It was this dimension of personal liberty that *Roe* sought to protect, and its holding invoked the reasoning and the tradition of the precedents we have discussed, granting protection to substantive liberties of the person. *Roe* was, of course, an extension of those cases. . . .

III

A

[I]t is common wisdom that the rule of *stare decisis* is not an "inexorable command," and certainly it is not such in every constitutional case. Rather, when this Court reexamines a prior holding, its judgment is customarily informed by a series of prudential and pragmatic considerations designed to test the consistency of overruling a prior decision with the ideal of the rule of law, and to gauge the respective costs of reaffirming and overruling a prior case. Thus, for example, we may ask whether the rule has proven to be intolerable simply in defying practical workability; whether the rule is subject to a kind of reliance that would lend a special hardship to the consequences of overruling and add inequity to the cost of repudiation; whether related principles of law have so far developed as to have left the old rule no more than a remnant of abandoned doctrine; or whether facts have so changed, or come to be seen so differently, as to have robbed the old rule of significant application or justification. . . .

1

Although *Roe* has engendered opposition, it has in no sense proven "unworkable," representing as it does a simple limitation beyond which a state law is unenforceable. While *Roe* has, of course, required judicial assessment of state laws affecting the exercise of the choice guaranteed against government infringement, and although the need for such review will remain as a consequence of today's decision, the required determinations fall within judicial competence.

2

The inquiry into reliance counts the cost of a rule's repudiation as it would fall on those who have relied reasonably on the rule's continued application. . . .

[F]or two decades of economic and social developments, people have organized intimate relationships and made choices that define their views of themselves and their places in society, in reliance on the availability of abortion in the event that contraception should fail. The ability of women to participate equally in the economic and social life of the Nation has been facilitated by their ability to control their reproductive lives. The Constitution serves human values, and while the effect of reliance on *Roe* cannot be exactly measured, neither can the certain cost of overruling *Roe* for people who have ordered their thinking and living around that case be dismissed.

3

No evolution of legal principle has left *Roe* 's doctrinal footings weaker than they were in 1973. No development of constitutional law since the case was decided has implicitly or explicitly left *Roe* behind as a mere survivor of obsolete constitutional thinking. . . .

4

We have seen how time has overtaken some of *Roe*'s factual assumptions: advances in maternal health care allow for abortions safe to the mother later in pregnancy than was true in 1973, and advances in neonatal care have advanced viability to a point somewhat earlier. But these facts go only to the scheme of time limits on the realization of competing interests, and the divergences from the factual premises of 1973 have no bearing on the validity of *Roe* 's central holding, that viability marks the earliest point at which the State's interest in fetal life is constitutionally adequate to justify a legislative ban on nontherapeutic abortions. The soundness or unsoundness of that constitutional judgment in no sense turns on whether viability occurs at approximately 28 weeks, as was usual at the time of *Roe*, at 23 to 24 weeks, as it sometimes does today, or at some moment even slightly earlier in pregnancy, as it may if fetal respiratory capacity can somehow be enhanced in the future. Whenever it may occur, the attainment of viability may continue to serve as the critical fact, just as it has done since *Roe* was decided; which is to say that no change in *Roe* 's factual underpinning has left its central holding obsolete, and none supports an argument for overruling it. . . .

B

In a less significant case, *stare decisis* analysis could, and would, stop at the point we have reached. But the sustained and widespread debate *Roe* has provoked calls for some comparison between that case and others of comparable dimension that have responded to national controversies and taken on the impress of the controversies addressed. . . .

C

. . . .

Where, in the performance of its judicial duties, the Court decides a case in such a way as to resolve the sort of intensely divisive controversy reflected in *Roe* and those rare, comparable cases, its decision has a dimension that the resolution of the normal case does not carry. It is the dimension present whenever the Court's interpretation of the Constitution calls the contending sides of a national controversy to end their national division by accepting a common mandate rooted in the Constitution.

The Court is not asked to do this very often, having thus addressed the Nation only twice in our lifetime, in the decisions of *Brown* [*v. Board of Education*] and *Roe.* But when the Court does act in this way, its decision requires an equally rare precedential force to counter the inevitable efforts to overturn it and to thwart its implementation. Some of those efforts may be mere unprincipled emotional reactions; others may proceed from principles worthy of profound respect. But whatever the premises of opposition may be, only the most convincing justification under accepted standards of precedent could suffice to demonstrate that a later decision overruling the first was anything but a surrender to political pressure, and an unjustified repudiation of the principle on which the Court staked its authority in the first instance. So to overrule under fire in the absence of the most compelling reason to reexamine a watershed decision would subvert the Court's legitimacy beyond any serious question. . . .

IV

From what we have said so far it follows that it is a constitutional liberty of the woman to have some freedom to terminate her pregnancy. We conclude that the basic decision in *Roe* was based on a constitutional analysis which we cannot now repudiate. The woman's liberty is not so unlimited, however, that from the outset the State cannot show its concern for the life of the unborn, and at a later point in fetal development the State's interest in life has sufficient force so that the right of the woman to terminate the pregnancy can be restricted. . . .

We conclude the line should be drawn at viability, so that before that time the woman has a right to choose to terminate her pregnancy. . . .

Roe established a trimester framework to govern abortion regulations. Under this elaborate but rigid construct, almost no regulation at all is permitted during the first trimester of pregnancy; regulations designed to protect the woman's health, but not to further the State's interest in potential life, are permitted during the second trimester; and during the third trimester, when the fetus is viable, prohibitions are permitted provided the life or health of the mother is not at stake. . . .

We reject the trimester framework, which we do not consider to be part of the essential holding of *Roe* . . . . The trimester framework suffers from these basic flaws: in its formulation it misconceives the nature of the pregnant woman's interest; and in practice it undervalues the State's interest in potential life, as recognized in *Roe* . . . .

Numerous forms of state regulation might have the incidental effect of increasing the cost or decreasing the availability of medical care, whether for abortion or any other medical procedure. The fact that a law which serves a valid purpose, one not designed to strike at the right itself, has the incidental effect of making it more difficult or more expensive to procure an abortion cannot be enough to invalidate it. Only where state regulation imposes an undue burden on a woman's ability to make this decision does the power of the State reach into the heart of the liberty protected by the Due Process Clause. . . .

The very notion that the State has a substantial interest in potential life leads to the conclusion that not all regulations must be deemed unwarranted. Not all burdens on the right to decide whether to terminate a pregnancy will be undue. In our view, the undue burden standard is the appropriate means of reconciling the State's interest with the woman's constitutionally protected liberty. . . .

A finding of an undue burden is a shorthand for the conclusion that a state regulation has the purpose or effect of placing a substantial obstacle in the path of a woman seeking an abortion of a nonviable fetus. A statute with this purpose is invalid because the means chosen by the State to further the interest in potential life must be calculated to inform the woman's free choice, not hinder it. And a statute which, while furthering the interest in potential life or some other valid state interest, has the effect of placing a substantial obstacle in the path of a woman's choice cannot be considered a permissible means of serving its legitimate ends. . . .

Some guiding principles should emerge. What is at stake is the woman's right to make the ultimate decision, not a right to be insulated from all others in doing so. Regulations which do no more than create a structural mechanism by which the State, or the parent or guardian of a minor, may express profound respect for the life of the unborn are permitted, if they are not a substantial obstacle to the woman's exercise of the right to choose. Unless it has that effect on her right of choice, a state measure designed to persuade her to choose childbirth over abortion will be upheld if reasonably related to that goal. Regulations designed to foster the health of a woman seeking an abortion are valid if they do not constitute an undue burden. . . .

V

. . . .

B

We next consider the informed consent requirement. Except in a medical emergency, the statute requires that at least 24 hours before performing an abortion a physician inform the woman of the nature of the procedure, the health risks of the abortion and of childbirth, and the "probable gestational age of the unborn child." The physician or a qualified nonphysician must inform the woman of the availability of printed materials published by the State describing the fetus and providing information about medical assistance for childbirth, information about child support from the father, and a list of agencies which provide adoption and other services as alternatives to abortion. An abortion may not be performed unless the woman certifies in writing that she has been informed of the availability of these printed materials and has been provided them if she chooses to view them. . . .

It cannot be questioned that psychological well-being is a facet of health. Nor can it be doubted that most women considering an abortion would deem the impact on the fetus relevant, if not dispositive, to the decision. In attempting to ensure that a woman apprehend the full consequences of her decision, the State furthers the legitimate purpose of reducing the risk that a woman may elect an abortion, only to discover later, with devastating psychological consequences, that her decision was not fully informed. If the information the State requires to be made available to the woman is truthful and not misleading, the requirement may be permissible. . . .

Since there is no evidence on this record that requiring a doctor to give the information as provided by the statute would amount in practical terms to a substantial obstacle to a woman seeking an abortion, we conclude that it is not an undue burden. Our cases reflect the fact that the Constitution gives the States broad latitude to decide that particular functions may be performed only by licensed professionals, even if an objective assessment might suggest that those same tasks could be performed by others. See *Williamson v. Lee Optical of Okla., Inc.*, 348 U.S. 483 (1955). Thus, we uphold the provision as a reasonable means to ensure that the woman's consent is informed.

Our analysis of Pennsylvania's 24–hour waiting period between the provision of the information deemed necessary to informed consent and the performance of an abortion under the undue burden standard requires us to reconsider the premise behind the decision in *Akron I* invalidating a parallel requirement. In *Akron I* we said: "Nor are we convinced that the State's legitimate concern that the woman's decision be informed is reasonably served by requiring a 24–hour delay as a matter of course." 462 U.S., at 450. We consider that conclusion to be wrong. The idea that important decisions will be more informed and deliberate if they follow some period of reflection does not strike us as unreasonable, particularly where the statute directs that important information become part of the background of the decision. The statute, as construed by the Court of Appeals, permits avoidance of the waiting period in the event of a medical emergency and the record evidence shows that in the vast majority of cases, a 24–hour delay does not create any appreciable health risk. In theory, at least, the waiting period is a reasonable measure to implement the State's interest in protecting the life of the unborn, a measure that does not amount to an undue burden.

Whether the mandatory 24–hour waiting period is nonetheless invalid because in practice it is a substantial obstacle to a woman's choice to terminate her pregnancy is a closer question. The findings of fact by the District Court indicate that because of the distances many women must travel to reach an abortion provider, the practical effect will often be a delay of much more than a day because the waiting period requires that a woman seeking an abortion make at least two visits to the doctor. The District Court also found that in many instances this will increase the exposure of women seeking abortions to "the harassment and hostility of anti-abortion protestors demonstrating outside a clinic." As a result, the District Court found that for those women who have the fewest financial resources, those who must travel long distances, and those who have difficulty explaining their whereabouts to husbands, employers, or others, the 24–hour waiting period will be "particularly burdensome."

These findings are troubling in some respects, but they do not demonstrate that the waiting period constitutes an undue burden. We do not doubt that, as the District Court held, the waiting period has the effect of "increasing the cost and risk of delay of abortions," but the District Court did not conclude that the increased costs and potential delays amount to substantial obstacles. . . .

We also disagree with the District Court's conclusion that the "particularly burdensome" effects of the waiting period on some women require its invalidation. A particular burden is not of necessity a substantial obstacle. Whether a burden falls on a particular group is a distinct inquiry from whether it is a substantial obstacle even as to the women in that group. And the District Court did not conclude that the waiting period is such an obstacle even for the women who are most burdened by it. Hence, on the record before us, and in the context of this facial challenge, we are not convinced that the 24–hour waiting period constitutes an undue burden. . . .

C

Section 3209 of Pennsylvania's abortion law provides, except in cases of medical emergency, that no physician shall perform an abortion on a married woman without receiving a signed statement from the woman that she has notified her spouse that she is about to undergo an abortion. The woman has the option of providing an alternative signed statement certifying that her husband is not the man who impregnated her; that her husband could not be located; that the pregnancy is the result of spousal sexual assault which she has reported; or that the woman believes that notifying her husband will cause him or someone else to inflict bodily injury upon her. A physician who performs an abortion on a married woman without receiving the appropriate signed statement will have his or her license revoked, and is liable to the husband for damages. . . .

The vast majority of women notify their male partners of their decision to obtain an abortion. In many cases in which married women do not notify their husbands, the pregnancy is the result of an extramarital affair. Where the husband is the father, the primary reason women do not notify their husbands is that the husband

and wife are experiencing marital difficulties, often accompanied by incidents of violence. . . .

The spousal notification requirement is thus likely to prevent a significant number of women from obtaining an abortion. It does not merely make abortions a little more difficult or expensive to obtain; for many women, it will impose a substantial obstacle. We must not blind ourselves to the fact that the significant number of women who fear for their safety and the safety of their children are likely to be deterred from procuring an abortion as surely as if the Commonwealth had outlawed abortion in all cases. . . .

If these cases concerned a State's ability to require the mother to notify the father before taking some action with respect to a living child raised by both, therefore, it would be reasonable to conclude as a general matter that the father's interest in the welfare of the child and the mother's interest are equal.

Before birth, however, the issue takes on a very different cast. It is an inescapable biological fact that state regulation with respect to the child a woman is carrying will have a far greater impact on the mother's liberty than on the father's. The effect of state regulation on a woman's protected liberty is doubly deserving of scrutiny in such a case, as the State has touched not only upon the private sphere of the family but upon the very bodily integrity of the pregnant woman. . . . The Court has held that "when the wife and the husband disagree on this decision, the view of only one of the two marriage partners can prevail. Inasmuch as it is the woman who physically bears the child and who is the more directly and immediately affected by the pregnancy, as between the two, the balance weighs in her favor." *Danforth, supra,* 428 U.S., at 71 . . . .

There was a time, not so long ago, when a different understanding of the family and of the Constitution prevailed. In *Bradwell v. State,* 16 Wall. 130 (1873), three Members of this Court reaffirmed the common-law principle that "a woman had no legal existence separate from her husband, who was regarded as her head and representative in the social state; and, notwithstanding some recent modifications of this civil status, many of the special rules of law flowing from and dependent upon this cardinal principle still exist in full force in most States." *Id.,* at 141 (Bradley, J., joined by Swayne and Field, JJ., concurring in judgment). Only one generation has passed since this Court observed that "woman is still regarded as the center of home and family life," with attendant "special responsibilities" that precluded full and independent legal status under the Constitution. *Hoyt v. Florida,* 368 U.S. 57, 62 (1961). These views, of course, are no longer consistent with our understanding of the family, the individual, or the Constitution.

In keeping with our rejection of the common-law understanding of a woman's role within the family, the Court held in *Danforth* that the Constitution does not permit a State to require a married woman to obtain her husband's consent before undergoing an abortion. The principles that guided the Court in *Danforth* should be our guides today. For the great many women who are victims of abuse inflicted by their husbands, or whose children are the victims of such abuse, a spousal notice requirement enables the husband to wield an effective veto over his wife's decision. . . .

Section 3209 embodies a view of marriage consonant with the common-law status of married women but repugnant to our present understanding of marriage and of the nature of the rights secured by the Constitution. Women do not lose their constitutionally protected liberty when they marry. The Constitution protects all individuals, male or female, married or unmarried, from the abuse of governmental power, even where that power is employed for the supposed benefit of a member of the individual's family. These considerations confirm our conclusion that § 3209 is invalid.

D

We next consider the parental consent provision. Except in a medical emergency, an unemancipated young woman under 18 may not obtain an abortion unless she and one of her parents (or guardian) provides informed consent as defined above. If neither a parent nor a guardian provides consent, a court may authorize the performance of an abortion upon a determination that the young woman is mature and capable of giving informed consent and has in fact given her informed consent, or that an abortion would be in her best interests.

We have been over most of this ground before. Our cases establish, and we reaffirm today, that a State may require a minor seeking an abortion to obtain the consent of a parent or guardian, provided that there is an adequate judicial bypass procedure. Under these precedents, in our view, the one-parent consent requirement and judicial bypass procedure are constitutional.

The only argument made by petitioners respecting this provision and to which our prior decisions do not speak is the contention that the parental consent requirement is invalid because it requires informed parental consent. For the most part, petitioners' argument is a reprise of their argument with respect to the informed consent requirement in general, and we reject it for the reasons given above. Indeed, some of the provisions regarding informed consent have particular force with respect to minors: the waiting period, for example, may provide the parent or parents of a pregnant young woman the opportunity to consult with her in private, and to discuss the consequences of her decision in the context of the values and moral or religious principles of their family.

E

Under the recordkeeping and reporting requirements of the statute, every facility which performs abortions is required to file a report stating its name and address as well as the name and address of any related entity, such as a controlling or subsidiary organization. In the case of state-funded institutions, the information becomes public.

For each abortion performed, a report must be filed identifying: the physician (and the second physician where required); the facility; the referring physician or agency;

the woman's age; the number of prior pregnancies and prior abortions she has had; gestational age; the type of abortion procedure; the date of the abortion; whether there were any pre-existing medical conditions which would complicate pregnancy; medical complications with the abortion; where applicable, the basis for the determination that the abortion was medically necessary; the weight of the aborted fetus; and whether the woman was married, and if so, whether notice was provided or the basis for the failure to give notice. Every abortion facility must also file quarterly reports showing the number of abortions performed broken down by trimester. In all events, the identity of each woman who has had an abortion remains confidential.

In *Danforth,* 428 U.S., at 80, we held that recordkeeping and reporting provisions "that are reasonably directed to the preservation of maternal health and that properly respect a patient's confidentiality and privacy are permissible." We think that under this standard, all the provisions at issue here, except that relating to spousal notice, are constitutional. Although they do not relate to the State's interest in informing the woman's choice, they do relate to health. The collection of information with respect to actual patients is a vital element of medical research, and so it cannot be said that the requirements serve no purpose other than to make abortions more difficult. Nor do we find that the requirements impose a substantial obstacle to a woman's choice. At most they might increase the cost of some abortions by a slight amount. While at some point increased cost could become a substantial obstacle, there is no such showing on the record before us. . . .

VI

Our Constitution is a covenant running from the first generation of Americans to us and then to future generations. It is a coherent succession. Each generation must learn anew that the Constitution's written terms embody ideas and aspirations that must survive more ages than one. We accept our responsibility not to retreat from interpreting the full meaning of the covenant in light of all of our precedents. We invoke it once again to define the freedom guaranteed by the Constitution's own promise, the promise of liberty. . . .

Justice Scalia, with whom The Chief Justice, Justice White, and Justice Thomas join, concurring in the judgment in part and dissenting in part.

My views on this matter are unchanged from those I set forth in my separate opinions in *Webster v. Reproductive Health Services,* 492 U.S. 490, 532 (1989) (opinion concurring in part and concurring in judgment), and *Ohio v. Akron Center for Reproductive Health,* 497 U.S. 502, 520 (1990) (*Akron II*) (concurring opinion). The States may, if they wish, permit abortion on demand, but the Constitution does not *require* them to do so. The permissibility of abortion, and the limitations upon it, are to be resolved like most important questions in our democracy: by citizens trying to persuade one another and then voting. . . . A State's choice between two positions on which reasonable people can disagree is constitutional even when (as is often the case) it intrudes upon a "liberty" in the absolute sense. Laws against bigamy, for example—with which entire societies of reasonable people disagree—intrude upon men and women's liberty to marry and live with one another. But bigamy happens not to be a liberty specially "protected" by the Constitution.

That is, quite simply, the issue in these cases: not whether the power of a woman to abort her unborn child is a "liberty" in the absolute sense; or even whether it is a liberty of great importance to many women. Of course it is both. The issue is whether it is a liberty protected by the Constitution of the United States. I am sure it is not. I reach that conclusion not because of anything so exalted as my views concerning the "concept of existence, of meaning, of the universe, and of the mystery of human life." Rather, I reach it for the same reason I reach the conclusion that bigamy is not constitutionally protected—because of two simple facts: (1) the Constitution says absolutely nothing about it, and (2) the longstanding traditions of American society have permitted it to be legally proscribed. . . .

* * *

There is a poignant aspect to today's opinion. Its length, and what might be called its epic tone, suggest that its authors believe they are bringing to an end a troublesome era in the history of our Nation and of our Court. "It is the dimension" of authority, they say, to "cal[l] the contending sides of national controversy to end their national division by accepting a common mandate rooted in the Constitution."

There comes vividly to mind a portrait by Emanuel Leutze that hangs in the Harvard Law School: Roger Brooke Taney, painted in 1859, the 82d year of his life, the 24th of his Chief Justiceship, the second after his opinion in *Dred Scott.* He is all in black, sitting in a shadowed red armchair, left hand resting upon a pad of paper in his lap, right hand hanging limply, almost lifelessly, beside the inner arm of the chair. He sits facing the viewer and staring straight out. There seems to be on his face, and in his deep-set eyes, an expression of profound sadness and disillusionment. Perhaps he always looked that way, even when dwelling upon the happiest of thoughts. But those of us who know how the lustre of his great Chief Justiceship came to be eclipsed by *Dred Scott* cannot help believing that he had that case—its already apparent consequences for the Court and its soon-to-be-played-out consequences for the Nation—burning on his mind. I expect that two years earlier he, too, had thought himself "call[ing] the contending sides of national controversy to end their national division by accepting a common mandate rooted in the Constitution."

It is no more realistic for us in this litigation, than it was for him in that, to think that an issue of the sort they both involved—an issue involving life and death, freedom and subjugation—can be "speedily and finally settled" by the Supreme Court, as President James Buchanan in his inaugural address said the issue of slavery in the territories would be. Quite to the contrary, by foreclosing all democratic outlet for the deep passions this issue arouses, by banishing the issue from the political forum that gives all participants, even the losers, the satisfaction of a fair hearing and an honest fight, by continuing the imposition of a rigid national rule instead of allowing for regional differences, the Court merely prolongs and intensifies the anguish.

We should get out of this area, where we have no right to be, and where we do neither ourselves nor the country any good by remaining.

[The opinions of Justices Stevens, Blackmun, and Chief Justice Rehnquist, concurring in part and dissenting in part, are omitted.]

Notes and Questions

1. Recall that in *Griswold*, *Roe*, and *Bowers*, the Court spoke about a right to "privacy." Does the term "privacy" appear anywhere within the excerpt from *Casey*? How, if at all, is the switch in terminology relevant?

2. *Casey* at times uses breathtakingly broad language to describe the scope of the due process right at issue in the case. How does that compare with the more narrow focus of *Bowers*, which preceded it? With Justice Scalia's proposed approach in the *Michael H.* case? Are the decisions reconcilable? Is there language in *Casey* that is more focused in nature and thus more consistent with those earlier decisions?

3. In *Casey*, the Court sets forth a series of factors to consider in deciding whether to overturn existing precedent. If the Court were asked to reconsider *Bowers*, in which way would these factors point?

4. The Court states that it is re-affirming *Roe*'s essential holding, but it nonetheless makes significant changes to the constitutional standards for abortion restrictions. In what way do *Roe* and *Casey* differ with respect to the state's ability to discourage or restrict abortions?

5. As contrasted with the "strict scrutiny" standard employed in *Roe*, how protective is the "undue burden" standard of the abortion right articulated in *Casey*? In this regard, consider that the Court had—after *Roe* but prior to *Casey*—struck down informed consent provisions and waiting periods. *See Akron v. Akron Center for Reproductive Health, Inc.*, 462 U.S. 416 (1983).

6. Where does the "undue burden" come from? The standard had appeared only in very rudimentary form in concurring opinions in abortion cases, primarily those penned by Justice O'Connor writing for herself. In *Casey*, only three Justices endorse the standard; the remaining Justices endorse either strict scrutiny or rational basis review. Is the invocation of this new, less stringent standard a signal that abortion is being downgraded from a fundamental right to a less protected one, or is the plurality signaling a general change in the level of scrutiny for all fundamental rights from strict scrutiny to something less exacting?

7. The materials in the previous chapter raised the question whether proof of discriminatory purpose is required where infringements upon fundamental rights are involved. Does the language used in *Casey* in describing the undue burden standard shed light on the answer to this question?

Washington v. Glucksberg

521 U.S. 702 (1997)

Chief Justice Rehnquist delivered the opinion of the Court.

[The Chief Justice summarizes the facts of the case, which involves a group of physicians and terminally ill patients as well as a nonprofit organization bringing suit against the State of Washington, seeking a declaration that its law banning physician-assisted suicide violates the Due Process Clause of the Fourteenth Amendment.]

Our established method of substantive-due-process analysis has two primary features: First, we have regularly observed that the Due Process Clause specially protects those fundamental rights and liberties which are, objectively, "deeply rooted in this Nation's history and tradition," and "implicit in the concept of ordered liberty," such that "neither liberty nor justice would exist if they were sacrificed." Second, we have required in substantive-due-process cases a "careful description" of the asserted fundamental liberty interest. . . .

Turning to the claim at issue here, the Court of Appeals stated that "[p]roperly analyzed, the first issue to be resolved is whether there is a liberty interest in determining the time and manner of one's death," or, in other words, "[i]s there a right to die?" Similarly, respondents assert a "liberty to choose how to die" and a right to "control of one's final days," and describe the asserted liberty as "the right to choose a humane, dignified death," and "the liberty to shape death." As noted above, we have a tradition of carefully formulating the interest at stake in substantive-due-process cases. For example, although *Cruzan* [*v. Director, Mo. Dept. of Health*] is often described as a "right to die" case, we were, in fact, more precise: We assumed that the Constitution granted competent persons a "constitutionally protected right to refuse lifesaving hydration and nutrition." The Washington statute at issue in this case prohibits "aid[ing] another person to attempt suicide," and, thus, the question before us is whether the "liberty" specially protected by the Due Process Clause includes a right to commit suicide which itself includes a right to assistance in doing so.

We now inquire whether this asserted right has any place in our Nation's traditions. Here . . . we are confronted with a consistent and almost universal tradition that has long rejected the asserted right, and continues explicitly to reject it today, even for terminally ill, mentally competent adults. To hold for respondents, we would have to reverse centuries of legal doctrine and practice, and strike down the considered policy choice of almost every State. . . .

Respondents contend, however, that the liberty interest they assert *is* consistent with this Court's substantive-due-process line of cases, if not with this Nation's history and practice. Pointing to *Casey* and *Cruzan*, respondents read our jurisprudence in this area as reflecting a general tradition of "self-sovereignty," and as teaching that the "liberty" protected by the Due Process Clause includes "basic and intimate exercises of personal autonomy," see *Casey*, 505 U.S., at 847 ("It is a promise of the Constitution that there is a realm of personal liberty which the government may not enter"). According to respondents, our liberty jurisprudence, and the broad, individualistic principles it reflects, protects the "liberty of competent, terminally ill adults to make end-of-life decisions free of undue government interference." The question presented in this case, however, is whether the protections of the Due Process Clause include a right to commit suicide with another's assistance. With this "careful description" of respondents' claim in mind, we turn to *Casey* and *Cruzan*.

In *Cruzan*, we considered whether Nancy Beth Cruzan, who had been severely injured in an automobile accident and was in a persistive vegetative state, "ha[d] a right under the United States Constitution which would require the hospital to withdraw life-sustaining treatment" at her parents' request. We began with the observation that "[a]t common law, even the touching of one person by another without consent and without legal justification was a battery." We then discussed the related rule that "informed consent is generally required for medical treatment." After reviewing a long line of relevant state cases, we concluded that "the common-law doctrine of informed consent is viewed as generally encompassing the right of a competent individual to refuse medical treatment." Next, we reviewed our own cases on the subject, and stated that "[t]he principle that a competent person has a constitutionally protected liberty interest in refusing unwanted medical treatment may be inferred from our prior decisions." Therefore, "for purposes of [that] case, we assume[d] that the United States Constitution would grant a competent person a constitutionally protected right to refuse lifesaving hydration and nutrition." We concluded that, notwithstanding this right, the Constitution permitted Missouri to require clear and convincing evidence of an incompetent patient's wishes concerning the withdrawal of life-sustaining treatment. . . .

The right assumed in *Cruzan* . . . was not simply deduced from abstract concepts of personal autonomy. Given the common-law rule that forced medication was a battery, and the long legal tradition protecting the decision to refuse unwanted medical treatment, our assumption was entirely consistent with this Nation's history and constitutional traditions. The decision to commit suicide with the assistance of another may be just as personal and profound as the decision to refuse unwanted medical treatment, but it has never enjoyed similar legal protection. . . .

Respondents also rely on *Casey*. . . .

[R]espondents emphasize the statement in *Casey* that:

> "At the heart of liberty is the right to define one's own concept of existence, of meaning, of the universe, and of the mystery of human life. Beliefs about these matters could not define the attributes of personhood were they formed under compulsion of the State."

By choosing this language, the Court's opinion in *Casey* described, in a general way and in light of our prior cases, those personal activities and decisions that this Court has identified as so deeply rooted in our history and traditions, or so fundamental to our concept of constitutionally ordered liberty, that they are protected by the Fourteenth Amendment. The opinion moved from the recognition that liberty necessarily includes freedom of conscience and belief about ultimate considerations to the observation that "though the abortion decision may originate within the zone of conscience and belief, it is *more than a philosophic exercise*." That many of the rights and liberties protected by the Due Process Clause sound in personal autonomy does not warrant the sweeping conclusion that any and all important, intimate, and personal decisions are so protected, and *Casey* did not suggest otherwise.

The history of the law's treatment of assisted suicide in this country has been and continues to be one of the rejection of nearly all efforts to permit it. That being the case, our decisions lead us to conclude that the asserted "right" to assistance in committing suicide is not a fundamental liberty interest protected by the Due Process Clause. The Constitution also requires, however, that Washington's assisted-suicide ban be rationally related to legitimate government interests. This requirement is unquestionably met here. . . .

First, Washington has an "unqualified interest in the preservation of human life." *Cruzan*, 497 U.S., at 282. The State's prohibition on assisted suicide, like all homicide laws, both reflects and advances its commitment to this interest. This interest is symbolic and aspirational as well as practical. . . .

Relatedly, all admit that suicide is a serious public-health problem, especially among persons in otherwise vulnerable groups. The State has an interest in preventing suicide, and in studying, identifying, and treating its causes.

Those who attempt suicide-terminally ill or not-often suffer from depression or other mental disorders. Research indicates, however, that many people who request physician-assisted suicide withdraw that request if their depression and pain are treated. The New York Task Force, however, expressed its concern that, because depression is difficult to diagnose, physicians and medical professionals often fail to respond adequately to seriously ill patients' needs. Thus, legal physician-assisted suicide could make it more difficult for the State to protect depressed or mentally ill persons, or those who are suffering from untreated pain, from suicidal impulses.

The State also has an interest in protecting the integrity and ethics of the medical profession.... [T]he American Medical Association, like many other medical and physicians' groups, has concluded that "[p]hysician-assisted suicide is fundamentally incompatible with the physician's role as healer." And physician-assisted suicide could, it is argued, undermine the trust that is essential to the doctor-patient relationship by blurring the time-honored line between healing and harming.

Next, the State has an interest in protecting vulnerable groups—including the poor, the elderly, and disabled persons-from abuse, neglect, and mistakes.... If physician-assisted suicide were permitted, many might resort to it to spare their families the substantial financial burden of end-of-life health-care costs.

The State's interest here goes beyond protecting the vulnerable from coercion; it extends to protecting disabled and terminally ill people from prejudice, negative and inaccurate stereotypes, and "societal indifference." The State's assisted-suicide ban reflects and reinforces its policy that the lives of terminally ill, disabled, and elderly people must be no less valued than the lives of the young and healthy, and that a seriously disabled person's suicidal impulses should be interpreted and treated the same way as anyone else's.

Finally, the State may fear that permitting assisted suicide will start it down the path to voluntary and perhaps even involuntary euthanasia....

We need not weigh exactingly the relative strengths of these various interests. They are unquestionably important and legitimate, and Washington's ban on assisted suicide is at least reasonably related to their promotion and protection....

Throughout the Nation, Americans are engaged in an earnest and profound debate about the morality, legality, and practicality of physician-assisted suicide. Our holding permits this debate to continue, as it should in a democratic society....

[The concurring opinions of Justices O'Connor, Breyer, Souter, Stevens, and Ginsburg are omitted.]

Notes and Questions

1. Recall that in *Griswold*, *Roe*, and *Bowers*, the Court spoke about a right to "privacy," while the *Casey* plurality used somewhat different language. Which language does *Glucksberg* employ, and how, if at all, is the switch in terminology relevant?

2. *Glucksberg* sets forth what it describes as a two-part test for evaluating substantive due process claims. The first part requires framing the right. How narrowly or broadly does the Court require that the right be framed? How does this compare with the various methods suggested by the Justices in the *Michael H.* case? With the framing employed in *Bowers*, *Roe*, and *Casey*? In contemplating the answer to this question, keep in mind that Justices Kennedy and O'Connor, who wrote separately in *Michael H.*, are members of the majority in *Glucksberg*.

3. The second part of the *Glucksberg* test requires a determination whether the right, appropriately framed, exists. To what does the *Glucksberg* test look to in making

that determination? How does that compare with the approach employed by the Court in its earlier fundamental rights cases?

4. Although *Glucksberg* describes the test as a two-part test, in reality, the key step in the test is the framing part, is it not? After all, the more narrowly the right is framed, the less likely one is to find support for their right in historical or contemporary sources. Similarly, the more abstractly the right is framed, the more likely it is one can find support for the right at stake, broadly described.

Chapter 17

The "Reverse Discrimination" Cases

A. General Methodological Questions

For most of American history, government action drawing distinctions on the basis of race has been one-sided, with laws enacted by the white majority for the purpose of disadvantaging minority groups, particularly African Americans. As demonstrated in earlier chapters, the U.S. Supreme Court now subjects such laws to strict scrutiny under the Equal Protection Clause.

Yet does that same level of judicial scrutiny apply to laws designed to *benefit* minority groups? Beginning in the latter part of the twentieth century, federal and state lawmakers enacted programs—often denominated "affirmative action" programs—designed to offset the effects of prior discrimination in employment and education by providing members of minority groups with a preference when making hiring and admissions decisions. In more recent decades, such programs have been established to promote additional goals, including diversity.

Recall from Chapter 2 that there was language in the Court's first decision interpreting the Equal Protection Clause suggesting that it might only apply to laws discriminating *against* African Americans:

> We doubt very much whether any action of a State not directed by way of discrimination against the negroes as a class, or on account of their race, will ever be held to come within the purview of this provision. It is so clearly a provision for that race and that emergency, that a strong case would be necessary for its application to any other.

The Slaughter-House Cases, 83 U.S. 36, 81 (1873).

To be sure, dicta in another early case suggested otherwise, at least where African Americans were in the majority:

> If in those States where the colored people constitute a majority of the entire population a law should be enacted excluding all white men from jury service, thus denying to them the privilege of participating equally with the blacks in the administration of justice, we apprehend no one would be heard to claim that it would not be a denial to white men of the equal protection of the laws.

Strauder v. West Virginia, 100 U.S. 303, 308 (1880).

Yet these decisions do little to answer the question whether the Equal Protection Clause applies when the white majority decides to enact a program designed to benefit the African American minority.

The issue has reached the U.S. Supreme Court on several occasions since the 1970s. On each occasion, the Court has been strongly divided, and indeed, often failed to produce a majority opinion. First, in *Regents of University of California v. Bakke*, 438 U.S. 265 (1978), the Court struck down an affirmative action program at a state medical school in which 16 of the 100 positions in the class were reserved for members of disadvantaged groups, but there was no consensus on whether strict or intermediate scrutiny applied to racial classifications employed for remedial purposes.

Two years later, in *Fullilove v. Klutznick*, 448 U.S. 448 (1980), the Court upheld a federal program that provided grants to state and local governments for use in public works projects that contained a requirement that 10 percent of the funds be used to support minority business enterprises, without deciding the level of scrutiny that would be applied. But six years after that, the Court, in *Wygant v. Jackson Bd. of Educ.*, 476 U.S. 267 (1986), struck down a provision in a public sector collective bargaining agreement in which layoffs—although normally done on the basis of seniority—were subject to a proviso under which at "no time will there be a greater percentage of minority personnel laid off than the current percentage of minority personnel employed at the time of the layoff." Again in *Wygant*, the Court failed to produce a majority on the question whether strict scrutiny or some lower level of scrutiny was applicable.

In the cases that follow, the Court begins to reach consensus on a number of questions. Chief among these is the question whether the same level of scrutiny—strict—applies to laws designed to help racial minorities as applies to those designed to invidiously discriminate against them. In these cases, the Court also addresses the question whether the federal government is subject to the same level of scrutiny when it enacts such laws, or whether it has somewhat greater freedom. Finally, the cases begin to identify the sorts of governmental interests that are deemed sufficiently strong to justify enacting such laws.

City of Richmond v. J.A. Croson Co.

488 U.S. 469 (1989)

Justice O'Connor announced the judgment of the Court and delivered the opinion of the Court with respect to Parts I, III-B, and IV, an opinion with respect to Part II, in which The Chief Justice and Justice White join, and an opinion with respect to Parts III-A and V, in which The Chief Justice, Justice White, and Justice Kennedy join.

In this case, we confront once again the tension between the Fourteenth Amendment's guarantee of equal treatment to all citizens, and the use of race-based measures to ameliorate the effects of past discrimination on the opportunities enjoyed by members of minority groups in our society. In *Fullilove v. Klutznick*, 448 U.S. 448

(1980), we held that a congressional program requiring that 10% of certain federal construction grants be awarded to minority contractors did not violate the equal protection principles embodied in the Due Process Clause of the Fifth Amendment. Relying largely on our decision in *Fullilove,* some lower federal courts have applied a similar standard of review in assessing the constitutionality of state and local minority set-aside provisions under the Equal Protection Clause of the Fourteenth Amendment. . . .

I

On April 11, 1983, the Richmond City Council adopted the Minority Business Utilization Plan (the Plan). The Plan required prime contractors to whom the city awarded construction contracts to subcontract at least 30% of the dollar amount of the contract to one or more Minority Business Enterprises (MBE's). The 30% set-aside did not apply to city contracts awarded to minority-owned prime contractors.

The Plan defined an MBE as "[a] business at least fifty-one (51) percent of which is owned and controlled . . . by minority group members." § 12-23, p. 941. "Minority group members" were defined as "[c]itizens of the United States who are Blacks, Spanish-speaking, Orientals, Indians, Eskimos, or Aleuts." *Ibid.* There was no geographic limit to the Plan; an otherwise qualified MBE from anywhere in the United States could avail itself of the 30% set-aside. The Plan declared that it was "remedial" in nature, and enacted "for the purpose of promoting wider participation by minority business enterprises in the construction of public projects." § 12-158(a). The Plan expired on June 30, 1988, and was in effect for approximately five years. . . .

II

The parties and their supporting *amici* fight an initial battle over the scope of the city's power to adopt legislation designed to address the effects of past discrimination. Relying on our decision in *Wygant,* appellee argues that the city must limit any race-based remedial efforts to eradicating the effects of its own prior discrimination. . . . Appellant argues that our decision in *Fullilove* is controlling, and that as a result the city of Richmond enjoys sweeping legislative power to define and attack the effects of prior discrimination in its local construction industry. We find that neither of these two rather stark alternatives can withstand analysis.

In *Fullilove,* we upheld the minority set-aside contained in § 103(f)(2) of the Public Works Employment Act of 1977 (Act) against a challenge based on the equal protection component of the Due Process Clause. . . .

The principal opinion in *Fullilove,* written by Chief Justice Burger, did not employ "strict scrutiny" or any other traditional standard of equal protection review. The Chief Justice noted at the outset that although racial classifications call for close examination, the Court was at the same time "bound to approach [its] task with appropriate deference to the Congress, a co-equal branch charged by the Constitution with the power to 'provide for the . . . general Welfare of the United States' and 'to enforce by appropriate legislation,' the equal protection guarantees of the Fourteenth Amendment." 448 U.S., at 472 . . . .

His opinion stressed two factors in upholding the MBE set-aside. First was the unique remedial powers of Congress under § 5 of the Fourteenth Amendment. . . .

Because of these unique powers, the Chief Justice concluded that "Congress not only may induce voluntary action to assure compliance with existing federal statutory or constitutional antidiscrimination provisions, but also, where Congress has authority to *declare certain conduct unlawful,* it may, as here, authorize and induce state action to avoid such conduct." *Id.,* at 483-484 (emphasis added).

In reviewing the legislative history behind the Act, the principal opinion focused on the evidence before Congress that a nationwide history of past discrimination had reduced minority participation in federal construction grants. . . .

The second factor emphasized by the principal opinion in *Fullilove* was the flexible nature of the 10% set-aside. Two "congressional assumptions" underlay the MBE program: first, that the effects of past discrimination had impaired the competitive position of minority businesses, and second, that "adjustment for the effects of past discrimination" would assure that at least 10% of the funds from the federal grant program would flow to minority businesses. The Chief Justice noted that both of these "assumptions" could be "rebutted" by a grantee seeking a waiver of the 10% requirement. Thus a waiver could be sought where minority businesses were not available to fill the 10% requirement or, more importantly, where an MBE attempted "to exploit the remedial aspects of the program by charging an unreasonable price, *i.e.,* a price not attributable to the present effects of prior discrimination." The Chief Justice indicated that without this fine tuning to remedial purpose, the statute would not have "pass[ed] muster." . . . .

Appellant and its supporting *amici* rely heavily on *Fullilove* for the proposition that a city council, like Congress, need not make specific findings of discrimination to engage in race-conscious relief. . . .

What appellant ignores is that Congress, unlike any State or political subdivision, has a specific constitutional mandate to enforce the dictates of the Fourteenth Amendment. The power to "enforce" may at times also include the power to define situations which *Congress* determines threaten principles of equality and to adopt prophylactic rules to deal with those situations. See *Katzenbach v. Morgan,* 384 U.S., at 651 ("Correctly viewed, § 5 is a positive grant of legislative power authorizing Congress to exercise its discretion in determining whether and what legislation is needed to secure the guarantees of the Fourteenth Amendment"). See also *South Carolina v. Katzenbach,* 383 U.S. 301, 326 (1966) (similar interpretation of congressional power under § 2 of the Fifteenth Amendment) . . . .

That Congress may identify and redress the effects of society-wide discrimination does not mean that, *a fortiori,* the States and their political subdivisions are free to decide that such remedies are appropriate. Section 1 of the Fourteenth Amendment is an explicit *constraint* on state power, and the States must undertake any remedial efforts in accordance with that provision. To hold otherwise would be to cede control over the content of the Equal Protection Clause to the 50 state legislatures and their myriad political subdivisions. The mere recitation of a benign or compensatory purpose for the use of a racial classification would essentially entitle the States to exercise the full power of Congress under § 5 of the Fourteenth Amendment and insulate any racial classification from judicial scrutiny under § 1. We believe that such a result would be contrary to the intentions of the Framers of the Fourteenth Amendment, who desired to place clear limits on the States' use of race as a criterion for legislative action, and to have the federal courts enforce those limitations....

It would seem equally clear, however, that a state or local subdivision (if delegated the authority from the State) has the authority to eradicate the effects of private discrimination within its own legislative jurisdiction. This authority must, of course, be exercised within the constraints of § 1 of the Fourteenth Amendment. Our decision in *Wygant* is not to the contrary. *Wygant* addressed the constitutionality of the use of racial quotas by local school authorities pursuant to an agreement reached with the local teachers' union. It was in the context of addressing the school board's power to adopt a race-based layoff program affecting its own work force that the *Wygant* plurality indicated that the Equal Protection Clause required "some showing of prior discrimination by the governmental unit involved." *Wygant,* 476 U.S., at 274. As a matter of state law, the city of Richmond has legislative authority over its procurement policies, and can use its spending powers to remedy private discrimination, if it identifies that discrimination with the particularity required by the Fourteenth Amendment....

Thus, if the city could show that it had essentially become a "passive participant" in a system of racial exclusion practiced by elements of the local construction industry, we think it clear that the city could take affirmative steps to dismantle such a system. It is beyond dispute that any public entity, state or federal, has a compelling interest in assuring that public dollars, drawn from the tax contributions of all citizens, do not serve to finance the evil of private prejudice.

III

A

The Equal Protection Clause of the Fourteenth Amendment provides that "[n]o State shall ... deny to *any person* within its jurisdiction the equal protection of the laws." (Emphasis added.) As this Court has noted in the past, the "rights created by the first section of the Fourteenth Amendment are, by its terms, guaranteed to the individual. The rights established are personal rights." *Shelley v. Kraemer,* 334 U.S. 1 (1948). The Richmond Plan denies certain citizens the opportunity to compete for a fixed percentage of public contracts based solely upon their race. To whatever racial group these citizens belong, their "personal rights" to be treated with equal dignity and respect are implicated by a rigid rule erecting race as the sole criterion in an aspect of public decisionmaking.

Absent searching judicial inquiry into the justification for such race-based measures, there is simply no way of determining what classifications are "benign" or "remedial" and what classifications are in fact motivated by illegitimate notions of racial inferiority or simple racial politics. Indeed, the purpose of strict scrutiny is to "smoke out" illegitimate uses of race by assuring that the legislative body is pursuing a goal important enough to warrant use of a highly suspect tool. The test also ensures that the means chosen "fit" this compelling goal so closely that there is little or no possibility that the motive for the classification was illegitimate racial prejudice or stereotype.

Classifications based on race carry a danger of stigmatic harm. Unless they are strictly reserved for remedial settings, they may in fact promote notions of racial inferiority and lead to a politics of racial hostility. We thus reaffirm the view expressed by the plurality in *Wygant* that the standard of review under the Equal Protection Clause is not dependent on the race of those burdened or benefited by a particular classification. . . .

Even were we to accept a reading of the guarantee of equal protection under which the level of scrutiny varies according to the ability of different groups to defend their interests in the representative process, heightened scrutiny would still be appropriate in the circumstances of this case. One of the central arguments for applying a less exacting standard to "benign" racial classifications is that such measures essentially involve a choice made by dominant racial groups to disadvantage themselves. If one aspect of the judiciary's role under the Equal Protection Clause is to protect "discrete and insular minorities" from majoritarian prejudice or indifference, see *United States v. Carolene Products Co.*, 304 U.S. 144, 153, n. 4 (1938), some maintain that these concerns are not implicated when the "white majority" places burdens upon itself. See J. Ely, Democracy and Distrust 170 (1980).

In this case, blacks constitute approximately 50% of the population of the city of Richmond. Five of the nine seats on the city council are held by blacks. The concern that a political majority will more easily act to the disadvantage of a minority based on unwarranted assumptions or incomplete facts would seem to militate for, not against, the application of heightened judicial scrutiny in this case.

In *Bakke, supra,* the Court confronted a racial quota employed by the University of California at Davis Medical School. Under the plan, 16 out of 100 seats in each entering class at the school were reserved exclusively for certain minority groups. Among the justifications offered in support of the plan were the desire to "reduc[e] the historic deficit of traditionally disfavored minorities in medical school and the medical profession" and the need to "counte[r] the effects of societal discrimination." . . . .

Justice Powell's opinion applied heightened scrutiny under the Equal Protection Clause to the racial classification at issue. His opinion decisively rejected the first justification for the racially segregated admissions plan. The desire to have more black medical students or doctors, standing alone, was not merely insufficiently compelling to justify a racial classification, it was "discrimination for its own sake," forbidden by the Constitution. Nor could the second concern, the history of discrimination in society at large, justify a racial quota in medical school admissions. Justice Powell contrasted the "focused" goal of remedying "wrongs worked by specific instances of racial discrimination" with "the remedying of the effects of 'societal discrimination,' an amorphous concept of injury that may be ageless in its reach into the past." He indicated that for the governmental interest in remedying past discrimination to be triggered "judicial, legislative, or administrative findings of constitutional or statutory violations" must be made. Only then does the government have a compelling interest in favoring one race over another.

In *Wygant,* 476 U.S. 267 (1986), four Members of the Court applied heightened scrutiny to a race-based system of employee layoffs. Justice Powell, writing for the plurality, again drew the distinction between "societal discrimination" which is an inadequate basis for race-conscious classifications, and the type of identified discrimination that can support and define the scope of race-based relief. The challenged classification in that case tied the layoff of minority teachers to the percentage of minority students enrolled in the school district. The lower courts had upheld the scheme, based on the theory that minority students were in need of "role models" to alleviate the effects of prior discrimination in society. This Court reversed, with a plurality of four Justices reiterating the view expressed by Justice Powell in *Bakke* that "[s]ocietal discrimination, without more, is too amorphous a basis for imposing a racially classified remedy."

The role model theory employed by the lower courts failed for two reasons. First, the statistical disparity between students and teachers had no probative value in demonstrating the kind of prior discrimination in hiring or promotion that would justify race-based relief. Second, because the role model theory had no relation to some basis for believing a constitutional or statutory violation had occurred, it could be used to "justify" race-based decisionmaking essentially limitless in scope and duration.

B

We think it clear that the factual predicate offered in support of the Richmond Plan suffers from the same two defects identified as fatal in *Wygant.* The District Court found the city council's "findings sufficient to ensure that, in adopting the Plan, it was remedying the present effects of past discrimination in the *construction industry.*" Like the "role model" theory employed in *Wygant,* a generalized assertion that there has been past discrimination in an entire industry provides no guidance for a legislative body to determine the precise scope of the injury it seeks to remedy. It "has no logical stopping point." *Wygant, supra,* at 275 (plurality opinion). "Relief" for such an ill-defined wrong could extend until the percentage of public contracts awarded to MBE's in Richmond mirrored the percentage of minorities in the population as a whole.

Appellant argues that it is attempting to remedy various forms of past discrimination that are alleged to be responsible for the small number of minority businesses in the local contracting industry. Among these the city cites the exclusion of blacks from skilled construction trade unions and training programs. . . . The city also lists a host of nonracial factors which would seem to face a member of any racial group attempting to establish a new business enterprise, such as deficiencies in working capital, inability to meet bonding requirements, unfamiliarity with bidding procedures, and disability caused by an inadequate track record.

While there is no doubt that the sorry history of both private and public discrimination in this country has contributed to a lack of opportunities for black entrepreneurs, this observation, standing alone, cannot justify a rigid racial quota in the awarding of public contracts in Richmond, Virginia. Like the claim that discrimination in primary and secondary schooling justifies a rigid racial preference in medical school admissions, an amorphous claim that there has been past discrimination in a particular industry cannot justify the use of an unyielding racial quota.

It is sheer speculation how many minority firms there would be in Richmond absent past societal discrimination, just as it was sheer speculation how many minority medical students would have been admitted to the medical school at Davis absent past discrimination in educational opportunities. Defining these sorts of injuries as "identified discrimination" would give local governments license to create a patchwork of racial preferences based on statistical generalizations about any particular field of endeavor.

These defects are readily apparent in this case. The 30% quota cannot in any realistic sense be tied to any injury suffered by anyone. The District Court relied upon five predicate "facts" in reaching its conclusion that there was an adequate basis for the 30% quota: (1) the ordinance declares itself to be remedial; (2) several proponents of the measure stated their views that there had been past discrimination in the construction industry; (3) minority businesses received 0.67% of prime contracts from the city while minorities constituted 50% of the city's population; (4) there were very few minority contractors in local and state contractors' associations; and (5) in 1977, Congress made a determination that the effects of past discrimination had stifled minority participation in the construction industry nationally.

None of these "findings," singly or together, provide the city of Richmond with a "strong basis in evidence for its conclusion that remedial action was necessary." *Wygant*, 476 U.S., at 277 (plurality opinion). There is nothing approaching a *prima facie* case of a constitutional or statutory violation by *anyone* in the Richmond construction industry. . . .

The District Court also relied on the highly conclusionary statement of a proponent of the Plan that there was racial discrimination in the construction industry "in this area, and the State, and around the nation." It also noted that the city manager had related his view that racial discrimination still plagued the construction industry in his home city of Pittsburgh. These statements are of little probative value in establishing identified discrimination in the Richmond construction industry. The factfinding process of legislative bodies is generally entitled to a presumption of regularity and deferential review by the judiciary. See *Williamson v. Lee Optical of Oklahoma, Inc.*, 348 U.S. 483, 488–489 (1955). But when a legislative body chooses to employ a suspect classification, it cannot rest upon a generalized assertion as to the classification's relevance to its goals. A governmental actor cannot render race a legitimate proxy for a particular condition merely by declaring that the condition exists. The history of racial classifications in this country suggests that blind judicial deference to legislative or executive pronouncements of necessity has no place in equal protection analysis. . . .

Reliance on the disparity between the number of prime contracts awarded to minority firms and the minority population of the city of Richmond is similarly misplaced. . . .

In the employment context, we have recognized that for certain entry level positions or positions requiring minimal training, statistical comparisons of the racial composition of an employer's work force to the racial composition of the relevant population may be probative of a pattern of discrimination. But where special qualifications are necessary, the relevant statistical pool for purposes of demonstrating discriminatory exclusion must be the number of minorities qualified to undertake the particular task. . . .

The city and the District Court also relied on evidence that MBE membership in local contractors' associations was extremely low. Again, standing alone this evidence is not probative of any discrimination in the local construction industry. There are numerous explanations for this dearth of minority participation, including past societal discrimination in education and economic opportunities as well as both black and white career and entrepreneurial choices. Blacks may be disproportionately attracted to industries other than construction. The mere fact that black membership in these trade organizations is low, standing alone, cannot establish a *prima facie* case of discrimination.

For low minority membership in these associations to be relevant, the city would have to link it to the number of local MBE's eligible for membership. If the statistical disparity between eligible MBE's and MBE membership were great enough, an inference of discriminatory exclusion could arise. In such a case, the city would have a compelling interest in preventing its tax dollars from assisting these organizations in maintaining a racially segregated construction market.

Finally, the city and the District Court relied on Congress' finding in connection with the set-aside approved in *Fullilove* that there had been nationwide discrimination in the construction industry. The probative value of these findings for demonstrating the existence of discrimination in Richmond is extremely limited. By its inclusion of a waiver procedure in the national program addressed in *Fullilove*, Congress explicitly recognized that the scope of the problem would vary from market area to market area.

Moreover, as noted above, Congress was exercising its powers under § 5 of the Fourteenth Amendment in making a finding that past discrimination would cause federal funds to be distributed in a manner which reinforced prior patterns of discrimination. While the States and their subdivisions may take remedial action when they possess evidence that their own spending practices are exacerbating a pattern of prior discrimination, they must identify that discrimination, public or private, with some specificity before they may use race-conscious relief. Congress has made national findings that there has been societal discrimination in a host of fields. If all a state or local government need do is find a congressional report on the subject to enact a set-aside program, the constraints of the Equal Protection Clause will, in effect, have been rendered a nullity. . . .

In sum, none of the evidence presented by the city points to any identified discrimination in the Richmond construction industry. We, therefore, hold that the city has failed to demonstrate a compelling interest in apportioning public contracting opportunities on the basis of race. To accept Richmond's claim that past societal discrimination alone can serve as the basis for rigid racial preferences would be to open the door to competing claims for "remedial relief" for every disadvantaged group. The dream of a Nation of equal citizens in a society where race is irrelevant to personal opportunity and achievement would be lost in a mosaic of shifting preferences based on inherently unmeasurable claims of past wrongs. . . . We think such a result would be contrary to both the letter and spirit of a constitutional provision whose central command is equality.

The foregoing analysis applies only to the inclusion of blacks within the Richmond set-aside program. There is *absolutely no evidence* of past discrimination against Spanish-speaking, Oriental, Indian, Eskimo, or Aleut persons in any aspect of the Richmond construction industry. The District Court took judicial notice of the fact that the vast majority of "minority" persons in Richmond were black. It may well be that Richmond has never had an Aleut or Eskimo citizen. The random inclusion of racial groups that, as a practical matter, may never have suffered from discrimination in the construction industry in Richmond suggests that perhaps the city's purpose was not in fact to remedy past discrimination.

If a 30% set-aside was "narrowly tailored" to compensate black contractors for past discrimination, one may legitimately ask why they are forced to share this "remedial relief" with an Aleut citizen who moves to Richmond tomorrow? The gross overinclusiveness of Richmond's racial preference strongly impugns the city's claim of remedial motivation.

IV

As noted by the court below, it is almost impossible to assess whether the Richmond Plan is narrowly tailored to remedy prior discrimination since it is not linked to identified discrimination in any way. We limit ourselves to two observations in this regard.

First, there does not appear to have been any consideration of the use of race-neutral means to increase minority business participation in city contracting. Many of the barriers to minority participation in the construction industry relied upon by the city to justify a racial classification appear to be race neutral. If MBE's disproportionately lack capital or cannot meet bonding requirements, a race-neutral program of city financing for small firms would, *a fortiori,* lead to greater minority participation. The principal opinion in *Fullilove* found that Congress had carefully examined and rejected race-neutral alternatives before enacting the MBE set-aside. . . .

Second, the 30% quota cannot be said to be narrowly tailored to any goal, except perhaps outright racial balancing. It rests upon the "completely unrealistic" assumption that minorities will choose a particular trade in lockstep proportion to their representation in the local population.

Since the city must already consider bids and waivers on a case-by-case basis, it is difficult to see the need for a rigid numerical quota. As noted above, the congressional scheme upheld in *Fullilove* allowed for a waiver of the set-aside provision where an MBE's higher price was not attributable to the effects of past discrimination. Based upon proper findings, such programs are less problematic from an equal protection standpoint because they treat all candidates individually, rather than making the color of an applicant's skin the sole relevant consideration. Unlike the program upheld in *Fullilove,* the Richmond Plan's waiver system focuses solely on the availability of MBE's; there is no inquiry into whether or not the particular MBE seeking a racial preference has suffered from the effects of past discrimination by the city or prime contractors.

Given the existence of an individualized procedure, the city's only interest in maintaining a quota system rather than investigating the need for remedial action in particular cases would seem to be simple administrative convenience. But the interest in avoiding the bureaucratic effort necessary to tailor remedial relief to those who truly have suffered the effects of prior discrimination cannot justify a rigid line drawn on the basis of a suspect classification. Under Richmond's scheme, a successful black, Hispanic, or Oriental entrepreneur from anywhere in the country enjoys an absolute preference over other citizens based solely on their race. We think it obvious that such a program is not narrowly tailored to remedy the effects of prior discrimination.

V

Nothing we say today precludes a state or local entity from taking action to rectify the effects of identified discrimination within its jurisdiction. If the city of Richmond had evidence before it that nonminority contractors were systematically excluding minority businesses from subcontracting opportunities it could take action to end the discriminatory exclusion. Where there is a significant statistical disparity between the number of qualified minority contractors willing and able to perform a particular service and the number of such contractors actually engaged by the locality or the locality's prime contractors, an inference of discriminatory exclusion could arise. Under such circumstances, the city could act to dismantle the closed business system by taking appropriate measures against those who discriminate on the basis of race or other illegitimate criteria. In the extreme case, some form of narrowly tailored racial preference might be necessary to break down patterns of deliberate exclusion.

Nor is local government powerless to deal with individual instances of racially motivated refusals to employ minority contractors. Where such discrimination occurs, a city would be justified in penalizing the discriminator and providing appropriate relief to the victim of such discrimination. Moreover, evidence of a pattern of individual discriminatory acts can, if supported by appropriate statistical proof, lend support to a local government's determination that broader remedial relief is justified.

Even in the absence of evidence of discrimination, the city has at its disposal a whole array of race-neutral devices to increase the accessibility of city contracting opportunities to small entrepreneurs of all races. Simplification of bidding procedures, relaxation of bonding requirements, and training and financial aid for disadvantaged entrepreneurs of all races would open the public contracting market to all those who have suffered the effects of past societal discrimination or neglect. Many of the formal barriers to new entrants may be the product of bureaucratic inertia more than actual necessity, and may have a disproportionate effect on the opportunities open to new minority firms. Their elimination or modification would have little detrimental effect on the city's interests and would serve to increase the opportunities available to minority business without classifying individuals on the basis of race. The city may also act to prohibit discrimination in the provision of credit or bonding by local suppliers and banks. Business as usual should not mean business pursuant to the unthinking exclusion of certain members of our society from its rewards....

Justice Stevens, concurring in part and concurring in the judgment.

A central purpose of the Fourteenth Amendment is to further the national goal of equal opportunity for all our citizens. In order to achieve that goal we must learn from our past mistakes, but I believe the Constitution requires us to evaluate our policy decisions-including those that govern the relationships among different racial and ethnic groups-primarily by studying their probable impact on the future. I therefore do not agree with the premise that seems to underlie today's decision ... that a governmental decision that rests on a racial classification is never permissible except as a remedy for a past wrong.[1] I do, however, agree with the Court's explanation of why the Richmond ordinance cannot be justified as a remedy for past discrimination, and therefore join Parts I, III-B, and IV of its opinion....

Justice Kennedy, concurring in part and concurring in the judgment.

I join all but Part II of Justice O'Connor's opinion and give this further explanation....

1. In my view the Court's approach to this case gives unwarranted deference to race-based legislative action that purports to serve a purely remedial goal, and overlooks the potential value of race-based determinations that may serve other valid purposes....

With the acknowledgment that the summary in Part II is both precise and fair, I must decline to join it. The process by which a law that is an equal protection violation when enacted by a State becomes transformed to an equal protection guarantee when enacted by Congress poses a difficult proposition for me; but as it is not before us, any reconsideration of that issue must await some further case. . . .

Justice Scalia, concurring in the judgment.

I agree with much of the Court's opinion, and, in particular, with Justice O'Connor's conclusion that strict scrutiny must be applied to all governmental classification by race, whether or not its asserted purpose is "remedial" or "benign." I do not agree, however, with Justice O'Connor's dictum suggesting that, despite the Fourteenth Amendment, state and local governments may in some circumstances discriminate on the basis of race in order (in a broad sense) "to ameliorate the effects of past discrimination." . . . .

We have in some contexts approved the use of racial classifications by the Federal Government to remedy the effects of past discrimination. I do not believe that we must or should extend those holdings to the States. . . . As Justice O'Connor acknowledges, however, it is one thing to permit racially based conduct by the Federal Government-whose legislative powers concerning matters of race were explicitly enhanced by the Fourteenth Amendment, see U.S. Const., Amdt. 14, § 5—and quite another to permit it by the precise entities against whose conduct in matters of race that Amendment was specifically directed, see Amdt. 14, § 1 . . . .

A sound distinction between federal and state (or local) action based on race rests not only upon the substance of the Civil War Amendments, but upon social reality and governmental theory. It is a simple fact that what Justice Stewart described in *Fullilove* as "the dispassionate objectivity [and] the flexibility that are needed to mold a race-conscious remedy around the single objective of eliminating the effects of past or present discrimination"—political qualities already to be doubted in a national legislature—are substantially less likely to exist at the state or local level. The struggle for racial justice has historically been a struggle by the national society against oppression in the individual States. What the record shows, in other words, is that racial discrimination against any group finds a more ready expression at the state and local than at the federal level. To the children of the Founding Fathers, this should come as no surprise. An acute awareness of the heightened danger of oppression from political factions in small, rather than large, political units dates to the very beginning of our national history. . . .

In my view there is only one circumstance in which the States may act *by race* to "undo the effects of past discrimination": where that is necessary to eliminate their own maintenance of a system of unlawful racial classification. If, for example, a state agency has a discriminatory pay scale compensating black employees in all positions at 20% less than their nonblack counterparts, it may assuredly promulgate an order raising the salaries of "all black employees" to eliminate the differential. . . .

[The dissenting opinions of Justices Marshall and Blackmun are omitted.]

Notes and Questions

1. The *City of Richmond* Court identifies a number of different proffered justifications for affirmative action programs raised in both the case itself and in earlier cases. Which, if any, of the justifications does the Court indicate may potentially satisfy strict scrutiny? If they do not satisfy strict scrutiny, is it because the identified objectives are not compelling, because the means employed to carry out the objectives are not narrowly tailored, or both?

2. One year after *City of Richmond*, the Court, in *Metro Broadcasting, Inc. v. Federal Communications Commission*, 497 U.S. 547 (1990), upheld the constitutionality of a federal statute providing that a limited category of existing radio and television broadcasting stations be transferred only to minority-controlled firms. The Court held that where the *federal* government is involved, intermediate scrutiny applies to "benign race-conscious measures." *Id.* at 564-565. Moreover, the Court held that valid governmental interests extended beyond mere "remedial" measures designed to compensate victims of past governmental or societal discrimination, and concluded that the interest in furthering broadcasting diversity sufficed to uphold the statute. *Id.* at 564-68. Is such a holding consistent with the Court's decision in *City of Richmond*?

3. In considering the constitutionality of affirmative action under the Fourteenth Amendment, consider the following evidence that the drafters endorsed an early form of affirmative action:

> It is plain that the Fourteenth Amendment was not intended to prohibit measures designed to remedy the effects of the Nation's past treatment of Negroes. The Congress that passed the Fourteenth Amendment is the same Congress that passed the 1866 Freedmen's Bureau Act, an Act that provided many of its benefits only to Negroes. Although the Freedmen's Bureau legislation provided aid for refugees, thereby including white persons within some of the relief measures, the bill was regarded, to the dismay of many Congressmen, as "solely and entirely for the freedmen, and to the exclusion of all other persons. . . ." Cong.Globe, 39th Cong., 1st Sess., 544 (1866) (remarks of Rep. Taylor). Indeed, the bill was bitterly opposed on the ground that it "undertakes to make the negro in some respects . . . superior . . . and gives them favors that the poor white boy in the North cannot get." Id., at 401 (remarks of Sen. McDougall). The bill's supporters defended it—not by rebutting the claim of special treatment—but by pointing to the need for such treatment. . . .
>
> Despite the objection to the special treatment the bill would provide for Negroes, it was passed by Congress. President Johnson vetoed this bill and also a subsequent bill that contained some modifications; one of his principal objections to both bills was that they gave special benefits to Negroes. Rejecting the concerns of the President and the bill's opponents, Congress overrode the President's second veto.

> Since the Congress that considered and rejected the objections to the 1866 Freedmen's Bureau Act concerning special relief to Negroes also proposed the Fourteenth Amendment, it is inconceivable that the Fourteenth Amendment was intended to prohibit all race-conscious relief measures.... Such a result would pervert the intent of the Framers by substituting abstract equality for the genuine equality the Amendment was intended to achieve.

Regents of University of California v. Bakke, 438 U.S. 265, 396–98 (1978) (separate opinion of Marshall, J.). *See also Metro Broadcasting, Inc. v. Federal Communications Commission*, 497 U.S. 547, 564 n.12 (1990) ("The concept of benign race-conscious measures—even those with at least some nonremedial purposes—is as old as the Fourteenth Amendment. For example, the Freedman's Bureau Acts authorized the provision of land, education, medical care, and other assistance to Afro-Americans.").

Might the evidence of the Freedmen's Bureau Acts justify lower scrutiny for programs enacted by the federal government even if it does not justify lower scrutiny for programs enacted by state and local governments?

4. Is there a way to limit *City of Richmond* to the unusual facts of the case itself? Recall that the population of Richmond was 50 percent African American, and a majority of the seats on the city council were held by African Americans. Is there reason to be suspicious of the program enacted in *City of Richmond* but not to similar programs enacted in other cities in which African Americans are a population and political minority?

Adarand Constructors, Inc. v. Pena

515 U.S. 200 (1995)

Justice O'Connor announced the judgment of the Court and delivered an opinion with respect to Parts I, II, III–A, III–B, III–D, and IV, which is for the Court except insofar as it might be inconsistent with the views expressed in Justice Scalia's concurrence, and an opinion with respect to Part III-C in which Justice Kennedy joins.

Petitioner Adarand Constructors, Inc., claims that the Federal Government's practice of giving general contractors on Government projects a financial incentive to hire subcontractors controlled by "socially and economically disadvantaged individuals," and in particular, the Government's use of race-based presumptions in identifying such individuals, violates the equal protection component of the Fifth Amendment's Due Process Clause....

Adarand's claim arises under the Fifth Amendment to the Constitution, which provides that "No person shall ... be deprived of life, liberty, or property, without due process of law." Although this Court has always understood that Clause to provide some measure of protection against *arbitrary* treatment by the Federal Government, it is not as explicit a guarantee of *equal* treatment as the Fourteenth Amendment, which provides that "No *State* shall ... deny to any person within its jurisdiction the equal protection of the laws" (emphasis added). Our cases have accorded varying degrees of significance to the difference in the language of those two Clauses. We think it necessary to revisit the issue here.

Through the 1940's, this Court had routinely taken the view in non-race-related cases that, "[u]nlike the Fourteenth Amendment, the Fifth contains no equal protection clause and it provides no guaranty against discriminatory legislation by Congress." *Detroit Bank v. United States,* 317 U.S. 329, 337 (1943). When the Court first faced a Fifth Amendment equal protection challenge to a federal racial classification, it adopted a similar approach, with most unfortunate results. In *Hirabayashi v. United States,* 320 U.S. 81 (1943), the Court considered a curfew applicable only to persons of Japanese ancestry. The Court. . . . cited *Detroit Bank* for the proposition that the Fifth Amendment "restrains only such discriminatory legislation by Congress as amounts to a denial of due process," and upheld the curfew because "circumstances within the knowledge of those charged with the responsibility for maintaining the national defense afforded a rational basis for the decision which they made." . . . .

In *Bolling v. Sharpe,* 347 U.S. 497 (1954), the Court for the first time explicitly questioned the existence of any difference between the obligations of the Federal Government and the States to avoid racial classifications. *Bolling* did note that "[t]he 'equal protection of the laws' is a more explicit safeguard of prohibited unfairness than 'due process of law.'" But *Bolling* then concluded that, "[i]n view of [the] decision that the Constitution prohibits the states from maintaining racially segregated public schools, it would be unthinkable that the same Constitution would impose a lesser duty on the Federal Government." . . . .

Later cases in contexts other than school desegregation did not distinguish between the duties of the States and the Federal Government to avoid racial classifications. . . .

[I]n 1975, the Court stated explicitly that "[t]his Court's approach to Fifth Amendment equal protection claims has always been precisely the same as to equal protection claims under the Fourteenth Amendment." *Weinberger v. Wiesenfeld,* 420 U.S. 636, 638, n. 2 . . . .

Most of the cases discussed above involved classifications burdening groups that have suffered discrimination in our society. In 1978, the Court confronted the question whether race-based governmental action designed to *benefit* such groups should also be subject to "the most rigid scrutiny." *Regents of Univ. of Cal. v. Bakke,* 438 U.S. 265, involved an equal protection challenge to a state-run medical school's practice of reserving a number of spaces in its entering class for minority students. . . .

The Court's failure to produce a majority opinion in *Bakke* [as well as in subsequent cases] left unresolved the proper analysis for remedial race-based governmental action. . . .

The Court resolved the issue, at least in part, in 1989. *Richmond v. J.A. Croson Co.,* 488 U.S. 469 (1989), concerned a city's determination that 30% of its contracting work should go to minority-owned businesses. A majority of the Court in *Croson* held that "the standard of review under the Equal Protection Clause is not dependent on the race of those burdened or benefited by a particular classification," and that the single standard of review for racial classifications should be "strict scrutiny." . . . .

With *Croson,* the Court finally agreed that the Fourteenth Amendment requires strict scrutiny of all race-based action by state and local governments. But *Croson* of course had no occasion to declare what standard of review the Fifth Amendment requires for such action taken by the Federal Government. . . .

Despite lingering uncertainty in the details, however, the Court's cases through *Croson* had established three general propositions with respect to governmental racial classifications. First, skepticism: "'Any preference based on racial or ethnic criteria must necessarily receive a most searching examination.'" Second, consistency: "[T]he standard of review under the Equal Protection Clause is not dependent on the race of those burdened or benefited by a particular classification," *i.e.,* all racial classifications reviewable under the Equal Protection Clause must be strictly scrutinized. And third, congruence: "Equal protection analysis in the Fifth Amendment area is the same as that under the Fourteenth Amendment." Taken together, these three propositions lead to the conclusion that any person, of whatever race, has the right to demand that any governmental actor subject to the Constitution justify any racial classification subjecting that person to unequal treatment under the strictest judicial scrutiny. . . .

A year later, however, the Court took a surprising turn. *Metro Broadcasting, Inc. v. FCC,* involved a Fifth Amendment challenge to two race-based policies of the Federal Communications Commission (FCC). In *Metro Broadcasting,* the Court repudiated the long-held notion that "it would be unthinkable that the same Constitution would impose a lesser duty on the Federal Government" than it does on a State to afford equal protection of the laws, *Bolling, supra,* at 500. It did so by holding that "benign" federal racial classifications need only satisfy intermediate scrutiny, even though *Croson* had recently concluded that such classifications enacted by a State must satisfy strict scrutiny. "[B]enign" federal racial classifications, the Court said, "—even if those measures are not 'remedial' in the sense of being designed to compensate victims of past governmental or societal discrimination—are constitutionally permissible to the extent that they serve *important* governmental objectives within the power of Congress and are *substantially related* to achievement of those objectives." *Metro Broadcasting,* 497 U.S., at 564-565 (emphasis added) . . . .

Applying this test, the Court first noted that the FCC policies at issue did not serve as a remedy for past discrimination. Proceeding on the assumption that the policies were nonetheless "benign," it concluded that they served the "important governmental objective" of "enhancing broadcast diversity," *id.,* at 566-567, and that they were "substantially related" to that objective, *id.,* at 569. It therefore upheld the policies.

By adopting intermediate scrutiny as the standard of review for congressionally mandated "benign" racial classifications, *Metro Broadcasting* departed from prior cases in two significant respects. First, it turned its back on *Croson*'s explanation of why strict scrutiny of all governmental racial classifications is essential:

> "Absent searching judicial inquiry into the justification for such race-based measures, there is simply no way of determining what classifications are 'benign' or 'remedial' and what classifications are in fact motivated by illegitimate notions of racial inferiority or simple racial politics. Indeed, the purpose of strict scrutiny is to 'smoke out' illegitimate uses of race by assuring that the legislative body is pursuing a goal important enough to warrant use of a highly suspect tool. The test also ensures that the means chosen 'fit' this compelling goal so closely that there is little or no possibility that the motive for the classification was illegitimate racial prejudice or stereotype."

We adhere to that view today, despite the surface appeal of holding "benign" racial classifications to a lower standard, because "it may not always be clear that a so-called preference is in fact benign." *Bakke, supra,* at 298 (opinion of Powell, J.) . . . .

Second, *Metro Broadcasting* squarely rejected one of the three propositions established by the Court's earlier equal protection cases, namely, congruence between the standards applicable to federal and state racial classifications, and in so doing also undermined the other two—skepticism of all racial classifications and consistency of treatment irrespective of the race of the burdened or benefited group. . . .

The three propositions undermined by *Metro Broadcasting* all derive from the basic principle that the Fifth and Fourteenth Amendments to the Constitution protect *persons,* not *groups.* It follows from that principle that all governmental action based on race—a *group* classification long recognized as "in most circumstances irrelevant and therefore prohibited," *Hirabayashi,* 320 U.S., at 100—should be subjected to detailed judicial inquiry to ensure that the *personal* right to equal protection of the laws has not been infringed. These ideas have long been central to this Court's understanding of equal protection, and holding "benign" state and federal racial classifications to different standards does not square with them. . . . Accordingly, we hold today that all racial classifications, imposed by whatever federal, state, or local governmental actor, must be analyzed by a reviewing court under strict scrutiny. In other words, such classifications are constitutional only if they are narrowly tailored measures that further compelling governmental interests. To the extent that *Metro Broadcasting* is inconsistent with that holding, it is overruled.

In dissent, Justice Stevens criticizes us for "deliver[ing] a disconcerting lecture about the evils of governmental racial classifications." With respect, we believe his criticisms reflect a serious misunderstanding of our opinion.

Justice Stevens concurs in our view that courts should take a skeptical view of all governmental racial classifications. He also allows that "[n]othing is inherently wrong with applying a single standard to fundamentally different situations, as long as that standard takes relevant differences into account." What he fails to recognize is that strict scrutiny *does* take "relevant differences" into account—indeed, that is its fundamental purpose. The point of carefully examining the interest asserted by the government in support of a racial classification, and the evidence offered to show that the classification is needed, is precisely to distinguish legitimate from illegitimate uses of race in governmental decisionmaking. And JUSTICE STEVENS concedes that "some cases may be difficult to classify"; all the more reason, in our view, to examine all racial classifications carefully. Strict scrutiny does not "trea[t] dissimilar race-based decisions as though they were equally objectionable"; to the contrary, it evaluates carefully all governmental race-based decisions *in order to decide* which are constitutionally objectionable and which are not. By requiring strict scrutiny of racial classifications, we require courts to make sure that a governmental classification based on race, which "so seldom provide[s] a relevant basis for disparate treatment," is legitimate, before permitting unequal treatment based on race to proceed.

JUSTICE STEVENS chides us for our "supposed inability to differentiate between 'invidious' and 'benign' discrimination," because it is in his view sufficient that "people understand the difference between good intentions and bad." But, as we have just explained, the point of strict scrutiny is to "differentiate between" permissible and impermissible governmental use of race. . . .

Perhaps it is not the standard of strict scrutiny itself, but our use of the concepts of "consistency" and "congruence" in conjunction with it, that leads JUSTICE STEVENS to dissent. According to JUSTICE STEVENS, our view of consistency "equate[s] remedial preferences with invidious discrimination," and ignores the difference between "an engine of oppression" and an effort "to foster equality in society," or, more colorfully, "between a 'No Trespassing' sign and a welcome mat." It does nothing of the kind. The principle of consistency simply means that whenever the government treats any person unequally because of his or her race, that person has suffered an injury that falls squarely within the language and spirit of the Constitution's guarantee of equal protection. It says nothing about the ultimate validity of any particular law; that determination is the job of the court applying strict scrutiny. The principle of consistency explains the circumstances in which the injury requiring strict scrutiny occurs. The application of strict scrutiny, in turn, determines whether a compelling governmental interest justifies the infliction of that injury.

Consistency *does* recognize that any individual suffers an injury when he or she is disadvantaged by the government because of his or her race, whatever that race may be. . . .

JUSTICE STEVENS also claims that we have ignored any difference between federal and state legislatures. But requiring that Congress, like the States, enact racial classifications only when doing so is necessary to further a "compelling interest" does not contravene any principle of appropriate respect for a coequal branch of the Government. It is true that various Members of this Court have taken different views of the authority § 5 of the Fourteenth Amendment confers upon Congress to deal with the problem of racial discrimination, and the extent to which courts should defer to Congress' exercise of that authority. We need not, and do not, address these differences today....

"Although adherence to precedent is not rigidly required in constitutional cases, any departure from the doctrine of *stare decisis* demands special justification." *Arizona v. Rumsey,* 467 U.S. 203, 212 (1984). In deciding whether this case presents such justification, we recall Justice Frankfurter's admonition that "*stare decisis* is a principle of policy and not a mechanical formula of adherence to the latest decision, however recent and questionable, when such adherence involves collision with a prior doctrine more embracing in its scope, intrinsically sounder, and verified by experience." *Helvering v. Hallock,* 309 U.S. 106, 119 (1940). Remaining true to an "intrinsically sounder" doctrine established in prior cases better serves the values of *stare decisis* than would following a more recently decided case inconsistent with the decisions that came before it; the latter course would simply compound the recent error and would likely make the unjustified break from previously established doctrine complete. In such a situation, "special justification" exists to depart from the recently decided case.

As we have explained, *Metro Broadcasting* undermined important principles of this Court's equal protection jurisprudence, established in a line of cases stretching back over 50 years. Those principles together stood for an "embracing" and "intrinsically soun[d]" understanding of equal protection "verified by experience," namely, that the Constitution imposes upon federal, state, and local governmental actors the same obligation to respect the personal right to equal protection of the laws. This case therefore presents precisely the situation described by Justice Frankfurter in *Helvering:* We cannot adhere to our most recent decision without colliding with an accepted and established doctrine. We also note that *Metro Broadcasting*'s application of different standards of review to federal and state racial classifications has been consistently criticized by commentators....

It is worth pointing out the difference between the applications of *stare decisis* in this case and in *Planned Parenthood of Southeastern Pa. v. Casey,* 505 U.S. 833 (1992). *Casey* explained how considerations of *stare decisis* inform the decision whether to overrule a long-established precedent that has become integrated into the fabric of the law. Overruling precedent of that kind naturally may have consequences for "the ideal of the rule of law," *id.,* at 854. In addition, such precedent is likely to have engendered substantial reliance, as was true in *Casey* itself, *id.,* at 856. But in this case, as we have explained, we do not face a precedent of that kind, because *Metro Broadcasting* itself *departed* from our prior cases-and did so quite recently. By refusing to follow *Metro Broadcasting,* then, we do not depart from the fabric of the law; we restore it. We also note that reliance on a case that has recently departed from precedent is likely to be minimal, particularly where, as here, the rule set forth in that case is unlikely to affect primary conduct in any event....

Of course, it follows that to the extent (if any) that *Fullilove* held federal racial classifications to be subject to a less rigorous standard, it is no longer controlling. But we need not decide today whether the program upheld in *Fullilove* would survive strict scrutiny as our more recent cases have defined it.

Some have questioned the importance of debating the proper standard of review of race-based legislation. . . .We think that requiring strict scrutiny is the best way to ensure that courts will consistently give racial classifications that kind of detailed examination, both as to ends and as to means. . . .

Finally, we wish to dispel the notion that strict scrutiny is "strict in theory, but fatal in fact." The unhappy persistence of both the practice and the lingering effects of racial discrimination against minority groups in this country is an unfortunate reality, and government is not disqualified from acting in response to it. . . . When race-based action is necessary to further a compelling interest, such action is within constitutional constraints if it satisfies the "narrow tailoring" test this Court has set out in previous cases. . . .

Justice Scalia, concurring in part and concurring in the judgment.

I join the opinion of the Court . . . except insofar as it may be inconsistent with the following: In my view, government can never have a "compelling interest" in discriminating on the basis of race in order to "make up" for past racial discrimination in the opposite direction. Individuals who have been wronged by unlawful racial discrimination should be made whole; but under our Constitution there can be no such thing as either a creditor or a debtor race. That concept is alien to the Constitution's focus upon the individual. To pursue the concept of racial entitlement—even for the most admirable and benign of purposes—is to reinforce and preserve for future mischief the way of thinking that produced race slavery, race privilege and race hatred. In the eyes of government, we are just one race here. It is American.

It is unlikely, if not impossible, that the challenged program would survive under this understanding of strict scrutiny, but I am content to leave that to be decided on remand.

Justice Thomas, concurring in part and concurring in the judgment. . . .

These programs not only raise grave constitutional questions, they also undermine the moral basis of the equal protection principle. Purchased at the price of immeasurable human suffering, the equal protection principle reflects our Nation's understanding that such classifications ultimately have a destructive impact on the individual and our society. . . . So-called "benign" discrimination teaches many that because of chronic and apparently immutable handicaps, minorities cannot compete with them without their patronizing indulgence. Inevitably, such programs engender attitudes of superiority or, alternatively, provoke resentment among those who believe that they have been wronged by the government's use of race. These programs stamp minorities with a badge of inferiority and may cause them to develop dependencies or to adopt an attitude that they are "entitled" to preferences.

Indeed, JUSTICE STEVENS once recognized the real harms stemming from seemingly "benign" discrimination. See *Fullilove v. Klutznick,* 448 U.S. 448, 545 (1980) (STEVENS, J., dissenting) (noting that "remedial" race legislation "is perceived by many as resting on an assumption that those who are granted this special preference are less qualified in some respect that is identified purely by their race").

In my mind, government-sponsored racial discrimination based on benign prejudice is just as noxious as discrimination inspired by malicious prejudice. In each instance, it is racial discrimination, plain and simple....

JUSTICE STEVENS, with whom JUSTICE GINSBURG joins, dissenting....

The consistency that the Court espouses would disregard the difference between a "No Trespassing" sign and a welcome mat. It would treat a Dixiecrat Senator's decision to vote against Thurgood Marshall's confirmation in order to keep African-Americans off the Supreme Court as on a par with President Johnson's evaluation of his nominee's race as a positive factor. It would equate a law that made black citizens ineligible for military service with a program aimed at recruiting black soldiers. An attempt by the majority to exclude members of a minority race from a regulated market is fundamentally different from a subsidy that enables a relatively small group of newcomers to enter that market. An interest in "consistency" does not justify treating differences as though they were similarities.

The Court's explanation for treating dissimilar race-based decisions as though they were equally objectionable is a supposed inability to differentiate between "invidious" and "benign" discrimination. But the term "affirmative action" is common and well understood. Its presence in everyday parlance shows that people understand the difference between good intentions and bad. As with any legal concept, some cases may be difficult to classify, but our equal protection jurisprudence has identified a critical difference between state action that imposes burdens on a disfavored few and state action that benefits the few "in spite of" its adverse effects on the many. *Feeney,* 442 U.S., at 279.

Indeed, our jurisprudence has made the standard to be applied in cases of invidious discrimination turn on whether the discrimination is "intentional," or whether, by contrast, it merely has a discriminatory "effect." *Washington v. Davis,* 426 U.S. 229 (1976). Surely this distinction is at least as subtle, and at least as difficult to apply, as the usually obvious distinction between a measure intended to benefit members of a particular minority race and a measure intended to burden a minority race. A state actor inclined to subvert the Constitution might easily hide bad intentions in the guise of unintended "effects"; but I should think it far more difficult to enact a law intending to preserve the majority's hegemony while casting it plausibly in the guise of affirmative action for minorities....

Moreover, the Court may find that its new "consistency" approach to race-based classifications is difficult to square with its insistence upon rigidly separate categories for discrimination against different classes of individuals. For example, as the law currently stands, the Court will apply "intermediate scrutiny" to cases of invidious gender discrimination and "strict scrutiny" to cases of invidious race discrimination, while applying the same standard for benign classifications as for invidious ones. If this remains the law, then today's lecture about "consistency" will produce the anomalous result that the Government can more easily enact affirmative-action programs to remedy discrimination against women than it can enact affirmative-action programs to remedy discrimination against African-Americans—even though the primary purpose of the Equal Protection Clause was to end discrimination against the former slaves. When a court becomes pre-occupied with abstract standards, it risks sacrificing common sense at the altar of formal consistency.

As a matter of constitutional and democratic principle, a decision by representatives of the majority to discriminate against the members of a minority race is fundamentally different from those same representatives' decision to impose incidental costs on the majority of their constituents in order to provide a benefit to a disadvantaged minority. . . .

[P]rior to *Metro Broadcasting,* the interest in diversity had been mentioned in a few opinions, but it is perfectly clear that the Court had not yet decided whether that interest had sufficient magnitude to justify a racial classification. *Metro Broadcasting,* of course, answered that question in the affirmative. The majority today overrules *Metro Broadcasting* only insofar as it is "inconsistent with [the] holding" that strict scrutiny applies to "benign" racial classifications promulgated by the Federal Government. The proposition that fostering diversity may provide a sufficient interest to justify such a program is *not* inconsistent with the Court's holding today—indeed, the question is not remotely presented in this case—and I do not take the Court's opinion to diminish that aspect of our decision in *Metro Broadcasting* . . . .

[The dissenting opinions of Justices Souter and Ginsburg are omitted.]

Problem 17-A: Racial Preferences in Foster and Adoption Placements

A state legislature recently enacted a statute governing foster and adoption placements. In pertinent part, the statute provides that—when placing a child who is African American, Asian, or Hispanic/Latino—a preference will be given to prospective parents who share the child's race or ethnicity.

According to the statute's legislative history, the preference is grounded in a belief that parents who share a child's racial or ethnic heritage are in a superior position to familiarize those children with their racial or ethnic heritage. It is further justified by a belief that parents who share a child's minority status can best teach her healthy ways to protect herself from discrimination.

Shortly after the statute is enacted, a lawsuit challenging its constitutionality on equal protection grounds is filed in federal court by a group of Caucasian prospective foster and adoptive parents.

Is the challenged statutory preference constitutional?

Notes and Questions

1. *Adarand* introduces the concept of "congruence" between the equal protection standards applicable to the federal government and that applicable to state and local governments. Is that principle consistent with the court's alienage line of cases, considered in Chapter 13? If not, is there a principled basis for distinguishing that line of cases, or does *Adarand* overrule them *sub silentio*?

2. Is *Adarand* consistent with *City of Richmond*, which distinguished *Fullilove* on the basis of Congress's powers pursuant to Section 5 of the Fourteenth Amendment? Is *Adarand* subtly cutting back on the scope of Congress's powers under that provision?

3. Is the Court's decision to overrule *Metro Broadcasting* consistent with the principles of *stare decisis* articulated by the Court in *Casey*?

4. *Metro Broadcasting* identified the interest in diversity as a sufficiently strong justification for affirmative action laws. Does *Adarand* close the door to that interest as a justification for such laws?

5. Is the *Adarand* Court's announcement of the consistency principle really that much of a surprise? Is it not implicit in the Court's sex-based equal protection cases as well as its opinion in *Cleburne*?

6. Note that not every affirmative action program is subject to strict scrutiny. Rather, the level of scrutiny is tied to the classification at issue. Thus, as Justice Stevens points out in his dissent in *Adarand*, while a *race*-based affirmative action program is subject to strict scrutiny, a sex-based one would be subject only to intermediate scrutiny, while an age-based or intellectual disability-based one would be subject only to rational basis review. Thus when an affirmative action program is based on a classification other than race, ethnicity or (in most instances) alienage, justifications for the program—such as providing role models—that have been deemed insufficiently compelling in cases involving race-based affirmative action may nonetheless be deemed "important" or legitimate when a lower level of scrutiny is in play. Moreover, when an affirmative action program is based on a quasi-suspect or non-suspect classification, a less demanding fit between the goal and the means used to accomplish it are permissible. *See generally* Peter Nicolas, *Gayffirmative Action: The Constitutionality of Sexual Orientation-Based Affirmative Action Policies*, 92 Wash. U.L. Rev. 733 (2015).

7. Is there a tension between *Adarand*'s consistency principle and the *Frontiero* factors? The latter looks at such things as political powerlessness and a history of

discrimination to decide whether to accord heightened scrutiny to discrimination against a given class. Why those factors if *Adarand* calls for applying the same level of scrutiny to the class's opposite, which lacks either of those characteristics?

B. Race-Conscious Electoral Redistricting

At the same time that the Court's decisions through *Adarand* were firming up strict scrutiny as the standard applicable to laws that on their face took race into account, albeit for so-called benign purposes, another line of cases was developing regarding the level of judicial scrutiny for race-conscious electoral redistricting designed to make it easier to for racial minorities to achieve political representation. The following two cases address the appropriate level of scrutiny applicable to such laws, and arguably are in some tension with the *Adarand* line of cases.

Shaw v. Reno

509 U.S. 630 (1993)

Justice O'Connor delivered the opinion of the Court.

This case involves two of the most complex and sensitive issues this Court has faced in recent years: the meaning of the constitutional "right" to vote, and the propriety of race-based state legislation designed to benefit members of historically disadvantaged racial minority groups. As a result of the 1990 census, North Carolina became entitled to a 12th seat in the United States House of Representatives. The General Assembly enacted a reapportionment plan that included one majority-black congressional district. After the Attorney General of the United States objected to the plan pursuant to § 5 of the Voting Rights Act of 1965, the General Assembly passed new legislation creating a second majority-black district. Appellants allege that the revised plan, which contains district boundary lines of dramatically irregular shape, constitutes an unconstitutional racial gerrymander. The question before us is whether appellants have stated a cognizable claim....

The first of the two majority-black districts contained in the revised plan, District 1, is somewhat hook shaped. Centered in the northeast portion of the State, it moves southward until it tapers to a narrow band; then, with finger-like extensions, it reaches far into the southern-most part of the State near the South Carolina border. District 1 has been compared to a "Rorschach ink-blot test," and a "bug splattered on a windshield."

The second majority-black district, District 12, is even more unusually shaped. It is approximately 160 miles long and, for much of its length, no wider than the I–85 corridor. It winds in snakelike fashion through tobacco country, financial centers, and manufacturing areas "until it gobbles in enough enclaves of black neighborhoods." Northbound and southbound drivers on I–85 sometimes find themselves in separate districts in one county, only to "trade" districts when they enter the next county. Of the 10 counties through which District 12 passes, 5 are cut into 3 different districts; even towns are divided. At one point the district remains contiguous only because it intersects at a single point with two other districts before crossing over them. One state legislator has remarked that "'[i]f you drove down the interstate with both car doors open, you'd kill most of the people in the district.'" . . . .

"The right to vote freely for the candidate of one's choice is of the essence of a democratic society. . . ." *Reynolds v. Sims,* 377 U.S., at 555. For much of our Nation's history, that right sadly has been denied to many because of race. The Fifteenth Amendment, ratified in 1870 after a bloody Civil War, promised unequivocally that "[t]he right of citizens of the United States to vote" no longer would be "denied or abridged . . . by any State on account of race, color, or previous condition of servitude." U.S. Const., Amdt. 15, § 1.

But "[a] number of states . . . refused to take no for an answer and continued to circumvent the fifteenth amendment's prohibition through the use of both subtle and blunt instruments, perpetuating ugly patterns of pervasive racial discrimination." Ostensibly race-neutral devices such as literacy tests with "grandfather" clauses and "good character" provisos were devised to deprive black voters of the franchise. Another of the weapons in the States' arsenal was the racial gerrymander—"the deliberate and arbitrary distortion of district boundaries . . . for [racial] purposes." In the 1870's, for example, opponents of Reconstruction in Mississippi "concentrated the bulk of the black population in a 'shoestring' Congressional district running the length of the Mississippi River, leaving five others with white majorities." Some 90 years later, Alabama redefined the boundaries of the city of Tuskegee "from a square to an uncouth twenty-eight-sided figure" in a manner that was alleged to exclude black voters, and only black voters, from the city limits. *Gomillion v. Lightfoot,* 364 U.S. 339, 340 (1960) . . . .

[I]t soon became apparent that guaranteeing equal access to the polls would not suffice to root out other racially discriminatory voting practices. Drawing on the "one person, one vote" principle, this Court recognized that "[t]he right to vote can be affected by a *dilution* of voting power as well as by an absolute prohibition on casting a ballot." *Allen v. State Bd. of Elections,* 393 U.S. 544, 569 (1969) (emphasis added). Where members of a racial minority group vote as a cohesive unit, practices such as multimember or at-large electoral systems can reduce or nullify minority voters' ability, as a group, "to elect the candidate of their choice." *Ibid.* Accordingly, the Court held that such schemes violate the Fourteenth Amendment when they are adopted with a discriminatory purpose and have the effect of diluting minority voting strength. See, *e.g., Rogers v. Lodge,* 458 U.S. 613, 616–617 (1982); *White v. Regester,* 412 U.S. 755, 765–766 (1973) . . . .

Our focus is on appellants' claim that the State engaged in unconstitutional racial gerrymandering. That argument strikes a powerful historical chord: It is unsettling how closely the North Carolina plan resembles the most egregious racial gerrymanders of the past.

An understanding of the nature of appellants' claim is critical to our resolution of the case. In their complaint, appellants did not claim that the General Assembly's reapportionment plan unconstitutionally "diluted" white voting strength. They did not even claim to be white. Rather, appellants' complaint alleged that the deliberate segregation of voters into separate districts on the basis of race violated their constitutional right to participate in a "color-blind" electoral process.

Despite their invocation of the ideal of a "color-blind" Constitution, appellants appear to concede that race-conscious redistricting is not always unconstitutional. That concession is wise: This Court never has held that race-conscious state decisionmaking is impermissible in *all* circumstances. What appellants object to is redistricting legislation that is so extremely irregular on its face that it rationally can be viewed only as an effort to segregate the races for purposes of voting, without regard for traditional districting principles and without sufficiently compelling justification. . . .

The Equal Protection Clause provides that "[n]o State shall . . . deny to any person within its jurisdiction the equal protection of the laws." Its central purpose is to prevent the States from purposefully discriminating between individuals on the basis of race. . . .

Express racial classifications are immediately suspect because, "[a]bsent searching judicial inquiry . . . , there is simply no way of determining what classifications are 'benign' or 'remedial' and what classifications are in fact motivated by illegitimate notions of racial inferiority or simple racial politics." *Richmond v. J.A. Croson Co.,* 488 U.S. 469, 493 (1989) (plurality opinion); *id.,* at 520 (Scalia, J., concurring in judgment).

Classifications of citizens solely on the basis of race "are by their very nature odious to a free people whose institutions are founded upon the doctrine of equality." *Hirabayashi v. United States,* 320 U.S. 81, 100 (1943). Accord, *Loving v. Virginia,* 388 U.S. 1, 11 (1967). They threaten to stigmatize individuals by reason of their membership in a racial group and to incite racial hostility. . . .

These principles apply not only to legislation that contains explicit racial distinctions, but also to those "rare" statutes that, although race neutral, are, on their face, "unexplainable on grounds other than race." *Arlington Heights v. Metropolitan Housing Development Corp.,* 429 U.S. 252, 266 (1977) . . . .

Appellants contend that redistricting legislation that is so bizarre on its face that it is "unexplainable on grounds other than race," *Arlington Heights, supra,* 429 U.S., at 266, demands the same close scrutiny that we give other state laws that classify citizens by race. Our voting rights precedents support that conclusion.

In *Guinn v. United States,* 238 U.S. 347 (1915), the Court invalidated under the Fifteenth Amendment a statute that imposed a literacy requirement on voters but contained a "grandfather clause" applicable to individuals and their lineal descendants entitled to vote "on [or prior to] January 1, 1866." *Id.,* at 357. The determinative consideration for the Court was that the law, though ostensibly race neutral, on its face "embod[ied] no exercise of judgment and rest[ed] upon no discernible reason" other than to circumvent the prohibitions of the Fifteenth Amendment. *Id.,* at 363. In other words, the statute was invalid because, on its face, it could not be explained on grounds other than race.

The Court applied the same reasoning to the "uncouth twenty-eight-sided" municipal boundary line at issue in *Gomillion.* Although the statute that redrew the city limits of Tuskegee was race neutral on its face, plaintiffs alleged that its effect was impermissibly to remove from the city virtually all black voters and no white voters. . . .

The majority resolved the case under the Fifteenth Amendment. Justice Whittaker, however, concluded that the "unlawful segregation of races of citizens" into different voting districts was cognizable under the Equal Protection Clause. This Court's subsequent reliance on *Gomillion* in other Fourteenth Amendment cases suggests the correctness of Justice Whittaker's view. *Gomillion* thus supports appellants' contention that district lines obviously drawn for the purpose of separating voters by race require careful scrutiny under the Equal Protection Clause regardless of the motivations underlying their adoption.

The Court extended the reasoning of *Gomillion* to congressional districting in *Wright v. Rockefeller,* 376 U.S. 52 (1964). At issue in *Wright* were four districts contained in a New York apportionment statute. The plaintiffs alleged that the statute excluded nonwhites from one district and concentrated them in the other three. Every Member of the Court assumed that the plaintiffs' allegation that the statute "segregate[d] eligible voters by race and place of origin" stated a constitutional claim. . . . The majority, however, accepted the District Court's finding that the plaintiffs had failed to establish that the districts were in fact drawn on racial lines. Although the boundary lines were somewhat irregular, the majority reasoned, they were not so bizarre as to permit of no other conclusion. Indeed, because most of the nonwhite voters lived together in one area, it would have been difficult to construct voting districts without concentrations of nonwhite voters.

Wright illustrates the difficulty of determining from the face of a single-member districting plan that it purposefully distinguishes between voters on the basis of race. A reapportionment statute typically does not classify persons at all; it classifies tracts of land, or addresses. Moreover, redistricting differs from other kinds of state decisionmaking in that the legislature always is *aware* of race when it draws district lines, just as it is aware of age, economic status, religious and political persuasion, and a variety of other demographic factors. That sort of race consciousness does not lead inevitably to impermissible race discrimination. As *Wright* demonstrates, when members of a racial group live together in one community, a reapportionment plan that concentrates members of the group in one district and excludes them from others may reflect wholly legitimate purposes. The district lines may be drawn, for example, to provide for compact districts of contiguous territory, or to maintain the integrity of political subdivisions.

The difficulty of proof, of course, does not mean that a racial gerrymander, once established, should receive less scrutiny under the Equal Protection Clause than other state legislation classifying citizens by race. Moreover, it seems clear to us that proof sometimes will not be difficult at all. In some exceptional cases, a reapportionment plan may be so highly irregular that, on its face, it rationally cannot be understood as anything other than an effort to "segregat[e] . . . voters" on the basis of race. *Gomillion, supra,* 364 U.S., at 341. *Gomillion,* in which a tortured municipal boundary line was drawn to exclude black voters, was such a case. So, too, would be a case in which a State concentrated a dispersed minority population in a single district by disregarding traditional districting principles such as compactness, contiguity, and respect for political subdivisions. We emphasize that these criteria are important not because they are constitutionally required—they are not—but because they are objective factors that may serve to defeat a claim that a district has been gerrymandered on racial lines.

Put differently, we believe that reapportionment is one area in which appearances do matter. A reapportionment plan that includes in one district individuals who belong to the same race, but who are otherwise widely separated by geographical and political boundaries, and who may have little in common with one another but the color of their skin, bears an uncomfortable resemblance to political apartheid. It reinforces the perception that members of the same racial group—regardless of their age, education, economic status, or the community in which they live—think alike, share the same political interests, and will prefer the same candidates at the polls. . . . By perpetuating such notions, a racial gerrymander may exacerbate the very patterns of racial bloc voting that majority-minority districting is sometimes said to counteract.

The message that such districting sends to elected representatives is equally pernicious. When a district obviously is created solely to effectuate the perceived common interests of one racial group, elected officials are more likely to believe that their primary obligation is to represent only the members of that group, rather than their constituency as a whole. This is altogether antithetical to our system of representative democracy. . . .

For these reasons, we conclude that a plaintiff challenging a reapportionment statute under the Equal Protection Clause may state a claim by alleging that the legislation, though race-neutral on its face, rationally cannot be understood as anything other than an effort to separate voters into different districts on the basis of race, and that the separation lacks sufficient justification. It is unnecessary for us to decide whether or how a reapportionment plan that, on its face, can be explained in nonracial terms successfully could be challenged. Thus, we express no view as to whether "the intentional creation of majority-minority districts, without more," always gives rise to an equal protection claim. . . .

[The dissenting opinions of Justices White, Blackmun, Stevens, and Souter are omitted.]

Bush v. Vera

517 U.S. 952 (1996)

Justice O'Connor announced the judgment of the Court and delivered an opinion, in which The Chief Justice and Justice Kennedy join.

This is the latest in a series of appeals involving racial gerrymandering challenges to state redistricting efforts in the wake of the 1990 census. That census revealed a population increase, largely in urban minority populations, that entitled Texas to three additional congressional seats. In response, and with a view to complying with the Voting Rights Act of 1965 (VRA), the Texas Legislature promulgated a redistricting plan that, among other things, created District 30, a new majority-African-American district in Dallas County; created District 29, a new majority-Hispanic district in and around Houston in Harris County; and reconfigured District 18, which is adjacent to District 29, to make it a majority-African-American district. The Department of Justice precleared that plan under VRA § 5 in 1991, and it was used in the 1992 congressional elections.

The plaintiffs, six Texas voters, challenged the plan, alleging that 24 of Texas' 30 congressional districts constitute racial gerrymanders in violation of the Fourteenth Amendment. . . .

We must now determine whether those districts are subject to strict scrutiny. Our precedents have used a variety of formulations to describe the threshold for the application of strict scrutiny. Strict scrutiny applies where "redistricting legislation . . . is so extremely irregular on its face that it rationally can be viewed only as an effort to segregate the races for purposes of voting, without regard for traditional districting principles," *Shaw I, supra,* 509 U.S., at 642, or where "race for its own sake, and not other districting principles, was the legislature's dominant and controlling rationale in drawing its district lines," *Miller,* 515 U.S., at 913, and "the legislature subordinated traditional race-neutral districting principles . . . to racial considerations," *id.,* at 916. See also *id.,* at 928 (O'Connor, J., concurring) (strict scrutiny only applies where "the State has relied on race in substantial disregard of customary and traditional districting practices").

Strict scrutiny does not apply merely because redistricting is performed with consciousness of race. See *Shaw I, supra,* at 646. Nor does it apply to all cases of intentional creation of majority-minority districts. Electoral district lines are "facially race neutral," so a more searching inquiry is necessary before strict scrutiny can be found applicable in redistricting cases than in cases of "classifications based explicitly on race." See *Adarand Constructors, Inc. v. Peña,* 515 U.S. 200, 213. For strict scrutiny to apply, the plaintiffs must prove that other, legitimate districting principles were "subordinated" to race. *Miller,* 515 U.S., at 916. By that, we mean that race must be "*the predominant* factor motivating the legislature's [redistricting] decision." *Ibid.* (emphasis added). We thus differ from Justice Thomas, who would apparently hold that it suffices that racial considerations be *a* motivation for the drawing of a majority-minority district....

[The opinion proceeds to find that race was the predominant consideration, and thus subjects the redistricting plan to strict scrutiny.]

Justice Thomas, with whom Justice Scalia joins, concurring in the judgment.

In my view, application of strict scrutiny in this suit was never a close question. I cannot agree with Justice O'Connor's assertion that strict scrutiny is not invoked by the intentional creation of majority-minority districts. Though *Shaw v. Reno,* 509 U.S. 630, 649 (1993) *(Shaw I),* expressly reserved that question, we effectively resolved it in subsequent cases. Only last Term, in *Adarand Constructors, Inc. v. Peña,* 515 U.S. 200, 227 (1995), we vigorously asserted that all governmental racial classifications must be strictly scrutinized....

We have said that impermissible racial classifications do not follow inevitably from a legislature's mere awareness of racial demographics. But the intentional creation of a majority-minority district certainly means more than mere awareness that application of traditional, race-neutral districting principles will result in the creation of a district in which a majority of the district's residents are members of a particular minority group. See *Personnel Administrator of Mass. v. Feeney,* 442 U.S. 256, 279 (1979) (distinguishing discriminatory intent from "intent as volition" or "intent as awareness of consequences"). In my view, it means that the legislature affirmatively undertakes to create a majority-minority district that would not have existed but for the express use of racial classifications-in other words, that a majority-minority district is created "because of," and not merely "in spite of," racial demographics. See *ibid.* When that occurs, traditional race-neutral districting principles are necessarily subordinated (and race necessarily predominates), and the legislature has classified persons on the basis of race....

In this suit, Texas readily admits that it intentionally created majority-minority districts and that those districts would not have existed but for its affirmative use of racial demographics....

That is enough to require application of strict scrutiny in this suit. I am content to reaffirm our holding in *Adarand* that all racial classifications by government must be strictly scrutinized and, even in the sensitive area of state legislative redistricting, I would make no exceptions....

[The concurring opinions of Justice O'Connor and Justice Kennedy, and the dissenting opinions of Justices Stevens and Souter, are omitted.]

Notes and Questions

1. What distinguishes the laws at issue in *Shaw* and *Bush* from the laws at issue in *City of Richmond* and *Adarand* such that laws of the sort at issue in the latter are *always* subject to strict scrutiny but laws of the sort at issue in the former are not? Is it that the redistricting laws are facially neutral on the issue of race, while the affirmative action programs are explicit in taking race into account? However, is that not inconsistent with the Court's decisions involving facially neutral laws enacted for the purpose of discriminating against or administered in a manner that discriminates against racial minorities, which were held subject to strict scrutiny? Does the combination of being facially race neutral *and* being benign result in a lower level of scrutiny? Or is there something unique about the electoral redistricting process that necessitates a different standard?

2. In *Shaw*, Justice O'Connor notes that "reapportionment is one area in which appearances do matter." In what other lines of cases involving the Reconstruction Amendments has the Court focused on appearances? What makes appearances so important as a matter of constitutional law?

C. Public Education

Recall from the start of this chapter that the Court first considered the constitutionality of race-conscious laws designed to benefit racial minorities in *Bakke*, a case involving admission to a public university. The deeply fractured *Bakke* Court failed to reach a consensus on the applicable level of scrutiny for classifications employed for remedial purposes. Although the Court's cases through *Adarand* resolved the debate over the appropriate level of scrutiny, they left open a number of questions relevant to the educational context, including the question whether the interest in diversity—as contrasted with remedying past discrimination—qualifies as a compelling governmental interest. The cases that follow consider these questions in the context of both university admissions as well as primary and secondary public school assignments.

Grutter v. Bollinger

539 U.S. 306 (2003)

Justice O'Connor delivered the opinion of the Court.

This case requires us to decide whether the use of race as a factor in student admissions by the University of Michigan Law School (Law School) is unlawful.

The Law School ranks among the Nation's top law schools. It receives more than 3,500 applications each year for a class of around 350 students. Seeking to "admit a group of students who individually and collectively are among the most capable," the Law School looks for individuals with "substantial promise for success in law school" and "a strong likelihood of succeeding in the practice of law and contributing in diverse ways to the well-being of others." More broadly, the Law School seeks "a mix of students with varying backgrounds and experiences who will respect and learn from each other." In 1992, the dean of the Law School charged a faculty committee with crafting a written admissions policy to implement these goals. In particular, the Law School sought to ensure that its efforts to achieve student body diversity complied with this Court's most recent ruling on the use of race in university admissions. See *Regents of Univ. of Cal. v. Bakke,* 438 U.S. 265 (1978). Upon the unanimous adoption of the committee's report by the Law School faculty, it became the Law School's official admissions policy.

The hallmark of that policy is its focus on academic ability coupled with a flexible assessment of applicants' talents, experiences, and potential "to contribute to the learning of those around them." The policy requires admissions officials to evaluate each applicant based on all the information available in the file, including a personal statement, letters of recommendation, and an essay describing the ways in which the applicant will contribute to the life and diversity of the Law School. In reviewing an applicant's file, admissions officials must consider the applicant's undergraduate grade point average (GPA) and Law School Admission Test (LSAT) score because they are important (if imperfect) predictors of academic success in law school. The policy stresses that "no applicant should be admitted unless we expect that applicant to do well enough to graduate with no serious academic problems."

The policy makes clear, however, that even the highest possible score does not guarantee admission to the Law School. Nor does a low score automatically disqualify an applicant. Rather, the policy requires admissions officials to look beyond grades and test scores to other criteria that are important to the Law School's educational objectives. So-called "'soft' variables" such as "the enthusiasm of recommenders, the quality of the undergraduate institution, the quality of the applicant's essay, and the areas and difficulty of undergraduate course selection" are all brought to bear in assessing an "applicant's likely contributions to the intellectual and social life of the institution."

The policy aspires to "achieve that diversity which has the potential to enrich everyone's education and thus make a law school class stronger than the sum of its parts." The policy does not restrict the types of diversity contributions eligible for "substantial weight" in the admissions process, but instead recognizes "many possible bases for diversity admissions." The policy does, however, reaffirm the Law School's longstanding commitment to "one particular type of diversity," that is, "racial and ethnic diversity with special reference to the inclusion of students from groups which have been historically discriminated against, like African-Americans, Hispanics and Native Americans, who without this commitment might not be represented in our student body in meaningful numbers." By enrolling a "'critical mass' of [underrepresented] minority students," the Law School seeks to "ensur[e] their ability to make unique contributions to the character of the Law School." . . . .

Petitioner Barbara Grutter is a white Michigan resident who applied to the Law School in 1996 with a 3.8 GPA and 161 LSAT score. The Law School initially placed petitioner on a waiting list, but subsequently rejected her application. In December 1997, petitioner filed suit in the United States District Court for the Eastern District of Michigan.... Petitioner alleged that respondents discriminated against her on the basis of race in violation of the Fourteenth Amendment....

During the 15-day bench trial, the parties introduced extensive evidence concerning the Law School's use of race in the admissions process. Dennis Shields, Director of Admissions when petitioner applied to the Law School, testified that he did not direct his staff to admit a particular percentage or number of minority students, but rather to consider an applicant's race along with all other factors. Shields testified that at the height of the admissions season, he would frequently consult the so-called "daily reports" that kept track of the racial and ethnic composition of the class (along with other information such as residency status and gender). This was done, Shields testified, to ensure that a critical mass of underrepresented minority students would be reached so as to realize the educational benefits of a diverse student body. *Ibid.* Shields stressed, however, that he did not seek to admit any particular number or percentage of underrepresented minority students.

Erica Munzel, who succeeded Shields as Director of Admissions, testified that "'critical mass'" means "'meaningful numbers'" or "'meaningful representation,'" which she understood to mean a number that encourages underrepresented minority students to participate in the classroom and not feel isolated. Munzel stated there is no number, percentage, or range of numbers or percentages that constitute critical mass. Munzel also asserted that she must consider the race of applicants because a critical mass of underrepresented minority students could not be enrolled if admissions decisions were based primarily on undergraduate GPAs and LSAT scores.

The current Dean of the Law School, Jeffrey Lehman, also testified. Like the other Law School witnesses, Lehman did not quantify critical mass in terms of numbers or percentages. He indicated that critical mass means numbers such that underrepresented minority students do not feel isolated or like spokespersons for their race. When asked about the extent to which race is considered in admissions, Lehman testified that it varies from one applicant to another. In some cases, according to Lehman's testimony, an applicant's race may play no role, while in others it may be a "'determinative'" factor....

Dr. Stephen Raudenbush, the Law School's expert, focused on the predicted effect of eliminating race as a factor in the Law School's admission process. In Dr. Raudenbush's view, a race-blind admissions system would have a "'very dramatic,'" negative effect on underrepresented minority admissions. He testified that in 2000, 35 percent of underrepresented minority applicants were admitted. Dr. Raudenbush predicted that if race were not considered, only 10 percent of those applicants would have been admitted. Under this scenario, underrepresented minority students would have constituted 4 percent of the entering class in 2000 instead of the actual figure of 14.5 percent....

We last addressed the use of race in public higher education over 25 years ago. In the landmark *Bakke* case, we reviewed a racial set-aside program that reserved 16 out of 100 seats in a medical school class for members of certain minority groups. The decision produced six separate opinions, none of which commanded a majority of the Court. Four Justices would have upheld the program against all attack on the ground that the government can use race to "remedy disadvantages cast on minorities by past racial prejudice." Four other Justices avoided the constitutional question altogether and struck down the program on statutory grounds. Justice Powell provided a fifth vote not only for invalidating the set-aside program, but also for reversing the state court's injunction against any use of race whatsoever. The only holding for the Court in *Bakke* was that a "State has a substantial interest that legitimately may be served by a properly devised admissions program involving the competitive consideration of race and ethnic origin." Thus, we reversed that part of the lower court's judgment that enjoined the university "from any consideration of the race of any applicant."

Since this Court's splintered decision in *Bakke,* Justice Powell's opinion announcing the judgment of the Court has served as the touchstone for constitutional analysis of race-conscious admissions policies. Public and private universities across the Nation have modeled their own admissions programs on Justice Powell's views on permissible race-conscious policies. We therefore discuss Justice Powell's opinion in some detail.

Justice Powell began by stating that "[t]he guarantee of equal protection cannot mean one thing when applied to one individual and something else when applied to a person of another color. If both are not accorded the same protection, then it is not equal." *Bakke,* 438 U.S., at 289-290. In Justice Powell's view, when governmental decisions "touch upon an individual's race or ethnic background, he is entitled to a judicial determination that the burden he is asked to bear on that basis is precisely tailored to serve a compelling governmental interest." *Id.,* at 299. Under this exacting standard, only one of the interests asserted by the university survived Justice Powell's scrutiny.

First, Justice Powell rejected an interest in "'reducing the historic deficit of traditionally disfavored minorities in medical schools and in the medical profession'" as an unlawful interest in racial balancing. *Id.,* at 306-307. Second, Justice Powell rejected an interest in remedying societal discrimination because such measures would risk placing unnecessary burdens on innocent third parties "who bear no responsibility for whatever harm the beneficiaries of the special admissions program are thought to have suffered." *Id.,* at 310. Third, Justice Powell rejected an interest in "increasing the number of physicians who will practice in communities currently underserved," concluding that even if such an interest could be compelling in some circumstances the program under review was not "geared to promote that goal." *Id.,* at 306, 310.

Justice Powell approved the university's use of race to further only one interest: "the attainment of a diverse student body." *Id.,* at 311 . . . .

Justice Powell was, however, careful to emphasize that in his view race "is only one element in a range of factors a university properly may consider in attaining the goal of a heterogeneous student body." *Id.*, at 314. For Justice Powell, "[i]t is not an interest in simple ethnic diversity, in which a specified percentage of the student body is in effect guaranteed to be members of selected ethnic groups," that can justify the use of race. *Id.*, at 315. Rather, "[t]he diversity that furthers a compelling state interest encompasses a far broader array of qualifications and characteristics of which racial or ethnic origin is but a single though important element." *Ibid.*

In the wake of our fractured decision in *Bakke*, courts have struggled to discern whether Justice Powell's diversity rationale, set forth in part of the opinion joined by no other Justice, is nonetheless binding precedent. . . .

We do not find it necessary to decide whether Justice Powell's opinion is binding. . . . [F]or the reasons set out below, today we endorse Justice Powell's view that student body diversity is a compelling state interest that can justify the use of race in university admissions. . . .

Context matters when reviewing race-based governmental action under the Equal Protection Clause. In *Adarand Constructors, Inc. v. Peña*, we made clear that strict scrutiny must take "'relevant differences' into account." 515 U.S., at 228. Indeed, as we explained, that is its "fundamental purpose." *Ibid.* Not every decision influenced by race is equally objectionable, and strict scrutiny is designed to provide a framework for carefully examining the importance and the sincerity of the reasons advanced by the governmental decisionmaker for the use of race in that particular context. . . .

[R]espondents assert only one justification for their use of race in the admissions process: obtaining "the educational benefits that flow from a diverse student body." In other words, the Law School asks us to recognize, in the context of higher education, a compelling state interest in student body diversity.

We first wish to dispel the notion that the Law School's argument has been foreclosed, either expressly or implicitly, by our affirmative-action cases decided since *Bakke*. It is true that some language in those opinions might be read to suggest that remedying past discrimination is the only permissible justification for race-based governmental action. See, *e.g.*, *Richmond v. J.A. Croson Co.*, *supra*, at 493 (plurality opinion) (stating that unless classifications based on race are "strictly reserved for remedial settings, they may in fact promote notions of racial inferiority and lead to a politics of racial hostility"). But we have never held that the only governmental use of race that can survive strict scrutiny is remedying past discrimination. Nor, since *Bakke*, have we directly addressed the use of race in the context of public higher education. Today, we hold that the Law School has a compelling interest in attaining a diverse student body.

The Law School's educational judgment that such diversity is essential to its educational mission is one to which we defer. The Law School's assessment that diversity will, in fact, yield educational benefits is substantiated by respondents and their *amici*. Our scrutiny of the interest asserted by the Law School is no less strict for taking into account complex educational judgments in an area that lies primarily within the expertise of the university. Our holding today is in keeping with our tradition of giving a degree of deference to a university's academic decisions, within constitutionally prescribed limits.

We have long recognized that, given the important purpose of public education and the expansive freedoms of speech and thought associated with the university environment, universities occupy a special niche in our constitutional tradition. In announcing the principle of student body diversity as a compelling state interest, Justice Powell invoked our cases recognizing a constitutional dimension, grounded in the First Amendment, of educational autonomy: "The freedom of a university to make its own judgments as to education includes the selection of its student body." *Bakke, supra,* at 312. From this premise, Justice Powell reasoned that by claiming "the right to select those students who will contribute the most to the 'robust exchange of ideas,'" a university "seek[s] to achieve a goal that is of paramount importance in the fulfillment of its mission." 438 U.S., at 313. Our conclusion that the Law School has a compelling interest in a diverse student body is informed by our view that attaining a diverse student body is at the heart of the Law School's proper institutional mission, and that "good faith" on the part of a university is "presumed" absent "a showing to the contrary." 438 U.S., at 318-319.

As part of its goal of "assembling a class that is both exceptionally academically qualified and broadly diverse," the Law School seeks to "enroll a 'critical mass' of minority students." The Law School's interest is not simply "to assure within its student body some specified percentage of a particular group merely because of its race or ethnic origin." *Bakke,* 438 U.S., at 307 (opinion of Powell, J.). That would amount to outright racial balancing, which is patently unconstitutional. Rather, the Law School's concept of critical mass is defined by reference to the educational benefits that diversity is designed to produce.

These benefits are substantial. As the District Court emphasized, the Law School's admissions policy promotes "cross-racial understanding," helps to break down racial stereotypes, and "enables [students] to better understand persons of different races." These benefits are "important and laudable," because "classroom discussion is livelier, more spirited, and simply more enlightening and interesting" when the students have "the greatest possible variety of backgrounds."

The Law School's claim of a compelling interest is further bolstered by its *amici,* who point to the educational benefits that flow from student body diversity. In addition to the expert studies and reports entered into evidence at trial, numerous studies show that student body diversity promotes learning outcomes, and "better prepares students for an increasingly diverse workforce and society, and better prepares them as professionals." Brief for American Educational Research Association et al. as *Amici Curiae* 3.

These benefits are not theoretical but real, as major American businesses have made clear that the skills needed in today's increasingly global marketplace can only be developed through exposure to widely diverse people, cultures, ideas, and viewpoints. Brief for 3M et al. as *Amici Curiae* 5; Brief for General Motors Corp. as *Amicus Curiae* 3–4. What is more, high-ranking retired officers and civilian leaders of the United States military assert that, "[b]ased on [their] decades of experience," a "highly qualified, racially diverse officer corps . . . is essential to the military's ability to fulfill its principle mission to provide national security." Brief for Julius W. Becton, Jr., et al. as *Amici Curiae* 5. The primary sources for the Nation's officer corps are the service academies and the Reserve Officers Training Corps (ROTC), the latter comprising students already admitted to participating colleges and universities. *Ibid.* At present, "the military cannot achieve an officer corps that is *both* highly qualified *and* racially diverse unless the service academies and the ROTC used limited race-conscious recruiting and admissions policies." *Ibid.* To fulfill its mission, the military "must be selective in admissions for training and education for the officer corps, *and* it must train and educate a highly qualified, racially diverse officer corps in a racially diverse educational setting." *Id.*, at 29. We agree that "[i]t requires only a small step from this analysis to conclude that our country's other most selective institutions must remain both diverse and selective." *Ibid.*

We have repeatedly acknowledged the overriding importance of preparing students for work and citizenship, describing education as pivotal to "sustaining our political and cultural heritage" with a fundamental role in maintaining the fabric of society. *Plyler v. Doe,* 457 U.S. 202, 221 (1982). This Court has long recognized that "education . . . is the very foundation of good citizenship." *Brown v. Board of Education,* 347 U.S. 483, 493 (1954). For this reason, the diffusion of knowledge and opportunity through public institutions of higher education must be accessible to all individuals regardless of race or ethnicity. The United States, as *amicus curiae,* affirms that "[e]nsuring that public institutions are open and available to all segments of American society, including people of all races and ethnicities, represents a paramount government objective." And, "[n]owhere is the importance of such openness more acute than in the context of higher education." Effective participation by members of all racial and ethnic groups in the civic life of our Nation is essential if the dream of one Nation, indivisible, is to be realized.

Moreover, universities, and in particular, law schools, represent the training ground for a large number of our Nation's leaders. *Sweatt v. Painter,* 339 U.S. 629, 634 (1950) (describing law school as a "proving ground for legal learning and practice"). Individuals with law degrees occupy roughly half the state governorships, more than half the seats in the United States Senate, and more than a third of the seats in the United States House of Representatives. The pattern is even more striking when it comes to highly selective law schools. A handful of these schools accounts for 25 of the 100 United States Senators, 74 United States Courts of Appeals judges, and nearly 200 of the more than 600 United States District Court judges.

In order to cultivate a set of leaders with legitimacy in the eyes of the citizenry, it is necessary that the path to leadership be visibly open to talented and qualified individuals of every race and ethnicity. All members of our heterogeneous society must have confidence in the openness and integrity of the educational institutions that provide this training.... Access to legal education (and thus the legal profession) must be inclusive of talented and qualified individuals of every race and ethnicity, so that all members of our heterogeneous society may participate in the educational institutions that provide the training and education necessary to succeed in America.

The Law School does not premise its need for critical mass on "any belief that minority students always (or even consistently) express some characteristic minority viewpoint on any issue." To the contrary, diminishing the force of such stereotypes is both a crucial part of the Law School's mission, and one that it cannot accomplish with only token numbers of minority students. Just as growing up in a particular region or having particular professional experiences is likely to affect an individual's views, so too is one's own, unique experience of being a racial minority in a society, like our own, in which race unfortunately still matters. The Law School has determined, based on its experience and expertise, that a "critical mass" of underrepresented minorities is necessary to further its compelling interest in securing the educational benefits of a diverse student body....

Since *Bakke,* we have had no occasion to define the contours of the narrow-tailoring inquiry with respect to race-conscious university admissions programs. That inquiry must be calibrated to fit the distinct issues raised by the use of race to achieve student body diversity in public higher education....

To be narrowly tailored, a race-conscious admissions program cannot use a quota system—it cannot "insulat[e] each category of applicants with certain desired qualifications from competition with all other applicants." *Bakke,* 438 U.S., at 315 (opinion of Powell, J.). Instead, a university may consider race or ethnicity only as a "'plus' in a particular applicant's file," without "insulat[ing] the individual from comparison with all other candidates for the available seats." *Id.,* at 317. In other words, an admissions program must be "flexible enough to consider all pertinent elements of diversity in light of the particular qualifications of each applicant, and to place them on the same footing for consideration, although not necessarily according them the same weight." *Ibid.*

We find that the Law School's admissions program bears the hallmarks of a narrowly tailored plan. As Justice Powell made clear in *Bakke,* truly individualized consideration demands that race be used in a flexible, nonmechanical way. It follows from this mandate that universities cannot establish quotas for members of certain racial groups or put members of those groups on separate admissions tracks. Nor can universities insulate applicants who belong to certain racial or ethnic groups from the competition for admission. Universities can, however, consider race or ethnicity more flexibly as a "plus" factor in the context of individualized consideration of each and every applicant.

We are satisfied that the Law School's admissions program, like the Harvard plan described by Justice Powell, does not operate as a quota. Properly understood, a "quota" is a program in which a certain fixed number or proportion of opportunities are "reserved exclusively for certain minority groups." *Richmond v. J.A. Croson Co., supra,* at 496 (plurality opinion) .... In contrast, "a permissible goal ... require[s] only a good-faith effort ... to come within a range demarcated by the goal itself," *Sheet Metal Workers v. EEOC, supra,* at 495, and permits consideration of race as a "plus" factor in any given case while still ensuring that each candidate "compete[s] with all other qualified applicants," *Johnson v. Transportation Agency, Santa Clara Cty.,* 480 U.S. 616 (1987).

Justice Powell's distinction between the medical school's rigid 16-seat quota and Harvard's flexible use of race as a "plus" factor is instructive. Harvard certainly had minimum *goals* for minority enrollment, even if it had no specific number firmly in mind. What is more, Justice Powell flatly rejected the argument that Harvard's program was "the functional equivalent of a quota" merely because it had some "'plus'" for race, or gave greater "weight" to race than to some other factors, in order to achieve student body diversity.

The Law School's goal of attaining a critical mass of underrepresented minority students does not transform its program into a quota. ... "[S]ome attention to numbers," without more, does not transform a flexible admissions system into a rigid quota. Nor, as Justice KENNEDY posits, does the Law School's consultation of the "daily reports," which keep track of the racial and ethnic composition of the class (as well as of residency and gender), "sugges[t] there was no further attempt at individual review save for race itself" during the final stages of the admissions process. To the contrary, the Law School's admissions officers testified without contradiction that they never gave race any more or less weight based on the information contained in these reports. Moreover, as Justice Kennedy concedes, between 1993 and 1998, the number of African-American, Latino, and Native-American students in each class at the Law School varied from 13.5 to 20.1 percent, a range inconsistent with a quota.

The Chief Justice believes that the Law School's policy conceals an attempt to achieve racial balancing, and cites admissions data to contend that the Law School discriminates among different groups within the critical mass. But, as The Chief Justice concedes, the number of underrepresented minority students who ultimately enroll in the Law School differs substantially from their representation in the applicant pool and varies considerably for each group from year to year.

That a race-conscious admissions program does not operate as a quota does not, by itself, satisfy the requirement of individualized consideration. When using race as a "plus" factor in university admissions, a university's admissions program must remain flexible enough to ensure that each applicant is evaluated as an individual and not in a way that makes an applicant's race or ethnicity the defining feature of his or her application. The importance of this individualized consideration in the context of a race-conscious admissions program is paramount.

Here, the Law School engages in a highly individualized, holistic review of each applicant's file, giving serious consideration to all the ways an applicant might contribute to a diverse educational environment. The Law School affords this individualized consideration to applicants of all races. There is no policy, either *de jure* or *de facto,* of automatic acceptance or rejection based on any single "soft" variable. Unlike the program at issue in *Gratz v. Bollinger, post,* 539 U.S. 244, the Law School awards no mechanical, predetermined diversity "bonuses" based on race or ethnicity. See *post,* 539 U.S., at 271-272 (distinguishing a race-conscious admissions program that automatically awards 20 points based on race from the Harvard plan, which considered race but "did not contemplate that any single characteristic automatically ensured a specific and identifiable contribution to a university's diversity"). Like the Harvard plan, the Law School's admissions policy "is flexible enough to consider all pertinent elements of diversity in light of the particular qualifications of each applicant, and to place them on the same footing for consideration, although not necessarily according them the same weight." *Bakke, supra,* at 317 (opinion of Powell, J.).

We also find that, like the Harvard plan Justice Powell referenced in *Bakke,* the Law School's race-conscious admissions program adequately ensures that all factors that may contribute to student body diversity are meaningfully considered alongside race in admissions decisions. With respect to the use of race itself, all underrepresented minority students admitted by the Law School have been deemed qualified. By virtue of our Nation's struggle with racial inequality, such students are both likely to have experiences of particular importance to the Law School's mission, and less likely to be admitted in meaningful numbers on criteria that ignore those experiences.

The Law School does not, however, limit in any way the broad range of qualities and experiences that may be considered valuable contributions to student body diversity. To the contrary, the 1992 policy makes clear "[t]here are many possible bases for diversity admissions," and provides examples of admittees who have lived or traveled widely abroad, are fluent in several languages, have overcome personal adversity and family hardship, have exceptional records of extensive community service, and have had successful careers in other fields. The Law School seriously considers each "applicant's promise of making a notable contribution to the class by way of a particular strength, attainment, or characteristic—*e.g.,* an unusual intellectual achievement, employment experience, nonacademic performance, or personal background." All applicants have the opportunity to highlight their own potential diversity contributions through the submission of a personal statement, letters of recommendation, and an essay describing the ways in which the applicant will contribute to the life and diversity of the Law School.

What is more, the Law School actually gives substantial weight to diversity factors besides race. The Law School frequently accepts nonminority applicants with grades and test scores lower than underrepresented minority applicants (and other nonminority applicants) who are rejected. This shows that the Law School seriously weighs many other diversity factors besides race that can make a real and dispositive difference for nonminority applicants as well. By this flexible approach, the Law School sufficiently takes into account, in practice as well as in theory, a wide variety of characteristics besides race and ethnicity that contribute to a diverse student body....

Petitioner and the United States argue that the Law School's plan is not narrowly tailored because race-neutral means exist to obtain the educational benefits of student body diversity that the Law School seeks. We disagree. Narrow tailoring does not require exhaustion of every conceivable race-neutral alternative. Nor does it require a university to choose between maintaining a reputation for excellence or fulfilling a commitment to provide educational opportunities to members of all racial groups. Narrow tailoring does, however, require serious, good faith consideration of workable race-neutral alternatives that will achieve the diversity the university seeks.

We agree with the Court of Appeals that the Law School sufficiently considered workable race-neutral alternatives. The District Court took the Law School to task for failing to consider race-neutral alternatives such as "using a lottery system" or "decreasing the emphasis for all applicants on undergraduate GPA and LSAT scores." But these alternatives would require a dramatic sacrifice of diversity, the academic quality of all admitted students, or both.

The Law School's current admissions program considers race as one factor among many, in an effort to assemble a student body that is diverse in ways broader than race. Because a lottery would make that kind of nuanced judgment impossible, it would effectively sacrifice all other educational values, not to mention every other kind of diversity. So too with the suggestion that the Law School simply lower admissions standards for all students, a drastic remedy that would require the Law School to become a much different institution and sacrifice a vital component of its educational mission. The United States advocates "percentage plans," recently adopted by public undergraduate institutions in Texas, Florida, and California, to guarantee admission to all students above a certain class-rank threshold in every high school in the State. The United States does not, however, explain how such plans could work for graduate and professional schools. Moreover, even assuming such plans are race-neutral, they may preclude the university from conducting the individualized assessments necessary to assemble a student body that is not just racially diverse, but diverse along all the qualities valued by the university. We are satisfied that the Law School adequately considered race-neutral alternatives currently capable of producing a critical mass without forcing the Law School to abandon the academic selectivity that is the cornerstone of its educational mission.

We acknowledge that "there are serious problems of justice connected with the idea of preference itself." *Bakke,* 438 U.S., at 298 (opinion of Powell, J.). Narrow tailoring, therefore, requires that a race-conscious admissions program not unduly harm members of any racial group. Even remedial race-based governmental action generally "remains subject to continuing oversight to assure that it will work the least harm possible to other innocent persons competing for the benefit." *Id.,* at 308.

To be narrowly tailored, a race-conscious admissions program must not "unduly burden individuals who are not members of the favored racial and ethnic groups." *Metro Broadcasting, Inc. v. FCC,* 497 U.S. 547, 630 (1990) (O'Connor, J., dissenting).

We are satisfied that the Law School's admissions program does not. Because the Law School considers "all pertinent elements of diversity," it can (and does) select nonminority applicants who have greater potential to enhance student body diversity over underrepresented minority applicants. . . .

We are mindful, however, that "[a] core purpose of the Fourteenth Amendment was to do away with all governmentally imposed discrimination based on race." *Palmore v. Sidoti,* 466 U.S. 429, 432 (1984). Accordingly, race-conscious admissions policies must be limited in time. This requirement reflects that racial classifications, however compelling their goals, are potentially so dangerous that they may be employed no more broadly than the interest demands. Enshrining a permanent justification for racial preferences would offend this fundamental equal protection principle. We see no reason to exempt race-conscious admissions programs from the requirement that all governmental use of race must have a logical end point. The Law School, too, concedes that all "race-conscious programs must have reasonable durational limits."

In the context of higher education, the durational requirement can be met by sunset provisions in race-conscious admissions policies and periodic reviews to determine whether racial preferences are still necessary to achieve student body diversity. Universities in California, Florida, and Washington State, where racial preferences in admissions are prohibited by state law, are currently engaged in experimenting with a wide variety of alternative approaches. Universities in other States can and should draw on the most promising aspects of these race-neutral alternatives as they develop.

The requirement that all race-conscious admissions programs have a termination point "assure[s] all citizens that the deviation from the norm of equal treatment of all racial and ethnic groups is a temporary matter, a measure taken in the service of the goal of equality itself." *Richmond v. J.A. Croson Co.,* 488 U.S., at 510 (plurality opinion).

We take the Law School at its word that it would "like nothing better than to find a race-neutral admissions formula" and will terminate its race-conscious admissions program as soon as practicable. It has been 25 years since Justice Powell first approved the use of race to further an interest in student body diversity in the context of public higher education. Since that time, the number of minority applicants with high grades and test scores has indeed increased. We expect that 25 years from now, the use of racial preferences will no longer be necessary to further the interest approved today. . . .

[The concurring opinion of Justice Ginsburg, the opinions of Justices Scalia and Thomas, concurring in part and dissenting in part, and the dissenting opinions of Chief Justice Rehnquist and Justice Kennedy are omitted].

Notes and Questions

1. In the last paragraph of the opinion, Justice O'Connor writes that "[w]e expect that 25 years from now, the use of racial preferences will no longer be necessary." Is that a firm ending point? Justice Ginsburg wrote a separate concurring opinion in which she characterized the statement as a "hope" but not a "firm[] forecast." *Grutter v. Bollinger*, 539 U.S. 306, 346 (2003) (Ginsburg, J., concurring). In contrast, Justice Thomas—who otherwise generally dissented from the opinion—wrote, "I agree with the Court's holding that racial discrimination in higher education will be illegal in 25 years." *Id.* at 351 (Thomas, J., concurring in part and dissenting in part).

2. In his dissenting opinion, Chief Justice Rehnquist cited admissions data to support his conclusion that the law school was engaged in "racial balancing" rather than the achievement of a "critical mass":

> From 1995 through 2000, the Law School admitted between 1,130 and 1,310 students. Of those, between 13 and 19 were Native American, between 91 and 108 were African-American, and between 47 and 56 were Hispanic. If the Law School is admitting between 91 and 108 African-Americans in order to achieve "critical mass," thereby preventing African-American students from feeling "isolated or like spokespersons for their race," one would think that a number of the same order of magnitude would be necessary to accomplish the same purpose for Hispanics and Native Americans. Similarly, even if all of the Native American applicants admitted in a given year matriculate, which the record demonstrates is not at all the case, how can this possibly constitute a "critical mass" of Native Americans in a class of over 350 students? In order for this pattern of admission to be consistent with the Law School's explanation of "critical mass," one would have to believe that the objectives of "critical mass" offered by respondents are achieved with only half the number of Hispanics and one-sixth the number of Native Americans as compared to African-Americans. But respondents offer no race-specific reasons for such disparities. Instead, they simply emphasize the importance of achieving "critical mass," without any explanation of why that concept is applied differently among the three underrepresented minority groups.
>
> These different numbers, moreover, come only as a result of substantially different treatment among the three underrepresented minority groups, as is apparent in an example offered by the Law School and highlighted by the Court: The school asserts that it "frequently accepts nonminority applicants with grades and test scores lower than underrepresented minority applicants (and other nonminority applicants) who are rejected." . . . .
>
> Review of the record reveals only 67 such individuals. Of these 67 individuals, *56* were Hispanic, while only 6 were African-American, and only 5 were Native American. This discrepancy reflects a consistent practice. For

example, in 2000, 12 Hispanics who scored between a 159-160 on the LSAT and earned a GPA of 3.00 or higher applied for admission and only 2 were admitted. Meanwhile, 12 African-Americans in the same range of qualifications applied for admission and all 12 were admitted. Likewise, that same year, 16 Hispanics who scored between a 151-153 on the LSAT and earned a 3.00 or higher applied for admission and only 1 of those applicants was admitted. Twenty-three similarly qualified African-Americans applied for admission and 14 were admitted.

These statistics have a significant bearing on petitioner's case. Respondents have *never* offered any race-specific arguments explaining why significantly more individuals from one underrepresented minority group are needed in order to achieve "critical mass" or further student body diversity. They certainly have not explained why Hispanics, who they have said are among "the groups most isolated by racial barriers in our country," should have their admission capped out in this manner. True, petitioner is neither Hispanic nor Native American. But the Law School's disparate admissions practices with respect to these minority groups demonstrate that its alleged goal of "critical mass" is simply a sham. Petitioner may use these statistics to expose this sham, which is the basis for the Law School's admission of less qualified underrepresented minorities in preference to her. Surely strict scrutiny cannot permit these sorts of disparities without at least some explanation.

Only when the "critical mass" label is discarded does a likely explanation for these numbers emerge. The Court states that the Law School's goal of attaining a "critical mass" of underrepresented minority students is not an interest in merely "'assur[ing] within its student body some specified percentage of a particular group merely because of its race or ethnic origin.'" The Court recognizes that such an interest "would amount to outright racial balancing, which is patently unconstitutional." The Court concludes, however, that the Law School's use of race in admissions, consistent with Justice Powell's opinion in *Bakke*, only pays "'[s]ome attention to numbers.'"

But the correlation between the percentage of the Law School's pool of applicants who are members of the three minority groups and the percentage of the admitted applicants who are members of these same groups is far too precise to be dismissed as merely the result of the school paying "some attention to [the] numbers." ... [F]rom 1995 through 2000 the percentage of admitted applicants who were members of these minority groups closely tracked the percentage of individuals in the school's applicant pool who were from the same groups.

For example, in 1995, when 9.7% of the applicant pool was African-American, 9.4% of the admitted class was African-American. By 2000, only 7.5% of the applicant pool was African-American, and 7.3% of the

> admitted class was African-American. This correlation is striking. Respondents themselves emphasize that the number of underrepresented minority students admitted to the Law School would be significantly smaller if the race of each applicant were not considered. But, as the examples above illustrate, the measure of the decrease would differ dramatically among the groups. The tight correlation between the percentage of applicants and admittees of a given race, therefore, must result from careful race based planning by the Law School. It suggests a formula for admission based on the aspirational assumption that all applicants are equally qualified academically, and therefore that the proportion of each group admitted should be the same as the proportion of that group in the applicant pool.
>
> Not only do respondents fail to explain this phenomenon, they attempt to obscure it. But the divergence between the percentages of underrepresented minorities in the applicant pool and in the *enrolled* classes is not the only relevant comparison. In fact, it may not be the most relevant comparison. The Law School cannot precisely control which of its admitted applicants decide to attend the university. But it can and, as the numbers demonstrate, clearly does employ racial preferences in extending offers of admission. Indeed, the ostensibly flexible nature of the Law School's admissions program that the Court finds appealing appears to be, in practice, a carefully managed program designed to ensure proportionate representation of applicants from selected minority groups.

Grutter v. Bollinger, 539 U.S. 306, 381–386 (2003) (Rehnquist, C.J., dissenting). The majority contends that there is a distinction between a "quota" and a "critical mass." Can you articulate that distinction?

3. The majority in *Grutter* wrote that "The Law School's educational judgment that such diversity is essential to its educational mission is one to which we defer." Does this sound like the language of strict scrutiny? In his dissenting opinion, Justice Kennedy wrote that the deference that the majority gave to the law school amounted to a "refusal to apply meaningful strict scrutiny." *Grutter v. Bollinger*, 539 U.S. 306, 393 (2003) (Kennedy, J., dissenting). Do you agree with Justice Kennedy that the scrutiny applied by the majority was something less than traditional strict scrutiny? In subsequent decisions, the Court has clarified that although deference is given to the University's conclusion that a diverse student body would further its educational goals, *no* deference is owed to a university in determining whether the use of race is narrowly tailored to achieve the university's permissible goals. *See Fisher v. University of Texas (Fisher II)*, 136 S.Ct. 2198, 2208 (2016); *Fisher v. University of Texas (Fisher I)*, 570 U.S. 297, 312 (2013).

4. In *Grutter*, the Court referenced another decision issued that day, *Gratz v. Bollinger*, 539 U.S. 244 (2003). At issue in *Gratz*, was the constitutionality of the undergraduate admissions program at The University of Michigan. Under that program, applicants were awarded points for different aspects of their application, including grade point average, standardized test scores, in-state residency, alumni

relationship, and the like. The maximum number of points a student could earn was 150, and any student earning 100 points was automatically admitted. Under the scoring scheme, 20 points were awarded to an applicant if they were a member of an underrepresented racial or ethnic minority group. The majority held this scheme unconstitutional:

> We find that the University's policy, which automatically distributes 20 points, or one-fifth of the points needed to guarantee admission, to every single "underrepresented minority" applicant solely because of race, is not narrowly tailored to achieve the interest in educational diversity that respondents claim justifies their program....
>
> Justice Powell's opinion in *Bakke* emphasized the importance of considering each particular applicant as an individual, assessing all of the qualities that individual possesses, and in turn, evaluating that individual's ability to contribute to the unique setting of higher education. The admissions program Justice Powell described, however, did not contemplate that any single characteristic automatically ensured a specific and identifiable contribution to a university's diversity. Instead, under the approach Justice Powell described, each characteristic of a particular applicant was to be considered in assessing the applicant's entire application.
>
> The current LSA policy does not provide such individualized consideration. The LSA's policy automatically distributes 20 points to every single applicant from an "underrepresented minority" group, as defined by the University. The only consideration that accompanies this distribution of points is a factual review of an application to determine whether an individual is a member of one of these minority groups. Moreover, unlike Justice Powell's example, where the race of a "particular black applicant" could be considered without being decisive, the LSA's automatic distribution of 20 points has the effect of making "the factor of race ... decisive" for virtually every minimally qualified underrepresented minority applicant.

Id. at 270-72. *See also id.* at 280 (O'Connor, J., concurring) (describing the system of undergraduate admissions as "a nonindividualized, mechanical one," and distinguishing it from the law school admissions policy upheld in *Grutter*).

5. The *Grutter* majority identifies a number of factors in support of its conclusion that the program under review is narrowly tailored. What are those factors? Moreover, does an admissions program have to define diversity as broadly as the program in *Grutter* did, or could it be more narrowly focused on racial and ethnic diversity and still pass constitutional muster?

6. One of the arguments made in *Grutter* is that race neutral alternatives should be exhausted, including so called "top 10 percent" programs. Under these programs, the top 10 percent of students at *each* high school in the state receive automatic admission into the university, even if their grades and test scores are worse than students at other high schools who are not in the top 10 percent of their class. The

majority, in referencing these programs, writes "even assuming such plans are race-neutral." What do they mean by that? Consider the following:

> [O]nly an ostrich could regard the supposedly neutral alternatives as race unconscious....
>
> Texas' percentage plan was adopted with racially segregated neighborhoods and schools front and center stage. See House Research Organization, Bill Analysis, HB 588, pp. 4–5 (Apr. 15, 1997) ("Many regions of the state, school districts, and high schools in Texas are still predominantly composed of people from a single racial or ethnic group. Because of the persistence of this segregation, admitting the top 10 percent of all high schools would provide a diverse population and ensure that a large, well qualified pool of minority students was admitted to Texas universities."). It is race consciousness, not blindness to race, that drives such plans.

Fisher I, 570 U.S. at 335 (Ginsburg, J., dissenting). *Accord Fisher II*, 136 S.Ct. at 2213. Do you agree? If so, does that not call into question the Court's holdings in *Shaw* and *Bush*?

7. Does the interest in diversity apply only in the university setting? Or is the Court's holding in *Grutter* broad enough to encompass diversity in primary and secondary education?

Parents Involved in Community Schools v. Seattle School District No. 1

551 U.S. 701 (2007)

Chief Justice Roberts announced the judgment of the Court, and delivered the opinion of the Court with respect to Parts I, II, III–A, and III–C, and an opinion with respect to Parts III–B and IV, in which Justice Scalia, Justice Thomas, and Justice Alito join.

The school districts in these cases voluntarily adopted student assignment plans that rely upon race to determine which public schools certain children may attend. The Seattle school district classifies children as white or nonwhite; the Jefferson County school district as black or "other." In Seattle, this racial classification is used to allocate slots in oversubscribed high schools. In Jefferson County, it is used to make certain elementary school assignments and to rule on transfer requests. In each case, the school district relies upon an individual student's race in assigning that student to a particular school, so that the racial balance at the school falls within a predetermined range based on the racial composition of the school district as a whole. Parents of students denied assignment to particular schools under these plans solely because of their race brought suit, contending that allocating children to different public schools on the basis of race violated the Fourteenth Amendment guarantee of equal protection....

I

Both cases present the same underlying legal question—whether a public school that had not operated legally segregated schools or has been found to be unitary may choose to classify students by race and rely upon that classification in making school assignments. Although we examine the plans under the same legal framework, the specifics of the two plans, and the circumstances surrounding their adoption, are in some respects quite different.

A

Seattle School District No. 1 operates 10 regular public high schools. In 1998, it adopted the plan at issue in this case for assigning students to these schools. The plan allows incoming ninth graders to choose from among any of the district's high schools, ranking however many schools they wish in order of preference.

Some schools are more popular than others. If too many students list the same school as their first choice, the district employs a series of "tiebreakers" to determine who will fill the open slots at the oversubscribed school. The first tiebreaker selects for admission students who have a sibling currently enrolled in the chosen school. The next tiebreaker depends upon the racial composition of the particular school and the race of the individual student. . . . If an oversubscribed school is not within 10 percentage points of the district's overall white/nonwhite racial balance, it is what the district calls "integration positive," and the district employs a tiebreaker that selects for assignment students whose race "will serve to bring the school into balance." . . . .

Seattle has never operated segregated schools—legally separate schools for students of different races—nor has it ever been subject to court-ordered desegregation. It nonetheless employs the racial tiebreaker in an attempt to address the effects of racially identifiable housing patterns on school assignments. . . .

B

Jefferson County Public Schools operates the public school system in metropolitan Louisville, Kentucky. In 1973 a federal court found that Jefferson County had maintained a segregated school system, and in 1975 the District Court entered a desegregation decree. Jefferson County operated under this decree until 2000, when the District Court dissolved the decree after finding that the district had achieved unitary status by eliminating "[t]o the greatest extent practicable" the vestiges of its prior policy of segregation.

In 2001, after the decree had been dissolved, Jefferson County adopted the voluntary student assignment plan at issue in this case. . . . The plan requires all nonmagnet schools to maintain a minimum black enrollment of 15 percent, and a maximum black enrollment of 50 percent.

At the elementary school level, based on his or her address, each student is designated a "resides" school to which students within a specific geographic area are assigned; elementary resides schools are "grouped into clusters in order to facilitate integration." The district assigns students to nonmagnet schools in one of two ways: Parents of kindergartners, first graders, and students new to the district may submit an application indicating a first and second choice among the schools within their cluster; students who do not submit such an application are assigned within the cluster by the district. "Decisions to assign students to schools within each cluster are based on available space within the schools and the racial guidelines in the District's current student assignment plan." If a school has reached the "extremes of the racial guidelines," a student whose race would contribute to the school's racial imbalance will not be assigned there. After assignment, students at all grade levels are permitted to apply to transfer between nonmagnet schools in the district. Transfers may be requested for any number of reasons, and may be denied because of lack of available space or on the basis of the racial guidelines. . . .

III

A

It is well established that when the government distributes burdens or benefits on the basis of individual racial classifications, that action is reviewed under strict scrutiny. . . . In order to satisfy this searching standard of review, the school districts must demonstrate that the use of individual racial classifications in the assignment plans here under review is "narrowly tailored" to achieve a "compelling" government interest.

Without attempting in these cases to set forth all the interests a school district might assert, it suffices to note that our prior cases, in evaluating the use of racial classifications in the school context, have recognized two interests that qualify as compelling. The first is the compelling interest of remedying the effects of past intentional discrimination. See *Freeman v. Pitts,* 503 U.S. 467, 494 (1992). Yet the Seattle public schools have not shown that they were ever segregated by law, and were not subject to court-ordered desegregation decrees. The Jefferson County public schools were previously segregated by law and were subject to a desegregation decree entered in 1975. In 2000, the District Court that entered that decree dissolved it, finding that Jefferson County had "eliminated the vestiges associated with the former policy of segregation and its pernicious effects," and thus had achieved "unitary" status. Jefferson County accordingly does not rely upon an interest in remedying the effects of past intentional discrimination in defending its present use of race in assigning students.

Nor could it. We have emphasized that the harm being remedied by mandatory desegregation plans is the harm that is traceable to segregation, and that "the Constitution is not violated by racial imbalance in the schools, without more." *Milliken v. Bradley,* 433 U.S. 267, 280, n. 14 (1977). Once Jefferson County achieved unitary status, it had remedied the constitutional wrong that allowed race-based assignments. Any continued use of race must be justified on some other basis.

The second government interest we have recognized as compelling for purposes of strict scrutiny is the interest in diversity in higher education upheld in *Grutter,* 539

U.S., at 328. The specific interest found compelling in *Grutter* was student body diversity "in the context of higher education." The diversity interest was not focused on race alone but encompassed "all factors that may contribute to student body diversity." *Id.*, at 337 . . . .

The entire gist of the analysis in *Grutter* was that the admissions program at issue there focused on each applicant as an individual, and not simply as a member of a particular racial group. The classification of applicants by race upheld in *Grutter* was only as part of a "highly individualized, holistic review," 539 U.S., at 337 . . . . The point of the narrow tailoring analysis in which the *Grutter* Court engaged was to ensure that the use of racial classifications was indeed part of a broader assessment of diversity, and not simply an effort to achieve racial balance, which the Court explained would be "patently unconstitutional." *Id.*, at 330.

In the present cases, by contrast, race is not considered as part of a broader effort to achieve "exposure to widely diverse people, cultures, ideas, and viewpoints," *ibid.*; race, for some students, is determinative standing alone. . . . [U]nder each plan when race comes into play, it is decisive by itself. It is not simply one factor weighed with others in reaching a decision, as in *Grutter*; it is *the* factor. Like the University of Michigan undergraduate plan struck down in *Gratz,* 539 U.S., at 275, the plans here "do not provide for a meaningful individualized review of applicants" but instead rely on racial classifications in a "nonindividualized, mechanical" way, *id.*, at 276, 280 (O'Connor, J., concurring).

Even when it comes to race, the plans here employ only a limited notion of diversity, viewing race exclusively in white/nonwhite terms in Seattle and black/"other" terms in Jefferson County. . . .

Prior to *Grutter,* the courts of appeals rejected as unconstitutional attempts to implement race-based assignment plans—such as the plans at issue here—in primary and secondary schools. After *Grutter,* however, the two Courts of Appeals in these cases, and one other, found that race-based assignments were permissible at the elementary and secondary level, largely in reliance on that case.

In upholding the admissions plan in *Grutter,* though, this Court relied upon considerations unique to institutions of higher education, noting that in light of "the expansive freedoms of speech and thought associated with the university environment, universities occupy a special niche in our constitutional tradition." 539 U.S., at 329. See also *Bakke,* 438 U.S., at 312, 313 (opinion of Powell, J.). The Court explained that "[c]ontext matters" in applying strict scrutiny, and repeatedly noted that it was addressing the use of race "in the context of higher education." *Grutter, supra,* at 327, 328, 334. The Court in *Grutter* expressly articulated key limitations on its holding—defining a specific type of broad-based diversity and noting the unique context of higher education—but these limitations were largely disregarded by the lower courts in extending *Grutter* to uphold race-based assignments in elementary and secondary schools. The present cases are not governed by *Grutter.*

B

Perhaps recognizing that reliance on *Grutter* cannot sustain their plans, both school districts assert additional interests, distinct from the interest upheld in *Grutter,* to justify their race-based assignments. . . . Seattle contends that its use of race helps to reduce racial concentration in schools and to ensure that racially concentrated housing patterns do not prevent nonwhite students from having access to the most desirable schools. Jefferson County has articulated a similar goal. . . .[12] Each school district argues that educational and broader socialization benefits flow from a racially diverse learning environment, and each contends that because the diversity they seek is racial diversity—not the broader diversity at issue in *Grutter*—it makes sense to promote that interest directly by relying on race alone.

The parties and their *amici* dispute whether racial diversity in schools in fact has a marked impact on test scores and other objective yardsticks or achieves intangible socialization benefits. The debate is not one we need to resolve, however, because it is clear that the racial classifications employed by the districts are not narrowly tailored to the goal of achieving the educational and social benefits asserted to flow from racial diversity. In design and operation, the plans are directed only to racial balance, pure and simple, an objective this Court has repeatedly condemned as illegitimate.

The plans are tied to each district's specific racial demographics, rather than to any pedagogic concept of the level of diversity needed to obtain the asserted educational benefits. . . .

The districts offer no evidence that the level of racial diversity necessary to achieve the asserted educational benefits happens to coincide with the racial demographics of the respective school districts—or rather the white/nonwhite or black/"other" balance of the districts, since that is the only diversity addressed by the plans. . . .

In *Grutter,* the number of minority students the school sought to admit was an undefined "meaningful number" necessary to achieve a genuinely diverse student body. 539 U.S., at 316, 335–336. Although the matter was the subject of disagreement on the Court, the majority concluded that the law school did not count back from its applicant pool to arrive at the "meaningful number" it regarded as necessary to diversify its student body. *Id.,* at 335–336. Here the racial balance the districts seek is a defined range set solely by reference to the demographics of the respective school districts.

---

12. Jefferson County also argues that it would be incongruous to hold that what was constitutionally required of it one day—race-based assignments pursuant to the desegregation decree—can be constitutionally prohibited the next. But what was constitutionally required of the district prior to 2000 was the elimination of the vestiges of prior segregation—not racial proportionality in its own right. See *Freeman v. Pitts,* 503 U.S. 467, 494–496 (1992). Once those vestiges were eliminated, Jefferson County was on the same footing as any other school district, and its use of race must be justified on other grounds.

This working backward to achieve a particular type of racial balance, rather than working forward from some demonstration of the level of diversity that provides the purported benefits, is a fatal flaw under our existing precedent....

The Ninth Circuit below stated that it "share[d] in the hope" expressed in *Grutter* that in 25 years racial preferences would no longer be necessary to further the interest identified in that case. But in Seattle the plans are defended as necessary to address the consequences of racially identifiable housing patterns. The sweep of the mandate claimed by the district is contrary to our rulings that remedying past societal discrimination does not justify race-conscious government action....

C

The districts assert, as they must, that the way in which they have employed individual racial classifications is necessary to achieve their stated ends. The minimal effect these classifications have on student assignments, however, suggests that other means would be effective. Seattle's racial tiebreaker results, in the end, only in shifting a small number of students between schools....

While we do not suggest that *greater* use of race would be preferable, the minimal impact of the districts' racial classifications on school enrollment casts doubt on the necessity of using racial classifications.... Classifying and assigning schoolchildren according to a binary conception of race is an extreme approach in light of our precedents and our Nation's history of using race in public schools, and requires more than such an amorphous end to justify it.

The districts have also failed to show that they considered methods other than explicit racial classifications to achieve their stated goals. Narrow tailoring requires "serious, good faith consideration of workable race-neutral alternatives," *Grutter, supra,* at 339, and yet in Seattle several alternative assignment plans—many of which would not have used express racial classifications—were rejected with little or no consideration. Jefferson County has failed to present any evidence that it considered alternatives, even though the district already claims that its goals are achieved primarily through means other than the racial classifications....

* * *

If the need for the racial classifications embraced by the school districts is unclear, even on the districts' own terms, the costs are undeniable. "[D]istinctions between citizens solely because of their ancestry are by their very nature odious to a free people whose institutions are founded upon the doctrine of equality." *Adarand,* 515 U.S., at 214. Government action dividing us by race is inherently suspect because such classifications promote "notions of racial inferiority and lead to a politics of racial hostility," *Croson,* 488 U.S., at 493 (plurality opinion), "reinforce the belief, held by too many for too much of our history, that individuals should be judged by the color of their skin," *Shaw v. Reno,* 509 U.S. 630, 657 (1993), and "endorse race-based reasoning and the conception of a Nation divided into racial blocs, thus contributing to an escalation of racial hostility and conflict." *Metro Broadcasting,* 497 U.S., at 603 (O'Connor, J., dissenting)....

All this is true enough in the contexts in which these statements were made—government contracting, voting districts, allocation of broadcast licenses, and electing state officers—but when it comes to using race to assign children to schools, history will be heard. In *Brown v. Board of Education,* 347 U.S. 483 (1954) (*Brown I*), we held that segregation deprived black children of equal educational opportunities regardless of whether school facilities and other tangible factors were equal, because government classification and separation on grounds of race themselves denoted inferiority. It was not the inequality of the facilities but the fact of legally separating children on the basis of race on which the Court relied to find a constitutional violation in 1954. The next Term, we accordingly stated that "full compliance" with *Brown I* required school districts "to achieve a system of determining admission to the public schools *on a nonracial basis.*" *Brown II,* 349 U.S., at 300–301 (emphasis added).

The parties and their *amici* debate which side is more faithful to the heritage of *Brown,* but the position of the plaintiffs in *Brown* was spelled out in their brief and could not have been clearer: "[T]he Fourteenth Amendment prevents states from according differential treatment to American children on the basis of their color or race." . . . . What do the racial classifications do in these cases, if not determine admission to a public school on a racial basis?

Before *Brown,* schoolchildren were told where they could and could not go to school based on the color of their skin. The school districts in these cases have not carried the heavy burden of demonstrating that we should allow this once again—even for very different reasons. . . . The way to stop discrimination on the basis of race is to stop discriminating on the basis of race. . . .

Justice Kennedy, concurring in part and concurring in the judgment. . . .

Our Nation from the inception has sought to preserve and expand the promise of liberty and equality on which it was founded. Today we enjoy a society that is remarkable in its openness and opportunity. Yet our tradition is to go beyond present achievements, however significant, and to recognize and confront the flaws and injustices that remain. This is especially true when we seek assurance that opportunity is not denied on account of race. The enduring hope is that race should not matter; the reality is that too often it does.

This is by way of preface to my respectful submission that parts of the opinion by The Chief Justice imply an all-too-unyielding insistence that race cannot be a factor in instances when, in my view, it may be taken into account. The plurality opinion is too dismissive of the legitimate interest government has in ensuring all people have equal opportunity regardless of their race. The plurality's postulate that "[t]he way to stop discrimination on the basis of race is to stop discriminating on the basis of race," is not sufficient to decide these cases. Fifty years of experience since *Brown v. Board of Education,* 347 U.S. 483 (1954), should teach us that the problem before us defies so easy a solution. School districts can seek to reach *Brown*'s objective of equal educational opportunity. The plurality opinion is at least open to the interpretation that the Constitution requires school districts to ignore the problem of *de facto* resegregation in schooling. I cannot endorse that conclusion. To the extent the plurality opinion suggests the Constitution mandates that state and local school authorities must accept the status quo of racial isolation in schools, it is, in my view, profoundly mistaken.

The statement by Justice Harlan that "[o]ur Constitution is color-blind" was most certainly justified in the context of his dissent in *Plessy v. Ferguson,* 163 U.S. 537, 559 (1896). The Court's decision in that case was a grievous error it took far too long to overrule. *Plessy,* of course, concerned official classification by race applicable to all persons who sought to use railway carriages. And, as an aspiration, Justice Harlan's axiom must command our assent. In the real world, it is regrettable to say, it cannot be a universal constitutional principle.

In the administration of public schools by the state and local authorities it is permissible to consider the racial makeup of schools and to adopt general policies to encourage a diverse student body, one aspect of which is its racial composition. If school authorities are concerned that the student-body compositions of certain schools interfere with the objective of offering an equal educational opportunity to all of their students, they are free to devise race-conscious measures to address the problem in a general way and without treating each student in different fashion solely on the basis of a systematic, individual typing by race.

School boards may pursue the goal of bringing together students of diverse backgrounds and races through other means, including strategic site selection of new schools; drawing attendance zones with general recognition of the demographics of neighborhoods; allocating resources for special programs; recruiting students and faculty in a targeted fashion; and tracking enrollments, performance, and other statistics by race. These mechanisms are race conscious but do not lead to different treatment based on a classification that tells each student he or she is to be defined by race, so it is unlikely any of them would demand strict scrutiny to be found permissible. See *Bush v. Vera,* 517 U.S. 952, 958 (1996) (plurality opinion) ("Strict scrutiny does not apply merely because redistricting is performed with consciousness of race.... Electoral district lines are 'facially race neutral,' so a more searching inquiry is necessary before strict scrutiny can be found applicable in redistricting cases than in cases of 'classifications based explicitly on race'"). Executive and legislative branches, which for generations now have considered these types of policies and procedures, should be permitted to employ them with candor and with confidence that a constitutional violation does not occur whenever a decisionmaker considers the impact a given approach might have on students of different races. Assigning to each student a personal designation according to a crude system of individual racial classifications is quite a different matter; and the legal analysis changes accordingly.

Each respondent has asserted that its assignment of individual students by race is permissible because there is no other way to avoid racial isolation in the school districts. Yet, as explained, each has failed to provide the support necessary for that proposition. And individual racial classifications employed in this manner may be considered legitimate only if they are a last resort to achieve a compelling interest.

In the cases before us it is noteworthy that the number of students whose assignment depends on express racial classifications is limited. I join Part III–C of the Court's opinion because I agree that in the context of these plans, the small number of assignments affected suggests that the schools could have achieved their stated ends through different means. These include the facially race-neutral means set forth above or, if necessary, a more nuanced, individual evaluation of school needs and student characteristics that might include race as a component. The latter approach would be informed by *Grutter*, though of course the criteria relevant to student placement would differ based on the age of the students, the needs of the parents, and the role of the schools. . . .

This Nation has a moral and ethical obligation to fulfill its historic commitment to creating an integrated society that ensures equal opportunity for all of its children. A compelling interest exists in avoiding racial isolation, an interest that a school district, in its discretion and expertise, may choose to pursue. Likewise, a district may consider it a compelling interest to achieve a diverse student population. Race may be one component of that diversity, but other demographic factors, plus special talents and needs, should also be considered. What the government is not permitted to do, absent a showing of necessity not made here, is to classify every student on the basis of race and to assign each of them to schools based on that classification. Crude measures of this sort threaten to reduce children to racial chits valued and traded according to one school's supply and another's demand.

That statement, to be sure, invites this response: A sense of stigma may already become the fate of those separated out by circumstances beyond their immediate control. But to this the replication must be: Even so, measures other than differential treatment based on racial typing of individuals first must be exhausted.

The decision today should not prevent school districts from continuing the important work of bringing together students of different racial, ethnic, and economic backgrounds. Due to a variety of factors—some influenced by government, some not—neighborhoods in our communities do not reflect the diversity of our Nation as a whole. Those entrusted with directing our public schools can bring to bear the creativity of experts, parents, administrators, and other concerned citizens to find a way to achieve the compelling interests they face without resorting to widespread governmental allocation of benefits and burdens on the basis of racial classifications.

With this explanation I concur in the judgment of the Court.

Justice Breyer, with whom Justice Stevens, Justice Souter, and Justice Ginsburg join, dissenting. . . .

In both Seattle and Louisville, the local school districts began with schools that were highly segregated in fact. In both cities, plaintiffs filed lawsuits claiming unconstitutional segregation. In Louisville, a Federal District Court found that school segregation reflected pre-*Brown* state laws separating the races. In Seattle, the plaintiffs alleged that school segregation unconstitutionally reflected not only generalized societal discrimination and residential housing patterns, but also *school board policies and actions* that had helped to create, maintain, and aggravate racial segregation. In Louisville, a federal court entered a remedial decree. In Seattle, the parties settled after the school district pledged to undertake a desegregation plan. . . .

No one here disputes that Louisville's segregation was *de jure*. But what about Seattle's? Was it *de facto? De jure?* A mixture? Opinions differed. Or is it that a prior federal court had not adjudicated the matter? Does that make a difference? Is Seattle free on remand to say that its schools were *de jure* segregated, just as in 1956 a memo for the school board admitted? The plurality does not seem confident as to the answer. . . .

Are courts really to treat as merely *de facto* segregated those school districts that avoided a federal order by voluntarily complying with *Brown*'s requirements? . . . . Because the Constitution emphatically does not forbid the use of race-conscious measures by districts in the South that voluntarily desegregated their schools, on what basis does the plurality claim that the law forbids Seattle to do the same? . . . .

[The concurring opinion of Justice Thomas, and the dissenting opinion of Justice Stevens, are omitted.]

Notes and Questions

1. Both of the interests invoked in this case have been approved of in other cases: remedying past discrimination and promoting diversity. Why does the plurality nonetheless find those justifications insufficient? Are you persuaded by its rationales for so holding?

2. The plurality finds a number of ways to distinguish *Grutter*. In what ways are the two cases distinguishable, and are those distinctions as significant as the plurality suggests?

3. In his concurring opinion, Justice Kennedy suggests a number of alternatives that he characterizes as "race neutral," including: strategic site location of new schools; drawing attendance zones with general recognition of the demographics of neighborhoods; and recruiting students and faculty in a targeted fashion. He contends that, although these are race conscious, they would not be subject to strict scrutiny. What does he cite in support of that conclusion? Can that be reconciled with the Court's holdings in *Grutter* and *Fisher II*? Would the Court apply anything less than strict scrutiny to the use of such allegedly "race neutral" tactics if they were intentionally employed to *segregate* students on the basis of race?

Chapter 18

The Gay Rights Cases

In Chapter 16, you examined the Court's 1986 decision in *Bowers*, which upheld the constitutionality of a state law criminalizing consensual sodomy between adults, as applied to persons of the same sex. The *Bowers* Court decided the case on substantive due process grounds, and did not address the possibility that the law might be unconstitutional on equal protection grounds (although the law in *Bowers* in terms applied equally to same-sex and opposite-sex sodomy, in practice it was enforced only against the former).

This chapter closely examines a series of four cases decided between 1996 and 2015 addressing both due process and equal protection challenges to a variety of different laws impacting the rights of gays, lesbians, and bisexual persons (to date, the Court has not addressed the constitutionality of laws impacting the rights of transgender persons). Part A focuses on class-based equal protection claims. Part B involves a reconsideration of *Bowers* with a dual focus on both class-based equal protection and substantive due process. Part C takes a look at the Court's cases involving marriage rights for same-sex couples.

The four main cases in this chapter share three common characteristics. First, all four decisions were authored by Justice Kennedy, who has since retired from the Court. Second, all four decisions resulted in a victory for those challenging the constitutionality of the laws. Third, all four decisions contain significant ambiguities, not only on the level of scrutiny but even the constitutional basis for the decision.

A. Sexual Minorities and Equal Protection

What level of scrutiny applies to laws that discriminate on the basis of sexual orientation or gender identity? As an initial matter, recall from Chapter 15 that to even make out such a claim, one must show that the government acted with a discriminatory purpose against a particular class. In the case of a law that is discriminatory on its face—such as a law that in terms specifies that "gays, lesbians, and bisexuals" or "transgender persons" shall be denied a particular right or treated in a different way—the intent to discriminate is clear.

However, as noted in Chapter 15, some courts have held that laws targeting same-sex conduct—such as laws prohibiting same-sex sexual intimacy, adoption, or marriage—are facially neutral on sexual orientation because, in theory, two heterosexuals can engage in an act of same-sex sexual intimacy, seek to adopt a child together, or opt to legally marry one another for practical reasons. There are three potential responses to this argument. First, one can try to identify record evidence, akin to that in *Hunter v. Underwood*, of an intent to discriminate against sexual minorities. Second, one can treat this scenario as a case of extreme discriminatory effects akin to that found in *Yick Wo* and *Gomillion*, in which case discriminatory purpose might be inferred. Finally, one can reject the effort to treat such a law as facially neutral, relying on *Hernandez* and treating the targeted conduct as a proxy for sexual orientation.

Yet even if one overcomes those hurdles, the next question is to determine the appropriate level of scrutiny. As you saw in Chapter 4, traditional rational basis review under the *Railway Express-Lee Optical-Beach Communications* line of cases is extraordinarily deferential and is thus unlikely to result in the striking down of such laws. Are sexual minorities entitled to heightened scrutiny under the *Frontiero* factors? If not, are there nonetheless circumstances in which a law targeting sexual minorities will be struck down by the Court applying its unwritten fleeting rational basis plus review, as in *Moreno* and *Cleburne*?

After reading the facts of the case that follows, pause and take a few moments to sketch out the various ways in which a court *could* resolve the constitutional question. Then resume reading and try to determine what the Court in fact did.

Romer v. Evans

517 U.S. 620 (1996)

Justice Kennedy delivered the opinion of the Court.

One century ago, the first Justice Harlan admonished this Court that the Constitution "neither knows nor tolerates classes among citizens." *Plessy v. Ferguson*, 163 U.S. 537, 559 (1896) (dissenting opinion). Unheeded then, those words now are understood to state a commitment to the law's neutrality where the rights of persons are at stake. The Equal Protection Clause enforces this principle and today requires us to hold invalid a provision of Colorado's Constitution.

I

The enactment challenged in this case is an amendment to the Constitution of the State of Colorado, adopted in a 1992 statewide referendum. The parties and the state courts refer to it as "Amendment 2," its designation when submitted to the voters. The impetus for the amendment and the contentious campaign that preceded its adoption came in large part from ordinances that had been passed in various Colorado municipalities. For example, the cities of Aspen and Boulder and the city and County of Denver each had enacted ordinances which banned discrimination in many transactions and activities, including housing, employment, education, public accommodations, and health and welfare services. What gave rise to the statewide controversy was the protection the ordinances afforded to persons discriminated against by reason of their sexual orientation. Amendment 2 repeals these ordinances to the extent they prohibit discrimination on the basis of "homosexual, lesbian or bisexual orientation, conduct, practices or relationships."

Yet Amendment 2, in explicit terms, does more than repeal or rescind these provisions. It prohibits all legislative, executive or judicial action at any level of state or local government designed to protect the named class, a class we shall refer to as homosexual persons or gays and lesbians. The amendment reads:

> "No Protected Status Based on Homosexual, Lesbian or Bisexual Orientation. Neither the State of Colorado, through any of its branches or departments, nor any of its agencies, political subdivisions, municipalities or school districts, shall enact, adopt or enforce any statute, regulation, ordinance or policy whereby homosexual, lesbian or bisexual orientation, conduct, practices or relationships shall constitute or otherwise be the basis of or entitle any person or class of persons to have or claim any minority status, quota preferences, protected status or claim of discrimination. This Section of the Constitution shall be in all respects self-executing."

Soon after Amendment 2 was adopted, this litigation to declare its invalidity and enjoin its enforcement was commenced in the District Court for the City and County of Denver. Among the plaintiffs (respondents here) were homosexual persons, some of them government employees. They alleged that enforcement of Amendment 2 would subject them to immediate and substantial risk of discrimination on the basis of their sexual orientation. . . .

The trial court granted a preliminary injunction to stay enforcement of Amendment 2, and an appeal was taken to the Supreme Court of Colorado. Sustaining the interim injunction and remanding the case for further proceedings, the State Supreme Court held that Amendment 2 was subject to strict scrutiny under the Fourteenth Amendment because it infringed the fundamental right of gays and lesbians to participate in the political process. *Evans v. Romer,* 854 P.2d 1270 (Colo.1993) (*Evans I*). To reach this conclusion, the state court relied on our voting rights cases, and on our precedents involving discriminatory restructuring of governmental decisionmaking. On remand, the State advanced various arguments in an effort to show that Amendment 2 was narrowly tailored to serve compelling interests, but the trial court found none sufficient. It enjoined enforcement of Amendment 2, and the Supreme Court of Colorado, in a second opinion, affirmed the ruling. 882 P.2d 1335 (1994) (*Evans II*). We granted certiorari, and now affirm the judgment, but on a rationale different from that adopted by the State Supreme Court.

II

The State's principal argument in defense of Amendment 2 is that it puts gays and lesbians in the same position as all other persons. So, the State says, the measure does no more than deny homosexuals special rights. This reading of the amendment's language is implausible. We rely not upon our own interpretation of the amendment but upon the authoritative construction of Colorado's Supreme Court.

The state court, deeming it unnecessary to determine the full extent of the amendment's reach, found it invalid even on a modest reading of its implications. The critical discussion of the amendment, set out in *Evans I,* is as follows:

> "The immediate objective of Amendment 2 is, at a minimum, to repeal existing statutes, regulations, ordinances, and policies of state and local entities that barred discrimination based on sexual orientation.
>
> "The 'ultimate effect' of Amendment 2 is to prohibit any governmental entity from adopting similar, or more protective statutes, regulations, ordinances, or policies in the future unless the state constitution is first amended to permit such measures."

Sweeping and comprehensive is the change in legal status effected by this law. So much is evident from the ordinances the Colorado Supreme Court declared would be void by operation of Amendment 2. Homosexuals, by state decree, are put in a solitary class with respect to transactions and relations in both the private and governmental spheres. The amendment withdraws from homosexuals, but no others, specific legal protection from the injuries caused by discrimination, and it forbids reinstatement of these laws and policies.

The change Amendment 2 works in the legal status of gays and lesbians in the private sphere is far reaching, both on its own terms and when considered in light of the structure and operation of modern anti-discrimination laws. That structure is well illustrated by contemporary statutes and ordinances prohibiting discrimination by providers of public accommodations. "At common law, innkeepers, smiths, and others who 'made profession of a public employment,' were prohibited from refusing, without good reason, to serve a customer." *Hurley v. Irish-American Gay, Lesbian and Bisexual Group of Boston, Inc.,* 515 U.S. 557, 571 (1995). The duty was a general one and did not specify protection for particular groups. The common-law rules, however, proved insufficient in many instances, and it was settled early that the Fourteenth Amendment did not give Congress a general power to prohibit discrimination in public accommodations, *Civil Rights Cases,* 109 U.S. 3, 25 (1883). In consequence, most States have chosen to counter discrimination by enacting detailed statutory schemes.

Colorado's state and municipal laws typify this emerging tradition of statutory protection and follow a consistent pattern. The laws first enumerate the persons or entities subject to a duty not to discriminate. The list goes well beyond the entities covered by the common law. The Boulder ordinance, for example, has a comprehensive definition of entities deemed places of "public accommodation." They include "any place of business engaged in any sales to the general public and any place that offers services, facilities, privileges, or advantages to the general public or that receives financial support through solicitation of the general public or through governmental subsidy of any kind." The Denver ordinance is of similar breadth, applying, for example, to hotels, restaurants, hospitals, dental clinics, theaters, banks, common carriers, travel and insurance agencies, and "shops and stores dealing with goods or services of any kind."

These statutes and ordinances also depart from the common law by enumerating the groups or persons within their ambit of protection. Enumeration is the essential device used to make the duty not to discriminate concrete and to provide guidance for those who must comply. In following this approach, Colorado's state and local governments have not limited antidiscrimination laws to groups that have so far been given the protection of heightened equal protection scrutiny under our cases. Rather, they set forth an extensive catalog of traits which cannot be the basis for discrimination, including age, military status, marital status, pregnancy, parenthood, custody of a minor child, political affiliation, physical or mental disability of an individual or of his or her associates—and, in recent times, sexual orientation.

Amendment 2 bars homosexuals from securing protection against the injuries that these public-accommodations laws address. That in itself is a severe consequence, but there is more. Amendment 2, in addition, nullifies specific legal protections for this targeted class in all transactions in housing, sale of real estate, insurance, health and welfare services, private education, and employment.

Not confined to the private sphere, Amendment 2 also operates to repeal and forbid all laws or policies providing specific protection for gays or lesbians from discrimination by every level of Colorado government. The State Supreme Court cited two examples of protections in the governmental sphere that are now rescinded and may not be reintroduced. The first is Colorado Executive Order D0035 (1990), which forbids employment discrimination against "'all state employees, classified and exempt' on the basis of sexual orientation." Also repealed, and now forbidden, are "various provisions prohibiting discrimination based on sexual orientation at state colleges." The repeal of these measures and the prohibition against their future reenactment demonstrate that Amendment 2 has the same force and effect in Colorado's governmental sector as it does elsewhere and that it applies to policies as well as ordinary legislation.

Amendment 2's reach may not be limited to specific laws passed for the benefit of gays and lesbians. It is a fair, if not necessary, inference from the broad language of the amendment that it deprives gays and lesbians even of the protection of general laws and policies that prohibit arbitrary discrimination in governmental and private settings. At some point in the systematic administration of these laws, an official must determine whether homosexuality is an arbitrary and, thus, forbidden basis for decision. Yet a decision to that effect would itself amount to a policy prohibiting discrimination on the basis of homosexuality, and so would appear to be no more valid under Amendment 2 than the specific prohibitions against discrimination the state court held invalid.

If this consequence follows from Amendment 2, as its broad language suggests, it would compound the constitutional difficulties the law creates. The state court did not decide whether the amendment has this effect, however, and neither need we. In the course of rejecting the argument that Amendment 2 is intended to conserve resources to fight discrimination against suspect classes, the Colorado Supreme Court made the limited observation that the amendment is not intended to affect many anti-discrimination laws protecting nonsuspect classes. In our view that does not resolve the issue. In any event, even if, as we doubt, homosexuals could find some safe harbor in laws of general application, we cannot accept the view that Amendment 2's prohibition on specific legal protections does no more than deprive homosexuals of special rights. To the contrary, the amendment imposes a special disability upon those persons alone. Homosexuals are forbidden the safeguards that others enjoy or may seek without constraint. They can obtain specific protection against discrimination only by enlisting the citizenry of Colorado to amend the State Constitution or perhaps, on the State's view, by trying to pass helpful laws of general applicability. This is so no matter how local or discrete the harm, no matter how public and widespread the injury. We find nothing special in the protections Amendment 2 withholds. These are protections taken for granted by most people either because they already have them or do not need them; these are protections against exclusion from an almost limitless number of transactions and endeavors that constitute ordinary civic life in a free society.

III

The Fourteenth Amendment's promise that no person shall be denied the equal protection of the laws must coexist with the practical necessity that most legislation classifies for one purpose or another, with resulting disadvantage to various groups or persons. We have attempted to reconcile the principle with the reality by stating that, if a law neither burdens a fundamental right nor targets a suspect class, we will uphold the legislative classification so long as it bears a rational relation to some legitimate end. See, *e.g., Heller v. Doe*, 509 U.S. 312, 319–320 (1993).

Amendment 2 fails, indeed defies, even this conventional inquiry. First, the amendment has the peculiar property of imposing a broad and undifferentiated disability on a single named group, an exceptional and, as we shall explain, invalid form of legislation. Second, its sheer breadth is so discontinuous with the reasons offered for it that the amendment seems inexplicable by anything but animus toward the class it affects; it lacks a rational relationship to legitimate state interests.

Taking the first point, even in the ordinary equal protection case calling for the most deferential of standards, we insist on knowing the relation between the classification adopted and the object to be attained. The search for the link between classification and objective gives substance to the Equal Protection Clause; it provides guidance and discipline for the legislature, which is entitled to know what sorts of laws it can pass; and it marks the limits of our own authority. In the ordinary case, a law will be sustained if it can be said to advance a legitimate government interest, even if the law seems unwise or works to the disadvantage of a particular group, or if the rationale for it seems tenuous. See *Williamson v. Lee Optical of Okla., Inc.*, 348 U.S. 483 (1955) (assumed health concerns justified law favoring optometrists over opticians); *Railway Express Agency, Inc. v. New York,* 336 U.S. 106 (1949) (potential traffic hazards justified exemption of vehicles advertising the owner's products from general advertising ban). The laws challenged in the cases just cited were narrow enough in scope and grounded in a sufficient factual context for us to ascertain some relation between the classification and the purpose it served. By requiring that the classification bear a rational relationship to an independent and legitimate legislative end, we ensure that classifications are not drawn for the purpose of disadvantaging the group burdened by the law.

Amendment 2 confounds this normal process of judicial review. It is at once too narrow and too broad. It identifies persons by a single trait and then denies them protection across the board. The resulting disqualification of a class of persons from the right to seek specific protection from the law is unprecedented in our jurisprudence. The absence of precedent for Amendment 2 is itself instructive; "[d]iscriminations of an unusual character especially suggest careful consideration to determine whether they are obnoxious to the constitutional provision." *Louisville Gas & Elec. Co. v. Coleman,* 277 U.S. 32, 37–38 (1928).

It is not within our constitutional tradition to enact laws of this sort. Central both to the idea of the rule of law and to our own Constitution's guarantee of equal protection is the principle that government and each of its parts remain open on impartial terms to all who seek its assistance. "'Equal protection of the laws is not achieved through indiscriminate imposition of inequalities.'" *Sweatt v. Painter,* 339 U.S. 629, 635 (1950) (quoting *Shelley v. Kraemer,* 334 U.S. 1, 22 (1948)). Respect for this principle explains why laws singling out a certain class of citizens for disfavored legal status or general hardships are rare. A law declaring that in general it shall be more difficult for one group of citizens than for all others to seek aid from the government is itself a denial of equal protection of the laws in the most literal sense. "The guaranty of 'equal protection of the laws is a pledge of the protection of equal laws.'" *Skinner v. Oklahoma ex rel. Williamson,* 316 U.S. 535, 541 (1942) (quoting *Yick Wo v. Hopkins,* 118 U.S. 356, 369 (1886)).

Davis v. Beason, 133 U.S. 333 (1890), not cited by the parties but relied upon by the dissent, is not evidence that Amendment 2 is within our constitutional tradition, and any reliance upon it as authority for sustaining the amendment is misplaced. In *Davis,* the Court approved an Idaho territorial statute denying Mormons, polygamists, and advocates of polygamy the right to vote and to hold office because, as the Court construed the statute, it "simply excludes from the privilege of voting, or of holding any office of honor, trust or profit, those who have been convicted of certain offences, and those who advocate a practical resistance to the laws of the Territory and justify and approve the commission of crimes forbidden by it." To the extent *Davis* held that persons advocating a certain practice may be denied the right to vote, it is no longer good law. *Brandenburg v. Ohio,* 395 U.S. 444 (1969) *(per curiam).* To the extent it held that the groups designated in the statute may be deprived of the right to vote because of their status, its ruling could not stand without surviving strict scrutiny, a most doubtful outcome. To the extent *Davis* held that a convicted felon may be denied the right to vote, its holding is not implicated by our decision and is unexceptionable. See *Richardson v. Ramirez,* 418 U.S. 24 (1974).

A second and related point is that laws of the kind now before us raise the inevitable inference that the disadvantage imposed is born of animosity toward the class of persons affected. "[I]f the constitutional conception of 'equal protection of the laws' means anything, it must at the very least mean that a bare . . . desire to harm a politically unpopular group cannot constitute a *legitimate* governmental interest." *Department of Agriculture v. Moreno,* 413 U.S. 528, 534 (1973). Even laws enacted for broad and ambitious purposes often can be explained by reference to legitimate public policies which justify the incidental disadvantages they impose on certain persons. Amendment 2, however, in making a general announcement that gays and lesbians shall not have any particular protections from the law, inflicts on them immediate, continuing, and real injuries that outrun and belie any legitimate justifications that may be claimed for it. We conclude that, in addition to the far-reaching deficiencies of Amendment 2 that we have noted, the principles it offends, in another sense, are conventional and venerable; a law must bear a rational relationship to a legitimate governmental purpose, and Amendment 2 does not.

The primary rationale the State offers for Amendment 2 is respect for other citizens' freedom of association, and in particular the liberties of landlords or employers who have personal or religious objections to homosexuality. Colorado also cites its interest in conserving resources to fight discrimination against other groups. The breadth of the amendment is so far removed from these particular justifications that we find it impossible to credit them. We cannot say that Amendment 2 is directed to any identifiable legitimate purpose or discrete objective. It is a status-based enactment divorced from any factual context from which we could discern a relationship to legitimate state interests; it is a classification of persons undertaken for its own sake, something the Equal Protection Clause does not permit. "[C]lass legislation . . . [is] obnoxious to the prohibitions of the Fourteenth Amendment. . . ." *Civil Rights Cases,* 109 U.S., at 24.

We must conclude that Amendment 2 classifies homosexuals not to further a proper legislative end but to make them unequal to everyone else. This Colorado cannot do. A State cannot so deem a class of persons a stranger to its laws. Amendment 2 violates the Equal Protection Clause. . . .

Justice Scalia, with whom The Chief Justice and Justice Thomas join, dissenting.

The Court has mistaken a Kulturkampf for a fit of spite. The constitutional amendment before us here is not the manifestation of a "'bare . . . desire to harm'" homosexuals, but is rather a modest attempt by seemingly tolerant Coloradans to preserve traditional sexual mores against the efforts of a politically powerful minority to revise those mores through use of the laws. That objective, and the means chosen to achieve it, are not only unimpeachable under any constitutional doctrine hitherto pronounced (hence the opinion's heavy reliance upon principles of righteousness rather than judicial holdings); they have been specifically approved by the Congress of the United States and by this Court.

In holding that homosexuality cannot be singled out for disfavorable treatment, the Court contradicts a decision, unchallenged here, pronounced only 10 years ago, see *Bowers v. Hardwick,* 478 U.S. 186 (1986), and places the prestige of this institution behind the proposition that opposition to homosexuality is as reprehensible as racial or religious bias. Whether it is or not is *precisely* the cultural debate that gave rise to the Colorado constitutional amendment (and to the preferential laws against which the amendment was directed). Since the Constitution of the United States says nothing about this subject, it is left to be resolved by normal democratic means, including the democratic adoption of provisions in state constitutions. This Court has no business imposing upon all Americans the resolution favored by the elite class from which the Members of this institution are selected, pronouncing that "animosity" toward homosexuality is evil. I vigorously dissent.

I

Let me first discuss Part II of the Court's opinion, its longest section, which is devoted to rejecting the State's arguments that Amendment 2 "puts gays and lesbians in the same position as all other persons," and "does no more than deny homosexuals special rights." The Court concludes that this reading of Amendment 2's language is "implausible" under the "authoritative construction" given Amendment 2 by the Supreme Court of Colorado.

In reaching this conclusion, the Court considers it unnecessary to decide the validity of the State's argument that Amendment 2 does not deprive homosexuals of the "protection [afforded by] general laws and policies that prohibit arbitrary discrimination in governmental and private settings." I agree that we need not resolve that dispute, because the Supreme Court of Colorado has resolved it for us. In the case below, the Colorado court stated:

> "[I]t is significant to note that Colorado law currently proscribes discrimination against persons who are not suspect classes, including discrimination based on age, § 24–34–402(1)(a), 10A C.R.S. (1994 Supp.); marital or family status, § 24–34–502(1)(a), 10A C.R.S. (1994 Supp.); veterans' status, § 28–3–506, 11B C.R.S. (1989); and for any legal, off-duty conduct such as smoking tobacco, § 24–34–402.5, 10A C. R.S. (1994 Supp.). *Of course Amendment 2 is not intended to have any effect on this legislation, but seeks only to prevent the adoption of antidiscrimination laws intended to protect gays, lesbians, and bisexuals.*" *Id.*, at 1346, n. 9 (emphasis added).

The Court utterly fails to distinguish this portion of the Colorado court's opinion. Colorado Rev. Stat. § 24–34–402.5 (Supp.1995), which this passage authoritatively declares *not* to be affected by Amendment 2, was respondents' primary example of a generally applicable law whose protections would be unavailable to homosexuals under Amendment 2. The clear import of the Colorado court's conclusion that it is not affected is that "general laws and policies that prohibit arbitrary discrimination" would continue to prohibit discrimination on the basis of homosexual conduct as well. This analysis, which is fully in accord with (indeed, follows inescapably from) the text of the constitutional provision, lays to rest such horribles, raised in the course of oral argument, as the prospect that assaults upon homosexuals could not be prosecuted. The amendment prohibits *special treatment* of homosexuals, and nothing more. It would not affect, for example, a requirement of state law that pensions be paid to all retiring state employees with a certain length of service; homosexual employees, as well as others, would be entitled to that benefit. But it would prevent the State or any municipality from making death-benefit payments to the "life partner" of a homosexual when it does not make such payments to the long-time roommate of a nonhomosexual employee. Or again, it does not affect the requirement of the State's general insurance laws that customers be afforded coverage without discrimination unrelated to anticipated risk. Thus, homosexuals could not be denied coverage, or charged a greater premium, with respect to auto collision insurance; but neither the State nor any municipality could require that distinctive health insurance risks associated with homosexuality (if there are any) be ignored.

Despite all of its hand wringing about the potential effect of Amendment 2 on general antidiscrimination laws, the Court's opinion ultimately does not dispute all this, but assumes it to be true. The only denial of equal treatment it contends homosexuals have suffered is this: They may not obtain *preferential* treatment without amending the State Constitution. That is to say, the principle underlying the Court's opinion is that one who is accorded equal treatment under the laws, but cannot as readily as others obtain *preferential* treatment under the laws, has been denied equal protection of the laws. If merely stating this alleged "equal protection" violation does not suffice to refute it, our constitutional jurisprudence has achieved terminal silliness.

The central thesis of the Court's reasoning is that any group is denied equal protection when, to obtain advantage (or, presumably, to avoid disadvantage), it must have recourse to a more general and hence more difficult level of political decisionmaking than others. The world has never heard of such a principle, which is why the Court's opinion is so long on emotive utterance and so short on relevant legal citation. And it seems to me most unlikely that any multilevel democracy can function under such a principle. For *whenever* a disadvantage is imposed, or conferral of a benefit is prohibited, at one of the higher levels of democratic decisionmaking (*i.e.*, by the state legislature rather than local government, or by the people at large in the state constitution rather than the legislature), the affected group has (under this theory) been denied equal protection. To take the simplest of examples, consider a state law prohibiting the award of municipal contracts to relatives of mayors or city councilmen. Once such a law is passed, the group composed of such relatives must, in order to get the benefit of city contracts, persuade the state legislature—unlike all other citizens, who need only persuade the municipality. It is ridiculous to consider this a denial of equal protection, which is why the Court's theory is unheard of.

The Court might reply that the example I have given is *not* a denial of equal protection only because the same "rational basis" (avoidance of corruption) which renders constitutional the *substantive discrimination* against relatives (*i.e.*, the fact that they alone cannot obtain city contracts) also automatically suffices to sustain what might be called the *electoral-procedural discrimination* against them (*i.e.*, the fact that they must go to the state level to get this changed). This is of course a perfectly reasonable response, and would explain why "electoral-procedural discrimination" has not hitherto been heard of: A law that is valid in its substance is automatically valid in its level of enactment. But the Court cannot afford to make this argument, for as I shall discuss next, there is no doubt of a rational basis for the substance of the prohibition at issue here. The Court's entire novel theory rests upon the proposition that there is something *special*—something that cannot be justified by normal "rational basis" analysis—in making a disadvantaged group (or a nonpreferred group) resort to a higher decisionmaking level. That proposition finds no support in law or logic.

II

I turn next to whether there was a legitimate rational basis for the substance of the constitutional amendment—for the prohibition of special protection for homosexuals.[1] It is unsurprising that the Court avoids discussion of this question, since the answer is so obviously yes. The case most relevant to the issue before us today is not even mentioned in the Court's opinion: In *Bowers v. Hardwick*, 478 U.S. 186 (1986), we held that the Constitution does not prohibit what virtually all States had done from the founding of the Republic until very recent years—making homosexual conduct a crime. That holding is unassailable, except by those who think that the Constitution changes to suit current fashions. But in any event it is a given in the present case: Respondents' briefs did not urge overruling *Bowers*, and at oral argument respondents' counsel expressly disavowed any intent to seek such overruling. If it is constitutionally permissible for a State to make homosexual conduct criminal, surely it is constitutionally permissible for a State to enact other laws merely *disfavoring* homosexual conduct. (As the Court of Appeals for the District of Columbia Circuit has aptly put it: "If the Court [in *Bowers*] was unwilling to object to state laws that criminalize the behavior that defines the class, it is hardly open . . . to conclude that state sponsored discrimination against the class is invidious. After all, there can hardly be more palpable discrimination against a class than making the conduct that defines the class criminal." *Padula v. Webster*, 822 F.2d 97, 103 (1987).) And *a fortiori* it is constitutionally permissible for a State to adopt

---

1. The Court evidently agrees that "rational basis"—the normal test for compliance with the Equal Protection Clause—is the governing standard. The trial court rejected respondents' argument that homosexuals constitute a "suspect" or "quasi-suspect" class, and respondents elected not to appeal that ruling to the Supreme Court of Colorado. And the Court implicitly rejects the Supreme Court of Colorado's holding that Amendment 2 infringes upon a "fundamental right" of "independently identifiable class[es]" to "participate equally in the political process."

a provision *not even* disfavoring homosexual conduct, but merely prohibiting all levels of state government from bestowing *special protections* upon homosexual conduct. Respondents (who, unlike the Court, cannot afford the luxury of ignoring inconvenient precedent) counter *Bowers* with the argument that a greater-includes-the-lesser rationale cannot justify Amendment 2's application to individuals who do not engage in homosexual acts, but are merely of homosexual "orientation." Some Courts of Appeals have concluded that, with respect to laws of this sort at least, that is a distinction without a difference....

But assuming that, in Amendment 2, a person of homosexual "orientation" is someone who does not engage in homosexual conduct but merely has a tendency or desire to do so, *Bowers* still suffices to establish a rational basis for the provision. If it is rational to criminalize the conduct, surely it is rational to deny special favor and protection to those with a self-avowed tendency or desire to engage in the conduct. Indeed, where criminal sanctions are not involved, homosexual "orientation" is an acceptable stand-in for homosexual conduct. A State "does not violate the Equal Protection Clause merely because the classifications made by its laws are imperfect," *Dandridge v. Williams,* 397 U.S. 471 (1970). Just as a policy barring the hiring of methadone users as transit employees does not violate equal protection simply because *some* methadone users pose no threat to passenger safety, see *New York City Transit Authority v. Beazer,* 440 U.S. 568 (1979), and just as a mandatory retirement age of 50 for police officers does not violate equal protection even though it prematurely ends the careers of many policemen over 50 who still have the capacity to do the job, see *Massachusetts Bd. of Retirement v. Murgia,* 427 U.S. 307 (1976) *(per curiam),* Amendment 2 is not constitutionally invalid simply because it could have been drawn more precisely so as to withdraw special antidiscrimination protections only from those of homosexual "orientation" who actually engage in homosexual conduct. As Justice KENNEDY wrote, when he was on the Court of Appeals, in a case involving discharge of homosexuals from the Navy: "Nearly any statute which classifies people may be irrational as applied in particular cases. Discharge of the particular plaintiffs before us would be rational, under minimal scrutiny, not because their particular cases present the dangers which justify Navy policy, but instead because the general policy of discharging all homosexuals is rational." *Beller v. Middendorf,* 632 F.2d 788, 808-809, n. 20 (C.A.9 1980) (citation omitted).

Moreover, even if the provision regarding homosexual "orientation" *were* invalid, respondents' challenge to Amendment 2—which is a facial challenge—must fail. "A facial challenge to a legislative Act is, of course, the most difficult challenge to mount successfully, since the challenger must establish that no set of circumstances exists under which the Act would be valid." *United States v. Salerno,* 481 U.S. 739, 745 (1987). It would not be enough for respondents to establish (if they could) that Amendment 2 is unconstitutional as applied to those of homosexual "orientation"; since, under *Bowers,* Amendment 2 is unquestionably constitutional as applied to those who engage in homosexual conduct, the facial challenge cannot succeed. Some individuals of homosexual "orientation" who do not engage in homosexual acts might successfully bring an as-applied challenge to Amendment 2, but so far as the record indicates, none of the respondents is such a person.

III

The foregoing suffices to establish what the Court's failure to cite any case remotely in point would lead one to suspect: No principle set forth in the Constitution, nor even any imagined by this Court in the past 200 years, prohibits what Colorado has done here. But the case for Colorado is much stronger than that. What it has done is not only unprohibited, but eminently reasonable, with close, congressionally approved precedent in earlier constitutional practice.

First, as to its eminent reasonableness. The Court's opinion contains grim, disapproving hints that Coloradans have been guilty of "animus" or "animosity" toward homosexuality, as though that has been established as un-American. Of course it is our moral heritage that one should not hate any human being or class of human beings. But I had thought that one could consider certain conduct reprehensible—murder, for example, or polygamy, or cruelty to animals—and could exhibit even "animus" toward such conduct. Surely that is the only sort of "animus" at issue here: moral disapproval of homosexual conduct, the same sort of moral disapproval that produced the centuries-old criminal laws that we held constitutional in *Bowers.* The Colorado amendment does not, to speak entirely precisely, prohibit giving favored status to people who are *homosexuals;* they can be favored for many reasons—for example, because they are senior citizens or members of racial minorities. But it prohibits giving them favored status *because of their homosexual conduct*—that is, it prohibits favored status *for homosexuality.*

But though Coloradans are, as I say, *entitled* to be hostile toward homosexual conduct, the fact is that the degree of hostility reflected by Amendment 2 is the smallest conceivable. The Court's portrayal of Coloradans as a society fallen victim to pointless, hate-filled "gay-bashing" is so false as to be comical. Colorado not only is one of the 25 States that have repealed their antisodomy laws, but was among the first to do so. But the society that eliminates criminal punishment for homosexual acts does not necessarily abandon the view that homosexuality is morally wrong and socially harmful; often, abolition simply reflects the view that enforcement of such criminal laws involves unseemly intrusion into the intimate lives of citizens.

There is a problem, however, which arises when criminal sanction of homosexuality is eliminated but moral and social disapprobation of homosexuality is meant to be retained. The Court cannot be unaware of that problem; it is evident in many cities of the country, and occasionally bubbles to the surface of the news, in heated political disputes over such matters as the introduction into local schools of books teaching that homosexuality is an optional and fully acceptable "alternative life style." The problem (a problem, that is, for those who wish to retain social disapprobation of homosexuality) is that, because those who engage in homosexual conduct tend to reside in disproportionate numbers in certain communities, and, of course, care about homosexual-rights issues much more ardently than the public at large, they possess political power much greater than their numbers, both locally and statewide. Quite understandably, they devote this political power to achieving not merely a grudging social toleration, but full social acceptance, of homosexuality.

By the time Coloradans were asked to vote on Amendment 2, their exposure to homosexuals' quest for social endorsement was not limited to newspaper accounts of happenings in places such as New York, Los Angeles, San Francisco, and Key West. Three Colorado cities—Aspen, Boulder, and Denver—had enacted ordinances that listed "sexual orientation" as an impermissible ground for discrimination, equating the moral disapproval of homosexual conduct with racial and religious bigotry. The phenomenon had even appeared statewide: The Governor of Colorado had signed an executive order pronouncing that "in the State of Colorado we recognize the diversity in our pluralistic society and strive to bring an end to discrimination in any form," and directing state agency-heads to "ensure non-discrimination" in hiring and promotion based on, among other things, "sexual orientation." I do not mean to be critical of these legislative successes; homosexuals are as entitled to use the legal system for reinforcement of their moral sentiments as is the rest of society. But they are subject to being countered by lawful, democratic countermeasures as well.

That is where Amendment 2 came in. It sought to counter both the geographic concentration and the disproportionate political power of homosexuals by (1) resolving the controversy at the statewide level, and (2) making the election a single-issue contest for both sides. It put directly, to all the citizens of the State, the question: Should homosexuality be given special protection? They answered no. The Court today asserts that this most democratic of procedures is unconstitutional. Lacking any cases to establish that facially absurd proposition, it simply asserts that it *must* be unconstitutional, because it has never happened before....

As I have noted above, this is proved false every time a state law prohibiting or disfavoring certain conduct is passed, because such a law prevents the adversely affected group—whether drug addicts, or smokers, or gun owners, or motorcyclists—from changing the policy thus established in "each of [the] parts" of the State. What the Court says is even demonstrably false at the constitutional level. The Eighteenth Amendment to the Federal Constitution, for example, deprived those who drank alcohol not only of the power to alter the policy of prohibition *locally* or through *state legislation,* but even of the power to alter it through *state constitutional amendment* or *federal legislation.* The Establishment Clause of the First Amendment prevents theocrats from having their way by converting their fellow citizens at the local, state, or federal statutory level; as does the Republican Form of Government Clause prevent monarchists.

But there is a much closer analogy, one that involves precisely the effort by the majority of citizens to preserve its view of sexual morality statewide, against the efforts of a geographically concentrated and politically powerful minority to undermine it. The Constitutions of the States of Arizona, Idaho, New Mexico, Oklahoma, and Utah *to this day* contain provisions stating that polygamy is "forever prohibited."

Polygamists, and those who have a polygamous "orientation," have been "singled out" by these provisions for much more severe treatment than merely denial of favored status; and that treatment can only be changed by achieving amendment of the state constitutions. The Court's disposition today suggests that these provisions are unconstitutional, and that polygamy must be permitted in these States on a state-legislated, or perhaps even local-option, basis—unless, of course, polygamists for some reason have fewer constitutional rights than homosexuals.

The United States Congress, by the way, *required* the inclusion of these antipolygamy provisions in the Constitutions of Arizona, New Mexico, Oklahoma, and Utah, as a condition of their admission to statehood. (For Arizona, New Mexico, and Utah, moreover, the Enabling Acts required that the antipolygamy provisions be "irrevocable without the consent of the United States and the people of said State"—so that not only were "each of [the] parts" of these States not "open on impartial terms" to polygamists, but even the States as a whole were not; polygamists would have to persuade the whole country to their way of thinking.) Idaho adopted the constitutional provision on its own, but the 51st Congress, which admitted Idaho into the Union, found its Constitution to be "republican in form *and . . . in conformity with the Constitution of the United States.*" Act of Admission of Idaho, 26 Stat. 215 (emphasis added). Thus, this "singling out" of the sexual practices of a single group for statewide, democratic vote—so utterly alien to our constitutional system, the Court would have us believe—has not only happened, but has received the explicit approval of the United States Congress.

I cannot say that this Court has explicitly approved any of these state constitutional provisions; but it has approved a territorial statutory provision that went even further, depriving polygamists of the ability even to achieve a constitutional amendment, by depriving them of the power to vote. In *Davis v. Beason,* 133 U.S. 333 (1890), Justice Field wrote for a unanimous Court:

> "In our judgment, § 501 of the Revised Statutes of Idaho Territory, which provides that 'no person . . . who is a bigamist or polygamist or who teaches, advises, counsels, or encourages any person or persons to become bigamists or polygamists, or to commit any other crime defined by law, or to enter into what is known as plural or celestial marriage, or who is a member of any order, organization or association which teaches, advises, counsels, or encourages its members or devotees or any other persons to commit the crime of bigamy or polygamy, or any other crime defined by law . . . is permitted to vote at any election, or to hold any position or office of honor, trust, or profit within this Territory,' *is not open to any constitutional or legal objection.*" *Id.,* at 346-347 (emphasis added).

To the extent, if any, that this opinion permits the imposition of adverse consequences upon mere abstract advocacy of polygamy, it has, of course, been overruled by later cases. See *Brandenburg v. Ohio,* 395 U.S. 444 (1969) *(per curiam).* But the proposition that polygamy can be criminalized, and those engaging in that crime deprived of the vote, remains good law. See *Richardson v. Ramirez,* 418 U.S. 24, 53

(1974). *Beason* rejected the argument that "such discrimination is a denial of the equal protection of the laws." Among the Justices joining in that rejection were the two whose views in other cases the Court today treats as equal protection lodestars—Justice Harlan, who was to proclaim in *Plessy v. Ferguson,* 163 U.S. 537, 559 (1896) (dissenting opinion), that the Constitution "neither knows nor tolerates classes among citizens," and Justice Bradley, who had earlier declared that "class legislation . . . [is] obnoxious to the prohibitions of the Fourteenth Amendment," *Civil Rights Cases,* 109 U.S. 3, 24 (1883).[3]

This Court cited *Beason* with approval as recently as 1993, in an opinion authored by the same Justice who writes for the Court today. . . . It remains to be explained how § 501 of the Idaho Revised Statutes was not an "impermissible targeting" of polygamists, but (the much more mild) Amendment 2 is an "impermissible targeting" of homosexuals. Has the Court concluded that the perceived social harm of polygamy is a "legitimate concern of government," and the perceived social harm of homosexuality is not?

IV

I strongly suspect that the answer to the last question is yes, which leads me to the last point I wish to make: The Court today, announcing that Amendment 2 "defies . . . conventional [constitutional] inquiry," and "confounds [the] normal process of judicial review," employs a constitutional theory heretofore unknown to frustrate Colorado's reasonable effort to preserve traditional American moral values. The Court's stern disapproval of "animosity" towards homosexuality might be compared with what an earlier Court (including the revered Justices Harlan and Bradley) said in *Murphy v. Ramsey,* 114 U.S. 15 (1885), rejecting a constitutional challenge to a United States statute that denied the franchise in federal territories to those who engaged in polygamous cohabitation:

---

3. The Court labors mightily to get around *Beason,* but cannot escape the central fact that this Court found the statute at issue—which went much further than Amendment 2, denying polygamists not merely special treatment but the right *to vote*—"not open to any constitutional or legal objection," rejecting the appellant's argument (much like the argument of respondents today) that the statute impermissibly "single[d] him out." The Court adopts my conclusions that (a) insofar as *Beason* permits the imposition of adverse consequences based upon mere advocacy, it has been overruled by subsequent cases, and (b) insofar as *Beason* holds that convicted felons may be denied the right to vote, it remains good law. To these conclusions, it adds something new: the claim that "[t]o the extent [*Beason*] held that the groups designated in the statute may be deprived of the right to vote because of their status, its ruling could not stand without surviving strict scrutiny, a most doubtful outcome." But if that is so, it is only because we have declared the right *to vote* to be a "fundamental political right," deprivation of which triggers strict scrutiny. Amendment 2, of course, does not deny the fundamental right to vote, and the Court rejects the Colorado court's view that there exists a fundamental right to participate in the political process. Strict scrutiny is thus not in play here. Finally, the Court's suggestion that § 501 of the Revised Statutes of Idaho, and Amendment 2, deny rights on account of "status" (rather than conduct) opens up a broader debate involving the significance of *Bowers* to this case, a debate which the Court is otherwise unwilling to join.

> "[C]ertainly no legislation can be supposed more wholesome and necessary in the founding of a free, self-governing commonwealth, fit to take rank as one of the co-ordinate States of the Union, than that which seeks to establish it on the basis of the idea of the family, as consisting in and springing from the union for life of one man and one woman in the holy estate of matrimony; the sure foundation of all that is stable and noble in our civilization; the best guaranty of that reverent morality which is the source of all beneficent progress in social and political improvement."

I would not myself indulge in such official praise for heterosexual monogamy, because I think it no business of the courts (as opposed to the political branches) to take sides in this culture war.

But the Court today has done so, not only by inventing a novel and extravagant constitutional doctrine to take the victory away from traditional forces, but even by verbally disparaging as bigotry adherence to traditional attitudes. To suggest, for example, that this constitutional amendment springs from nothing more than "'a bare . . . desire to harm a politically unpopular group,'" quoting *Department of Agriculture v. Moreno,* 413 U.S. 528, 534 (1973), is nothing short of insulting. (It is also nothing short of preposterous to call "politically unpopular" a group which enjoys enormous influence in American media and politics, and which, as the trial court here noted, though composing no more than 4% of the population had the support of 46% of the voters on Amendment 2.)

When the Court takes sides in the culture wars, it tends to be with the knights rather than the villeins—and more specifically with the Templars, reflecting the views and values of the lawyer class from which the Court's Members are drawn. How that class feels about homosexuality will be evident to anyone who wishes to interview job applicants at virtually any of the Nation's law schools. The interviewer may refuse to offer a job because the applicant is a Republican; because he is an adulterer; because he went to the wrong prep school or belongs to the wrong country club; because he eats snails; because he is a womanizer; because she wears real-animal fur; or even because he hates the Chicago Cubs. But if the interviewer should wish not to be an associate or partner of an applicant because he disapproves of the applicant's homosexuality, *then* he will have violated the pledge which the Association of American Law Schools requires all its member schools to exact from job interviewers: "assurance of the employer's willingness" to hire homosexuals. Bylaws of the Association of American Law Schools, Inc. § 6–4(b); Executive Committee Regulations of the Association of American Law Schools § 6.19, in 1995 Handbook, Association of American Law Schools. This law-school view of what "prejudices" must be stamped out may be contrasted with the more plebeian attitudes that apparently still prevail in the United States Congress, which has been unresponsive to repeated attempts to extend to homosexuals the protections of federal civil rights laws, see, *e.g.,* Employment Non-Discrimination Act of 1994, S. 2238, 103d Cong., 2d Sess. (1994); Civil Rights Amendments of 1975, H.R. 5452, 94th Cong., 1st Sess. (1975), and which took the pains to exclude them specifically from the Americans with Disabilities Act of 1990, see 42 U.S.C. § 12211(a) (1988 ed., Supp. V).

* * *

Today's opinion has no foundation in American constitutional law, and barely pretends to. The people of Colorado have adopted an entirely reasonable provision which does not even disfavor homosexuals in any substantive sense, but merely denies them preferential treatment. Amendment 2 is designed to prevent piecemeal deterioration of the sexual morality favored by a majority of Coloradans, and is not only an appropriate means to that legitimate end, but a means that Americans have employed before. Striking it down is an act, not of judicial judgment, but of political will. I dissent.

Problem 18-A: Affirmative Action for Sexual Minorities

Assume that a public medical school—concerned with its low percentage of openly gay, lesbian, bisexual, or transgender students (hereinafter, "sexual minorities")—decides to establish an affirmative action program designed to address this concern. The rationale for the program is a belief that sexual minorities have special health concerns that are often misunderstood or undervalued by doctors, and that increasing the number of sexual minorities who are doctors will alleviate this problem, both because these individuals will naturally be more attuned to these concerns when they serve patients from their respective groups, and because they will raise these issues in their medical school classes, thus exposing other future doctors to these concerns. Under the school's current admissions scheme, every applicant receives an index score ranging from 0–100 based on a composite of their grade-point average and MCAT score, with those with the highest index scores being admitted. Under the new affirmative action program, 15 points are added to the index score of applicants who are sexual minorities. David Preston, a heterosexual, cisgender male who applied for and was denied admission in the year following the adoption of the new policy, decides to bring an equal protection challenge to the constitutionality of the affirmative action policy.

Assess the likelihood that David will succeed on his equal protection challenge. How, if at all, would your answer be impacted if there were a recording of the faculty meeting at which the policy was adopted in which one faculty member stated—immediately prior to the vote—that "the best thing about this policy is that I will no longer have to stare into a sea of straight people each time I walk into a classroom," followed by a mix of laughter and applause by some members of the faculty?

Notes and Questions

1. As with most other cases in which the Court strikes down a law under the rational basis standard, the form of rational basis applied in *Romer* does not seem like

that applied in cases such as *Beach Communications*. Thus far, we have identified two types of "rational basis plus" review: transitional (*e.g.*, *Reed* and *Weber*) and fleeting (*e.g.*, *Moreno* and *Cleburne*). Which of these forms of rational basis plus review seems to be at play here? Does Justice Kennedy suggest an answer to that question in *Romer*?

2. Justice Scalia is quick to limit the reach of *Romer*, making clear that the majority only applied rational basis scrutiny, and did not hold that sexual orientation is a suspect or quasi-suspect classification. Does the Court in fact foreclose the possibility of heightened scrutiny? Would the *Frontiero* factors result in a conclusion that heightened scrutiny is appropriate for discrimination on the basis of sexual orientation?

Although neither the Colorado Supreme Court nor the U.S. Supreme Court considered this issue in *Romer*, the state trial court considered and rejected a claim that sexual orientation is a suspect or quasi-suspect classification. While acknowledging that there is a history of discrimination against gays and lesbians, the trial court concluded that there was inconclusive evidence of whether sexual orientation is immutable. As for political powerlessness, the trial court noted that gays and lesbians, while representing only 4 percent of the population, were able to persuade 46 percent of Colorado voters to reject Amendment 2, suggesting that they have significant political power relative to their size. Did the trial court consider all of the *Frontiero* factors, and did it apply the ones it considered correctly? Could it have instead treated the sexual orientation discrimination in this case as a subset of sex discrimination and applied intermediate scrutiny?

3. As the majority notes in *Romer*, the Colorado Supreme Court relied on the U.S. Supreme Court's decisions treating voting as a fundamental right, coupled with its cases involving discriminatory restructuring of governmental decisionmaking, to conclude that strict scrutiny applied to Amendment 2. The case law treating voting as a fundamental right under the equal protection clause was examined in Chapter 8. The cases involving discriminatory restructuring of governmental decisionmaking—all of which arose in the context of race—were considered in Chapter 10. To what extent is reliance on the latter set of cases undermined by the Court's subsequent post-*Romer* decision in *Schuette*? In her dissenting opinion in *Schuette*, Justice Sotomayor contended that *Romer* was implicitly a case about discriminatory restructuring of governmental decisionmaking:

> Although the Court did not apply the political-process doctrine in *Romer*, the case resonates with the principles undergirding the political-process doctrine. The Court rejected an attempt by the majority to transfer decisionmaking authority from localities (where the targeted minority group could influence the process) to state government (where it had less ability to participate effectively).

Schuette v. Coalition to Defend Affirmative Action, 572 U.S. 291, 371–72 (2014) (Sotomayor, J., dissenting). Do you agree?

4. Is it possible that the *Romer* Court is neither applying transitional nor fleeting rational basis plus review, but is instead ushering in a new era of equal protection review in which the Court applies a single standard of "rational basis," akin to that advocated by Justice Stevens in *Cleburne*? In other words, is it possible that *Romer* kicks off a new method for assessing *all* Equal Protection Clause claims?

In thinking about this possibility, consider this: the Court has not identified *any* new classifications subject to heightened scrutiny since it recognized intermediate scrutiny for sex and legitimacy classifications. Moreover, as indicated earlier in this chapter, the *Frontiero* factors are in significant tension with the *Adarand* approach to equal protection. Might this new method be a way of resolving that tension?

5. Separate and apart from methodological concerns, why might the Court be reluctant in this case to declare sexual orientation a classification entitled to heightened equal protection scrutiny? What consequences would such a holding likely that have?

6. In his dissenting opinion, Justice Scalia rejects the idea of drawing a distinction—for equal protection purposes—between homosexual conduct on the one hand and homosexual orientation or status on the other. Is this thus a tacit acceptance of the idea, raised in *Hernandez*, that something can be so closely correlated with a class that discrimination on that basis is tantamount to discrimination against that class? To what extent, if any, does that help to resolve the question whether bans on same-sex marriage, sexual intimacy, and adoption are a form of sexual orientation discrimination?

7. What counts as unconstitutional "animus" under *Romer*? After all, isn't Justice Scalia correct to note that numerous types of criminal laws are grounded in a form of animus towards certain types of individuals, namely those who commit heinous crimes such as murder or child molestation? How is a court to determine what forms of animus are permissible and what forms are not?

8. Recall that in *Cleburne*, Justice Marshall wrote separately to express his concern that the Court applying "second order" rational basis review leads to inconsistency in lower courts. That prediction came true in the context of sexual orientation discrimination, with some post-*Romer* lower court decisions interpreting the decision broadly to strike down other types of discriminatory legislation, *see, e.g.*, *Brewer v. Diaz*, 656 F.3d 1008 (9th Cir. 2011), and others interpreting the decision narrowly to uphold similar measures, *see e.g.*, *Equality Foundation of Greater Cincinnati, Inc. v. City of Cincinnati*, 128 F.3d 289 (6th Cir. 1997),

B. *Bowers* Reconsidered

In upholding Georgia's law criminalizing sodomy, the *Bowers* Court considered only a substantive due process challenge to the law, and applied traditional rational basis scrutiny. Under that standard, it found moral disapproval of homosexuality a sufficient justification for the law. Although there was a colorable equal protection claim in that case—the statute, while written in general terms, was in practice enforced only against same-sex, not opposite-sex, couples—the Court did not address that claim. Moreover, even had it done so, it is not clear that it would have resulted in a different outcome: no decision had established heightened scrutiny for sexual orientation discrimination, and arguably the same moral disapproval that satisfied rational basis due process review would satisfy rational basis equal protection review.

In *Lawrence v. Texas*, the case that follows, the Court considers a challenge to Texas's law criminalizing sodomy seventeen years after its decision in *Bowers*. In terms, the Texas law applied only to same-sex, not opposite-sex, sodomy. Moreover, unlike in *Bowers*, the challengers in *Lawrence* were in fact prosecuted for violating the law. *Lawrence* thus not only presented a more clear-cut equal protection claim than was present in *Bowers*, but also gave the Court a chance to reconsider its due process holding in *Bowers* in light of subsequent developments in the Court's substantive due process line of cases.

Lawrence v. Texas

539 U.S. 558 (2003)

Justice Kennedy delivered the opinion of the Court.

Liberty protects the person from unwarranted government intrusions into a dwelling or other private places. In our tradition the State is not omnipresent in the home. And there are other spheres of our lives and existence, outside the home, where the State should not be a dominant presence. Freedom extends beyond spatial bounds. Liberty presumes an autonomy of self that includes freedom of thought, belief, expression, and certain intimate conduct. The instant case involves liberty of the person both in its spatial and in its more transcendent dimensions.

The question before the Court is the validity of a Texas statute making it a crime for two persons of the same sex to engage in certain intimate sexual conduct.

In Houston, Texas, officers of the Harris County Police Department were dispatched to a private residence in response to a reported weapons disturbance. They entered an apartment where one of the petitioners, John Geddes Lawrence, resided. The right of the police to enter does not seem to have been questioned. The officers observed Lawrence and another man, Tyron Garner, engaging in a sexual act. The two petitioners were arrested, held in custody overnight, and charged and convicted before a Justice of the Peace.

The complaints described their crime as "deviate sexual intercourse, namely anal sex, with a member of the same sex (man)." The applicable state law is Tex. Penal Code Ann. § 21.06(a) (2003). It provides: "A person commits an offense if he engages in deviate sexual intercourse with another individual of the same sex." The statute defines "[d]eviate sexual intercourse" as follows:

> "(A) any contact between any part of the genitals of one person and the mouth or anus of another person; or

> "(B) the penetration of the genitals or the anus of another person with an object." § 21.01(1).

The petitioners exercised their right to a trial *de novo* in Harris County Criminal Court. They challenged the statute as a violation of the Equal Protection Clause of the Fourteenth Amendment and of a like provision of the Texas Constitution. Tex. Const., Art. 1, § 3a. Those contentions were rejected. The petitioners, having entered a plea of *nolo contendere,* were each fined $200 and assessed court costs of $141.25.

The Court of Appeals for the Texas Fourteenth District considered the petitioners' federal constitutional arguments under both the Equal Protection and Due Process Clauses of the Fourteenth Amendment. After hearing the case en banc the court, in a divided opinion, rejected the constitutional arguments and affirmed the convictions. The majority opinion indicates that the Court of Appeals considered our decision in *Bowers v. Hardwick,* 478 U.S. 186 (1986), to be controlling on the federal due process aspect of the case. *Bowers* then being authoritative, this was proper.

We granted certiorari to consider three questions:

> 1. Whether petitioners' criminal convictions under the Texas 'Homosexual Conduct' law—which criminalizes sexual intimacy by same-sex couples, but not identical behavior by different-sex couples—violate the Fourteenth Amendment guarantee of equal protection of the laws.
>
> 2. Whether petitioners' criminal convictions for adult consensual sexual intimacy in the home violate their vital interests in liberty and privacy protected by the Due Process Clause of the Fourteenth Amendment.
>
> 3. Whether *Bowers v. Hardwick, supra,* should be overruled. See Pet. for Cert. i.

The petitioners were adults at the time of the alleged offense. Their conduct was in private and consensual.

We conclude the case should be resolved by determining whether the petitioners were free as adults to engage in the private conduct in the exercise of their liberty under the Due Process Clause of the Fourteenth Amendment to the Constitution. For this inquiry we deem it necessary to reconsider the Court's holding in *Bowers.*

There are broad statements of the substantive reach of liberty under the Due Process Clause in earlier cases, including *Pierce v. Society of Sisters,* 268 U.S. 510 (1925), and *Meyer v. Nebraska,* 262 U.S. 390 (1923); but the most pertinent beginning point is our decision in *Griswold v. Connecticut,* 381 U.S. 479 (1965).

In *Griswold* the Court invalidated a state law prohibiting the use of drugs or devices of contraception and counseling or aiding and abetting the use of contraceptives. The Court described the protected interest as a right to privacy and placed emphasis on the marriage relation and the protected space of the marital bedroom.

After *Griswold* it was established that the right to make certain decisions regarding sexual conduct extends beyond the marital relationship. In *Eisenstadt v. Baird,* 405 U.S. 438 (1972), the Court invalidated a law prohibiting the distribution of contraceptives to unmarried persons. The case was decided under the Equal Protection Clause; but with respect to unmarried persons, the Court went on to state the fundamental proposition that the law impaired the exercise of their personal rights. It quoted from the statement of the Court of Appeals finding the law to be in conflict with fundamental human rights, and it followed with this statement of its own:

> "It is true that in *Griswold* the right of privacy in question inhered in the marital relationship.... If the right of privacy means anything, it is the right of the *individual,* married or single, to be free from unwarranted governmental intrusion into matters so fundamentally affecting a person as the decision whether to bear or beget a child."

The opinions in *Griswold* and *Eisenstadt* were part of the background for the decision in *Roe v. Wade,* 410 U.S. 113 (1973) .... The Court cited cases that protect spatial freedom and cases that go well beyond it. *Roe* recognized the right of a woman to make certain fundamental decisions affecting her destiny and confirmed once more that the protection of liberty under the Due Process Clause has a substantive dimension of fundamental significance in defining the rights of the person.

In *Carey v. Population Services Int'l,* 431 U.S. 678 (1977), the Court confronted a New York law forbidding sale or distribution of contraceptive devices to persons under 16 years of age. Although there was no single opinion for the Court, the law was invalidated. Both *Eisenstadt* and *Carey,* as well as the holding and rationale in *Roe,* confirmed that the reasoning of *Griswold* could not be confined to the protection of rights of married adults. This was the state of the law with respect to some of the most relevant cases when the Court considered *Bowers v. Hardwick.*

The facts in *Bowers* had some similarities to the instant case.... One difference between the two cases is that the Georgia statute prohibited the conduct whether or not the participants were of the same sex, while the Texas statute, as we have seen, applies only to participants of the same sex....

The Court began its substantive discussion in *Bowers* as follows: "The issue presented is whether the Federal Constitution confers a fundamental right upon homosexuals to engage in sodomy and hence invalidates the laws of the many States that still make such conduct illegal and have done so for a very long time." That statement, we now conclude, discloses the Court's own failure to appreciate the extent of the liberty at stake. To say that the issue in *Bowers* was simply the right to engage in certain sexual conduct demeans the claim the individual put forward, just as it would demean a married couple were it to be said marriage is simply about the right to have sexual intercourse. The laws involved in *Bowers* and here are, to be sure, statutes that purport to do no more than prohibit a particular sexual act. Their penalties and purposes, though, have more far-reaching consequences, touching upon the most private human conduct, sexual behavior, and in the most private of places, the home. The statutes do seek to control a personal relationship that, whether or not entitled to formal recognition in the law, is within the liberty of persons to choose without being punished as criminals.

This, as a general rule, should counsel against attempts by the State, or a court, to define the meaning of the relationship or to set its boundaries absent injury to a person or abuse of an institution the law protects. It suffices for us to acknowledge that adults may choose to enter upon this relationship in the confines of their homes and their own private lives and still retain their dignity as free persons. When sexuality finds overt expression in intimate conduct with another person, the conduct can be but one element in a personal bond that is more enduring. The liberty protected by the Constitution allows homosexual persons the right to make this choice.

Having misapprehended the claim of liberty there presented to it, and thus stating the claim to be whether there is a fundamental right to engage in consensual sodomy, the *Bowers* Court said: "Proscriptions against that conduct have ancient roots." In academic writings, and in many of the scholarly *amicus* briefs filed to assist the Court in this case, there are fundamental criticisms of the historical premises relied upon by the majority and concurring opinions in *Bowers*. We need not enter this debate in the attempt to reach a definitive historical judgment, but the following considerations counsel against adopting the definitive conclusions upon which *Bowers* placed such reliance.

At the outset it should be noted that there is no longstanding history in this country of laws directed at homosexual conduct as a distinct matter. Beginning in colonial times there were prohibitions of sodomy derived from the English criminal laws passed in the first instance by the Reformation Parliament of 1533. The English prohibition was understood to include relations between men and women as well as relations between men and men. Nineteenth-century commentators similarly read American sodomy, buggery, and crime-against-nature statutes as criminalizing certain relations between men and women and between men and men. The absence of legal prohibitions focusing on homosexual conduct may be explained in part by noting that according to some scholars the concept of the homosexual as a distinct category of person did not emerge until the late 19th century. Thus early American sodomy laws were not directed at homosexuals as such but instead sought to prohibit nonprocreative sexual activity more generally. This does not suggest approval of homosexual conduct. It does tend to show that this particular form of conduct was not thought of as a separate category from like conduct between heterosexual persons.

Laws prohibiting sodomy do not seem to have been enforced against consenting adults acting in private. A substantial number of sodomy prosecutions and convictions for which there are surviving records were for predatory acts against those who could not or did not consent, as in the case of a minor or the victim of an assault. As to these, one purpose for the prohibitions was to ensure there would be no lack of coverage if a predator committed a sexual assault that did not constitute rape as defined by the criminal law. Thus the model sodomy indictments presented in a 19th-century treatise, addressed the predatory acts of an adult man against a minor girl or minor boy. Instead of targeting relations between consenting adults in private, 19th-century sodomy prosecutions typically involved relations between men and minor girls or minor boys, relations between adults involving force, relations between adults implicating disparity in status, or relations between men and animals.

To the extent that there were any prosecutions for the acts in question, 19th-century evidence rules imposed a burden that would make a conviction more difficult to obtain even taking into account the problems always inherent in prosecuting consensual acts committed in private. Under then-prevailing standards, a man could not be convicted of sodomy based upon testimony of a consenting partner, because the partner was considered an accomplice. A partner's testimony, however, was admissible if he or she had not consented to the act or was a minor, and therefore incapable of consent. The rule may explain in part the infrequency of these prosecutions. In all events that infrequency makes it difficult to say that society approved of a rigorous and systematic punishment of the consensual acts committed in private and by adults. The longstanding criminal prohibition of homosexual sodomy upon which the *Bowers* decision placed such reliance is as consistent with a general condemnation of nonprocreative sex as it is with an established tradition of prosecuting acts because of their homosexual character.

The policy of punishing consenting adults for private acts was not much discussed in the early legal literature. We can infer that one reason for this was the very private nature of the conduct. Despite the absence of prosecutions, there may have been periods in which there was public criticism of homosexuals as such and an insistence that the criminal laws be enforced to discourage their practices. But far from possessing "ancient roots," American laws targeting same-sex couples did not develop until the last third of the 20th century. The reported decisions concerning the prosecution of consensual, homosexual sodomy between adults for the years 1880–1995 are not always clear in the details, but a significant number involved conduct in a public place.

It was not until the 1970's that any State singled out same-sex relations for criminal prosecution, and only nine States have done so. Post-*Bowers* even some of these States did not adhere to the policy of suppressing homosexual conduct. Over the course of the last decades, States with same-sex prohibitions have moved toward abolishing them.

In summary, the historical grounds relied upon in *Bowers* are more complex than the majority opinion and the concurring opinion by Chief Justice Burger indicate. Their historical premises are not without doubt and, at the very least, are overstated.

It must be acknowledged, of course, that the Court in *Bowers* was making the broader point that for centuries there have been powerful voices to condemn homosexual conduct as immoral. The condemnation has been shaped by religious beliefs, conceptions of right and acceptable behavior, and respect for the traditional family. For many persons these are not trivial concerns but profound and deep convictions accepted as ethical and moral principles to which they aspire and which thus determine the course of their lives. These considerations do not answer the question before us, however. The issue is whether the majority may use the power of the State to enforce these views on the whole society through operation of the criminal law. "Our obligation is to define the liberty of all, not to mandate our own moral code." *Planned Parenthood of Southeastern Pa. v. Casey*, 505 U.S. 833, 850 (1992).

Chief Justice Burger joined the opinion for the Court in *Bowers* and further explained his views as follows: "Decisions of individuals relating to homosexual conduct have been subject to state intervention throughout the history of Western civilization. Condemnation of those practices is firmly rooted in Judeao-Christian moral and ethical standards." As with Justice White's assumptions about history, scholarship casts some doubt on the sweeping nature of the statement by Chief Justice Burger as it pertains to private homosexual conduct between consenting adults. In all events we think that our laws and traditions in the past half century are of most relevance here. These references show an emerging awareness that liberty gives substantial protection to adult persons in deciding how to conduct their private lives in matters pertaining to sex. "[H]istory and tradition are the starting point but not in all cases the ending point of the substantive due process inquiry." *County of Sacramento v. Lewis*, 523 U.S. 833, 857 (1998) (Kennedy, J., concurring).

This emerging recognition should have been apparent when *Bowers* was decided. In 1955 the American Law Institute promulgated the Model Penal Code and made clear that it did not recommend or provide for "criminal penalties for consensual sexual relations conducted in private." It justified its decision on three grounds: (1) The prohibitions undermined respect for the law by penalizing conduct many people engaged in; (2) the statutes regulated private conduct not harmful to others; and (3) the laws were arbitrarily enforced and thus invited the danger of blackmail. In 1961 Illinois changed its laws to conform to the Model Penal Code. Other States soon followed.

In *Bowers* the Court referred to the fact that before 1961 all 50 States had outlawed sodomy, and that at the time of the Court's decision 24 States and the District of Columbia had sodomy laws. Justice Powell pointed out that these prohibitions often were being ignored, however. Georgia, for instance, had not sought to enforce its law for decades.

The sweeping references by Chief Justice Burger to the history of Western civilization and to Judeo-Christian moral and ethical standards did not take account of other authorities pointing in an opposite direction. A committee advising the British Parliament recommended in 1957 repeal of laws punishing homosexual conduct. Parliament enacted the substance of those recommendations 10 years later.

Of even more importance, almost five years before *Bowers* was decided the European Court of Human Rights considered a case with parallels to *Bowers* and to today's case. An adult male resident in Northern Ireland alleged he was a practicing homosexual who desired to engage in consensual homosexual conduct. The laws of Northern Ireland forbade him that right. He alleged that he had been questioned, his home had been searched, and he feared criminal prosecution. The court held that the laws proscribing the conduct were invalid under the European Convention on Human Rights. *Dudgeon v. United Kingdom,* 45 Eur. Ct. H.R. (1981) & ¶ 52. Authoritative in all countries that are members of the Council of Europe (21 nations then, 45 nations now), the decision is at odds with the premise in *Bowers* that the claim put forward was insubstantial in our Western civilization.

In our own constitutional system the deficiencies in *Bowers* became even more apparent in the years following its announcement. The 25 States with laws prohibiting the relevant conduct referenced in the *Bowers* decision are reduced now to 13, of which 4 enforce their laws only against homosexual conduct. In those States where sodomy is still proscribed, whether for same-sex or heterosexual conduct, there is a pattern of nonenforcement with respect to consenting adults acting in private. The State of Texas admitted in 1994 that as of that date it had not prosecuted anyone under those circumstances.

Two principal cases decided after *Bowers* cast its holding into even more doubt. In *Planned Parenthood of Southeastern Pa. v. Casey,* 505 U.S. 833 (1992), the Court reaffirmed the substantive force of the liberty protected by the Due Process Clause. The *Casey* decision again confirmed that our laws and tradition afford constitutional protection to personal decisions relating to marriage, procreation, contraception, family relationships, child rearing, and education. In explaining the respect the Constitution demands for the autonomy of the person in making these choices, we stated as follows:

> "These matters, involving the most intimate and personal choices a person may make in a lifetime, choices central to personal dignity and autonomy, are central to the liberty protected by the Fourteenth Amendment. At the heart of liberty is the right to define one's own concept of existence, of meaning, of the universe, and of the mystery of human life. Beliefs about these matters could not define the attributes of personhood were they formed under compulsion of the State."

Persons in a homosexual relationship may seek autonomy for these purposes, just as heterosexual persons do. The decision in *Bowers* would deny them this right.

The second post-*Bowers* case of principal relevance is *Romer v. Evans,* 517 U.S. 620 (1996). There the Court struck down class-based legislation directed at homosexuals as a violation of the Equal Protection Clause. *Romer* invalidated an amendment to Colorado's Constitution which named as a solitary class persons who were homosexuals, lesbians, or bisexual either by "orientation, conduct, practices or relationships," and deprived them of protection under state antidiscrimination laws. We concluded that the provision was "born of animosity toward the class of persons affected" and further that it had no rational relation to a legitimate governmental purpose.

As an alternative argument in this case, counsel for the petitioners and some *amici* contend that *Romer* provides the basis for declaring the Texas statute invalid under the Equal Protection Clause. That is a tenable argument, but we conclude the instant case requires us to address whether *Bowers* itself has continuing validity. Were we to hold the statute invalid under the Equal Protection Clause some might question whether a prohibition would be valid if drawn differently, say, to prohibit the conduct both between same-sex and different-sex participants.

Equality of treatment and the due process right to demand respect for conduct protected by the substantive guarantee of liberty are linked in important respects, and a decision on the latter point advances both interests. If protected conduct is made criminal and the law which does so remains unexamined for its substantive validity, its stigma might remain even if it were not enforceable as drawn for equal protection reasons. When homosexual conduct is made criminal by the law of the State, that declaration in and of itself is an invitation to subject homosexual persons to discrimination both in the public and in the private spheres. The central holding of *Bowers* has been brought in question by this case, and it should be addressed. Its continuance as precedent demeans the lives of homosexual persons.

The stigma this criminal statute imposes, moreover, is not trivial. The offense, to be sure, is but a class C misdemeanor, a minor offense in the Texas legal system. Still, it remains a criminal offense with all that imports for the dignity of the persons charged. The petitioners will bear on their record the history of their criminal convictions. . . . We are advised that if Texas convicted an adult for private, consensual homosexual conduct under the statute here in question the convicted person would come within the registration laws of at least four States were he or she to be subject to their jurisdiction. This underscores the consequential nature of the punishment and the state-sponsored condemnation attendant to the criminal prohibition. Furthermore, the Texas criminal conviction carries with it the other collateral consequences always following a conviction, such as notations on job application forms, to mention but one example.

The foundations of *Bowers* have sustained serious erosion from our recent decisions in *Casey* and *Romer.* When our precedent has been thus weakened, criticism from other sources is of greater significance. In the United States criticism of *Bowers* has been substantial and continuing, disapproving of its reasoning in all respects, not just as to its historical assumptions. The courts of five different States have declined to follow it in interpreting provisions in their own state constitutions parallel to the Due Process Clause of the Fourteenth Amendment.

To the extent *Bowers* relied on values we share with a wider civilization, it should be noted that the reasoning and holding in *Bowers* have been rejected elsewhere. The European Court of Human Rights has followed not *Bowers* but its own decision in *Dudgeon v. United Kingdom.* Other nations, too, have taken action consistent with an affirmation of the protected right of homosexual adults to engage in intimate, consensual conduct. The right the petitioners seek in this case has been accepted as an integral part of human freedom in many other countries. There has been no showing that in this country the governmental interest in circumscribing personal choice is somehow more legitimate or urgent.

The doctrine of *stare decisis* is essential to the respect accorded to the judgments of the Court and to the stability of the law. It is not, however, an inexorable command. In *Casey* we noted that when a court is asked to overrule a precedent recognizing a constitutional liberty interest, individual or societal reliance on the existence of that liberty cautions with particular strength against reversing course. 505 U.S., at 855-856; see also *id.*, at 844 ("Liberty finds no refuge in a jurisprudence of doubt"). The holding in *Bowers,* however, has not induced detrimental reliance comparable to some instances where recognized individual rights are involved. Indeed, there has been no individual or societal reliance on *Bowers* of the sort that could counsel against overturning its holding once there are compelling reasons to do so. *Bowers* itself causes uncertainty, for the precedents before and after its issuance contradict its central holding.

The rationale of *Bowers* does not withstand careful analysis. In his dissenting opinion in Bowers JUSTICE STEVENS came to these conclusions:

> "Our prior cases make two propositions abundantly clear. First, the fact that the governing majority in a State has traditionally viewed a particular practice as immoral is not a sufficient reason for upholding a law prohibiting the practice; neither history nor tradition could save a law prohibiting miscegenation from constitutional attack. Second, individual decisions by married persons, concerning the intimacies of their physical relationship, even when not intended to produce offspring, are a form of 'liberty' protected by the Due Process Clause of the Fourteenth Amendment. Moreover, this protection extends to intimate choices by unmarried as well as married persons."

JUSTICE STEVENS' analysis, in our view, should have been controlling in *Bowers* and should control here.

Bowers was not correct when it was decided, and it is not correct today. It ought not to remain binding precedent. *Bowers v. Hardwick* should be and now is overruled.

The present case does not involve minors. It does not involve persons who might be injured or coerced or who are situated in relationships where consent might not easily be refused. It does not involve public conduct or prostitution. It does not involve whether the government must give formal recognition to any relationship that homosexual persons seek to enter. The case does involve two adults who, with full and mutual consent from each other, engaged in sexual practices common to a homosexual lifestyle. The petitioners are entitled to respect for their private lives. The State cannot demean their existence or control their destiny by making their private sexual conduct a crime. Their right to liberty under the Due Process Clause gives them the full right to engage in their conduct without intervention of the government. "It is a promise of the Constitution that there is a realm of personal liberty which the government may not enter." The Texas statute furthers no legitimate state interest which can justify its intrusion into the personal and private life of the individual.

Had those who drew and ratified the Due Process Clauses of the Fifth Amendment or the Fourteenth Amendment known the components of liberty in its manifold possibilities, they might have been more specific. They did not presume to have this insight. They knew times can blind us to certain truths and later generations can see that laws once thought necessary and proper in fact serve only to oppress. As the Constitution endures, persons in every generation can invoke its principles in their own search for greater freedom. . . .

Justice O'Connor, concurring in the judgment.

The Court today overrules *Bowers v. Hardwick,* 478 U.S. 186 (1986). I joined *Bowers,* and do not join the Court in overruling it. Nevertheless, I agree with the Court that Texas' statute banning same-sex sodomy is unconstitutional. Rather than relying on the substantive component of the Fourteenth Amendment's Due Process Clause, as the Court does, I base my conclusion on the Fourteenth Amendment's Equal Protection Clause.

The Equal Protection Clause of the Fourteenth Amendment "is essentially a direction that all persons similarly situated should be treated alike." Under our rational basis standard of review, "legislation is presumed to be valid and will be sustained if the classification drawn by the statute is rationally related to a legitimate state interest."

Laws such as economic or tax legislation that are scrutinized under rational basis review normally pass constitutional muster, since "the Constitution presumes that even improvident decisions will eventually be rectified by the democratic processes." We have consistently held, however, that some objectives, such as "a bare . . . desire to harm a politically unpopular group," are not legitimate state interests. *Department of Agriculture v. Moreno, supra,* at 534. See also *Cleburne v. Cleburne Living Center, supra,* at 446-447; *Romer v. Evans, supra,* at 632. When a law exhibits such a desire to harm a politically unpopular group, we have applied a more searching form of rational basis review to strike down such laws under the Equal Protection Clause.

We have been most likely to apply rational basis review to hold a law unconstitutional under the Equal Protection Clause where, as here, the challenged legislation inhibits personal relationships. In *Department of Agriculture v. Moreno,* for example, we held that a law preventing those households containing an individual unrelated to any other member of the household from receiving food stamps violated equal protection because the purpose of the law was to "'discriminate against hippies.'" The asserted governmental interest in preventing food stamp fraud was not deemed sufficient to satisfy rational basis review. In *Eisenstadt v. Baird,* 405 U.S. 438, 447–455 (1972), we refused to sanction a law that discriminated between married and unmarried persons by prohibiting the distribution of contraceptives to single persons. Likewise, in *Cleburne v. Cleburne Living Center,* we held that it was irrational for a State to require a home for the mentally disabled to obtain a special use permit when other residences—like fraternity houses and apartment buildings—did not have to obtain such a permit. And in *Romer v. Evans,* we disallowed a state statute that "impos[ed] a broad and undifferentiated disability on a single named group"—specifically, homosexuals.

The statute at issue here makes sodomy a crime only if a person "engages in deviate sexual intercourse with another individual of the same sex." Tex. Penal Code Ann. § 21.06(a) (2003). Sodomy between opposite-sex partners, however, is not a crime in Texas. That is, Texas treats the same conduct differently based solely on the participants. Those harmed by this law are people who have a same-sex sexual orientation and thus are more likely to engage in behavior prohibited by § 21.06.

The Texas statute makes homosexuals unequal in the eyes of the law by making particular conduct—and only that conduct—subject to criminal sanction. It appears that prosecutions under Texas' sodomy law are rare. This case shows, however, that prosecutions under § 21.06 *do* occur. And while the penalty imposed on petitioners in this case was relatively minor, the consequences of conviction are not. It appears that petitioners' convictions, if upheld, would disqualify them from or restrict their ability to engage in a variety of professions, including medicine, athletic training, and interior design. Indeed, were petitioners to move to one of four States, their convictions would require them to register as sex offenders to local law enforcement.

And the effect of Texas' sodomy law is not just limited to the threat of prosecution or consequence of conviction. Texas' sodomy law brands all homosexuals as criminals, thereby making it more difficult for homosexuals to be treated in the same manner as everyone else. Indeed, Texas itself has previously acknowledged the collateral effects of the law, stipulating in a prior challenge to this action that the law "legally sanctions discrimination against [homosexuals] in a variety of ways unrelated to the criminal law," including in the areas of "employment, family issues, and housing." *State v. Morales,* 826 S.W.2d 201, 203 (Tex.App.1992).

Texas attempts to justify its law, and the effects of the law, by arguing that the statute satisfies rational basis review because it furthers the legitimate governmental interest of the promotion of morality. In *Bowers,* we held that a state law criminalizing sodomy as applied to homosexual couples did not violate substantive due process. We rejected the argument that no rational basis existed to justify the law, pointing to the government's interest in promoting morality. The only question in front of the Court in *Bowers* was whether the substantive component of the Due Process Clause protected a right to engage in homosexual sodomy. *Bowers* did not hold that moral disapproval of a group is a rational basis under the Equal Protection Clause to criminalize homosexual sodomy when heterosexual sodomy is not punished.

This case raises a different issue than *Bowers:* whether, under the Equal Protection Clause, moral disapproval is a legitimate state interest to justify by itself a statute that bans homosexual sodomy, but not heterosexual sodomy. It is not. Moral disapproval of this group, like a bare desire to harm the group, is an interest that is insufficient to satisfy rational basis review under the Equal Protection Clause. See, *e.g., Department of Agriculture v. Moreno,* 413 U.S., at 534; *Romer v. Evans,* 517 U.S., at 634-635. Indeed, we have never held that moral disapproval, without any other asserted state interest, is a sufficient rationale under the Equal Protection Clause to justify a law that discriminates among groups of persons.

Moral disapproval of a group cannot be a legitimate governmental interest under the Equal Protection Clause because legal classifications must not be "drawn for the purpose of disadvantaging the group burdened by the law." *Id.,* at 633. Texas' invocation of moral disapproval as a legitimate state interest proves nothing more than Texas' desire to criminalize homosexual sodomy. But the Equal Protection Clause prevents a State from creating "a classification of persons undertaken for its own sake." *Id.,* at 635. And because Texas so rarely enforces its sodomy law as applied to private, consensual acts, the law serves more as a statement of dislike and disapproval against homosexuals than as a tool to stop criminal behavior. The Texas sodomy law "raise[s] the inevitable inference that the disadvantage imposed is born of animosity toward the class of persons affected." *Id.,* at 634.

Texas argues, however, that the sodomy law does not discriminate against homosexual persons. Instead, the State maintains that the law discriminates only against homosexual conduct. While it is true that the law applies only to conduct, the conduct targeted by this law is conduct that is closely correlated with being homosexual. Under such circumstances, Texas' sodomy law is targeted at more than conduct. It is instead directed toward gay persons as a class. "After all, there can hardly be more palpable discrimination against a class than making the conduct that defines the class criminal." *Id.,* at 641 (Scalia, J., dissenting). When a State makes homosexual conduct criminal, and not "deviate sexual intercourse" committed by persons of different sexes, "that declaration in and of itself is an invitation to subject homosexual persons to discrimination both in the public and in the private spheres."

Indeed, Texas law confirms that the sodomy statute is directed toward homosexuals as a class. In Texas, calling a person a homosexual is slander *per se* because the word "homosexual" "impute[s] the commission of a crime." The State has admitted that because of the sodomy law, *being* homosexual carries the presumption of being a criminal. Texas' sodomy law therefore results in discrimination against homosexuals as a class in an array of areas outside the criminal law. In *Romer v. Evans,* we refused to sanction a law that singled out homosexuals "for disfavored legal status." The same is true here. The Equal Protection Clause "'neither knows nor tolerates classes among citizens.'"

A State can of course assign certain consequences to a violation of its criminal law. But the State cannot single out one identifiable class of citizens for punishment that does not apply to everyone else, with moral disapproval as the only asserted state interest for the law. The Texas sodomy statute subjects homosexuals to "a lifelong penalty and stigma. A legislative classification that threatens the creation of an underclass . . . cannot be reconciled with" the Equal Protection Clause. *Plyler v. Doe,* 457 U.S., at 239 (Powell, J., concurring).

Whether a sodomy law that is neutral both in effect and application, see *Yick Wo v. Hopkins,* 118 U.S. 356 (1886), would violate the substantive component of the Due Process Clause is an issue that need not be decided today. I am confident, however, that so long as the Equal Protection Clause requires a sodomy law to apply equally to the private consensual conduct of homosexuals and heterosexuals alike, such a law would not long stand in our democratic society. In the words of Justice Jackson:

> "The framers of the Constitution knew, and we should not forget today, that there is no more effective practical guaranty against arbitrary and unreasonable government than to require that the principles of law which officials would impose upon a minority be imposed generally. Conversely, nothing opens the door to arbitrary action so effectively as to allow those officials to pick and choose only a few to whom they will apply legislation and thus to escape the political retribution that might be visited upon them if larger numbers were affected." *Railway Express Agency, Inc. v. New York,* 336 U.S. 106, 112–113 (1949) (concurring opinion).

That this law as applied to private, consensual conduct is unconstitutional under the Equal Protection Clause does not mean that other laws distinguishing between heterosexuals and homosexuals would similarly fail under rational basis review. Texas cannot assert any legitimate state interest here, such as national security or preserving the traditional institution of marriage. Unlike the moral disapproval of same-sex relations—the asserted state interest in this case—other reasons exist to promote the institution of marriage beyond mere moral disapproval of an excluded group.

A law branding one class of persons as criminal based solely on the State's moral disapproval of that class and the conduct associated with that class runs contrary to the values of the Constitution and the Equal Protection Clause, under any standard of review. I therefore concur in the Court's judgment that Texas' sodomy law banning "deviate sexual intercourse" between consenting adults of the same sex, but not between consenting adults of different sexes, is unconstitutional.

Justice Scalia, with whom The Chief Justice and Justice Thomas join, dissenting.

"Liberty finds no refuge in a jurisprudence of doubt." *Planned Parenthood of Southeastern Pa. v. Casey,* 505 U.S. 833, 844 (1992). That was the Court's sententious response, barely more than a decade ago, to those seeking to overrule *Roe v. Wade,* 410 U.S. 113 (1973). The Court's response today, to those who have engaged in a 17-year crusade to overrule *Bowers v. Hardwick,* 478 U.S. 186 (1986), is very different. The need for stability and certainty presents no barrier. . . .

I begin with the Court's surprising readiness to reconsider a decision rendered a mere 17 years ago in *Bowers v. Hardwick.* I do not myself believe in rigid adherence to *stare decisis* in constitutional cases; but I do believe that we should be consistent rather than manipulative in invoking the doctrine. Today's opinions in support of reversal do not bother to distinguish—or indeed, even bother to mention—the paean to *stare decisis* coauthored by three Members of today's majority in *Planned Parenthood v. Casey.* There, when *stare decisis* meant preservation of judicially invented abortion rights, the widespread criticism of *Roe* was strong reason to *reaffirm* it. . . .

Today, however, the widespread opposition to *Bowers,* a decision resolving an issue as "intensely divisive" as the issue in *Roe,* is offered as a reason in favor of *overruling* it. Gone, too, is any "enquiry" (of the sort conducted in *Casey*) into whether the decision sought to be overruled has "proven 'unworkable.'" . . . .

The Court's claim that *Planned Parenthood v. Casey, supra,* "casts some doubt" upon the holding in *Bowers* (or any other case, for that matter) does not withstand analysis. As far as its holding is concerned, *Casey* provided a *less* expansive right to abortion than did *Roe, which was already on the books when* Bowers *was decided.* And if the Court is referring not to the holding of *Casey,* but to the dictum of its famed sweet-mystery-of-life passage ("'At the heart of liberty is the right to define one's own concept of existence, of meaning, of the universe, and of the mystery of human life'"): That "casts some doubt" upon either the totality of our jurisprudence or else (presumably the right answer) nothing at all. I have never heard of a law that attempted to restrict one's "right to define" certain concepts; and if the passage calls into question the government's power to regulate *actions based on* one's self-defined "concept of existence, etc.," it is the passage that ate the rule of law.

I do not quarrel with the Court's claim that *Romer v. Evans,* 517 U.S. 620 (1996), "eroded" the "foundations" of *Bowers*' rational-basis holding. See *Romer, supra,* at 640-643 (SCALIA, J., dissenting). But *Roe* and *Casey* have been equally "eroded" by *Washington v. Glucksberg,* 521 U.S. 702, 721 (1997), which held that *only* fundamental rights which are "'deeply rooted in this Nation's history and tradition'" qualify for anything other than rational-basis scrutiny under the doctrine of "substantive due process." . . . .

Bowers, the Court says, has been subject to "substantial and continuing [criticism], disapproving of its reasoning in all respects, not just as to its historical assumptions." Exactly what those nonhistorical criticisms are, and whether the Court even agrees with them, are left unsaid, although the Court does cite two books. Of course, *Roe* too (and by extension *Casey*) had been (and still is) subject to unrelenting criticism, including criticism from the two commentators cited by the Court today. . . .

"[T]here has been," the Court says, "no individual or societal reliance on *Bowers* of the sort that could counsel against overturning its holding. . . ." It seems to me that the "societal reliance" on the principles confirmed in *Bowers* and discarded today has been overwhelming. Countless judicial decisions and legislative enactments have relied on the ancient proposition that a governing majority's belief that certain sexual behavior is "immoral and unacceptable" constitutes a rational basis for regulation. State laws against bigamy, same-sex marriage, adult incest, prostitution, masturbation, adultery, fornication, bestiality, and obscenity are likewise sustainable only in light of *Bowers'* validation of laws based on moral choices. Every single one of these laws is called into question by today's decision; the Court makes no effort to cabin the scope of its decision to exclude them from its holding. The impossibility of distinguishing homosexuality from other traditional "morals" offenses is precisely why *Bowers* rejected the rational-basis challenge. . . .

To tell the truth, it does not surprise me, and should surprise no one, that the Court has chosen today to revise the standards of *stare decisis* set forth in *Casey.* It has thereby exposed *Casey's* extraordinary deference to precedent for the result-oriented expedient that it is.

Having decided that it need not adhere to *stare decisis,* the Court still must establish that *Bowers* was wrongly decided and that the Texas statute, as applied to petitioners, is unconstitutional. . . .

Our opinions applying the doctrine known as "substantive due process" hold that the Due Process Clause prohibits States from infringing *fundamental* liberty interests, unless the infringement is narrowly tailored to serve a compelling state interest. We have held repeatedly, in cases the Court today does not overrule, that *only* fundamental rights qualify for this so-called "heightened scrutiny" protection—that is, rights which are "'deeply rooted in this Nation's history and tradition.'"[3] All other liberty interests may be abridged or abrogated pursuant to a validly enacted state law if that law is rationally related to a legitimate state interest.

Bowers held, first, that criminal prohibitions of homosexual sodomy are not subject to heightened scrutiny because they do not implicate a "fundamental right" under the Due Process Clause. . . .

The Court today does not overrule this holding. Not once does it describe homosexual sodomy as a "fundamental right" or a "fundamental liberty interest," nor does it subject the Texas statute to strict scrutiny. Instead, having failed to establish that the right to homosexual sodomy is "'deeply rooted in this Nation's history and tradition,'" the Court concludes that the application of Texas's statute to petitioners' conduct fails the rational-basis test, and overrules *Bowers'* holding to the contrary. . . .

I shall address that rational-basis holding presently. First, however, I address some aspersions that the Court casts upon *Bowers'* conclusion that homosexual sodomy is not a "fundamental right"—even though, as I have said, the Court does not have the boldness to reverse that conclusion.

---

3. The Court is quite right that "'[h]istory and tradition are the starting point but not in all cases the ending point of the substantive due process inquiry.'" An asserted "fundamental liberty interest" must not only be "'deeply rooted in this Nation's history and tradition,'" but it must *also* be "'implicit in the concept of ordered liberty,'" so that "'neither liberty nor justice would exist if [it] were sacrificed.'" Moreover, liberty interests unsupported by history and tradition, though not deserving of "heightened scrutiny," are *still* protected from state laws that are not rationally related to any legitimate state interest. As I proceed to discuss, it is this latter principle that the Court applies in the present case.

The Court's description of "the state of the law" at the time of *Bowers* only confirms that *Bowers* was right. The Court points to *Griswold v. Connecticut,* 381 U.S. 479 (1965). But that case *expressly disclaimed* any reliance on the doctrine of "substantive due process," and grounded the so-called "right to privacy" in penumbras of constitutional provisions *other than* the Due Process Clause. *Eisenstadt v. Baird,* 405 U.S. 438 (1972), likewise had nothing to do with "substantive due process"; it invalidated a Massachusetts law prohibiting the distribution of contraceptives to unmarried persons solely on the basis of the Equal Protection Clause. . . .

Roe v. Wade recognized that the right to abort an unborn child was a "fundamental right" protected by the Due Process Clause. The *Roe* Court, however, made no attempt to establish that this right was "'deeply rooted in this Nation's history and tradition'" . . . . We have since rejected *Roe's* holding that regulations of abortion must be narrowly tailored to serve a compelling state interest—and thus, by logical implication, *Roe's* holding that the right to abort an unborn child is a "fundamental right."

After discussing the history of antisodomy laws, the Court proclaims that, "it should be noted that there is no longstanding history in this country of laws directed at homosexual conduct as a distinct matter." This observation in no way casts into doubt the "definitive [historical] conclusio[n]," on which *Bowers* relied: that our Nation has a longstanding history of laws prohibiting *sodomy in general*—regardless of whether it was performed by same-sex or opposite-sex couples. . . .

Next the Court makes the claim, again unsupported by any citations, that "[l]aws prohibiting sodomy do not seem to have been enforced against consenting adults acting in private." . . . . If all the Court means by "acting in private" is "on private premises, with the doors closed and windows covered," it is entirely unsurprising that evidence of enforcement would be hard to come by (Imagine the circumstances that would enable a search warrant to be obtained for a residence on the ground that there was probable cause to believe that consensual sodomy was then and there occurring.) . . . . There are 203 prosecutions for consensual, adult homosexual sodomy reported in the West Reporting system and official state reporters from the years 1880–1995. There are also records of 20 sodomy prosecutions and 4 executions during the colonial period. *Bowers'* conclusion that homosexual sodomy is not a fundamental right "deeply rooted in this Nation's history and tradition" is utterly unassailable.

Realizing that fact, the Court instead says: "[W]e think that our laws and traditions in the past half century are of most relevance here. These references show *an emerging awareness* that liberty gives substantial protection to adult persons in deciding how to conduct their private lives *in matters pertaining to sex.*" Apart from the fact that such an "emerging awareness" does not establish a "fundamental right," the statement is factually false. States continue to prosecute all sorts of crimes by adults "in matters pertaining to sex": prostitution, adult incest, adultery, obscenity, and child pornography. Sodomy laws, too, have been enforced "in the past half century," in which there have been 134 reported cases involving prosecutions for consensual, adult, homosexual sodomy....

In any event, an "emerging awareness" is by definition not "deeply rooted in this Nation's history and tradition[s]," as we have said "fundamental right" status requires. Constitutional entitlements do not spring into existence because some States choose to lessen or eliminate criminal sanctions on certain behavior. Much less do they spring into existence, as the Court seems to believe, because *foreign nations* decriminalize conduct.... The Court's discussion of these foreign views (ignoring, of course, the many countries that have retained criminal prohibitions on sodomy) is therefore meaningless dicta. Dangerous dicta, however, since "this Court ... should not impose foreign moods, fads, or fashions on Americans."

I turn now to the ground on which the Court squarely rests its holding: the contention that there is no rational basis for the law here under attack. This proposition is so out of accord with our jurisprudence—indeed, with the jurisprudence of *any* society we know—that it requires little discussion.

The Texas statute undeniably seeks to further the belief of its citizens that certain forms of sexual behavior are "immoral and unacceptable,"—the same interest furthered by criminal laws against fornication, bigamy, adultery, adult incest, bestiality, and obscenity. *Bowers* held that this *was* a legitimate state interest. The Court today reaches the opposite conclusion. The Texas statute, it says, "furthers *no legitimate state interest* which can justify its intrusion into the personal and private life of the individual." The Court embraces instead JUSTICE STEVENS' declaration in his *Bowers* dissent, that "'the fact that the governing majority in a State has traditionally viewed a particular practice as immoral is not a sufficient reason for upholding a law prohibiting the practice.'" This effectively decrees the end of all morals legislation. If, as the Court asserts, the promotion of majoritarian sexual morality is not even a *legitimate* state interest, none of the above-mentioned laws can survive rational-basis review....

Finally, I turn to petitioners' equal-protection challenge, which no Member of the Court save JUSTICE O'CONNOR (opinion concurring in judgment), embraces: On its face § 21.06(a) applies equally to all persons. Men and women, heterosexuals and homosexuals, are all subject to its prohibition of deviate sexual intercourse with someone of the same sex. To be sure, § 21.06 does distinguish between the sexes insofar as concerns the partner with whom the sexual acts are performed: men can violate the law only with other men, and women only with other women. But this cannot itself be a denial of equal protection, since it is precisely the same distinction regarding partner that is drawn in state laws prohibiting marriage with someone of the same sex while permitting marriage with someone of the opposite sex.

The objection is made, however, that the antimiscegenation laws invalidated in *Loving v. Virginia*, 388 U.S. 1, 8 (1967), similarly were applicable to whites and blacks alike, and only distinguished between the races insofar as the *partner* was concerned.

In *Loving*, however, we correctly applied heightened scrutiny, rather than the usual rational-basis review, because the Virginia statute was "designed to maintain White Supremacy." *Id.*, at 6, 11. A racially discriminatory purpose is always sufficient to subject a law to strict scrutiny, even a facially neutral law that makes no mention of race. See *Washington v. Davis*, 426 U.S. 229, 241–242 (1976). No purpose to discriminate against men or women as a class can be gleaned from the Texas law, so rational-basis review applies. That review is readily satisfied here by the same rational basis that satisfied it in *Bowers*—society's belief that certain forms of sexual behavior are "immoral and unacceptable." This is the same justification that supports many other laws regulating sexual behavior that make a distinction based upon the identity of the partner—for example, laws against adultery, fornication, and adult incest, and laws refusing to recognize homosexual marriage.

Justice O'Connor argues that the discrimination in this law which must be justified is not its discrimination with regard to the sex of the partner but its discrimination with regard to the sexual proclivity of the principal actor.

> "While it is true that the law applies only to conduct, the conduct targeted by this law is conduct that is closely correlated with being homosexual. Under such circumstances, Texas' sodomy law is targeted at more than conduct. It is instead directed toward gay persons as a class."

Of course the same could be said of any law. A law against public nudity targets "the conduct that is closely correlated with being a nudist," and hence "is targeted at more than conduct"; it is "directed toward nudists as a class." But be that as it may. Even if the Texas law *does* deny equal protection to "homosexuals as a class," that denial *still* does not need to be justified by anything more than a rational basis, which our cases show is satisfied by the enforcement of traditional notions of sexual morality.

Justice O'Connor simply decrees application of "a more searching form of rational basis review" to the Texas statute. The cases she cites do not recognize such a standard, and reach their conclusions only after finding, as required by conventional rational-basis analysis, that no conceivable legitimate state interest supports the classification at issue. Nor does Justice O'Connor explain precisely what her "more searching form" of rational-basis review consists of. It must at least mean, however, that laws exhibiting "a desire to harm a politically unpopular group" are invalid *even though* there may be a conceivable rational basis to support them.

This reasoning leaves on pretty shaky grounds state laws limiting marriage to opposite-sex couples. Justice O'Connor seeks to preserve them by the conclusory statement that "preserving the traditional institution of marriage" is a legitimate state interest. But "preserving the traditional institution of marriage" is just a kinder way of describing the State's *moral disapproval* of same-sex couples. Texas's interest in § 21.06 could be recast in similarly euphemistic terms: "preserving the traditional sexual mores of our society." In the jurisprudence Justice O'Connor has seemingly created, judges can validate laws by characterizing them as "preserving the traditions of society" (good); or invalidate them by characterizing them as "expressing moral disapproval" (bad) . . . .

JUSTICE THOMAS, dissenting.

I join JUSTICE SCALIA's dissenting opinion. I write separately to note that the law before the Court today "is . . . uncommonly silly." *Griswold v. Connecticut,* 381 U.S. 479, 527 (1965) (Stewart, J., dissenting). If I were a member of the Texas Legislature, I would vote to repeal it. Punishing someone for expressing his sexual preference through noncommercial consensual conduct with another adult does not appear to be a worthy way to expend valuable law enforcement resources.

Notwithstanding this, I recognize that as a Member of this Court I am not empowered to help petitioners and others similarly situated. My duty, rather, is to "decide cases 'agreeably to the Constitution and laws of the United States.'" *Id.,* at 530. And, just like Justice Stewart, I "can find [neither in the Bill of Rights nor any other part of the Constitution a] general right of privacy," or as the Court terms it today, the "liberty of the person both in its spatial and more transcendent dimensions."

Problem 18-B: Scoping Out Lawrence*'s Scope*

Assess the constitutionality of the following laws in light of *Lawrence v. Texas:*

(1) A law that makes it a crime for two soldiers of different ranks to engage in consensual sodomy.

(2) A law that makes it a crime to commit adultery as applied in the following contexts:

  (a) the offending spouse and his wife have children;

  (b) the offending spouse and her husband have no children, and the husband consented to her engaging in adultery;

  (c) the offender is a single man in the military, and the act involved the wife of another soldier.

(3) A state law that criminalizes solicitation to commit sodomy, applied in the situation in which the defendant approaches an undercover officer in a public restroom and proposes that they go back to his place to engage in sexual activity.

(4) A law that makes it a crime to engage in consensual sexual acts that involve the infliction of pain or injury.

(5) A law that makes it a crime for three or more individuals to engage in sexual activity together.

(6) A law that makes it a crime to engage in sexual activity with an animal.

(7) A law that makes it a crime for first cousins to have sexual intercourse with one another.

(8) A law that makes it a crime to engage in prostitution.

Notes and Questions

1. The *Lawrence* majority notes a number of what in which the facts and laws at issue in *Bowers* and *Lawrence* were similar and different. What impact, if any, did those differences likely have on the outcome of the case?

2. To what extent is the majority in *Lawrence* influenced by the dissenting opinions of Justices Blackmun and Stevens in *Bowers*? Does the *Lawrence* majority adopt those dissents wholesale, or does it only rely selectively on them?

3. *Lawrence* differs from *Bowers* in two key ways: it frames the right claimed and its prior holdings in much broader terms, and history plays a different role. How does this compare with the Court's earlier decision in *Glucksberg*? Does *Lawrence* overrule *Glucksberg sub silentio*? If not, how can the two cases be reconciled?

4. Is *Lawrence* a fundamental rights substantive due process case applying strict scrutiny, or a run-of-the-mill substantive due process case applying rational basis? Or is it applying something more akin to the "undue burden" standard of *Casey*, or a form of rational basis plus review, treating the right at issue as not a fundamental one but perhaps a quasi-fundamental one? Are *Lawrence* and *Romer* together ushering in a new method for assessing both equal protection and due process claims that parallels Justice Steven's proposed approach to equal protection claims in *Cleburne*?

5. After *Lawrence*, can public moral disapproval ever suffice to justify a law when challenged on substantive due process grounds? Is the Court's opinion clear in that regard, or is there an ambiguity? If it cannot justify a law challenged on substantive due process grounds, is Justice Scalia right in suggesting that the decision casts doubt on the constitutionality of laws criminalizing or banning bigamy, same-sex marriage, adult incest, prostitution, masturbation, adultery, fornication, bestiality, and obscenity? Or are there ways to distinguish these laws from laws criminalizing consensual sexual activity between two persons of the same sex?

6. In one sense, the majority opinion in *Lawrence*—like that in *Casey*—is breathtakingly broad, describing the right at issue in sweeping terms. Yet other aspects of the majority opinion appear to substantially constrain its scope. From the standpoint of the Court, what are the advantages of this framework coupled with its silence on the level of scrutiny being applied? From the standpoint of those seeking to litigate future gay rights cases (or other cases falling within the zone of liberty identified in *Lawrence*), what disadvantages are there with this approach?

7. In his opinion in *Lawrence*, Justice Kennedy notes that "the concept of the homosexual as a distinct category of person did not emerge until the late 19th century." If homosexuals as a distinct category of persons did not emerge until the late 19th century, can laws that predate that emergence ever be deemed to violate the Equal Protection Clause? In this regard, recall a key limitation on the scope of the Equal Protection Clause: it only encompasses discrimination that is *intentional*; it does not encompass discrimination that merely has a disparate impact on a given group.

8. Is the *Lawrence* Court's decision to overrule *Bowers* consistent with the *Casey* Court's decision *not* to overrule *Roe*?

9. What is the relationship between equal protection and due process in the majority's opinion? In this regard, recall that *Skinner*, *Eisenstadt*, and *Romer* were all formally decided on equal protection grounds.

10. Justice O'Connor's concurring opinion in *Lawrence* is important because it is the only Supreme Court opinion—save for Justice Marshall's separate opinion in *Cleburne*—to acknowledge the existence of "a more searching form of rational basis review." Yet, does she articulate when this more searching form of review is triggered and how, exactly, it differs from traditional rational basis review?

11. Justice O'Connor in her concurring opinion in *Lawrence* rejects the idea of drawing a distinction—for equal protection purposes—between homosexual conduct on the one hand and homosexual orientation or status on the other. Is this thus a tacit acceptance of the idea, raised in *Hernandez*, that something can be so closely correlated with a class that discrimination on that basis is tantamount to discrimination against that class?

12. Which resolution of *Lawrence* do you find more satisfying, the majority's application of rational basis review under the Due Process Clause, or Justice O'Connor's application of "a more searching form of rational basis review" under the Equal Protection Clause? Had Justice O'Connor's approach been the approach adopted by the majority, how would the Court have resolved a challenge to a sodomy law—akin to that in *Bowers*—that criminalized both same-sex and opposite-sex sodomy? In this regard, consider Justice O'Connor's citation to *Yick Wo v. Hopkins*, 118 U.S. 356 (1886).

13. Justice O'Connor treats moral disapproval differently for due process and equal protection purposes, deeming it a legitimate governmental interest under the former but not under the latter. Although the majority in *Lawrence* held—or at least strongly implied—that moral disapproval was not a legitimate governmental interest for due process purposes, it did not address its legitimacy under the Equal Protection Clause. Nonetheless, do you see why Justice O'Connor's conclusion that moral disapproval is never a legitimate governmental interest is a necessary conclusion if the Equal Protection Clause is to have any meaning?

14. In *Lawrence*, both the majority and Justice O'Connor seek to cabin the reach of their holdings, alluding to such issues as same-sex marriage and Don't Ask, Don't Tell and noting that the decision does not address those issues. Yet, as Justice Scalia points out in his dissent, it seems hard to draw a principled line between the issue before the Court in *Lawrence* and those other issues. To be sure, had the Court come out and held in either *Romer* or *Lawrence* that intermediate or strict scrutiny applied to sexual orientation discrimination, it would have virtually answered the question whether prohibitions on same-sex marriage or military service by sexual minorities are constitutional, would it not? Might this be the virtue (or vice, depending upon your perspective) of not clearly articulating which standard of review is being applied?

15. In his dissenting opinion in *Lawrence*, Justice Scalia makes clear his view that the law at issue in *Lawrence* does not discriminate on the basis of *sex* because it treats men and women alike in that both are equally prohibited from engaging in sexual intercourse with someone of the same sex. Justice Scalia cites *Loving v. Virginia*, 388 U.S. 1 (1967) in support of his conclusion. Are you persuaded by Justice Scalia's characterization of the Court's holding in *Loving*?

C. Same-Sex Marriage

From the 1990s through the 2010s, a large percentage of states enacted laws that both barred same-sex couples from marrying and that refused to recognize same-sex marriages entered into in other states or countries. In addition, in 1996, Congress enacted a law, entitled the Defense of Marriage Act (DOMA), that provided that the federal government would not recognize marriages between persons of the same sex entered into in states that permitted it.

Challenges were brought to these laws in both state and federal courts, raising both federal substantive due process and equal protection claims as well as claims under analogous provisions of state constitutions. Many of these challenges succeeded, and legal same-sex marriage slowly spread throughout the United States.

In 2012, the U.S. Court of Appeals for the Second Circuit, in *Windsor v. United States*, 699 F.3d 169 (2d Cir. 2012), declared DOMA's refusal to recognize same-sex marriages lawfully entered into in states that permitted it unconstitutional. Applying the *Frontiero* factors, the Second Circuit concluded that intermediate scrutiny was applicable to discrimination on the basis of sexual orientation. After easily concluding that gays and lesbians suffered from a history of discrimination and that the characteristic bears no relation to ability to perform or contribute to society, the court turned its attention to what it described as the two remaining factors: "whether the class exhibits 'obvious, immutable, or distinguishing characteristics that define them as a discrete group;'" and "whether the class is 'a minority or politically powerless.'" With respect to the first of these remaining factors, the court wrote:

> This consideration is often couched in terms of "immutability." . . . . But the test is broader: whether there are "obvious, immutable, *or* distinguishing characteristics that define . . . a discrete group." No "obvious badge" is necessary. Classifications based on alienage, illegitimacy, and national origin are all subject to heightened scrutiny, even though these characteristics do not declare themselves, and often may be disclosed or suppressed as a matter of preference. What seems to matter is whether the characteristic of the class calls down discrimination when it is manifest.
>
> Thus a person of illegitimate birth may keep that status private, and ensure that no outward sign discloses the status in social settings or in the workplace, or on the subway. But when such a person applies for Social Security benefits

> on the death of a parent (for example), the illegitimate status becomes manifest. The characteristic is necessarily revealed in order to exercise a legal right. Similarly, sexual preference is necessarily disclosed when two persons of the same sex apply for a marriage license (as they are legally permitted to do in New York), or when a surviving spouse of a same-sex marriage seeks the benefit of the spousal deduction (as Windsor does here).

Windsor, 699 F.3d, at 183-84. As for the final factor, in addition to noting that it is presented in the disjunctive ("minority *or* politically powerless"), the court held that "The question is not whether homosexuals have achieved political successes over the years; they clearly have. The question is whether they have the strength to politically protect themselves from wrongful discrimination." *Id.* at 184. Drawing parallels to the inability of women to fully protect themselves politically despite their numerical majority, the court concluded that this factor also weighed in favor of applying heightened scrutiny.

The U.S. government appealed to the U.S. Supreme Court. In the first of the two decisions that follows, the Court considers the constitutionality of DOMA. In the second decision, decided two years later, the Court considers whether *state* bans on same-sex marriage also violate the U.S. Constitution.

United States v. Windsor

570 U.S. 744 (2013)

[At issue in this case is a challenge to the constitutionality of Section 3 of the Defense of Marriage Act. In an earlier section of the opinion, the Court found that both it and the Court of Appeals had jurisdiction to review the trial court's decision declaring Section 3 to be unconstitutional. In the excerpt that follows, the Court addresses the merits of the challenge.]

Justice Kennedy delivered the opinion of the Court....

When at first Windsor and Spyer longed to marry, neither New York nor any other State granted them that right. After waiting some years, in 2007 they traveled to Ontario to be married there....

Slowly at first and then in rapid course, the laws of New York came to acknowledge the urgency of this issue for same-sex couples who wanted to affirm their commitment to one another before their children, their family, their friends, and their community. And so New York recognized same-sex marriages performed elsewhere; and then it later amended its own marriage laws to permit same-sex marriage. New York, in common with, as of this writing, 11 other States and the District of Columbia, decided that same-sex couples should have the right to marry and so live with pride in themselves and their union and in a status of equality with all other married persons....

Against this background of lawful same-sex marriage in some States, the design, purpose, and effect of DOMA should be considered as the beginning point in deciding whether it is valid under the Constitution. By history and tradition the definition and regulation of marriage, as will be discussed in more detail, has been treated as being within the authority and realm of the separate States. Yet it is further established that Congress, in enacting discrete statutes, can make determinations that bear on marital rights and privileges. . . . Congress has the power both to ensure efficiency in the administration of its programs and to choose what larger goals and policies to pursue. . . .

In addressing the interaction of state domestic relations and federal immigration law Congress determined that marriages "entered into for the purpose of procuring an alien's admission [to the United States] as an immigrant" will not qualify the noncitizen for that status, even if the noncitizen's marriage is valid and proper for state-law purposes. And in establishing income-based criteria for Social Security benefits, Congress decided that although state law would determine in general who qualifies as an applicant's spouse, common-law marriages also should be recognized, regardless of any particular State's view on these relationships.

Though these discrete examples establish the constitutionality of limited federal laws that regulate the meaning of marriage in order to further federal policy, DOMA has a far greater reach; for it enacts a directive applicable to over 1,000 federal statutes and the whole realm of federal regulations. And its operation is directed to a class of persons that the laws of New York, and of 11 other States, have sought to protect. . . .

In order to assess the validity of that intervention it is necessary to discuss the extent of the state power and authority over marriage as a matter of history and tradition. State laws defining and regulating marriage, of course, must respect the constitutional rights of persons, see, *e.g., Loving v. Virginia,* 388 U.S. 1 (1967); but, subject to those guarantees, "regulation of domestic relations" is "an area that has long been regarded as a virtually exclusive province of the States." *Sosna v. Iowa,* 419 U.S. 393, 404 (1975) . . . .

Consistent with this allocation of authority, the Federal Government, through our history, has deferred to state-law policy decisions with respect to domestic relations. In *De Sylva v. Ballentine,* 351 U.S. 570 (1956), for example, the Court held that, "[t]o decide who is the widow or widower of a deceased author, or who are his executors or next of kin," under the Copyright Act "requires a reference to the law of the State which created those legal relationships" because "there is no federal law of domestic relations." In order to respect this principle, the federal courts, as a general rule, do not adjudicate issues of marital status even when there might otherwise be a basis for federal jurisdiction. . . .

Marriage laws vary in some respects from State to State. For example, the required minimum age is 16 in Vermont, but only 13 in New Hampshire. Likewise the permissible degree of consanguinity can vary (most States permit first cousins to marry, but a handful—such as Iowa and Washington—prohibit the practice). But these rules are in every event consistent within each State.

Against this background DOMA rejects the long-established precept that the incidents, benefits, and obligations of marriage are uniform for all married couples within each State, though they may vary, subject to constitutional guarantees, from one State to the next. Despite these considerations, it is unnecessary to decide whether this federal intrusion on state power is a violation of the Constitution because it disrupts the federal balance. The State's power in defining the marital relation is of central relevance in this case quite apart from principles of federalism. Here the State's decision to give this class of persons the right to marry conferred upon them a dignity and status of immense import. When the State used its historic and essential authority to define the marital relation in this way, its role and its power in making the decision enhanced the recognition, dignity, and protection of the class in their own community. DOMA, because of its reach and extent, departs from this history and tradition of reliance on state law to define marriage. "'[D]iscriminations of an unusual character especially suggest careful consideration to determine whether they are obnoxious to the constitutional provision.'" *Romer v. Evans,* 517 U.S. 620, 633 (1996).

The Federal Government uses this state-defined class for the opposite purpose—to impose restrictions and disabilities. That result requires this Court now to address whether the resulting injury and indignity is a deprivation of an essential part of the liberty protected by the Fifth Amendment....

The States' interest in defining and regulating the marital relation, subject to constitutional guarantees, stems from the understanding that marriage is more than a routine classification for purposes of certain statutory benefits. Private, consensual sexual intimacy between two adult persons of the same sex may not be punished by the State, and it can form "but one element in a personal bond that is more enduring." *Lawrence v. Texas,* 539 U.S. 558, 567 (2003). By its recognition of the validity of same-sex marriages performed in other jurisdictions and then by authorizing same-sex unions and same-sex marriages, New York sought to give further protection and dignity to that bond....

DOMA seeks to injure the very class New York seeks to protect. By doing so it violates basic due process and equal protection principles applicable to the Federal Government. See U.S. Const., Amdt. 5; *Bolling v. Sharpe,* 347 U.S. 497 (1954). The Constitution's guarantee of equality "must at the very least mean that a bare congressional desire to harm a politically unpopular group cannot" justify disparate treatment of that group. *Department of Agriculture v. Moreno,* 413 U.S. 528, 534–535 (1973). In determining whether a law is motived by an improper animus or purpose, "'[d]iscriminations of an unusual character'" especially require careful consideration. *Supra,* at 19 (quoting *Romer, supra,* at 633). DOMA cannot survive under these principles. The responsibility of the States for the regulation of domestic relations is an important indicator of the substantial societal impact the State's classifications have in the daily lives and customs of its people. DOMA's unusual deviation from the usual tradition of recognizing and accepting state definitions of marriage here operates to deprive same-sex couples of the benefits and responsibilities that come with the federal recognition of their marriages. This is strong evidence of a law having the purpose and effect of disapproval of that class. The avowed purpose and practical effect of the law here in question are to impose a disadvantage, a separate status, and so a stigma upon all who enter into same-sex marriages made lawful by the unquestioned authority of the States.

The history of DOMA's enactment and its own text demonstrate that interference with the equal dignity of same-sex marriages, a dignity conferred by the States in the exercise of their sovereign power, was more than an incidental effect of the federal statute. It was its essence. . . . The House concluded that DOMA expresses "both moral disapproval of homosexuality, and a moral conviction that heterosexuality better comports with traditional (especially Judeo–Christian) morality." The stated purpose of the law was to promote an "interest in protecting the traditional moral teachings reflected in heterosexual-only marriage laws." Were there any doubt of this far-reaching purpose, the title of the Act confirms it: The Defense of Marriage.

The arguments put forward by BLAG are just as candid about the congressional purpose to influence or interfere with state sovereign choices about who may be married. As the title and dynamics of the bill indicate, its purpose is to discourage enactment of state same-sex marriage laws and to restrict the freedom and choice of couples married under those laws if they are enacted. The congressional goal was "to put a thumb on the scales and influence a state's decision as to how to shape its own marriage laws." The Act's demonstrated purpose is to ensure that if any State decides to recognize same-sex marriages, those unions will be treated as second-class marriages for purposes of federal law. This raises a most serious question under the Constitution's Fifth Amendment.

DOMA's operation in practice confirms this purpose. When New York adopted a law to permit same-sex marriage, it sought to eliminate inequality; but DOMA frustrates that objective through a system-wide enactment with no identified connection to any particular area of federal law. DOMA writes inequality into the entire United States Code. The particular case at hand concerns the estate tax, but DOMA is more than a simple determination of what should or should not be allowed as an estate tax refund. Among the over 1,000 statutes and numerous federal regulations that DOMA controls are laws pertaining to Social Security, housing, taxes, criminal sanctions, copyright, and veterans' benefits.

DOMA's principal effect is to identify a subset of state-sanctioned marriages and make them unequal. The principal purpose is to impose inequality, not for other reasons like governmental efficiency. . . . By creating two contradictory marriage regimes within the same State, DOMA forces same-sex couples to live as married for the purpose of state law but unmarried for the purpose of federal law, thus diminishing the stability and predictability of basic personal relations the State has found it proper to acknowledge and protect. By this dynamic DOMA undermines both the public and private significance of state-sanctioned same-sex marriages; for it tells those couples, and all the world, that their otherwise valid marriages are unworthy of federal recognition. This places same-sex couples in an unstable position of being in a second-tier marriage. The differentiation demeans the couple, whose moral and sexual choices the Constitution protects, see *Lawrence,* 539 U.S. 558, and whose relationship the State has sought to dignify. And it humiliates tens of thousands of children now being raised by same-sex couples. The law in question makes it even more difficult for the children to understand the integrity and closeness of their own family and its concord with other families in their community and in their daily lives.

Under DOMA, same-sex married couples have their lives burdened, by reason of government decree, in visible and public ways. By its great reach, DOMA touches many aspects of married and family life, from the mundane to the profound. . . .

DOMA also brings financial harm to children of same-sex couples. It raises the cost of health care for families by taxing health benefits provided by employers to their workers' same-sex spouses. And it denies or reduces benefits allowed to families upon the loss of a spouse and parent, benefits that are an integral part of family security. . . .

The power the Constitution grants it also restrains. And though Congress has great authority to design laws to fit its own conception of sound national policy, it cannot deny the liberty protected by the Due Process Clause of the Fifth Amendment.

What has been explained to this point should more than suffice to establish that the principal purpose and the necessary effect of this law are to demean those persons who are in a lawful same-sex marriage. This requires the Court to hold, as it now does, that DOMA is unconstitutional as a deprivation of the liberty of the person protected by the Fifth Amendment of the Constitution.

The liberty protected by the Fifth Amendment's Due Process Clause contains within it the prohibition against denying to any person the equal protection of the laws. While the Fifth Amendment itself withdraws from Government the power to degrade or demean in the way this law does, the equal protection guarantee of the Fourteenth Amendment makes that Fifth Amendment right all the more specific and all the better understood and preserved.

The class to which DOMA directs its restrictions and restraints are those persons who are joined in same-sex marriages made lawful by the State. DOMA singles out a class of persons deemed by a State entitled to recognition and protection to enhance their own liberty. It imposes a disability on the class by refusing to acknowledge a status the State finds to be dignified and proper. DOMA instructs all federal officials, and indeed all persons with whom same-sex couples interact, including their own children, that their marriage is less worthy than the marriages of others. The federal statute is invalid, for no legitimate purpose overcomes the purpose and effect to disparage and to injure those whom the State, by its marriage laws, sought to protect in personhood and dignity. By seeking to displace this protection and treating those persons as living in marriages less respected than others, the federal statute is in violation of the Fifth Amendment. This opinion and its holding are confined to those lawful marriages. . . .

Chief Justice Roberts, dissenting. . . .

[W]hile I disagree with the result to which the majority's analysis leads it in this case, I think it more important to point out that its analysis leads no further. The Court does not have before it, and the logic of its opinion does not decide, the distinct question whether the States, in the exercise of their "historic and essential authority to define the marital relation," may continue to utilize the traditional definition of marriage.

The majority goes out of its way to make this explicit in the penultimate sentence of its opinion. . . . In my view, though, the disclaimer is a logical and necessary consequence of the argument the majority has chosen to adopt. The dominant theme of the majority opinion is that the Federal Government's intrusion into an area "central to state domestic relations law applicable to its residents and citizens" is sufficiently "unusual" to set off alarm bells. I think the majority goes off course, as I have said, but it is undeniable that its judgment is based on federalism. . . .

We may in the future have to resolve challenges to state marriage definitions affecting same-sex couples. That issue, however, is not before us in this case. . . . I write only to highlight the limits of the majority's holding and reasoning today, lest its opinion be taken to resolve not only a question that I believe is not properly before us—DOMA's constitutionality—but also a question that all agree, and the Court explicitly acknowledges, is not at issue.

Justice Scalia, with whom Justice Thomas joins, and with whom The Chief Justice joins as to Part I, dissenting. . . .

There are many remarkable things about the majority's merits holding. The first is how rootless and shifting its justifications are. For example, the opinion starts with seven full pages about the traditional power of States to define domestic relations—initially fooling many readers, I am sure, into thinking that this is a federalism opinion. . . . Even after the opinion has formally disclaimed reliance upon principles of federalism, mentions of "the usual tradition of recognizing and accepting state definitions of marriage" continue. What to make of this? The opinion never explains. My guess is that the majority, while reluctant to suggest that defining the meaning of "marriage" in federal statutes is unsupported by any of the Federal Government's enumerated powers, nonetheless needs some rhetorical basis to support its pretense that today's prohibition of laws excluding same-sex marriage is confined to the Federal Government (leaving the second, state-law shoe to be dropped later, maybe next Term). But I am only guessing.

Equally perplexing are the opinion's references to "the Constitution's guarantee of equality." Near the end of the opinion, we are told that although the "equal protection guarantee of the Fourteenth Amendment makes [the] Fifth Amendment [due process] right all the more specific and all the better understood and preserved"—what can *that* mean?—"the Fifth Amendment itself withdraws from Government the power to degrade or demean in the way this law does." The only possible interpretation of this statement is that the Equal Protection Clause, even the Equal

Protection Clause as incorporated in the Due Process Clause, is not the basis for today's holding. But the portion of the majority opinion that explains why DOMA is unconstitutional (Part IV) begins by citing *Bolling v. Sharpe,* 347 U.S. 497 (1954), *Department of Agriculture v. Moreno,* 413 U.S. 528 (1973), and *Romer v. Evans,* 517 U.S. 620 (1996)—*all* of which are equal-protection cases. And those three cases are the *only* authorities that the Court cites in Part IV about the Constitution's meaning, except for its citation of *Lawrence v. Texas,* 539 U.S. 558 (2003) (not an equal-protection case) to support its passing assertion that the Constitution protects the "moral and sexual choices" of same-sex couples.

Moreover, if this is meant to be an equal-protection opinion, it is a confusing one. The opinion does not resolve and indeed does not even mention what had been the central question in this litigation: whether, under the Equal Protection Clause, laws restricting marriage to a man and a woman are reviewed for more than mere rationality. ... In accord with my previously expressed skepticism about the Court's "tiers of scrutiny" approach, I would review this classification only for its rationality. As nearly as I can tell, the Court agrees with that; its opinion does not apply strict scrutiny, and its central propositions are taken from rational-basis cases like *Moreno.* But the Court certainly does not *apply* anything that resembles that deferential framework.

The majority opinion need not get into the strict-vs.-rational-basis scrutiny question, and need not justify its holding under either, because it says that DOMA is unconstitutional as "a deprivation of the liberty of the person protected by the Fifth Amendment of the Constitution"; that it violates "basic due process" principles; and that it inflicts an "injury and indignity" of a kind that denies "an essential part of the liberty protected by the Fifth Amendment." The majority never utters the dread words "substantive due process," perhaps sensing the disrepute into which that doctrine has fallen, but that is what those statements mean. ...

The sum of all the Court's nonspecific hand-waving is that this law is invalid (maybe on equal-protection grounds, maybe on substantive-due-process grounds, and perhaps with some amorphous federalism component playing a role) because it is motivated by a "'bare ... desire to harm'" couples in same-sex marriages. ...

The penultimate sentence of the majority's opinion is a naked declaration that "[t]his opinion and its holding are confined" to those couples "joined in same-sex marriages made lawful by the State." I have heard such "bald, unreasoned disclaimer[s]" before. *Lawrence,* 539 U.S., at 604. When the Court declared a constitutional right to homosexual sodomy, we were assured that the case had nothing, nothing at all to do with "whether the government must give formal recognition to any relationship that homosexual persons seek to enter." *Id.,* at 578. Now we are told that DOMA is invalid because it "demeans the couple, whose moral and sexual choices the Constitution protects"—with an accompanying citation of *Lawrence.* ...

[T]he real rationale of today's opinion, whatever disappearing trail of its legalistic argle-bargle one chooses to follow, is that DOMA is motivated by "'bare ... desire to harm'" couples in same-sex marriages. How easy it is, indeed how inevitable, to reach the same conclusion with regard to state laws denying same-sex couples marital status. . . .

[T]hat Court which finds it so horrific that Congress irrationally and hatefully robbed same-sex couples of the "personhood and dignity" which state legislatures conferred upon them, will of a certitude be similarly appalled by state legislatures' irrational and hateful failure to acknowledge that "personhood and dignity" in the first place. As far as this Court is concerned, no one should be fooled; it is just a matter of listening and waiting for the other shoe. . . .

[The dissenting opinion of Justice Alito is omitted.]

Notes and Questions

1. What is the constitutional basis for the decision? Is it federalism? Substantive due process? Rights-based equal protection? Class-based equal protection? An amalgam of all of these? If federalism concerns are a not a formal basis for the decision, what role do they play?

2. Without regard to the precise constitutional ground for the decision, what level of scrutiny is the Court applying? The Court speaks of no "legitimate" purpose—the lingo of rational basis—but it feels like something more potent, does it not?

3. To the extent that the decision is focused on class-based equal protection concerns, what is the nature of the classification involved, according to the Court? And how does the Court's choice of how to describe the classification avoid having to deal with the question whether laws targeting same-sex conduct are facially neutral with respect to sexual orientation?

4. How if at all, is DOMA distinguishable from state laws that prohibit same-sex couples from marrying and that refuse to recognize out-of-state same-sex marriages?

Obergefell v. Hodges

135 S. Ct. 2584 (2015)

Justice Kennedy delivered the opinion of the Court. . . .

These cases come from Michigan, Kentucky, Ohio, and Tennessee, States that define marriage as a union between one man and one woman. The petitioners are 14 same-sex couples and two men whose same-sex partners are deceased. The respondents are state officials responsible for enforcing the laws in question. The petitioners claim the respondents violate the Fourteenth Amendment by denying them the right to marry or to have their marriages, lawfully performed in another State, given full recognition. . . .

This Court granted review, limited to two questions. The first, presented by the cases from Michigan and Kentucky, is whether the Fourteenth Amendment requires a State to license a marriage between two people of the same sex. The second, presented by the cases from Ohio, Tennessee, and, again, Kentucky, is whether the Fourteenth Amendment requires a State to recognize a same-sex marriage licensed and performed in a State which does grant that right. . . .

Under the Due Process Clause of the Fourteenth Amendment, no State shall "deprive any person of life, liberty, or property, without due process of law." The fundamental liberties protected by this Clause include most of the rights enumerated in the Bill of Rights. See *Duncan v. Louisiana,* 391 U.S. 145, 147–149 (1968). In addition these liberties extend to certain personal choices central to individual dignity and autonomy, including intimate choices that define personal identity and beliefs. See, *e.g., Eisenstadt v. Baird,* 405 U.S. 438, 453 (1972); *Griswold v. Connecticut,* 381 U.S. 479, 484–486 (1965).

The identification and protection of fundamental rights is an enduring part of the judicial duty to interpret the Constitution. That responsibility, however, "has not been reduced to any formula." *Poe v. Ullman,* 367 U.S. 497, 542 (1961) (Harlan, J., dissenting). Rather, it requires courts to exercise reasoned judgment in identifying interests of the person so fundamental that the State must accord them its respect. See *ibid.* That process is guided by many of the same considerations relevant to analysis of other constitutional provisions that set forth broad principles rather than specific requirements. History and tradition guide and discipline this inquiry but do not set its outer boundaries. See *Lawrence, supra,* at 572. That method respects our history and learns from it without allowing the past alone to rule the present.

The nature of injustice is that we may not always see it in our own times. The generations that wrote and ratified the Bill of Rights and the Fourteenth Amendment did not presume to know the extent of freedom in all of its dimensions, and so they entrusted to future generations a charter protecting the right of all persons to enjoy liberty as we learn its meaning. When new insight reveals discord between the Constitution's central protections and a received legal stricture, a claim to liberty must be addressed.

Applying these established tenets, the Court has long held the right to marry is protected by the Constitution. In *Loving v. Virginia,* 388 U.S. 1, 12 (1967), which invalidated bans on interracial unions, a unanimous Court held marriage is "one of the vital personal rights essential to the orderly pursuit of happiness by free men." The Court reaffirmed that holding in *Zablocki v. Redhail,* 434 U.S. 374, 384 (1978), which held the right to marry was burdened by a law prohibiting fathers who were behind on child support from marrying. The Court again applied this principle in *Turner v. Safley,* 482 U.S. 78, 95 (1987), which held the right to marry was abridged by regulations limiting the privilege of prison inmates to marry. Over time and in other contexts, the Court has reiterated that the right to marry is fundamental under the Due Process Clause. See, *e.g., Griswold, supra,* at 486; *Skinner v. Oklahoma ex rel. Williamson,* 316 U.S. 535, 541 (1942); *Meyer v. Nebraska,* 262 U.S. 390, 399 (1923).

It cannot be denied that this Court's cases describing the right to marry presumed a relationship involving opposite-sex partners. . . .

Still, there are other, more instructive precedents. This Court's cases have expressed constitutional principles of broader reach. In defining the right to marry these cases have identified essential attributes of that right based in history, tradition, and other constitutional liberties inherent in this intimate bond. See, *e.g., Lawrence,* 539 U.S., at 574; *Turner, supra,* at 95; *Zablocki, supra,* at 384; *Loving, supra,* at 12; *Griswold, supra,* at 486. And in assessing whether the force and rationale of its cases apply to same-sex couples, the Court must respect the basic reasons why the right to marry has been long protected. See, *e.g., Eisenstadt, supra,* at 453–454; *Poe, supra,* at 542–553 (Harlan, J., dissenting).

This analysis compels the conclusion that same-sex couples may exercise the right to marry. The four principles and traditions to be discussed demonstrate that the reasons marriage is fundamental under the Constitution apply with equal force to same-sex couples.

A first premise of the Court's relevant precedents is that the right to personal choice regarding marriage is inherent in the concept of individual autonomy. This abiding connection between marriage and liberty is why *Loving* invalidated interracial marriage bans under the Due Process Clause. Like choices concerning contraception, family relationships, procreation, and childrearing, all of which are protected by the Constitution, decisions concerning marriage are among the most intimate that an individual can make. See *Lawrence, supra,* at 574 . . . .

The nature of marriage is that, through its enduring bond, two persons together can find other freedoms, such as expression, intimacy, and spirituality. This is true for all persons, whatever their sexual orientation. See *Windsor,* 570 U.S., at 770-73. There is dignity in the bond between two men or two women who seek to marry and in their autonomy to make such profound choices.

A second principle in this Court's jurisprudence is that the right to marry is fundamental because it supports a two-person union unlike any other in its importance to the committed individuals. This point was central to *Griswold v. Connecticut,* which held the Constitution protects the right of married couples to use contraception. 381 U.S., at 485. Suggesting that marriage is a right "older than the Bill of Rights," *Griswold* described marriage this way:

> "Marriage is a coming together for better or for worse, hopefully enduring, and intimate to the degree of being sacred. It is an association that promotes a way of life, not causes; a harmony in living, not political faiths; a bilateral loyalty, not commercial or social projects. Yet it is an association for as noble a purpose as any involved in our prior decisions. " *Id.,* at 486.

And in *Turner,* the Court again acknowledged the intimate association protected by this right, holding prisoners could not be denied the right to marry because their committed relationships satisfied the basic reasons why marriage is a fundamental right. See 482 U.S., at 95–96. The right to marry thus dignifies couples who "wish to define themselves by their commitment to each other." *Windsor, supra,* at 763-64. Marriage responds to the universal fear that a lonely person might call out only to find no one there. It offers the hope of companionship and understanding and assurance that while both still live there will be someone to care for the other.

As this Court held in *Lawrence,* same-sex couples have the same right as opposite-sex couples to enjoy intimate association. *Lawrence* invalidated laws that made same-sex intimacy a criminal act. And it acknowledged that "[w]hen sexuality finds overt expression in intimate conduct with another person, the conduct can be but one element in a personal bond that is more enduring." 539 U.S., at 567. But while *Lawrence* confirmed a dimension of freedom that allows individuals to engage in intimate association without criminal liability, it does not follow that freedom stops there. Outlaw to outcast may be a step forward, but it does not achieve the full promise of liberty.

A third basis for protecting the right to marry is that it safeguards children and families and thus draws meaning from related rights of childrearing, procreation, and education. See *Pierce v. Society of Sisters,* 268 U.S. 510 (1925); *Meyer,* 262 U.S., at 399. The Court has recognized these connections by describing the varied rights as a unified whole: "[T]he right to 'marry, establish a home and bring up children' is a central part of the liberty protected by the Due Process Clause." *Zablocki,* 434 U.S., at 384 (quoting *Meyer, supra,* at 399). Under the laws of the several States, some of marriage's protections for children and families are material. But marriage also confers more profound benefits. By giving recognition and legal structure to their parents' relationship, marriage allows children "to understand the integrity and closeness of their own family and its concord with other families in their community and in their daily lives." *Windsor, supra,* at 771-74. Marriage also affords the permanency and stability important to children's best interests.

As all parties agree, many same-sex couples provide loving and nurturing homes to their children, whether biological or adopted. And hundreds of thousands of children are presently being raised by such couples. Most States have allowed gays and lesbians to adopt, either as individuals or as couples, and many adopted and foster children have same-sex parents. This provides powerful confirmation from the law itself that gays and lesbians can create loving, supportive families.

Excluding same-sex couples from marriage thus conflicts with a central premise of the right to marry. Without the recognition, stability, and predictability marriage offers, their children suffer the stigma of knowing their families are somehow lesser. They also suffer the significant material costs of being raised by unmarried parents, relegated through no fault of their own to a more difficult and uncertain family life. The marriage laws at issue here thus harm and humiliate the children of same-sex couples. See *Windsor, supra,* at 771-74.

That is not to say the right to marry is less meaningful for those who do not or cannot have children. An ability, desire, or promise to procreate is not and has not been a prerequisite for a valid marriage in any State. In light of precedent protecting the right of a married couple not to procreate, it cannot be said the Court or the States have conditioned the right to marry on the capacity or commitment to procreate. The constitutional marriage right has many aspects, of which childbearing is only one.

Fourth and finally, this Court's cases and the Nation's traditions make clear that marriage is a keystone of our social order. . . .

For that reason, just as a couple vows to support each other, so does society pledge to support the couple, offering symbolic recognition and material benefits to protect and nourish the union. Indeed, while the States are in general free to vary the benefits they confer on all married couples, they have throughout our history made marriage the basis for an expanding list of governmental rights, benefits, and responsibilities. . . . Valid marriage under state law is also a significant status for over a thousand provisions of federal law. See *Windsor*, 570 U.S., at 764-67. The States have contributed to the fundamental character of the marriage right by placing that institution at the center of so many facets of the legal and social order.

There is no difference between same- and opposite-sex couples with respect to this principle. Yet by virtue of their exclusion from that institution, same-sex couples are denied the constellation of benefits that the States have linked to marriage. This harm results in more than just material burdens. Same-sex couples are consigned to an instability many opposite-sex couples would deem intolerable in their own lives. As the State itself makes marriage all the more precious by the significance it attaches to it, exclusion from that status has the effect of teaching that gays and lesbians are unequal in important respects. It demeans gays and lesbians for the State to lock them out of a central institution of the Nation's society. Same-sex couples, too, may aspire to the transcendent purposes of marriage and seek fulfillment in its highest meaning. . . .

Objecting that this does not reflect an appropriate framing of the issue, the respondents refer to *Washington v. Glucksberg*, 521 U.S. 702, 721 (1997), which called for a "'careful description'" of fundamental rights. They assert the petitioners do not seek to exercise the right to marry but rather a new and nonexistent "right to same-sex marriage." *Glucksberg* did insist that liberty under the Due Process Clause must be defined in a most circumscribed manner, with central reference to specific historical practices. Yet while that approach may have been appropriate for the asserted right there involved (physician-assisted suicide), it is inconsistent with the approach this Court has used in discussing other fundamental rights, including marriage and intimacy. *Loving* did not ask about a "right to interracial marriage"; *Turner* did not ask about a "right of inmates to marry"; and *Zablocki* did not ask about a "right of fathers with unpaid child support duties to marry." Rather, each case inquired about the right to marry in its comprehensive sense, asking if there was a sufficient justification for excluding the relevant class from the right.

That principle applies here. If rights were defined by who exercised them in the past, then received practices could serve as their own continued justification and new groups could not invoke rights once denied. This Court has rejected that approach, both with respect to the right to marry and the rights of gays and lesbians. See *Loving* 388 U.S., at 12; *Lawrence,* 539 U.S., at 566–567.

The right to marry is fundamental as a matter of history and tradition, but rights come not from ancient sources alone. They rise, too, from a better informed understanding of how constitutional imperatives define a liberty that remains urgent in our own era. Many who deem same-sex marriage to be wrong reach that conclusion based on decent and honorable religious or philosophical premises, and neither they nor their beliefs are disparaged here. But when that sincere, personal opposition becomes enacted law and public policy, the necessary consequence is to put the imprimatur of the State itself on an exclusion that soon demeans or stigmatizes those whose own liberty is then denied. Under the Constitution, same-sex couples seek in marriage the same legal treatment as opposite-sex couples, and it would disparage their choices and diminish their personhood to deny them this right.

The right of same-sex couples to marry that is part of the liberty promised by the Fourteenth Amendment is derived, too, from that Amendment's guarantee of the equal protection of the laws. The Due Process Clause and the Equal Protection Clause are connected in a profound way, though they set forth independent principles. Rights implicit in liberty and rights secured by equal protection may rest on different precepts and are not always co-extensive, yet in some instances each may be instructive as to the meaning and reach of the other. In any particular case one Clause may be thought to capture the essence of the right in a more accurate and comprehensive way, even as the two Clauses may converge in the identification and definition of the right. This interrelation of the two principles furthers our understanding of what freedom is and must become.

The Court's cases touching upon the right to marry reflect this dynamic. In *Loving* the Court invalidated a prohibition on interracial marriage under both the Equal Protection Clause and the Due Process Clause. The Court first declared the prohibition invalid because of its unequal treatment of interracial couples. It stated: "There can be no doubt that restricting the freedom to marry solely because of racial classifications violates the central meaning of the Equal Protection Clause." 388 U.S., at 12. With this link to equal protection the Court proceeded to hold the prohibition offended central precepts of liberty: "To deny this fundamental freedom on so unsupportable a basis as the racial classifications embodied in these statutes, classifications so directly subversive of the principle of equality at the heart of the Fourteenth Amendment, is surely to deprive all the State's citizens of liberty without due process of law." *Ibid.* The reasons why marriage is a fundamental right became more clear and compelling from a full awareness and understanding of the hurt that resulted from laws barring interracial unions.

The synergy between the two protections is illustrated further in *Zablocki.* There the Court invoked the Equal Protection Clause as its basis for invalidating the challenged law, which, as already noted, barred fathers who were behind on child-support payments from marrying without judicial approval. The equal protection analysis depended in central part on the Court's holding that the law burdened a right "of fundamental importance." 434 U.S., at 383. It was the essential nature of the marriage right, discussed at length in *Zablocki,* see *id.,* at 383–387, that made apparent the law's incompatibility with requirements of equality. Each concept—liberty and equal protection—leads to a stronger understanding of the other.

Indeed, in interpreting the Equal Protection Clause, the Court has recognized that new insights and societal understandings can reveal unjustified inequality within our most fundamental institutions that once passed unnoticed and unchallenged. To take but one period, this occurred with respect to marriage in the 1970's and 1980's. Notwithstanding the gradual erosion of the doctrine of coverture, invidious sex-based classifications in marriage remained common through the mid–20th century. These classifications denied the equal dignity of men and women.... Responding to a new awareness, the Court invoked equal protection principles to invalidate laws imposing sex-based inequality on marriage. Like *Loving* and *Zablocki,* these precedents show the Equal Protection Clause can help to identify and correct inequalities in the institution of marriage, vindicating precepts of liberty and equality under the Constitution.

Other cases confirm this relation between liberty and equality.... In *Eisenstadt v. Baird,* the Court invoked both principles to invalidate a prohibition on the distribution of contraceptives to unmarried persons but not married persons. See 405 U.S., at 446–454. And in *Skinner v. Oklahoma ex rel. Williamson,* the Court invalidated under both principles a law that allowed sterilization of habitual criminals. See 316 U.S., at 538–543.

In *Lawrence* the Court acknowledged the interlocking nature of these constitutional safeguards in the context of the legal treatment of gays and lesbians. See 539 U.S., at 575. Although *Lawrence* elaborated its holding under the Due Process Clause, it acknowledged, and sought to remedy, the continuing inequality that resulted from laws making intimacy in the lives of gays and lesbians a crime against the State. See *ibid. Lawrence* therefore drew upon principles of liberty and equality to define and protect the rights of gays and lesbians, holding the State "cannot demean their existence or control their destiny by making their private sexual conduct a crime." *Id.,* at 578.

This dynamic also applies to same-sex marriage. It is now clear that the challenged laws burden the liberty of same-sex couples, and it must be further acknowledged that they abridge central precepts of equality. Here the marriage laws enforced by the respondents are in essence unequal: same-sex couples are denied all the benefits afforded to opposite-sex couples and are barred from exercising a fundamental right. Especially against a long history of disapproval of their relationships, this denial to same-sex couples of the right to marry works a grave and continuing harm. The imposition of this disability on gays and lesbians serves to disrespect and subordinate them. And the Equal Protection Clause, like the Due Process Clause, prohibits this unjustified infringement of the fundamental right to marry. See, *e.g., Zablocki, supra,* at 383–388; *Skinner,* 316 U.S., at 541.

These considerations lead to the conclusion that the right to marry is a fundamental right inherent in the liberty of the person, and under the Due Process and Equal Protection Clauses of the Fourteenth Amendment couples of the same-sex may not be deprived of that right and that liberty. The Court now holds that same-sex couples may exercise the fundamental right to marry. No longer may this liberty be denied to them. . . .

These cases also present the question whether the Constitution requires States to recognize same-sex marriages validly performed out of State. . . .

As counsel for the respondents acknowledged at argument, if States are required by the Constitution to issue marriage licenses to same-sex couples, the justifications for refusing to recognize those marriages performed elsewhere are undermined. The Court, in this decision, holds same-sex couples may exercise the fundamental right to marry in all States. It follows that the Court also must hold—and it now does hold—that there is no lawful basis for a State to refuse to recognize a lawful same-sex marriage performed in another State on the ground of its same-sex character. . . .

Chief Justice Roberts, with whom Justice Scalia and Justice Thomas join, dissenting. . . .

Petitioners first contend that the marriage laws of their States violate the Due Process Clause. The Solicitor General of the United States, appearing in support of petitioners, expressly disowned that position before this Court. The majority nevertheless resolves these cases for petitioners based almost entirely on the Due Process Clause. . . .

Perhaps recognizing how little support it can derive from precedent, the majority goes out of its way to jettison the "careful" approach to implied fundamental rights taken by this Court in *Glucksberg*. It is revealing that the majority's position requires it to effectively overrule *Glucksberg*, the leading modern case setting the bounds of substantive due process. At least this part of the majority opinion has the virtue of candor. Nobody could rightly accuse the majority of taking a careful approach.

Ultimately, only one precedent offers any support for the majority's methodology: *Lochner v. New York*, 198 U.S. 45 . . . .

One immediate question invited by the majority's position is whether States may retain the definition of marriage as a union of two people. *Cf. Brown v. Buhman*, 947 F.Supp.2d 1170 (Utah 2013), appeal pending, No. 14–4117 (CA10). Although the majority randomly inserts the adjective "two" in various places, it offers no reason at all why the two-person element of the core definition of marriage may be preserved while the man-woman element may not. Indeed, from the standpoint of history and tradition, a leap from opposite-sex marriage to same-sex marriage is much greater than one from a two-person union to plural unions, which have deep roots in some cultures around the world. If the majority is willing to take the big leap, it is hard to see how it can say no to the shorter one.

It is striking how much of the majority's reasoning would apply with equal force to the claim of a fundamental right to plural marriage. If "[t]here is dignity in the bond between two men or two women who seek to marry and in their autonomy to make such profound choices," why would there be any less dignity in the bond between three people who, in exercising their autonomy, seek to make the profound choice to marry? If a same-sex couple has the constitutional right to marry because their children would otherwise "suffer the stigma of knowing their families are somehow lesser," why wouldn't the same reasoning apply to a family of three or more persons raising children? If not having the opportunity to marry "serves to disrespect and subordinate" gay and lesbian couples, why wouldn't the same "imposition of this disability" serve to disrespect and subordinate people who find fulfillment in polyamorous relationships?

I do not mean to equate marriage between same-sex couples with plural marriages in all respects. There may well be relevant differences that compel different legal analysis. But if there are, petitioners have not pointed to any. When asked about a plural marital union at oral argument, petitioners asserted that a State "doesn't have such an institution." But that is exactly the point: the States at issue here do not have an institution of same-sex marriage, either. . . .

In addition to their due process argument, petitioners contend that the Equal Protection Clause requires their States to license and recognize same-sex marriages. The majority does not seriously engage with this claim. Its discussion is, quite frankly, difficult to follow. The central point seems to be that there is a "synergy between" the Equal Protection Clause and the Due Process Clause, and that some precedents relying on one Clause have also relied on the other. Absent from this portion of the opinion, however, is anything resembling our usual framework for deciding equal protection cases. It is casebook doctrine that the "modern Supreme Court's treatment of equal protection claims has used a means-ends methodology in which judges ask whether the classification the government is using is sufficiently related to the goals it is pursuing." G. Stone, L. Seidman, C. Sunstein, M. Tushnet, & P. Karlan, Constitutional Law 453 (7th ed.2013). The majority's approach today is different. . . .

The majority goes on to assert in conclusory fashion that the Equal Protection Clause provides an alternative basis for its holding. Yet the majority fails to provide even a single sentence explaining how the Equal Protection Clause supplies independent weight for its position, nor does it attempt to justify its gratuitous violation of the canon against unnecessarily resolving constitutional questions. In any event, the marriage laws at issue here do not violate the Equal Protection Clause, because distinguishing between opposite-sex and same-sex couples is rationally related to the States' "legitimate state interest" in "preserving the traditional institution of marriage." *Lawrence*, 539 U.S., at 585 (O'Connor, J., concurring in judgment).

It is important to note with precision which laws petitioners have challenged. Although they discuss some of the ancillary legal benefits that accompany marriage, such as hospital visitation rights and recognition of spousal status on official documents, petitioners' lawsuits target the laws defining marriage generally rather than those allocating benefits specifically. The equal protection analysis might be different, in my view, if we were confronted with a more focused challenge to the denial of certain tangible benefits. Of course, those more selective claims will not arise now that the Court has taken the drastic step of requiring every State to license and recognize marriages between same-sex couples. . . .

Justice Thomas, with whom Justice Scalia joins, dissenting. . . .

As used in the Due Process Clauses, "liberty" most likely refers to "the power of locomotion, of changing situation, or removing one's person to whatsoever place one's own inclination may direct; without imprisonment or restraint, unless by due course of law." 1 W. Blackstone, Commentaries on the Laws of England 130 (1769) (Blackstone). That definition is drawn from the historical roots of the Clauses and is consistent with our Constitution's text and structure. . . .

Even assuming that the "liberty" in those Clauses encompasses something more than freedom from physical restraint, it would not include the types of rights claimed by the majority. In the American legal tradition, liberty has long been understood as individual freedom from governmental action, not as a right to a particular governmental entitlement. . . .

Whether we define "liberty" as locomotion or freedom from governmental action more broadly, petitioners have in no way been deprived of it.

Petitioners cannot claim, under the most plausible definition of "liberty," that they have been imprisoned or physically restrained by the States for participating in same-sex relationships. To the contrary, they have been able to cohabitate and raise their children in peace. They have been able to hold civil marriage ceremonies in States that recognize same-sex marriages and private religious ceremonies in all States. They have been able to travel freely around the country, making their homes where they please. Far from being incarcerated or physically restrained, petitioners have been left alone to order their lives as they see fit.

Nor, under the broader definition, can they claim that the States have restricted their ability to go about their daily lives as they would be able to absent governmental restrictions. Petitioners do not ask this Court to order the States to stop restricting their ability to enter same-sex relationships, to engage in intimate behavior, to make vows to their partners in public ceremonies, to engage in religious wedding ceremonies, to hold themselves out as married, or to raise children. The States have imposed no such restrictions. Nor have the States prevented petitioners from approximating a number of incidents of marriage through private legal means, such as wills, trusts, and powers of attorney.

Instead, the States have refused to grant them governmental entitlements. Petitioners claim that as a matter of "liberty," they are entitled to access privileges and benefits that exist solely *because* of the government. They want, for example, to receive the State's *imprimatur* on their marriages—on state issued marriage licenses, death certificates, or other official forms. And they want to receive various monetary benefits, including reduced inheritance taxes upon the death of a spouse, compensation if a spouse dies as a result of a work-related injury, or loss of consortium damages in tort suits. But receiving governmental recognition and benefits has nothing to do with any understanding of "liberty" that the Framers would have recognized.

To the extent that the Framers would have recognized a natural right to marriage that fell within the broader definition of liberty, it would not have included a right to governmental recognition and benefits. Instead, it would have included a right to engage in the very same activities that petitioners have been left free to engage in—making vows, holding religious ceremonies celebrating those vows, raising children, and otherwise enjoying the society of one's spouse—without governmental interference. At the founding, such conduct was understood to predate government, not to flow from it. . . . Petitioners misunderstand the institution of marriage when they say that it would "mean little" absent governmental recognition.

Petitioners' misconception of liberty carries over into their discussion of our precedents identifying a right to marry, not one of which has expanded the concept of "liberty" beyond the concept of negative liberty. Those precedents all involved absolute prohibitions on private actions associated with marriage. *Loving v. Virginia*, 388 U.S. 1 (1967), for example, involved a couple who was criminally prosecuted for marrying in the District of Columbia and cohabiting in Virginia, *id.*, at 2–3. They were each sentenced to a year of imprisonment, suspended for a term of 25 years on the condition that they not reenter the Commonwealth together during that time. *Id.*, at 3. In a similar vein, *Zablocki v. Redhail*, 434 U.S. 374 (1978), involved a man who was prohibited, on pain of criminal penalty, from "marry[ing] in Wisconsin or elsewhere" because of his outstanding child-support obligations, *id.*, at 387; *see id.*, at 377–378. And *Turner v. Safley*, 482 U.S. 78 (1987), involved state inmates who were prohibited from entering marriages without the permission of the superintendent of the prison, permission that could not be granted absent compelling reasons, *id.*, at 82. In none of those cases were individuals denied solely governmental recognition and benefits associated with marriage. . . .

[The dissenting opinions of Justices Scalia and Alito are omitted].

*Problem 18-C: Fundamental Rights in a Post-*Obergefell *World*

Assess the constitutionality of the following laws in light of *Obergefell v. Hodges:*

(1) A state law that prohibits adoption by couples of the same sex.

(2) A state law that does not prohibit adoption by couples of the same sex, but that contains a preference for placing children with opposite-sex couples if available.

(3) A state law that provides that when a gay or transgender child is up for adoption, there is a preference for placing the child with gay or transgender parents, respectively.

(4) A state law that prohibits plural marriage (*i.e.*, marriage involving more than two persons).

(5) A state family court decree denying custody to the biological parent of a child—who is in the process of divorcing the child's other biological parent—because the parent identifies as transgender and is currently in the process of socially and medically transitioning from male to female. In denying custody, the state family court judge identified two rationales: (a) the child may be subject to ridicule by other children and adults; and (b) the parent's transition may confuse the child as he sexually develops.

(6) A state law that gets the state "out of the marriage business" by prohibiting the issuance of marriage licenses to same-sex and opposite-sex couples alike. The law does not, however, "undo" existing marriages.

Notes and Questions

1. To the extent that the decision is grounded in substantive due process, is the majority's opinion consistent with the approach to framing rights set forth in *Glucksberg*? If not, are the two cases reconcilable?

2. What role does equal protection play in this case? Is the majority treating marriage as a fundamental right partially protected by equal protection? Is it a concern with the classification? Or does this case signal a convergence of the Due Process and Equal Protection Clauses?

3. Is the right sought by the plaintiffs in this case a positive right or a negative right, and why does that matter? Does the Due Process Clause protect positive rights? What about the Equal Protection Clause?

4. Whether decided under the Due Process Clause, the Equal Protection Clause, or both, what level of scrutiny is the *Obergefell* Court applying?

5. Why did the *Obergefell* majority not decide the case by simply declaring sexual orientation to be a suspect or a quasi-suspect classification? With *Obergefell* itself declaring bans on same-sex marriage unconstitutional and Congress having repealed the ban on military service by gays, lesbians, and bisexuals, what unintended consequences of applying heightened scrutiny to hot-button social issues involving gays, lesbians, and bisexuals did the majority fear?

6. What is encompassed within the right to marry recognized in *Obergefell*? In *Pavan v. Smith*, 137 S.Ct 2075 (2017), the Court considered a constitutional challenge to Arkansas's system for placing the names of a child's parents on their birth certificate. Under Arkansas law, when a married woman gives birth, her male

spouse's name generally appears on the birth certificate regardless of his actual biological relationship to the child. However, if a married woman gives birth, her *female* spouse's name does not appear on the birth certificate. Reasoning that the state has thus "denied married same-sex couples access to the 'constellation of benefits that the Stat[e] ha[s] linked to marriage.'" *Obergefell*, 135 S.Ct., at 2601," the Court declared the Arkansas scheme unconstitutional.

Chapter 19

The Abortion Rights Cases Revisited

It should come as no surprise that the question of abortion rights in the United States is a contested one, not merely as a political matter but also a constitutional one. *Roe* recognized the right to procure an abortion as a fundamental right subject to strict scrutiny, and made most efforts by the government to restrict or even discourage procuring an abortion unconstitutional. The *Casey* plurality re-affirmed the constitutional right at stake, but introduced a new level of scrutiny—the undue burden standard—that gave the government somewhat more flexibility to restrict or discourage abortion.

Yet the undue burden standard—which was ultimately endorsed in a majority opinion in *Stenberg v. Carhart,* 530 U.S. 914 (2000)—is very different from any of the standards that the Court has applied in any other context under the Equal Protection and Due Process Clauses. The established levels of scrutiny assess constitutionality along two axes. First, they assess the strength of the governmental interest, requiring it to be either legitimate, important, or compelling. And second, they assess the means-end fit, requiring it to be either rationally related, substantially related, or narrowly tailored.

In contrast, the undue burden standard asks a single question: does the law have the purpose or effect of placing a substantial obstacle in the path of a woman seeking an abortion of a non-viable fetus? The standard provides no method of assessing the strength of new interests that the government might invoke for justifying an abortion law beyond the previously recognized interests of preserving the life and health of the pregnant woman and the life of the unborn child. Second, it does not delineate how tight the fit must be between the end the government is trying to achieve and the means employed to achieve it. Finally, it is unclear whether the strength of the government's interest matters in determining whether a burden is undue.

The three cases that follow begin to delineate the contours of the undue burden standard. As you read these cases, see if you can answer the following questions:

- Does the Court stick with some of its firm rules from *Roe*, such as the distinction between pre-viability and post-viability abortions, and the requirement of an exception for the life or health of the pregnant woman, or does it relax those rules to any extent?
- Does the Court address the question of how to assess governmental interests other than health of woman and life of the unborn fetus?

- Does the undue burden standard require a balancing of a law's benefits against its burdens? If so, must benefits outweigh burdens, and if so, by how much? And is the Court supposed to measure the cumulative burden of multiple abortion laws, or just assess each challenged law's individual or incremental effect?
- How does the undue burden standard stack up against the other levels of scrutiny? Is it closer to rational basis, intermediate, or strict scrutiny?

Gonzales v. Carhart

550 U.S. 124 (2007)

Justice Kennedy delivered the opinion of the Court.

These cases require us to consider the validity of the Partial–Birth Abortion Ban Act of 2003 (Act), a federal statute regulating abortion procedures. In recitations preceding its operative provisions the Act refers to the Court's opinion in *Stenberg v. Carhart,* 530 U.S. 914 (2000), which also addressed the subject of abortion procedures used in the later stages of pregnancy. Compared to the state statute at issue in *Stenberg,* the Act is more specific concerning the instances to which it applies and in this respect more precise in its coverage. We conclude the Act should be sustained against the objections lodged by the broad, facial attack brought against it. . . .

The Act proscribes a particular manner of ending fetal life, so it is necessary here, as it was in *Stenberg,* to discuss abortion procedures in some detail. . . .

Between 85 and 90 percent of the approximately 1.3 million abortions performed each year in the United States take place in the first three months of pregnancy, which is to say in the first trimester. . . . The Act does not regulate these procedures.

Of the remaining abortions that take place each year, most occur in the second trimester. The surgical procedure referred to as "dilation and evacuation" or "D & E" is the usual abortion method in this trimester. . . .

A doctor must first dilate the cervix at least to the extent needed to insert surgical instruments into the uterus and to maneuver them to evacuate the fetus. . . .

After sufficient dilation the surgical operation can commence. The woman is placed under general anesthesia or conscious sedation. The doctor, often guided by ultrasound, inserts grasping forceps through the woman's cervix and into the uterus to grab the fetus. The doctor grips a fetal part with the forceps and pulls it back through the cervix and vagina, continuing to pull even after meeting resistance from the cervix. The friction causes the fetus to tear apart. For example, a leg might be ripped off the fetus as it is pulled through the cervix and out of the woman. The process of evacuating the fetus piece by piece continues until it has been completely removed. A doctor may make 10 to 15 passes with the forceps to evacuate the fetus in its entirety, though sometimes removal is completed with fewer passes. Once the fetus has been evacuated, the placenta and any remaining fetal material are suctioned or scraped out of the uterus. . . .

Some doctors, especially later in the second trimester, may kill the fetus a day or two before performing the surgical evacuation. They inject digoxin or potassium chloride into the fetus, the umbilical cord, or the amniotic fluid. Fetal demise may cause contractions and make greater dilation possible. Once dead, moreover, the fetus' body will soften, and its removal will be easier. . . .

The abortion procedure that was the impetus for the numerous bans on "partial-birth abortion," including the Act, is a variation of this standard D & E. The medical community has not reached unanimity on the appropriate name for this D & E variation. It has been referred to as "intact D & E," "dilation and extraction" (D & X), and "intact D & X." For discussion purposes this D & E variation will be referred to as intact D & E. The main difference between the two procedures is that in intact D & E a doctor extracts the fetus intact or largely intact with only a few passes. . . .

In an intact D & E procedure the doctor extracts the fetus in a way conducive to pulling out its entire body, instead of ripping it apart. . . .

Intact D & E gained public notoriety when, in 1992, Dr. Martin Haskell gave a presentation describing his method of performing the operation. In the usual intact D & E the fetus' head lodges in the cervix, and dilation is insufficient to allow it to pass. Haskell explained the next step as follows:

> "'At this point, the right-handed surgeon slides the fingers of the left [hand] along the back of the fetus and "hooks" the shoulders of the fetus with the index and ring fingers (palm down).
>
> "'While maintaining this tension, lifting the cervix and applying traction to the shoulders with the fingers of the left hand, the surgeon takes a pair of blunt curved Metzenbaum scissors in the right hand. He carefully advances the tip, curved down, along the spine and under his middle finger until he feels it contact the base of the skull under the tip of his middle finger.
>
> "'[T]he surgeon then forces the scissors into the base of the skull or into the foramen magnum. Having safely entered the skull, he spreads the scissors to enlarge the opening.
>
> "'The surgeon removes the scissors and introduces a suction catheter into this hole and evacuates the skull contents. With the catheter still in place, he applies traction to the fetus, removing it completely from the patient.'"

This is an abortion doctor's clinical description. Here is another description from a nurse who witnessed the same method performed on a 26½-week fetus and who testified before the Senate Judiciary Committee:

> "'Dr. Haskell went in with forceps and grabbed the baby's legs and pulled them down into the birth canal. Then he delivered the baby's body and the arms—everything but the head. The doctor kept the head right inside the uterus. . . .
>
> "'The baby's little fingers were clasping and unclasping, and his little feet were kicking. Then the doctor stuck the scissors in the back of his head, and

> the baby's arms jerked out, like a startle reaction, like a flinch, like a baby does when he thinks he is going to fall.
>
> "'The doctor opened up the scissors, stuck a high-powered suction tube into the opening, and sucked the baby's brains out. Now the baby went completely limp....
>
> "'He cut the umbilical cord and delivered the placenta. He threw the baby in a pan, along with the placenta and the instruments he had just used.'"

Dr. Haskell's approach is not the only method of killing the fetus once its head lodges in the cervix, and "the process has evolved" since his presentation. Another doctor, for example, squeezes the skull after it has been pierced "so that enough brain tissue exudes to allow the head to pass through." Still other physicians reach into the cervix with their forceps and crush the fetus' skull. Others continue to pull the fetus out of the woman until it disarticulates at the neck, in effect decapitating it. These doctors then grasp the head with forceps, crush it, and remove it.

Some doctors performing an intact D & E attempt to remove the fetus without collapsing the skull. Yet one doctor would not allow delivery of a live fetus younger than 24 weeks because "the objective of [his] procedure is to perform an abortion," not a birth.... Another doctor testified he crushes a fetus' skull not only to reduce its size but also to ensure the fetus is dead before it is removed. For the staff to have to deal with a fetus that has "some viability to it, some movement of limbs," according to this doctor, "[is] always a difficult situation."

D & E and intact D & E are not the only second-trimester abortion methods. Doctors also may abort a fetus through medical induction. The doctor medicates the woman to induce labor, and contractions occur to deliver the fetus.... Doctors turn to two other methods of second-trimester abortion, hysterotomy and hysterectomy, only in emergency situations because they carry increased risk of complications....

After Dr. Haskell's procedure received public attention, with ensuing and increasing public concern, bans on "'partial birth abortion'" proliferated. By the time of the *Stenberg* decision, about 30 States had enacted bans designed to prohibit the procedure.... In 2003, after this Court's decision in *Stenberg*, Congress passed the Act at issue here....

The Act responded to *Stenberg* in two ways. First, Congress made factual findings.... Congress found, among other things, that "[a] moral, medical, and ethical consensus exists that the practice of performing a partial-birth abortion ... is a gruesome and inhumane procedure that is never medically necessary and should be prohibited."

Second, and more relevant here, the Act's language differs from that of the Nebraska statute struck down in *Stenberg*....

The principles set forth in the joint opinion in *Planned Parenthood of Southeastern Pa. v. Casey*, 505 U.S. 833 (1992), did not find support from all those who join the instant opinion. Whatever one's views concerning the *Casey* joint opinion, it is evident a premise central to its conclusion—that the government has a legitimate and substantial interest in preserving and promoting fetal life—would be repudiated were the Court now to affirm the judgments of the Courts of Appeals. . . .

To implement its holding, *Casey* rejected both *Roe's* rigid trimester framework and the interpretation of *Roe* that considered all previability regulations of abortion unwarranted. On this point *Casey* overruled the holdings in two cases because they undervalued the State's interest in potential life.

We assume the following principles for the purposes of this opinion. Before viability, a State "may not prohibit any woman from making the ultimate decision to terminate her pregnancy." 505 U.S., at 879 (plurality opinion). It also may not impose upon this right an undue burden, which exists if a regulation's "purpose or effect is to place a substantial obstacle in the path of a woman seeking an abortion before the fetus attains viability." *Id.*, at 878. On the other hand, "[r]egulations which do no more than create a structural mechanism by which the State, or the parent or guardian of a minor, may express profound respect for the life of the unborn are permitted, if they are not a substantial obstacle to the woman's exercise of the right to choose." *Id.*, at 877. *Casey*, in short, struck a balance. The balance was central to its holding. We now apply its standard to the cases at bar.

We begin with a determination of the Act's operation and effect. A straightforward reading of the Act's text demonstrates its purpose and the scope of its provisions: It regulates and proscribes, with exceptions or qualifications to be discussed, performing the intact D & E procedure. . . .

The Act punishes "knowingly perform[ing]" a "partial-birth abortion." It defines the unlawful abortion in explicit terms.

First, the person performing the abortion must "vaginally delive[r] a living fetus." The Act does not restrict an abortion procedure involving the delivery of an expired fetus. The Act, furthermore, is inapplicable to abortions that do not involve vaginal delivery (for instance, hysterotomy or hysterectomy). The Act does apply both previability and postviability because, by common understanding and scientific terminology, a fetus is a living organism while within the womb, whether or not it is viable outside the womb. We do not understand this point to be contested by the parties.

Second, the Act's definition of partial-birth abortion requires the fetus to be delivered "until, in the case of a head-first presentation, the entire fetal head is outside the body of the mother, or, in the case of breech presentation, any part of the fetal trunk past the navel is outside the body of the mother.". The Attorney General concedes, and we agree, that if an abortion procedure does not involve the delivery of a living fetus to one of these "anatomical 'landmarks'"—where, depending on the presentation, either the fetal head or the fetal trunk past the navel is outside the body of the mother—the prohibitions of the Act do not apply.

Third, to fall within the Act, a doctor must perform an "overt act, other than completion of delivery, that kills the partially delivered living fetus." For purposes of criminal liability, the overt act causing the fetus' death must be separate from delivery. And the overt act must occur after the delivery to an anatomical landmark. This is because the Act proscribes killing "the partially delivered" fetus, which, when read in context, refers to a fetus that has been delivered to an anatomical landmark.

Fourth, the Act contains scienter requirements concerning all the actions involved in the prohibited abortion. To begin with, the physician must have "deliberately and intentionally" delivered the fetus to one of the Act's anatomical landmarks. If a living fetus is delivered past the critical point by accident or inadvertence, the Act is inapplicable. In addition, the fetus must have been delivered "for the purpose of performing an overt act that the [doctor] knows will kill [it]." If either intent is absent, no crime has occurred. . . .

We next determine whether the Act imposes an undue burden, as a facial matter, because its restrictions on second-trimester abortions are too broad. A review of the statutory text discloses the limits of its reach. The Act prohibits intact D & E; and, notwithstanding respondents' arguments, it does not prohibit the D & E procedure in which the fetus is removed in parts.

The Act prohibits a doctor from intentionally performing an intact D & E. The dual prohibitions of the Act, both of which are necessary for criminal liability, correspond with the steps generally undertaken during this type of procedure. First, a doctor delivers the fetus until its head lodges in the cervix, which is usually past the anatomical landmark for a breech presentation. Second, the doctor proceeds to pierce the fetal skull with scissors or crush it with forceps. This step satisfies the overt-act requirement because it kills the fetus and is distinct from delivery. The Act's intent requirements, however, limit its reach to those physicians who carry out the intact D & E after intending to undertake both steps at the outset.

The Act excludes most D & Es in which the fetus is removed in pieces, not intact. If the doctor intends to remove the fetus in parts from the outset, the doctor will not have the requisite intent to incur criminal liability. A doctor performing a standard D & E procedure can often "tak[e] about 10–15 'passes' through the uterus to remove the entire fetus." Removing the fetus in this manner does not violate the Act because the doctor will not have delivered the living fetus to one of the anatomical landmarks or committed an additional overt act that kills the fetus after partial delivery.

A comparison of the Act with the Nebraska statute struck down in *Stenberg* confirms this point. The statute in *Stenberg* prohibited "'deliberately and intentionally delivering into the vagina a living unborn child, or a substantial portion thereof, for the purpose of performing a procedure that the person performing such procedure knows will kill the unborn child and does kill the unborn child.'" 530 U.S., at 922. The Court concluded that this statute encompassed D & E because "D & E will often involve a physician pulling a 'substantial portion' of a still living fetus, say, an arm or leg, into the vagina prior to the death of the fetus." 530 U.S., at 939. The Court also rejected the limiting interpretation urged by Nebraska's Attorney General that the statute's reference to a "procedure" that "'kill[s] the unborn child'" was to a distinct procedure, not to the abortion procedure as a whole. *Id.*, at 943.

Congress, it is apparent, responded to these concerns because the Act departs in material ways from the statute in *Stenberg*. It adopts the phrase "delivers a living fetus," instead of "'delivering . . . a living unborn child, or a substantial portion thereof,'" 530 U.S., at 938. The Act's language, unlike the statute in *Stenberg*, expresses the usual meaning of "deliver" when used in connection with "fetus," namely, extraction of an entire fetus rather than removal of fetal pieces. . . . D & E does not involve the delivery of a fetus because it requires the removal of fetal parts that are ripped from the fetus as they are pulled through the cervix.

The identification of specific anatomical landmarks to which the fetus must be partially delivered also differentiates the Act from the statute at issue in *Stenberg*. The Court in *Stenberg* interpreted "'substantial portion'" of the fetus to include an arm or a leg. The Act's anatomical landmarks, by contrast, clarify that the removal of a small portion of the fetus is not prohibited. The landmarks also require the fetus to be delivered so that it is partially "outside the body of the mother." To come within the ambit of the Nebraska statute, on the other hand, a substantial portion of the fetus only had to be delivered into the vagina; no part of the fetus had to be outside the body of the mother before a doctor could face criminal sanctions.

By adding an overt-act requirement Congress sought further to meet the Court's objections to the state statute considered in *Stenberg*. The Act makes the distinction the Nebraska statute failed to draw (but the Nebraska Attorney General advanced) by differentiating between the overall partial-birth abortion and the distinct overt act that kills the fetus. The fatal overt act must occur after delivery to an anatomical landmark, and it must be something "other than [the] completion of delivery." This distinction matters because, unlike intact D & E, standard D & E does not involve a delivery followed by a fatal act. . . .

Under the principles accepted as controlling here, the Act, as we have interpreted it, would be unconstitutional "if its purpose or effect is to place a substantial obstacle in the path of a woman seeking an abortion before the fetus attains viability." *Casey*, 505 U.S., at 878 (plurality opinion). The abortions affected by the Act's regulations take place both previability and postviability; so the quoted language and the undue burden analysis it relies upon are applicable. The question is whether the Act, measured by its text in this facial attack, imposes a substantial obstacle to late-term, but previability, abortions. The Act does not on its face impose a substantial obstacle, and we reject this further facial challenge to its validity.

The Act's purposes are set forth in recitals preceding its operative provisions. A description of the prohibited abortion procedure demonstrates the rationale for the congressional enactment. The Act proscribes a method of abortion in which a fetus is killed just inches before completion of the birth process. Congress stated as follows: "Implicitly approving such a brutal and inhumane procedure by choosing not to prohibit it will further coarsen society to the humanity of not only newborns, but all vulnerable and innocent human life, making it increasingly difficult to protect such life." The Act expresses respect for the dignity of human life.

Congress was concerned, furthermore, with the effects on the medical community and on its reputation caused by the practice of partial-birth abortion. The findings in the Act explain:

> "Partial-birth abortion . . . confuses the medical, legal, and ethical duties of physicians to preserve and promote life, as the physician acts directly against the physical life of a child, whom he or she had just delivered, all but the head, out of the womb, in order to end that life."

There can be no doubt the government "has an interest in protecting the integrity and ethics of the medical profession." *Washington v. Glucksberg*, 521 U.S. 702, 731 (1997). Under our precedents it is clear the State has a significant role to play in regulating the medical profession.

Casey reaffirmed these governmental objectives. The government may use its voice and its regulatory authority to show its profound respect for the life within the woman. . . . The three premises of *Casey* must coexist. The third premise, that the State, from the inception of the pregnancy, maintains its own regulatory interest in protecting the life of the fetus that may become a child, cannot be set at naught by interpreting *Casey's* requirement of a health exception so it becomes tantamount to allowing a doctor to choose the abortion method he or she might prefer. Where it has a rational basis to act, and it does not impose an undue burden, the State may use its regulatory power to bar certain procedures and substitute others, all in furtherance of its legitimate interests in regulating the medical profession in order to promote respect for life, including life of the unborn.

The Act's ban on abortions that involve partial delivery of a living fetus furthers the Government's objectives. No one would dispute that, for many, D & E is a procedure itself laden with the power to devalue human life. Congress could nonetheless conclude that the type of abortion proscribed by the Act requires specific regulation because it implicates additional ethical and moral concerns that justify a special prohibition. Congress determined that the abortion methods it proscribed had a "disturbing similarity to the killing of a newborn infant," and thus it was concerned with "draw[ing] a bright line that clearly distinguishes abortion and infanticide." The Court has in the past confirmed the validity of drawing boundaries to prevent certain practices that extinguish life and are close to actions that are condemned. *Glucksberg* found reasonable the State's "fear that permitting assisted suicide will start it down the path to voluntary and perhaps even involuntary euthanasia." 521 U.S., at 732–735, and n. 23.

Respect for human life finds an ultimate expression in the bond of love the mother has for her child. The Act recognizes this reality as well. Whether to have an abortion requires a difficult and painful moral decision. While we find no reliable data to measure the phenomenon, it seems unexceptionable to conclude some women come to regret their choice to abort the infant life they once created and sustained. Severe depression and loss of esteem can follow.

In a decision so fraught with emotional consequence some doctors may prefer not to disclose precise details of the means that will be used, confining themselves to the required statement of risks the procedure entails. . . .

It is, however, precisely this lack of information concerning the way in which the fetus will be killed that is of legitimate concern to the State. The State has an interest in ensuring so grave a choice is well informed. It is self-evident that a mother who comes to regret her choice to abort must struggle with grief more anguished and sorrow more profound when she learns, only after the event, what she once did not know: that she allowed a doctor to pierce the skull and vacuum the fast-developing brain of her unborn child, a child assuming the human form.

It is a reasonable inference that a necessary effect of the regulation and the knowledge it conveys will be to encourage some women to carry the infant to full term, thus reducing the absolute number of late-term abortions. The medical profession, furthermore, may find different and less shocking methods to abort the fetus in the second trimester, thereby accommodating legislative demand. The State's interest in respect for life is advanced by the dialogue that better informs the political and legal systems, the medical profession, expectant mothers, and society as a whole of the consequences that follow from a decision to elect a late-term abortion.

It is objected that the standard D & E is in some respects as brutal, if not more, than the intact D & E, so that the legislation accomplishes little. What we have already said, however, shows ample justification for the regulation. Partial-birth abortion, as defined by the Act, differs from a standard D & E because the former occurs when the fetus is partially outside the mother to the point of one of the Act's anatomical landmarks. It was reasonable for Congress to think that partial-birth abortion, more than standard D & E, "undermines the public's perception of the appropriate role of a physician during the delivery process, and perverts a process during which life is brought into the world." . . . .

The Act's furtherance of legitimate government interests bears upon, but does not resolve, the next question: whether the Act has the effect of imposing an unconstitutional burden on the abortion right because it does not allow use of the barred procedure where "'necessary, in appropriate medical judgment, for the preservation of the . . . health of the mother.'" *Ayotte,* 546 U.S., at 327–328 (quoting *Casey, supra,* at 879 (plurality opinion)). The prohibition in the Act would be unconstitutional, under precedents we here assume to be controlling, if it "subject[ed] [women] to significant health risks." *Ayotte, supra,* at 328; see also *Casey, supra,* at 880 (opinion of the Court). In *Ayotte* the parties agreed a health exception to the challenged parental-involvement statute was necessary "to avert serious and often irreversible damage to [a pregnant minor's] health." 546 U.S., at 328. Here, by contrast, whether the Act creates significant health risks for women has been a contested factual question. The evidence presented in the trial courts and before Congress demonstrates both sides have medical support for their position....

The question becomes whether the Act can stand when this medical uncertainty persists. The Court's precedents instruct that the Act can survive this facial attack. The Court has given state and federal legislatures wide discretion to pass legislation in areas where there is medical and scientific uncertainty.

This traditional rule is consistent with *Casey,* which confirms the State's interest in promoting respect for human life at all stages in the pregnancy. Physicians are not entitled to ignore regulations that direct them to use reasonable alternative procedures. The law need not give abortion doctors unfettered choice in the course of their medical practice, nor should it elevate their status above other physicians in the medical community....

Medical uncertainty does not foreclose the exercise of legislative power in the abortion context any more than it does in other contexts. The medical uncertainty over whether the Act's prohibition creates significant health risks provides a sufficient basis to conclude in this facial attack that the Act does not impose an undue burden.

The conclusion that the Act does not impose an undue burden is supported by other considerations. Alternatives are available to the prohibited procedure. As we have noted, the Act does not proscribe D & E.... In addition the Act's prohibition only applies to the delivery of "a living fetus." If the intact D & E procedure is truly necessary in some circumstances, it appears likely an injection that kills the fetus is an alternative under the Act that allows the doctor to perform the procedure....

The considerations we have discussed support our further determination that these facial attacks should not have been entertained in the first instance. In these circumstances the proper means to consider exceptions is by as-applied challenge. The Government has acknowledged that preenforcement, as-applied challenges to the Act can be maintained. This is the proper manner to protect the health of the woman if it can be shown that in discrete and well-defined instances a particular condition has or is likely to occur in which the procedure prohibited by the Act must be used. In an as-applied challenge the nature of the medical risk can be better quantified and balanced than in a facial attack....

Justice Thomas, with whom Justice Scalia joins, concurring.

I join the Court's opinion because it accurately applies current jurisprudence, including *Planned Parenthood of Southeastern Pa. v. Casey,* 505 U.S. 833 (1992). I write separately to reiterate my view that the Court's abortion jurisprudence, including *Casey* and *Roe v. Wade,* 410 U.S. 113 (1973), has no basis in the Constitution. I also note that whether the Partial–Birth Abortion Ban Act of 2013 constitutes a permissible exercise of Congress' power under the Commerce Clause is not before the Court. The parties did not raise or brief that issue; it is outside the question presented; and the lower courts did not address it.

Justice Ginsburg, with whom Justice Stevens, Justice Souter, and Justice Breyer join, dissenting....

Today's decision is alarming. It refuses to take *Casey* and *Stenberg* seriously. It tolerates, indeed applauds, federal intervention to ban nationwide a procedure found necessary and proper in certain cases by the American College of Obstetricians and Gynecologists (ACOG). It blurs the line, firmly drawn in *Casey,* between previability and postviability abortions. And, for the first time since *Roe,* the Court blesses a prohibition with no exception safeguarding a woman's health. . . .

The Court offers flimsy and transparent justifications for upholding a nationwide ban on intact D & E *sans* any exception to safeguard a woman's health. Today's ruling, the Court declares, advances "a premise central to [*Casey's*] conclusion"—*i.e.,* the Government's "legitimate and substantial interest in preserving and promoting fetal life." But the Act scarcely furthers that interest: The law saves not a single fetus from destruction, for it targets only a *method* of performing abortion. And surely the statute was not designed to protect the lives or health of pregnant women. . . .

As another reason for upholding the ban, the Court emphasizes that the Act does not proscribe the nonintact D & E procedure. But why not, one might ask. Nonintact D & E could equally be characterized as "brutal," involving as it does "tear[ing] [a fetus] apart" and "ripp[ing] off" its limbs. . . . Never mind that the procedures deemed acceptable might put a woman's health at greater risk.

Ultimately, the Court admits that "moral concerns" are at work, concerns that could yield prohibitions on any abortion. Notably, the concerns expressed are untethered to any ground genuinely serving the Government's interest in preserving life. By allowing such concerns to carry the day and case, overriding fundamental rights, the Court dishonors our precedent.

Revealing in this regard, the Court invokes an antiabortion shibboleth for which it concededly has no reliable evidence: Women who have abortions come to regret their choices, and consequently suffer from "[s]evere depression and loss of esteem." Because of women's fragile emotional state and because of the "bond of love the mother has for her child," the Court worries, doctors may withhold information about the nature of the intact D & E procedure. The solution the Court approves, then, is *not* to require doctors to inform women, accurately and adequately, of the different procedures and their attendant risks. Instead, the Court deprives women of the right to make an autonomous choice, even at the expense of their safety.

This way of thinking reflects ancient notions about women's place in the family and under the Constitution—ideas that have long since been discredited. . . .

In cases on a "woman's liberty to determine whether to [continue] her pregnancy," this Court has identified viability as a critical consideration. . . .

Today, the Court blurs that line, maintaining that "[t]he Act [legitimately] appl[ies] both previability and postviability because . . . a fetus is a living organism while within the womb, whether or not it is viable outside the womb." Instead of drawing the line at viability, the Court refers to Congress' purpose to differentiate "abortion and infanticide" based not on whether a fetus can survive outside the womb, but on where a fetus is anatomically located when a particular medical procedure is performed.

One wonders how long a line that saves no fetus from destruction will hold in face of the Court's "moral concerns." The Court's hostility to the right *Roe* and *Casey* secured is not concealed. Throughout, the opinion refers to obstetrician-gynecologists and surgeons who perform abortions not by the titles of their medical specialties, but by the pejorative label "abortion doctor." A fetus is described as an "unborn child," and as a "baby"; second-trimester, previability abortions are referred to as "late-term"; and the reasoned medical judgments of highly trained doctors are dismissed as "preferences" motivated by "mere convenience." Instead of the heightened scrutiny we have previously applied, the Court determines that a "rational" ground is enough to uphold the Act. And, most troubling, *Casey's* principles, confirming the continuing vitality of "the essential holding of *Roe*," are merely "assume[d]" for the moment, rather than "retained" or "reaffirmed," *Casey*, 505 U.S., at 846 . . . .

Whole Woman's Health v. Hellerstedt

136 S.Ct. 2292 (2016)

Justice Breyer delivered the opinion of the court.

In *Planned Parenthood of Southeastern Pa. v. Casey*, 505 U.S. 833, 878 (1992), a plurality of the Court concluded that there "exists" an "undue burden" on a woman's right to decide to have an abortion, and consequently a provision of law is constitutionally invalid, if the "*purpose or effect*" of the provision "*is to place a substantial obstacle* in the path of a woman seeking an abortion before the fetus attains viability." (Emphasis added.) The plurality added that "[u]nnecessary health regulations that have the purpose or effect of presenting a substantial obstacle to a woman seeking an abortion impose an undue burden on the right." *Ibid.*

We must here decide whether two provisions of Texas' House Bill 2 violate the Federal Constitution as interpreted in *Casey*. The first provision, which we shall call the "*admitting-privileges requirement*," says that

> "[a] physician performing or inducing an abortion . . . must, on the date the abortion is performed or induced, have active admitting privileges at a hospital that . . . is located not further than 30 miles from the location at which the abortion is performed or induced."

This provision amended Texas law that had previously required an abortion facility to maintain a written protocol "for managing medical emergencies and the transfer of patients requiring further emergency care to a hospital."

The second provision, which we shall call the "*surgical-center requirement*," says that

> "the minimum standards for an abortion facility must be equivalent to the minimum standards adopted under [the Texas Health and Safety Code section] for ambulatory surgical centers."

We conclude that neither of these provisions confers medical benefits sufficient to justify the burdens upon access that each imposes. Each places a substantial obstacle in the path of women seeking a previability abortion, each constitutes an undue burden on abortion access, *Casey, supra,* at 878 (plurality opinion), and each violates the Federal Constitution. Amdt. 14, § 1 . . . .

Undue Burden—Legal Standard

We begin with the standard, as described in *Casey.* We recognize that the "State has a legitimate interest in seeing to it that abortion, like any other medical procedure, is performed under circumstances that insure maximum safety for the patient." *Roe v. Wade,* 410 U.S. 113, 150 (1973). But, we added, "a statute which, while furthering [a] valid state interest, has the effect of placing a substantial obstacle in the path of a woman's choice cannot be considered a permissible means of serving its legitimate ends." *Casey,* 505 U.S., at 877 (plurality opinion). Moreover, "[u]nnecessary health regulations that have the purpose or effect of presenting a substantial obstacle to a woman seeking an abortion impose an undue burden on the right." *Id.,* at 878.

The Court of Appeals wrote that a state law is "constitutional if: (1) it does not have the purpose or effect of placing a substantial obstacle in the path of a woman seeking an abortion of a nonviable fetus; and (2) it is reasonably related to (or designed to further) a legitimate state interest." 790 F.3d, at 572. The Court of Appeals went on to hold that "the district court erred by substituting its own judgment for that of the legislature" when it conducted its "undue burden inquiry," in part because "medical uncertainty underlying a statute is for resolution by legislatures, not the courts." *Id.,* at 587 (citing *Gonzales v. Carhart,* 550 U.S. 124, 163 (2007)).

The Court of Appeals' articulation of the relevant standard is incorrect. The first part of the Court of Appeals' test may be read to imply that a district court should not consider the existence or nonexistence of medical benefits when considering whether a regulation of abortion constitutes an undue burden. The rule announced in *Casey,* however, requires that courts consider the burdens a law imposes on abortion access together with the benefits those laws confer. See 505 U.S., at 887–898, 112 S.Ct. 2791 (opinion of the Court) (performing this balancing with respect to a spousal notification provision); *id.,* at 899–901 (joint opinion of O'Connor, KENNEDY, and Souter, JJ.) (same balancing with respect to a parental notification provision). And the second part of the test is wrong to equate the judicial review applicable to the regulation of a constitutionally protected personal liberty with the less strict review applicable where, for example, economic legislation is at issue. See, *e.g., Williamson v. Lee Optical of Okla., Inc.,* 348 U.S. 483, 491 (1955). The Court of Appeals' approach simply does not match the standard that this Court laid out in *Casey,* which asks courts to consider whether any burden imposed on abortion access is "undue."

The statement that legislatures, and not courts, must resolve questions of medical uncertainty is also inconsistent with this Court's case law. Instead, the Court, when determining the constitutionality of laws regulating abortion procedures, has placed considerable weight upon evidence and argument presented in judicial proceedings. In *Casey*, for example, we relied heavily on the District Court's factual findings and the research-based submissions of *amici* in declaring a portion of the law at issue unconstitutional. 505 U.S., at 888–894 (opinion of the Court) (discussing evidence related to the prevalence of spousal abuse in determining that a spousal notification provision erected an undue burden to abortion access). And, in *Gonzales* the Court, while pointing out that we must review legislative "factfinding under a deferential standard," added that we must not "place dispositive weight" on those "findings." 550 U.S., at 165. *Gonzales* went on to point out that the "*Court retains an independent constitutional duty to review factual findings where constitutional rights are at stake.*" *Ibid.* (emphasis added). Although there we upheld a statute regulating abortion, we did not do so solely on the basis of legislative findings explicitly set forth in the statute, noting that "evidence presented in the District Courts contradicts" some of the legislative findings. *Id.*, at 166. In these circumstances, we said, "[u]ncritical deference to Congress' factual findings . . . is inappropriate." *Ibid.*

Unlike in *Gonzales*, the relevant statute here does not set forth any legislative findings. Rather, one is left to infer that the legislature sought to further a constitutionally acceptable objective (namely, protecting women's health). For a district court to give significant weight to evidence in the judicial record in these circumstances is consistent with this Court's case law. As we shall describe, the District Court did so here. It did not simply substitute its own judgment for that of the legislature. It considered the evidence in the record—including expert evidence, presented in stipulations, depositions, and testimony. It then weighed the asserted benefits against the burdens. We hold that, in so doing, the District Court applied the correct legal standard.

Undue Burden—Admitting–Privileges Requirement

Turning to the lower courts' evaluation of the evidence, we first consider the admitting-privileges requirement. Before the enactment of H.B. 2, doctors who provided abortions were required to "have admitting privileges *or* have a working arrangement with a physician(s) who has admitting privileges at a local hospital in order to ensure the necessary back up for medical complications." (emphasis added). The new law changed this requirement by requiring that a "physician performing or inducing an abortion . . . must, on the date the abortion is performed or induced, have active admitting privileges at a hospital that . . . is located not further than 30 miles from the location at which the abortion is performed or induced." The District Court held that the legislative change imposed an "undue burden" on a woman's right to have an abortion. We conclude that there is adequate legal and factual support for the District Court's conclusion.

The purpose of the admitting-privileges requirement is to help ensure that women have easy access to a hospital should complications arise during an abortion procedure. But the District Court found that it brought about no such health-related benefit. The court found that "[t]he great weight of evidence demonstrates that, before the act's passage, abortion in Texas was extremely safe with particularly low rates of serious complications and virtually no deaths occurring on account of the procedure." Thus, there was no significant health-related problem that the new law helped to cure. . . .

We have found nothing in Texas' record evidence that shows that, compared to prior law (which required a "working arrangement" with a doctor with admitting privileges), the new law advanced Texas' legitimate interest in protecting women's health.

We add that, when directly asked at oral argument whether Texas knew of a single instance in which the new requirement would have helped even one woman obtain better treatment, Texas admitted that there was no evidence in the record of such a case. . . .

At the same time, the record evidence indicates that the admitting-privileges requirement places a "substantial obstacle in the path of a woman's choice." *Casey*, 505 U.S., at 877 (plurality opinion). The District Court found, as of the time the admitting-privileges requirement began to be enforced, the number of facilities providing abortions dropped in half, from about 40 to about 20. Eight abortion clinics closed in the months leading up to the requirement's effective date. Eleven more closed on the day the admitting-privileges requirement took effect. . . .

In our view, the record contains sufficient evidence that the admitting-privileges requirement led to the closure of half of Texas' clinics, or thereabouts. Those closures meant fewer doctors, longer waiting times, and increased crowding. Record evidence also supports the finding that after the admitting-privileges provision went into effect, the "number of women of reproductive age living in a county . . . more than 150 miles from a provider increased from approximately 86,000 to 400,000 . . . and the number of women living in a county more than 200 miles from a provider from approximately 10,000 to 290,000." We recognize that increased driving distances do not always constitute an "undue burden." See *Casey*, 505 U.S., at 885–887 (joint opinion of O'Connor, Kennedy, and Souter, JJ.). But here, those increases are but one additional burden, which, when taken together with others that the closings brought about, and when viewed in light of the virtual absence of any health benefit, lead us to conclude that the record adequately supports the District Court's "undue burden" conclusion. Cf. *id.*, at 895 (opinion of the Court) (finding burden "undue" when requirement places "substantial obstacle to a woman's choice" in "a large fraction of the cases in which" it "is relevant") . . . .

Undue Burden—Surgical-Center Requirement

The second challenged provision of Texas' new law sets forth the surgical-center requirement. Prior to enactment of the new requirement, Texas law required abortion facilities to meet a host of health and safety requirements. . . .

H.B. 2 added the requirement that an "abortion facility" meet the "minimum standards . . . for ambulatory surgical centers" under Texas law. The surgical-center regulations include, among other things, detailed specifications relating to the size of the nursing staff, building dimensions, and other building requirements. . . .

There is considerable evidence in the record supporting the District Court's findings indicating that the statutory provision requiring all abortion facilities to meet all surgical-center standards does not benefit patients and is not necessary. The District Court found that "risks are not appreciably lowered for patients who undergo abortions at ambulatory surgical centers as compared to nonsurgical-center facilities." The court added that women "will not obtain better care or experience more frequent positive outcomes at an ambulatory surgical center as compared to a previously licensed facility." And these findings are well supported.

The record makes clear that the surgical-center requirement provides no benefit when complications arise in the context of an abortion produced through medication. That is because, in such a case, complications would almost always arise only after the patient has left the facility. The record also contains evidence indicating that abortions taking place in an abortion facility are safe—indeed, safer than numerous procedures that take place outside hospitals and to which Texas does not apply its surgical-center requirements. The total number of deaths in Texas from abortions was five in the period from 2001 to 2012, or about one every two years (that is to say, one out of about 120,000 to 144,000 abortions). Nationwide, childbirth is 14 times more likely than abortion to result in death, but Texas law allows a midwife to oversee childbirth in the patient's own home. Colonoscopy, a procedure that typically takes place outside a hospital (or surgical center) setting, has a mortality rate 10 times higher than an abortion. Medical treatment after an incomplete miscarriage often involves a procedure identical to that involved in a nonmedical abortion, but it often takes place outside a hospital or surgical center. And Texas partly or wholly grandfathers (or waives in whole or in part the surgical-center requirement for) about two-thirds of the facilities to which the surgical-center standards apply. But it neither grandfathers nor provides waivers for any of the facilities that perform abortions. These facts indicate that the surgical-center provision imposes "a requirement that simply is not based on differences" between abortion and other surgical procedures "that are reasonably related to" preserving women's health, the asserted "purpos[e] of the Act in which it is found." *Doe,* 410 U.S., at 194 (quoting *Morey v. Doud,* 354 U.S. 457, 465 (1957)).

Moreover, many surgical-center requirements are inappropriate as applied to surgical abortions. Requiring scrub facilities; maintaining a one-way traffic pattern through the facility; having ceiling, wall, and floor finishes; separating soiled utility and sterilization rooms; and regulating air pressure, filtration, and humidity control can help reduce infection where doctors conduct procedures that penetrate the skin. But abortions typically involve either the administration of medicines or procedures performed through the natural opening of the birth canal, which is itself not sterile. Nor do provisions designed to safeguard heavily sedated patients (unable to help themselves) during fire emergencies provide any help to abortion patients, as abortion facilities do not use general anesthesia or deep sedation. Further, since the few instances in which serious complications do arise following an abortion almost always require hospitalization, not treatment at a surgical center, surgical-center standards will not help in those instances either.

The upshot is that this record evidence, along with the absence of any evidence to the contrary, provides ample support for the District Court's conclusion that "[m]any of the building standards mandated by the act and its implementing rules have such a tangential relationship to patient safety in the context of abortion as to be nearly arbitrary." That conclusion, along with the supporting evidence, provides sufficient support for the more general conclusion that the surgical-center requirement "will not [provide] better care or . . . more frequent positive outcomes." The record evidence thus supports the ultimate legal conclusion that the surgical-center requirement is not necessary.

At the same time, the record provides adequate evidentiary support for the District Court's conclusion that the surgical-center requirement places a substantial obstacle in the path of women seeking an abortion. The parties stipulated that the requirement would further reduce the number of abortion facilities available to seven or eight facilities, located in Houston, Austin, San Antonio, and Dallas/Fort Worth. In the District Court's view, the proposition that these "seven or eight providers could meet the demand of the entire State stretches credulity." We take this statement as a finding that these few facilities could not "meet" that "demand." . . . .

[I]n the face of no threat to women's health, Texas seeks to force women to travel long distances to get abortions in crammed-to-capacity superfacilities. Patients seeking these services are less likely to get the kind of individualized attention, serious conversation, and emotional support that doctors at less taxed facilities may have offered. Healthcare facilities and medical professionals are not fungible commodities. Surgical centers attempting to accommodate sudden, vastly increased demand may find that quality of care declines. Another commonsense inference that the District Court made is that these effects would be harmful to, not supportive of, women's health.

Finally, the District Court found that the costs that a currently licensed abortion facility would have to incur to meet the surgical-center requirements were considerable, ranging from $1 million per facility (for facilities with adequate space) to $3 million per facility (where additional land must be purchased). This evidence supports the conclusion that more surgical centers will not soon fill the gap when licensed facilities are forced to close.

We agree with the District Court that the surgical-center requirement, like the admitting-privileges requirement, provides few, if any, health benefits for women, poses a substantial obstacle to women seeking abortions, and constitutes an "undue burden" on their constitutional right to do so.

[T]exas claims that the provisions at issue here do not impose a substantial obstacle because the women affected by those laws are not a "large fraction" of Texan women "of reproductive age," which Texas reads *Casey* to have required. But *Casey* used the language "large fraction" to refer to "a large fraction of cases in which [the provision at issue] is *relevant,*" a class narrower than "all women," "pregnant women," or even "the class of *women seeking abortions* identified by the State." 505 U.S., at 894–895 (opinion of the Court) (emphasis added). Here, as in *Casey,* the relevant denominator is "those [women] for whom [the provision] is an actual rather than an irrelevant restriction." *Id.*, at 895 . . . .

Justice Thomas, dissenting. . . .

This case [] underscores the Court's increasingly common practice of invoking a given level of scrutiny—here, the abortion-specific undue burden standard—while applying a different standard of review entirely. Whatever scrutiny the majority applies to Texas' law, it bears little resemblance to the undue-burden test the Court articulated in *Planned Parenthood of Southeastern Pa. v. Casey,* 505 U.S. 833 (1992), and its successors. Instead, the majority eviscerates important features of that test to return to a regime like the one that *Casey* repudiated. . . .

The majority's furtive reconfiguration of the standard of scrutiny applicable to abortion restrictions also points to a deeper problem. The undue-burden standard is just one variant of the Court's tiers-of-scrutiny approach to constitutional adjudication. And the label the Court affixes to its level of scrutiny in assessing whether the government can restrict a given right—be it "rational basis," intermediate, strict, or something else—is increasingly a meaningless formalism. As the Court applies whatever standard it likes to any given case, nothing but empty words separates our constitutional decisions from judicial fiat.

Though the tiers of scrutiny have become a ubiquitous feature of constitutional law, they are of recent vintage. Only in the 1960's did the Court begin in earnest to speak of "strict scrutiny" versus reviewing legislation for mere rationality, and to develop the contours of these tests. In short order, the Court adopted strict scrutiny as the standard for reviewing everything from race-based classifications under the Equal Protection Clause to restrictions on constitutionally protected speech. *Roe v. Wade,* 410 U.S. 113, then applied strict scrutiny to a purportedly "fundamental" substantive due process right for the first time. Then the tiers of scrutiny proliferated into ever more gradations. See, *e.g., Craig,* 429 U.S., at 197–198 (intermediate scrutiny for sex-based classifications); *Lawrence v. Texas,* 539 U.S. 558, 580 (2003) (O'Connor, J., concurring in judgment) ("a more searching form of rational basis review" applies to laws reflecting "a desire to harm a politically unpopular group"); *Buckley v. Valeo,* 424 U.S. 1, 25 (1976) (*per curiam*) (applying "'closest scrutiny'" to campaign-finance contribution limits). *Casey*'s undue-burden test added yet another right-specific test on the spectrum between rational-basis and strict-scrutiny review.

The illegitimacy of using "made-up tests" to "displace longstanding national traditions as the primary determinant of what the Constitution means" has long been apparent. The Constitution does not prescribe tiers of scrutiny. The three basic tiers—"rational basis," intermediate, and strict scrutiny—"are no more scientific than their names suggest, and a further element of randomness is added by the fact that it is largely up to us which test will be applied in each case."

But the problem now goes beyond that. If our recent cases illustrate anything, it is how easily the Court tinkers with levels of scrutiny to achieve its desired result. This Term, it is easier for a State to survive strict scrutiny despite discriminating on the basis of race in college admissions than it is for the same State to regulate how abortion doctors and clinics operate under the putatively less stringent undue-burden test. All the State apparently needs to show to survive strict scrutiny is a list of aspirational educational goals (such as the "cultivat[ion of] a set of leaders with legitimacy in the eyes of the citizenry") and a "reasoned, principled explanation" for why it is pursuing them—then this Court defers. *Fisher v. University of Tex. at Austin*, 136 S.Ct. 2198, — — (2016). Yet the same State gets no deference under the undue-burden test, despite producing evidence that abortion safety, one rationale for Texas' law, is medically debated. Likewise, it is now easier for the government to restrict judicial candidates' campaign speech than for the Government to define marriage—even though the former is subject to strict scrutiny and the latter was supposedly subject to some form of rational-basis review. Compare *Williams–Yulee v. Florida Bar*, 575 U.S. 433, 443–43 (2015), with *United States v. Windsor*, 570 U.S. 744, 768–71 (2013).

These more recent decisions reflect the Court's tendency to relax purportedly higher standards of review for less-preferred rights. Meanwhile, the Court selectively applies rational-basis review—under which the question is supposed to be whether "any state of facts reasonably may be conceived to justify" the law, *McGowan v. Maryland*, 366 U.S. 420, 426 (1961)—with formidable toughness. *E.g., Lawrence*, 539 U.S., at 580 (O'Connor, J., concurring in judgment) (at least in equal protection cases, the Court is "most likely" to find no rational basis for a law if "the challenged legislation inhibits personal relationships"); see *id.*, at 586 (Scalia, J., dissenting) (faulting the Court for applying "an unheard-of form of rational-basis review").

These labels now mean little.... The Court should abandon the pretense that anything other than policy preferences underlies its balancing of constitutional rights and interests in any given case....

[The concurring opinion of Justice Ginsburg and the dissenting opinion of Justice Alito are omitted.]

Box v. Planned Parenthood of Indiana and Kentucky, Inc.

139 S.Ct. 1780 (2019)

Per Curiam.

Indiana's petition for certiorari argues that the Court of Appeals for the Seventh Circuit incorrectly invalidated two new provisions of Indiana law: the first relating to the disposition of fetal remains by abortion providers; and the second barring the knowing provision of sex-, race-, or disability-selective abortions by abortion providers. We reverse the judgment of the Seventh Circuit with respect to the first question presented, and we deny the petition with respect to the second question presented.

The first challenged provision altered the manner in which abortion providers may dispose of fetal remains. Among other changes, it excluded fetal remains from the definition of infectious and pathological waste, thereby preventing incineration of fetal remains along with surgical byproducts. It also authorized simultaneous cremation of fetal remains, which Indiana does not generally allow for human remains. The law did not affect a woman's right under existing law "to determine the final disposition of the aborted fetus."

Respondents have never argued that Indiana's law creates an undue burden on a woman's right to obtain an abortion. Respondents have instead litigated this case on the assumption that the law does not implicate a fundamental right and is therefore subject only to ordinary rational basis review. To survive under that standard, a state law need only be "rationally related to legitimate government interests." *Washington v. Glucksberg*, 521 U. S. 702, 728 (1997) . . . .

This Court has already acknowledged that a State has a "legitimate interest in proper disposal of fetal remains." *Akron v. Akron Center for Reproductive Health, Inc.*, 462 U. S. 416, 452, n. 45 (1983) . . . . The only remaining question, then, is whether Indiana's law is rationally related to the State's interest in proper disposal of fetal remains. We conclude that it is, even if it is not perfectly tailored to that end. We therefore uphold Indiana's law under rational basis review.

We reiterate that, in challenging this provision, respondents have never argued that Indiana's law imposes an undue burden on a woman's right to obtain an abortion. This case, as litigated, therefore does not implicate our cases applying the undue burden test to abortion regulations. Other courts have analyzed challenges to similar disposition laws under the undue burden standard. Our opinion expresses no view on the merits of those challenges.

Our opinion likewise expresses no view on the merits of the second question presented, i.e., whether Indiana may prohibit the knowing provision of sex-, race-, and disability-selective abortions by abortion providers. . . .

Justice Thomas, concurring. . . .

I write separately to address the other aspect of Indiana law at issue here—the "Sex Selective and Disability Abortion Ban." This statute makes it illegal for an abortion provider to perform an abortion in Indiana when the provider knows that the mother is seeking the abortion solely because of the child's race, sex, diagnosis of Down syndrome, disability, or related characteristics. The law requires that the mother be advised of this restriction and given information about financial assistance and adoption alternatives, but it imposes liability only on the provider. Each of the immutable characteristics protected by this law can be known relatively early in a pregnancy, and the law prevents them from becoming the sole criterion for deciding whether the child will live or die. Put differently, this law and other laws like it promote a State's compelling interest in preventing abortion from becoming a tool of modern-day eugenics.

The use of abortion to achieve eugenic goals is not merely hypothetical. The foundations for legalizing abortion in America were laid during the early 20th-century birth-control movement. That movement developed alongside the American eugenics movement. And significantly, Planned Parenthood founder Margaret Sanger recognized the eugenic potential of her cause. . . .

This Court threw its prestige behind the eugenics movement in its 1927 decision upholding the constitutionality of Virginia's forced-sterilization law, *Buck v. Bell*, 274 U. S. 200. The plaintiff, Carrie Buck, had been found to be "a feeble minded white woman" who was "the daughter of a feeble minded mother . . . and the mother of an illegitimate feeble minded child." *Id.*[3] In an opinion written by Justice Oliver Wendell Holmes, Jr., and joined by seven other Justices, the Court offered a full-throated defense of forced sterilization. . . .

The Court's decision to allow further percolation should not be interpreted as agreement with the decisions below. Enshrining a constitutional right to an abortion based solely on the race, sex, or disability of an unborn child, as Planned Parenthood advocates, would constitutionalize the views of the 20th-century eugenics movement. In other contexts, the Court has been zealous in vindicating the rights of people even potentially subjected to race, sex, and disability discrimination.

Although the Court declines to wade into these issues today, we cannot avoid them forever. Having created the constitutional right to an abortion, this Court is dutybound to address its scope. . . .

[The opinion of Justice Ginsburg, concurring in part and dissenting in part, is omitted.]

Problem 19-A: Fetal Pain Prevention Acts

Assume that the legislatures of three states—State A, State B, and State C—each enact laws regulating abortion in an effort to prevent fetal pain. Each of the three states rely on two recent studies indicating that a fetus can feel pain at or after 20 weeks of gestation. The studies—although published in well-respected journals—are nonetheless strongly contested, with most other studies suggesting that a fetus is not capable of experiencing pain until later in pregnancy.

3. The finding that Buck was "feeble minded" was apparently wrong.

State A's law consists of a fetal pain notification requirement. For those women seeking an abortion at or after 20 weeks of gestation, the statute requires that the doctor make the following statement to her:

> By 20 weeks of gestational age, a fetus has the physical structures necessary to experience pain, and there is some evidence that by that age a fetus seeks to avoid certain stimuli in a manner that in an infant or adult would be interpreted as a response to pain. Accordingly, medical evidence suggests that your unborn child may experience pain during the abortion procedure if you choose to proceed with it.

After being so informed, the woman must wait at least 24 hours before obtaining an abortion. The stated legislative purpose for State A's fetal pain notification requirement is to provide women seeking an abortion with notice of the possibility that the fetus might experience pain as a result of the procedure, with the goal of encouraging her to pursue an alternative to abortion.

State B's law requires that doctors performing abortions at or after 20 weeks of gestation administer (via the woman) an anesthetic or analgesic designed to eliminate or alleviate pain to the unborn fetus caused by the abortion procedure. The stated legislative purpose for this requirement is the state's interest in preventing fetuses from experiencing pain.

Finally, State C's law relies on the same studies as States A and B to prohibit all abortions performed at or after 20 weeks except where necessary to preserve the life or health of the pregnant woman. The stated legislative purpose for this prohibition is the state's interest in preventing fetuses from experiencing pain.

You are employed as a staff attorney at an organization that advocates in favor of abortion rights. You have been asked by your supervisor to provide an unbiased assessment of the arguments in favor of and against the constitutionality of each of the three state laws in light of existing precedent so that the organization's leadership can decide whether or not to bring a legal challenge to the laws.

What is your assessment of the constitutionality of the laws enacted by States A, B, and C?

Problem 19-B: Steinem-Milk Prenatal Anti-Discrimination Act

Assume that the legislature of a U.S. state recently enacted a law entitled the "Gloria Steinem and Harvey Milk Prenatal Anti-Discrimination Act" (hereinafter, "the Act"). The Act makes it a crime for a physician to perform an abortion with the knowledge that the woman is seeking the abortion because of the sex or sexual orientation of the fetus. The statute makes clear that if a physician is unaware of the woman's unlawful purpose in seeking the abortion, the physician will not be held criminally liable. The Act applies at all stages of a woman's pregnancy. The statute does not impose criminal liability on the pregnant woman seeking the abortion. The legislative findings state, in relevant part, as follows:

> Current medical science makes it possible to determine the sex of an unborn child, while research is underway that might make it possible to determine the sexual orientation of an unborn child.
>
> There is evidence that some unborn children are targeted for abortion in our country based solely on their sex—overwhelmingly, because the unborn child is female—as well as evidence that gay or lesbian unborn children will be targeted for abortion in the future if a test for identifying sexual orientation is perfected.
>
> Permitting people to seek and physicians to perform abortions sought for these purposes reinforces negative stereotypes about the equal worth of women and sexual minorities that the state has a strong interest in combatting.

You are employed as a staff attorney at an organization that advocates in favor of abortion rights. You have been asked by your supervisor to provide an unbiased assessment of the arguments in favor of and against the Act's constitutionality in light of existing precedent so that the organization's leadership can decide whether or not to bring a legal challenge against the Act.

What is your assessment of the Act's constitutionality?

Problem 19-C: Abortion and COVID-19

In 2020, in the midst of the COVID-19 crisis, governors throughout the nation issued orders temporarily halting medical procedures deemed "non-essential." These orders were typically issued in conjunction with general "shelter in place" orders and were designed to serve two purposes. First, the orders were designed to shield healthy people from exposure to COVID-19 by preventing them from leaving their homes to receive non-essential medical treatment. Second, the orders were designed to preserve scarce medical resources needed to treat COVID-19 patients.

Among the procedures included in these orders—either explicitly or by means of executive interpretation—were abortions, including those occurring pre-viability, save for limited exceptions where necessary to preserve the life of the pregnant woman.

Lawsuits were filed challenging these orders, contending that they are inconsistent with the right to an abortion recognized in *Roe v. Wade* and its progeny.

What is your assessment of the constitutionality of the orders? If you need more information, what would you need to know, and how it would impact your analysis?

Notes and Questions

1. As Justice Ginsburg notes in her *Gonzales* dissent, the majority permits the government to prohibit a particular *type* of abortion pre-viability. Might that same rationale justify prohibiting a pre-viability abortion that is sought out for specific purposes, such as sex selection?

2. Does the *Gonzales* Court recognize new interests beyond the life and health of the pregnant woman and the life of the unborn fetus? If so, must those interests be compelling? Important? Rational? In answering this question, of what significance is it that the *Gonzales* Court relies on a justification for the law that was endorsed by the *Glucksberg* Court?

3. How does *Whole Woman's Health* address the questions whether and how the Court must balance the benefits of a law against its burdens? How clear is the guidance for application in future cases?

4. Do the *Gonzales* and *Whole Woman's Health* decisions provide any insight into how the undue burden standard compares with traditional rational basis review? Are they consistent in how they characterize the standard?

5. What do you make of Justice Thomas's critique in his *Whole Woman's Health* dissent of both the tiered levels of scrutiny and their application by the Court? Whether or not you endorse his preferred outcomes in the cases he describes, do you agree with his essential claim that the Court first decides whether or not it wants to uphold or strike down a challenged law and then manipulates the doctrine to support its desired conclusion? In other words, do you agree that the tiered levels of scrutiny are window dressing for what is in fact unfettered judicial discretion?

6. *Whole Woman's Health* was decided by a narrow 5–3 margin, with Justice Kennedy in the majority and Chief Justice Roberts and Justices Thomas and Alito in the dissent (Justice Scalia died while the decision was pending). In the years that followed, the Court moved in what most court observers viewed as a more conservative direction — with Justice Kennedy replaced by Justice Kavanaugh and Justice Gorsuch appointed to fill the vacancy created by Justice Scalia's death — resulting in a solid court majority with actual or perceived records hostile to *Roe* and its progeny. Yet in 2020, in a case that many pundits saw as a vehicle for overruling or cutting back on *Roe*, the Court, by a 5–4 margin, declared unconstitutional a Louisiana law that was largely identical to the Texas law struck down in *Whole Woman's Health*. In *June Medical Services L.L.C. v. Russo*, 591 U.S. ____ (2020), Justice Breyer penned a plurality opinion (for four Justices) that largely reiterated the Court's holding in *Whole Woman's Health*. Chief Justice Roberts provided the crucial fifth vote, writing a separate opinion concurring in the judgment only. While reiterating his dissenting view from *Whole Woman's Health* that the decision was wrongly decided, the Chief Justice viewed the two cases as indistinguishable from one another and relied on *stare decisis* as a basis for striking down the Louisiana law. *See id.* at ____, slip op. at 2–4 (Roberts, C.J., concurring in judgment).

Two aspects of the Court's decision in *June Medical Services L.L.C.* are noteworthy. First, a majority of the Court agreed that the abortion providers had third-party standing to raise the constitutional rights of their patients, and thus that the Court had jurisdiction to adjudicate the case. *See June Medical Services L.L.C.*, 591 U.S. at ___, slip op. at 11–16; *id.* at ___, slip op. at 12 n.4 (Roberts, C.J., concurring in judgment). And second, in language that may prove to be critical in future cases, Chief Justice Roberts rejected those parts of the plurality opinion (as well as those parts of *Whole Woman's Health*) that appeared to require a *weighing* or *balancing* of a law's benefits against its costs, reasoning that the task of weighing a woman's liberty interest on the one hand and the state interests in protecting potential human life and the health of a pregnant woman on the other was akin to "judging whether a particular line is longer than a particular rock is heavy." *Id.* at ___, slip op. at 6 (Roberts, C.J., concurring in judgment) (quoting *Bendix Autolite Corp. v. Midwesco Enterprises, Inc.*, 486 U.S. 888, 897 (1988) (Scalia, J., concurring in judgment). Rather, Chief Justice Roberts characterized the Court's prior decisions addressing a law's benefits (including *Whole Woman's Health*) as relevant only to the threshold requirement that the law have a "legitimate purpose" and be "reasonably related" to that purpose, with an assessment of the law's costs alone relevant to the subsequent inquiry whether the law places a "substantial obstacle" in the path of a woman seeking an abortion of a nonviable fetus. *See id.* at ___, slip op. at 5–11 (Roberts, C.J., concurring in judgment).

Indeed, just days after issuing its opinion in *June Medical Services L.L.C.*, the Court vacated a lower court decision that had declared unconstitutional a law requiring a woman to undergo an ultrasound at least 18 hours before obtaining an abortion, and directed the lower court to reconsider its decision in light of *June Medical Services L.L.C. See Box v. Planned Parenthood of Indiana and Kentucky*, 591 U.S. ___ (2020). The lower court had balanced the law's benefits and costs in a manner condemned by Chief Justice Roberts in his concurring opinion in *June Medical Services L.L.C. See Planned Parenthood of Indiana and Kentucky v. Indiana State Department of Health*, 896 F.3d 809 (2018). Does this turn of events suggest that *June Medical Services L.L.C.* will lead to a narrowing of the abortion right in future cases with facts distinguishable from *Whole Woman's Health*?

7. Assume that in *Box*, the challengers *did* argue that the fetal disposition law infringes upon the fundamental right to an abortion. Do you agree that this would be a fair characterization, and if so, how would the law fare under the undue burden standard?

Chapter 20

The Privileges or Immunities Clause Revisited

Recall from Chapter 2 that the Court's first decision interpreting the Reconstruction Amendments, *The Slaughter-House Cases*, narrowly interpreted the Fourteenth Amendment's Privileges or Immunities Clause so as to make it virtually dead letter. Not only did the four dissenters in that case view that as a mistake, but so do many constitutional law scholars. The Court's subsequent use of the ill-fitting Equal Protection and Due Process Clauses to enforce unenumerated fundamental rights has been viewed by many as a messy way to undo the mistake made by the Court in *The Slaughter-House Cases.*

Yet in recent years, the Court—or at least some individual Justices—have called for re-considering the vitality of the Privileges or Immunities Clause. The following case excerpts explore that idea in further detail.

Saenz v. Roe

526 U.S. 489 (1999)

Justice Stevens delivered the opinion of the Court.

In 1992, California enacted a statute limiting the maximum welfare benefits available to newly arrived residents. The scheme limits the amount payable to a family that has resided in the State for less than 12 months to the amount payable by the State of the family's prior residence. . . .

The word "travel" is not found in the text of the Constitution. Yet the "constitutional right to travel from one State to another" is firmly embedded in our jurisprudence. . . .

In *Shapiro,* we reviewed the constitutionality of three statutory provisions that denied welfare assistance to residents of Connecticut, the District of Columbia, and Pennsylvania, who had resided within those respective jurisdictions less than one year immediately preceding their applications for assistance. Without pausing to identify the specific source of the right, we began by noting that the Court had long "recognized that the nature of our Federal Union and our constitutional concepts of personal liberty unite to require that all citizens be free to travel throughout the length and breadth of our land uninhibited by statutes, rules, or regulations which unreasonably burden or restrict this movement." *Id.,* at 629. We squarely held that it was "constitutionally impermissible" for a State to enact durational residency requirements for the purpose of inhibiting the migration by needy persons into the State. We further held that a classification that had the effect of imposing a penalty on the exercise of the right to travel violated the Equal Protection Clause "unless shown to be necessary to promote a *compelling* governmental interest," *id.,* at 634, and that no such showing had been made.

In this case California argues that § 11450.03 was not enacted for the impermissible purpose of inhibiting migration by needy persons and that, unlike the legislation reviewed in *Shapiro,* it does not penalize the right to travel because new arrivals are not ineligible for benefits during their first year of residence. California submits that, instead of being subjected to the strictest scrutiny, the statute should be upheld if it is supported by a rational basis and that the State's legitimate interest in saving over $10 million a year satisfies that test. . . . The debate about the appropriate standard of review . . . persuades us that it will be useful to focus on the source of the constitutional right on which respondents rely.

The "right to travel" discussed in our cases embraces at least three different components. It protects the right of a citizen of one State to enter and to leave another State, the right to be treated as a welcome visitor rather than an unfriendly alien when temporarily present in the second State, and, for those travelers who elect to become permanent residents, the right to be treated like other citizens of that State.

It was the right to go from one place to another, including the right to cross state borders while en route, that was vindicated in *Edwards v. California,* 314 U.S. 160 (1941), which invalidated a state law that impeded the free interstate passage of the indigent. We reaffirmed that right in *United States v. Guest,* 383 U.S. 745 (1966), which afforded protection to the "'right to travel freely to and from the State of Georgia and to use highway facilities and other instrumentalities of interstate commerce within the State of Georgia.'" *Id.,* at 757. Given that § 11450.03 imposed no obstacle to respondents' entry into California, we think the State is correct when it argues that the statute does not directly impair the exercise of the right to free interstate movement. For the purposes of this case, therefore, we need not identify the source of that particular right in the text of the Constitution. . . .

The second component of the right to travel is, however, expressly protected by the text of the Constitution. The first sentence of Article IV, § 2, provides:

> "The Citizens of each State shall be entitled to all Privileges and Immunities of Citizens in the several States."

Thus, by virtue of a person's state citizenship, a citizen of one State who travels in other States, intending to return home at the end of his journey, is entitled to enjoy the "Privileges and Immunities of Citizens in the several States" that he visits. . . . It provides important protections for nonresidents who enter a State whether to obtain employment, *Hicklin v. Orbeck,* 437 U.S. 518 (1978), to procure medical services, *Doe v. Bolton,* 410 U.S. 179, 200 (1973), or even to engage in commercial shrimp fishing, *Toomer v. Witsell,* 334 U.S. 385 (1948). Those protections are not "absolute," but the Clause "does bar discrimination against citizens of other States where there is no substantial reason for the discrimination beyond the mere fact that they are citizens of other States." *Id.*, at 396. There may be a substantial reason for requiring the nonresident to pay more than the resident for a hunting license, see *Baldwin v. Fish and Game Comm'n of Mont.*, 436 U.S. 371, 390–391 (1978), or to enroll in the state university, see *Vlandis v. Kline*, 412 U.S. 441, 445 (1973), but our cases have not identified any acceptable reason for qualifying the protection afforded by the Clause for "the 'citizen of State A who ventures into State B' to settle there and establish a home." *Zobel*, 457 U.S., at 74 (O'CONNOR, J., concurring in judgment). Permissible justifications for discrimination between residents and nonresidents are simply inapplicable to a nonresident's exercise of the right to move into another State and become a resident of that State.

What is at issue in this case, then, is this third aspect of the right to travel-the right of the newly arrived citizen to the same privileges and immunities enjoyed by other citizens of the same State. That right is protected not only by the new arrival's status as a state citizen, but also by her status as a citizen of the United States.[15] That additional source of protection is plainly identified in the opening words of the Fourteenth Amendment:

> "All persons born or naturalized in the United States, and subject to the jurisdiction thereof, are citizens of the United States and of the State wherein they reside. No State shall make or enforce any law which shall abridge the privileges or immunities of citizens of the United States; . . . ."

Despite fundamentally differing views concerning the coverage of the Privileges or Immunities Clause of the Fourteenth Amendment, most notably expressed in the majority and dissenting opinions in the *Slaughter-House Cases*, 16 Wall. 36 (1872), it has always been common ground that this Clause protects the third component of the right to travel. Writing for the majority in the *Slaughter-House Cases*, Justice Miller explained that one of the privileges conferred by this Clause "is that a citizen of the United States can, of his own volition, become a citizen of any State of the Union by a *bonâ fide* residence therein, with the same rights as other citizens of that State." *Id.*, at 80. Justice Bradley, in dissent, used even stronger language to make the same point. . . .

That newly arrived citizens "have two political capacities, one state and one federal," adds special force to their claim that they have the same rights as others who share their citizenship. Neither mere rationality nor some intermediate standard of review should be used to judge the constitutionality of a state rule that discriminates

15. The Framers of the Fourteenth Amendment modeled this Clause upon the "Privileges and Immunities" Clause found in Article IV. In *Dred Scott v. Sandford*, 19 How. 393 (1856), this Court had limited the protection of Article IV to rights under state law and concluded that free blacks could not claim citizenship. The Fourteenth Amendment overruled this decision. The Amendment's Privileges or Immunities Clause and Citizenship Clause guaranteed the rights of newly freed black citizens by ensuring that they could claim the state citizenship of any State in which they resided and by precluding that State from abridging their rights of national citizenship.

against some of its citizens because they have been domiciled in the State for less than a year. The appropriate standard may be more categorical than that articulated in *Shapiro,* but it is surely no less strict.

Because this case involves discrimination against citizens who have completed their interstate travel, the State's argument that its welfare scheme affects the right to travel only "incidentally" is beside the point. Were we concerned solely with actual deterrence to migration, we might be persuaded that a partial withholding of benefits constitutes a lesser incursion on the right to travel than an outright denial of all benefits. But since the right to travel embraces the citizen's right to be treated equally in her new State of residence, the discriminatory classification is itself a penalty.

It is undisputed that respondents and the members of the class that they represent are citizens of California and that their need for welfare benefits is unrelated to the length of time that they have resided in California. We thus have no occasion to consider what weight might be given to a citizen's length of residence if the bona fides of her claim to state citizenship were questioned. Moreover, because whatever benefits they receive will be consumed while they remain in California, there is no danger that recognition of their claim will encourage citizens of other States to establish residency for just long enough to acquire some readily portable benefit, such as a divorce or a college education, that will be enjoyed after they return to their original domicile. See, *e.g., Sosna v. Iowa,* 419 U.S. 393 (1975); *Vlandis v. Kline,* 412 U.S. 441 (1973).

The classifications challenged in this case-and there are many-are defined entirely by (a) the period of residency in California and (b) the location of the prior residences of the disfavored class members. The favored class of beneficiaries includes all eligible California citizens who have resided there for at least one year, plus those new arrivals who last resided in another country or in a State that provides benefits at least as generous as California's. Thus, within the broad category of citizens who resided in California for less than a year, there are many who are treated like lifetime residents. And within the broad subcategory of new arrivals who are treated less favorably, there are many smaller classes whose benefit levels are determined by the law of the States from whence they came. To justify § 11450.03, California must therefore explain not only why it is sound fiscal policy to discriminate against those who have been citizens for less than a year, but also why it is permissible to apply such a variety of rules within that class.

These classifications may not be justified by a purpose to deter welfare applicants from migrating to California for three reasons. First, although it is reasonable to assume that some persons may be motivated to move for the purpose of obtaining higher benefits, the empirical evidence reviewed by the District Judge, which takes into account the high cost of living in California, indicates that the number of such persons is quite small—surely not large enough to justify a burden on those who had no such motive. Second, California has represented to the Court that the legislation was not enacted for any such reason. Third, even if it were, as we squarely held in *Shapiro v. Thompson,* 394 U.S. 618 (1969), such a purpose would be unequivocally impermissible.

Disavowing any desire to fence out the indigent, California has instead advanced an entirely fiscal justification for its multitiered scheme. The enforcement of § 11450.03 will save the State approximately $10.9 million a year. The question is not whether such saving is a legitimate purpose but whether the State may accomplish that end by the discriminatory means it has chosen. An evenhanded, across-the-board reduction of about 72 cents per month for every beneficiary would produce the same result. But our negative answer to the question does not rest on the weakness of the State's purported fiscal justification. It rests on the fact that the Citizenship Clause of the Fourteenth Amendment expressly equates citizenship with residence: "That Clause does not provide for, and does not allow for, degrees of citizenship based on length of residence." *Zobel,* 457 U.S., at 69. It is equally clear that the Clause does not tolerate a hierarchy of 45 subclasses of similarly situated citizens based on the location of their prior residence. Thus § 11450.03 is doubly vulnerable: Neither the duration of respondents' California residence, nor the identity of their prior States of residence, has any relevance to their need for benefits. Nor do those factors bear any relationship to the State's interest in making an equitable allocation of the funds to be distributed among its needy citizens. As in *Shapiro,* we reject any contributory rationale for the denial of benefits to new residents. . . .

* * *

Citizens of the United States, whether rich or poor, have the right to choose to be citizens "of the State wherein they reside." U.S. Const., Amdt. 14, § 1. The States, however, do not have any right to select their citizens. The Fourteenth Amendment, like the Constitution itself, was, as Justice Cardozo put it, "framed upon the theory that the peoples of the several states must sink or swim together, and that in the long run prosperity and salvation are in union and not division." *Baldwin v. G.A.F. Seelig, Inc.,* 294 U.S. 511, 523 (1935) . . . .

Chief Justice Rehnquist, with whom Justice Thomas joins, dissenting.

The Court today breathes new life into the previously dormant Privileges or Immunities Clause of the Fourteenth Amendment—a Clause relied upon by this Court in only one other decision overruled five years later. . . . Because I do not think any provision of the Constitution—and surely not a provision relied upon for only the second time since its enactment 130 years ago—requires this result, I dissent.

Much of the Court's opinion is unremarkable and sound. The right to travel clearly embraces the right to go from one place to another, and prohibits States from impeding the free interstate passage of citizens. . . .

The Court wisely holds that because Cal. Welf. & Inst.Code Ann. § 11450.03 imposes no obstacle to respondents' entry into California, the statute does not infringe upon the right to travel. Thus, the traditional conception of the right to travel is simply not an issue in this case.

I also have no difficulty with aligning the right to travel with the protections afforded by the Privileges and Immunities Clause of Article IV, § 2, to nonresidents who enter other States "intending to return home at the end of [their] journey." Nonresident visitors of other States should not be subject to discrimination solely because they live out of State. Like the traditional right-to-travel guarantees discussed above, however, this Clause has no application here, because respondents expressed a desire to stay in California and become citizens of that State. Respondents therefore plainly fall outside the protections of Article IV, § 2.

Finally, I agree with the proposition that a "citizen of the United States can, of his own volition, become a citizen of any State of the Union by a *bonâ fide* residence therein, with the same rights as other citizens of that State." *Slaughter-House Cases,* 16 Wall. 36, 80 (1872).

But I cannot see how the right to become a citizen of another State is a necessary "component" of the right to travel, or why the Court tries to marry these separate and distinct rights. A person is no longer "traveling" in any sense of the word when he finishes his journey to a State which he plans to make his home. Indeed, under the Court's logic, the protections of the Privileges or Immunities Clause recognized in this case come into play only when an individual *stops* traveling with the intent to remain and become a citizen of a new State. The right to travel and the right to become a citizen are distinct, their relationship is not reciprocal, and one is not a "component" of the other. . . . At most, restrictions on an individual's right to become a citizen indirectly affect his calculus in deciding whether to exercise his right to travel in the first place, but such an attenuated and uncertain relationship is no ground for folding one right into the other.

No doubt the Court has, in the past 30 years, essentially conflated the right to travel with the right to equal state citizenship in striking down durational residence requirements similar to the one challenged here. These cases marked a sharp departure from the Court's prior right-to-travel cases because in none of them was travel itself prohibited.

Instead, the Court in these cases held that restricting the provision of welfare benefits, votes, or certain medical benefits to new citizens for a limited time impermissibly "penalized" them under the Equal Protection Clause of the Fourteenth Amendment for having exercised their right to travel. The Court thus settled for deciding what restrictions amounted to "deprivations of very important benefits and rights" that operated to indirectly "penalize" the right to travel. In other cases, the Court recognized that laws dividing new and old residents had little to do with the right to travel and merely triggered an inquiry into whether the resulting classification rationally furthered a legitimate government purpose. . . .

The Court today tries to clear much of the underbrush created by these prior right-to-travel cases, abandoning its effort to define what residence requirements deprive individuals of "important rights and benefits" or "penalize" the right to travel. Under its new analytical framework, a State, outside certain ill-defined circumstances, cannot classify its citizens by the length of their residence in the State without offending the Privileges or Immunities Clause of the Fourteenth Amendment. The Court thus departs from *Shapiro* and its progeny, and, while paying lipservice to the right to travel, the Court does little to explain how the right to travel is involved at all. Instead, as the Court's analysis clearly demonstrates, this case is only about respondents' right to immediately enjoy all the privileges of being a California citizen in relation to that State's ability to test the good-faith assertion of this right. The Court has thus come full circle by effectively disavowing the analysis of *Shapiro,* segregating the right to travel and the rights secured by Article IV from the right to become a citizen under the Privileges or Immunities Clause, and then testing the residence requirement here against this latter right. For all its misplaced efforts to fold the right to become a citizen into the right to travel, the Court has essentially returned to its original understanding of the right to travel.

In unearthing from its tomb the right to become a state citizen and to be treated equally in the new State of residence, however, the Court ignores a State's need to assure that only persons who establish a bona fide residence receive the benefits provided to current residents of the State. The *Slaughter-House* dicta at the core of the Court's analysis specifically condition a United States citizen's right to "become a citizen of any state of the Union" and to enjoy the "same rights as other citizens of that State" on the establishment of a "*bonâ fide residence therein.*" 16 Wall., at 80 (emphasis added) . . . .

While the physical presence element of a bona fide residence is easy to police, the subjective intent element is not. It is simply unworkable and futile to require States to inquire into each new resident's subjective intent to remain. Hence, States employ objective criteria such as durational residence requirements to test a new resident's resolve to remain before these new citizens can enjoy certain in-state benefits. Recognizing the practical appeal of such criteria, this Court has repeatedly sanctioned the State's use of durational residence requirements before new residents receive in-state tuition rates at state universities. . . . The Court has done the same in upholding a 1-year residence requirement for eligibility to obtain a divorce in state courts, see *Sosna v. Iowa,* 419 U.S. 393, 406–409 (1975), and in upholding political party registration restrictions that amounted to a durational residency requirement for voting in primary elections, see *Rosario v. Rockefeller,* 410 U.S. 752, 760–762 (1973).

If States can require individuals to reside in-state for a year before exercising the right to educational benefits, the right to terminate a marriage, or the right to vote in primary elections that all other state citizens enjoy, then States may surely do the same for welfare benefits. Indeed, there is no material difference between a 1-year residence requirement applied to the level of welfare benefits given out by a State, and the same requirement applied to the level of tuition subsidies at a state university. The welfare payment here and in-state tuition rates are cash subsidies provided to a limited class of people, and California's standard of living and higher education system make both subsidies quite attractive. . . .

The Court today recognizes that States retain the ability to determine the bona fides of an individual's claim to residence, but then tries to avoid the issue. It asserts that because respondents' need for welfare benefits is unrelated to the length of time they have resided in California, it has "no occasion to consider what weight might be given to a citizen's length of residence if the bona fides of her claim to state citizenship were questioned." See *ibid.* But I do not understand how the absence of a link between need and length of residency bears on the State's ability to objectively test respondents' resolve to stay in California. There is no link between the need for an education or for a divorce and the length of residence, and yet States may use length of residence as an objective yardstick to channel their benefits to those whose intent to stay is legitimate. . . .

The Court tries to distinguish education and divorce benefits by contending that the welfare payment here will be consumed in California, while a college education or a divorce produces benefits that are "portable" and can be enjoyed after individuals return to their original domicile. But this "you can't take it with you" distinction is more apparent than real, and offers little guidance to lower courts who must apply this rationale in the future. Welfare payments are a form of insurance, giving impoverished individuals and their families the means to meet the demands of daily life while they receive the necessary training, education, and time to look for a job. The cash itself will no doubt be spent in California, but the benefits from receiving this income and having the opportunity to become employed or employable will stick with the welfare recipients if they stay in California or go back to their true domicile. Similarly, tuition subsidies are "consumed" in-state but the recipient takes the benefits of a college education with him wherever he goes. A welfare subsidy is thus as much an investment in human capital as is a tuition subsidy, and their attendant benefits are just as "portable." [FN3] More importantly, this foray into social economics demonstrates that the line drawn by the Court borders on the metaphysical, and requires lower courts to plumb the policies animating certain benefits like welfare to define their "essence" and hence their "portability." . . . .

Justice Thomas, with whom The Chief Justice joins, dissenting. . . .

The Privileges or Immunities Clause of the Fourteenth Amendment provides that "[n]o State shall make or enforce any law which shall abridge the privileges or immunities of citizens of the United States." U.S. Const., Amdt. 14, § 1. Unlike the Equal Protection and Due Process Clauses, which have assumed near-talismanic status in modern constitutional law, the Court all but read the Privileges or Immunities Clause out of the Constitution in the *Slaughter-House Cases,* 16 Wall. 36 (1872) . . . .

As The Chief Justice points out, it comes as quite a surprise that the majority relies on the Privileges or Immunities Clause at all in this case. That is because, as I have explained, the *Slaughter-House Cases* sapped the Clause of any meaning. Although the majority appears to breathe new life into the Clause today, it fails to address its historical underpinnings or its place in our constitutional jurisprudence. Because I believe that the demise of the Privileges or Immunities Clause has contributed in no small part to the current disarray of our Fourteenth Amendment jurisprudence, I would be open to reevaluating its meaning in an appropriate case. Before invoking the Clause, however, we should endeavor to understand what the Framers of the Fourteenth Amendment thought that it meant. We should also consider whether the Clause should displace, rather than augment, portions of our equal protection and substantive due process jurisprudence. The majority's failure to consider these important questions raises the specter that the Privileges or Immunities Clause will become yet another convenient tool for inventing new rights, limited solely by the "predilections of those who happen at the time to be Members of this Court." *Moore v. East Cleveland,* 431 U.S. 494, 502 (1977) . . . .

Problem 20-A: COVID-19 Self-Quarantine

In 2020, in the midst of the COVID-19 crisis, governors in individual states—such as Alaska, Florida, Hawaii and Texas—issued orders requiring people arriving in their states to "self-quarantine" for a period of time (typically 2 weeks) before moving about the state. Some of the orders, such as those in Alaska and Hawaii, applied to anyone entering their states, while others, such as those in Florida and Texas, applied only to those arriving from states such as New York that were experiencing major COVID-19 outbreaks. All of the laws applied equally to out-of-state citizens and returning in-state citizens.

Did such orders violate any aspect of the "right to travel" identified in Saenz v. Roe?

McDonald v. City of Chicago

561 U.S. 742 (2010)

[In this decision—excerpted in greater detail in Chapter 3—the Court held the Second Amendment applicable to the states via "incorporation" pursuant to the Due Process Clause. In a concurring opinion, Justice Thomas agreed that the Second Amendment was applicable to the states, but viewed the Privileges or Immunities Clause as the appropriate conduit.]

Justice Thomas, concurring in part and concurring in the judgment.

I agree with the Court that the Fourteenth Amendment makes the right to keep and bear arms set forth in the Second Amendment "fully applicable to the States." I write separately because I believe there is a more straightforward path to this conclusion, one that is more faithful to the Fourteenth Amendment's text and history. . . .

In the *Slaughter-House Cases,* 16 Wall. 36 (1873), decided just five years after the Fourteenth Amendment's adoption, the Court interpreted this text, now known as the Privileges or Immunities Clause, for the first time. In a closely divided decision, the Court drew a sharp distinction between the privileges and immunities of state citizenship and those of federal citizenship, and held that the Privileges or Immunities Clause protected only the latter category of rights from state abridgment. The Court defined that category to include only those rights "which owe their existence to the Federal government, its National character, its Constitution, or its laws." *Id.*, at 79. This arguably left open the possibility that certain individual rights enumerated in the Constitution could be considered privileges or immunities of federal citizenship. See *ibid.* (listing "[t]he right to peaceably assemble" and "the privilege of the writ of *habeas corpus* " as rights potentially protected by the Privileges or Immunities Clause). But the Court soon rejected that proposition, interpreting the Privileges or Immunities Clause even more narrowly in its later cases.

Chief among those cases is *United States v. Cruikshank,* 92 U.S. 542 (1876). There, the Court held that members of a white militia who had brutally murdered as many as 165 black Louisianians congregating outside a courthouse had not deprived the victims of their privileges as American citizens to peaceably assemble or to keep and bear arms. According to the Court, the right to peaceably assemble codified in the First Amendment was not a privilege of United States citizenship because "[t]he right . . . existed long *before* the adoption of the Constitution." 92 U.S., at 551 (emphasis added). Similarly, the Court held that the right to keep and bear arms was not a privilege of United States citizenship because it was not "in any manner dependent upon that instrument for its existence." *Id.*, at 553. In other words, the reason the Framers codified the right to bear arms in the Second Amendment—its nature as an inalienable right that pre-existed the Constitution's adoption—was the very reason citizens could not enforce it against States through the Fourteenth.

That circular reasoning effectively has been the Court's last word on the Privileges or Immunities Clause. In the intervening years, the Court has held that the Clause prevents state abridgment of only a handful of rights, such as the right to travel, see *Saenz v. Roe,* 526 U.S. 489, 503 (1999), that are not readily described as essential to liberty.

As a consequence of this Court's marginalization of the Clause, litigants seeking federal protection of fundamental rights turned to the remainder of § 1 in search of an alternative fount of such rights. They found one in a most curious place—that section's command that every State guarantee "due process" to any person before depriving him of "life, liberty, or property." . . . .

All of this is a legal fiction. The notion that a constitutional provision that guarantees only "process" before a person is deprived of life, liberty, or property could define the substance of those rights strains credulity for even the most casual user of words. Moreover, this fiction is a particularly dangerous one. The one theme that links the Court's substantive due process precedents together is their lack of a guiding principle to distinguish "fundamental" rights that warrant protection from nonfundamental rights that do not. Today's decision illustrates the point. Replaying a debate that has endured from the inception of the Court's substantive due process jurisprudence, the dissents laud the "flexibility" in this Court's substantive due process doctrine, while the plurality makes yet another effort to impose principled restraints on its exercise. But neither side argues that the meaning they attribute to the Due Process Clause was consistent with public understanding at the time of its ratification.

To be sure, the plurality's effort to cabin the exercise of judicial discretion under the Due Process Clause by focusing its inquiry on those rights deeply rooted in American history and tradition invites less opportunity for abuse than the alternatives. But any serious argument over the scope of the Due Process Clause must acknowledge that neither its text nor its history suggests that it protects the many substantive rights this Court's cases now claim it does.

I cannot accept a theory of constitutional interpretation that rests on such tenuous footing. This Court's substantive due process framework fails to account for both the text of the Fourteenth Amendment and the history that led to its adoption, filling that gap with a jurisprudence devoid of a guiding principle. I believe the original meaning of the Fourteenth Amendment offers a superior alternative, and that a return to that meaning would allow this Court to enforce the rights the Fourteenth Amendment is designed to protect with greater clarity and predictability than the substantive due process framework has so far managed....

The Privileges or Immunities Clause of the Fourteenth Amendment declares that "[n]o State ... shall abridge the privileges or immunities of citizens of the United States." In interpreting this language, it is important to recall that constitutional provisions are "'written to be understood by the voters.'" *Heller,* 128 S.Ct., at 2788 (quoting *United States v. Sprague,* 282 U.S. 716, 731 (1931)). Thus, the objective of this inquiry is to discern what "ordinary citizens" at the time of ratification would have understood the Privileges or Immunities Clause to mean.

At the time of Reconstruction, the terms "privileges" and "immunities" had an established meaning as synonyms for "rights." The two words, standing alone or paired together, were used interchangeably with the words "rights," "liberties," and "freedoms," and had been since the time of Blackstone. In addition, dictionary definitions confirm that the public shared this understanding.

The fact that a particular interest was designated as a "privilege" or "immunity," rather than a "right," "liberty," or "freedom," revealed little about its substance. Blackstone, for example, used the terms "privileges" and "immunities" to describe both the inalienable rights of individuals and the positive-law rights of corporations....

The group of rights-bearers to whom the Privileges or Immunities Clause applies is, of course, "citizens." By the time of Reconstruction, it had long been established that both the States and the Federal Government existed to preserve their citizens' inalienable rights, and that these rights were considered "privileges" or "immunities" of citizenship.

This tradition begins with our country's English roots. Parliament declared the basic liberties of English citizens in a series of documents ranging from the Magna Carta to the Petition of Right and the English Bill of Rights.... These rights included many that later would be set forth in our Federal Bill of Rights, such as the right to petition for redress of grievances, the right to a jury trial, and the right of "Protestants" to "have arms for their defence."

As English subjects, the colonists considered themselves to be vested with the same fundamental rights as other Englishmen. They consistently claimed the rights of English citizenship in their founding documents, repeatedly referring to these rights as "privileges" and "immunities." . . . .

As tensions between England and the Colonies increased, the colonists adopted protest resolutions reasserting their claim to the inalienable rights of Englishmen. Again, they used the terms "privileges" and "immunities" to describe these rights. . . .

After declaring their independence, the newly formed States replaced their colonial charters with constitutions and state bills of rights, almost all of which guaranteed the same fundamental rights that the former colonists previously had claimed by virtue of their English heritage.

Several years later, the Founders amended the Constitution to expressly protect many of the same fundamental rights against interference by the Federal Government. Consistent with their English heritage, the founding generation generally did not consider many of the rights identified in these amendments as new entitlements, but as inalienable rights of all men, given legal effect by their codification in the Constitution's text. The Court's subsequent decision in *Barron,* however, made plain that the codification of these rights in the Bill made them legally enforceable only against the Federal Government, not the States.

Even though the Bill of Rights did not apply to the States, other provisions of the Constitution did limit state interference with individual rights. Article IV, § 2, cl. 1 provides that "[t]he Citizens of each State shall be entitled to all Privileges and Immunities of Citizens in the several States." The text of this provision resembles the Privileges or Immunities Clause, and it can be assumed that the public's understanding of the latter was informed by its understanding of the former.

Article IV, § 2 was derived from a similar clause in the Articles of Confederation, and reflects the dual citizenship the Constitution provided to all Americans after replacing that "league" of separate sovereign States. By virtue of a person's citizenship in a particular State, he was guaranteed whatever rights and liberties that State's constitution and laws made available. Article IV, § 2 vested citizens of each State with an additional right: the assurance that they would be afforded the "privileges and immunities" of citizenship in any of the several States in the Union to which they might travel.

What were the "Privileges and Immunities of Citizens in the several States"? That question was answered perhaps most famously by Justice Bushrod Washington sitting as Circuit Justice in *Corfield v. Coryell,* 6 F. Cas. 546, 551-552 (No. 3,230) (CC ED Pa. 1825). In that case, a Pennsylvania citizen claimed that a New Jersey law prohibiting nonresidents from harvesting oysters from the State's waters violated Article IV, § 2 because it deprived him, as an out-of-state citizen, of a right New Jersey availed to its own citizens. *Id.,* at 550. Justice Washington rejected that argument, refusing to "accede to the proposition" that Article IV, § 2 entitled "citizens of the several states . . . to participate in *all* the rights which belong exclusively to the citizens of any other particular state." *Id.,* at 552 (emphasis added). In his view, Article IV, § 2 did not guarantee equal access to all public benefits a State might choose to make available to its citizens. See *id.,* at 552. Instead, it applied only to those rights "which are, in their nature, *fundamental*; which belong, of right, to the citizens of all free governments." *Id.,* at 551 (emphasis added). Other courts generally agreed with this principle.

When describing those "fundamental" rights, Justice Washington thought it "would perhaps be more tedious than difficult to enumerate" them all, but suggested that they could "be all comprehended under" a broad list of "general heads," such as "[p]rotection by the government," "the enjoyment of life and liberty, with the right to acquire and possess property of every kind," "the benefit of the writ of habeas corpus," and the right of access to "the courts of the state," among others.[6] *Corfield, supra,* at 551-552.

Notably, Justice Washington did not indicate whether Article IV, § 2 *required* States to recognize these fundamental rights in their own citizens and thus in sojourning citizens alike, or whether the Clause simply prohibited the States from discriminating against sojourning citizens with respect to whatever fundamental rights state law happened to recognize. On this question, the weight of legal authorities at the time of Reconstruction indicated that Article IV, § 2 prohibited States from discriminating against sojourning citizens when recognizing fundamental rights, but did not require States to recognize those rights and did not prescribe their content. . . . This Court adopted the same conclusion in a unanimous opinion just one year after the Fourteenth Amendment was ratified. See *Paul v. Virginia,* 8 Wall. 168, 180 (1869).

* * *

The text examined so far demonstrates three points about the meaning of the Privileges or Immunities Clause in § 1. First, "privileges" and "immunities" were synonyms for "rights." Second, both the States and the Federal Government had long recognized the inalienable rights of their citizens. Third, Article IV, § 2 of the

---

6. Justice Washington's complete list was as follows:

"Protection by the government; the enjoyment of life and liberty, with the right to acquire and possess property of every kind, and to pursue and obtain happiness and safety; subject nevertheless to such restraints as the government may justly prescribe for the general good of the whole. The right of a citizen of one state to pass through, or to reside in any other state, for purposes of trade, agriculture, professional pursuits, or otherwise; to claim the benefit of the writ of habeas corpus; to institute and maintain actions of any kind in the courts of the state; to take, hold and dispose of property, either real or personal; and an exemption from higher taxes or impositions than are paid by the other citizens of the state; may be mentioned as some of the particular privileges and immunities of citizens, which are clearly embraced by the general description of privileges deemed to be fundamental: to which may be added, the elective franchise, as regulated and established by the laws or constitution of the state in which it is to be exercised." 6 Fed. Cas., at 551-552.

Constitution protected traveling citizens against state discrimination with respect to the fundamental rights of state citizenship.

Two questions still remain, both provoked by the textual similarity between § 1's Privileges or Immunities Clause and Article IV, § 2. The first involves the nature of the rights at stake: Are the privileges or immunities of "citizens of the United States" recognized by § 1 the same as the privileges and immunities of "citizens in the several States" to which Article IV, § 2 refers? The second involves the restriction imposed on the States: Does § 1, like Article IV, § 2, prohibit only discrimination with respect to certain rights *if* the State chooses to recognize them, or does it require States to recognize those rights? I address each question in turn....

Evidence from the political branches in the years leading to the Fourteenth Amendment's adoption demonstrates broad public understanding that the privileges and immunities of United States citizenship included rights set forth in the Constitution....

When interpreting constitutional text, the goal is to discern the most likely public understanding of a particular provision at the time it was adopted. Statements by legislators can assist in this process to the extent they demonstrate the manner in which the public used or understood a particular word or phrase. They can further assist to the extent there is evidence that these statements were disseminated to the public. In other words, this evidence is useful not because it demonstrates what the draftsmen of the text may have been thinking, but only insofar as it illuminates what the public understood the words chosen by the draftsmen to mean.

[Justice Thomas proceeds to quote from various speeches by members of Congress during debates over the Fourteenth Amendment indicating that the effect of the Privileges or Immunities Clause of the Fourteenth Amendment would be to make the enumerated rights found in the Bill of Rights enforceable against the States. He also relies on other historical evidence, including legislation enacted by Congress following its approval of the Fourteenth Amendment, as well as early interpretations of the Clause.]

This evidence plainly shows that the ratifying public understood the Privileges or Immunities Clause to protect constitutionally enumerated rights, including the right to keep and bear arms....

The next question is whether the Privileges or Immunities Clause merely prohibits States from discriminating among citizens if they recognize the Second Amendment's right to keep and bear arms, or whether the Clause requires States to recognize the right....

I begin, again, with the text. The Privileges or Immunities Clause opens with the command that "*No State shall*" abridge the privileges or immunities of citizens of the United States. Amdt. 14, § 1 (emphasis added). The very same phrase opens Article I, § 10 of the Constitution, which prohibits the States from "pass[ing] any Bill of Attainder" or "ex post facto Law," among other things. Article I, § 10 is one of the few constitutional provisions that limits state authority. In *Barron,* when Chief

Justice Marshall interpreted the Bill of Rights as lacking "plain and intelligible language" restricting state power to infringe upon individual liberties, he pointed to Article I, § 10 as an example of text that would have accomplished that task. 7 Pet., at 250. Indeed, Chief Justice Marshall would later describe Article I, § 10 as "a bill of rights for the people of each state." *Fletcher v. Peck,* 6 Cranch 87, 138 (1810). Thus, the fact that the Privileges or Immunities Clause uses the command "[n]o State shall"—which Article IV, § 2 does not—strongly suggests that the former imposes a greater restriction on state power than the latter.

This interpretation is strengthened when one considers that the Privileges or Immunities Clause uses the verb "abridge," rather than "discriminate," to describe the limit it imposes on state authority. The Webster's dictionary in use at the time of Reconstruction defines the word "abridge" to mean "[t]o deprive; to cut off; . . . as, to *abridge* one of his rights." The Clause is thus best understood to impose a limitation on state power to infringe upon pre-existing substantive rights. It raises no indication that the Framers of the Clause used the word "abridge" to prohibit only discrimination.

This most natural textual reading is underscored by a well-publicized revision to the Fourteenth Amendment that the Reconstruction Congress rejected. After several Southern States refused to ratify the Amendment, President Johnson met with their Governors to draft a compromise. . . .

Significantly, this proposal removed the "[n]o State shall" directive and the verb "abridge" from § 1, and also changed the class of rights to be protected from those belonging to "citizens of the United States" to those of the "citizens in the several States." This phrasing is materially indistinguishable from Article IV, § 2, which generally was understood as an antidiscrimination provision alone. The proposal thus strongly indicates that at least the President of the United States and several southern Governors thought that the Privileges or Immunities Clause, which they unsuccessfully tried to revise, prohibited more than just state-sponsored discrimination. . . .

[The majority opinion of Justice Alito, the concurring opinion of Justice Scalia, and the dissenting opinion of Justices Stevens and Breyer are omitted].

Notes and Questions

1. Other than perhaps correcting a likely historical error made by the Court in *The Slaughter-House Cases,* what virtue is there in recognizing fundamental rights under the Privileges or Immunities Clause instead of the Due Process and Equal Protection Clauses? Do you not still face the same quandary of how to determine the existence and scope of those rights? How is Justice Thomas's analysis under the Privileges or Immunities Clause any different from the analysis performed by the Court in its existing fundamental rights lines of cases?

2. Would fundamental rights recognized under the Privileges or Immunities Clause be available to non-citizens? How, if at all, does that differ from fundamental

rights recognized under the Due Process and Equal Protection Clauses? Does the text of those provisions answer that question? Might the answer to that question explain why some Justices may be reluctant to shift fundamental rights jurisprudence from the Due Process and Equal Protection Clauses to the Privileges or Immunities Clause?

Chapter 21

Refining the Scope of Congressional Power to Enforce the Reconstruction Amendments

Recall from Chapters 2 and 9 that each of the three Reconstruction Amendments empowers Congress with the ability to "enforce" the constitutional provision by "appropriate legislation." The cases that you have read thus far have raised and at least provisionally answered two questions regarding the relationship between the enforcement provision and the self-executing provision of each Amendment. First, can Congress regulate conduct pursuant to one of the enforcement provisions that does not, standing alone, violate the corresponding self-executing provision? And second, is that relationship the same across all three of the Reconstruction Amendments?

The cases that you examined in Chapter 9 seemed to give Congress virtually unchecked authority to act pursuant to the enforcement provisions, with legislation enacted to enforce the Reconstruction Amendments subject only to rationality review. Indeed, the cases suggested even more sweeping congressional authority, with not only broad power to enact legislation that was only loosely designed to further the underlying self-executing rights protected by the Reconstruction Amendments, but also the power to *define* the scope and nature of the rights protected by those Amendments.

In earlier chapters, you saw that a more conservative Court in the late 20th century began to cut back on the vitality of the Reconstruction Amendments by taking a narrower view of the concept of state action; enforcing a rather strict discriminatory purpose requirement; subjecting reverse-discrimination scenarios to heightened scrutiny; cabining the Court's discretion to recognize and enforce fundamental rights; and narrowing the reordering of the political process doctrine. In that same period, the Court also began to cut back on the scope of congressional power to enforce the Reconstruction Amendments. Part A of this chapter examines the Court's new and now relatively established approach under Section 5 of the 14th Amendment. Part B explores the likely impact that approach has on congressional power pursuant to Section 2 of the Thirteenth and Fifteenth Amendments.

A. The Fourteenth Amendment

City of Boerne v. Flores

521 U.S. 507 (1997)

Justice Kennedy delivered the opinion of the Court.

A decision by local zoning authorities to deny a church a building permit was challenged under the Religious Freedom Restoration Act of 1993 (RFRA or Act). The case calls into question the authority of Congress to enact RFRA. We conclude the statute exceeds Congress' power. . . .

Congress enacted RFRA in direct response to the Court's decision in *Employment Div., Dept. of Human Resources of Oregon v. Smith,* 494 U.S. 872 (1990). There we considered a Free Exercise Clause claim brought by members of the Native American Church who were denied unemployment benefits when they lost their jobs because they had used peyote. Their practice was to ingest peyote for sacramental purposes, and they challenged an Oregon statute of general applicability which made use of the drug criminal. In evaluating the claim, we declined to apply the balancing test set forth in *Sherbert v. Verner,* 374 U.S. 398 (1963), under which we would have asked whether Oregon's prohibition substantially burdened a religious practice and, if it did, whether the burden was justified by a compelling government interest. . . .

The application of the *Sherbert* test, the *Smith* decision explained, would have produced an anomaly in the law, a constitutional right to ignore neutral laws of general applicability. The anomaly would have been accentuated, the Court reasoned, by the difficulty of determining whether a particular practice was central to an individual's religion. . . .

Smith held that neutral, generally applicable laws may be applied to religious practices even when not supported by a compelling governmental interest.

Four Members of the Court disagreed. They argued the law placed a substantial burden on the Native American Church members so that it could be upheld only if the law served a compelling state interest and was narrowly tailored to achieve that end. . . .

These points of constitutional interpretation were debated by Members of Congress in hearings and floor debates. Many criticized the Court's reasoning, and this disagreement resulted in the passage of RFRA. . . .

The Act's stated purposes are:

> "(1) to restore the compelling interest test as set forth in *Sherbert v. Verner,* 374 U.S. 398 (1963) and *Wisconsin v. Yoder,* 406 U.S. 205 (1972) and to guarantee its application in all cases where free exercise of religion is substantially burdened; and
>
> "(2) to provide a claim or defense to persons whose religious exercise is substantially burdened by government."

RFRA prohibits "[g]overnment" from "substantially burden[ing]" a person's exercise of religion even if the burden results from a rule of general applicability unless the government can demonstrate the burden "(1) is in furtherance of a compelling governmental interest; and (2) is the least restrictive means of furthering that compelling governmental interest." The Act's mandate applies to any "branch, department, agency, instrumentality, and official (or other person acting under color of law) of the United States," as well as to any "State, or . . . subdivision of a State." . . . .

Congress relied on its Fourteenth Amendment enforcement power in enacting the most far-reaching and substantial of RFRA's provisions, those which impose its requirements on the States. . . .

The parties disagree over whether RFRA is a proper exercise of Congress' § 5 power "to enforce" by "appropriate legislation" the constitutional guarantee that no State shall deprive any person of "life, liberty, or property, without due process of law" nor deny any person "equal protection of the laws." . . . .

It is said the congressional decision to dispense with proof of deliberate or overt discrimination and instead concentrate on a law's effects accords with the settled understanding that § 5 includes the power to enact legislation designed to prevent, as well as remedy, constitutional violations. It is further contended that Congress' § 5 power is not limited to remedial or preventive legislation.

All must acknowledge that § 5 is "a positive grant of legislative power" to Congress, *Katzenbach v. Morgan,* 384 U.S. 641, 651 (1966). In *Ex parte Virginia,* 100 U.S. 339, 345–346 (1879), we explained the scope of Congress' § 5 power in the following broad terms:

> "Whatever legislation is appropriate, that is, adapted to carry out the objects the amendments have in view, whatever tends to enforce submission to the prohibitions they contain, and to secure to all persons the enjoyment of perfect equality of civil rights and the equal protection of the laws against State denial or invasion, if not prohibited, is brought within the domain of congressional power."

Legislation which deters or remedies constitutional violations can fall within the sweep of Congress' enforcement power even if in the process it prohibits conduct which is not itself unconstitutional and intrudes into "legislative spheres of autonomy previously reserved to the States." *Fitzpatrick v. Bitzer,* 427 U.S. 445, 455 (1976). For example, the Court upheld a suspension of literacy tests and similar voting requirements under Congress' parallel power to enforce the provisions of the Fifteenth Amendment, see U.S. Const., Amdt. 15, § 2, as a measure to combat racial discrimination in voting, *South Carolina v. Katzenbach,* 383 U.S. 301, 308 (1966), despite the facial constitutionality of the tests under *Lassiter v. Northampton County Bd. of Elections,* 360 U.S. 45 (1959). We have also concluded that other measures protecting voting rights are within Congress' power to enforce the Fourteenth and Fifteenth Amendments, despite the burdens those measures placed on the States.

It is also true, however, that "[a]s broad as the congressional enforcement power is, it is not unlimited." *Oregon v. Mitchell, supra,* at 128 (opinion of Black, J.). In assessing the breadth of § 5's enforcement power, we begin with its text. Congress has been given the power "to enforce" the "provisions of this article." We agree with respondent, of course, that Congress can enact legislation under § 5 enforcing the constitutional right to the free exercise of religion. The "provisions of this article," to which § 5 refers, include the Due Process Clause of the Fourteenth Amendment. Congress' power to enforce the Free Exercise Clause follows from our holding in *Cantwell v. Connecticut,* 310 U.S. 296, 303 (1940), that the "fundamental concept of liberty embodied in [the Fourteenth Amendment's Due Process Clause] embraces the liberties guaranteed by the First Amendment." . . . .

Congress' power under § 5, however, extends only to "enforc[ing]" the provisions of the Fourteenth Amendment. The Court has described this power as "remedial," *South Carolina v. Katzenbach, supra,* at 326. The design of the Amendment and the text of § 5 are inconsistent with the suggestion that Congress has the power to decree the substance of the Fourteenth Amendment's restrictions on the States. Legislation which alters the meaning of the Free Exercise Clause cannot be said to be enforcing the Clause. Congress does not enforce a constitutional right by changing what the right is. It has been given the power "to enforce," not the power to determine what constitutes a constitutional violation. Were it not so, what Congress would be enforcing would no longer be, in any meaningful sense, the "provisions of [the Fourteenth Amendment]."

While the line between measures that remedy or prevent unconstitutional actions and measures that make a substantive change in the governing law is not easy to discern, and Congress must have wide latitude in determining where it lies, the distinction exists and must be observed. There must be a congruence and proportionality between the injury to be prevented or remedied and the means adopted to that end. Lacking such a connection, legislation may become substantive in operation and effect. History and our case law support drawing the distinction, one apparent from the text of the Amendment.

[The Court proceeds to examine the drafting history of the Reconstruction Amendments, which suggest that Congress rejected earlier drafts that seemed to give Congress sweeping substantive power.]

As enacted, the Fourteenth Amendment confers substantive rights against the States which, like the provisions of the Bill of Rights, are self-executing. The power to interpret the Constitution in a case or controversy remains in the Judiciary.

The remedial and preventive nature of Congress' enforcement power, and the limitation inherent in the power, were confirmed in our earliest cases on the Fourteenth Amendment. In the *Civil Rights Cases,* 109 U.S. 3 (1883), the Court invalidated sections of the Civil Rights Act of 1875 which prescribed criminal penalties for denying to any person "the full enjoyment of" public accommodations and conveyances, on the grounds that it exceeded Congress' power by seeking to regulate private conduct. The Enforcement Clause, the Court said, did not authorize Congress to pass "general legislation upon the rights of the citizen, but corrective legislation, that is, such as may be necessary and proper for counteracting such laws as the States may adopt or enforce, and which, by the amendment, they are prohibited from making or enforcing. . . ." . . . .

Recent cases have continued to revolve around the question whether § 5 legislation can be considered remedial. In *South Carolina v. Katzenbach, supra,* we emphasized that "[t]he constitutional propriety of [legislation adopted under the Enforcement Clause] must be judged with reference to the historical experience . . . it reflects." 383 U.S., at 308. There we upheld various provisions of the Voting Rights Act of 1965, finding them to be "remedies aimed at areas where voting discrimination has been most flagrant," *id.,* at 315, and necessary to "banish the blight of racial discrimination in voting, which has infected the electoral process in parts of our country for nearly a century," *id.,* at 308. We noted evidence in the record reflecting the subsisting and pervasive discriminatory—and therefore unconstitutional—use of literacy tests. *Id.,* at 333–334. The Act's new remedies, which used the administrative resources of the Federal Government, included the suspension of both literacy tests and, pending federal review, all new voting regulations in covered jurisdictions, as well as the assignment of federal examiners to list qualified applicants enabling those listed to vote. The new, unprecedented remedies were deemed necessary given the ineffectiveness of the existing voting rights laws, see *id.,* at 313–315, and the slow, costly character of case-by-case litigation, *id.,* at 328 . . . .

There is language in our opinion in *Katzenbach v. Morgan,* 384 U.S. 641 (1966), which could be interpreted as acknowledging a power in Congress to enact legislation that expands the rights contained in § 1 of the Fourteenth Amendment. This is not a necessary interpretation, however, or even the best one. . . .

If Congress could define its own powers by altering the Fourteenth Amendment's meaning, no longer would the Constitution be "superior paramount law, unchangeable by ordinary means." It would be "on a level with ordinary legislative acts, and, like other acts, . . . alterable when the legislature shall please to alter it." *Marbury v. Madison,* 1 Cranch, at 177. Under this approach, it is difficult to conceive of a principle that would limit congressional power. Shifting legislative majorities could change the Constitution and effectively circumvent the difficult and detailed amendment process contained in Article V. . . .

Respondent contends that RFRA is a proper exercise of Congress' remedial or preventive power. The Act, it is said, is a reasonable means of protecting the free exercise of religion as defined by *Smith.* It prevents and remedies laws which are enacted with the unconstitutional object of targeting religious beliefs and practices. To avoid the difficulty of proving such violations, it is said, Congress can simply invalidate any law which imposes a substantial burden on a religious practice unless it is justified by a compelling interest and is the least restrictive means of accomplishing that interest. If Congress can prohibit laws with discriminatory effects in order to prevent racial discrimination in violation of the Equal Protection Clause, see *Fullilove v. Klutznick,* 448 U.S. 448, 477 (1980) (plurality opinion); *City of Rome,* 446 U.S., at 177, then it can do the same, respondent argues, to promote religious liberty.

While preventive rules are sometimes appropriate remedial measures, there must be a congruence between the means used and the ends to be achieved. The appropriateness of remedial measures must be considered in light of the evil presented. Strong measures appropriate to address one harm may be an unwarranted response to another, lesser one.

A comparison between RFRA and the Voting Rights Act is instructive. In contrast to the record which confronted Congress and the Judiciary in the voting rights cases, RFRA's legislative record lacks examples of modern instances of generally applicable laws passed because of religious bigotry. The history of persecution in this country detailed in the hearings mentions no episodes occurring in the past 40 years. . . . Rather, the emphasis of the hearings was on laws of general applicability which place incidental burdens on religion. . . . This lack of support in the legislative record, however, is not RFRA's most serious shortcoming. . . .

Regardless of the state of the legislative record, RFRA cannot be considered remedial, preventive legislation, if those terms are to have any meaning. RFRA is so out of proportion to a supposed remedial or preventive object that it cannot be understood as responsive to, or designed to prevent, unconstitutional behavior. It appears, instead, to attempt a substantive change in constitutional protections. Preventive measures prohibiting certain types of laws may be appropriate when there is reason to believe that many of the laws affected by the congressional enactment have a significant likelihood of being unconstitutional. . . .

RFRA is not so confined. Sweeping coverage ensures its intrusion at every level of government, displacing laws and prohibiting official actions of almost every description and regardless of subject matter. RFRA's restrictions apply to every agency and official of the Federal, State, and local Governments. RFRA applies to all federal and state law, statutory or otherwise, whether adopted before or after its enactment. RFRA has no termination date or termination mechanism. Any law is subject to challenge at any time by any individual who alleges a substantial burden on his or her free exercise of religion.

The reach and scope of RFRA distinguish it from other measures passed under Congress' enforcement power, even in the area of voting rights. In *South Carolina v. Katzenbach,* the challenged provisions were confined to those regions of the country where voting discrimination had been most flagrant, see 383 U.S., at 315, and affected a discrete class of state laws, *i.e.,* state voting laws. Furthermore, to ensure that the reach of the Voting Rights Act was limited to those cases in which constitutional violations were most likely (in order to reduce the possibility of overbreadth), the coverage under the Act would terminate "at the behest of States and political subdivisions in which the danger of substantial voting discrimination has not materialized during the preceding five years." *Id.,* at 331. The provisions restricting and banning literacy tests, upheld in *Katzenbach v. Morgan,* 384 U.S. 641 (1966), and

Oregon v. Mitchell, supra, attacked a particular type of voting qualification, one with a long history as a "notorious means to deny and abridge voting rights on racial grounds." *South Carolina v. Katzenbach,* 383 U.S., at 355 (Black, J., concurring and dissenting). In *City of Rome, supra,* the Court rejected a challenge to the constitutionality of a Voting Rights Act provision which required certain jurisdictions to submit changes in electoral practices to the Department of Justice for preimplementation review. The requirement was placed only on jurisdictions with a history of intentional racial discrimination in voting. *Id.,* at 177. Like the provisions at issue in *South Carolina v. Katzenbach,* this provision permitted a covered jurisdiction to avoid preclearance requirements under certain conditions and, moreover, lapsed in seven years. This is not to say, of course, that § 5 legislation requires termination dates, geographic restrictions, or egregious predicates. Where, however, a congressional enactment pervasively prohibits constitutional state action in an effort to remedy or to prevent unconstitutional state action, limitations of this kind tend to ensure Congress' means are proportionate to ends legitimate under § 5.

The stringent test RFRA demands of state laws reflects a lack of proportionality or congruence between the means adopted and the legitimate end to be achieved. If an objector can show a substantial burden on his free exercise, the State must demonstrate a compelling governmental interest and show that the law is the least restrictive means of furthering its interest. Claims that a law substantially burdens someone's exercise of religion will often be difficult to contest. Requiring a State to demonstrate a compelling interest and show that it has adopted the least restrictive means of achieving that interest is the most demanding test known to constitutional law. . . . Laws valid under *Smith* would fall under RFRA without regard to whether they had the object of stifling or punishing free exercise. We make these observations not to reargue the position of the majority in *Smith* but to illustrate the substantive alteration of its holding attempted by RFRA. Even assuming RFRA would be interpreted in effect to mandate some lesser test, say, one equivalent to intermediate scrutiny, the statute nevertheless would require searching judicial scrutiny of state law with the attendant likelihood of invalidation. This is a considerable congressional intrusion into the States' traditional prerogatives and general authority to regulate for the health and welfare of their citizens.

The substantial costs RFRA exacts, both in practical terms of imposing a heavy litigation burden on the States and in terms of curtailing their traditional general regulatory power, far exceed any pattern or practice of unconstitutional conduct under the Free Exercise Clause as interpreted in *Smith.* Simply put, RFRA is not designed to identify and counteract state laws likely to be unconstitutional because of their treatment of religion. In most cases, the state laws to which RFRA applies are not ones which will have been motivated by religious bigotry. If a state law disproportionately burdened a particular class of religious observers, this circumstance might be evidence of an impermissible legislative motive. Cf. *Washington v. Davis,* 426 U.S. 229, 241 (1976). RFRA's substantial-burden test, however, is not even a discriminatory effects or disparate-impact test. . . .

It is for Congress in the first instance to "determin[e] whether and what legislation is needed to secure the guarantees of the Fourteenth Amendment," and its conclusions are entitled to much deference. *Katzenbach v. Morgan,* 384 U.S., at 651. Congress' discretion is not unlimited, however, and the courts retain the power, as they have since *Marbury v. Madison,* to determine if Congress has exceeded its authority under the Constitution. Broad as the power of Congress is under the Enforcement Clause of the Fourteenth Amendment, RFRA contradicts vital principles necessary to maintain separation of powers and the federal balance. . . .

[The concurring opinions of Justices Stevens and Scalia, and the dissenting opinions of Justices O'Connor and Souter, are omitted.]

Notes and Questions

1. Do you understand why *Boerne* is a Fourteenth Amendment case, even though it appears at first blush to be about the First Amendment?

2. Congressional power under *Boerne* is clearly more constrained than it was under *Morgan.* Does *Boerne* nonetheless still leave room for Congress to prohibit conduct pursuant to Section 5 of the Fourteenth Amendment that does not, strictly speaking, violate Section 1 of that Amendment? If so, what is the theoretical justification for allowing Congress in any way to legislate beyond the scope of the self-executing portions of the Amendment?

3. The *Boerne* Court distinguishes between "substantive" and "remedial" legislation by Congress. What is the distinction between the two, and why is that distinction significant from the Court's perspective?

4. The *Boerne* Court speaks of "congruence" and "proportionality." What do those terms mean? Do they each refer to something distinct, or do they together constitute a single test?

5. Does it seem as though *Boerne*'s "congruence" and "proportionality" test likely applies to congressional legislation enacted pursuant to Section 2 of the Thirteenth and Fifteenth Amendments? Are there any clues in the decision itself that help to shed light on the answer to that question?

United States v. Morrison

529 U.S. 598 (2000)

Chief Justice Rehnquist delivered the opinion of the Court.

In these cases we consider the constitutionality of 42 U.S.C. § 13981, which provides a federal civil remedy for the victims of gender-motivated violence. . . .

Petitioner Christy Brzonkala enrolled at Virginia Polytechnic Institute (Virginia Tech) in the fall of 1994. In September of that year, Brzonkala met respondents Antonio Morrison and James Crawford, who were both students at Virginia Tech and members of its varsity football team. Brzonkala alleges that, within 30 minutes of meeting Morrison and Crawford, they assaulted and repeatedly raped her. After the attack, Morrison allegedly told Brzonkala, "You better not have any . . . diseases." In the months following the rape, Morrison also allegedly announced in the dormitory's dining room that he "like[d] to get girls drunk and. . . ." The omitted portions, quoted verbatim in the briefs on file with this Court, consist of boasting, debased remarks about what Morrison would do to women, vulgar remarks that cannot fail to shock and offend. . . .

In December 1995, Brzonkala sued Morrison, Crawford, and Virginia Tech in the United States District Court for the Western District of Virginia. Her complaint alleged that Morrison's and Crawford's attack violated § 13981 and that Virginia Tech's handling of her complaint violated Title IX of the Education Amendments of 1972 . . . .

The District Court dismissed Brzonkala's Title IX claims against Virginia Tech for failure to state a claim upon which relief can be granted. It then held that Brzonkala's complaint stated a claim against Morrison and Crawford under § 13981, but dismissed the complaint because it concluded that Congress lacked authority to enact the section under either the Commerce Clause or § 5 of the Fourteenth Amendment. . . .

Section 13981 was part of the Violence Against Women Act of 1994. It states that "[a]ll persons within the United States shall have the right to be free from crimes of violence motivated by gender." 42 U.S.C. § 13981(b). To enforce that right, subsection (c) declares:

> "A person (including a person who acts under color of any statute, ordinance, regulation, custom, or usage of any State) who commits a crime of violence motivated by gender and thus deprives another of the right declared in subsection (b) of this section shall be liable to the party injured, in an action for the recovery of compensatory and punitive damages, injunctive and declaratory relief, and such other relief as a court may deem appropriate."

Congress explicitly identified the sources of federal authority on which it relied in enacting § 13981. It said that a "Federal civil rights cause of action" is established "[p]ursuant to the affirmative power of Congress . . . under section 5 of the Fourteenth Amendment to the Constitution, as well as under section 8 of Article I of the Constitution." 42 U.S.C. § 13981(a). We address Congress' authority to enact this remedy under each of these constitutional provisions in turn.

[The Court first concludes that Congress lacked the power to enact Section 13981 pursuant to its Commerce Clause powers under Article I, Section 8 of the Constitution.]

Because we conclude that the Commerce Clause does not provide Congress with authority to enact § 13981, we address petitioners' alternative argument that the section's civil remedy should be upheld as an exercise of Congress' remedial power under § 5 of the Fourteenth Amendment. . . .

The principles governing an analysis of congressional legislation under § 5 are well settled. Section 5 states that Congress may "'enforce' by 'appropriate legislation' the constitutional guarantee that no State shall deprive any person of 'life, liberty, or property, without due process of law,' nor deny any person 'equal protection of the laws.'" *City of Boerne v. Flores,* 521 U.S. 507, 517 (1997). Section 5 is "a positive grant of legislative power," *Katzenbach v. Morgan,* 384 U.S. 641, 651 (1966), that includes authority to "prohibit conduct which is not itself unconstitutional and [to] intrud[e] into 'legislative spheres of autonomy previously reserved to the States.'" *Flores, supra,* at 518 (quoting *Fitzpatrick v. Bitzer,* 427 U.S. 445, 455 (1976)). However, "[a]s broad as the congressional enforcement power is, it is not unlimited." *Oregon v. Mitchell,* 400 U.S. 112 (1970). In fact, as we discuss in detail below, several limitations inherent in § 5's text and constitutional context have been recognized since the Fourteenth Amendment was adopted.

Petitioners' § 5 argument is founded on an assertion that there is pervasive bias in various state justice systems against victims of gender-motivated violence. This assertion is supported by a voluminous congressional record. Specifically, Congress received evidence that many participants in state justice systems are perpetuating an array of erroneous stereotypes and assumptions. Congress concluded that these discriminatory stereotypes often result in insufficient investigation and prosecution of gender-motivated crime, inappropriate focus on the behavior and credibility of the victims of that crime, and unacceptably lenient punishments for those who are actually convicted of gender-motivated violence. Petitioners contend that this bias denies victims of gender-motivated violence the equal protection of the laws and that Congress therefore acted appropriately in enacting a private civil remedy against the perpetrators of gender-motivated violence to both remedy the States' bias and deter future instances of discrimination in the state courts.

As our cases have established, state-sponsored gender discrimination violates equal protection unless it "'serves "important governmental objectives and . . . the discriminatory means employed" are "substantially related to the achievement of those objectives."'" *United States v. Virginia,* 518 U.S. 515, 533, 116 S.Ct. 2264, 135 L.Ed.2d 735 (1996). However, the language and purpose of the Fourteenth Amendment place certain limitations on the manner in which Congress may attack discriminatory conduct. These limitations are necessary to prevent the Fourteenth Amendment from obliterating the Framers' carefully crafted balance of power between the States and the National Government. Foremost among these limitations is the time-honored principle that the Fourteenth Amendment, by its very terms, prohibits only state action. . . .

Shortly after the Fourteenth Amendment was adopted, we decided two cases interpreting the Amendment's provisions, *United States v. Harris,* 106 U.S. 629 (1883), and the *Civil Rights Cases,* 109 U.S. 3 (1883). In *Harris,* the Court considered a challenge to § 2 of the Civil Rights Act of 1871. That section sought to punish "private persons" for "conspiring to deprive any one of the equal protection of the laws enacted by the State." 106 U.S., at 639. We concluded that this law exceeded Congress' § 5 power because the law was "directed exclusively against the action of private persons, without reference to the laws of the State, or their administration by her officers." *Id.*, at 640 . . . .

We reached a similar conclusion in the *Civil Rights Cases.* In those consolidated cases, we held that the public accommodation provisions of the Civil Rights Act of 1875, which applied to purely private conduct, were beyond the scope of the § 5 enforcement power. 109 U.S., at 11.

The force of the doctrine of *stare decisis* behind these decisions stems not only from the length of time they have been on the books, but also from the insight attributable to the Members of the Court at that time. Every Member had been appointed by President Lincoln, Grant, Hayes, Garfield, or Arthur—and each of their judicial appointees obviously had intimate knowledge and familiarity with the events surrounding the adoption of the Fourteenth Amendment. . . .

Petitioners alternatively argue that, unlike the situation in the *Civil Rights Cases,* here there has been gender-based disparate treatment by state authorities, whereas in those cases there was no indication of such state action. There is abundant evidence, however, to show that the Congresses that enacted the Civil Rights Acts of 1871 and 1875 had a purpose similar to that of Congress in enacting § 13981: There were state laws on the books bespeaking equality of treatment, but in the administration of these laws there was discrimination against newly freed slaves. . . .

But even if that distinction were valid, we do not believe it would save § 13981's civil remedy. For the remedy is simply not "corrective in its character, adapted to counteract and redress the operation of such prohibited [s]tate laws or proceedings of [s]tate officers." *Civil Rights Cases, supra,* at 18. Or, as we have phrased it in more recent cases, prophylactic legislation under § 5 must have a "congruence and proportionality between the injury to be prevented or remedied and the means adopted to that end." Section 13981 is not aimed at proscribing discrimination by officials which the Fourteenth Amendment might not itself proscribe; it is directed not at any State or state actor, but at individuals who have committed criminal acts motivated by gender bias.

In the present cases, for example, § 13981 visits no consequence whatever on any Virginia public official involved in investigating or prosecuting Brzonkala's assault. The section is, therefore, unlike any of the § 5 remedies that we have previously upheld. For example, in *Katzenbach v. Morgan,* 384 U.S. 641 (1966), Congress prohibited New York from imposing literacy tests as a prerequisite for voting because it found that such a requirement disenfranchised thousands of Puerto Rican immigrants who had been educated in the Spanish language of their home territory. That law, which we upheld, was directed at New York officials who administered the State's election law and prohibited them from using a provision of that law. In *South Carolina v. Katzenbach,* 383 U.S. 301 (1966), Congress imposed voting rights requirements on States that, Congress found, had a history of discriminating against blacks in voting. The remedy was also directed at state officials in those States. Similarly, in

Ex parte Virginia, 100 U.S. 339 (1879), Congress criminally punished state officials who intentionally discriminated in jury selection; again, the remedy was directed to the culpable state official.

Section 13981 is also different from these previously upheld remedies in that it applies uniformly throughout the Nation. Congress' findings indicate that the problem of discrimination against the victims of gender-motivated crimes does not exist in all States, or even most States. By contrast, the § 5 remedy upheld in *Katzenbach v. Morgan, supra,* was directed only to the State where the evil found by Congress existed, and in *South Carolina v. Katzenbach, supra,* the remedy was directed only to those States in which Congress found that there had been discrimination.

For these reasons, we conclude that Congress' power under § 5 does not extend to the enactment of § 13981 . . . .

[The concurring opinion of Justice Thomas and the dissenting opinions of Justices Breyer and Souter are omitted.]

Nevada Department of Human Resources v. Hibbs

538 U.S. 721 (2003)

CHIEF JUSTICE REHNQUIST delivered the opinion of the Court.

The Family and Medical Leave Act of 1993 (FMLA or Act) entitles eligible employees to take up to 12 work weeks of unpaid leave annually for any of several reasons, including the onset of a "serious health condition" in an employee's spouse, child, or parent. The Act creates a private right of action to seek both equitable relief and money damages "against any employer (including a public agency) in any Federal or State court of competent jurisdiction" should that employer "interfere with, restrain, or deny the exercise of" FMLA rights. We hold that employees of the State of Nevada may recover money damages in the event of the State's failure to comply with the family-care provision of the Act. . . .

For over a century now, we have made clear that the Constitution does not provide for federal jurisdiction over suits against nonconsenting States. . . .

Congress may, however, abrogate such immunity in federal court if it makes its intention to abrogate unmistakably clear in the language of the statute and acts pursuant to a valid exercise of its power under § 5 of the Fourteenth Amendment. The clarity of Congress' intent here is not fairly debatable. . . . This case turns, then, on whether Congress acted within its constitutional authority when it sought to abrogate the States' immunity for purposes of the FMLA's family-leave provision. . . .

Two provisions of the Fourteenth Amendment are relevant here: Section 5 grants Congress the power "to enforce" the substantive guarantees of § 1—among them, equal protection of the laws—by enacting "appropriate legislation." Congress may, in the exercise of its § 5 power, do more than simply proscribe conduct that we have held unconstitutional. "'Congress' power "to enforce" the Amendment includes the authority both to remedy and to deter violation of rights guaranteed thereunder by prohibiting a somewhat broader swath of conduct, including that which is not itself forbidden by the Amendment's text.'" *Garrett, supra,* at 365 (quoting *Kimel, supra,* at 81); *City of Boerne v. Flores,* 521 U.S. 507, 536 (1997); *Katzenbach v. Morgan,* 384 U.S. 641, 658 (1966). In other words, Congress may enact so-called prophylactic legislation that proscribes facially constitutional conduct, in order to prevent and deter unconstitutional conduct.

City of Boerne also confirmed, however, that it falls to this Court, not Congress, to define the substance of constitutional guarantees.... Section 5 legislation reaching beyond the scope of § 1's actual guarantees must be an appropriate remedy for identified constitutional violations, not "an attempt to substantively redefine the States' legal obligations." We distinguish appropriate prophylactic legislation from "substantive redefinition of the Fourteenth Amendment right at issue" by applying the test set forth in *City of Boerne:* Valid § 5 legislation must exhibit "congruence and proportionality between the injury to be prevented or remedied and the means adopted to that end."

The FMLA aims to protect the right to be free from gender-based discrimination in the workplace. We have held that statutory classifications that distinguish between males and females are subject to heightened scrutiny. For a gender-based classification to withstand such scrutiny, it must "serv[e] important governmental objectives," and "the discriminatory means employed [must be] substantially related to the achievement of those objectives." *United States v. Virginia,* 518 U.S. 515, 533 (1996). The State's justification for such a classification "must not rely on overbroad generalizations about the different talents, capacities, or preferences of males and females." *Ibid.* We now inquire whether Congress had evidence of a pattern of constitutional violations on the part of the States in this area.

The history of the many state laws limiting women's employment opportunities is chronicled in—and, until relatively recently, was sanctioned by—this Court's own opinions....

Congress responded to this history of discrimination by abrogating States' sovereign immunity in Title VII of the Civil Rights Act of 1964, and we sustained this abrogation in *Fitzpatrick.* But state gender discrimination did not cease.... According to evidence that was before Congress when it enacted the FMLA, States continue to rely on invalid gender stereotypes in the employment context, specifically in the administration of leave benefits. Reliance on such stereotypes cannot justify the States' gender discrimination in this area. *Virginia, supra,* at 533. The long and extensive history of sex discrimination prompted us to hold that measures that differentiate on the basis of gender warrant heightened scrutiny; here, as in *Fitzpatrick,* the persistence of such unconstitutional discrimination by the States justifies Congress' passage of prophylactic § 5 legislation.

As the FMLA's legislative record reflects, a 1990 Bureau of Labor Statistics (BLS) survey stated that 37 percent of surveyed private-sector employees were covered by maternity leave policies, while only 18 percent were covered by paternity leave policies. The corresponding numbers from a similar BLS survey the previous year were 33 percent and 16 percent, respectively. While these data show an increase in the percentage of employees eligible for such leave, they also show a widening of the gender gap during the same period. Thus, stereotype-based beliefs about the allocation of family duties remained firmly rooted, and employers' reliance on them in establishing discriminatory leave policies remained widespread.[3]

Congress also heard testimony that "[p]arental leave for fathers . . . is rare. Even . . . [w]here child-care leave policies do exist, men, *both in the public and private sectors,* receive notoriously discriminatory treatment in their requests for such leave." . . . . This and other differential leave policies were not attributable to any differential physical needs of men and women, but rather to the pervasive sex-role stereotype that caring for family members is women's work.

Finally, Congress had evidence that, even where state laws and policies were not facially discriminatory, they were applied in discriminatory ways. It was aware of the "serious problems with the discretionary nature of family leave," because when "the authority to grant leave and to arrange the length of that leave rests with individual supervisors," it leaves "employees open to discretionary and possibly unequal treatment." . . . .

In sum, the States' record of unconstitutional participation in, and fostering of, gender-based discrimination in the administration of leave benefits is weighty enough to justify the enactment of prophylactic § 5 legislation.

We reached the opposite conclusion in *Garrett* and *Kimel.* In those cases, the § 5 legislation under review responded to a purported tendency of state officials to make age- or disability-based distinctions. Under our equal protection case law, discrimination on the basis of such characteristics is not judged under a heightened review standard, and passes muster if there is "a rational basis for doing so at a class-based level, even if it 'is probably not true' that those reasons are valid in the majority of cases." Thus, in order to impugn the constitutionality of state discrimination against the disabled or the elderly, Congress must identify, not just the existence of age- or disability-based state decisions, but a "widespread pattern" of irrational reliance on such criteria. We found no such showing with respect to the ADEA and Title I of the Americans with Disabilities Act of 1990(ADA).

Here, however, Congress directed its attention to state gender discrimination, which triggers a heightened level of scrutiny. Because the standard for demonstrating the constitutionality of a gender-based classification is more difficult to meet than our rational-basis test—it must "serv[e] important governmental objectives" and be "substantially related to the achievement of those objectives," *Virginia,* 518 U.S., at 533—it was easier for Congress to show a pattern of state constitutional violations.

---

3. While this and other material described leave policies in the private sector, a 50–state survey also before Congress demonstrated that "[t]he proportion and construction of leave policies available to public sector employees differs little from those offered private sector employees."

Congress was similarly successful in *South Carolina v. Katzenbach,* 383 U.S. 301, 308–313 (1966), where we upheld the Voting Rights Act of 1965: Because racial classifications are presumptively invalid, most of the States' acts of race discrimination violated the Fourteenth Amendment.

The impact of the discrimination targeted by the FMLA is significant. Congress determined:

> "Historically, denial or curtailment of women's employment opportunities has been traceable directly to the pervasive presumption that women are mothers first, and workers second. This prevailing ideology about women's roles has in turn justified discrimination against women when they are mothers or mothers-to-be."

Stereotypes about women's domestic roles are reinforced by parallel stereotypes presuming a lack of domestic responsibilities for men. Because employers continued to regard the family as the woman's domain, they often denied men similar accommodations or discouraged them from taking leave. These mutually reinforcing stereotypes created a self-fulfilling cycle of discrimination that forced women to continue to assume the role of primary family caregiver, and fostered employers' stereotypical views about women's commitment to work and their value as employees. Those perceptions, in turn, Congress reasoned, lead to subtle discrimination that may be difficult to detect on a case-by-case basis.

We believe that Congress' chosen remedy, the family-care leave provision of the FMLA, is "congruent and proportional to the targeted violation." Congress had already tried unsuccessfully to address this problem through Title VII and the amendment of Title VII by the Pregnancy Discrimination Act. Here, as in *Katzenbach, supra,* Congress again confronted a "difficult and intractable proble[m]," where previous legislative attempts had failed. Such problems may justify added prophylactic measures in response.

By creating an across-the-board, routine employment benefit for all eligible employees, Congress sought to ensure that family-care leave would no longer be stigmatized as an inordinate drain on the workplace caused by female employees, and that employers could not evade leave obligations simply by hiring men. By setting a minimum standard of family leave for *all* eligible employees, irrespective of gender, the FMLA attacks the formerly state-sanctioned stereotype that only women are responsible for family caregiving, thereby reducing employers' incentives to engage in discrimination by basing hiring and promotion decisions on stereotypes.

The dissent characterizes the FMLA as a "substantive entitlement program" rather than a remedial statute because it establishes a floor of 12 weeks' leave. In the dissent's view, in the face of evidence of gender-based discrimination by the States in the provision of leave benefits, Congress could do no more in exercising its § 5 power than simply proscribe such discrimination. But this position cannot be squared with our recognition that Congress "is not confined to the enactment of legislation that merely parrots the precise wording of the Fourteenth Amendment," but may prohibit "a somewhat broader swath of conduct, including that which is not itself forbidden by the Amendment's text." *Kimel, supra,* at 81. For example, this Court has upheld certain prophylactic provisions of the Voting Rights Act as valid exercises of Congress' § 5 power, including the literacy test ban and preclearance requirements for changes in States' voting procedures. See, *e.g., Katzenbach v. Morgan,* 384 U.S. 641 (1966); *Oregon v. Mitchell,* 400 U.S. 112 (1970); *South Carolina v. Katzenbach, supra* . . . .

Unlike the statutes at issue in *City of Boerne, Kimel,* and *Garrett,* which applied broadly to every aspect of state employers' operations, the FMLA is narrowly targeted at the faultline between work and family—precisely where sex-based overgeneralization has been and remains strongest—and affects only one aspect of the employment relationship.

We also find significant the many other limitations that Congress placed on the scope of this measure. The FMLA requires only unpaid leave, and applies only to employees who have worked for the employer for at least one year and provided 1,250 hours of service within the last 12 months. Employees in high-ranking or sensitive positions are simply ineligible for FMLA leave; of particular importance to the States, the FMLA expressly excludes from coverage state elected officials, their staffs, and appointed policymakers. Employees must give advance notice of foreseeable leave, and employers may require certification by a health care provider of the need for leave. In choosing 12 weeks as the appropriate leave floor, Congress chose "a middle ground, a period long enough to serve 'the needs of families' but not so long that it would upset 'the legitimate interests of employers.'" Moreover, the cause of action under the FMLA is a restricted one: The damages recoverable are strictly defined and measured by actual monetary losses, and the accrual period for backpay is limited by the Act's 2–year statute of limitations (extended to three years only for willful violations).

For the above reasons, we conclude that [the FMLA] is congruent and proportional to its remedial object, and can "be understood as responsive to, or designed to prevent, unconstitutional behavior." *City of Boerne, supra,* at 532 . . . .

[The concurring opinions of Justices Souter and Stevens, and the dissenting opinions of Justices Scalia and Kennedy, are omitted.]

Tennessee v. Lane

541 U.S. 509 (2004)

Justice Stevens delivered the opinion of the Court.

Title II of the Americans with Disabilities Act of 1990 (ADA or Act) provides that "no qualified individual with a disability shall, by reason of such disability, be excluded from participation in or be denied the benefits of the services, programs or activities of a public entity, or be subjected to discrimination by any such entity." The question presented in this case is whether Title II exceeds Congress' power under § 5 of the Fourteenth Amendment.

In August 1998, respondents George Lane and Beverly Jones filed this action against the State of Tennessee and a number of Tennessee counties, alleging past and ongoing violations of Title II. Respondents, both of whom are paraplegics who use wheelchairs for mobility, claimed that they were denied access to, and the services of, the state court system by reason of their disabilities. Lane alleged that he was compelled to appear to answer a set of criminal charges on the second floor of a county courthouse that had no elevator. At his first appearance, Lane crawled up two flights of stairs to get to the courtroom. When Lane returned to the courthouse for a hearing, he refused to crawl again or to be carried by officers to the courtroom; he consequently was arrested and jailed for failure to appear. Jones, a certified court reporter, alleged that she has not been able to gain access to a number of county courthouses, and, as a result, has lost both work and an opportunity to participate in the judicial process. Respondents sought damages and equitable relief. . . .

Applying the *Boerne* test in *Garrett,* we concluded that Title I of the ADA was not a valid exercise of Congress' § 5 power to enforce the Fourteenth Amendment's prohibition on unconstitutional disability discrimination in public employment. . . .

In view of the significant differences between Titles I and II, however, *Garrett* left open the question whether Title II is a valid exercise of Congress' § 5 enforcement power. It is to that question that we now turn.

The first step of the *Boerne* inquiry requires us to identify the constitutional right or rights that Congress sought to enforce when it enacted Title II. In *Garrett* we identified Title I's purpose as enforcement of the Fourteenth Amendment's command that "all persons similarly situated should be treated alike." As we observed, classifications based on disability violate that constitutional command if they lack a rational relationship to a legitimate governmental purpose.

Title II, like Title I, seeks to enforce this prohibition on irrational disability discrimination. But it also seeks to enforce a variety of other basic constitutional guarantees, infringements of which are subject to more searching judicial review. See, *e.g.*, *Dunn v. Blumstein,* 405 U.S. 330, 336–337 (1972); *Shapiro v. Thompson,* 394 U.S. 618, 634 (1969); *Skinner v. Oklahoma ex rel. Williamson,* 316 U.S. 535, 541 (1942). These rights include some, like the right of access to the courts at issue in this case, that are protected by the Due Process Clause of the Fourteenth Amendment. The Due Process Clause and the Confrontation Clause of the Sixth Amendment, as applied to the States via the Fourteenth Amendment, both guarantee to a criminal defendant such as respondent Lane the "right to be present at all stages of the trial where his absence might frustrate the fairness of the proceedings." *Faretta v. California,* 422 U.S. 806, 819, n. 15 (1975). The Due Process Clause also requires the States to afford certain civil litigants a "meaningful opportunity to be heard" by removing obstacles to their full participation in judicial proceedings. *Boddie v. Connecticut,* 401 U.S. 371, 379 (1971); *M.L.B. v. S.L. J.,* 519 U.S. 102 (1996). We have held that the Sixth Amendment guarantees to criminal defendants the right to trial by a jury composed of a fair cross section of the community, noting that the exclusion of "identifiable segments playing major roles in the community cannot be squared with the constitutional concept of jury trial." *Taylor v. Louisiana,* 419 U.S. 522, 530 (1975). And, finally, we have recognized that members of the public have a right of access to criminal proceedings secured by the First Amendment. *Press-Enterprise Co. v. Superior Court of Cal., County of Riverside,* 478 U.S. 1, 8–15 (1986).

Whether Title II validly enforces these constitutional rights is a question that "must be judged with reference to the historical experience which it reflects." *South Carolina v. Katzenbach,* 383 U.S. 301, 308 (1966) . . . .

It is not difficult to perceive the harm that Title II is designed to address. Congress enacted Title II against a backdrop of pervasive unequal treatment in the administration of state services and programs, including systematic deprivations of fundamental rights. For example, "[a]s of 1979, most States . . . categorically disqualified 'idiots' from voting, without regard to individual capacity." The majority of these laws remain on the books, and have been the subject of legal challenge as recently as 2001. Similarly, a number of States have prohibited and continue to prohibit persons with disabilities from engaging in activities such as marrying and serving as jurors. The historical experience that Title II reflects is also documented in this Court's cases, which have identified unconstitutional treatment of disabled persons by state agencies in a variety of settings, including unjustified commitment; the abuse and neglect of persons committed to state mental health hospitals; and irrational discrimination in zoning decisions. The decisions of other courts, too, document a pattern of unequal treatment in the administration of a wide range of public services, programs, and activities, including the penal system, public education, and voting. Notably, these decisions also demonstrate a pattern of unconstitutional treatment in the administration of justice.

This pattern of disability discrimination persisted despite several federal and state legislative efforts to address it. In the deliberations that led up to the enactment of the ADA, Congress identified important shortcomings in existing laws that rendered them "inadequate to address the pervasive problems of discrimination that people with disabilities are facing." It also uncovered further evidence of those shortcomings, in the form of hundreds of examples of unequal treatment of persons with disabilities by States and their political subdivisions. As the Court's opinion in *Garrett* observed, the "overwhelming majority" of these examples concerned discrimination in the administration of public programs and services.

With respect to the particular services at issue in this case, Congress learned that many individuals, in many States across the country, were being excluded from courthouses and court proceedings by reason of their disabilities. . . .

Given the sheer volume of evidence demonstrating the nature and extent of unconstitutional discrimination against persons with disabilities in the provision of public services, the dissent's contention that the record is insufficient to justify Congress' exercise of its prophylactic power is puzzling, to say the least. Just last Term in *Hibbs,* we approved the family-care leave provision of the FMLA as valid §5 legislation based primarily on evidence of disparate provision of parenting leave, little of which concerned unconstitutional state conduct. We explained that because the FMLA was targeted at sex-based classifications, which are subject to a heightened standard of judicial scrutiny, "it was easier for Congress to show a pattern of state constitutional violations" than in *Garrett* or *Kimel*, both of which concerned legislation that targeted classifications subject to rational-basis review. Title II is aimed at the enforcement of a variety of basic rights, including the right of access to the courts at issue in this case, that call for a standard of judicial review at least as searching, and in some cases more searching, than the standard that applies to sex-based classifications. And in any event, the record of constitutional violations in this case-including judicial findings of unconstitutional state action, and statistical, legislative, and anecdotal evidence of the widespread exclusion of persons with disabilities from the enjoyment of public services-far exceeds the record in *Hibbs* . . . .

The only question that remains is whether Title II is an appropriate response to this history and pattern of unequal treatment. . . .

The remedy Congress chose is [] a limited one. . . . Title II does not require States to employ any and all means to make judicial services accessible to persons with disabilities, and it does not require States to compromise their essential eligibility criteria for public programs. It requires only "reasonable modifications" that would not fundamentally alter the nature of the service provided, and only when the individual seeking modification is otherwise eligible for the service. As Title II's implementing regulations make clear, the reasonable modification requirement can be satisfied in a number of ways. . . . And in no event is the entity required to undertake measures that would impose an undue financial or administrative burden, threaten historic preservation interests, or effect a fundamental alteration in the nature of the service. . . .

Title II's affirmative obligation to accommodate persons with disabilities in the administration of justice cannot be said to be "so out of proportion to a supposed remedial or preventive object that it cannot be understood as responsive to, or designed to prevent, unconstitutional behavior." *Boerne*, 521 U.S., at 532. It is, rather, a reasonable prophylactic measure, reasonably targeted to a legitimate end.

For these reasons, we conclude that Title II, as it applies to the class of cases implicating the fundamental right of access to the courts, constitutes a valid exercise of Congress' § 5 authority to enforce the guarantees of the Fourteenth Amendment. . . .

Justice Scalia, dissenting. . . .

I joined the Court's opinion in *Boerne* with some misgiving. I have generally rejected tests based on such malleable standards as "proportionality," because they have a way of turning into vehicles for the implementation of individual judges' policy preferences. . . .

I yield to the lessons of experience. The "congruence and proportionality" standard, like all such flabby tests, is a standing invitation to judicial arbitrariness and policy-driven decisionmaking. . . .

I would replace "congruence and proportionality" with another test-one that provides a clear, enforceable limitation supported by the text of § 5. Section 5 grants Congress the power "to *enforce,* by appropriate legislation," the other provisions of the Fourteenth Amendment. U.S. Const., Amdt. 14 (emphasis added). *Morgan* notwithstanding, one does not, within any normal meaning of the term, "enforce" a prohibition by issuing a still broader prohibition directed to the same end. One does not, for example, "enforce" a 55-mile-per-hour speed limit by imposing a 45-mile-per-hour speed limit—even though that is indeed directed to the same end of automotive safety and will undoubtedly result in many fewer violations of the 55-mile-per-hour limit. . . . Nothing in § 5 allows Congress to go *beyond* the provisions of the Fourteenth Amendment to proscribe, prevent, or "remedy" conduct that does not *itself* violate any provision of the Fourteenth Amendment. So-called "prophylactic legislation" is reinforcement rather than enforcement. . . .

The major impediment to the approach I have suggested is *stare decisis.* A lot of water has gone under the bridge since *Morgan,* and many important and well-accepted measures, such as the Voting Rights Act, assume the validity of *Morgan* and *South Carolina* . . . .

However, *South Carolina* and *Morgan,* all of our later cases except *Hibbs* that give an expansive meaning to "enforce" in § 5 of the Fourteenth Amendment, and all of our earlier cases that even suggest such an expansive meaning in dicta, involved congressional measures that were directed exclusively against, or were used in the particular case to remedy, *racial discrimination.* . . .

Giving § 5 more expansive scope with regard to measures directed against racial discrimination by the States accords to practices that are distinctively violative of the principal purpose of the Fourteenth Amendment a priority of attention that this Court envisioned from the beginning, and that has repeatedly been reflected in our opinions. In the *Slaughter-House Cases,* 16 Wall. 36, 81 (1873), the Court's first confrontation with the Fourteenth Amendment, we said the following with respect to the Equal Protection Clause:

> "We doubt very much whether any action of a State not directed by way of discrimination against the negroes as a class, or on account of their race, will ever be held to come within the purview of this provision. It is so clearly a provision for that race and that emergency, that a strong case would be necessary for its application to any other."

Racial discrimination was the practice at issue in the early cases (cited in *Morgan*) that gave such an expansive description of the effects of § 5. In those early days, bear in mind, the guarantee of equal protection had not been extended beyond race to sex, age, and the many other categories it now covers. Also still to be developed were the incorporation doctrine (which holds that the Fourteenth Amendment incorporates and applies against the States the Bill of Rights) and the doctrine of so-called "substantive due process" (which holds that the Fourteenth Amendment's Due Process Clause protects unenumerated liberties). Thus, the Fourteenth Amendment did not include the many guarantees that it now provides. In such a seemingly limited context, it did not appear to be a massive expansion of congressional power to interpret § 5 broadly. Broad interpretation was particularly appropriate with regard to racial discrimination, since that was the principal evil against which the Equal Protection Clause was directed, and the principal constitutional prohibition that some of the States stubbornly ignored. The former is still true, and the latter remained true at least as late as *Morgan* . . . .

Thus, principally for reasons of *stare decisis,* I shall henceforth apply the permissive *McCulloch* standard to congressional measures designed to remedy racial discrimination by the States. I would not, however, abandon the requirement that Congress may impose prophylactic § 5 legislation only upon those particular States in which there has been an identified history of relevant constitutional violations. I would also adhere to the requirement that the prophylactic remedy predicated upon such state violations must be directed against the States or state actors rather than the public at large. And I would not, of course, permit any congressional measures that violate other provisions of the Constitution. When those requirements have been met, however, I shall leave it to Congress, under constraints no tighter than those of the Necessary and Proper Clause, to decide what measures are appropriate under § 5 to prevent or remedy racial discrimination by the States.

I shall also not subject to "congruence and proportionality" analysis congressional action under § 5 that is *not* directed to racial discrimination. Rather, I shall give full effect to that action when it consists of "enforcement" of the provisions of the Fourteenth Amendment, within the broad but not unlimited meaning of that term I have described above. When it goes beyond enforcement to prophylaxis, however, I shall consider it ultra vires. The present legislation is plainly of the latter sort. . . .

[The concurring opinions of Justices Souter and Ginsburg, and the dissenting opinion of Chief Justice Rehnquist and Justice Thomas, are omitted.]

Problem 21-A: Reproductive Rights Restoration Act

Assume that in early 2021, pro-abortion rights candidates win the presidency as well as both houses of Congress. Shortly thereafter, Congress enacts—and the President signs into law—the Reproductive Rights Restoration Act ("RRRA"). RRRA recites findings by Congress that in recent years, state legislatures have enacted an extraordinary number of laws regulating and restricting abortion; that these laws have had the effect—particularly in certain parts of the country—of dramatically reducing the number of available abortion providers; that many of the enacted laws constitute clear violations of the right to an abortion outlined in the U.S. Supreme Court's precedents; and that private case-by-case litigation challenging such laws has proven insufficient to fully vindicate that right, due to the frequency with which such laws are enacted and the ingenuity of legislatures in trying to curtail the right. Invoking congressional power to enforce, by "appropriate legislation," the Fourteenth Amendment, RRRA sets forth a formula for determining which states are subject to its requirements, providing that any state in which the number of abortion providers has declined by more than 30 percent in the last 10 years is a "covered jurisdiction." RRRA further provides that a law regulating or restricting abortion enacted by a covered jurisdiction cannot take effect unless it is precleared by the Attorney General of the United States. Pursuant to RRRA, the Attorney General must deny preclearance to any law prohibiting abortion in any way prior to fetal viability, and can preclear laws regulating abortion only if she determines that they would not result in any woman in the state having to travel more than 100 miles to procure an abortion after the law takes effect (or if some women already have to travel that far, that it would not increase the distance any further). RRRA has a five-year sunset provision, and thus expires in 2026 unless reenacted by Congress.

Shortly after RRRA is enacted into law, the Kansas and Kentucky legislatures enact new abortion laws. Both states qualify as "covered jurisdictions" under RRRA. Moreover, the Kansas law prohibits abortion under certain circumstances prior to fetal viability, while the Kentucky law will result in the closure of abortion facilities such that some women in the state will have to travel more than 100 miles to procure an abortion after it takes effect. Finally, neither Kansas nor Kentucky sought pre-clearance. Lawsuits are filed in federal district courts in Kansas and Kentucky, seeking to enjoin the new abortion laws from taking effect. In their complaints, the plaintiffs contend that the new laws should be enjoined from taking effect until the states seek and receive preclearance from the Attorney General. Kansas and Kentucky contend in response that the laws should not be enjoined because Congress lacked the constitutional authority to enact RRRA.

Was the enactment of RRRA a lawful exercise of congressional power under the Fourteenth Amendment?

Notes and Questions

1. At first glance, it is somewhat difficult to reconcile *Hibbs*, *Lane*, and some of the cases cited therein, such as *Garrett* and *Kimel*. What explains the seemingly inconsistent outcomes in these cases? The Court appears to be focused on the underlying level of constitutional scrutiny that would be involved under the self-executing portions of the Reconstruction Amendments, but the relationship appears to be an inverse rather than a direct one. What does that mean, and why does that relationship exist? What would that inverse relationship look like if the legislation at issue were designed to enforce the abortion right recognized in *Roe* and its progeny? The right to sexual intimacy recognized in *Lawrence*?

2. Recall from some of our previous cases that appearances or optics sometimes seem to play a role in the outcome of the case. To what extent do you suppose appearances were a relevant consideration in *Lane*? Should they have been?

3. What do you make of Justice Scalia's dissent in *Lane*? If his proposed approach were adopted, how much of a practical difference would it make to the outcomes of decided cases?

B. The Thirteenth and Fifteenth Amendments

Shelby County v. Holder

570 U.S. 529 (2013)

Chief Justice Roberts delivered the opinion of the Court.

The Voting Rights Act of 1965 employed extraordinary measures to address an extraordinary problem. Section 5 of the Act required States to obtain federal permission before enacting any law related to voting—a drastic departure from basic principles of federalism. And §4 of the Act applied that requirement only to some States—an equally dramatic departure from the principle that all States enjoy equal sovereignty. This was strong medicine, but Congress determined it was needed to address entrenched racial discrimination in voting, "an insidious and pervasive evil which had been perpetuated in certain parts of our country through unremitting and ingenious defiance of the Constitution." *South Carolina v. Katzenbach*, 383 U.S. 301, 309 (1966). As we explained in upholding the law, "exceptional conditions can justify legislative measures not otherwise appropriate." *Id.*, at 334. Reflecting the unprecedented nature of these measures, they were scheduled to expire after five years.

Nearly 50 years later, they are still in effect; indeed, they have been made more stringent, and are now scheduled to last until 2031. There is no denying, however, that the conditions that originally justified these measures no longer characterize voting in the covered jurisdictions. . . . Census Bureau data indicate that African–American voter turnout has come to exceed white voter turnout in five of the six States originally covered by §5, with a gap in the sixth State of less than one half of one percent. . . .

The Fifteenth Amendment was ratified in 1870, in the wake of the Civil War. . . .

"The first century of congressional enforcement of the Amendment, however, can only be regarded as a failure." In the 1890s, Alabama, Georgia, Louisiana, Mississippi, North Carolina, South Carolina, and Virginia began to enact literacy tests for voter registration and to employ other methods designed to prevent African–Americans from voting. Congress passed statutes outlawing some of these practices and facilitating litigation against them, but litigation remained slow and expensive, and the States came up with new ways to discriminate as soon as existing ones were struck down. Voter registration of African–Americans barely improved.

Inspired to action by the civil rights movement, Congress responded in 1965 with the Voting Rights Act. Section 2 was enacted to forbid, in all 50 States, any "standard, practice, or procedure . . . imposed or applied . . . to deny or abridge the right of any citizen of the United States to vote on account of race or color." . . . . Section 2 is permanent, applies nationwide, and is not at issue in this case.

Other sections targeted only some parts of the country. At the time of the Act's passage, these "covered" jurisdictions were those States or political subdivisions that had maintained a test or device as a prerequisite to voting as of November 1, 1964, and had less than 50 percent voter registration or turnout in the 1964 Presidential election. . . .

In those jurisdictions, § 4 of the Act banned all such tests or devices. Section 5 provided that no change in voting procedures could take effect until it was approved by federal authorities in Washington, D.C.—either the Attorney General or a court of three judges. A jurisdiction could obtain such "preclearance" only by proving that the change had neither "the purpose [nor] the effect of denying or abridging the right to vote on account of race or color."

Sections 4 and 5 were intended to be temporary; they were set to expire after five years. . . .

In 1970, Congress reauthorized the Act for another five years, and extended the coverage formula in § 4(b) to jurisdictions that had a voting test and less than 50 percent voter registration or turnout as of 1968. Congress also extended the ban in § 4(a) on tests and devices nationwide.

In 1975, Congress reauthorized the Act for seven more years, and extended its coverage to jurisdictions that had a voting test and less than 50 percent voter registration or turnout as of 1972. Congress also amended the definition of "test or device" to include the practice of providing English-only voting materials in places where over five percent of voting-age citizens spoke a single language other than English. . . . Congress correspondingly amended sections 2 and 5 to forbid voting discrimination on the basis of membership in a language minority group, in addition to discrimination on the basis of race or color. Finally, Congress made the nationwide ban on tests and devices permanent.

In 1982, Congress reauthorized the Act for 25 years, but did not alter its coverage formula. . . .

We upheld each of these reauthorizations against constitutional challenge.

In 2006, Congress again reauthorized the Voting Rights Act for 25 years, again without change to its coverage formula. Section 5 now forbids voting changes with "any discriminatory purpose" as well as voting changes that diminish the ability of citizens, on account of race, color, or language minority status, "to elect their preferred candidates of choice." . . . .

Shelby County is located in Alabama, a covered jurisdiction. . . . [I]n 2010, the county sued the Attorney General in Federal District Court in Washington, D.C., seeking a declaratory judgment that sections 4(b) and 5 of the Voting Rights Act are facially unconstitutional, as well as a permanent injunction against their enforcement. . . .

In *Northwest Austin,* we stated that "the Act imposes current burdens and must be justified by current needs." 557 U.S., at 203. And we concluded that "a departure from the fundamental principle of equal sovereignty requires a showing that a statute's disparate geographic coverage is sufficiently related to the problem that it targets." *Ibid.* These basic principles guide our review of the question before us.

The Constitution and laws of the United States are "the supreme Law of the Land." U.S. Const., Art. VI, cl. 2. State legislation may not contravene federal law. The Federal Government does not, however, have a general right to review and veto state enactments before they go into effect. . . .

Outside the strictures of the Supremacy Clause, States retain broad autonomy in structuring their governments and pursuing legislative objectives. Indeed, the Constitution provides that all powers not specifically granted to the Federal Government are reserved to the States or citizens. Amdt. 10 . . . .

More specifically, "'the Framers of the Constitution intended the States to keep for themselves, as provided in the Tenth Amendment, the power to regulate elections.'" *Gregory v. Ashcroft,* 501 U.S. 452, 461–462 (1991). Of course, the Federal Government retains significant control over federal elections. . . .

Not only do States retain sovereignty under the Constitution, there is also a "fundamental principle of *equal* sovereignty" among the States. *Northwest Austin, supra,* at 203 . . . .

The Voting Rights Act sharply departs from these basic principles. It suspends "*all* changes to state election law—however innocuous—until they have been precleared by federal authorities in Washington, D.C." *Id.,* at 202. States must beseech the Federal Government for permission to implement laws that they would otherwise have the right to enact and execute on their own. . . .

And despite the tradition of equal sovereignty, the Act applies to only nine States (and several additional counties). While one State waits months or years and expends funds to implement a validly enacted law, its neighbor can typically put the same law into effect immediately, through the normal legislative process. . . .

[T]he Act constitutes "extraordinary legislation otherwise unfamiliar to our federal system." 557 U.S., at 211.

In 1966, we found these departures from the basic features of our system of government justified. The "blight of racial discrimination in voting" had "infected the electoral process in parts of our country for nearly a century." *Katzenbach,* 383 U.S., at 308. Several States had enacted a variety of requirements and tests "specifically designed to prevent" African-Americans from voting. *Id.,* at 310. Case-by-case litigation had proved inadequate to prevent such racial discrimination in voting, in part because States "merely switched to discriminatory devices not covered by the federal decrees," "enacted difficult new tests," or simply "defied and evaded court orders." *Id.,* at 314. Shortly before enactment of the Voting Rights Act, only 19.4 percent of African-Americans of voting age were registered to vote in Alabama, only 31.8 percent in Louisiana, and only 6.4 percent in Mississippi. *Id.*, at 313. Those figures were roughly 50 percentage points or more below the figures for whites. *Ibid.*

In short, we concluded that "[u]nder the compulsion of these unique circumstances, Congress responded in a permissibly decisive manner." *Id.*, at 334, 335. We also noted then and have emphasized since that this extraordinary legislation was intended to be temporary, set to expire after five years.

At the time, the coverage formula—the means of linking the exercise of the unprecedented authority with the problem that warranted it—made sense. We found that "Congress chose to limit its attention to the geographic areas where immediate action seemed necessary." *Katzenbach*, 383 U.S., at 328. The areas where Congress found "evidence of actual voting discrimination" shared two characteristics: "the use of tests and devices for voter registration, and a voting rate in the 1964 presidential election at least 12 points below the national average." *Id.*, at 330 . . . . We therefore concluded that "the coverage formula [was] rational in both practice and theory." *Ibid.* . . .

Nearly 50 years later, things have changed dramatically. Shelby County contends that the preclearance requirement, even without regard to its disparate coverage, is now unconstitutional. Its arguments have a good deal of force. In the covered jurisdictions, "[v]oter turnout and registration rates now approach parity. Blatantly discriminatory evasions of federal decrees are rare. And minority candidates hold office at unprecedented levels." *Northwest Austin,* 557 U.S., at 202 . . . .

There is no doubt that these improvements are in large part *because of* the Voting Rights Act. The Act has proved immensely successful at redressing racial discrimination and integrating the voting process. . . .

Yet the Act has not eased the restrictions in § 5 or narrowed the scope of the coverage formula in § 4(b) along the way. Those extraordinary and unprecedented features were reauthorized—as if nothing had changed. In fact, the Act's unusual remedies have grown even stronger. When Congress reauthorized the Act in 2006, it did so for another 25 years on top of the previous 40—a far cry from the initial five-year period. Congress also expanded the prohibitions in § 5. We had previously interpreted § 5 to prohibit only those redistricting plans that would have the purpose or effect of worsening the position of minority groups. In 2006, Congress amended § 5 to prohibit laws that could have favored such groups but did not do so because of a discriminatory purpose, even though we had stated that such broadening of § 5 coverage would "exacerbate the substantial federalism costs that the preclearance procedure already exacts, perhaps to the extent of raising concerns about § 5's constitutionality," *Bossier II, supra,* at 336. In addition, Congress expanded § 5 to prohibit any voting law "that has the purpose of or will have the effect of diminishing the ability of any citizens of the United States," on account of race, color, or language minority status, "to elect their preferred candidates of choice." In light of those two amendments, the bar that covered jurisdictions must clear has been raised even as the conditions justifying that requirement have dramatically improved.

We have also previously highlighted the concern that "the preclearance requirements in one State [might] be unconstitutional in another." *Northwest Austin,* 557 U.S., at 203; see *Georgia v. Ashcroft,* 539 U.S., at 491 (KENNEDY, J., concurring) ("considerations of race that would doom a redistricting plan under the Fourteenth Amendment or § 2 [of the Voting Rights Act] seem to be what save it under § 5"). Nothing has happened since to alleviate this troubling concern about the current application of § 5 . . . .

The provisions of § 5 apply only to those jurisdictions singled out by § 4. We now consider whether that coverage formula is constitutional in light of current conditions. . . .

Coverage today is based on decades-old data and eradicated practices. The formula captures States by reference to literacy tests and low voter registration and turnout in the 1960s and early 1970s. But such tests have been banned nationwide for over 40 years. And voter registration and turnout numbers in the covered States have risen dramatically in the years since. Racial disparity in those numbers was compelling evidence justifying the preclearance remedy and the coverage formula. There is no longer such a disparity. . . .

The Government's defense of the formula is limited. . . .

The Government [contends] that because the formula was relevant in 1965, its continued use is permissible so long as any discrimination remains in the States Congress identified back then — regardless of how that discrimination compares to discrimination in States unburdened by coverage. This argument does not look to "current political conditions," *Northwest Austin, supra,* at 203, but instead relies on a comparison between the States in 1965. That comparison reflected the different histories of the North and South. It was in the South that slavery was upheld by law until uprooted by the Civil War, that the reign of Jim Crow denied African–Americans the most basic freedoms, and that state and local governments worked tirelessly to disenfranchise citizens on the basis of race. The Court invoked that history — rightly so — in sustaining the disparate coverage of the Voting Rights Act in 1966.

But history did not end in 1965. By the time the Act was reauthorized in 2006, there had been 40 more years of it. In assessing the "current need [ ]" for a preclearance system that treats States differently from one another today, that history cannot be ignored. During that time, largely because of the Voting Rights Act, voting tests were abolished, disparities in voter registration and turnout due to race were erased, and African–Americans attained political office in record numbers. And yet the coverage formula that Congress reauthorized in 2006 ignores these developments, keeping the focus on decades-old data relevant to decades-old problems, rather than current data reflecting current needs.

The Fifteenth Amendment commands that the right to vote shall not be denied or abridged on account of race or color, and it gives Congress the power to enforce that command. The Amendment is not designed to punish for the past; its purpose is to ensure a better future. To serve that purpose, Congress—if it is to divide the States—must identify those jurisdictions to be singled out on a basis that makes sense in light of current conditions. It cannot rely simply on the past. We made that clear in *Northwest Austin,* and we make it clear again today.

In defending the coverage formula, the Government, the intervenors, and the dissent also rely heavily on data from the record that they claim justify disparate coverage. Congress compiled thousands of pages of evidence before reauthorizing the Voting Rights Act. . . . Regardless of how to look at the record, however, no one can fairly say that it shows anything approaching the "pervasive," "flagrant," "widespread," and "rampant" discrimination that faced Congress in 1965, and that clearly distinguished the covered jurisdictions from the rest of the Nation at that time. *Katzenbach, supra,* at 308, 315, 331; *Northwest Austin*, 557 U.S., at 201.

But a more fundamental problem remains: Congress did not use the record it compiled to shape a coverage formula grounded in current conditions. It instead reenacted a formula based on 40–year–old facts having no logical relation to the present day. . . .

There is no valid reason to insulate the coverage formula from review merely because it was previously enacted 40 years ago. If Congress had started from scratch in 2006, it plainly could not have enacted the present coverage formula. It would have been irrational for Congress to distinguish between States in such a fundamental way based on 40–year–old data, when today's statistics tell an entirely different story. And it would have been irrational to base coverage on the use of voting tests 40 years ago, when such tests have been illegal since that time. But that is exactly what Congress has done.

* * *

Striking down an Act of Congress "is the gravest and most delicate duty that this Court is called on to perform." *Blodgett v. Holden,* 275 U.S. 142, 148 (1927) (Holmes, J., concurring). We do not do so lightly. That is why, in 2009, we took care to avoid ruling on the constitutionality of the Voting Rights Act when asked to do so, and instead resolved the case then before us on statutory grounds. But in issuing that decision, we expressed our broader concerns about the constitutionality of the Act. Congress could have updated the coverage formula at that time, but did not do so. Its failure to act leaves us today with no choice but to declare § 4(b) unconstitutional. The formula in that section can no longer be used as a basis for subjecting jurisdictions to preclearance.

Our decision in no way affects the permanent, nationwide ban on racial discrimination in voting found in § 2. We issue no holding on § 5 itself, only on the coverage formula. Congress may draft another formula based on current conditions. Such a formula is an initial prerequisite to a determination that exceptional conditions still exist justifying such an "extraordinary departure from the traditional course of relations between the States and the Federal Government." *Presley,* 502 U.S., at 500–501. Our country has changed, and while any racial discrimination in voting is too much, Congress must ensure that the legislation it passes to remedy that problem speaks to current conditions. . . .

Justice Thomas, concurring.

I join the Court's opinion in full but write separately to explain that I would find § 5 of the Voting Rights Act unconstitutional as well. The Court's opinion sets forth the reasons.

"The Voting Rights Act of 1965 employed extraordinary measures to address an extraordinary problem." *Ante,* at 2618. In the face of "unremitting and ingenious defiance" of citizens' constitutionally protected right to vote, § 5 was necessary to give effect to the Fifteenth Amendment in particular regions of the country. *South Carolina v. Katzenbach,* 383 U.S. 301, 309 (1966). Though § 5's preclearance requirement represented a "shar[p] depart[ure]" from "basic principles" of federalism and the equal sovereignty of the States, *ante,* at 2622, 2623, the Court upheld the measure against early constitutional challenges because it was necessary at the time to address "voting discrimination where it persist[ed] on a pervasive scale." *Katzenbach, supra,* at 308.

Today, our Nation has changed. "[T]he conditions that originally justified [§ 5] no longer characterize voting in the covered jurisdictions." *Ante,* at 2618. As the Court explains: "'[V]oter turnout and registration rates now approach parity. Blatantly discriminatory evasions of federal decrees are rare. And minority candidates hold office at unprecedented levels.'" *Ante,* at 2625 (quoting *Northwest Austin Municipal Util. Dist. No. One v. Holder,* 557 U.S. 193, 202 (2009)).

In spite of these improvements, however, Congress *increased* the already significant burdens of § 5. Following its reenactment in 2006, the Voting Rights Act was amended to "prohibit more conduct than before." *Ante,* at 2621. "Section 5 now forbids voting changes with 'any discriminatory purpose' as well as voting changes that diminish the ability of citizens, on account of race, color, or language minority status, 'to elect their preferred candidates of choice.'" *Ante,* at 2621. While the pre–2006 version of the Act went well beyond protection guaranteed under the Constitution, it now goes even further.

It is, thus, quite fitting that the Court repeatedly points out that this legislation is "extraordinary" and "unprecedented" and recognizes the significant constitutional problems created by Congress' decision to raise "the bar that covered jurisdictions must clear," even as "the conditions justifying that requirement have dramatically improved." *Ante,* at 2627. However one aggregates the data compiled by Congress, it cannot justify the considerable burdens created by § 5. As the Court aptly notes: "[N]o one can fairly say that [the record] shows anything approaching the 'pervasive,' 'flagrant,' 'widespread,' and 'rampant' discrimination that faced Congress in 1965, and that clearly distinguished the covered jurisdictions from the rest of the Nation at that time." *Ante,* at 2629. Indeed, circumstances in the covered jurisdictions can no longer be characterized as "exceptional" or "unique." "The extensive pattern of discrimination that led the Court to previously uphold § 5 as enforcing the Fifteenth Amendment no longer exists." *Northwest Austin, supra,* at 226 (THOMAS, J., concurring in judgment in part and dissenting in part). Section 5 is, thus, unconstitutional.

While the Court claims to "issue no holding on § 5 itself," *ante,* at 2631, its own opinion compellingly demonstrates that Congress has failed to justify "'current burdens'" with a record demonstrating "'current needs.'" See *ante,* at 2622 (quoting *Northwest Austin, supra,* at 203). By leaving the inevitable conclusion unstated, the Court needlessly prolongs the demise of that provision. For the reasons stated in the Court's opinion, I would find § 5 unconstitutional.

[The dissenting opinion of Justice Ginsburg is omitted.]

Problem 21-B: Shepard-Byrd Hate Crimes Prevention Act of 2009

In 2009, Congress enacted the Matthew Shepard and James Byrd, Jr. Hate Crimes Prevention Act of 2009. Among its provisions is Section 249(a)(1), which makes it a federal crime to injure or attempt to injure a person anywhere in the United States "because of the actual or perceived race, color, religion, or national origin" of the person. Section 249(a)(2) also makes it a crime to commit such acts "because of the actual or perceived religion, national origin, gender, sexual orientation, gender identity, or disability" of the person, but the latter applies only if the crime somehow affected interstate commerce.

Congress invoked its Commerce Clause powers in enacting Section 249(a)(2), but invoked its power to "enforce" the Thirteenth Amendment in enacting Section 249(a)(1). With respect to the latter, Congress compiled statistics regarding the prevalence of hate crimes in the United States and the need for expanded federal jurisdiction over the problem, and wrote that "eliminating racially motivated violence is an important means of eliminating, to the extent possible, the badges, incidents, and relics of slavery and involuntary servitude."

Why did Congress rely on different constitutional provisions in enacting Sections 249(a)(1) and 249(a)(2)? Was the enactment of Section 249(a)(1) a valid exercise of congressional power under the Thirteenth Amendment?

Notes and Questions

1. Which test does the *Shelby County* Court apply, the rationality test of cases such as *South Carolina v. Katzenbach* or the congruence and proportionality test of *Boerne*? Is there language in *Shelby County* that sheds light on the answer to that question?

2. Together, do *Boerne* and *Shelby County* cast doubt on cases such as *Jones* involving congressional power pursuant to Section 2 of the Thirteenth Amendment? *See United States v. Cannon*, 750 F.3d 492 (5th Cir. 2014); *id.* at 509 (Elrod, J., specially concurring) (upholding a federal statute under the permissive test of *Jones*, but

noting the tension between that case and the recent cases interpreting the scope of the enforcement power of the Fourteenth and Fifteenth Amendments that will have to be resolved eventually by the U.S. Supreme Court).

3. Are there sound ways to distinguish congressional power pursuant to Section 5 of the Fourteenth Amendment and its powers pursuant to Section 2 of the Thirteenth and Fifteenth Amendments? Does Justice Scalia's dissent in *Lane* suggest a policy rationale for so doing?

4. As a practical matter, how significant would extension of the congruence and proportionality test to Section 2 of the Thirteenth and Fifteenth Amendments be? In this regard consider that legislation enacted pursuant to these two provisions, unlike that enacted pursuant to Section 5 of the Fourteenth Amendment, is virtually always about race.

Index